SAP Crystal Dashboard Design 2011 And Presentation Design 2011 For Beginners

By Dr. Indera E. Murphy

Tolana Publishing
Teaneck, New Jersey

SAP Crystal Dashboard Design 2011 And Presentation Design 2011 For Beginners

Published By:
Tolana Publishing
PO Box 719
Teaneck, NJ 07666 USA

Find us online at www.tolanapublishing.com
Inquiries may be sent to the publisher: tolanapub@yahoo.com

Our books are available online at www.barnesandnoble.com.
They can also be ordered from Ingram and Baker & Taylor.

Quantity discounts are available for corporations, non-profit organizations and educational institutions for educational purposes, fundraising or resale. www.tolana.com/wholesale.html

ISBN-13: 978-1-935208-11-2
ISBN-10: 1-935208-11-X

Library of Congress Control Number: 2011941907

Printed and bound in the United States Of America

Cover by Mary Kramer, owner of Milkweed Graphics, www.milkweedgraphics.com

v1.0

About The Series

SAP Crystal Dashboard Design 2011 And Presentation Design 2011 For Beginners, is part of the growing series of computer software books that are designed to be used in a classroom setting, an online class or as a self-paced learning tool. The books contain an abundance of step-by-step instructions and screen shots to help reduce the "stress" often associated with learning new software.

Titles In The Series

	ISBN
ACT! 2007	978-0-9773912-5-7
ACT! 2009	978-1-935208-07-5
ACT! 2010	978-1-935208-09-9
ACT! Pro 2011	978-1-935208-13-6
ACT! Pro 2012	978-1-935208-17-4
Using Crystal Reports 2008 With ACT! 2010 Databases	978-1-935208-10-5
Crystal Reports XI For Beginners (2nd Edition)	978-1-935208-00-6
What's New In Crystal Reports 2008	978-1-935208-01-3
Crystal Reports 2008 For Beginners	978-0-9773912-9-5
Crystal Reports 2011 For Beginners	978-1-935208-15-0
Crystal Reports For Visual Studio 2005	978-0-9773912-6-4
Crystal Reports Basic For Visual Studio 2008	978-0-9773912-8-8
Crystal Reports For Visual Studio 2010	978-1-935208-12-9
Crystal Xcelsius 4.5	978-1-935208-02-0
Xcelsius 2008	978-1-935208-05-1
Dashboard Design 2011 And Presentation Design 2011 For Beginners	978-1-935208-11-2
OpenOffice.org 2 Writer	978-0-9773912-4-0
OpenOffice.org 3 Writer	978-1-935208-08-2
Microsoft Office Starter 2010 (Word & Excel)	978-1-935208-14-3
Microsoft PowerPivot For Excel 2010	978-1-935208-16-7
Microsoft Works 7	978-0-9773912-2-6
Microsoft Works 8 & 8.5	978-0-9773912-1-9
Microsoft Works 9	978-0-9773912-7-1
Windows XP	978-0-9773912-0-2

About The Author

Dr. Indera E. Murphy is an author, educator and IT professional that has over 20 years of experience in the Information Technology field. She has held a variety of positions including technical writer, programmer, consultant, web designer, course developer and project leader. Indera has designed and developed software applications and web sites, as well as, manage technology driven projects in several industries. In addition to being an Executive Director and consultant, as an online adjunct professor, she has taught courses in a variety of areas including project management, technical writing, information processing, Access, HTML, Windows, Excel, Dreamweaver and critical thinking.

Thank you for purchasing this book!

Why A Book On Dashboard Design?

Over the years, I have come to realize that many people only use a small percent of the features that software has to offer. One of my goals in all of the books that I write is to point out as many features as possible. My theory is that if more people knew about more than 10% of the features that a software package has, at the very least, they would try a few of them.

After reading the Users Guide that comes with Dashboard Design and Presentation Design, I felt that new users of the software would prefer to have more assistance in learning how to get the most out of the software. In general, there are not a lot of beginner level books with hands-on exercises for complex software. As a professor and author, I do not feel that flipping between a book and the Help file in the software is the most ideal way to learn how to use software.

I know that many books claim to have "step-by-step instructions". If you have tried to follow books that make this claim and you got lost or could not complete a task as instructed, it may not have been your fault. When I decided to write computer books, I vowed to really have step-by-step instructions that actually included every step. This includes steps like which file to open, which menu option to select, when to save a file and more. In my opinion, it is this level of detail that makes a computer book easy to follow. I hope that you feel the same way. If not, this is probably not the book for you.

Who This Book Is For

This book is for everyone that wants to learn Dashboard Design or Presentation Design. People that are upgrading from a previous version of the software (Xcelsius) will have a refresher of the basics and then learn about the features and options that are new in this version.

This book is primarily for beginners and end-users that have never used either of these software packages. Business Intelligence consultants and professionals will find this book helpful in terms of how they can incorporate Dashboard Design into the projects that they work on.

CONTENTS

INTRODUCTION TO DASHBOARD DESIGN 2011 AND PRESENTATION DESIGN 2011

The goal of this chapter is to introduce you to two software products: Dashboard Design (formerly known as Xcelsius 2008) and Presentation Design (formerly known as Xcelsius Present) and what they offer. These software packages are similar. Please note that unless stated otherwise, when Dashboard Design is referenced, Presentation Design is also being referenced.

Dashboard Design is gaining in popularity as a way to present and analyze data in dashboard format. In a way, this software sits at the intersection of data presentation and data analysis. The other concept covered in this chapter is to explain the basics of Business Intelligence and how Dashboard Design can be used as a key tool for Business Intelligence analysis.

Excel has been around for a long time and has been a primary way to analyze data, provide data in chart format and provide what-if functionality. The good news is that Dashboard Design is not going to cause Excel to go away. In fact, Dashboard Design uses Excel spreadsheets. Dashboard Design is used to provide interactive functionality for data in spreadsheets, as well as, other data sources.

Having said all of that, please be assured that the focus of this book is teaching you how to use Dashboard Design. The extent that Excel and Business Intelligence are covered is in an overview format, so that you can start to understand how and why they work well together.

So sit back and lets get started!

What Is Dashboard Design?

Dashboard Design is a software package that is used to visually organize and present data from Excel spreadsheets and other data sources in a meaningful way. The primary goal of Dashboard Design is to take the data and put it in a visual format that will be used as part of a presentation or for business analysis purposes. The software provides several options for how the data can be viewed, including what-if analysis, drill-down charts and other interactive features.

While Excel allows you to present the data in chart format, Pivot Tables and even some types of dashboards, if you need to redisplay the data based on changing one of the variables, you could be stuck if you are in the middle of a live presentation or meeting. You may have to create another chart during the presentation in front of a roomful of people. For example, if the Excel chart displayed the mortgage data based on a specific interest rate, but people in the meeting ask to see the mortgage data in a chart based on several interest rates, you would have to modify the spreadsheet on the spot during the meeting to display the mortgage data with several interest rates instead of one. No stress there <smile>.

This is where Dashboard Design is very beneficial and the better tool for the task. You could add a component for the mortgage interest rate cell to accommodate a wide range of interest rates in one dashboard. By adding a component like the slider to the mortgage interest rate cell, different interest rates could be selected. Each time that a different interest rate is selected, the chart would change immediately to reflect the interest rate that is selected. With Dashboard Design you could go one step further and hide one of the charts initially displayed and allow users to display it when they want or need to, with the click of a button on the dashboard.

This functionality is done in real time in Dashboard Design, which makes the dashboard **DYNAMIC** (ever changing), instead of **STATIC** (never changing). Using Dashboard Design to present data in an interactive, visual format is the next level up from using Excel and PowerPoint to present data. Two of the biggest advantages Dashboard Design has over Excel are explained below.

① People using a dashboard that was created in Dashboard Design do not have to have Dashboard Design or Excel installed on their computer, nor do they have to know how to use either software package.

② A dashboard that is created in Dashboard Design can be distributed in several formats including HTML, Adobe PDF and Flash.

If you have been struggling trying to get your Excel data into a PowerPoint presentation or struggling to make the presentation look better or more professional, those days are just about over because the dashboards created in Dashboard Design can also be incorporated in a PowerPoint presentation.

In one sentence to answer what Dashboard Design software is, I would say "Dashboard Design is a software package that is used to visually spice up how data is presented and allow the person using the dashboard to control what data is displayed".

Dashboard Design Editions

There are three editions of this software. They all allow the creation of dashboards. The main differences are the data sources and components that can be used.

① The **DASHBOARD DESIGN DEPARTMENTAL EDITION** is the most popular edition. It supports Excel spreadsheets and options to link to data in SAP BusinessObjects repositories, as well as, link external data sources to the embedded spreadsheet. This edition has a maximum connection of two external data sources.

② The **PRESENTATION DESIGN EDITION** can only use Excel spreadsheets as the data source. Models cannot be exported to Flash. It has less components then the Dashboard Design edition.

③ The **ENTERPRISE EDITION** has all of the features that the Dashboard Design edition has. It also supports an unlimited number of data sources and connections, including Universe Connectivity, Reporting Services and Web Portals.

What's New In Dashboard Design 2011?

What you will notice that's new, depends on the version of Xcelsius that you are upgrading from, if any. The older the version of Xcelsius that you are upgrading from, the more new features you will notice. For example, if the previous version that you used was the version 4.5, you will see a lot more new features then if you are upgrading from the 2008 Engage version. Some of the new features are discussed below.

⇒ The software has been renamed from Xcelsius to Dashboard Design.
⇒ If you are upgrading from Xcelsius 4.5, the biggest difference that you will notice is that many of the options on the Properties panel have been renamed.
⇒ The workspace has a new look. Parts of the workspace can be hidden.
⇒ New components have been added, including: Sparkline chart, Bullets chart, Push Button selector and Canvas container.
⇒ A series of data can now be plotted on the primary and secondary axis on some chart types by using the new Dual Y axis option.

How This Book Is Organized

Topics and exercises build on ones covered in previous chapters. To get the most out of this book, it is not advised that you skip around unless you have used a previous version of the software. The first reason is because some of the files used in later chapters are created in exercises earlier in the book. The other reason is that a topic or option may have been covered in more detail earlier in the book. If you decide to skip around and cannot complete an exercise because there is something that you do not understand, you will have to go back and find the section that covers the topic in question. Below is an overview of what is covered in each chapter.

Chapter 1 covers the conventions used in this book, so that you will know what certain things mean. You will learn how to check for software updates. Some of the terms that are used extensively in the Business Intelligence community are explained in detail.

Chapter 2 introduces you to Dashboard Design by explaining the workspace environment and its options. This includes menu options, the toolbar, the Components Browser and Object Browser. The types of dashboards that Dashboard Design can produce are explained and illustrated.

Chapter 3 covers the Dashboard Design workspace in detail, including docking panels, Quick Views, resizing the canvas, printing dashboards and more.

Chapter 4 provides a walk through of the dashboard design process so that you have a foundation to build on for creating effective, more so than dazzling, dashboards. You will learn how to import data into a model. Common options on the Properties panel are explained. You will see that you cannot create a dashboard without these options, so pay attention <smile>. And probably most important to you, is that you will create your first dashboard if you have never used the software before.

Chapter 5 covers Excel topics that you need to understand so that you can ensure that the spreadsheets that you use will work smoothly in Dashboard Design. You will also learn how cells, rows and columns of data in the spreadsheet are linked to components in a dashboard. Don't worry, you do not need a scientific calculator to complete this chapter.

Chapter 6 covers Single Value components, like sliders and gauges in detail. These components are often used to control or select the data that appears in another component on the dashboard.

Chapters 7 and **8** probably cover more than you ever wanted to know about chart components. You will see that a large number of dashboards have charts. Some of the charts created in these chapters are the foundation for other features covered later in the book. So make sure that you complete all of these exercises.

Chapter 9 shows you how to create a variety of menus. Menus are used to control other components on a dashboard, like which chart to display. For all intensive purposes, if you needed to create 25 dashboards that each need two charts and used data from 25 spreadsheets, you could combine all of that data into one spreadsheet, using 25 tabs on the spreadsheet. You could create one menu that would have options for each of the 25 dashboards and display the dashboards one by one. Some may call this cheating, but I just wanted to let you know the possibilities that a good menu design can handle.

Chapter 10 covers alerts, which is a way to conditionally change the color of components at run time. Alerts are a visual technique used to emphasize certain data or make the data stand out.

Chapter 11 covers map components. You will learn how to create interactive maps to display data geographically.

Chapter 12 covers several ways to enhance dashboards, including refreshing the data, using the Art and Background components, as well as, linking information on the Internet to components on a dashboard. You will also learn how to let users update the data in a spreadsheet and have the changes that they make incorporated in the dashboard, the next time that the model is published.

Chapter 13 covers advanced menu and chart types, including drill down charts, interactive calendars and picture menus.

Chapter 14 goes beyond the basics and covers functionality that some would put in the advanced category. This includes password protecting dashboards and having the ability to display and hide components on a dashboard as needed. The secret behind many of the "cool" features is Dynamic Visibility, which is covered in detail.

Chapter 15 covers the following components: Panel Container, Tab Set, List Builder, History and Trend Analyzer.

Chapter 16 covers customization options and techniques. The export options to turn a model into a dashboard that can be distributed to other people to use are covered. Yes, I know that you are sad to see it end <smile>.

Helpful, But Not Required

This book is written to be used for self-paced training, as well as, accommodate classroom and online training. While there are no required prerequisites to successfully complete the exercises in this book, having a general knowledge of any of the following would be helpful, but not required.

- ☑ Using formulas and cell references in Excel.
- ☑ The purpose of dashboards.
- ☑ Business Intelligence.
- ☑ What-If analysis.

Objectives Of The Book

This book takes a hands-on, performance based approach to teaching you how to use Dashboard Design and provides the skills required to create pivot tables and pivot charts efficiently. While Dashboard Design may be considered very technical or "geeky", I explain the terms and concepts in a manner that is hopefully easy to understand. Examples and screen shots are also provided to help make sure that you understand the concepts and are completing the exercises correctly. After completing the exercises in this book, you will be able to perform the following tasks and more:

- ☑ Implement good dashboard design techniques.
- ☑ Add interactive and animated functionality to dashboards.
- ☑ Create charts and menus.
- ☑ Use features like drill-down charts, accordion menus and calendars.
- ☑ Use advanced options including password protection and creating help options in a dashboard.
- ☑ Incorporate maps in dashboards.
- ☑ Publish (export) dashboards to several output formats including PDF, HTML and PowerPoint.

Chapter 1 Objectives

After reading and completing the exercises in this chapter you will understand the following:

- ☑ What Dashboard Design is designed to do.
- ☑ What dashboards are.
- ☑ The requirements and the process of importing data into a Dashboard Design model.
- ☑ How to get help if you get stuck.
- ☑ What a visual model is and its purpose in Dashboard Design.

Conventions Used In This Book

I designed the following conventions to make it easier for you to follow the instructions in this book:

- ☑ The official name of the software is SAP Crystal Dashboard Design 2011 Departmental Edition. As you many have noticed, I refer to the software as Dashboard Design.
- ☑ The `Courier font` is used to indicate what you should type.
- ☑ **Drag** means to hold down the left mouse button while moving the mouse.
- ☑ **Click** means to press the left mouse button once, then release it immediately.
- ☑ **Double-click** means to quickly press the left mouse button twice, then release it.
- ☑ **Right-click** means to press the right mouse button once, which will open a shortcut menu.
- ☑ Press **CTRL+SHIFT** means to press and hold down the CTRL (Control) key, then press the Shift key.
- ☑ Click **OK** means to click the OK button on the dialog box.

- ☑ Press **Enter** means to press the Enter key on your keyboard.
- ☑ Press **Tab** means to press the Tab key on your keyboard.
- ☑ Click **Save** means to click the Save button on the toolbar or dialog box.
- ☑ This icon indicates a shortcut or another way to complete the task that is being discussed. It can also indicate a tip or additional information about the topic that is being discussed. Some of this information comes from my personal experience with Dashboard Design.
- ☑ This icon indicates a warning, like a feature that has been removed or information that you need to be aware of.

NEW This icon represents a new or modified feature in Dashboard Design.

- ☑ **SMALL CAPS** are used to indicate an option to click on or to bring something to your attention.
- ☑ Instead of repeating the phrase over and over, I use **BOE** in place of SAP Business Objects Enterprise Repository. Data from these systems can be accessed from within Dashboard Design.
- ☑ [See Chapter 3, Object Browser] refers to a section in a different chapter that you can use as a reference for the topic currently being covered.
- ☑ [See Chapter 2, Figure 2-8] refers to an illustration (screen shot) in a different chapter that you can use as a reference for the topic currently being covered.
- ☑ The section heading **EXERCISE X.Y:** (where X equals the chapter number and Y equals the exercise number) represents exercises that have step-by-step instructions that you should complete. You will also see sections that have step-by-step instructions that are not an exercise. Completing them as you go through the book is optional, but recommended.
- ☑ When you see the phrase "**YOU SHOULD HAVE THE OPTIONS SHOWN IN FIGURE X-X**", or something similar in the exercises, check to make sure that your screen does look like the figure. If it does, continue with the next set of instructions. If your screen does not look like the figure, redo the steps that you just completed so that your screen does match the figure. Not doing so may cause problems when trying to complete exercises later in the book.
- ☑ "Clear the (name of option)" means to remove the check mark from the option specified in the instruction.
- ☑ "Select the range" means to select the cells in the spreadsheet of the model that is currently open.
- ☑ "Save the (name of model) as" means to open the (name of model) file and save it with the new file name that is specified in the instruction. Doing this lets you keep the original file as is.
- ☑ Many of the dialog boxes in Dashboard Design have OK, Cancel and Help buttons. Viewing these buttons on all of the figures adds no value, so they are not shown.
- ☑ **FORMAT ⇒ ALIGN ⇒ TOP** means to open the **FORMAT** menu, select the **ALIGN** option, then select the **TOP** option, as illustrated in Figure 1-1.

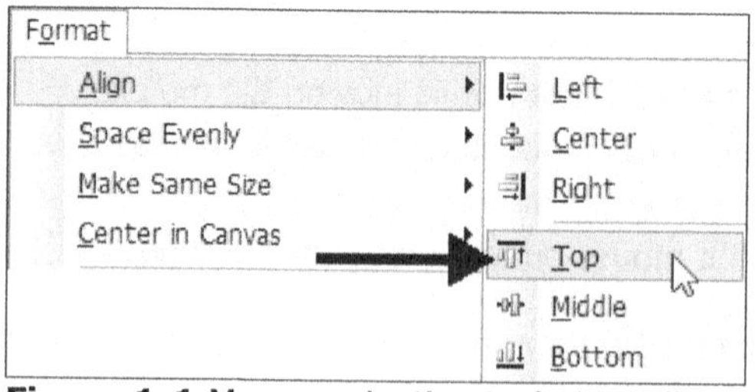

Figure 1-1 Menu navigation technique illustrated

Assumptions

(Yes, I know one should never assume anything, but the following assumptions have been made.)
It is assumed that . . . .

- ☑ You know that Dashboard Design Departmental is the edition used to write this book. You need to have Dashboard Design 2011 or Presentation Design 2011 installed to follow the exercises in this book. If you are using Presentation Design, you will not be able to complete all of the exercises in this book.
- ☑ You know that the operating system used to write this book is Windows 7. If you are using a different version of Windows, any or all of the following can apply:
  - ① Some of the screen shots may have a slightly different look
  - ② Some of the instructions for Windows tasks may be different.
  - ③ The path to folders and files on your computer may be different then the paths listed in this book.
- ☑ Microsoft Excel 2003 or higher has to be installed. Excel must be installed before installing Dashboard Design.
- ☑ You know that the version of Word, Excel, Outlook and PowerPoint used or referenced in this book is the 2010 version. Having Word, Outlook and PowerPoint installed will be helpful if you want to view some of the dashboards created in this book.
- ☑ You understand that if you have a different version of any of the software packages referenced above, that what you see on your computer screen will be slightly different then some of the illustrations in this book.
- ☑ You are familiar with the Windows environment including Windows Explorer and are comfortable using a mouse.
- ☑ When you see C1:E14, you know that it means to select (highlight) the range of cells from C1 to E14 on the Excel spreadsheet.
- ☑ You have access to the Internet to download the practice files needed to complete the exercises in this book and to download any updates to Dashboard Design that are available.
- ☑ When you see <smile>, it signifies my attempt at adding humor to the learning process.
- ☑ You know that Dashboard Design requires that the Flash Player version 9 or higher or plug-in be installed. When Dashboard Design is installed, there is a prompt to install the player if it is not already installed on your computer or if the version of the player or plug-in that is installed on your computer is too old. If an acceptable version of the player is installed, you will not be prompted to install it. If for some reason you discover that the Flash Player is not installed on your computer, you can download and install it for free from www.adobe.com.

How To Check For Software Updates

This exercise will show you how to check for and install updates for Dashboard Design.
The software does not have a built-in option that will notify you that an update is available.
This means that you will have to check the web site periodically, to see if there are any updates.

1. Go to www.sdn.sap.com/irj/boc/downloads. It would be nice to have a link on the Start Page of Dashboard Design for software updates. <smile>

2. Click on the link for Dashboard Design downloads, then open the **SOFTWARE PRODUCT** drop-down list and select Dashboard/Presentation Design (Xcelsius).

3. Open the **PRODUCT VERSION** drop-down list and select 2011, then click the Search button. (At the time that this book went to print, there was no option for 2011 in this drop-down list.) You will see a web page similar to the one shown in Figure 1-2.

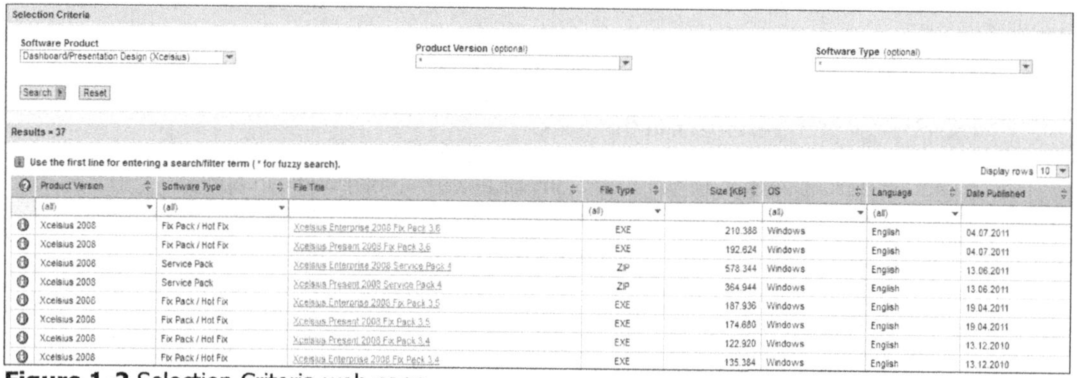

Figure 1-2 Selection Criteria web page

4. Click on the link for the update file that you need, then save it to your computers hard drive.

> I save update files to my desktop so that they are easier to find. After I install it, I remove it from my desktop, mainly because fewer items on the desktop means the computer will boot faster.

5. Extract the files from the zip file, then double-click on the **SETUP.EXE** file and follow the installation instructions.

Getting Help

As explained below, there are four primary ways to get help if you have a question on how to use a feature or option in Dashboard Design.

① Read this book from cover to cover. Many of the basic questions that you may have are probably covered in this book.

② The Online Help file. This is the electronic version of the Users Guide. It is helpful for the basic definitions of properties.

③ Dashboard Design forum. You can post questions and learn how other people are using the software. The forum is also a great way to keep up on the latest trends and getting ideas on how to enhance your dashboards.

④ Hire an Dashboard Design consultant. Need I say that this is the most expensive option and you probably will not get an answer to your question as fast as you would like.

Forum

If you have a question about Dashboard Design you can post a message in the forum listed below. This is the best place to go for help if you are having trouble installing the software or have a question on how to use an option. If you do not already have an account for the forum, you will be prompted to create one. The account is free.

The questions are answered by other users and forum moderators. Before posting your question, you should search the forum because the answer to your question may already be there.

Dashboard Design forum www.forums.sdn.sap.com/index.jspa
Scroll down to the Business Intelligence (Business Objects/Crystal Solutions) section, then click on the Dashboard and Presentation Design (Xcelsius) link.

Exercise 1.1: Create A Folder For Your Files

You will use several spreadsheets as the basis for the models and dashboards that you will create in this book. Some of these spreadsheets are ones that I created for this book and others are the spreadsheets for the sample dashboards that come with Dashboard Design.

All of the files that I created start with dd_. These files are in Excel 2003.xls format to accommodate people that have not upgraded to Excel 2007 or higher, which uses the .xlsx format. All of the files that you need for this book are in a zip file named dashboard2011.zip. I did this to make it easier for you to have all of the files needed for this book in one place, but you can use the spreadsheet files for the sample dashboards, from the folder that they are already in, on your computers hard drive, if you want. In addition to the spreadsheets, there are model files that I created and image files that you will need to complete some of the exercises. Some of the files that are in the zip file are used to demonstrate a concept.

Throughout the book I will refer to the folder that you will create in this exercise as "your folder". You will create the folder at the root of the C drive to store the files that you download, as well as, the models and dashboards that you create.

To obtain the files, send an email to dashboard2011@tolanapublishing.com. If you do not receive an email in a few minutes with the subject line Dashboard Design 2011 Files, check the spam folder in your email software.

1. Open Windows Explorer, then click on the C drive or the primary drive that you save files on.
2. File ⇒ New ⇒ Folder.
3. Type `Dashboard Design Book` as the folder name, then press Enter.
4. Go to the web page listed in the email that you received and download the zip file into the folder that you just created.
5. In Windows Explorer, click on the folder that you just created. Right-click on the zip file and extract the files to your folder.

File Naming Conventions

Like many things in life, there are rules that you have to follow. Below are the rules for the files that you will create.

① The file name cannot contain any of the following characters:
~ ! @ # $ % ^ & * ( ) + { } | : " < > ? ` - = [ ] \ ; ' , . /

② The file name can have a combination of letters, numbers and the under score. The underscore is often used in place of a space in the file name.

As you read earlier, the files that I created for this book have the underscore as part of the file name instead of spaces. I acquired this habit in my former life as a programmer. Many IT people still follow this practice today, especially for any file that will be accessed on the Internet.

The models and dashboards that you create will be saved with prefix "My". That way they will all be grouped together in the folder, so that you will know which files you created.

Okay Already, Can I See What Dashboard Design Can Do With Spreadsheet Data?

Given all of the types of databases, enterprise tools and reporting packages that are available, you have to admit that it is interesting that Excel is still being used as much as it is. I am by no means down playing Excel, just the opposite. I think that it is fantastic that for over 20 years Excel is still growing, holding its own and still going strong.

Even better that Dashboard Design came along and will take data from an Excel spreadsheet and turn it into something visually appealing to look at and use. Excel is a widely used software application. If you do not believe me, search the book section of Amazon's web site for books on Excel. Dashboard Design is a great boost to business intelligence analysis because it takes what many call "boring data" and transforms the data into an interactive dashboard, that can display the data in summary format, as well as, display the underlying detail data.

Usually, one PowerPoint slide would be created for each region shown in the first column in Figure 1-3, especially if you also needed to display a chart and show the detailed data for each region.

Using Dashboard Design, all of that data including the detail data and chart, can easily be incorporated into one dashboard.

If you wanted to go a step further, the dashboard could be exported to PowerPoint. In PowerPoint, the dashboard would only be one slide in the presentation.

	A	B	C
1	Actual Sales vs Projected		
2			
3		Last Years Actual Sales	Projected Sales
4			
5	North	$147,000	$150,000
6	South	$472,000	$375,000
7	East	$515,000	$500,000
8	West	$280,000	$405,000
9			
10		Current Actual Sales	Projected Sales
11			
12	North	$123,000	$150,000
13	South	$424,000	$400,000
14	East	$394,000	$375,000
15	West	$210,000	$225,000

Figure 1-3 Spreadsheet data

If you have ever come close to not wanting to create a PowerPoint presentation because of the large amount of spreadsheet data and charts that need to be placed in a format that is easy to use and understand, help is here. With Dashboard Design and this book, those days are just about over because this software will turn the static spreadsheet data into an interactive visual presentation that people will want to look at and use.

You can take some of the data in the spreadsheet and create a visualization like the one shown above in Figure 1-4.

You could also create a chart for the current and projected sales, create a menu with options to select the charts, all in one dashboard.

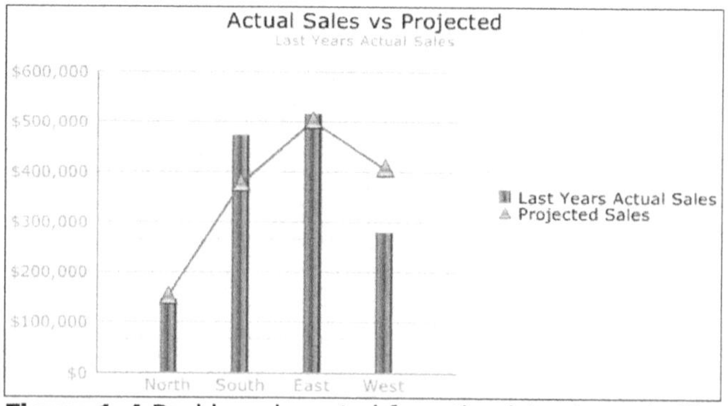

Figure 1-4 Dashboard created from the data shown in Figure 1-3

Figure 1-6 shown earlier is the way that a lot of people, display data in a spreadsheet. When the spreadsheet has a lot of data, it can be difficult to understand, interpret and see trends in the data. Being able to see large amounts of data in a relatively compact format, usually makes the data easier to understand. This is precisely what Dashboard Design was created to do an why people that work with large amounts of data to make business decisions really like dashboards.

Additionally, Dashboard Design has drill-down and dynamic functionality. The drill-down functionality allows the user to start off viewing summary data in the dashboard and then view the detail data if needed. There are components that are used to make the dashboard interactive.

In most chapters you will learn about different types of components that are used to create dashboards. I understand how easy it is to want to incorporate as many features as possible. That's fine as long as they are well placed and easy to understand. I hope that you keep in mind that the majority of dashboards that you create will be used to make business decisions.

Terms That You Need To Understand

Before you go any further, there are some terms that you need to understand to get a better idea of how dashboards can aid in the decision making process, display trends and much more. You will also start to understand how powerful Dashboard Design is. There are terms that you may have heard before, but are not exactly sure what they mean: Business Intelligence, Metric, Key Performance Indicators, What-If Analysis, Components, Visual Model and Dashboard. The goal of this section is to explain the terms and their relationship to Dashboard Design.

Business Intelligence is often called BI for short. Business intelligence is the process of analyzing data, raw or otherwise and converting the analysis into knowledge (intelligence). Business intelligence, in the broad sense, is a collection of technology and applications that are used to gather, store, access and analyze data. This process is usually used to make business decisions or track trends and changes. The typical business intelligence uses include querying, reporting, forecasting, data mining and statistical analysis.

Some of the goals of business intelligence analysis include being able to easily find new business opportunities, making decisions on existing processes, looking for ways to save money and having the ability to recognize where improvement is needed. Dashboard Design presents the data in a visual format. While not the traditional type of report, the dashboards that are created in Dashboard Design produce reports on a higher and more interactive level than what can be created in Excel. There are entire books on the Business Intelligence practices and techniques.

Metric A metric is one piece of data. Examples are the number of cars built in a month or quarterly sales per region. These values can be manually entered into a spreadsheet or a formula can be created to calculate the metric.

Key Performance Indicators are often called KPI's for short. KPI's are a way to measure the performance of a process. Alerts are often used to display KPI's. [See Chapter 10, Creating Dashboards That Have Alerts] The goal of KPI is to uncover performance that is not in the normal, acceptable range. Many dashboards are created around this concept because key performance indicators are one tool used to make business decisions, strategic or otherwise.

For example, during the course of a month, a car manufacturing plant may produce 10,000 cars. Each car needs a steering wheel. On a dashboard that monitors the quantity of steering wheels and other car parts on hand, one can monitor if the quantity of a product drops below the number of cars produced on any given day. If the quantity of steering wheels drop below the required on hand amount, the process of producing cars slows down.

The lack of a sufficient number of steering wheels indicates that at least one of the following is true: Enough steering wheels are not being ordered, the production of cars was increased without enough notice to the department or vendor that produces the steering wheels, the delivery time is too long or the product is not being ordered soon enough. Whatever the reason, the end result is the same, the car manufacturer loses revenue because production stops or at least slows down. Car dealers do not get the cars on time, so they can potentially lose sales. Should this happen, the KPI's need to be reviewed and a business decision has to be made that will prevent a shortage of car parts going forward.

Another way to explain KPI is that it is a metric that is tied to a target. This target can be a single value or a range of values. In the example above, the target (10,000 cars a month) is a single value. The metric is the current number of cars that have been produced. This metric can be presented by day or by week. On the 24th of the month, the metric value should be larger than the metric value for the fifth of the month because more cars should have been produced later in the month then in the first week.

What-If Analysis This type of analysis is used to see how changing the value in one field affects other values that are being used in the analysis. The example most used to explain what-if analysis is how changing the interest rate changes the monthly mortgage payment. In this example, the what-if value, if you will, is the interest rate. When the interest rate is changed, the monthly mortgage payment is automatically recalculated to show the new mortgage payment.

If you have used Excel for a while, you know that one of its strong points is being able to create what-if analysis scenarios. One of the ways that this is accomplished in Excel is through the use of Pivot Tables. The functionality in Dashboard Design will let you take what-if analysis to a completely different level and allow you to make changes to the what-if fields in the dashboard, in real-time. This means that during a presentation, you will have the ability to demonstrate what-if this or what-if that, without having to modify the Excel spreadsheet. For many, just being able to turn the what-if analysis functionality into a visual presentation is worth the price of learning Dashboard Design.

Visual Model or **Model** This is the working version file of what will become the dashboard when the model is compiled and published. This is the file that you import the spreadsheet data into, as well as, add components to. Visual models, or models, as I refer to them, make the raw spreadsheet data shown earlier in Figure 1-3, easier to understand. In Dashboard Design, you will spend almost all of your time working with visual model files. In addition to designing the dashboard layout, the model can be used for testing, before the actual dashboard is created and distributed.

What Is A Dashboard?

More than likely, if you have read any literature on Dashboard Design, it had the word "Dashboard" in it. In general, a dashboard is a visual or graphical representation of the data behind a performance indicator. In Dashboard Design, a dashboard is the finished product. Okay, I know what you are asking. You are asking "What is the finished product?" The finished product is the output of the **VISUAL MODEL**, which contains interactive objects like menus, sliders, charts and the data that these components represent. The finished product is a standalone file that can be distributed and used by people, which does not require Dashboard Design or the software that was used to create the data to be installed on their computer.

Unlike scorecards (1), dashboards are very closely tied to providing data (usually operational) in a visual format that is easy for the user to understand. From a high level perspective, a dashboard is one tool used to determine whether or not a business strategy is meeting expectations.

(1) The primary function of a **SCORECARD** is to aid in keeping the company (or a department) on track by monitoring the progress of KPI's that have been determined as necessary to meet a business objective. To me, scorecards are a type of project plan, which contains a list of tasks that must be completed, tested and implemented before the project can be considered complete.

Sample Dashboards

Figures 1-5 to 1-7 show some of the sample dashboards that come with Dashboard Design.

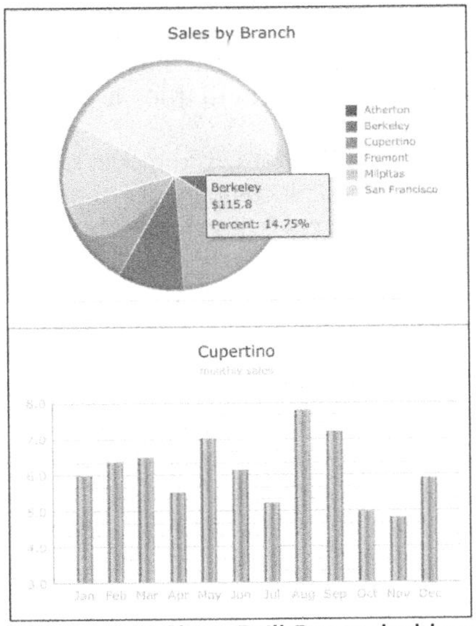

Figure 1-5 Chart-Drill Down dashboard

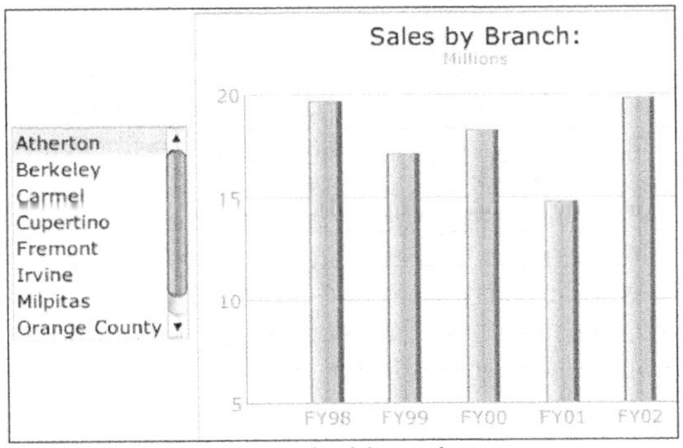

Figure 1-6 List Box dashboard

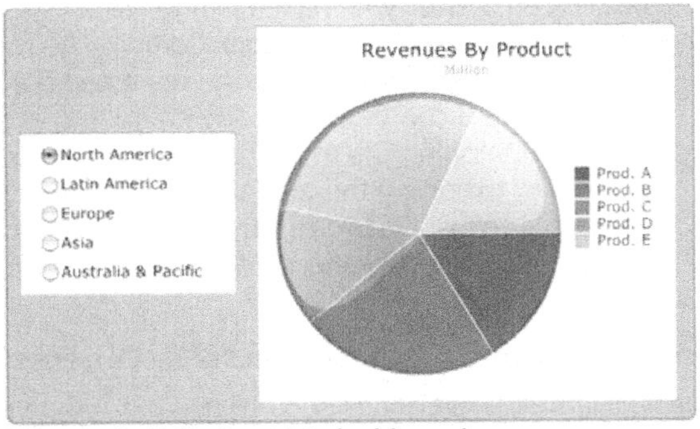

Figure 1-7 Status List dashboard

How Dashboard Design Does What It Does

The prior sections have explained what the software is and what it is capable of doing. Hopefully, you are somewhat excited about using Dashboard Design to create dashboards. I suspect though, that you are a bit curious about how Dashboard Design does what it does, especially because you can create a dashboard for the most part, using point and click techniques. Translated, that means very little typing is required to use Dashboard Design. What I find interesting is that for all that this software can incorporate in a dashboard, the file size of a dashboard is very small. The three main tasks that are needed to create a dashboard are explained below.

① **IMPORT THE DATA** from an Excel (**.XLS** or **.XLSX**) spreadsheet into a model. You can also connect to other data sources. A model can only use one spreadsheet. If the data that you want to use to create the dashboard is in another format, like a database or word processing document, you will have to export the data to an Excel spreadsheet. Yes, I know that it is often reported that Dashboard Design only uses data created in Excel spreadsheets, but trust me, as a lot of companies have data in Enterprise databases, they could not use Dashboard Design if they could not access and use some of their core data that is in other formats.

As long as you can import data from another source into Excel, you can use the data in Dashboard Design. Dashboard Design can use data that is pulled into Excel from an XML file format that Excel can recognize. Using XML is beyond the scope of this book. If you need to use enterprise data and cannot or do not want to set up an XML file to import the data into Excel, you can use a tool like Microsoft Query. You can also look into the Enterprise edition of Dashboard Design to see if it better meets your needs.

When the spreadsheet data is imported into the model, the import process creates a copy of the Excel spreadsheet and uses the copy in the model. The cell formatting and formulas in the spreadsheet are also imported. Nothing is changed in the original spreadsheet. If data is changed in the original spreadsheet, it is not automatically picked up by the model. The spreadsheet would have to be re-imported, so that the changes would be incorporated in the dashboard. This is how the dashboard can function as a stand alone file. Having said that, a dashboard can be configured to use live data at run time, through XML or the Enterprise edition of Dashboard Design. The closest solution to using live data is to refresh the data and publish the model again.

② **CREATE THE MODEL** by selecting the appropriate components for the data. The model is your dashboard in design mode. This is the file used to add and link components to the data in the model. The model is also the file that is used to edit and test what will become the finished product (the dashboard). If you need to change the dashboard or re-import data, the model is the file that you use. The dashboard file cannot be modified. It has to be recreated after you make changes to the model file that you want to publish.

③ **COMPILE AND PUBLISH THE MODEL** Compile the model for testing and previewing purposes to make sure that it produces the expected outcomes. The compiled file makes sure that the dashboard can be run on any computer, regardless of the computers operating system. Publishing the model is how the dashboard file is created. Publishing is the process of exporting the model file, into a stand alone file that does not require having the software installed to run the dashboard. As you will learn, there are several output formats that you can select from.

Dashboard Design Objects vs Xcelsius Objects

Dashboard Design models are designed to use the Adobe Flash Player, which supports the **SWF FILE FORMAT**. SWF supports vector-based graphics. This means that the graphics play back smoothly on any screen size, as well as on multiple platforms. The graphics are also scaleable in .swf files.

If a Dashboard Design file is saved locally, like to your hard drive, the file is saved in a zipped format with the XLF extension. The **XLF FILE** (the design document) contains the model information and the embedded spreadsheet file (the data used to create the model). If a Dashboard Design file is saved to a BOE, the model is saved as a Dashboard Design object. This object can contain the XLF file and the SWF file in the same object.

If the Dashboard Design object is modified in the Dashboard Design software, the SWF file is updated automatically with the changes. This means that the SWF file does not have to be exported after the changes have been made for users to get the changes. XLF and SWF files created in Xcelsius 2008 require the SWF file to be exported again for users to get the changes.

Backing Up Your Work

I cannot stress how important it is to back up your work frequently. Doing so will save you frustration in the event a power failure occurs or if your computer has a hardware failure. The majority of times that you lose work, it can't be recovered or if it can, it may cost you a few hundred dollars or more to recover it. I use to tell my students this and it never failed that a student lost some, if not all of their work. Don't say that I didn't warn you <smile>.

If you aren't already, you should also be saving a copy of your work to an external source like an external hard drive or USB drive. My favorite file backup device at the moment is the ClickFree C6 external drive.

What This Book Does Not Cover

As the title of this book indicates, this is a book primarily for beginners. However, that does not mean that this book does not cover the majority of functionality that the software has. The reason the word beginner is in the title is because the book has step-by-step instructions, which show you how to use the features of the software, opposed to paragraphs that just discuss the features and leave you to figure out how to use the features. Having said that, there are a few topics that are not covered in this book. They are listed below:

① Features only found in the Enterprise edition of Dashboard Design.
② XML functionality and connectivity.
③ Live Office connectivity.
④ Integrating dashboards into Crystal Reports.
⑤ Using Universes.

> **Attention Presentation Design Users**
> Presentation Design (formerly known as Xcelsius Present) does not have all of the components and functionality that Dashboard Design has. The list below contains the majority of components and functionality that Presentation Design does not have. Exercises that use any of these components or functionality cannot be completed in Presentation Design.

Accordion Menu component
Calendar component
Canvas Container component
Connection Refresh Button component
Data Manager dialog box
Export to AIR
Export to Flash
Export to HTML
Export to Outlook
Fisheye Picture menu component
Grid component
History component
List Builder component
Panel Container component
Panel Container 2 component
Panel Set component
Play Button options
Play Selector component
Reporting Services Button component
Slide Show component
Sliding Picture Menu component
Source Data component
SWF Loader component
Tab Set component
Trend Analyzer component

QUICK TOUR OF DASHBOARD DESIGN

In this chapter you will learn your way around Dashboard Design, by learning about the following:

- ☑ Start Page
- ☑ The workspace
- ☑ The canvas
- ☑ The menu
- ☑ Toolbars
- ☑ Formatting options
- ☑ Ordering components
- ☑ Selecting components

CHAPTER 2

NEW The Start Page

When you open Dashboard Design you will see the window shown in Figure 2-1. The Start Page has options to create new models and open recently opened models, as explained below.

New Section Options

The **BLANK MODEL** option is used to create a model and the data for the model.

The **MODEL WITH SPREADSHEET DATA** option is used to create a model from data in an existing spreadsheet.

The **MODEL FROM TEMPLATE** option opens the New From Template dialog box shown later in Figure 2-3, which lets you select a template for the model that you are going to create.

Recent Section Options

The files in this section display the last four models that you opened.

Open Section Options

The options in this section are used to open models from specific locations.

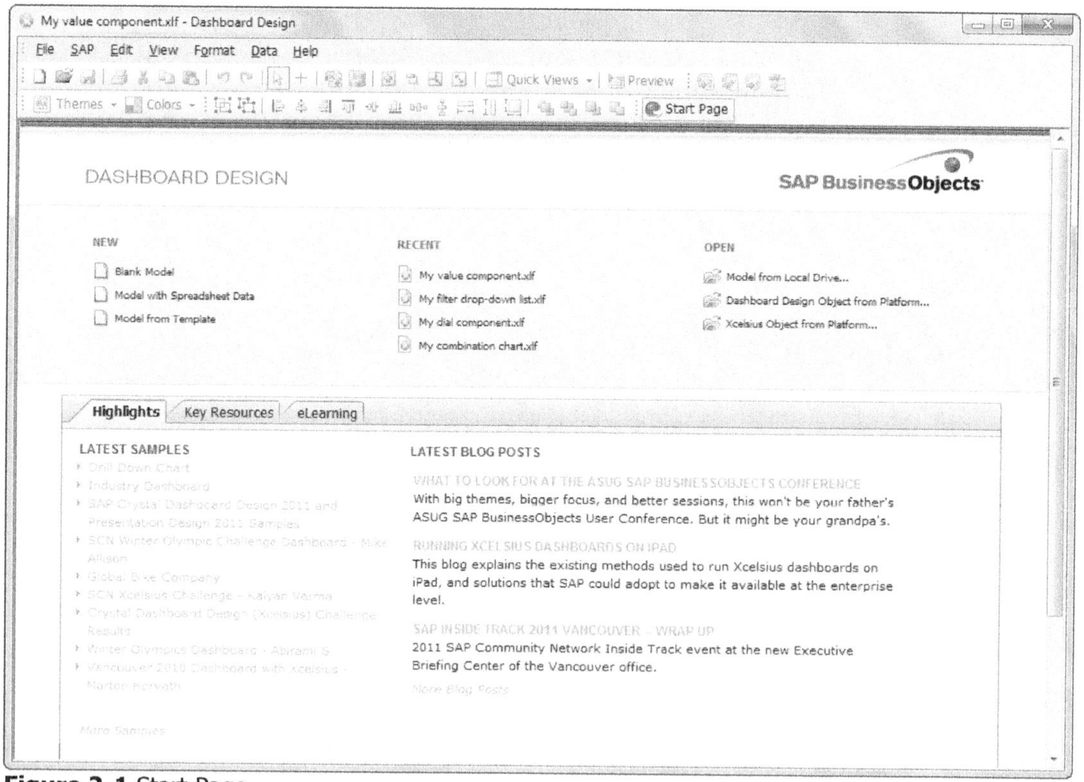

Figure 2-1 Start Page

In the middle of the window are three tabs. They are only available if the computer is connected to the Internet. The tabs are explained below.

① **HIGHLIGHTS** Provides links to sample reports, free product add-ons and blog posts.
② **KEY RESOURCES** Has links to newsletters, getting started information, forums and resources.
③ **ELEARNING** Has links to tutorials for Dashboard Design.

> The Start Page contains many of the options that were on the **QUICK START** panel in Xcelsius 2008.

The Workspace

When you open a model you will see the workspace shown in Figure 2-2. This is where you create or edit the model that will become the dashboard. To view the Start Page shown above in Figure 2-1, click the Start Page button circled in Figure 2-2.

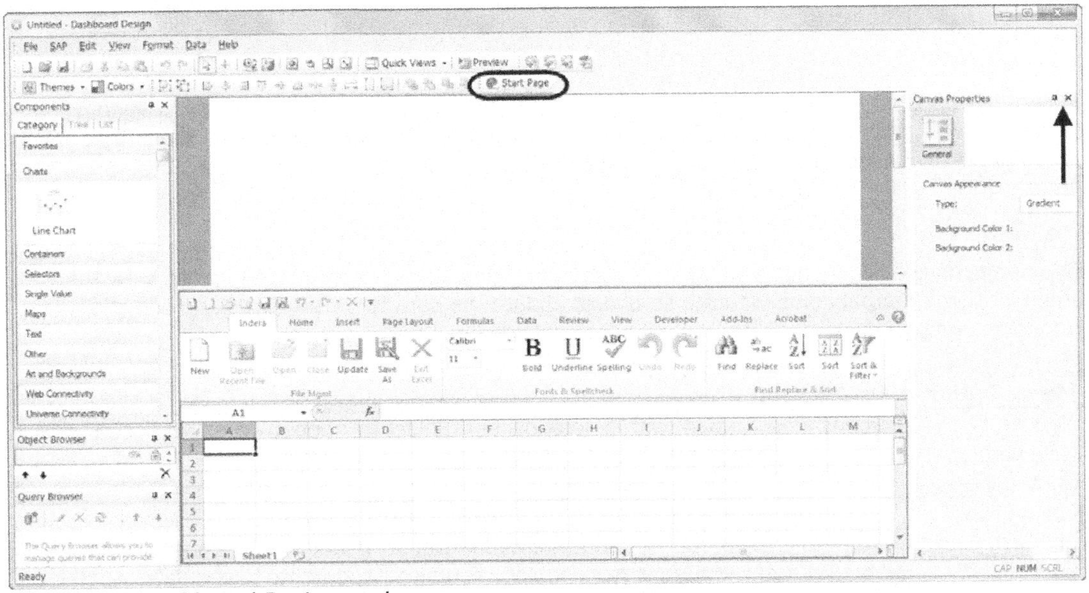

Figure 2-2 Dashboard Design workspace

By default, when a model is first opened the Components Browser, Object Browser and Canvas Properties panel are opened automatically, as shown above. To close a panel, click on the X at the top of the panel, as illustrated above, in the upper right corner of Figure 2-2.

The Canvas

The white space in the middle of the workspace is called the **CANVAS**. This is where you place the components, backgrounds and other objects needed to build the model for the dashboard.

Adding A Component To The Canvas

There are three ways to add a component to the canvas as explained below.

① Drag the component from the Components Browser and place it on the canvas.
② Click on the component in the Components Browser, then click on the canvas.
③ Copy the component from another model and paste it on the canvas.

Canvas Size

The canvas that you saw above in Figure 2-2 is the default canvas size. You can change the canvas size at any time. You can change it before you start creating the model, when you are finished creating the model or anytime in between. I tend to leave the canvas size large until I am finished creating and testing the model.

NEW

Platform Options
All options in the software that have the word "Platform" are new in Dashboard Design 2011.

What I find interesting is that there is no option to close a model. I suspect that the current file is automatically closed when you open another model.

The Menu

Many of the options on the menu are the same as options in spreadsheet or word processing software. The options explained below in Tables 2-1 to 2-6 are the options on each menu that are either specific to Dashboard Design or provide different functionality then what you may expect.

File Menu

The options on the File menu in addition to opening models are used to create models, view the sample dashboards that come with the software, update the data for dashboards and compile a model to create a dashboard. The options are explained in Table 2-1.

Menu Option	Description
New ⇒ New with Spreadsheet	Opens a new model with a spreadsheet. Select this option when you need to create the data for a new model.
Open From Platform	Is used to open an Xcelsius 2008 model (**.XLF**) or a Dashboard Design object file from a BOE. This option requires the Departmental or Enterprise edition, otherwise, this option is not enabled. You also need rights to the data.
Save to Platform	Is used to save the model to a BOE as a Dashboard Design object.
Save to Platform As	The options on this submenu are used to save an existing Dashboard Design object or save an Xcelsius object as a Dashboard Design object, with a new name in a BOE. The second option is used to save the open Xcelsius object as a Dashboard Design object and delete the existing Flash (swf) object.
Templates	Opens the dialog box shown in Figure 2-3. You can select a template to use as the basis for the dashboard that you want to create.
Samples	Opens the dialog box shown in Figure 2-4. The options in the **ITEMS** list are the sample dashboards that come with Dashboard Design.
Document Properties	Opens the dialog box shown in Figure 2-5. The options on this dialog box override the options set on the Preferences dialog box.
Translation Settings	Is used to select the data in the spreadsheet that you want to be translated into another language.
Preferences	The options on the Preferences dialog box are used to select defaults for the current model.

Table 2-1 File menu options explained

Menu Option	Description
Export Preview	Compiles the model, creates a temporary SWF file and displays the model in your web browser. This is one way that you can test the model.
Export	Displays the submenu shown in Figure 2-7. Each option compiles and exports (publishes) the model to a different file format. For example, if you select the PDF option, the model will be saved in a PDF file, which is the dashboard file that you would distribute.
Export Settings	Opens the dialog box shown in Figure 2-8. The options shown at the top of the figure are used to select how the data for the model will be updated (refreshed). ① **USE CURRENT EXCEL DATA** This is the default option. It will use the same spreadsheet that was last imported into the model. ② **USE ANOTHER EXCEL FILE** This option is used to select a spreadsheet, other then the last one imported into the model.
Snapshot	Exports the data that is currently displayed in the model in preview mode. This is a subset of the data that was imported into the model. I did not find this option to work as intended.
Manage Add-Ons	Opens the dialog box shown in Figure 2-9. Add-ons are charts, maps and other extensions that you can download and use in your dashboard. Some are free.
Print	Is used to print the dashboard to paper.
Print Preview	Is used to view how the dashboard will look when printed to paper.

Table 2-1 File menu options explained (Continued)

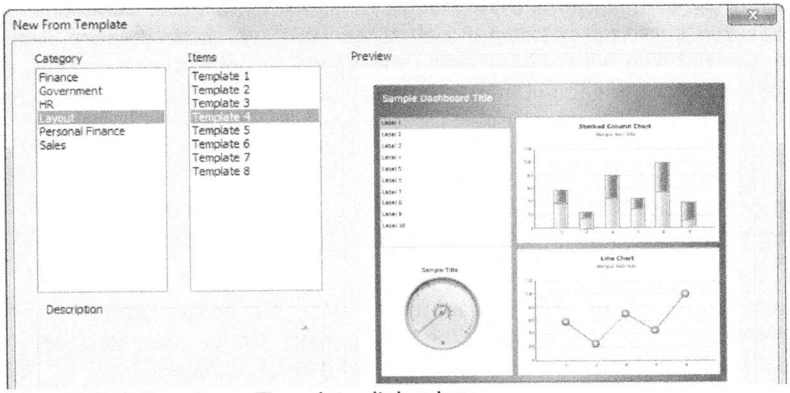

Figure 2-3 New From Template dialog box

If there is more than one category, select the category and the sample dashboards in the category will appear in the Items list.

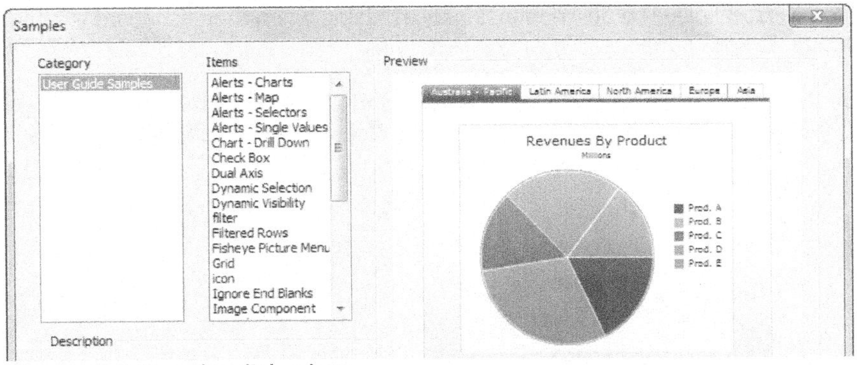

Figure 2-4 Samples dialog box

The options in the **PRESET SIZE** drop-down list are different display sizes.

The **USE GLOBAL FONT** options are used to change the fonts that the components use. The default font is Verdana. You can select a different font that will be used for all components or you can change the default font on a dashboard by dashboard basis.

The **USE DEVICE FONTS** option allows any font to be used. Selecting this option means that all of the fonts installed on your computer will be available on the Properties panel text tab. It also means that different fonts can be used for different components on the same dashboard.

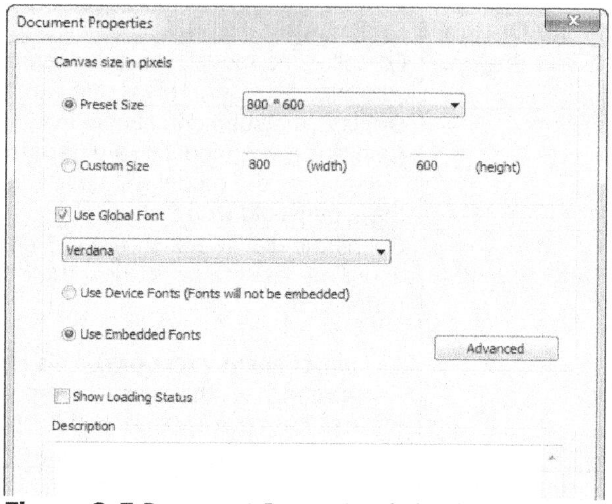

Figure 2-5 Document Properties dialog box

The downside is that if the font that you select is not on the computer running the dashboard, the dashboard will probably not have the look that you intended, because the fonts are not embedded when the model is exported. Instead, they will be substituted with fonts installed on the computer that the dashboard is being run from. This means that the text on the dashboard can vary from computer to computer.

The **USE EMBEDDED FONTS** option is the default option even though it increases the file size and load time of the dashboard. The file size is increased because a copy of the True Type fonts that are used in the model are placed in the SWF file. The benefit of selecting this option is that the fonts display properly in the dashboard whether or not the computer that the dashboard is run from has the fonts installed that you used. The downside is that the fonts used for the components cannot be changed on the Properties panel.

The **ADVANCED** button opens the dialog box shown in Figure 2-6. This is where you select the characters to embed in the dashboard. (1)

NEW Select the **SHOW LOADING STATUS** option if you want to display messages like "Start Calculations" or "Loading Components" when the dashboard is first opening. The problem with this option in my opinion, is that the messages go by so fast, they are very difficult to read.

You can enter any information about the model that you think is helpful or important in the **DESCRIPTION** field. The description is only available when the dashboard is opened in Dashboard Design. It does not appear in the exported file.

(1) The font options shown in Figures 2-5 and 2-6 were on the Font Menu option in Crystal Xcelsius 4.5 or earlier. They were moved to the Document Properties dialog box in Xcelsius 2008.

Not all components support these font options.

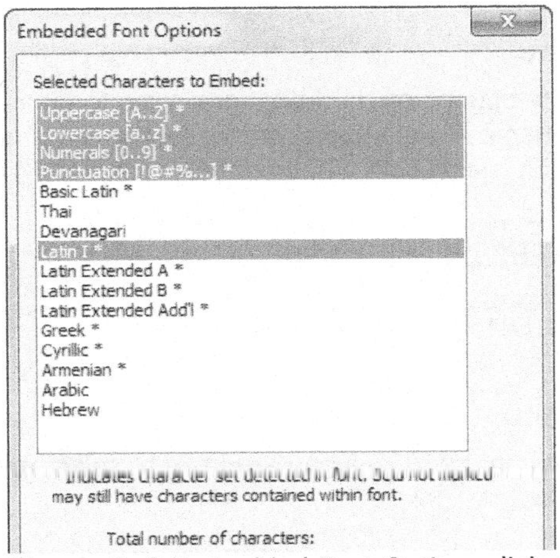

Figure 2-6 Embedded Font Options dialog box

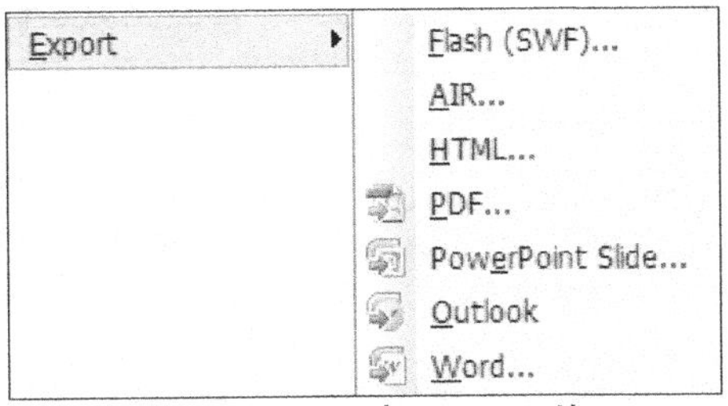

Figure 2-7 Export submenu options

Figure 2-8 Export Settings dialog box

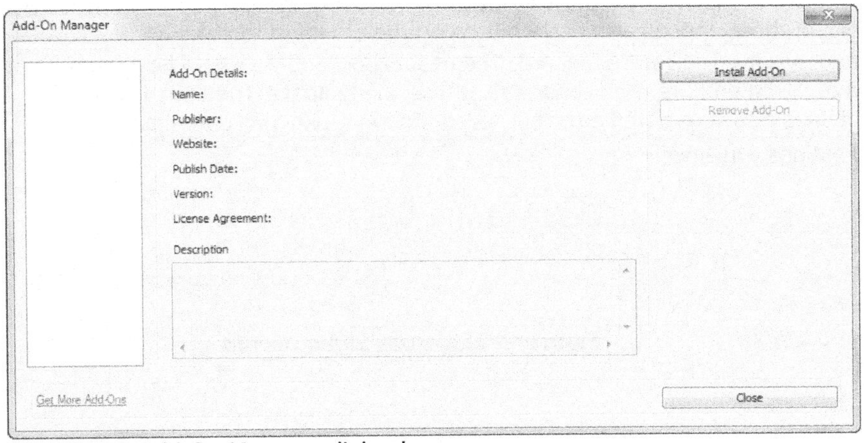

Figure 2-9 Add-On Manager dialog box

NEW SAP Menu

The options on this menu are only available if the model is connected to data in a BOE data source.

Edit Menu

Many of the options on the Edit menu may be familiar, especially if you have used word processing software. Some of the options on the Edit menu require a component to be selected before the menu option is available. The options are explained in Table 2-2.

Menu Option	Description
Select All	Selects all of the components on the model that are not hidden.

Table 2-2 Edit menu option explained

View Menu

The options on the View menu are used to select many of the tools in Dashboard Design. The options are explained in Table 2-3.

Menu Option	Description
Grid	Is used to align objects on the canvas.
Properties	Displays or hides the Properties panel.
Object Browser	Displays or hides the Object Browser.
Components	Displays the Components Browser.
NEW Query Browser	Displays or hides the Query Browser window, which is in the lower left corner of the workspace. This window is only activated when the model is connected to a BOE. This window displays a list of queries that can be run to retrieve data for the model.
Quick Views	The options shown in Figure 2-10 are used to select a different workspace view.
Canvas Sizing	The options shown in Figure 2-11 are used to change the size of the canvas. Each of these options also has a button on the Standard toolbar.
Toolbars	There are five toolbars: Standard, Themes, Export and Format. The options on the submenu are used to display or hide the toolbars. The Start Page option is also considered a toolbar, even though it only has one button.

Table 2-3 View menu options explained

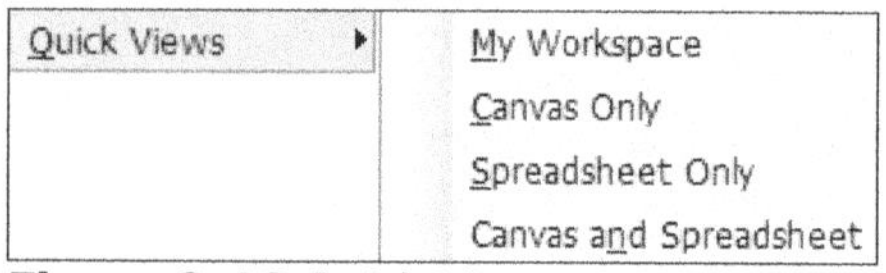

Figure 2-10 Quick Views options

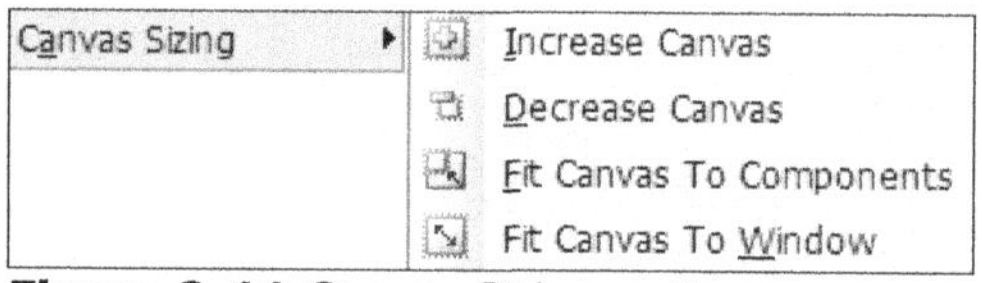

Figure 2-11 Canvas Sizing options

Format Menu

The options on the Format menu are used to modify the components in the model, including changing the size of the components. The first four options on this menu and the order options are explained later in this chapter. The remaining options are explained in Table 2-4.

Menu Option	Description
Theme	Opens the Themes dialog box. Themes are used to change the appearance of components.
Color Scheme	Opens the Color Schemes dialog box. The options on the dialog box are used to apply a different color scheme to components, edit an existing color scheme or create a new color scheme.
Order	The options on this submenu are used to reorder components that are layered on top of each other.
Group	Places the selected components in a folder in the Object Browser, as illustrated in Figure 2-12. This may make finding components easier, if the model has a lot of components.
Ungroup	Removes the components from the group.

Table 2-4 Format menu options explained

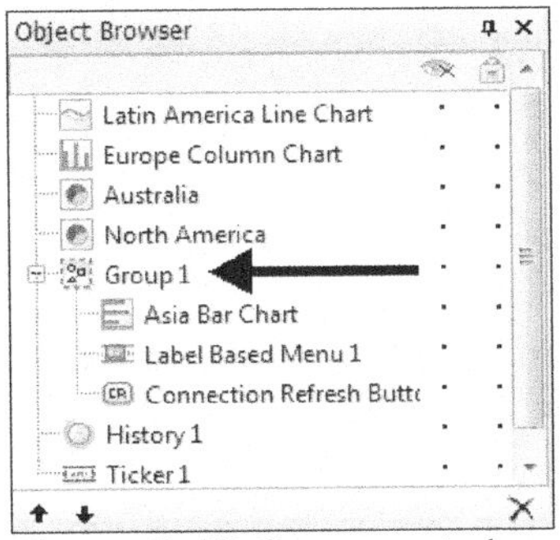

Figure 2-12 Components in a group illustrated

Data Menu

The options on the Data menu are used to work with the spreadsheet data. The options are explained in Table 2-5.

Menu Option	Description
Import	Adds the data from an Excel spreadsheet to the model.
NEW Import from Platform	Is used to import data from an Excel spreadsheet in the BOE to use for the model. Keep in mind that all of the worksheets in the workbook will be imported. This may or may not be what you want, but it is, what it is <smile>.
Export	Exports a copy of the Excel spreadsheet that was used to create the dashboard. It does not matter whether or not the model was created on your computer or another computer, because the data is part of the model.
Connections	Opens the dialog box shown in Figure 2-13. The options are used to connect to external data sources other than Excel.

Table 2-5 Data menu options explained

This dialog box is not available in Presentation Design.

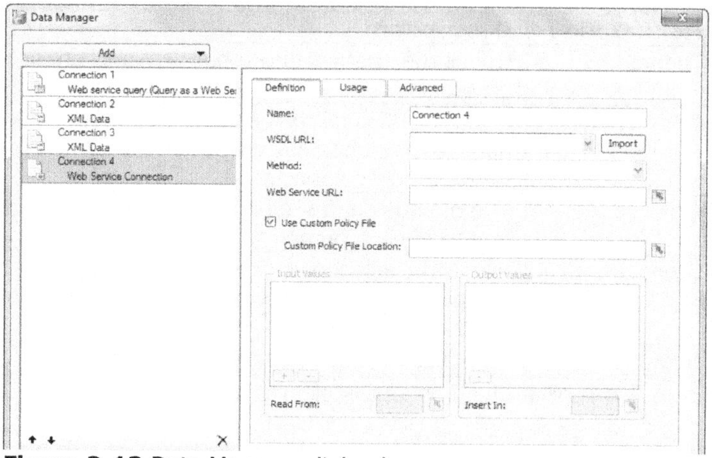

Figure 2-13 Data Manager dialog box

Help Menu

The options on the Help menu provide ways to get assistance, ass a license for the software. The options are explained in Table 2-6.

Option	Description
Dashboard Design Help	Opens the online help file.
Start Page	Displays the Start Page window shown earlier in Figure 2-1.
License Manager	Is used to enter a key code for the software.
About Dashboard Design	Opens the About dialog box, which displays the version number of Dashboard Design that is installed.

Table 2-6 Help menu options explained

The Online Help File

To open the Help file, follow the instructions below.

1. Help ⇒ Dashboard Design Help.

   You will see the window shown in Figure 2-14.

   Each of the tabs (Contents, Index, Search and Favorites) provide help in a different way.

   The **CONTENTS** tab is like a table of contents.

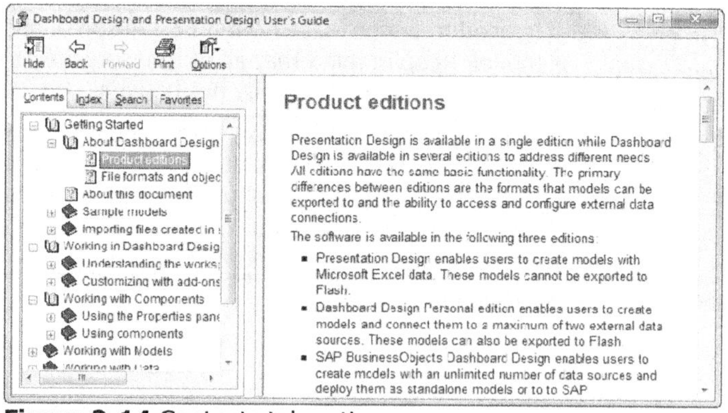

Figure 2-14 Contents tab options

2. Click on the **SEARCH** tab.

   If you type in a keyword on this tab and then click the **LIST TOPICS** button shown in Figure 2-15, you will see a list of topics that relate to the keyword that you typed in.

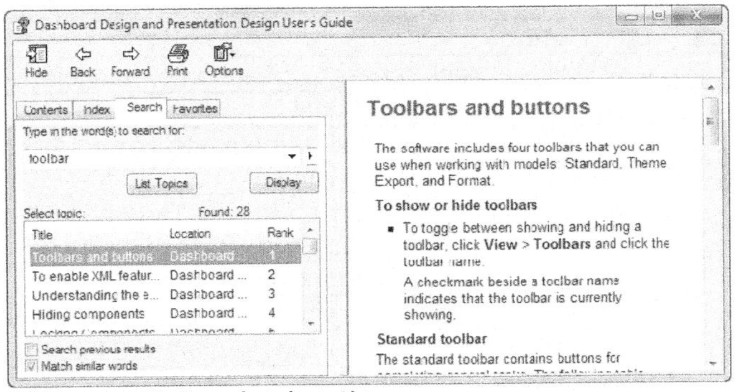

Figure 2-15 Search tab options

Boolean Search Options

The right arrow button after the Search field illustrated in Figure 2-16, is used to create a complex search. This allows for several terms or keywords to be searched for at the same time.

Type in the first keyword that you want to search for, then select one of the Boolean options in the drop-down list illustrated in Figure 2-16.

Type in the next keyword that you want to include (or exclude). Once you have entered all of the keywords, click the **LIST TOPICS** button.

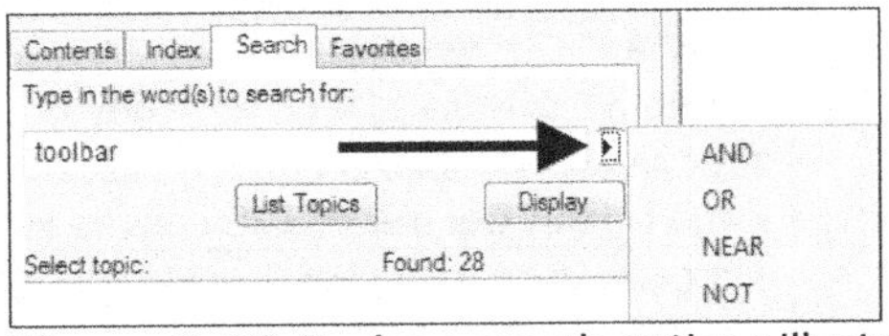

Figure 2-16 Boolean search options illustrated

3. Select the topic that is closest to what you are looking for, then click the **DISPLAY** button or double-click on the topic.

The advantage that the Search tab has over the Index tab is that you do not have to know the exact name or phrase of what you are looking for. You should try using both tabs and see which one gives you the best results.

Toolbars

Dashboard Design has four toolbars, which makes it easier to use many of the menu options. The options on the toolbars are explained in the next few sections.

Standard Toolbar

The toolbar shown in Figure 2-17 contains buttons for the menu options that you will probably use the most. The buttons on the toolbar are a subset of the menu options. Table 2-7 explains the buttons on the toolbar.

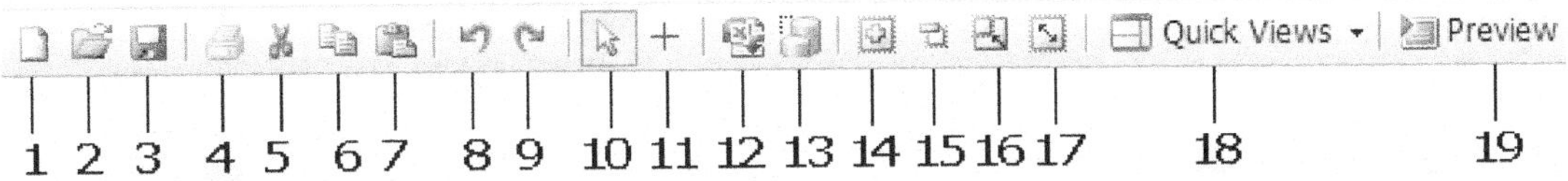

Figure 2-17 Standard toolbar

Button	Description
1	**NEW** Opens a blank canvas to create a new model.
2	**OPEN** Opens an existing model.
3	**SAVE** Saves the open model. If the model has not been saved before, you will be prompted to provide a file name.
4	**PRINT THE SWF FILE** Prints the SWF file. This option is disabled if the computer does not have a printer driver installed. This option is only available in preview mode.
5	**CUT** Deletes the selected components.
6	**COPY** Copies the selected components and places them in the Windows clipboard.
7	**PASTE** Places the components in the clipboard into the model.
8	**UNDO** Undoes the last action.
9	**REDO** Redoes the last action.
10	**SELECTION TOOL** Takes the focus to the selected components.
11	**COMPONENT TOOL** Takes the focus to the Components Browser.
12	**IMPORT SPREADSHEET** Adds the data from an external Excel spreadsheet (in Excel 2003, .xls or Excel 2007 .xlsx format) to the model that is open.
13	**MANAGE CONNECTIONS** Opens the Data Manager dialog box.
14	**INCREASE CANVAS** Makes the canvas size larger each time the button is clicked.
15	**DECREASE CANVAS** Makes the canvas size smaller each time the button is clicked.
16	**FIT CANVAS TO COMPONENTS** Resizes the canvas to the size of the components. Usually, this decreases the canvas size.
17	**FIT CANVAS TO WINDOW** Resizes the canvas to the size of the window. Usually, this increases the canvas size.
18	**CHANGES WINDOWS LAYOUT** (Quick Views button) Is used to select a different workspace view. Clicking this button displays the options shown earlier in Figure 2-10.
19	**TOGGLE PREVIEW MODE** (Preview button) Switches between the **PREVIEW MODE**, which is used for testing and printing the model and the **DESIGN MODE**, which is used to create and modify the model.

Table 2-7 Standard toolbar buttons explained

Themes Toolbar

The options on the toolbar shown in Figure 2-18 are used to modify the appearance of the model. The options were explained earlier. They are covered in detail in Chapter 16.

Figure 2-18 Themes toolbar

Export Toolbar

The options on the toolbar shown in Figure 2-19 are used to export the model. Table 2-8 explains the options on the toolbar.

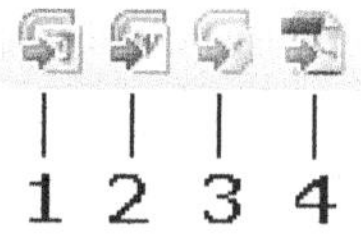

Figure 2-19 Export toolbar

Button	Description
1	**SEND TO POWERPOINT** Exports the model to a PowerPoint slide. (2)
2	**SEND TO MICROSOFT WORD** Exports the model to a Microsoft Word document. (2)

Table 2-8 Export toolbar buttons explained

Button	Description
3	**ATTACH THE SWF IN OUTLOOK** Creates a Flash file, then opens a new email window in Microsoft Outlook and attaches the Flash file to the email.
4	**SEND TO ADOBE ACROBAT PDF** Exports the model to an Adobe PDF file. This option will export the file to Acrobat 9.0 format. The PDF Export Option on the File menu will give you a choice of exporting to Acrobat 9.0 or Acrobat 6.0. (2)

Table 2-8 Export toolbar buttons explained (Continued)

(2) This toolbar button works differently then the same option on the File menu. You will not be prompted (prior to creating the dashboard file) to enter a file name for the dashboard by clicking on this toolbar button, like the File ⇒ Export menu option does. Clicking on this button creates a temporary SWF file, that can be used for testing purposes. Once the file is created, you can use the **SAVE AS** option on the File menu of PowerPoint, Word or Adobe to save the file with the name that you want.

Format Toolbar

The options on the toolbar shown in Figure 2-20 are used to modify the components. Table 2-9 explains the buttons on the toolbar.

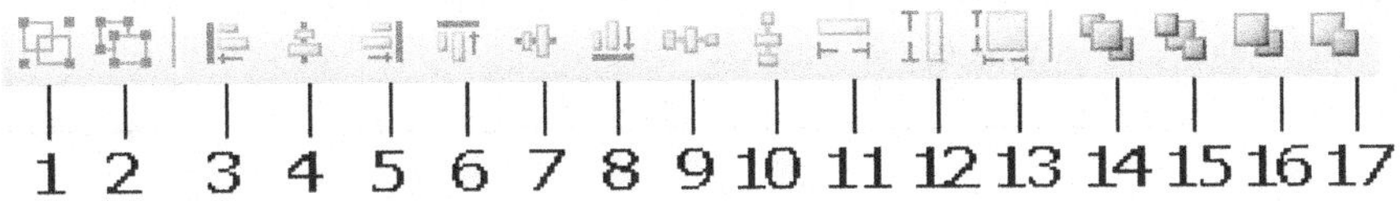

Figure 2-20 Format toolbar

Button	Description
1	**GROUP COMPONENTS** Places the selected components in a folder in the Object Browser, as shown earlier in Figure 2-12.
2	**UNGROUP COMPONENTS** Removes the components from the group.
3	**ALIGN LEFT** Aligns on the left side of the component.
4	**CENTER HORIZONTALLY** Aligns on the center of components horizontally.
5	**ALIGN RIGHT** Aligns on the right side of the component.
6	**ALIGN TOP** Aligns on the top of the component.
7	**CENTER VERTICALLY** Aligns on the middle of components vertically.
8	**ALIGN BOTTOM** Aligns on the bottom of the component.
9	**SPACE EVENLY ACROSS** Adds or removes space between the components from left to right.
10	**SPACE EVENLY DOWN** Adds or removes space between the components from top to bottom.
11	**MAKE SAME WIDTH** Makes the selected components the same width.
12	**MAKE SAME HEIGHT** Makes the selected components the same height.
13	**MAKE SAME SIZE** Makes the selected components the same width and height.
14	**BRING TO FRONT** Moves the selected components to the top layer.
15	**SEND TO BACK** Moves the selected components to the bottom layer.
16	**BRING FORWARD** Moves the selected components up one layer.
17	**SEND BACKWARD** Moves the selected components back one layer.

Table 2-9 Format toolbar buttons explained

File Types

Dashboard Design produces two types of files. Each file type has a different extension, as explained below.

① **.SWF TEMPORARY FILES** This is the model file in a compiled format.

② **.XLF FILES** This is the model file that is used to create the dashboard (also known as the dashboard definition file). XLF stands for **X**ce**L**sius **F**ile.

Temporary Files

Dashboard Design creates a variety of temporary files when data is imported and when models are compiled and previewed. Unfortunately, these files are not automatically deleted when you close the software or turn the computer off like some software packages do. You will have to delete them from the Temp folder on your computers hard drive manually. The location of the temp folder is C:\Users\Your account\AppData\Local\Temp. The majority of temp files end in .swf. Folders like xc_780 are also created that contain temp files. These folders and the files in them can also be deleted. In Xcelsius 2008 and earlier, many of the temp files started with the same first three characters, which made it easier to find the temp files. That feature has been removed, which makes it difficult to find the temp files that can be deleted. I think that it would be a good idea for the software to create one temp folder and place all files in it that can be deleted. This would make it easier for us to know what files can be deleted.

Dashboard Examples

This section discusses three examples of how dashboards can be used to take static data in a spreadsheet and turn it into interactive data in a dashboard.

Dashboard Example #1

Figure 2-21 shows a spreadsheet that has profit margin data for books. The Marketing department has a big book promotion project that they need to get approval for. The Vice President of Marketing asked to see the projected income if the number of copies sold increased by 500, 1,500 and 4,000 copies per region. Having this information would help determine if the book promotion project should be approved. Unless someone in the marketing department is a human calculator, they could not answer this question off the top of their head or while giving a presentation to pitch the promotion project.

If the data shown in Figure 2-21 was turned into the dashboard shown in Figure 2-22, it would be easy to answer what the projected income would be, based on the number of additional copies sold.

That is because the person could use the slider at the bottom of the dashboard to select the number of copies sold (the what-if). Changing the number of copies sold, increases or decreases the profits accordingly.

	A	B	C	D	E	F
1	Profit Margin For New Book			What if this many more books were sold?		
2	Projected Goal - $150,000		$24.95			
3						
4	Region	Qty Sold	Total Sales			
5						
6	North	280	$6,986.00			
7	South	172	$4,291.40			
8	East	397	$9,905.15			
9	West	743	$18,537.85			
10	Other countries	520	$12,974.00			
11						
12			Total Sales	$52,694.40		

Figure 2-21 Profit margin spreadsheet

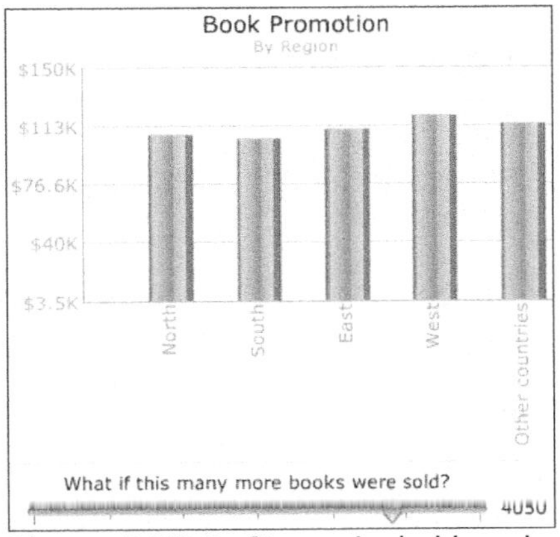

Figure 2-22 Profit margin dashboard

Dashboard Example #2

Figure 2-23 shows the revenues for five products that are sold in five parts of the world. A column chart like the one shown above in Figure 2-22 could be used to display all of the product data in the Revenues By Product spreadsheet at one time. A better solution in my opinion, would be to create five different charts, one for each region.

I know what you may be thinking. You are thinking that displaying five charts on the dashboard at the same time is too much. If that is what you are thinking, you are correct. Rather than display all five charts at one time on the dashboard, a menu could be added. The options on the menu shown in Figure 2-24 allow the user to click on a button to display the data for one region. Figure 2-24 shows the data for Latin America. Figure 2-25 shows the data for Asia.

	A	B	C	D	E	F	G
1	Revenues By Product		Rev				
2							
3		Status List	Prod. A	Prod. B	Prod. C	Prod. D	Prod. E
4	North America		$ 14.22	$ 20.12	$ 12.18	$ 25.49	$ 15.64
5	Latin America		$ 21.05	$ 19.54	$ 15.88	$ 18.73	$ 15.02
6	Europe		$ 21.06	$ 20.45	$ 14.49	$ 16.78	$ 13.61
7	Asia		$ 12.25	$ 17.12	$ 20.99	$ 16.79	$ 12.07
8	Australia & Pacific		$ 15.36	$ 25.74	$ 13.17	$ 19.42	$ 12.70

Figure 2-23 Revenues By Product spreadsheet

Figure 2-24 Latin America Revenues By Product dashboard

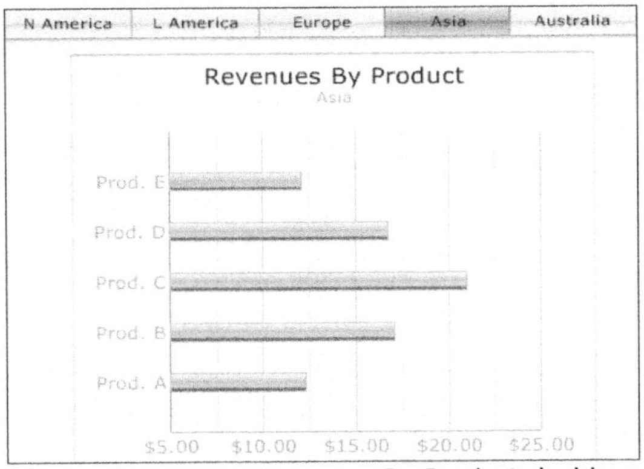

Figure 2-25 Asia Revenues By Product dashboard

Dashboard Example #3

1. Open Dashboard Design if it is not already open.

2. File ⇒ Samples. Click on the **USER GUIDE SAMPLES** category. Select the **ALERTS-SINGLE VALUES** option, then click OK.

The dashboard shown in Figure 2-26 allows the user to select a different dollar amount for three line items (sales, inventories and cost of goods sold) in the budget. The three colors on each gauge represent whether or not the forecast number is acceptable. Forecast numbers that are in the red section of the **GAUGE** component are not acceptable.

Numbers in the yellow section indicate that caution should be noted. Numbers in the green section are an acceptable forecast amount for the line item. Notice that the needle on each gauge changes color. To change the value on the gauge, use the sliders at the bottom of the dashboard. Can you believe that the dashboard shown in Figure 2-26 was created from the data in the spreadsheet shown in Figure 2-27?

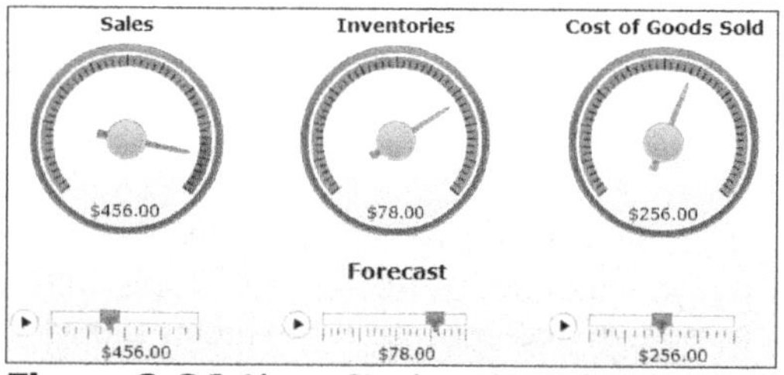

Figure 2-26 Alerts Single Values dashboard

	A	B		C		D	
1	Summary Report						
2	Corporate Health Measures						
3							
4			Sales		Inventories		Cost of Goods Sold
5	Actual Value	$	456.00	$	78.00	$	256.00
6	Target	$	435.00	$	54.00	$	220.00

Figure 2-27 Alerts Single Values spreadsheet

Formatting Options

There are four main ways that components can be formatted. The options are at the top of the Format menu shown in Figure 2-28. The Space Evenly option requires that at least three components be selected on the model. As you can see, each formatting option on the menu has a right arrow which means that there is a submenu of options. Tables 2-10 to 2-13 explain the options on each submenu.

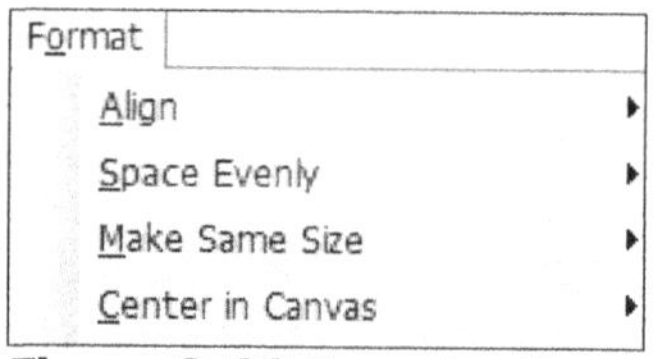

Figure 2-28 Format options

> When multiple components are selected, they are aligned or resized based on the first component that is selected.

Align Option	Aligns On The . . .
Left	Left side of the component.
Center	Center of components horizontally.
Right	Right side of the component.
Top	Top of the component.
Middle	Middle of components vertically.
Bottom	Bottom of the component.

Table 2-10 Align options explained

Space Evenly Option	Adds Or Removes Space Between The Components From . . .
Across	Left to right.
Down	Top to bottom.

Table 2-11 Space Evenly options explained

Make Same Size Option	Makes The Selected Components The Same . . .
Width	Width.
Height	Height.
Both	Width and height.

Table 2-12 Make Same Size options explained

Center Option	Centers The Component Between The . . .
Vertically	Top and bottom margins of the canvas vertically, where it is in the model. The component will not be moved left or right.
Horizontally	Left and right margins of the canvas horizontally, where it is in the model. The component will not be moved up or down.
Both	Top and bottom margins of the canvas vertically and the left and right margins horizontally.

Table 2-13 Center in Canvas options explained

The **CENTER IN CANVAS** options explained above in Table 2-13 do not move the components to the center of the model.

Order Options

The options shown in Figure 2-29 are used to rearrange the order of the components. Layers are invisible and are automatically created when components are stacked on top of each other on the canvas. These options are used to change the components position in the stack.

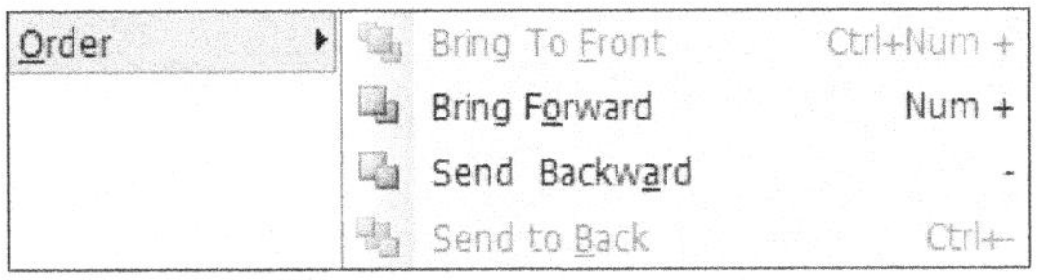

Figure 2-29 Order options

The only order option shown above in Figure 2-29 that I use is Send To Back, to place a background component behind the other components. Table 2-14 explains the order options.

Option	Moves The Selected Components . . .
Bring To Front	To the top layer.
Bring Forward	Up one layer, closer to the top.
Send Backward	Back one layer, closer to the bottom.
Send To Back	To the bottom layer.

Table 2-14 Order submenu options explained

Selecting Components

You will spend a lot of time selecting components on the canvas to create the perfect dashboard. Like many features, there is more than one way to select components on the canvas, as explained in the next two sections.

Selecting A Single Component

To select a single component on the canvas, click on it with the left mouse button.

When selected, you will see a (blue) frame around it, as illustrated in Figure 2-30. You will also see squares on the frame. These squares are called **RESIZE HANDLES**. They are used to change the size of the component to make it wider, longer, shorter or smaller.

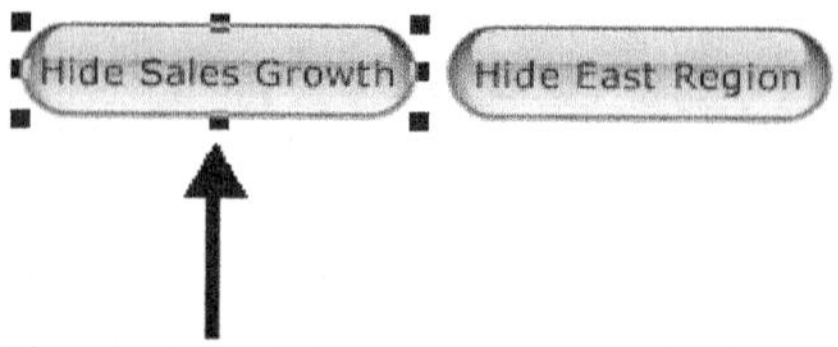

Figure 2-30 Component selected and resize handles illustrated

Selecting Multiple Components

There will probably be times when you need to apply the same option or formatting to more than one component in the model. A lot of the editing that you will do requires multiple components to be selected. There are two primary ways to select multiple components on the canvas, as explained below.

① Click on one component. Press and hold down the **CTRL** key, then click on the other components that you need to select.

② Draw what is called a **MARQUEE** or **LASSO** around the components with the mouse, as shown in Figure 2-31. To do this successfully, the components need to be near each other, either side by side or up and down from each other. To use this technique, no components can already be selected. Click outside of the first component. Hold the left mouse button down and draw around the components that you need to select. You will see a frame being drawn. When you are finished selecting the components and release the mouse button, you will see that several components have been selected.

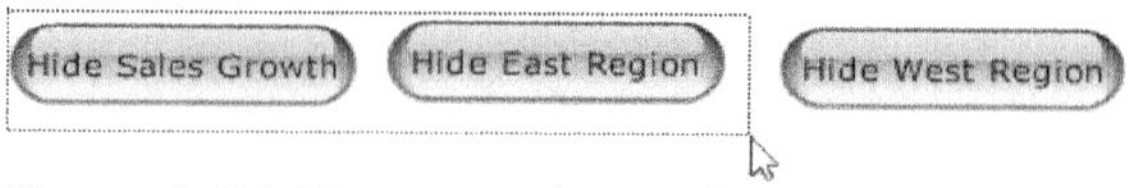

Figure 2-31 Marquee or lasso effect

Nudging Components

So far in this chapter you have learned how to move and resize components using the mouse. You can also move and resize components using the keyboard and touchpad. This is helpful if you use a laptop and do not use a mouse. Using the keyboard and touchpad to move or resize components is known as **NUDGING**.

How To Move A Component By Nudging It

1. Without using the mouse, select the component that you want to move.

2. Use one of the four arrow keys on the keyboard to move the component in the direction that you need to reposition it.

EXPLORING THE WORKSPACE

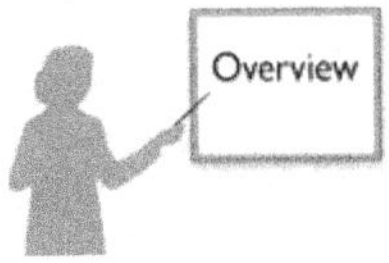

In this chapter you will learn more about the workspace by learning about the following features:

- ☑ Components Browser
- ☑ Object Browser
- ☑ Resize parts of the workspace
- ☑ Canvas Properties panel
- ☑ Docking panels
- ☑ Quick Views
- ☑ Preferences
- ☑ Printing dashboards
- ☑ Print Preview options
- ☑ Copy and paste components between models
- ☑ The built-in spreadsheet
- ☑ Importing models from previous versions of the software

CHAPTER 3

The Workspace

Chapter 2 covered the basics of the workspace. Because you will spend a lot of time pointing and clicking your way around the workspace, this chapter provides in-depth coverage of the workspace.

Components Browser

This is one of the most used tools in Dashboard Design. This tool contains the objects, which are called components, that are added to the canvas to create a dashboard. Each tab groups and displays the companies differently. If you are using Presentation Design, you will not see all of the folders and components shown in Figures 3-1 and 3-2.

Category View

As shown in Figure 3-1, the components are organized by category. They are grouped by their functionality. (1)

Tree View

Like the Category view, the components are organized by category and are grouped by functionality, as shown in Figure 3-2. (1)

The only difference between the Category and Tree views is that the Category view shows what the component looks like.

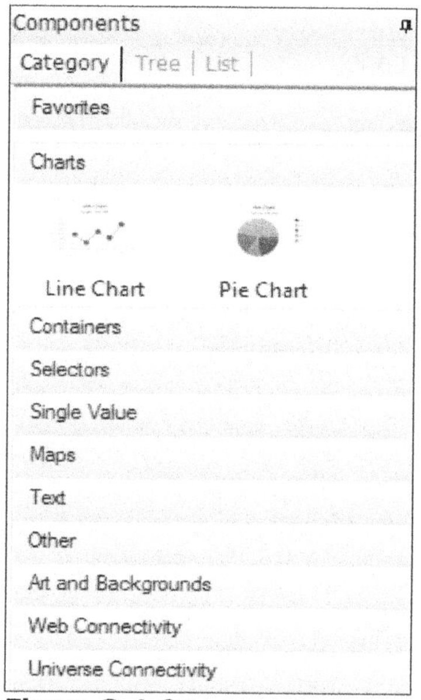

Figure 3-1 Category view

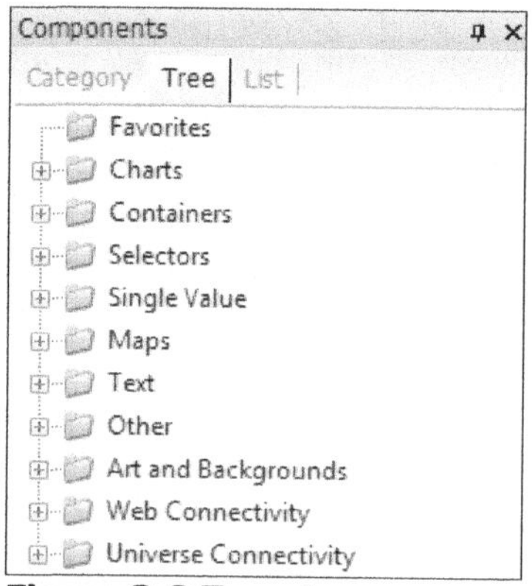

Figure 3-2 Tree view

(1) This view has the Add-Ons category. It contains the Add-ons that have been installed through the Add-On Manager dialog box. [See Chapter 2, Figure 2-9]

List View

If you do not want to memorize which folder a component is in, click on the **LIST** tab at the top of the Components Browser.

The components are listed in alphabetical order on this tab, as shown in Figure 3-3. You can scroll down the list to find the component that you want to use or you can click any place in the window, then type the first letter of the component to display that part of the list.

I personally think that this view would be more effective if the maps were not included or if they were at the bottom of the list.

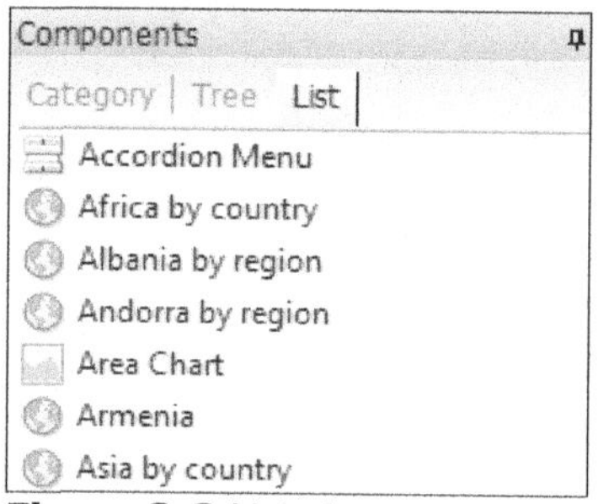

Figure 3-3 List view

Favorites Section

If there are components that you use on a regular basis, you can add them to the Favorites section of the Components Browser. The List View does not have the Favorites section.

To add a component to the Favorites section, right-click on it and select **ADD TO FAVORITES**, as shown in Figure 3-4. You will see the component in the Favorites section shown in Figure 3-5. To delete a component from the Favorites section, right-click on it and select **REMOVE FROM FAVORITES**.

Figure 3-4 Add To Favorites option

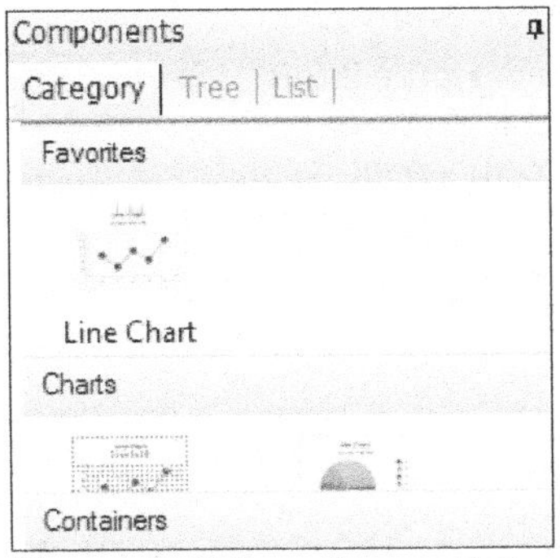

Figure 3-5 Favorites section

Components Browser Tab Shortcut Menu

If you right-click on any tab on the Component Browser, you will see the shortcut menu shown in Figure 3-6.

The options are used to display or hide a part of the workspace.

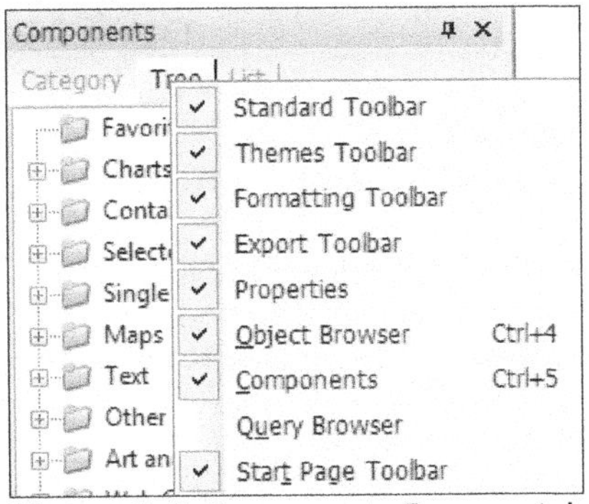

Figure 3-6 Components Browser tab shortcut menu

Object Browser

When you display a model, the Object Browser opens by default. It contains all of the components that have been added to the model. The order that components are added to the canvas is the order that they appear in the Object Browser. The Object Browser window is used to perform a variety of tasks like selecting, grouping, renaming or hiding components. If you want to keep this window from opening each time that you open the software, close the Object Browser window, then close the software. When you reopen the software, the Object Browser window will not open.

Selecting Components In The Object Browser

Below are two ways to select a component in the Object Browser.

① To **SELECT ONE COMPONENT** in the model, click on the icon or component name. You will see a frame around the component in the model.

② To **SELECT MORE THAN ONE COMPONENT**, click on the first component that you need, then press and hold down the CTRL key and click on the other components that you need to select. If the components that you want to select are next to each other, you can click on the first component, press and hold down the SHIFT key, then click on the last component that you want to select. Usually, the reason to select multiple components is because you need to make the same change to all of the selected components, like making all charts the same size or deleting all of the labels.

Object Browser Shortcut Menu

The shortcut menu shown in Figure 3-7 is the same shortcut menu that is available when you right-click on a component on the canvas.

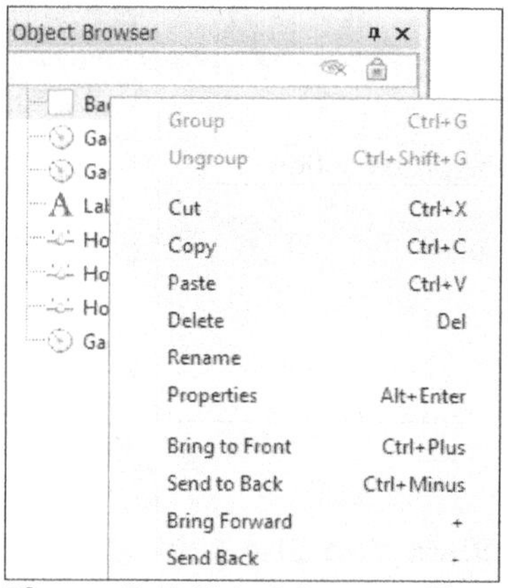

Figure 3-7 Object Browser Shortcut menu

Object Browser Features

The more popular tasks that can be accomplished in the Object Browser are explained below.

① **DELETING MULTIPLE COMPONENTS AT ONE TIME** Select all of the components that you want to delete, then press the Delete key or select Delete on the shortcut menu.

② **HIDING COMPONENTS** Clicking in the Hide column across from the component, will hide the component on the canvas. This may be useful if there are a lot of components on the canvas and you need more space to work. Hidden components are displayed when the model is previewed or exported.

③ **RENAMING COMPONENTS** The component names in the Object Browser shown in Figure 3-8 are the default component names that are automatically assigned when a component is added to the canvas. This is the same name that appears at the top of the Properties panel. If the dashboard only has a few components, using the default component names may not be such a bad thing.

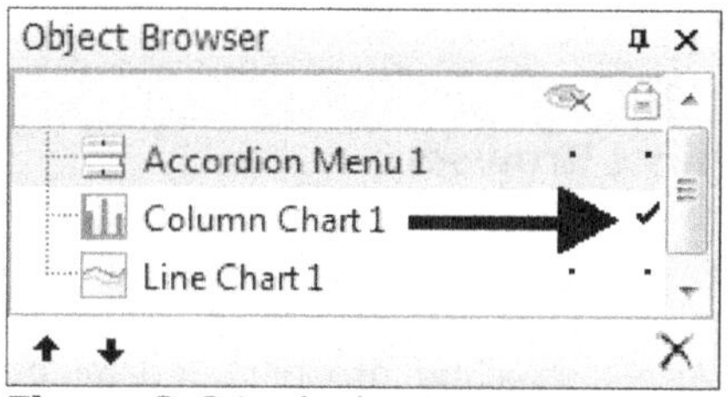

Figure 3-8 Locked component

If there are several of the same component in the model, it will be difficult to know which component is which. In that case, renaming the components is a good idea.

④ **LOCKING COMPONENTS** This option is used to lock components and groups so that they can only be selected from the Object Browser. To lock a component or group, click in the Lock column across from the component. You will see a check mark, as illustrated above in Figure 3-8.

⑤ **GROUPING COMPONENTS** While all types of components can be grouped, the best reasons that I can think of to group components is because they are the same component type and you need to change their properties. When you make a property change, it is changed for all of the components in the group. The other reason is for setting up Dynamic Visibility functionality.

Another reason to group components is if you will have the need to move several components at the same time. An example of this would be a dashboard that has several toggle buttons. The buttons may currently be at the top of the dashboard, but they now need to be moved to the bottom of the dashboard. You do not have to select each toggle button component individually. You can select the group, which allows all of the components in the group to be moved at the same time.

To group components, select the components that you want to group, then right-click on one of the selected components and select **GROUP**. When components are grouped, they appear in a group folder in a tree structure, like the one shown in Chapter 2, Figure 2-12. As you can see in the figure, the default group name does not indicate anything about the components in the group. You can change the group name by following the steps in the Renaming Components section below.

You do not have to group components in order to change an option for several components at one time. You can select all of the components on the canvas that you need to modify before opening the Properties panel.

The **QUICK START** panel that was available in Xcelsius 2008 has been removed.

Renaming Components

If there are several of the same type of component in the model, it will be confusing to know which component is which, when looking at them in the Object Browser. One time that I can think of when renaming components is a good idea is when you need to place several of the same type of component on top of each other in the model. An example would be if you had three charts and based on a condition, a different chart would be displayed. If this is the case, without moving the components around on the canvas, you have no way to access the second or third component because they are covered up. To rename a component that is not marked as hidden in the Object Browser, follow the steps below.

1. Right-click on the component name and select Rename on the shortcut menu.

2. Type in the new name, then press Enter.

How To Resize The Properties Panel, Components Browser Or Object Browser

You may have the need to change the size of one of these windows. To make the window wider, place the mouse pointer on the right edge of the window. The mouse pointer is in the right place when you see the arrow illustrated on the right side of Figure 3-9.

Drag the mouse pointer in the direction that you want to resize the window to.

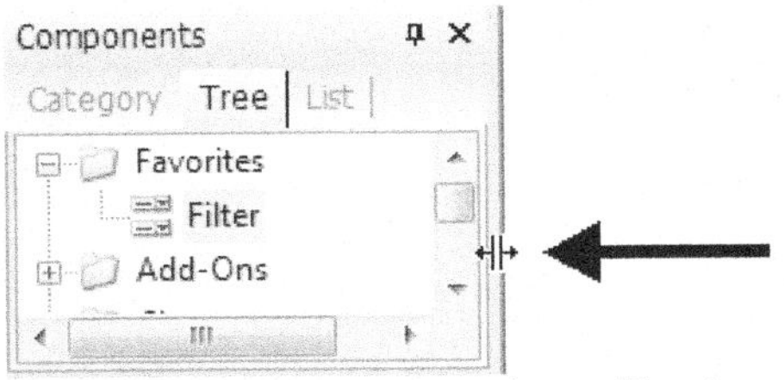

Figure 3-9 Mouse pointer in position to resize the window

If you want to make the window shorter or longer, place the mouse pointer at the top or bottom of the window, then drag the mouse pointer in the direction that you want to resize the window.

Resize The Canvas

In Chapter 2, you learned two ways (Fit canvas to components and Fit canvas to the window) to resize the canvas. When you read about the options, you learned about the Document Properties dialog box. It can be used to change the canvas size, either by selecting a preset size, modifying a preset size or selecting a width and height to create a custom size for the dashboard.

While you are creating and editing a model, the amount of space that it takes up on the canvas is not a problem because the larger it is, the easier it is to work with. Without giving it much thought, you would probably export it at the size that it currently is. I know that you do not know me, but with dashboards, size does matter! <smile>

When exporting a model, the entire canvas is exported, whether the components are using all of the space on the canvas or not. Usually, this is not what you want or need to happen. Mainly because it is more difficult to position and resize the SWF file inside of another file, like in a PowerPoint slide. In some cases, you cannot resize the SWF file that is embedded in another file, like in a PDF file.

If you exported any of the models that you create in this book to Word or PowerPoint, you will see what I am talking about. Often, you will find that the size of the final product is too small and when you try to resize the dashboard, you will see that the frame around it is an inch or more away from the dashboard. That is why it is very difficult to resize the dashboard the way that you need to. I have found it easier to always include the steps below for every model right before it is exported to a dashboard format.

1. Make sure that all components are the correct size and in the right location in the model.

2. With the model open, click the **FIT CANVAS TO COMPONENTS** button on the toolbar, then save the changes.

Figure 3-10 shows a dashboard that has been exported to Word without resizing the canvas. As you can see, it is small.

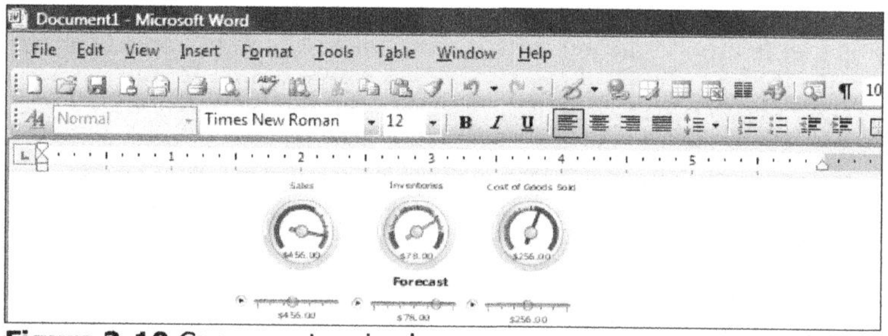

Figure 3-10 Canvas not resized

Figure 3-11 shows the same dashboard exported to Word after the Fit canvas to components option was applied. The dashboard in Figure 3-11 is easier to read.

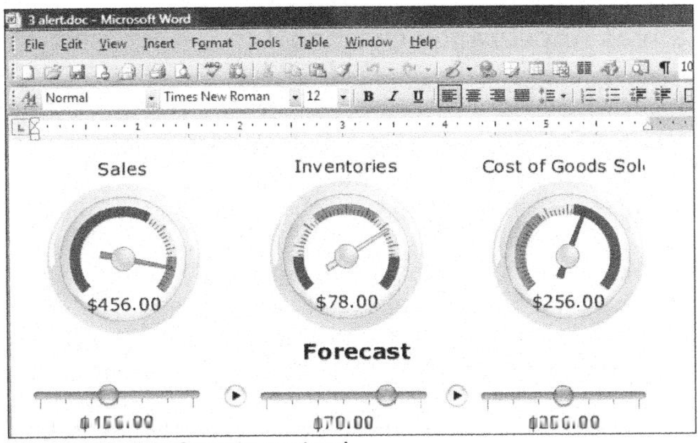

Figure 3-11 Canvas resized

Specific Size Dashboards

If the dashboard has to be a specific size for any reason, like having to accommodate a specific screen size like 14 inches, instead of 21 inches, the Fit canvas to components option may not work. Instead, use the **FIT CANVAS TO WINDOW** option or one of the options on the Document Properties dialog box.

Canvas Properties Panel

The options on this panel are used to change the background of the canvas. It uses the same window as the Properties panel, which is used to customize the components. The Canvas Properties panel is only available when no components are selected on the canvas.

To enable the canvas properties, click on a blank space on the canvas. There are four appearance types that you can select from: Solid Color, Gradient, Image and None. They are explained below.

Solid Color Canvas Appearance Options

Figure 3-12 shows the solid color appearance options.

BACKGROUND COLOR The default background color is white. You can select a different color by clicking on the Color selector button that is illustrated.

The color that you select will be the background color surrounding the components in the model and will be applied when the dashboard is created.

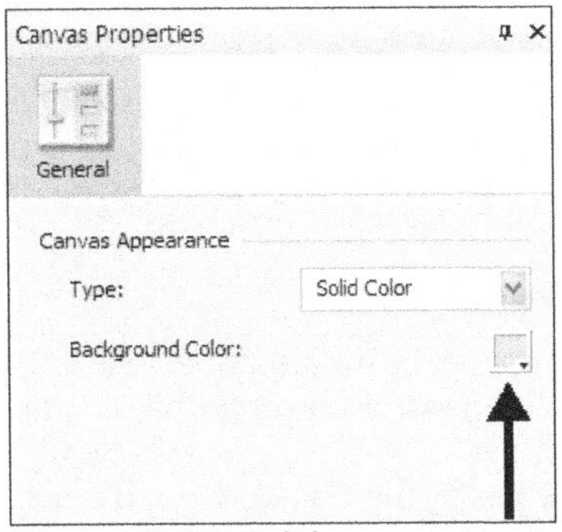

Figure 3-12 Solid canvas appearance color options

Gradient Canvas Appearance Options

Figure 3-13 shows the gradient appearance options.

BACKGROUND COLOR 1 Is used to select the background color that will be displayed at the top of the canvas. This color gets lighter towards the middle of the canvas.

BACKGROUND COLOR 2 Is used to select the background color that will be displayed from the middle of the canvas to the bottom of the canvas. This color starts off light at the top and gets darker at the bottom of the canvas.

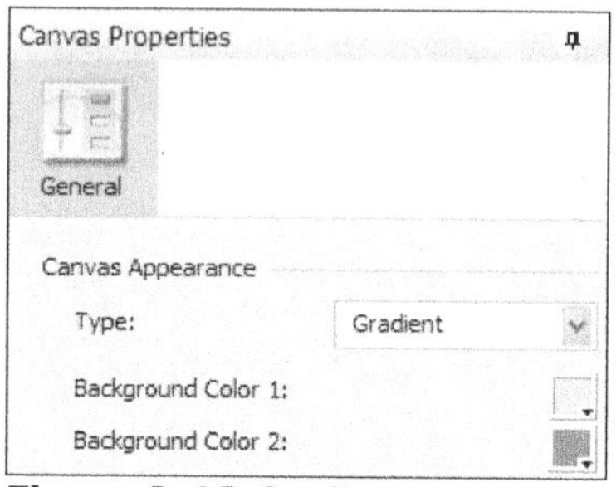

Figure 3-13 Gradient canvas appearance color options

Image Canvas Appearance Options

Figure 3-14 shows the image appearance options.

If you want to use an image as the background for the canvas, click the **IMPORT** button.

You can select an image file that is in one of the following formats: **.JPG**, **.PNG**, **.GIF** or **.BMP**.

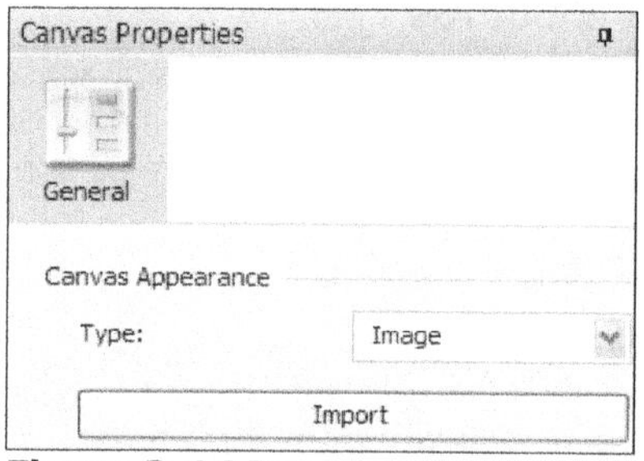

Figure 3-14 Image canvas appearance color options

None Canvas Appearance Option

Selecting None from the Type drop-down list shown above in Figure 3-14 creates a transparent background for the dashboard.

Docking Panels

The feature is helpful if you need more canvas space to create dashboards. The Properties panel, Components Browser, Query Browser and Object Browser panels can be docked, which will provide more canvas space. By default, these windows are docked.

How To Dock A Panel

If you want to dock a panel or dock a panel in a different location, follow the steps below. These steps use the Components Browser panel, but the steps work for the other panels also.

1. Click on the Title Bar of the Components Browser.

2. Drag the panel to the right side of the workspace, as shown in Figure 3-15. Below the panel you should see arrows, as shown at the bottom of Figure 3-15. Each arrow represents a dockable section of the workspace. If you see a fifth arrow, as shown in the right corner of the figure, that means that is the closest dockable section in the workspace.

3. To select the dockable area of the fifth arrow, drag the panel over to the fifth arrow. The panel is in the right place when you see a shaded background, as shown in Figure 3-16.

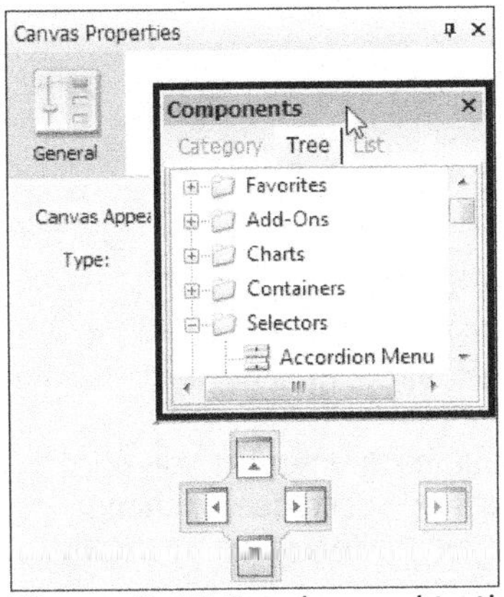

Figure 3-15 Panel moved to the right

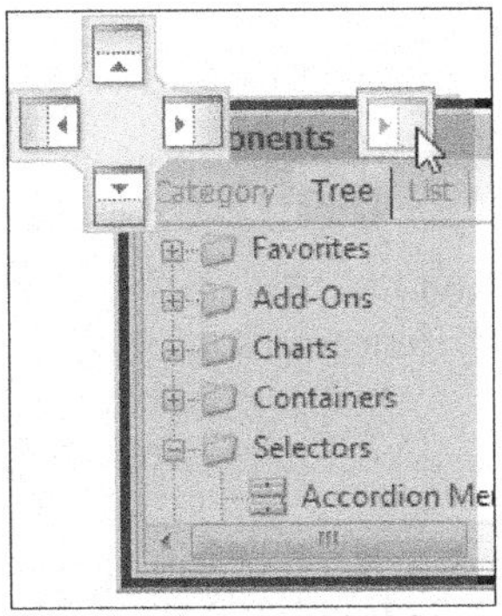

Figure 3-16 Dockable section selected

4. Release the mouse button. The panel will now be in a new location, as shown in Figure 3-17.

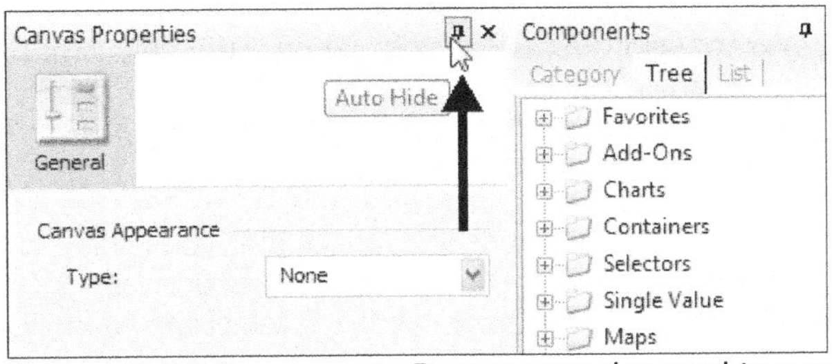

Figure 3-17 Components Browser panel moved to a new dockable location

Using The Auto Hide Option

This option is used to display and hide panels on the workspace.

Clicking the **AUTO HIDE** icon illustrated above in Figure 3-17 will hide the window and place a button for it on the border of the workspace, as illustrated in Figure 3-18.

Using the Auto Hide option provides a lot more space for the canvas. To display one of the windows, click the button for it.

If you decide that you do not want a panel to be hidden automatically, click the Auto Hide button shown above in Figure 3-17. This option works with the components, Object Browser, Properties and Query Browser panels.

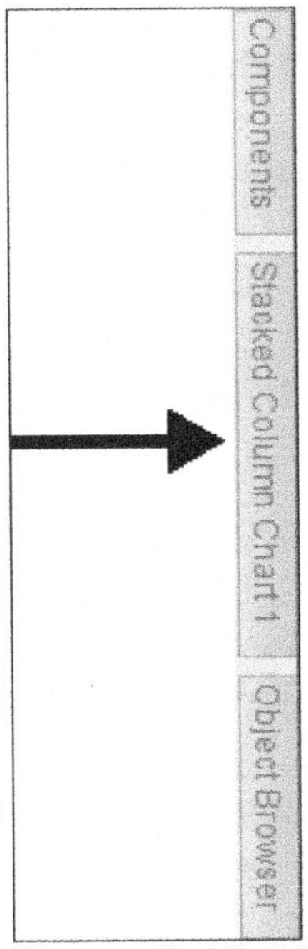

Figure 3-18 Windows with the Auto Hide option enabled

Quick Views

The options shown in Figure 3-19 are used to select a different layout for the workspace.

These options can also be accessed from the View menu. Each option provides a different workspace view, as explained below.

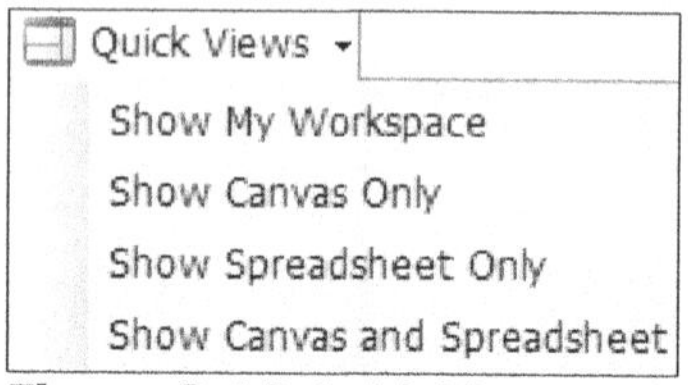

Figure 3-19 Quick Views options

① **MY WORKSPACE** This is the view that will be displayed by default each time that you open Dashboard Design. If the other three views do not meet your workspace needs, change the workspace layout to meet your needs. The changes that you make will automatically be saved to the My Workspace view, the next time that you close the software.

② **CANVAS ONLY** Select this option if the only item that you want to see on the workspace is the canvas. (2)

③ **SPREADSHEET ONLY** Select this option if the only item that you want to see on the workspace is the spreadsheet. (2)

④ **CANVAS AND SPREADSHEET** Select this option if you want to see the canvas and spreadsheet. (2)

(2) This view is preconfigured, which means that you cannot change it. By default, this option does not display the Properties panel, Components Browser or Object Browser. If you select this view and want to view any of these windows, select the window from the View menu.

Preferences

The options on the Preferences dialog box are used to modify the workspace and configure global preferences. File ⇒ Preferences, opens the Preferences dialog box. Unlike the options on the Document Properties dialog box, which are only for the current model, the options on the Preferences dialog box are global. They effect the current model and all future models that you create, until an option is changed again.

Document Options

The options shown in Figure 3-20 are used to select the default canvas size, theme and color scheme.

Canvas Size Options

The options in this section are used to select the default canvas size. These options do not change the model that you currently have open, or any existing models. These options are only for models that you create after the canvas size change is saved.

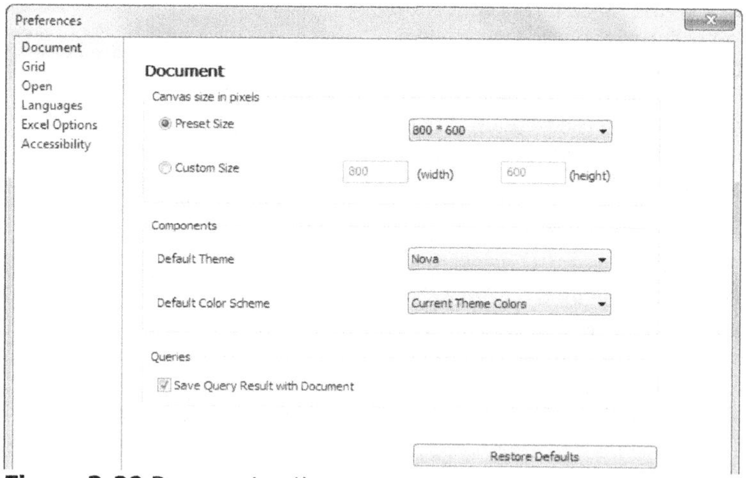

Figure 3-20 Document options

PRESET SIZE The options in this drop-down list are standard sizes for dashboards. If the size that you need is in the drop-down list, select it.

CUSTOM SIZE Is used to enter the width and height for the canvas.

Components Options

The options in this section are used to select the theme and color scheme that you want applied to new models that you create.

The **RESTORE DEFAULTS** button is helpful if you have saved changes, but do not like the changes and cannot remember what the default options are on the dialog box. Clicking this button will restore the options to what they were when the software was first installed.

Queries Options

The **SAVE QUERY RESULT WITH DOCUMENT** option is used to save the data from the query with the model.

Grid Options

The options shown in Figure 3-21 are used to customize the grid that can be displayed on the canvas.

Figure 3-21 Grid options

Using The Grid

Selecting options on the dialog box shown above in Figure 3-21 can help align components on the canvas. When you need to have greater precision over lining up objects on a model then doing it manually provides, you can enable the **SHOW GRID** option.

When components are added to the canvas and the **SNAP TO GRID** option is enabled, the components are automatically placed on the closest grid position to where you release the mouse button.

View ⇒ Grid, will display the grid on the model, as shown in Figure 3-22.

The grid is the line pattern in the background. The smaller the number that is entered in the **WIDTH** and **HEIGHT** options on the Preferences dialog box, the smaller the grid will be.

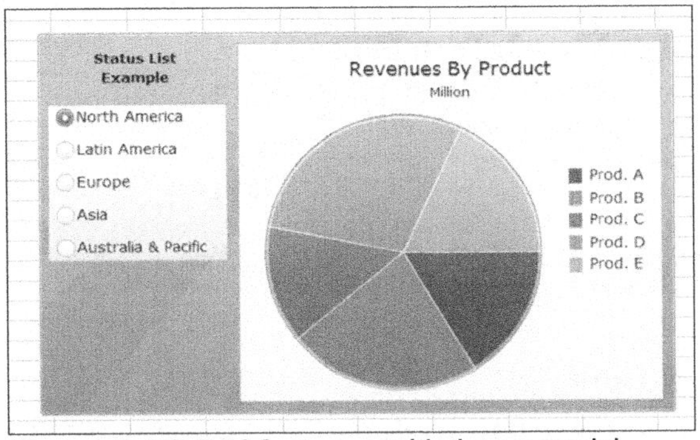

Figure 3-22 Grid feature enabled on a model

> When the Snap To Grid option is enabled, even if you do not display the grid on the canvas, components are still automatically placed on the closest grid position.

Open Options

The options shown in Figure 3-23 are used to select the default folder that will automatically be opened when the Open button (on the Standard toolbar) is clicked or the File ⇒ Open, menu option is selected.

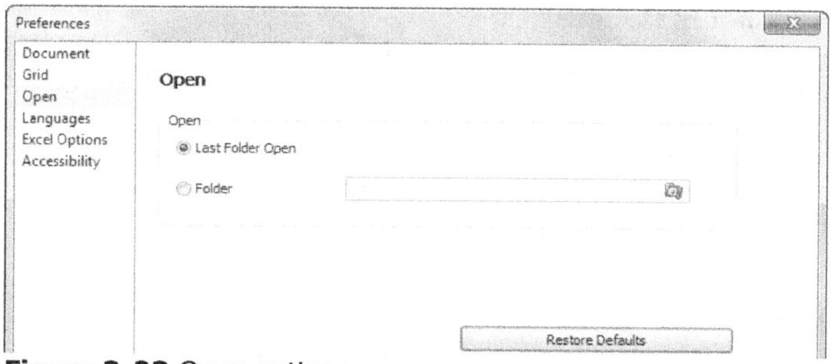

Figure 3-23 Open options

LAST FOLDER OPEN This is the default open option. Currently, the folder that opens is the folder that you created. If you opened a different folder, it would become the default folder that is opened if this is the Open option that is selected.

FOLDER Select this option if you want to always have the same folder open every time that you click the Open button on the toolbar, regardless of the last folder that was opened. Click on the icon at the end of the field to select a folder.

Languages Options

The option shown in Figure 3-24 is used to select a different language that the workspace will use. If the drop-down list is not enabled, it means that only one language was selected during the installation process.

If you need to use a language that is not in the **CURRENT LANGUAGE** drop-down list, you will have to uninstall Dashboard Design and re-install it. During the installation process, select the language that you need to use.

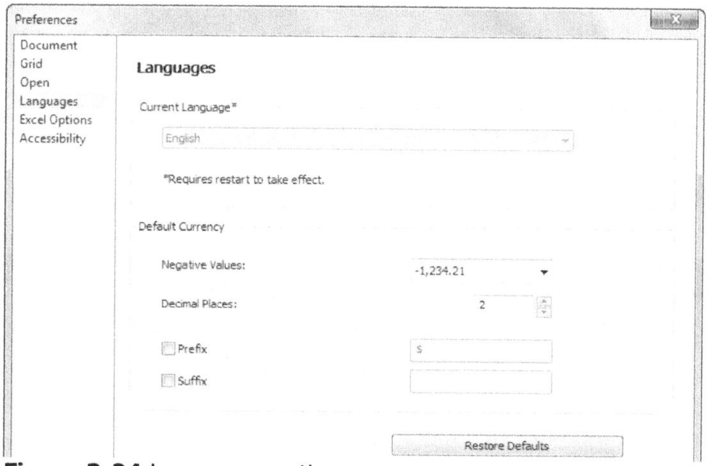

Figure 3-24 Languages options

The options in the Default currency section are used to select how you want currency values in the spreadsheet to be formatted.

Excel Options

The first option shown in Figure 3-25 is used to enable **LIVE OFFICE COMPATIBILITY**.

The **MAXIMUM NUMBER OF ROWS** option is used to select the maximum number of rows that can be bound to a component.

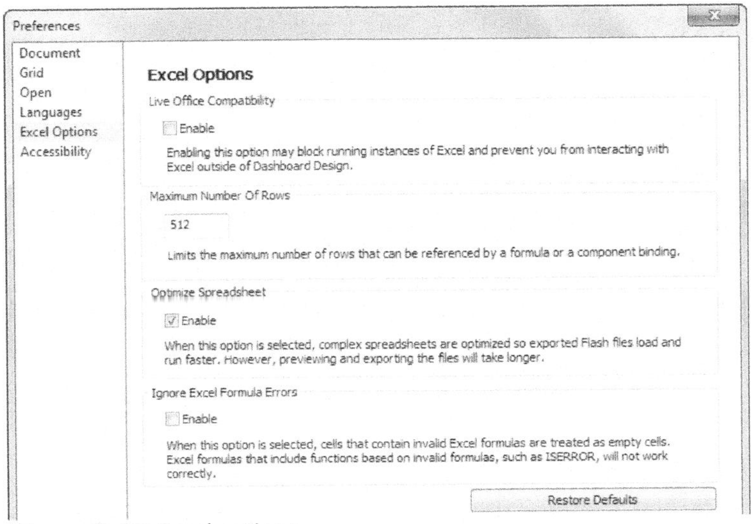

Figure 3-25 Excel options

If the model has a lot of components that are bound to 700 rows of data for example, the Maximum number of rows option would need to be increased. The recommendation is 512 rows or less, which is the default. The larger the number, the longer it will take for the model to open. If more than 512 rows of data are bound, you may see a warning message.

> **Excel Warning Messages**
> If your operating system is Windows 7 and you get Excel related errors, try turning off the **USER ACCOUNT CONTROL (UAC)** option in Windows, by following the steps below.

1. Open the Control Panel in Windows, then select the User Accounts option.
2. Select the Change User Account Control Settings option, then slide the bar down to Never.
3. Click OK, then close the Control Panel.

> **Excel Is Busy Message**
> The message shown in Figure 3-26 appears in Dashboard Design, when Excel is busy. Check to see if Excel is open by following the steps below.
> 1. Open the Task Manager in Windows by pressing the CTRL+ALT+DEL keys, while Dashboard Design is open.
> 2. On the Applications tab, look for Excel, as shown in Figure 3-27. If it's there, select it, then click the End Task button.
> 3. On the Processes tab, look for the Excel.exe, as shown in Figure 3-28. Select it, then click the End Process button.
>
> I had this problem when I used Windows Vista and Xcelsius 2008. With Windows 7 and Dashboard Design 2011, so far I have not had this issue, but decided to leave this section in the book in case someone does have the problem.

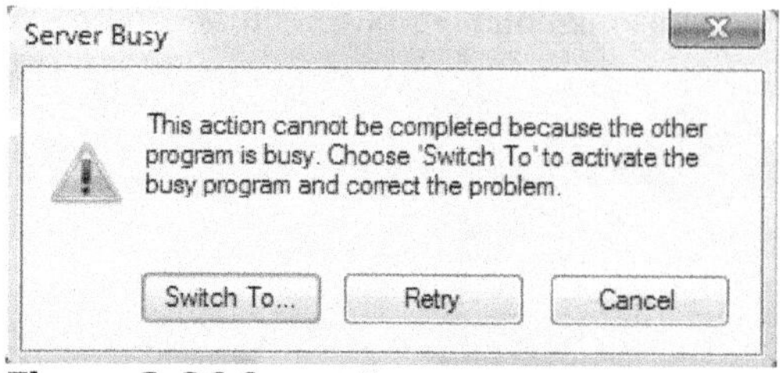

Figure 3-26 Server Busy message

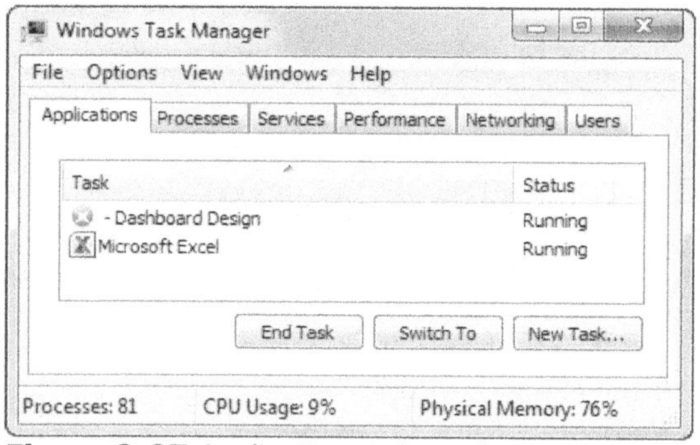

Figure 3-27 Applications tab on the Task Manager dialog box

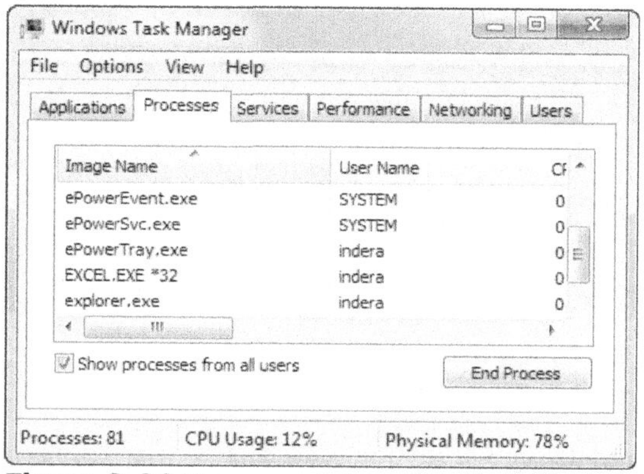

Figure 3-28 Processes tab on the Task Manager dialog box

NEW Accessibility Options

The options shown in Figure 3-29 are used to hide the **SWF** content like security options from applications like speech recognition software.

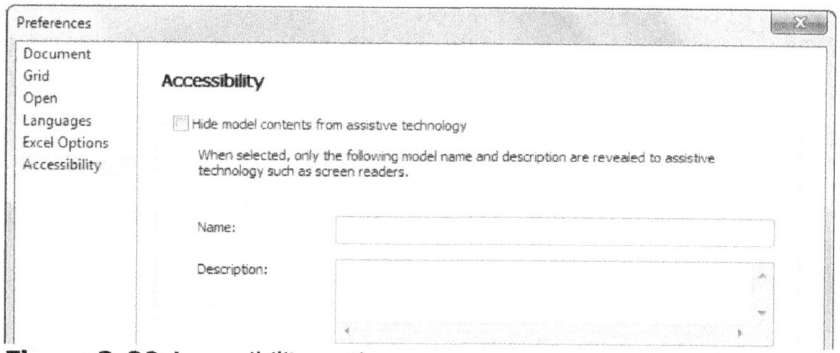

Figure 3-29 Accessibility options

Printing Dashboards

The File ⇒ Print option is used to print a copy of the model. You have to preview the model to enable the print option. Clicking the Print button or selecting the Print option on the File menu opens the Print dialog box. Select the printer and any printer options that you need before sending the model to the printer.

Print Preview

The File ⇒ Print Preview option is used to preview the model, as shown in Figure 3-30, as it will look when printed.

You have to preview the model to enable the Print Preview option.

If you want to print the model from this window, click the Print button on the toolbar in the Print Preview window.

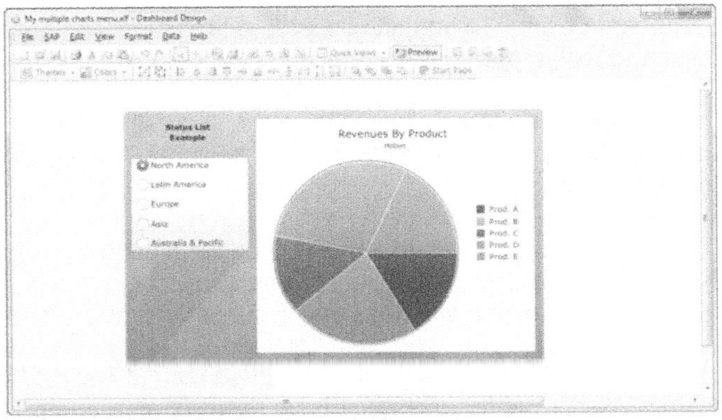

Figure 3-30 Print Preview window

Copy And Paste Components

This feature is used to copy a component (that you have configured) from one model to another. References on the Properties panel are retained if possible. In my opinion, this feature is really only useful when the model that you are copying the component to has the same or similar data as the model that you are copying the component from. Follow the steps below to copy a component from model to another.

1. Open the model that has the component that you want to copy.
2. Right-click on the component and select copy.
3. Open the existing model or a new model that you want to paste the component in.
4. Right-click in the model from step 3 and select Paste.

Using The Built In Spreadsheet

In addition to displaying imported data, the **EMBEDDED SPREADSHEET** illustrated at the bottom of the workspace shown in Figure 3-31 can be used to create, edit and delete data, instead of having to re-import the Excel spreadsheet.

Keep in mind that the embedded spreadsheet does not support all of the functionality that Excel has.

For example, the embedded spreadsheet does not support all of the formula functions, conditional formatting and macros that Excel has.

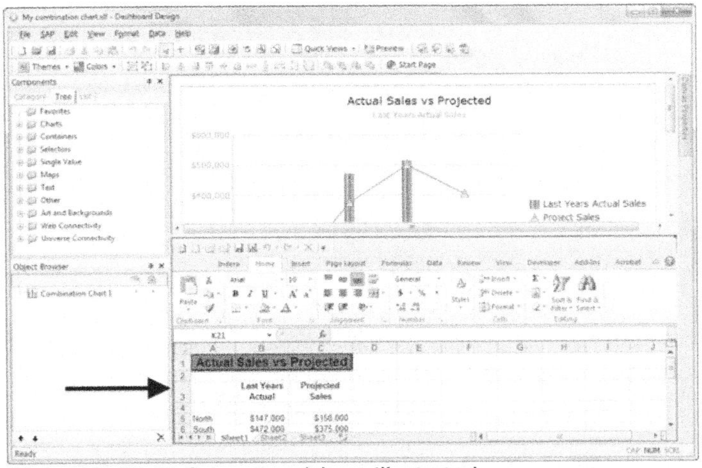

Figure 3-31 Built in spreadsheet illustrated

If you have Excel 2003 installed, you will see the default toolbars in the built in spreadsheet. You will notice that some buttons on the toolbars are disabled. That is because the functionality is handled by Dashboard Design. To add additional Excel functionality, right-click on a spreadsheet toolbar, then select the toolbar that has the functionality that you need.

If you have Excel 2007 or higher installed, you will see the ribbon. Some of the buttons like Open and Save are not enabled on the toolbars or ribbon, because the functionality is handled by Dashboard Design.

To save the changes that you make in the spreadsheet, click the Save button on the Standard Dashboard Design toolbar. If you add new rows or columns of data that you want a component to use, you may have to change some of the options on the Properties panel.

Being able to change data in the embedded spreadsheet is helpful for the person creating the dashboard, but not for users that have to maintain the data, unless they have the software installed on their computer. In my opinion, if the underlying data was imported from a spreadsheet, it is better to make the changes in the spreadsheet and re-import the spreadsheet with the changes. The reason I say that is because if you forget that you made changes via the built-in spreadsheet and then import a spreadsheet, the changes will be overwritten.

Importing Xcelsius 2008 And Crystal Xcelsius 4.5 Model Files

The feature is used to convert models created in previous versions of the software into the current file format. Keep in mind that imported models may look different then they did before they were imported. For example, custom colors may be different, the formatting of some components may be different or the size of the component may change slightly. In addition to backing up the model file before you import it, you should also back up external SWF and JPEG files before importing them.

How To Import Xcelsius 2008 And Crystal Xcelsius 4.5 Model Files

Crystal Xcelsius 3.0, 3.5 and 4.0 files cannot be imported directly into Dashboard Design. They have to be imported into Crystal Xcelsius 4.5 first. Once you import a Crystal Xcelsius 4.5 XLF file into Dashboard Design format, the newly imported file cannot be opened in Crystal Xcelsius 4.5. The steps below show you how to import Xcelsius 2008 and Crystal Xcelsius 4.5 XLF files into Dashboard Design.

1. In Dashboard Design, File ⇒ Open.

2. Navigate to and double-click on the Xcelsius 2008 or Crystal Xcelsius 4.5 XLF file that you want to import.

   You will see the message shown in Figure 3-32. This message warns that some features may not work as expected.

   Click OK. The XLF file will be imported and upgraded to Dashboard Design format.

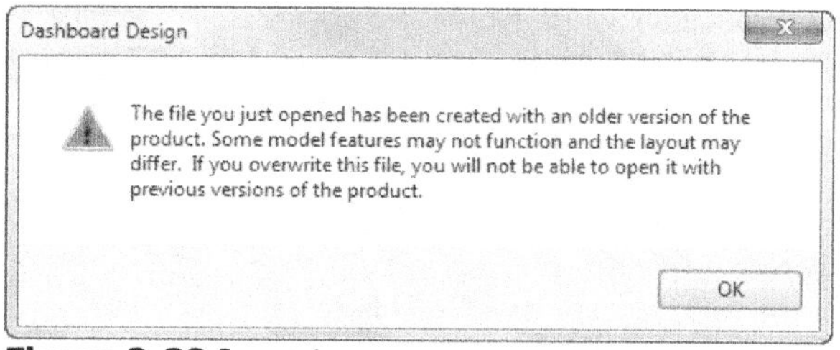

Figure 3-32 Import message

3. Save the model. If you have to save the file with the same file name, save it in a different folder then the 2008 or 4.5 version of the file, otherwise, you will overwrite the older version of the file.

CREATING YOUR FIRST DASHBOARD

In this chapter you will learn how to create a basic dashboard. While learning how to create a dashboard, you will learn about the following:

- ☑ The dashboard design process
- ☑ Properties panel for components
- ☑ Single Value components
- ☑ Other components

CHAPTER 4

Designing Dashboards Overview

Yes, I know that you are anxious to create your first dashboard, but having a foundation of effective dashboard layout and design principles and techniques is important because if you start off wrong, you will end up wrong or worse <smile>. Many of the layout and design concepts that I discuss in this chapter are very similar to those used for creating reports. However, keep in mind that reports are usually paper based and dashboards are not. If you have used a report writer like Crystal Reports, you may already be familiar with some of the design topics that are covered in this chapter.

Designing For Scalability

This term refers to the process of trying not to limit the functionality of the end product. Scalability allows a product to have modifications made without significantly altering the structure of the underlying data. Even though the user may only request the functionality for a, b and c, you should analyze their request and think "What-If", with each item that they are requesting. Some call this thinking outside of the box.

Even when you give the user exactly what they asked for, they will often come back and say "What about this?" or "What about that?". If the spreadsheet or dashboard design has limitations, you may find it difficult and at the very least, extremely time consuming, to make the changes needed to incorporate any new functionality that may be requested. If this happens, it means that you did not design with scalability.

Keep in mind that even though the data in a spreadsheet is in a **FLAT FILE** format, it can be designed to allow a dashboard to have the "relational" aspect that is often required. The reason that data in a spreadsheet is flat file is because often, the same information is entered in the same column for several records. If you are sitting there shaking your head, pay close attention in Chapter 5, because it sheds light on the differences between flat file and relational data.

Dashboard Design Process

There are several items that need to be addressed and worked out before you create a dashboard, whether this is your first dashboard or your 100th dashboard. This section is an overview of the dashboard design process. The design process could be an entire chapter or two all by itself, but I am giving you the abridged version. The dashboard design process is part of what is known as the "Business Requirements" phase of a project. As you gain experience, you will see that if you do not get the business requirements right, the project will be delayed, potentially be over budget and not produce the results that the business owner (requestor) or client is looking for. Many call this a "bad career move".

When you learn the concepts presented in this chapter, it will be easier for you to create dashboards. Out in the real world, you should write down the answers to the questions that will be covered in the dashboard design process sections of this chapter. The more planning that you do before you create the dashboard, the less that you will have to modify a dashboard after it is created. There are four primary steps to the dashboard design process. Each step can have multiple tasks.

You will see how these steps come together through the exercises in this book. When creating dashboards, especially ones that other people will use, it is imperative that you fully understand the requirements, which often includes asking a lot of questions. This is not a task that you can be bashful about. Not asking questions, or worse, asking the wrong questions, will more than likely cause you grief down the road.

Step 1: Define The Purpose Of The Dashboard

Yes, I know what you are saying; "How hard can it be to figure out the purpose of a dashboard?". The answer is that it depends on how well the person or group of people are able to explain what they want the dashboard to provide and how well you understand what they tell you.

It is possible that the majority of dashboards that you create will be used by someone else, which means that you should meet with the person or group of people that will use the dashboard. These meetings are part of the requirement gathering process. You may have to have more than one meeting to get a good idea of what the dashboard needs to include, because the users may not tell you or be able to clearly articulate their needs in one meeting.

Dashboards are often used as a decision making tool, which means that poor decisions will be made or the decision making process will be ineffective, due to missing or incorrect data that is presented on the dashboard. The data must be correct and presented in a logical manner in order to be an effective decision making tool.

> One dashboard can be used by people at different levels in the company. This means that at each level, people can have slightly different needs. If this is the case, you will have to plan and design the dashboard accordingly, so that it meets the needs for all of the users.

Your role as the dashboard designer is to gather the information needed, which will help the users of the dashboard to be able to use it easily, as well as, understand the data that is presented on the dashboard. If the information is not presented in a way that works for the users, trust me, they will let you know and you will be spending a lot of time modifying the dashboard.

In my opinion and based on the experiences that I have had, the more that users have you modify a dashboard, the faster your credibility goes down hill. That is not something that you want to happen. What I have discovered, is that if you create a prototype (which is explained later in this chapter) for the users, they can discuss what they like and do not like about the prototype. Usually, you will gain valuable information that is often hard to get users to discuss. The worst thing that you can do in many cases, is give the users the impression that you know more about their needs or data then they do. I am not saying that in some cases that you will not know more about their needs or data, just don't give them that impression, if you know what I mean.

To define the expected outcome of the dashboard, write a descriptive sentence or two about the purpose of the dashboard or what the dashboard needs to accomplish. Below are some sample purpose statements.

① The purpose of the dashboard is to compare last years sales data to this years sales data, by region.
② The purpose of the dashboard is to show products that are low on inventory and need to be reordered.

What I am about to say may sound a little off of the beaten path, but please hear me out. When you ask questions, try to think of the components that will be needed. For example, the first purpose statement above indicates that a chart is needed. At the very least, the dashboard needs a chart that can display a trend of two series of data.

The dashboard needs a combination or area chart. To allow the user to select the region (more than three or four regions could make the chart cluttered or hard to read), the dashboard needs a menu component or a toggle component that allows a specific region to be selected. Being able to narrow down the component options will help you understand how the data in the spreadsheet needs to be laid out.

In addition to defining the expected outcome of the dashboard, you have to take into consideration who will be using the dashboard. It is very possible that managers and their staff will request similar dashboards. In many cases, it is better to create separate dashboards, even if there is only one component that is different, then to try and get multiple parties to try and come up with one dashboard that works for both groups of users. If you are responsible for supporting the dashboards, the down side to creating multiple dashboards that are similar is that you may have to make future changes to multiple dashboards. As you gain dashboard design experience, understand business requirements and know the requestors, you will be able to quickly determine which is the best solution.

Step 2: Determine The Layout Of The Dashboard

Now that you have determined the purpose of the dashboard, you need to determine where each piece of data should be placed on the dashboard.

Task 1 In addition to determining where the data should be placed, you need to determine some or all of the following:

① Create a list of fields (cells) that need to be displayed on the dashboard. If you know what spreadsheet each field is in, include that on the list. If the data does not currently exist, include it on the list also. You will use this list to complete tasks in future steps in the design process.

② If necessary, create a list of fields that will be used to select what other components display.

③ An important question to answer during this step is what format the dashboard needs to be in. This is known as the **DELIVERY METHOD**. For example, does the dashboard need to be in PDF format or does it need to be web based. The way that a dashboard needs to be distributed can influence the layout of a dashboard. You should also determine if the dashboard needs to be distributed in more than one format.

④ What is the appropriate title for the dashboard? Is the title in a field or do you have to type it in?

⑤ Does the dashboard need dates? If so, what format should they be in and where should they be placed on the dashboard.

Task 2 If you are creative you will like this task. This task involves selecting the components, backgrounds etc. Yes, I know that it is early in the design process, but there is no point waiting, because making decisions like this can help structure the data in the spreadsheet better. If you followed my advice in step 1 about the components, you may be well on your way to completing the component selection process. Keep in mind that as fun and exciting as it is to create a dashboard in Dashboard Design, that it is a business decision tool, not something that can be framed as artwork.

Step 3: Find The Data For The Dashboard

This step is very important because without the data there is no dashboard. As the person creating the dashboard, life will be much easier for you if you are familiar with the data needed for the dashboard and how the data is organized. If you are not familiar with the data or are not technical, you may have to rely on the users or Information Technology specialists, to help you with the tasks in this step. There are three tasks that you have to work on to complete this step successfully.

Keep in mind that when you finish all of the tasks in this step, that you have all of the data in one spreadsheet. The data can be on more than one tab, as needed.

Task 1 The first task that you have to complete is to find out which spreadsheets and possibly other data repositories, like a database, contain the data for the dashboard. Use the list of fields that you created in Step 2, to find the spreadsheets and databases. You may also have to find out what servers the data is on. This task is known as finding the **DATA SOURCE**.

Task 2 This task involves selecting the actual fields in the spreadsheets that are needed for the dashboard. Use the list that you created in Step 2. Once the fields are selected, determine the formatting for each field and how the fields need to be displayed on the dashboard. You also have to determine if the current column or field names are the best choice for the dashboard. One example of when a column or field name needs to be changed on a dashboard is for fields that are known as ID fields. Using ID fields as the name on a dashboard will have no meaning to most users.

Task 3 Now that you have found some of the data, there may be fields left on the list that you created in Step 2 that you have not found. More than likely, many of the fields that are left on the list are calculated fields. This task involves writing out the formulas for the calculated fields. Some calculated fields may use a built-in Excel function and others will require you to write the formula. Examples of calculated fields include:

① Sales price times quantity.
② Number of days between the order date and the ship date.
③ How long the person has been employed at the company.

If you, as the dashboard designer, come to the conclusion that some data that the users are requesting does not exist, they or someone other then you, needs to create the data if the user plans to stick to their original request.

Step 4: Organize The Data

This step involves organizing all of the data. Many of the options that you decide on in Task 1 below will automatically dictate which type of component (i.e. chart, menu, slider) each field will have to use.

Task 1 To complete this task you have to organize all of the data, from the spreadsheets and calculated fields, as well as, any other data source. Organizing the data means that at a minimum, answering the following question is necessary.

Does the dashboard need to have any data flagged? If so, how should the data be flagged? The primary reason data would be flagged is so that it can be easily identified on a dashboard. Make a list of any data that needs to be flagged. Dashboard Design has several options including alerts, borders, symbols, changing the font size and other formatting techniques that can be used to indicate that the data is flagged.

Task 2 To complete this task you have to determine which type of component each field should use. Task 1 had you make decisions on how to organize the data at a high level. There are several types of components that can be used to display data. You also have to determine if the component should be an input (requests data from the user) or output (displays data) component.

Task 3 One way that you organize the data is selecting which rows of data will actually be used as the data source. This is important because it is not a requirement that all of the data in a spreadsheet appear on the dashboard. For example, if the dashboard needs to display sales (orders) for a specific sales rep, you would select a component that would allow the user to select the particular sales rep whose data will appear on the dashboard. Another example would be to display all customers that purchased a specific product or group of products.

In addition to data selection, it may be necessary to create filters which will make the dashboard more flexible in terms of record selection. Filters allow the user to select the criteria that will be used to retrieve the data that will appear on the dashboard. Filters allow one dashboard to be run with a variety of selection criteria. An example of this would be an order dashboard. This dashboard could have filters for the order date, order amount and sales rep fields. One dashboard could display all of the following.

① All orders on a specific date.

② All orders for a specific sales rep.

③ All orders for a specific product.

④ All orders on a certain date for a specific sales rep.

Task 4 Depending on the company, it may be necessary to have the person or group of people sign a document that states that all of the tasks explained above will produce the dashboard that they need.

Refreshing Data

Unlike reports that are run off of live data all the time, dashboards usually do not. While not a part of the actual dashboard design process this task must be addressed. As you have read, once the data is imported into the model, the spreadsheet is disconnected from the model.

Dashboards become outdated, when they use old data. If you will be the one responsible for re-exporting the model to get the revised data, you need to set up a schedule that works for you and the users. Remember, that they do not have Dashboard Design installed on their computer, so they cannot update the data in a dashboard on their own.

Dashboard Prototype

Even though you will go through the entire dashboard design process, it is very possible that the users are still somewhat unclear or cannot visualize what the finished dashboard will look like. No pun intended. If that is the case, creating a dashboard prototype will be a life saver. A prototype can be hand drawn on paper or you can create a sample dashboard that displays the data based on the information that you gather during the dashboard design process. This sample dashboard is known as a **PROTOTYPE**.

Some dashboard designers create this prototype as each of the steps and tasks that were explained above are completed. Other dashboard designers will create the prototype right after the dashboard design process is over. The reason prototypes are helpful is because the users will get a pretty good idea of what the finished dashboard will look like, based on the information that they have supplied.

The feedback that you receive from the users about the prototype is invaluable because users get to "see" what they asked for. I have found this process to be a very effective way for users to tell me what they like, don't like, need and don't need.

Dashboard Creation Options

There are two ways to create a dashboard: Using an existing model and from scratch. Each has pros and cons, as explained in the next two sections.

Create A Dashboard Based Off Of An Existing Model

If a dashboard exists that is similar to the dashboard that you now need to create, select this dashboard creation option. Save an existing model with a new file name, then make the necessary changes to create the new dashboard.

An example of when to create a dashboard based off of an existing dashboard would be when two groups of people need to see the majority of the same data and one group needs additional information that the other group does not need, or when one group needs the same data, just in a different layout. A different layout could be something as easy as using a different type of chart. You can also use one of the templates that come with Dashboard Design to format the dashboard differently.

Create A Dashboard From Scratch

This option provides the most flexibility to create a dashboard. You start with a blank canvas (no pun intended, again) and add the components.

Learning To Create Dashboards

For some, learning to create dashboards can be intimidating, especially in the beginning, but being the fearless person that you are, I am sure that you will do just fine. **LEARNING TO CREATE DASHBOARDS REQUIRES TIME, PATIENCE, DEDICATION, PRACTICE AND ATTENTION TO DETAIL**. Dashboard Design is a very robust package and has a lot of features and options. As you go through the hands-on exercises in this book, take your time and try to understand how the concepts that you are learning can be applied to dashboards that you will create on your own. It is possible to go through this entire book in a few days if you already have above average dashboard design experience or if you have used a previous version of the software.

The reality is that you will make some mistakes along the way. If you have a fear of making mistakes, this is the time to let go of that fear, because the fear will prevent you from learning. It is also normal to initially get confused on what to do next. Even though you may not understand why you are being instructed to do something, the steps in each exercise will allow you to achieve the expected result. This is how you will begin to build a foundation for creating dashboards and learning Dashboard Design.

The first time that a concept or technique is presented, a lot of information is provided. Each subsequent time that you have to perform the same task, less and less information (aka hand holding) will occur. As you will see, there are a lot of repetitious tasks involved in creating dashboards. These are the tasks that less and less information will be provided for as you go through the book. The purpose behind this learning technique is to allow you to start relying more on your knowledge, which in turn allows you to complete an exercise in less time, instead of flipping through this book to find the answer. Hopefully, after reading the previous pages in this chapter, you are much better prepared to create your first dashboard.

Component Properties Panel

The Component Properties panel is how a component is modified. I will refer to this tool as the Properties panel. There are common properties that all components have. The properties are on several views. Some views have properties on several tabs. The common properties are explained in this chapter.

The **GENERAL VIEW** contains the options that you will use most because they are used to select the data that the component displays. The options on this view are used to link a cell or range of cells to a component. All components have a General view.

The options on the General view provide the same functionality from one component type to another. Each component type uses different options to accomplish data linking tasks. Some of the options on this view are used to create or select titles for various parts of a component and link cells in the data source to the component. Each component type has options on the General view that are the same for the majority of components of that type. They are explained at the beginning of the chapter that the component type is covered in.

The **INSERTION VIEW** (formerly known as the **DRILL DOWN VIEW**) contains options that allow detail data to be displayed. Use the options on this view when you want the chart to be used as a selector. This detail data comes from summary data in another component on the dashboard. This view is only available for some charts and is covered in detail in Chapter 13. The reason to drill down to view the detail data is to gain a better understanding of the summary data. For example, in Exercise 13.5, you will create a dashboard that has a pie chart that displays the yearly sales by branch. Having this detail data could also help determine if there is a pattern of when branch sales will be high or low.

The **BEHAVIOR VIEW** contains properties that determine minimum and maximum data ranges, animation, default settings for the component, how the user can interact with the component on the dashboard and whether or not a component is visible when the dashboard is first opened.

The options on the Behavior view vary from one component type to another. Each component type has options on this view that are the same for the majority of components of that type. Many components have **DYNAMIC VISIBILITY** and **IGNORE BLANK CELLS** options. The Dynamic Visibility options are covered in Chapter 14 and the Ignore Blank Cells options are covered in Chapter 15. I do not reference them when explaining the options for any individual component. The exception is for the Accordion Menu because it has a different ignore blank cells option.

The **APPEARANCE VIEW** contains options that are used to change how the component looks. This includes changing the color, font size or location of where a part of the component is displayed. For example, there is an option to select where the charts legend will be displayed.

The **ALERTS VIEW** contains options that are used to dynamically change the colors on a component, based on values that are pre-selected. These dynamic color changes are used to bring data on the dashboard to the users attention.

The options on this view are used to set conditions, both positive and negative. These options cause different parts of the component to change colors. Every component that supports alerts has the same options on this view. Because the Alerts view is covered in detail in Chapter 10, I do not reference the view when explaining the components options.

All components do not have all five views shown at the top of Figure 4-1. The views have different options depending on the type of component.

For example, the Common tab options shown in Figure 4-2 are for a **LINE CHART** component.

Figure 4-3 shows the Common tab options for a **COMBO BOX** component.

Don't worry, the options for each component are explained in this book on a view by view, tab by tab basis, not in a glossary at the end. You can thank me later <smile>.

When you add a component to the canvas, more than likely, the default functionality on the Properties panel is not enough for the component to perform the way that you need it to. Selecting and changing options on the Properties panel gives the component additional functionality.

As you will see, there are a lot of options on the Properties panel. You do not have to try to memorize them.

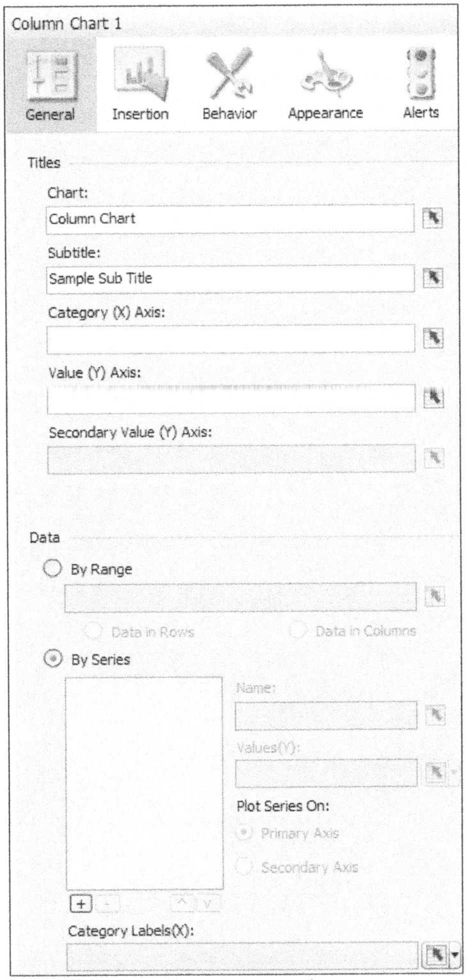

Figure 4-1 Properties panel

Tabs

In addition to the views shown above in Figure 4-1, the Behavior and Appearance views have tabs. The tabs vary from component to component. To help make it easier to find these tabs, Table 4-1 lists the view and its tabs. Hopefully, now you understand why earlier I said to pay attention to the Properties panel discussions.

View	Tabs
Behavior	Common, Scale, Animations and Effects, as shown in Figure 4-2.
Appearance	Layout, Series, Axes, Text and Color, as shown in Figure 4-4.

Table 4-1 Tabs on the views

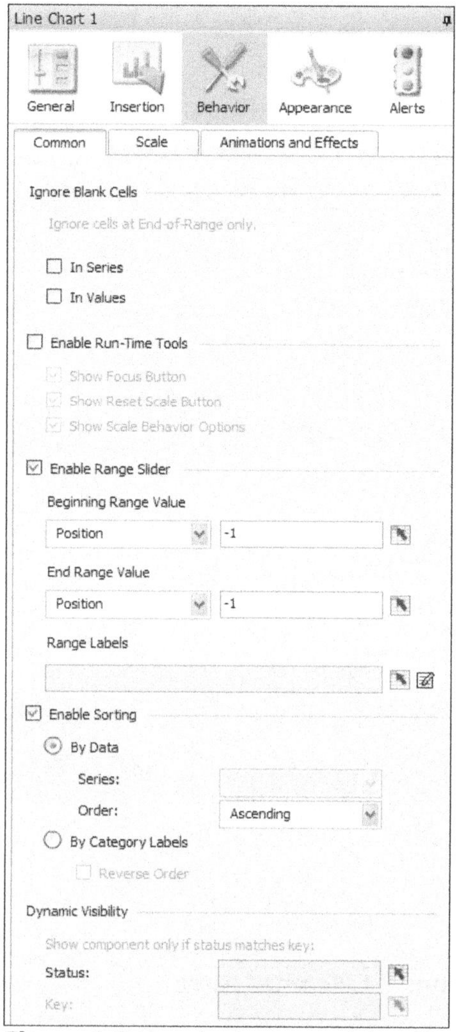

Figure 4-2 Line chart common tab options

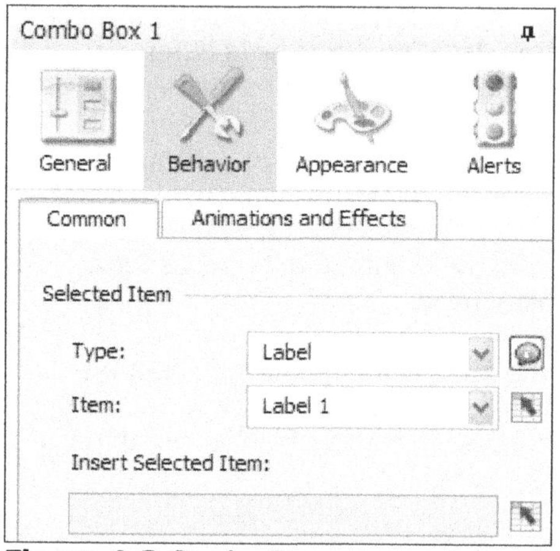

Figure 4-3 Combo Box common tab options

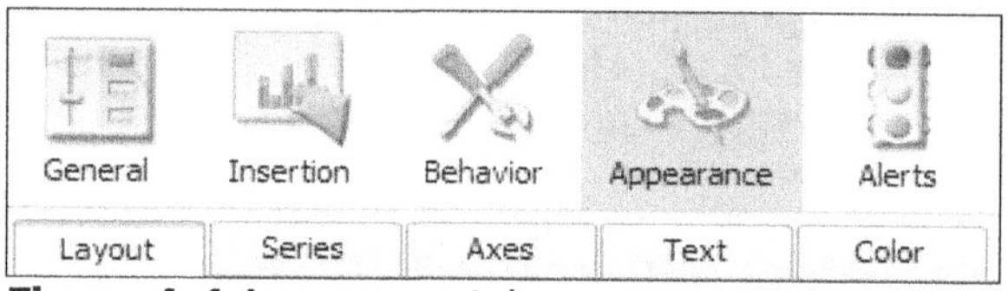

Figure 4-4 Appearance tabs

> Dashboard Design refers to each option, except for buttons, on the Properties panel as a property. I refer to each option on the Properties panel as an option or field. For example, in Figure 4-2 shown above, I would refer to the Status property as the Status option or Status field.

The sections below discuss the options on each tab that are the same or used often, regardless of the component type. As you have probably figured out, each category of components like charts and selectors have their own set of properties. Some components have properties that are specific to the component. These properties are also explained in the chapter that the component is covered in.

Common Buttons On The Properties Panel

The buttons explained in this section are available for most components.

Bind Button This is probably the most used option on the Properties panel. Clicking the button shown in Figure 4-5 or Figure 4-6 opens the **SELECT A RANGE** dialog box and shifts focus to the spreadsheet. This is how you select the cells that a component will use.

NEW The Bind button shown in Figure 4-6 has a drop-down list which allows you to select a query to use to import the data from for the field, instead of from the spreadsheet. Selecting the Query Data option opens the **SELECT FROM QUERY** dialog box.

Figure 4-5 Bind button

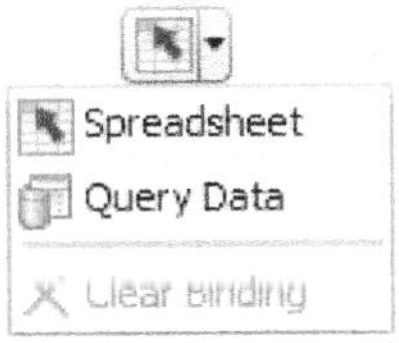

Figure 4-6 Bind button drop-down list

Manual Edit Button Clicking the button shown in Figure 4-7 will open a dialog box like the ones shown in Figures 4-8 and 4-9. This button was formerly called the **BROWSE BUTTON**.

Figure 4-7 Manual Edit button

The dialog boxes shown in Figures 4-8 and 4-9 are used to type in values for the option instead of selecting a cell in the spreadsheet that has the value. You can also change the default values on these dialog boxes.

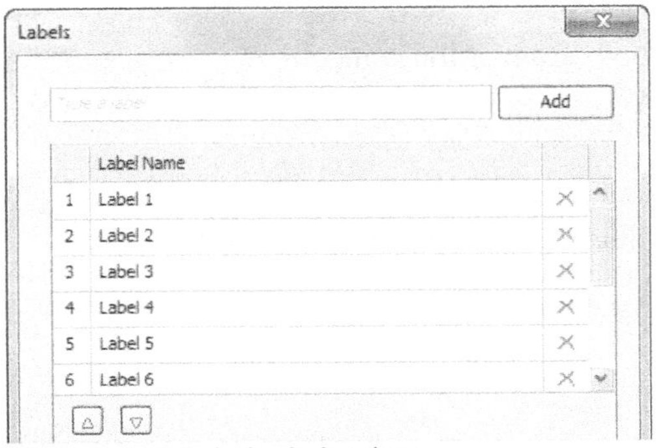

Figure 4-8 Labels dialog box

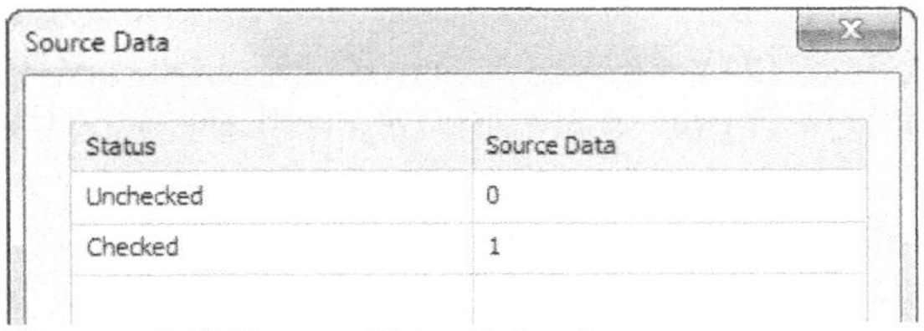

Figure 4-9 Source Data dialog box

Information Button At the end of some options you will see the button shown in Figure 4-10.

Figure 4-10 Information button

This button provides more information on how features on the Properties panel work together.

If you click this button, you will see a window similar to the one shown in Figure 4-11. You can view an animated demo of how the component works.

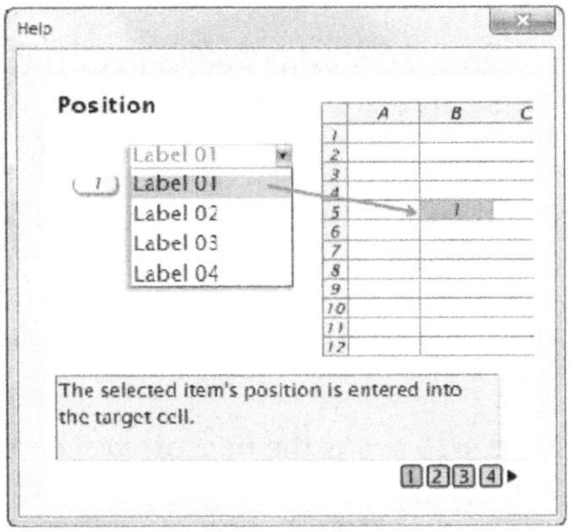

Figure 4-11 Help window

Color Selector Button

As its name suggests, clicking the button shown in Figure 4-12 will open the dialog box shown in Figure 4-13.

Figure 4-12
Color selector button

This is how you select the color that you want to use for a portion of the component.

If you want to create a custom color, click the **MORE COLORS** option.

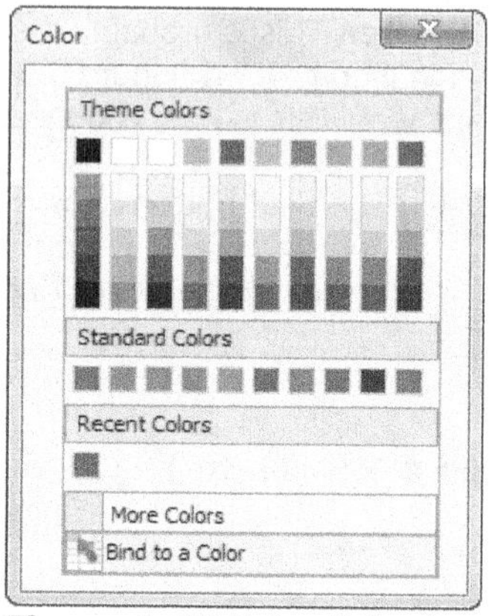

Figure 4-13 Color dialog box

Common Options On The Properties Panel

This section covers the options that are common on different tabs on the Properties panel. The options explained in this section are available for most components.

Axis Values

You will see several options on different views on the Properties panel that are for an axis on the component. They are explained below.

X Axis or **(X)** values are displayed horizontally across the bottom of the component.
Y Axis or **(Y)** values are displayed vertically along the left side of the component.

Common Appearance Options

The options explained in this section may appear in a different section of the Appearance view or one of the tabs below it, as listed earlier in Table 4-1, but they work the same from component to component. The options are used to customize how the component will look.

Transparency Option

This option is shown in Figure 4-14 and is used to select how see through a part of the component is.

You can select a value from zero to 100. Zero makes part of the component completely solid. Objects behind the component are not visible.

100 makes the component transparent and invisible.

Figure 4-15 shows the transparency option set to 50.

Figure 4-16 shows the transparency option set to 90.

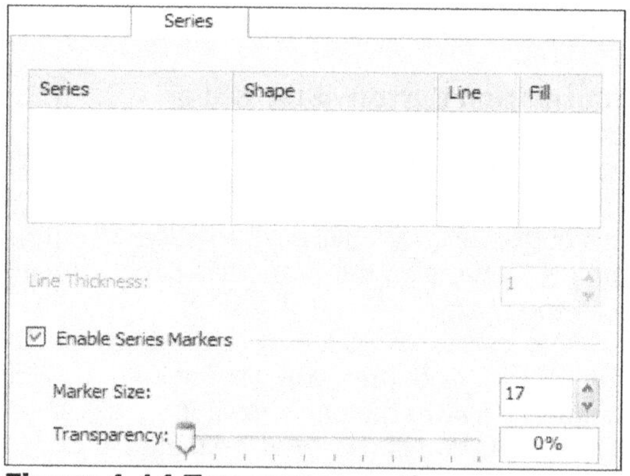

Figure 4-14 Transparency option

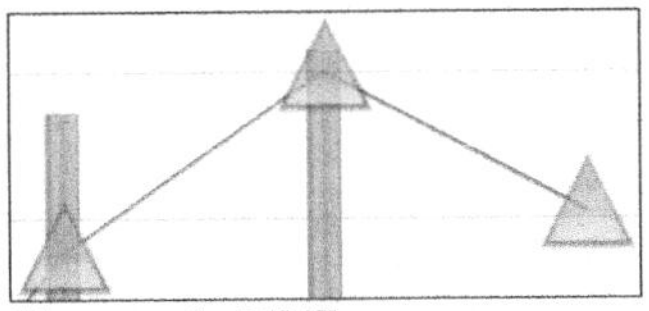

Figure 4-15 Transparency option set to 50

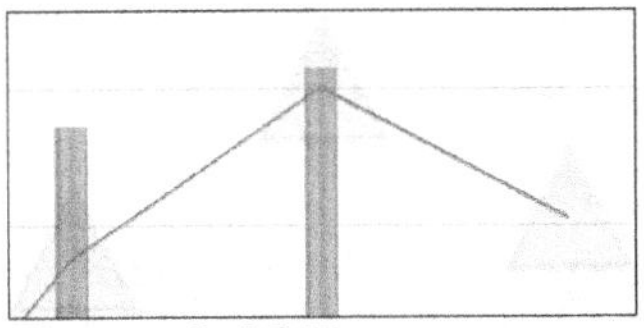

Figure 4-16 Transparency option set to 90

The **LIST TRANSPARENCY** option shown in Figure 4-17 is only applied to the list portion of the component.

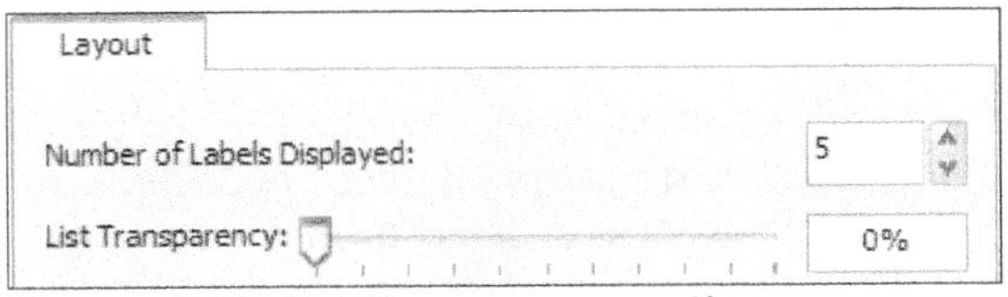

Figure 4-17 List Transparency option

Thickness Option

This option is shown twice in Figure 4-18 and is used to select the width of a line. Zero is the thinnest line size and 100 is the thickest size that the line can be. Figure 4-19 shows the horizontal axis weight option set to 10 and the vertical axis weight option set to 25.

> On some components, you will see **BORDER THICKNESS** instead of **THICKNESS**, as shown in Figure 4-20. Both options provide the same functionality.

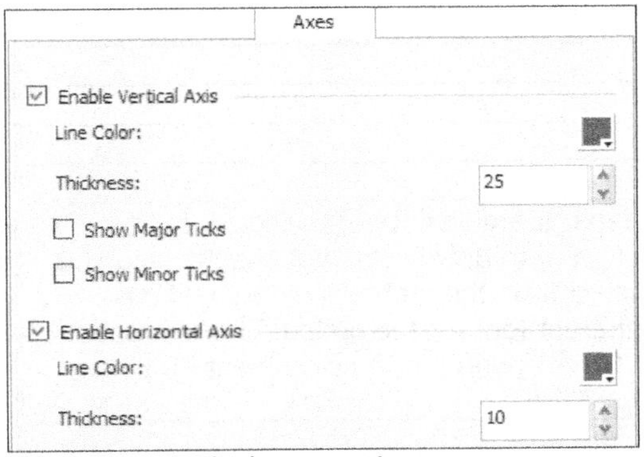

Figure 4-18 Thickness option

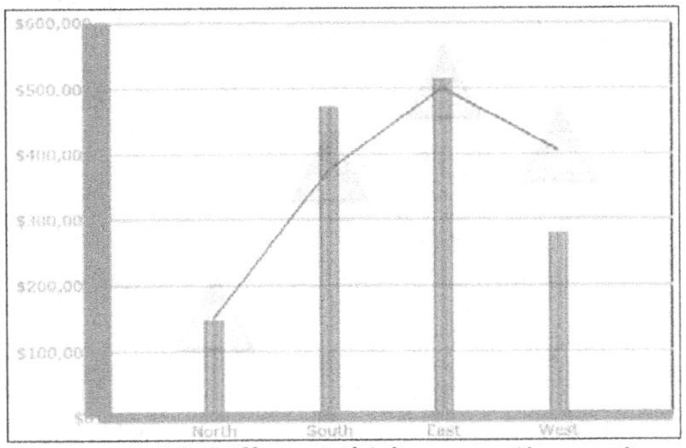

Figure 4-19 Different thickness options set

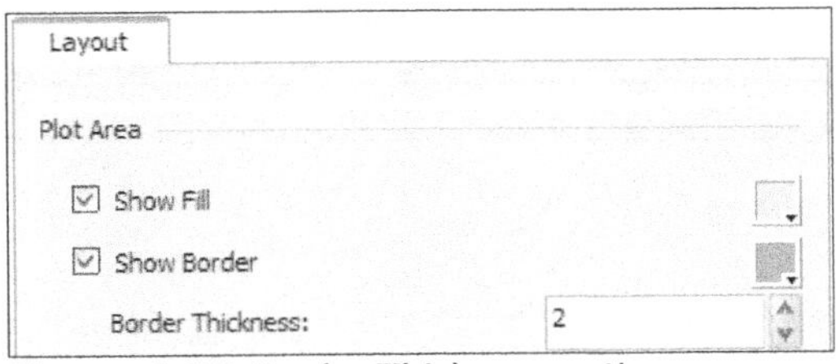

Figure 4-20 Border Thickness option

Common Text Tab Options

Show/Text Options

The options in this section are for the text items on the component that you can modify. Many of these options come from options selected on the General view.

The **SHOW** option determines whether or not the text item will be displayed on the component. Even if you enter text or select a cell for the corresponding option on another tab, the text will not appear on the component if the Show option is not checked.

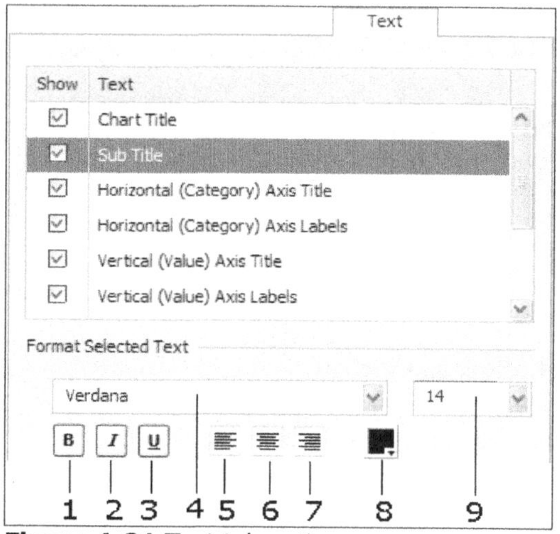

Figure 4-21 Text tab options

Format Selected Text Options

The options in this section are shown at the bottom of Figure 4-21. They are used to modify the option that is selected at the top of the tab. In this figure, the Sub Title option is selected. The changes made will be applied to the sub title. The options are explained in Table 4-2.

Button	Description
1	Makes the text bold.
2	Makes the text italic.
3	Underlines the text.
4	The default font for all components is Verdana. If a global font is selected, fonts cannot be selected for components. If the font drop-down list is not enabled and you want to use a different font, you have to select it on the Embedded Font Options dialog box. If available, you can select a different font for the option. The font option is only available if the Use Non-Embedded Fonts option (on the Document Properties dialog box) is selected. [See Chapter 2, Figure 2-5]
5	Is used to left align the text.
6	Is used to center the text.
7	Is used to right align the text.
8	Is used to select a color for the text. [See Color Selector button earlier in this chapter]
9	Is used to select the font size.

Table 4-2 Format Selected Text options explained

Position And Offset Options

The options shown in Figure 4-22 are used to select where the text that this option is associated to will appear. The position drop-down list can have some or all of the following nine options: Top left, top center, top right, left, right, center, bottom left, bottom center or bottom right. The options available depend on the component.

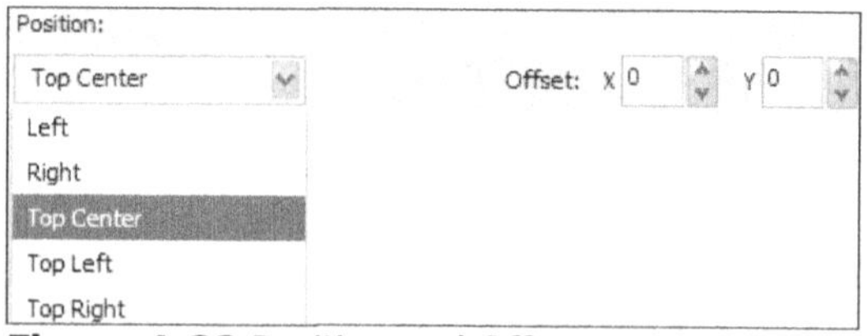

Figure 4-22 Position and Offset options

The **OFFSET X** option shown above in Figure 4-22 is used to move the selected text or values, right or left, based on the option selected in the **POSITION** option.

The **OFFSET Y** option is used to move the selected text or values, up or down, based on the option selected in the **POSITION** option shown above in Figure 4-22.

Numeric Format Options

The options in this section of the Text tab are built-in formats that can be applied to different types of numeric data. The numeric formats are explained below.

① The **GENERAL** format option shown in Figure 4-23 displays the data as it is. No formatting is applied. (1)

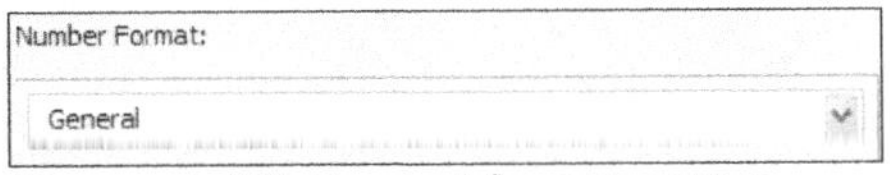

Figure 4-23 General format option

② The **NUMERIC** format options shown in Figure 4-24 are used to format numbers.

Select the **DEFAULT NUMBER FORMAT** option if you want to use the regional number format associated with the users computer. Selecting this option disables the other numeric format options.

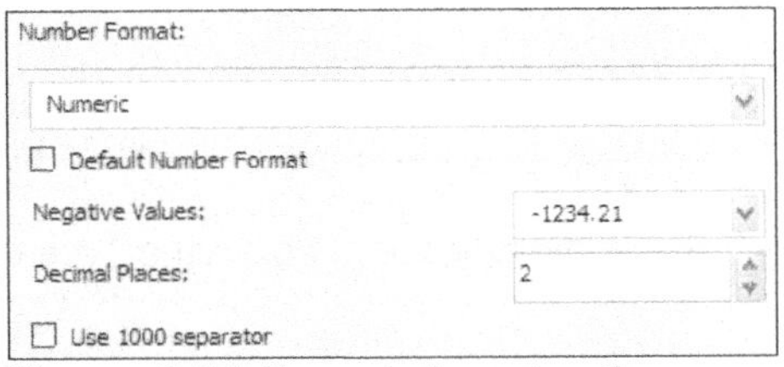

Figure 4-24 Numeric format options

The options in the **NEGATIVE VALUES** drop-down list are used to select how negative numbers should be displayed on the component.

DECIMAL PLACES Is used to select the number of decimal places to display.

Check the **USE 1000 SEPARATOR** option if you want numbers to display commas.

③ The **CURRENCY** format options shown in Figure 4-25 are used to format monetary values.

Select the **DEFAULT CURRENCY FORMAT** option if you want to use the regional currency format associated with the users computer. Selecting this option disables the other numeric format options.

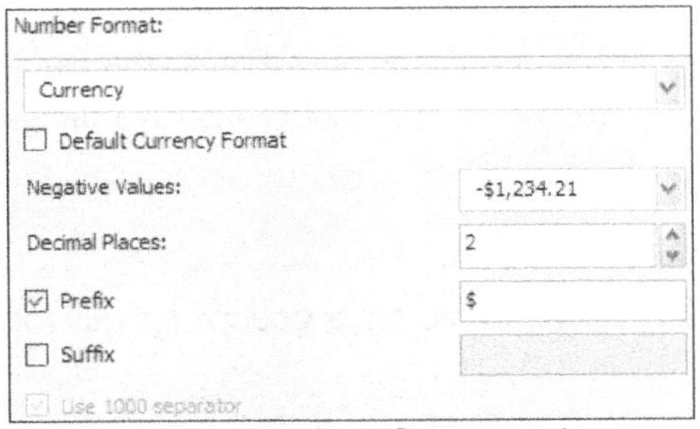

Figure 4-25 Currency format options

PREFIX Is used to select a symbol to place at the beginning of currency values. The default is a dollar sign. You can type in another symbol.

SUFFIX Is used to type in a symbol to place at the end of the currency value.

> The prefix and suffix options are mutually exclusive, meaning that you can select one or the other, but not both.

④ The **PERCENT** format options shown in Figure 4-26 are used to format percent values. You can select the number of decimal places the percent value should display.

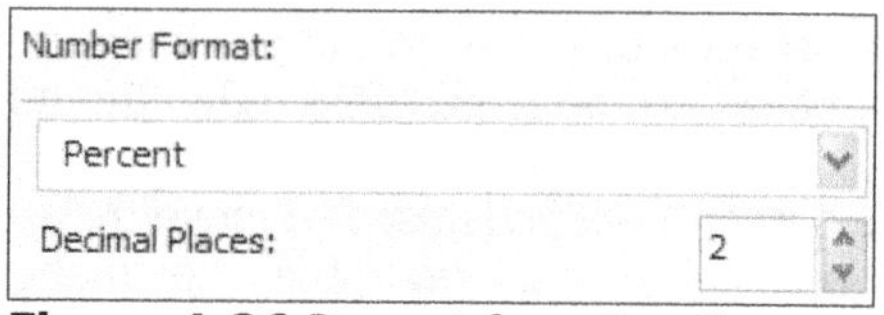

Figure 4-26 Percent format options

⑤ The **DATE** format options shown in Figure 4-27 are used to select how dates should be displayed.

Select the date format from the Type drop-down list.

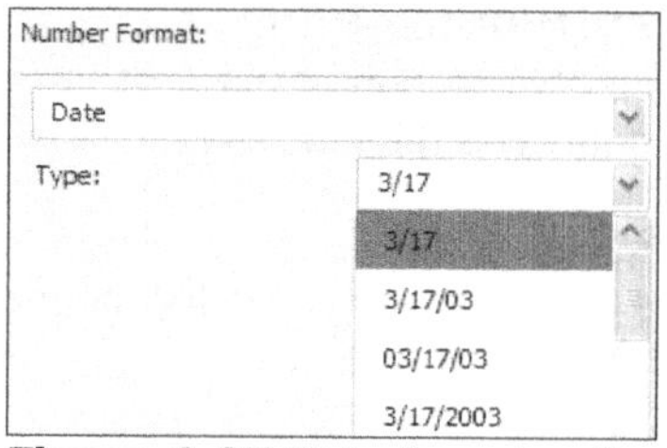

Figure 4-27 Date format options

⑥ The **TIME** format options shown in Figure 4-28 are used to select how times should be displayed.

Select the time format from the Type drop-down list.

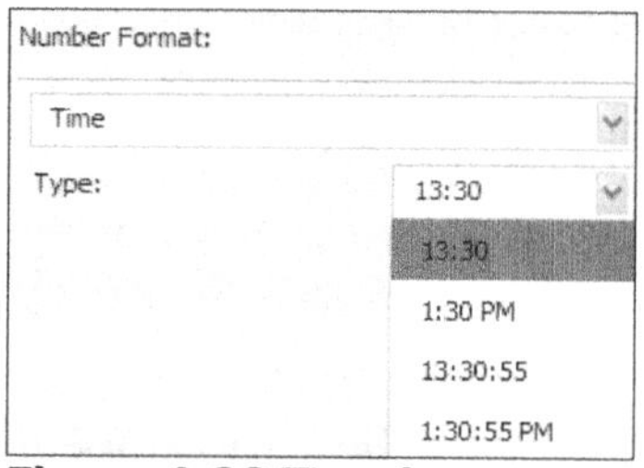

Figure 4-28 Time format options

⑦ The **BOOLEAN** format options shown in Figure 4-29 will display the data as Yes/No, On/Off or True/False. (1)

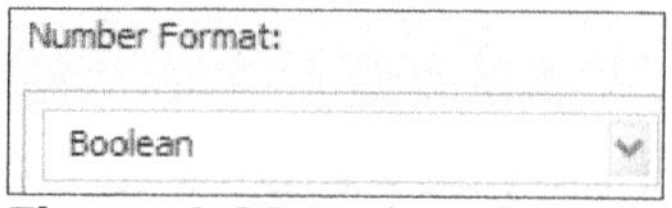

Figure 4-29 Boolean format options

⑧ The **TEXT** format option shown in Figure 4-30 is used when you want to display numeric values as plain text. (1)

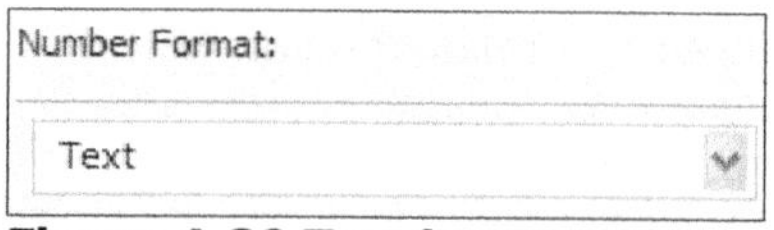

Figure 4-30 Text format option

(1) There are no other options for this format type.

What Are Components?

I have used the word component more than a few times already in this book, but have not taken the time to thoroughly explain what a component is until now. The reason is because you are about to create your first dashboard and I wanted this concept to be fresh in your mind.

Components are objects like gauges, maps, charts and toggle buttons that are used in Dashboard Design to add interactive functionality to dashboards. Some components are used to display data, while other components are used to select data or used to get data from the user at run time.

Components are the core of what makes Dashboard Design the tool that it is. Single Value components are just one type of component that you can use. All of the Single Value components basically provide the same functionality, meaning that if you connect a gauge or slider to the same cell, you will get the same data results and functionality. One component often looks better or is more appropriate for a particular layout then another.

Why Reinvent The Wheel?

I do not know what you think, but I think that the sample dashboards that come with Dashboard Design are very good. What I thought to myself when I was learning Dashboard Design was that it would be cool to learn how to create the dashboards that come with the software. Hopefully you agree, because they are some of the dashboards that you will learn how to create in this book. Did you ever try to recreate the sample files that come with software that you use? I have and sometimes it can be frustrating. This is your lucky day because I have suffered through deconstructing many of the sample dashboards. Well, I am exaggerating because they were not as bad as I thought they would be to figure out.

Your First Dashboard

Earlier, you learned about the three basic tasks that need to be completed to go from spreadsheet data to finished dashboard. [See Chapter 1, How Dashboard Design Does What It Does]
The primary goal of this chapter is to help you feel comfortable using Dashboard Design.

As the title of this chapter states, you will create your first fully functional dashboard. Along the way of creating the dashboard you will learn about the following: Importing data, creating and testing a model and Single Value components. Items and options that are not explained in detail in this exercise, are explained in detail in later chapters. I know how excited you are to create a dashboard and I do not want to slow the process down any further then I already have.

Exercise 4.1: Create A Basic Dashboard

This exercise shows you how to complete the following tasks, which are the basic requirements to create a dashboard.

① Import the data from an Excel spreadsheet.
② Select and configure the components for the model.
③ Test the model and publish it. You will need PowerPoint installed to view the dashboard created in this exercise.

In this exercise you will learn how to create the slider dashboard shown in Figure 4-31.

The dashboard displays the number of cars sold and the total sales amount per city (location).

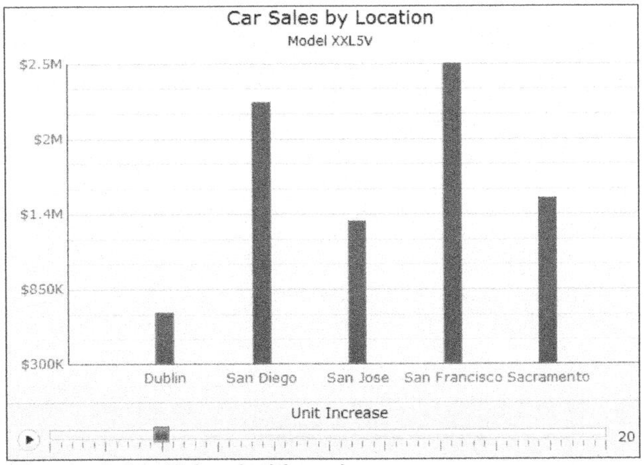

Figure 4-31 Slider dashboard

Import The Data

1. Open Dashboard Design, then click the Blank Model option on the Start Page.

2. Click the **IMPORT SPREADSHEET** button on the Standard toolbar. (The Excel icon)

   You may see the message shown in Figure 4-32. This message is letting you know that if the model has an existing spreadsheet, the changes will be lost.

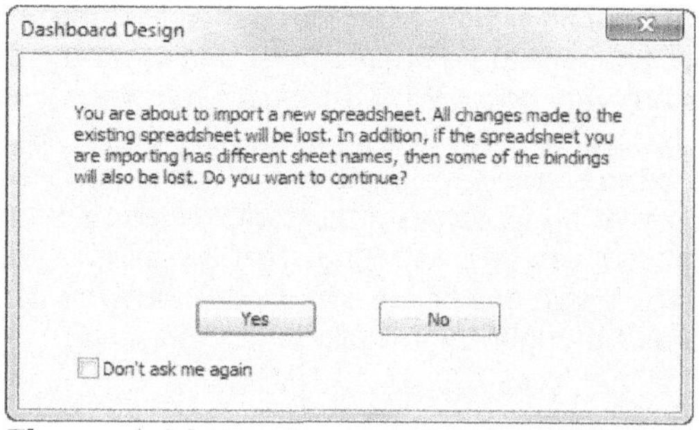

Figure 4-32 Import new spreadsheet message

3. If you do not want to see this message every time that you import a spreadsheet, check the Don't ask me again option, then click Yes to continue.

> **DATA ⇒ IMPORT**, will also let you import data.

4. Navigate to your folder and double-click on the Slider spreadsheet file. You will see the spreadsheet at the bottom of the workspace. Click on the Sheet 3 tab, if it is not already selected.

> The important thing to remember is that once the data from the spreadsheet has been imported, Dashboard Design detaches (or disconnects) from the spreadsheet. If the spreadsheet that the model is based on is updated, the new or revised data will not be part of the dashboard unless the spreadsheet is re-imported.

Create The Model

Creating the model is sometimes called "Building the visual model". You will add two components to the model, a chart and a slider.

Add The Chart Component To The Model

This component will be used to create a visual representation of the data in the spreadsheet. That is a sophisticated way of saying that the chart component will be used to display the data <smile>.

1. Open the Charts category folder in the Components Browser, then click on the Column Chart option.

2. With the Column Chart component still selected, drag it to the canvas. The Properties panel should have automatically opened. If not, double-click on the chart to open the Properties panel.

> If you right-click on the component on the canvas and select the Properties option, the Properties panel will also open.

Select The Options For The Column Chart

All of the options that have the **BIND** button shown earlier in Figures 4-5 or 4-6 have two options for adding the text, a cell or cell range to it, as explained below.

① You can type the data in the field. Use this option when the value that you need is not in the spreadsheet.

② Select the cells in the spreadsheet. It is best to use this option when the data that you need is in the spreadsheet because it helps reduce errors. If the data in the spreadsheet changes and you re-import the data, the data in the model will be updated.

Select The General View Options

1. Click the Bind button at the end of the Chart field.

2. Click in cell A1 in the spreadsheet, as illustrated in Figure 4-33, then click OK on the Select A Range dialog box.

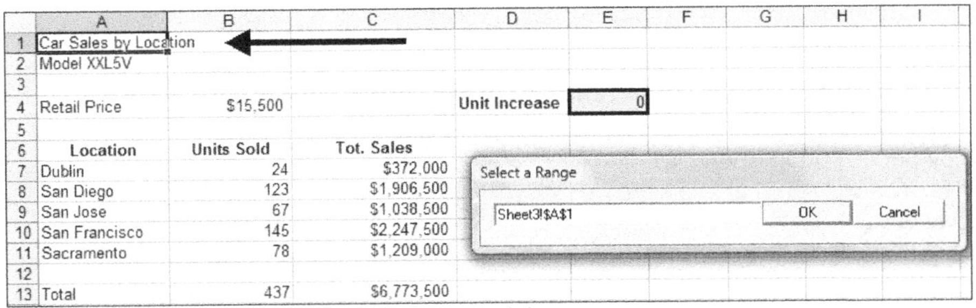

Figure 4-33 Spreadsheet data for the model

> The **SELECT A RANGE** dialog box, shown above on the right side of Figure 4-33, is the tool used to link (bind) cells in the spreadsheet to a component. One cell or multiple cells can be selected. Notice that the component has displayed the data that corresponds to the cell that you selected. In this exercise that is the chart title. If multiple components are selected, the Properties panel will only display Properties that are available for all of the selected components.

3. Type `Model XXL5V` in the Subtitle field. This is the same data that is in cell A2 in the spreadsheet. You could have selected cell A2 for the Subtitle field.

> **Binding Components**
> Dashboard Design supports an unlimited number of rows to be bound to a component. 512 rows can be selected by default. The maximum amount can be raised. [See Chapter 3, Excel Options]

Data Options

The options in this section of the Properties panel are used to select the values in the spreadsheet for the plot area section of the chart. In this exercise, the values that will be plotted are the total sales for all locations. The **DATA IN ROWS** and **DATA IN COLUMNS** options are used to indicate how the series of data is laid out in the data range that was selected.

1. Click the Bind button at the end of the By Range field.

2. Select the range C7:C11 in the spreadsheet, then click OK.

   You should have the options selected that are shown in Figure 4-34.

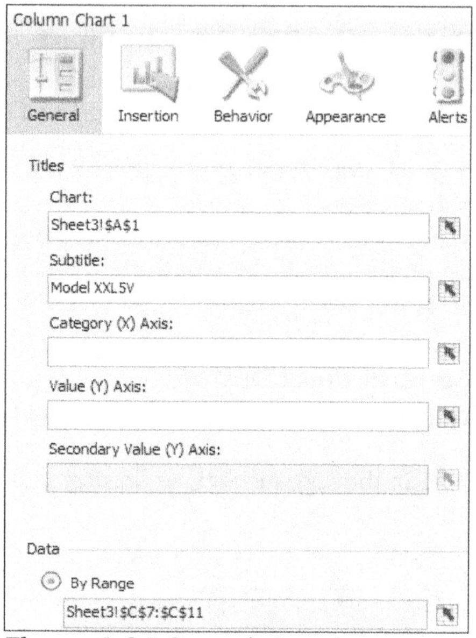

Figure 4-34 General view changes

3. Select the By Series option, then click on the series. You will see that the series **NAME** and **VALUES (Y)** fields were automatically filled in, as shown in Figure 4-35.

   You can change the series name by typing it in or by selecting the cell in the spreadsheet that has the name that you want to use.

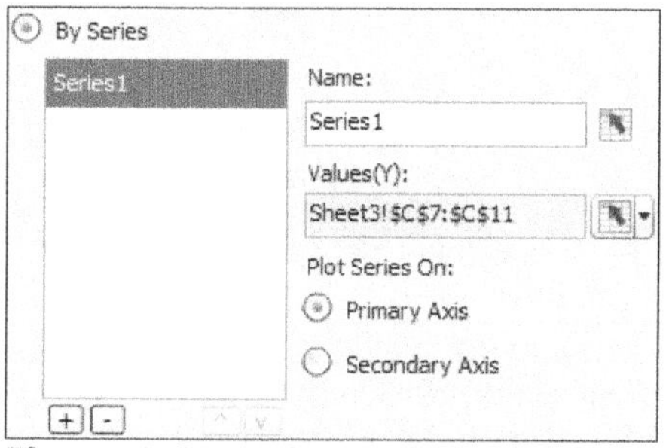

Figure 4-35 By Series changes

Notice the values on the X axis shown in Figure 4-36. They are different then the ones shown earlier in Figure 4-31. Also notice that the format of the values is different.

The options on the X axis shown earlier in Figure 4-31 are the default options that Dashboard Design automatically selected.

There is a specific range of values for the total sales, which limits the (range of) values that will be displayed on the dashboard.

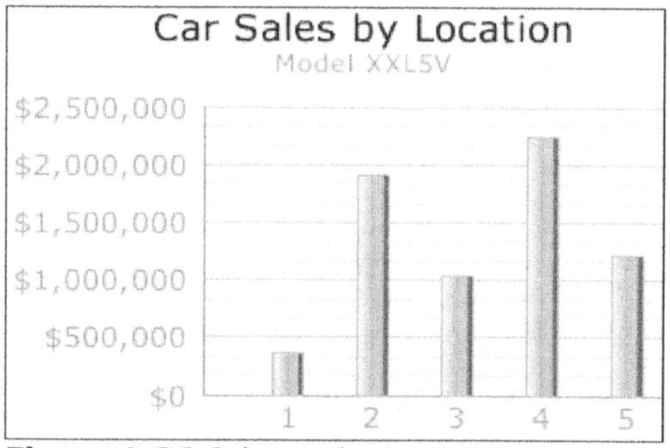

Figure 4-36 Column chart

If the spreadsheet that is being used to create the dashboard has a lot of data or data that does not need to be displayed, you could limit the range of values. I personally prefer **NOT** to limit values because doing so sometimes does not provide a true portrayal of the data in the spreadsheet. This could unintentionally be misleading to the people that use the dashboard.

If you need to put limits on a range of values, I think that it is a good practice to indicate that on the dashboard. Using the Subtitle field is a good place to put this information or you can use a label component. For example, putting a date range in the Subtitle field would let users know the dates that the data displayed in the dashboard is for.

In the spreadsheet shown earlier in Figure 4-33, I would put "For Jan 1, 2011 to Jan 31, 2011" in cell D1. In the Subtitle field, I would select cell D1. If the dashboard is updated and includes data from a different date range, I would change the date range in cell D1, so that when the data is refreshed, the date range in the Subtitle field would reflect the changes. Doing this is optional.

Category Labels (X) Option

This is the option that stores the values that will be displayed across the bottom of the chart. Currently, you see numbers across the bottom of the chart. The chart would be easier to understand if the locations were displayed, instead of the numbers.

1. Click the Bind button at the end of the Category Labels (X) option, at the bottom of the General view. You may have to scroll down to see this option.

2. Select the range A7:A11, then click OK.

Select The Scale Tab Options

The options on this tab are used to manipulate the data that is displayed on the dashboard and to select the run time options. To make your dashboard look like the one shown earlier, options on the Scale tab need to be changed.

The **MANUAL (Y) AXIS** option is used to change the values on the Y axis. You can type in the values that you want or you can select them from the spreadsheet. It is very possible that the values that you want to use are not in the spreadsheet.

1. Select the Behavior view. On the Scale tab, select the Manual (Y) Axis option.

2. Type `300000` in the **MINIMUM LIMIT** field, then type `2500000` in the **MAXIMUM LIMIT** field.

3. Check the **FIXED LABEL SIZE** option.

   Select the Number of Divisions option, then change the value to 4. You should have the options shown in Figure 4-37.

   The Fixed Label Size option makes the axis label values uniform, which should make the values on the axis easier to read. In this exercise, the range is $300,000 to $2.5 million.

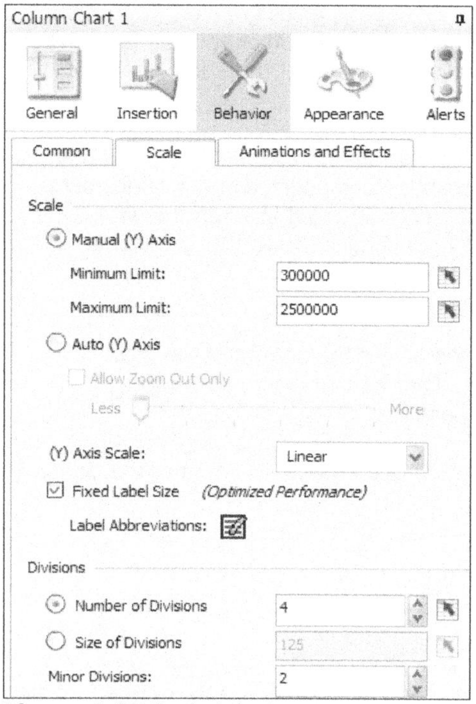

Figure 4-37 Scale tab changes

Add The Slider Component To The Model

The slider component that you add to the model will be used to increase or decrease the number of cars (units) sold.

1. Open the Single Value category folder in the Components Browser, then open the Horizontal Slider folder.

2. Drag the **HORIZONTAL SLIDER** component to the canvas and place it under the chart.

3. On the General view of the Properties panel, click the Bind button at the end of the Title field. Click in cell D4, then click OK.

4. Click the Bind button at the end of the **DATA** field. Click in cell E4, then click OK. You should have the options shown in Figure 4-38.

Yes, I know that cell E4 is empty. If you were going to use the spreadsheet to perform the analysis of "What If X more cars were sold per location", cell E4 is where you would type in X. In the dashboard, the slider will be used to select X.

The Total Sales field on the spreadsheet has the formula, Unit Increase plus Units Sold. Therefore, as the Unit Increase value becomes larger, the Total Sales cells in the spreadsheet and the bars in the chart will go up, as you will see shortly. The value selected on the slider is placed in cell E4 in this example, which then recalculates the values in the Total Sales column.

Figure 4-38 General view changes

5. Select the Behavior view. On the Common tab, select the **ENABLE PLAY BUTTON** option.

6. Select the Appearance view. On the Layout tab, select the **MANUAL** option.

   In the **NUMBER OF TICKS** section, change the Major option to 11.

   Change the **MINOR** option to 4, as shown in Figure 4-39.

   You can type the number in or you can use the arrow buttons at the end of the field to select the number.

   Earlier in Figure 4-31, you saw tick marks on the slider component.

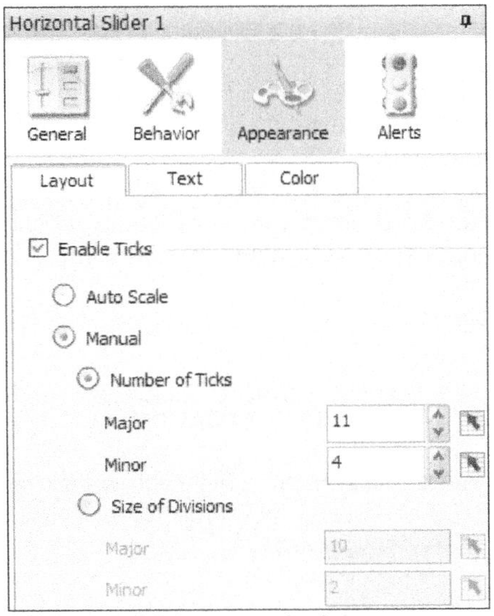

Figure 4-39 Layout tab changes

Save And Test The Model

In this part of the exercise you will test the model.

1. If necessary, make the chart larger and the slider as wide as the chart.

2. Click the Save button on the Standard toolbar. You should see your folder at the top of the Save As dialog box. Type `My slider model` as the file name, then press Enter.

3. Click the Preview button. The model should look like the one shown earlier in Figure 4-31. You can drag the blue button on the slider or click the **PLAY** button on the slider. Clicking the Play button a second time causes the slider to stop.

If you click the Play button and let the slider go all the way to the end, what you will notice is that the bars for some locations (cities) will reach the maximum value of $2.5 million before the slider reaches 100. This is an example of why I am not a fan of using a range for data, in particular, for the maximum amount.

4. If you need to make changes, click the Preview button to return to the design mode and make the changes. Save the changes.

Export And Publish The Model

In the previous part of the exercise you created and saved the model. In the file format that the model is currently in, the only people that could use it are people that have Dashboard Design installed. Most of the time, you will need to distribute dashboards to people that do not have Dashboard Design installed on their computer. The way that the dashboard is distributed is to export the model. A Flash file is automatically created and then added to the export option that you select. The Flash file can be run as is, saved in a PDF file or another output format.

In this part of the exercise you will learn how to export the model to a Flash file, which is the file that you can distribute to other people. This is probably the part of the exercise that you have been waiting for because you will be able to let other people use your dashboard. By now, I am sure that you understand that Dashboard Design provides several options for you to select from to distribute your dashboard. These options are pretty straight forward.

1. In design mode, File ⇒ Export.
   You will see the submenu shown in Figure 4-40.

   Options that are not enabled means that you cannot export your model to that format.

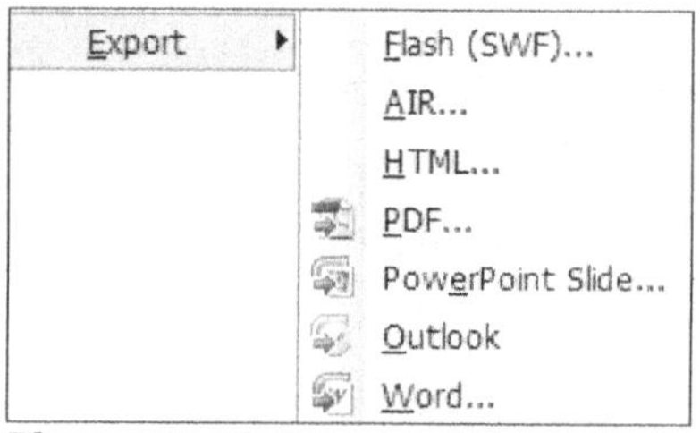

Figure 4-40 Export submenu

2. Select the **POWERPOINT SLIDE** option.

3. Navigate to the folder where you want to save the dashboard. In this exercise, navigate to your folder if necessary, then type `My slider dashboard` as the file name, as shown at the bottom of Figure 4-41.

   If you were going to distribute this dashboard, you will save it on a network drive instead of the hard drive on your computer. That way other people can access it.

   Press Enter or click the Save button. Once the dashboard is created, it will open in the format that you selected. In this exercise PowerPoint will open.

   As you can see, the dashboard is smaller in PowerPoint than it was in the model. In Chapter 3 you learned how to resize the canvas, which is how the size of the dashboard is changed. Hopefully, the process of creating the dashboard was not too painful.

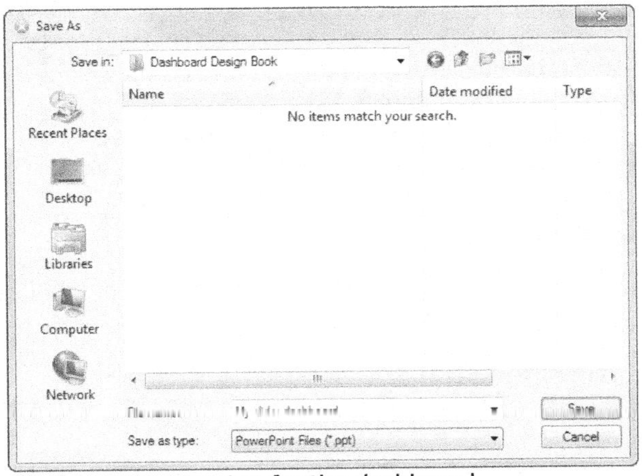

Figure 4-41 Location for the dashboard

If you have PowerPoint 2010 installed and want to save the slide, save it in 97-2003 .ppt format.

Other Component Types

As shown in Figure 4-42, Single Value components are just one type of component.

There are nine other types of components, which are explained in Table 4-3. The chapter that the component type is covered in is listed at the end of the description in brackets.

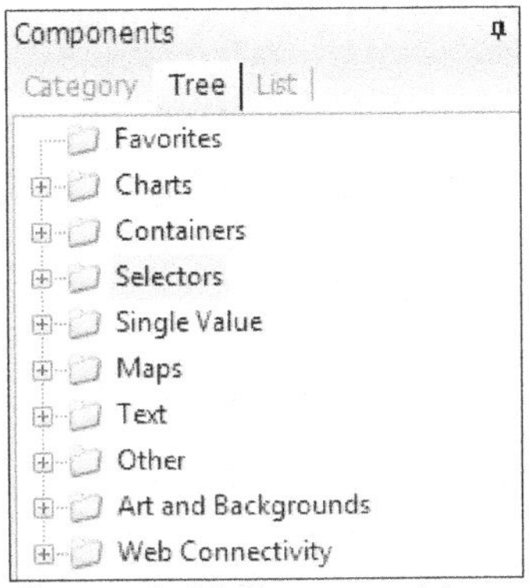

Figure 4-42 Component types

Component Type	Description
Charts	Displays the data from the spreadsheet in a chart. [Chapters 7 and 8]
Containers	Displays other components. [Chapter 15]
Selectors	Components that allow the user to change at least one variable, which causes the data displayed in another component on the dashboard to change. [Chapter 9]
Maps	Links data geographically to different parts of the map. [Chapter 11]
Text	Input and Label components that are used to pass data to the dashboard and to display text or data. [Chapter 12]
Other	Components that do not fit in any of the other categories. [Chapter 12]
Art and Backgrounds	Components that can be added to the model to make the dashboard look better. They have no effect on the data or functionality of the dashboard. [Chapter 12]

Table 4-3 Other component types explained

Component Type	Description
Web Connectivity	Adds Internet functionality and allows images and Flash files on the Internet to be used in the dashboard. [Chapter 12]
Universe Connectivity	These components allow users to enter prompt vales and refresh data through Universe connections. They are beyond the scope of this book. This component type is not available in Presentation Design.

Table 4-3 Other component types explained (Continued)

PREPARING EXCEL SPREADSHEETS FOR DASHBOARDS

In this chapter you will learn about topics that will help you create better Excel spreadsheets for dashboards, including the following:

- ☑ Excel functionality not supported in Dashboard Design
- ☑ Design principles
- ☑ Data modeling
- ☑ Connecting to external data sources
- ☑ Filtering data
- ☑ Formatting options

Shameless Book Plug
If after completing the exercises in this book, you have the need to use spreadsheets that have thousands or millions of rows of data or you need to use data from multiple spreadsheets or other data sources, you will find that PowerPivot for Excel 2010, a free add-on for Excel 2010, will let you work with spreadsheets that have a million rows of data to create sophisticated Pivot Tables and Pivot Charts that cannot be created in Excel.

If you have the need to create Pivot Tables or Pivot Charts that are beyond what Excel can handle, you may find my book, Getting Started With PowerPivot For Excel 2010 (ISBN 978-1-935208-13-6) helpful because PowerPivot supports spreadsheets with millions of rows of data.

Because you purchased this book on Dashboard Design, you can order the PowerPivot book for 50% off of the list price ($20 plus $5 for priority mail shipping). To order, go to www.tolana.com/books/dashboard.html.

CHAPTER 5

Excel Overview

Okay, now that you have created your first dashboard in Dashboard Design, this is a good time to go over topics in Excel that will help you structure that data in the spreadsheet to be more Dashboard Design friendly. If you are using Presentation Design, this chapter should be very beneficial because Excel is the only option available for importing data. Before you become too excited about Dashboard Design, I want to spend some time going over some Excel concepts that I think will help you create better dashboards.

As I have said earlier, Excel has been around for a long time and will be here for quite some time. Some of the first dashboards were created in Excel. Many still are today. Because you purchased this book, I can conclude that at the very least, you want to see what Dashboard Design has to offer that Excel doesn't, in terms of dashboard functionality.

If you have created dashboards in Excel, I think that the majority of topics covered in this chapter will be familiar. My primary goal for this chapter is to get you to start thinking about spreadsheet data and data in general, in terms of what is needed to be able to create an effective dashboard in Dashboard Design. In Chapter 4 you read about the dashboard design process. Some of the topics covered in this chapter expand on the topics presented in that chapter.

Another reason that at the 11th hour of writing my first book for this software package (Crystal Xcelsius 4.5) that I decided to add this chapter is to let you know that most of the time the spreadsheet will not come to you from the user in the layout needed to create a dashboard.

Having written more than 20 computer books that require sample files, every so often, I receive an email from a reader asking why is it that the data that they use at work is not ready to be used in a mail merge or a report like the sample files for the book are. Because I have or will, by the end of this chapter, addressed this topic thoroughly, I am not expecting any email like that from you. Instead, you can email me thanking me for the heads up <smile>.

I realize that some readers have already created dashboards in Excel. In this chapter, I try to point out as many similarities and differences as I can between creating dashboards in Excel and Dashboard Design, to help make your transition easier.

Dashboard Design Benefits

There are some benefits to using Dashboard Design to create dashboards that Excel does not provide, including the following:

① By default, users cannot view, change or delete the formulas in the spreadsheet used to create a dashboard because they do not have access to the spreadsheet.
② Security of the spreadsheet data. While you can hide or protect the data and formulas in an Excel dashboard, it is much easier for someone to gain access to the protected information in Excel. Dashboards created in Dashboard Design do not have this issue because the users only interaction with the data is via the dashboard. The formulas work in the dashboard but are not accessible via the dashboard.
③ Dashboards created in Dashboard Design can be exported to other formats like HTML or PowerPoint and the formulas still work.

Excel Functionality That Dashboard Design Does Not Support

For all that Dashboard Design offers, there are some Excel features and functionality that Dashboard Design does not support, as listed below:

① Active X Controls
② Auto Filters
③ Form Controls
④ Cells or spreadsheets that are linked to other spreadsheets
⑤ Macros
⑥ Rounding
⑦ Pivot Tables, but you can import the data displayed in a Pivot Table
⑧ Scientific formatted numbers

Excel Functions Supported In Dashboard Design

Thankfully, the Dashboard Design documentation team included a list of the supported Excel functions in the online users guide. I say thankfully, because I truly did not want to have to type them in <smile>. To view the list, follow the steps below.

1. Open Dashboard Design.

2. Help ⇒ Dashboard Design Help ⇒ Contents tab ⇒ Working with Data ⇒ Understanding the embedded spreadsheet ⇒ Supported Excel functions.

   You should see the list shown on the right side of Figure 5-1.

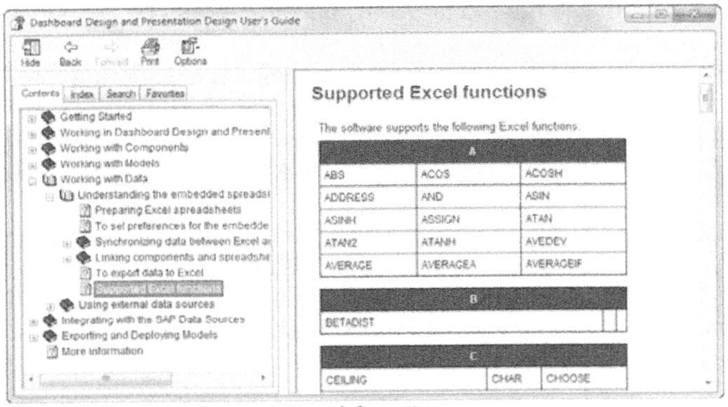

Figure 5-1 Supported Excel functions

> These functions should be used with small amounts of data because large data sets can slow down the performance of the dashboard. The work around for this is to do the processing from the database or on the server, instead of in the spreadsheet.

Reports vs Dashboards

I have heard people use these words interchangeably and often it drives me nuts because they are two different ways to display data. Never mind that fact that I have written several books on Crystal Reports, the most popular report writing software currently on the market, so I think I know a thing or two about reports.

Out of all of the Business Intelligence tools, reports are probably the most used. Reports allow data to be presented in an easy to read and understand format. Reports primarily display raw data if you will. Reports present data, usually with minimal interaction between the report and person running the report. Reports often lead to further analysis. Most reports are paper based and have a broad goal and are not intended to be used to slice and dice data, as they say.

Dashboards are primarily graphical. They are usually not paper based. The graphical representation of data makes it easier to see the trends and draw conclusions. Dashboards either have the analysis built-in or allows the user to display the analysis in more than one way. Dashboards tend to present summary information, while reports tend to display more detailed information.

Dashboard Design should be used to present data for analysis purposes. This means that often the data has already been summarized before it is imported into a model. Overall, Dashboard Design uses less rows of data then a traditional report. Now that I have cleared up the differences between reports and dashboards, lets move on.

Data Modeling

In Chapter 4, I explained the concept of designing for scalability. That is part of data modeling. A **DATA MODEL** is the structure or foundation for the data for a specific purpose. The purpose of a data model is to store data for analysis, not process data. In this case, the purpose is to import the spreadsheet data into a Dashboard Design model.

I am sure that there is a limit to how many rows of spreadsheet data Dashboard Design can work with, without coming to a screeching halt, but I could not find a definitive answer. For testing purposes, I imported a spreadsheet that had 15,000 rows of data. The import process took a while, but after that, I had no problems building the model.

If the data model is not correct and the data is imported into Dashboard Design, you will find that you cannot design the dashboard that you need. I understand that this concept may sound scary, but it is not as bad as you may be thinking. If you can visualize what the dashboard should look like and what functionality it should have, it will be easier to set up an appropriate data model.

Sometimes, trying to visualize what the data for the dashboard should look like does not work. When that happens, I work backwards and will create the prototype with the data however I have it set up and see where I run into a problem. Often, for me, this is quicker and less stressful then trying to figure out the data model first. I don't advise this though, especially for people that are just starting out, because it is easy to miss something.

In Chapter 4, you learned how to gather all of the fields needed for the dashboard. Once you have the fields, you have to put them in the correct structure for the data model. One thing that may help is to keep in mind that from left to right in a spreadsheet, the data needed for a menu or filter component and data that is repeated row after row, goes in the left most columns. The data that is unique to each row, like totals or quantities, are placed in the right most columns.

As shown in Figure 5-2, Columns A to C contain the data the repeats, row after row, while the data in columns D to G is different from row to row.

	A	B	C	D	E	F	G
1	Sales by Sales Representative						
2							
3	*Product*	*Sales Rep*	*Account Type*	Q1	Q2	Q3	Q4
4	Product 1	Sales Rep. 1	New Customer	$ 44.2	$ 64.4	$ 55.3	$ 50.7
5	Product 2	Sales Rep. 1	New Customer	$ 39.6	$ 38.3	$ 34.7	$ 47.2
6	Product 3	Sales Rep. 1	New Customer	$ 41.9	$ 66.8	$ 55.5	$ 54.2
7	Product 4	Sales Rep. 1	New Customer	$ 41.5	$ 66.9	$ 40.8	$ 59.4
8	Product 5	Sales Rep. 1	New Customer	$ 63.2	$ 40.2	$ 58.1	$ 46.7
9	Product 6	Sales Rep. 1	New Customer	$ 50.9	$ 44.3	$ 50.1	$ 51.9
10	Product 7	Sales Rep. 1	New Customer	$ 53.7	$ 54.8	$ 39.1	$ 54.7
11	Product 8	Sales Rep. 1	New Customer	$ 62.0	$ 58.7	$ 56.6	$ 62.6
12	Product 9	Sales Rep. 1	New Customer	$ 63.8	$ 37.6	$ 48.1	$ 53.3
13	Product 1	Sales Rep. 1	Existing Customer	$ 52.8	$ 43.5	$ 44.0	$ 63.6
14	Product 2	Sales Rep. 1	Existing Customer	$ 63.7	$ 41.0	$ 45.3	$ 40.4

Figure 5-2 Appropriate data structure for a dashboard

If you are creating the dashboard in Excel, you would have to be concerned about what is known as **DATA PRESENTATION**. This is a term used to describe how the data looks visually. A lot of the data presentation is handled for you in Dashboard Design. In a way, it doesn't matter what the data looks like in Excel, as much as it matters that the data model is correct.

How Metrics And KPI's Influence The Spreadsheet Structure

In Chapter 1 you read about these terms. Now it is time to dig deeper to understand how they will influence the spreadsheet structure. Following the KPI example in Chapter 1 of producing 10,000 cars a month, if the user needed to see the data by number of cars produced a day and by week, one section of the spreadsheet would need daily totals and another section would need weekly totals, as shown in Figure 5-3.

	A	B	C	D	E	F	G	H	I	J	K	L	M	N	O
1	Car Model	Feb. 1	Feb. 2	Feb. 3	Feb. 4	Feb. 5	Feb. 6	Feb. 7	Feb. 8	Feb. 9	Feb. 10	Feb. 11	Feb. 12	Feb. 13	Feb. 14
2															
3	Model A	12	50	40	99	130	80	50	40	99	111	68	77	52	67
4	Model B	12	123	200	99	13	81	50	200	99	333	89	49	83	15
5	Model C	8	45	75	99	110	82	50	75	99	222	79	37	95	150
6															
7	Daily Total	32	218	315	297	253	243	150	315	297	666	236	163	230	232
8															
9	Week 1 Total		1508												
10	Week 2 Total		2139												

Figure 5-3 Appropriate data structure for daily and weekly totals

Using Multiple Tabs

Many of the spreadsheets that you will come across will have one week or one month of data on a different tab. Often, spreadsheets like this have links between the tabs or links to other spreadsheets, which is not supported in Dashboard Design. You should be able to fit a years worth of data on one tab.

A good use of creating a dashboard from a spreadsheet that has data on multiple tabs is if the dashboard needs to display unrelated data. For example, a dashboard that would be used as part of a presentation to the Executive board could have the following requirements because you know how executives like to hear about several areas of the company at the same time <smile>.

① Display the detail and summary information for sales in North America.

② Display the healthcare costs for offices in the United States, Canada and Australia.

③ Display the number of laptops donated to charities by state.

To make it easier to keep the data needed for these three requests organized, each data set could go on a different tab. While the data for the requirements for the dashboard is unrelated, all of the data would probably not be displayed at the same time, but it could. A menu would be created in the dashboard that lets the user select which of these data sets they want to view.

Using Enterprise Data

If you are using Presentation Design and have been looking around Dashboard Design or Excel trying to figure out how you are going to get data from your Enterprise environment into Excel without having to get a Database Administrator to do it for you, this may be the section that you have been looking for. If the database is password protected, you will need the login information. You may also need rights to the server that the database is on.

Connecting To External Data Sources

By now you know that Excel is the tool that Dashboard Design uses to import data. Many companies keep their data in databases like SQL and Microsoft Access. There are two tools that come to mind that you can use to import data into Excel, as listed below. The basics of each tool are covered in this chapter.

① The Get External Data options in Excel.
② Microsoft Query.

Using The Import External Data Option In Excel

Excel has built in functionality that is used to connect to external data sources to import data into a spreadsheet.

The **IMPORT EXTERNAL DATA** option shown in Figure 5-4 is a wizard that walks you through selecting the database and tables that you want to import.

In Excel 2007, this option was renamed to Get External Data.

The steps below show you how to import data from a Microsoft Access database into an Excel 2010 spreadsheet. You can connect to other data sources in addition to Microsoft Access using this wizard.

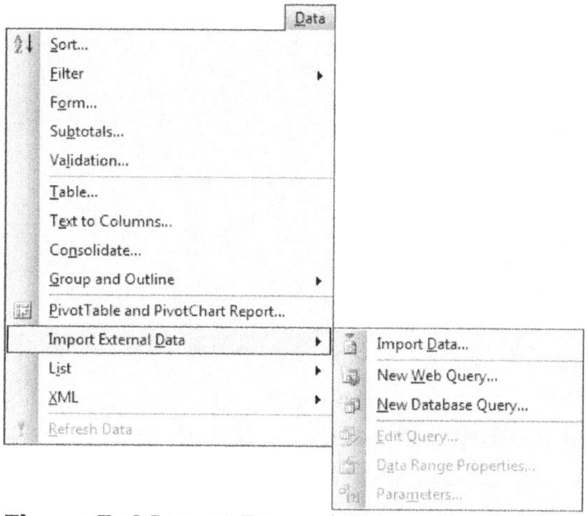

Figure 5-4 Import External Data option in Excel 2003

1. Open a new Excel workbook, unless you want to import data into an existing workbook.

2. Data Tab ⇒ Get External Data ⇒ From Access.

Database Connections
If you have never connected to a database that is the same type as the one that you want to connect to now (on the computer that you are currently using), you have to set up a connection for that type of database. For example, if you want to connect to an SQL database, but have never created a connection to any SQL database, you have to create a connection for SQL databases before you can import data from that data type.

3. If you need to create a Connection and see a connection to the database and table in Figure 5-5 that you need select it, then click the Open button, otherwise go to step 4 if you do not need to create or select a connection.

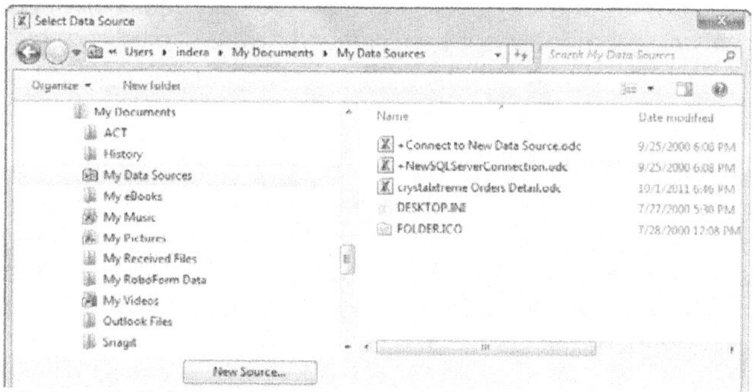

Figure 5-5 Select Data Source dialog box

4. Navigate to the folder that the database is in, then double-click on the database. You will see the dialog box shown in Figure 5-6. If the database has queries or views, they will be listed on this dialog box also. You can select one of these as the data source to import. Select the table, then click OK.

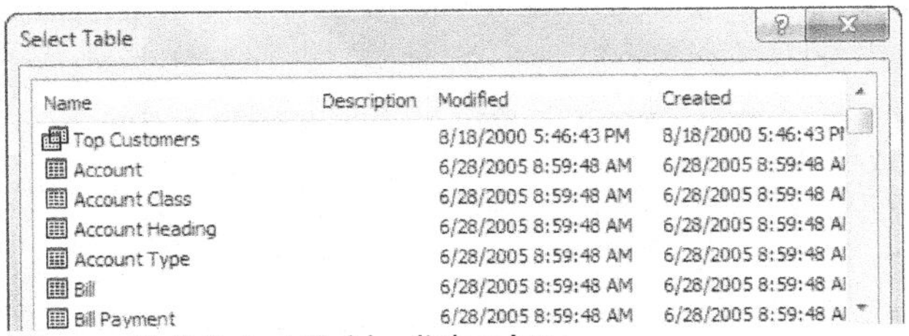

Figure 5-6 Select Table dialog box

Import Data Dialog Box Options

On the dialog box shown in Figure 5-7, select **EXISTING WORKSHEET** if you want the data from the table to be imported to the current worksheet.

If you want the data to be imported to a **NEW WORKSHEET**, select this option.

The **PROPERTIES** button opens the dialog box shown in Figure 5-8. The options selected are the default options. If you need to change any option, you can.

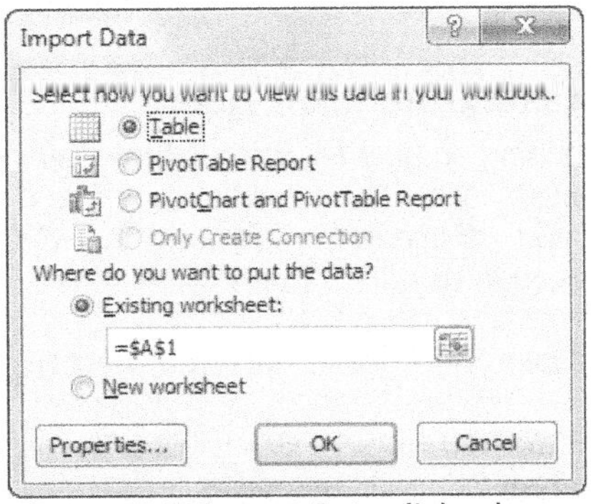

Figure 5-7 Import Data dialog box

5. If you made changes on the dialog box shown in Figure 5-8, click OK.

   Once you have made your selections on the Import Data dialog box shown above in Figure 5-7, click OK. The data will be imported into the spreadsheet.

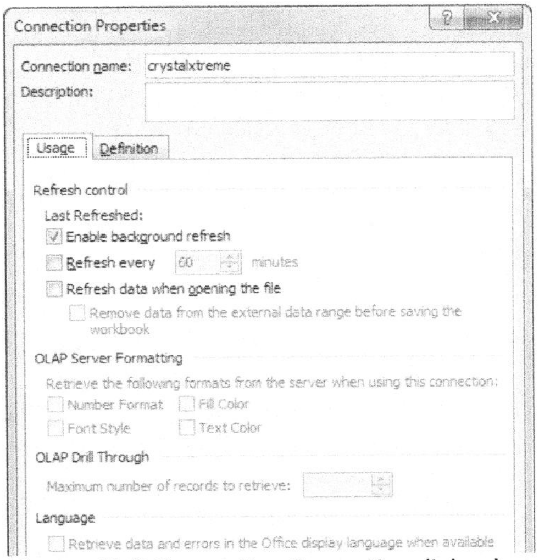

Figure 5-8 Connection Properties dialog box

External Table Data Options

After the data is imported, you should see the Table Tools Design tab. When you need to refresh the data from the external data source, click the Refresh button in the External Table Data section shown in Figure 5-9.

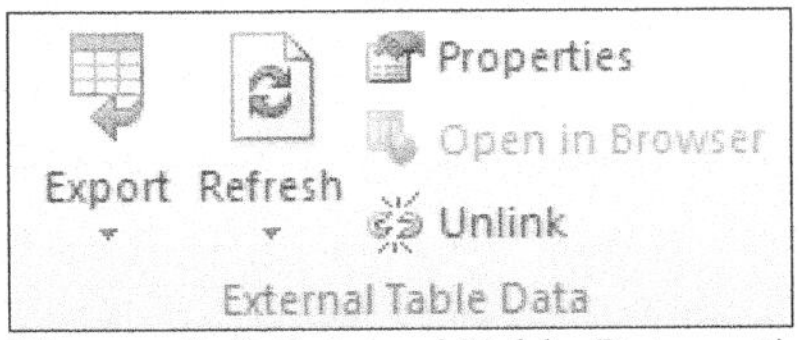

Figure 5-9 External Table Data options

Microsoft Query Wizard

This is a program that comes on the Microsoft Office installation CD. One of the features of the Query Wizard is to create connections to external data sources and import data into Excel. The advantage that this tool has over the Import External Data option in Excel is that you can modify the structure of the data that will be imported. By that I mean that you can do any of the following, prior to importing the data.

① Create a query to select specific records to import from the tables.
② Join several tables.
③ Sort the data before it is imported.

Installing Microsoft Query

Depending on how Microsoft Office was installed, the MS Query Wizard may or may not already be installed. Follow the steps below to see if MS Query is installed and if it isn't, install it, if you know that you will use it. If you know that MS Query is installed, go to the section "Create A Database Connection Using MS Query".

1. Open Excel, if it is not already open.

2. Data Tab ⇒ Get External Data ⇒ From Other Data Sources ⇒ From Microsoft Query, as shown in Figure 5-10.

   If you see the Choose Data Source dialog box shown in Figure 5-12, MS Query is already installed.

   Go to the section, "Create A Database Connection Using MS Query".

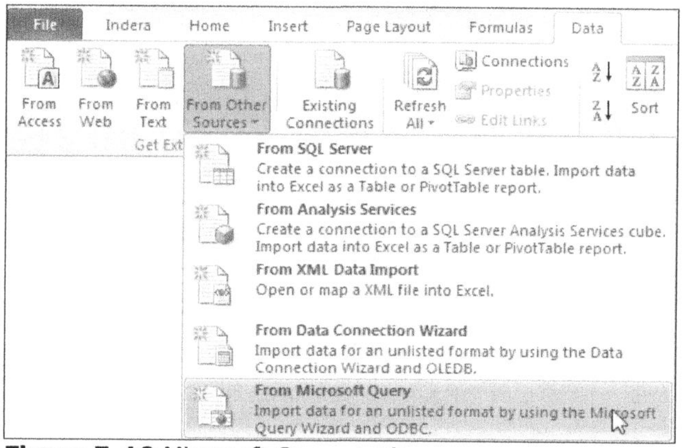

Figure 5-10 Microsoft Query option

3. If you see the message shown in Figure 5-11, click Yes, to start the installation process.

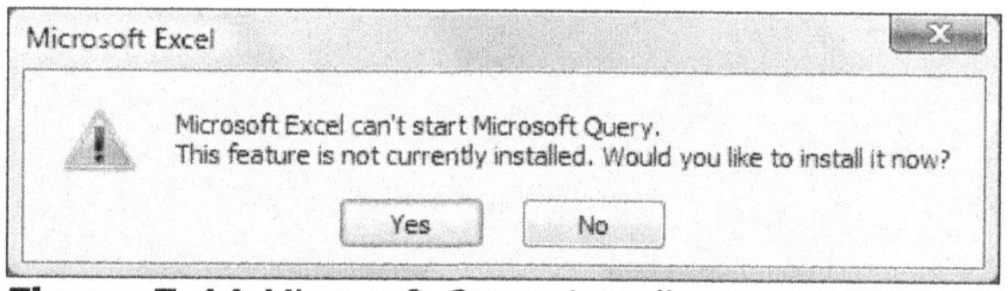

Figure 5-11 Microsoft Query install message

You may be prompted to put the Microsoft Office CD into the drive. When the installation is completed you will see the Choose Data Source dialog box.

Create A Database Connection Using MS Query

The steps below show you how to create a connection to a Microsoft Access database.

1. In Excel, Data ⇒ Get External Data ⇒ From Other Data Sources ⇒ From Microsoft Query. You will see the dialog box shown in Figure 5-12.

   It is very possible that you will see different file types then the ones shown. The options that you have are from connections that you have already set up.

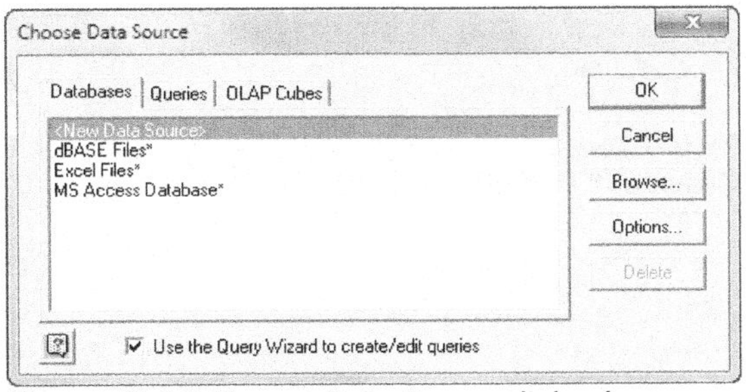

Figure 5-12 Choose Data Source dialog box

To connect to a database that has a file type (dBase Files, Excel Files and MS Access Database) in the list shown above in Figure 5-12, select the file type, then click OK. If you need to connect to an SQL or Oracle database or a database that does not have a corresponding file type in the list, select the **NEW DATA SOURCE** option, then click OK.

2. Select the MS Access Database option, then click OK.

3. If the database is not on your computers hard drive, open the **DRIVES** drop-down list, shown at the bottom of Figure 5-13 and select the drive that the database is on. You may also see the message box shown in Figure 5-14. This lets you know that you are in the process of creating a connection to a database.

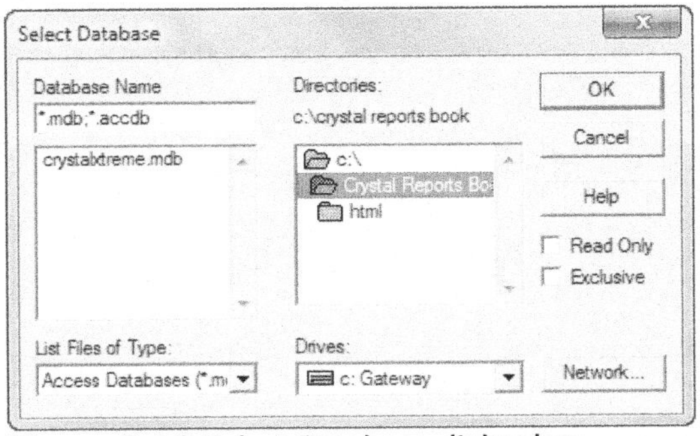

Figure 5-13 Select Database dialog box

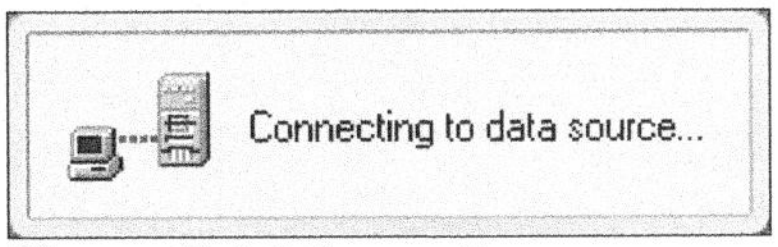

Figure 5-14 Connection message

4. In the **DIRECTORIES** section of the Select Database dialog box, navigate to and double-click on the folder that has the database with the tables that you want to import.

5. In the **DATABASE NAME** list you will see a list of the databases that are in the folder that you selected. Click on the database that you want to create a connection to, then click OK.

Query Wizard

You will now see the Query Wizard screen shown in Figure 5-15. This is where you select the fields from the tables that you want to import. If you click on the plus sign in front of a table name in the **AVAILABLE TABLES AND COLUMNS** list, you will see all of the fields in that table, as shown in Figure 5-16.

If you are not sure of the data that is in a field (which the Query Wizard refers to as a column), click on the field in the Available tables and columns list or Columns in your query list, then click the

PREVIEW NOW button. In the **PREVIEW OF DATA IN SELECTED COLUMN** field, you will see the data that is in that field.

The **OPTIONS** button opens the dialog box shown in Figure 5-17. These options control what is displayed in the Available tables and columns list.

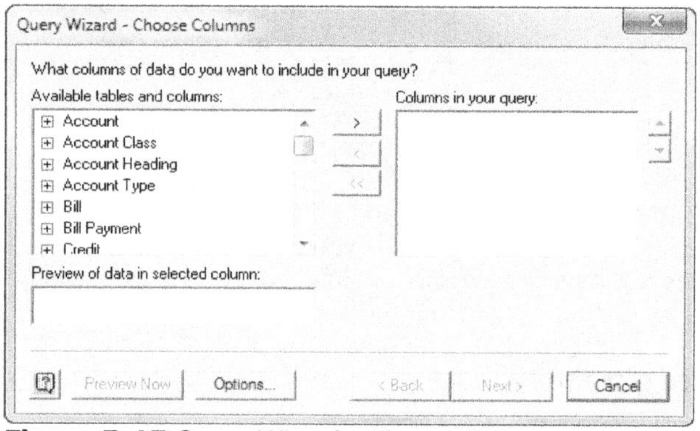

Figure 5-15 Query Wizard - Choose Columns screen

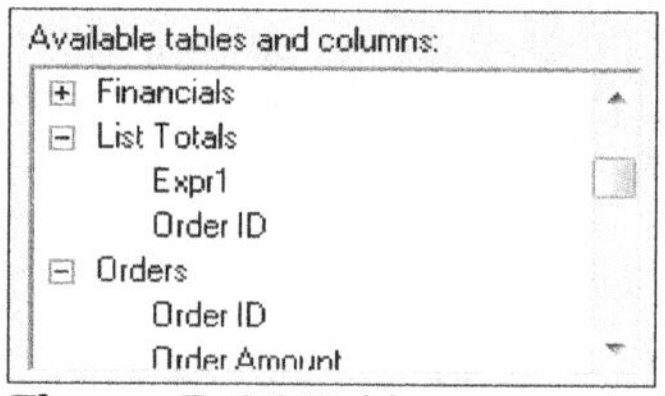

Figure 5-16 Tables expanded

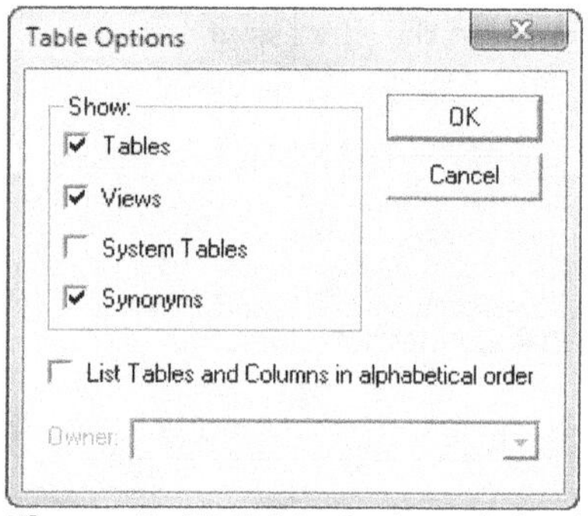

Figure 5-17 Table Options dialog box

Use The Query Wizard To Select The Data To Import

There are four steps to selecting and importing data using the Query Wizard. Steps 2 and 3 are optional.

Step 1: Choose The Columns

1. Select a field that you want to import, then click the right arrow button. You should see the field that you selected in the **COLUMNS IN YOUR QUERY** list.

> **How To Add All Fields From A Table**
> If you want to import all of the fields from a table, click on the name of the table, then click the right arrow button.

> **How To Change The Order Of Fields Being Imported**
> If you need to rearrange the order of the fields in the Columns in your query list, click on the field that you want to move, then click the Up or Down button to the right of the list box.

2. When you have selected all of the fields that you need, click Next.

Step 2: Filter The Data

The options on this screen are used to select the criteria to filter (reduce) the number of records that will be imported into Excel. If you need to create criteria for another field, select the field name on the left, then select the criteria for the field.

Figure 5-18 shows sample filter criteria. Fields in bold in the **COLUMN TO FILTER** list indicate that you have already selected criteria for the field.

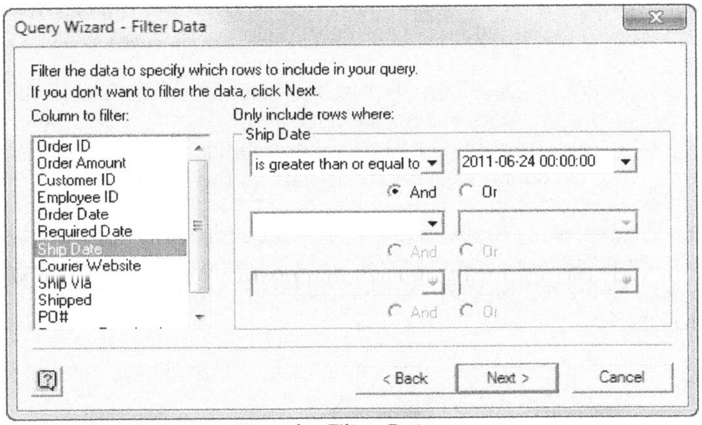

Figure 5-18 Query Wizard - Filter Data screen

1. Select the filter criteria for each field that you need, then click Next.

Step 3: Sort The Records

The options shown in Figure 5-19 are used to sort the records that will be imported into Excel.

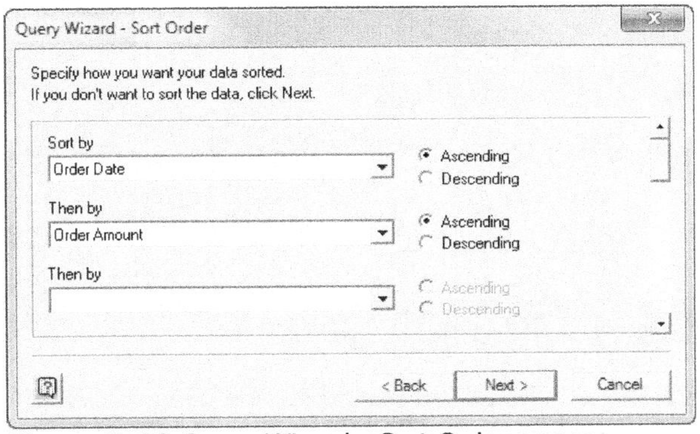

Figure 5-19 Query Wizard - Sort Order screen

1. Select the Sort Order, then click Next.

Step 4: Finish The Import

The options shown in Figure 5-20 are used to select what you want to do with the records that will be imported.

The **SAVE QUERY** button saves the query that you just created.

Queries that you save will appear on the Queries tab on the Choose Data Source dialog box.

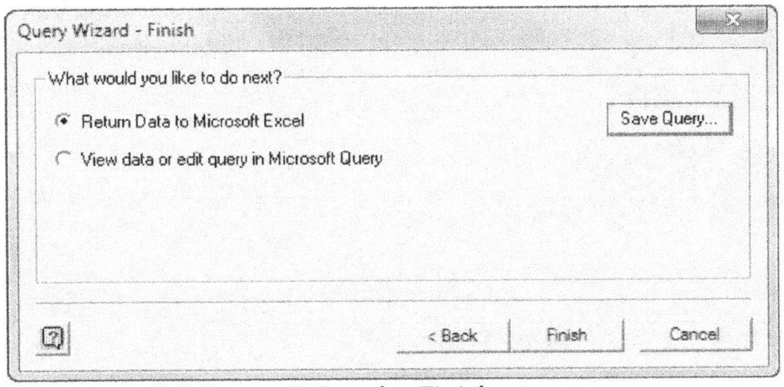

Figure 5-20 Query Wizard - Finish screen

The **RETURN DATA TO MICROSOFT EXCEL** option imports the data into the current worksheet.

The **VIEW DATA OR EDIT QUERY IN MICROSOFT QUERY** option is used to view the data that will be imported or to edit the query that you created in the Query Wizard, as shown in Figure 5-21. The options explained below are how to close the Query Tool.

① File ⇒ Cancel and Return to Microsoft Office Excel, will close the query tool and query wizard. Data will not be imported.
② File ⇒ Return Data to Microsoft Office Excel, is used to view and modify the query. This option will import the data to the spreadsheet.

The **CREATE AN OLAP CUBE FROM THIS QUERY** option will appear if you have already set up a connection to a database that supports OLAP Cubes. You will see the wizard shown in Figure 5-22. This wizard is used to import the data into an OLAP Cube structure. **OLAP** stands for On-Line Analytical Processing.

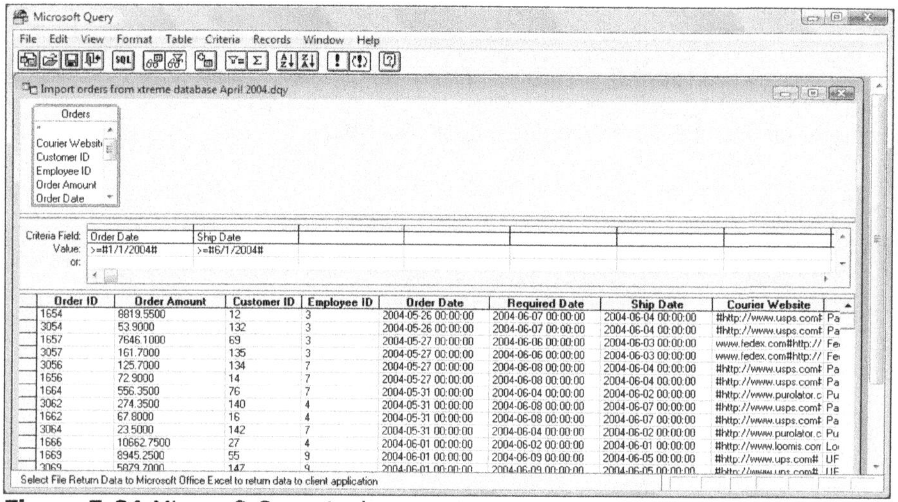

Figure 5-21 Microsoft Query tool

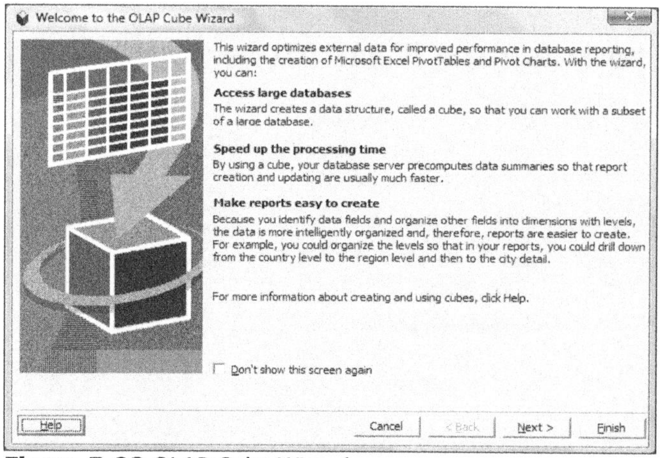

Figure 5-22 OLAP Cube Wizard

1. Click the Finish button on the Query Wizard dialog box.

Check The Data Model

There are several tasks that need to be completed before the spreadsheet is imported into Dashboard Design, as explained below.

① Make sure that all of the data is in the spreadsheet. I know that sounds funny, but it is very easy to leave off a row or column of data.
② Check and test the formulas and functions to make sure that they reference the correct cells and are not producing any errors.
③ Include as much numeric formatting as needed. Also make sure that the numeric formatting is correct for each field.
④ For testing purposes (in Dashboard Design), in the spreadsheet you should include negative numbers and data that does not belong, to see how Dashboard Design handles it.

Importing Data Into Dashboard Design Tips

When you start creating dashboards on your own, it is very possible that the layout of the spreadsheet data will need to be changed to be able to get the dashboard to work the way that you need it to. If you find this to be the case, don't panic because this is part of the learning curve. Hopefully, the tips below will help you.

① The data and formulas in the spreadsheet need to be correct before the import takes place.
② If there is a function in the spreadsheet that is not supported in Dashboard Design, it needs to be replaced in the spreadsheet or deleted before the data is imported.
③ As best you can, make sure that the layout of the spreadsheet is correct. If you add, modify or delete rows or columns in the spreadsheet to be able to create the dashboard and then re-import the data, some of the references to cells on the Properties panel in Dashboard Design may not work. If this type of change occurs, you will have to manually change the links in the model so that the dashboard will work with the structure changes in the spreadsheet.
④ When you import a spreadsheet, all of the tabs in the Excel workbook are imported. This allows you to select data on any tab, to link a component to in the model. If there are tabs with data in the spreadsheet that you will not use to create the dashboard, you should delete the tabs of data or copy the tabs of data that are needed to a new spreadsheet before starting the import process.

Once the data is imported into the model in Dashboard Design, any changes made to the data on the spreadsheet will not be captured in the dashboard unless the spreadsheet data is re-imported into the model. If it seems that you have read this already in this book, you are not crazy, you have. I have purposely written it more than once because it seems to be a step that people just learning Dashboard Design forget.

How Many Rows And Columns Is Too Many?

The honest answer to that question is it depends on the following:

① The number of rows and columns in the spreadsheet.
② The number of complex formulas the spreadsheet has.

I have created a model that has 15,000 plus rows, but only four columns of data and a few SUM formulas. I haven't tried it, but I suspect that a spreadsheet that has 15,000 rows and 12 or more columns of data will cause the dashboard to run slow.

After reading a lot of messages in forums, I found out that formulas cause a performance hit (1), more than a large number of rows of data. The more complex the formulas are, the quicker the performance of the dashboard will degrade. Excel does not process the formulas in a dashboard. Remember that once you import the data into the model, Excel is disconnected from the model. Flash actually processes the formulas in the dashboard, which is probably why all of Excels functions are not supported in Dashboard Design. (I did not verify that, it is just my educated guess.)

The one function that I noticed when reading the messages in the forums that people had trouble with is VLOOKUP. Too many formulas with the VLOOKUP function in a model, causes the dashboard to take a performance hit.

(1) A **PERFORMANCE HIT** comes from a process that causes something, in this case, a dashboard to run slower then it would if the process was not being used.

VLOOKUP Function

VLOOKUP is an Excel function that is used to look for a specific value in the left most column of data. The value found is used to retrieve data in another cell in the row.

Filtering Data

If you need to filter data you need to know what fields the filters are for and what component will be used. The component that comes to mind is the Filter component.

If you are or were a programmer at any time, this is one area of the dashboard design process that will truly make you cringe <smile>. In order to be able to filter data for components, each row of data must have the same information in certain columns.

For example, Figure 5-23 shows the quarterly sales per rep, per product, per account type.

Fellow programmers, so far, so good. Unfortunately, Dashboard Design cannot use this layout to populate the Filter component shown in Figure 5-24.

	A	B	C	D	E	F	G
1	Sales by Sales Representative						
2							
3	***Sales Rep***	***Account Type***	***Product***	**Q1**	**Q2**	**Q3**	**Q4**
4	Sales Rep. 1	New Customer	Product 1	$44.2	$64.4	$55.3	$50.7
5			Product 2	$39.6	$38.3	$34.7	$47.2
6			Product 3	$41.9	$66.8	$55.5	$54.2
7	Sales Rep. 1	Existing Customer	Product 1	$52.8	$43.5	$44.0	$63.6
8			Product 2	$63.7	$41.0	$45.3	$40.4
9	Sales Rep. 2	New Customer	Product 1	$58.1	$38.3	$56.7	$61.0
10			Product 2	$48.5	$54.3	$43.3	$38.1
11			Product 3	$52.6	$26.9	$40.6	$60.1
12			Product 4	$42.5	$66.5	$44.0	$44.7

Figure 5-23 Quarterly sales

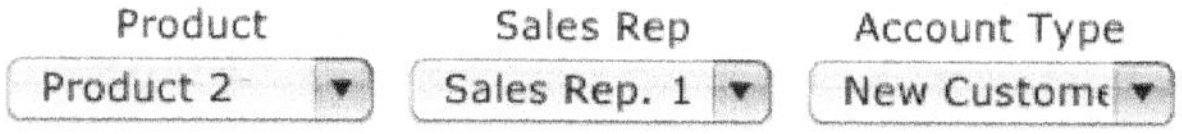

Figure 5-24 Filter component

I understand that in Excel the layout shown earlier in Figure 5-23 is a very popular format for creating reports. It is very common to use empty space for repetitive data. To populate the Filter component, the data must look like the spreadsheet shown earlier in Figure 5-2, which contains data for a three level filter component.

Programmers, you may cringe now. For all of the non programmers reading this book, the reason that we are cringing at the data structure shown earlier in Figure 5-2 is because if we created a database that stored data this way (repeating the same data over and over, row by row), we would be fired! Sadly, this is a perfect example of what I meant earlier when I stated that you have to use an Excel structure that Dashboard Design can support.

Until Dashboard Design can directly support relational databases, this is how the data must be structured in a spreadsheet.

Flat File vs Relational Data Structures
For as long as I can remember, someone will state that Excel is relational. If you are one of those people, this will hopefully clarify it for you. Relational data is stored in more than one table in a database. To display relational data, more than one table is required. In order for a table to be relational, each record in the table **MUST** have a unique identifier. This identifier is usually system generated, which means that us mere mortals do not add data to the field. Excel does not have the ability to create a unique system generated field or another type of unique identifier, therefore, Excel is not relational, it is flat file.

How To Filter Data In Excel

If filtering data is a new concept to you, follow the steps below to get a feel for how filtering data works in Excel. It is very similar to how it works in Dashboard Design. My goal is to help you become familiar with the data for the Filter component in Dashboard Design. The steps below are based on Excel 2010.

1. Open the Filter spreadsheet in Excel.

2. Data Tab ⇒ Sort & Filter ⇒ Filter. At the top of the spreadsheet, each column should have a drop-down list.

3. Open the drop-down list for the Account Type column. Clear all of the options except the New Customer option.

You should only see rows of data that have New Customer, as shown in Figure 5-25.

The Filter component shown earlier in Figure 5-24, works the same way.

	A	B	C	D		E		F		G	
1	Sales by Sales Repr	entative									
4	Product 1	Sales Rep. 1	New Customer	$	44.2	$	64.4	$	55.3	$	50.7
5	Product 2	Sales Rep. 1	New Customer	$	39.6	$	38.3	$	34.7	$	47.2
6	Product 3	Sales Rep. 1	New Customer	$	41.9	$	66.8	$	55.5	$	54.2
7	Product 4	Sales Rep. 1	New Customer	$	41.5	$	66.9	$	40.8	$	59.4
8	Product 5	Sales Rep. 1	New Customer	$	63.2	$	40.2	$	58.1	$	46.7
9	Product 6	Sales Rep. 1	New Customer	$	50.9	$	44.3	$	50.1	$	51.9
10	Product 7	Sales Rep. 1	New Customer	$	53.7	$	54.8	$	39.1	$	54.7
11	Product 8	Sales Rep. 1	New Customer	$	62.0	$	58.7	$	56.6	$	62.6
12	Product 9	Sales Rep. 1	New Customer	$	63.8	$	37.6	$	48.1	$	53.3
22	Product 1	Sales Rep. 2	New Customer	$	58.1	$	38.3	$	56.7	$	61.0
23	Product 2	Sales Rep. 2	New Customer	$	48.5	$	54.3	$	43.3	$	38.1

Figure 5-25 Data filtered in the spreadsheet

4. Open the Sales Rep drop-down list and select Sales rep 2. Only new customers for Sales rep 2 are displayed in the spreadsheet. All of the other records are hidden.

Before you fall out of the chair, as the dashboard designer, you do not have to change the spreadsheet shown earlier in Figure 5-23 to the one shown earlier in Figure 5-2. You can tell the spreadsheet owner to change the data to the required layout. What I learned a long time ago, is that as the developer of a data driven project, you are much safer by having the data owners make changes to the data, then doing it yourself. Yes, as IT people we could probably do it faster, but that is not the point. If you do not touch a users data, they cannot attempt to blame you for data errors down the road <smile>!

If it is discovered that any of the following needs to be done after you have finished the dashboard and put it into production, the spreadsheet and model will require modifications after you finish yelling. (Can you say scope creep?) If you skimmed over the Dashboard Design Process section in Chapter 4, you may want to revisit it before venturing out on your own to create a dashboard.

① At least one filter, as shown earlier in Figure 5-24, is in the wrong order. For example, if the sales rep filter should come before the product filter, the spreadsheet would have to be changed and Column B would have to be moved to Column A. No change would have to be made to the Properties panel options in the model, only the data would have to be refreshed.

② A new filter is needed. For example, the filter options shown earlier in Figure 5-24, also need an option to select the customers state. A new column would have to be added to the spreadsheet in the appropriate location. This change, in addition to having to refresh the data in the model would at the very minimum require changes to the options on the General view on the Properties panel in Dashboard Design to include the addition of the new column of data.

③ An existing column of data that is being used in the filter needs to be deleted. If the column of data for the filter that needs to be deleted is between other columns that are being used as filters, the column would have to be deleted and options on the General view would have to be modified after the data has been refreshed. If the column that is no longer needed for the filter is the first or last column in the filter range in the spreadsheet, you can leave the spreadsheet as is and just change the options on the General view to not reference the column.

Cells With And Without Formulas

When cells are linked to a component, they behave differently depending on whether or not they have a formula. Single Value components that are linked to a value can be used to select other data in the dashboard. For example, a slider component that is linked to a cell with a value, as shown in Figure 5-26 can be used to select values that display in a chart. Figure 5-27 shows the spreadsheet used for the component.

A component that is linked to a cell with a formula can only be used as an output component. You need to make sure that cells that will be linked to a Single Value component that will be used to select or control data in another component on the dashboard do not have formulas.

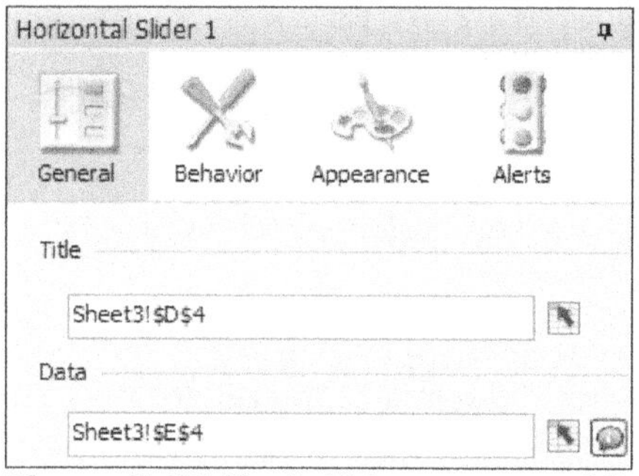

Figure 5-26 Single Value component linked to a cell with a value

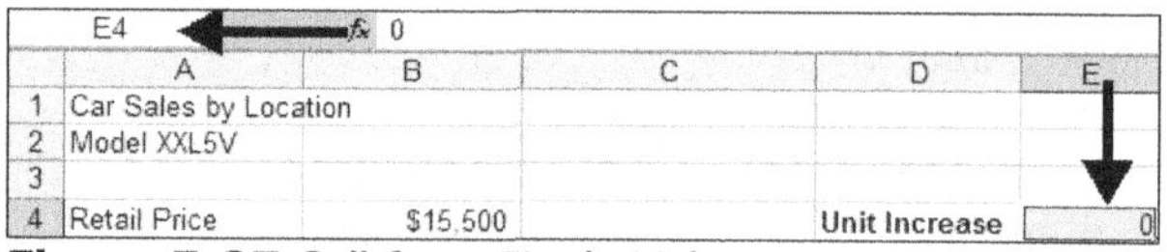

Figure 5-27 Cell for a Single Value component illustrated

Charts

Charts are the core of dashboards in Excel and Dashboard Design. The majority of chart types in Dashboard Design and Excel are the same. The differences in charts in Excel and Dashboard Design that I have observed are explained below.

① The biggest difference is that the data that is displayed in charts in Dashboard Design can be changed by other components in the dashboard.
② In Excel you can modify individual parts of a chart, like a data series. While charts created in Dashboard Design have data series, they cannot be customized as much. In Dashboard Design, a chart does not have individual parts, other then the titles, labels and legend.
③ Dashboard Design does not allow you to change the chart type once the component has been added to the canvas.
④ Combination charts in Dashboard Design only use line and column charts, unlike Combination charts in Excel, which can use an area chart as one of the chart types in a Combination chart.

Demystifying Chart Data

As if going through the dashboard design process in Chapter 4 was not bad enough and having to figure out the appropriate data model didn't push you to the edge, now you have to know how to set up the data, depending on the chart type <smile>.

The reason that I am covering this information is based on an Introduction to Excel class that I taught. I do not know what it is, but students that have an A average in the class will all of a sudden have a C average after completing the assignments on charts. It took me a while to figure out why. What I concluded was that students truly did not understand that different types of charts require the data to be set up in a specific way. I believe this is because they do not know which values in a spreadsheet, Excel uses to plot data. If you fall into this category, you are not alone.

The goal of this section is to help get you familiar with how the data layout should be for some of the more common chart types. The spreadsheets and charts used in the examples come from exercises that you will complete later in this book.

Pie Chart Data

Pie charts represent a series of data at a specific time. Figure 5-28 shows data that will allow you to create a pie chart. To create a pie chart for all products in Europe, the data range would be C6:G6. Each value in the data range represents a slice of the pie.

The (Category Axis) labels would be C3:G3. The column headings are the category labels. There is no rule that column headings have to be in row A. The chart would look like the one shown in Figure 5-29.

	A	B	C	D	E	F	G
1	Revenues By Product		Rev				
2							
3		Status List	Prod. A	Prod. B	Prod. C	Prod. D	Prod. E
4	North America		$ 14.22	$ 20.12	$ 12.18	$ 25.49	$ 15.64
5	Latin America		$ 21.05	$ 19.54	$ 15.88	$ 18.73	$ 15.02
6	Europe		$ 21.06	$ 20.45	$ 14.49	$ 16.78	$ 13.61
7	Asia		$ 12.25	$ 17.12	$ 20.99	$ 16.79	$ 12.07
8	Australia & Pacific		$ 15.36	$ 25.74	$ 13.17	$ 19.42	$ 12.70

Figure 5-28 Data for a pie chart

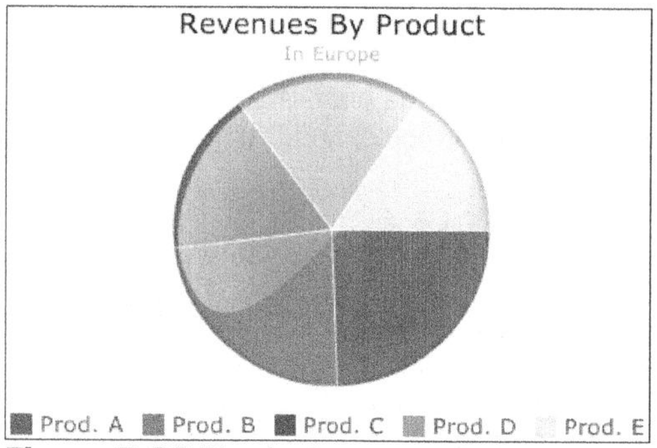

Figure 5-29 Pie chart

Line Chart Data

Line charts represent data over a period of time. Figure 5-30 shows data that can be used to create a line chart. Bar, area and column charts can also be created from the data in Figure 5-30.

A line chart can be created to show one series of data, as shown in Figure 5-31. Figure 5-32 shows two series of data in an area chart. The data range for the market growth series is B4:I4. The data range for the sales growth series is B5:I5. If you were going to create a Line chart with two series, you would select the same data range.

	A	B	C	D	E	F	G	H	I
1	Sales Growth vs Market Growth								
2									
3		**1995**	**1996**	**1997**	**1998**	**1999**	**2000**	**2001**	**2002**
4	Market Growth	7.00%	5.00%	5.00%	3.50%	7.00%	8.00%	5.00%	2.50%
5	Sales Growth	9.00%	7.00%	6.00%	5.00%	8.00%	10.00%	11.00%	13.00%

Figure 5-30 Data for a line chart

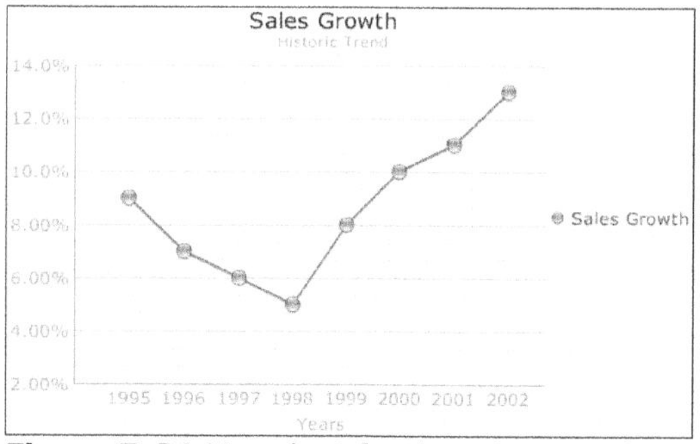

Figure 5-31 Line chart for the sales growth series of data

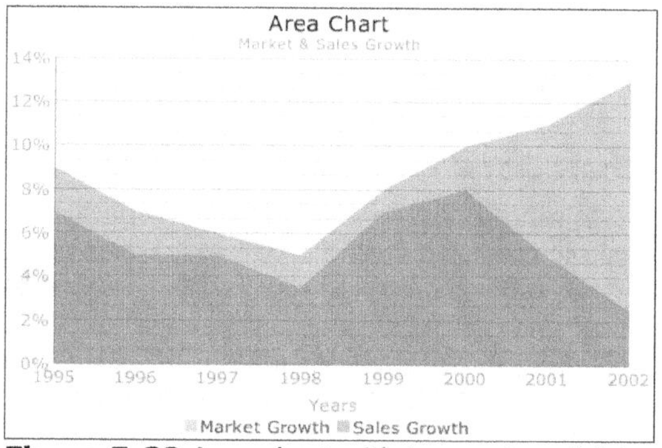

Figure 5-32 Area chart with two series of data

Figure 5-33 shows the same two series of data in a bar chart that were used to create the area chart, shown above in Figure 5-32.

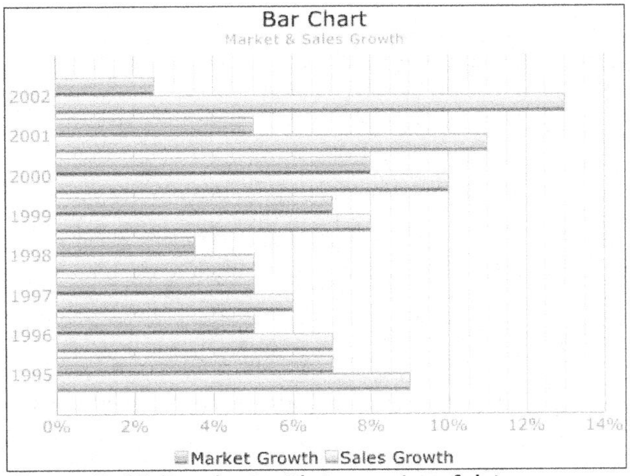

Figure 5-33 Bar chart with two series of data

Bubble, XY And Radar Chart Data

These chart types are similar in terms of data structure. All three chart types plot data based on the X and Y axis. Where the X value and Y value intersect is where the marker is placed on the chart.

Bubble charts go one step further by also using a Z value, which is used to determine the size of the bubble on the chart.

Figure 5-34 shows data that can be used to create these three chart types.

	A	B	C
1	Months on market	Asking Price	Qty
2	35	$355,000	78
3	12	$160,000	19
4	6	$150,000	89
5	25	$400,000	36
6	28	$210,000	100
7	8	$175,000	47
8	22	$360,000	51
9	15	$223,000	22
10	33	$316,000	53
11	10	$500,000	10
12	8	$429,000	44
13	4	$279,900	77

Figure 5-34 Data for several chart types

Column A is the data for the X axis. Column B is the data for the Y axis. Column C is the data that will determine the size of the bubble. The larger the number in Column C, the larger the bubble size will be. XY and Radar charts would not use this column of data in this scenario.

Figure 5-35 shows the Bubble chart from the data shown in above in Figure 5-34.

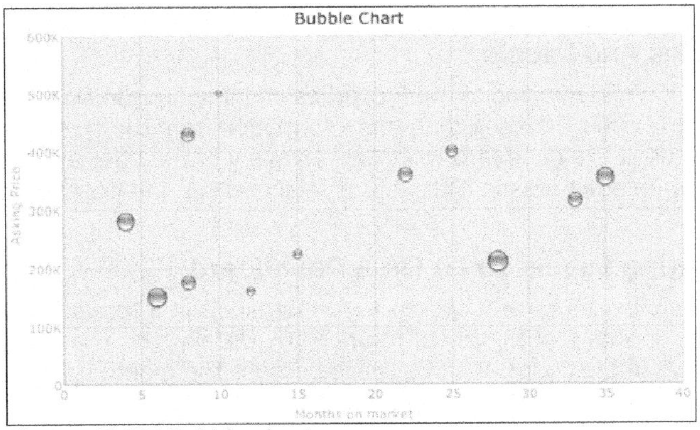

Figure 5-35 Bubble chart

Figure 5-36 shows an XY chart that could be created from the data shown earlier in Figure 5-34.

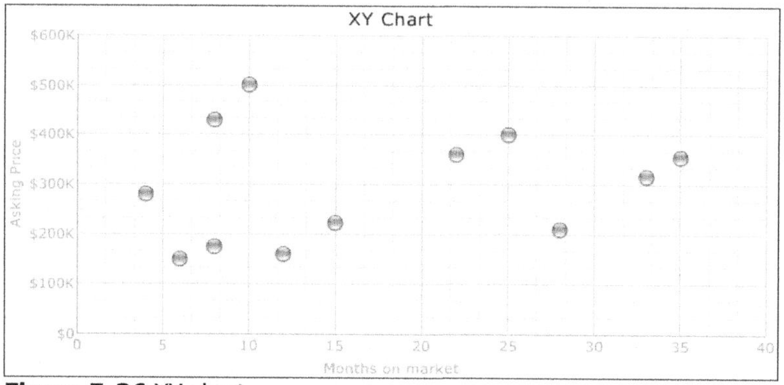

Figure 5-36 XY chart

Bubble Charts vs XY And Radar Charts

While these chart types appear similar, there are some differences, as explained below.

① Bubble charts can only use numeric data. Usually, the X axis data for XY and Radar charts is text.
② Bubble charts require three columns of data. XY and Radar only use two columns of data.

Form Controls

As you read earlier in this chapter, Dashboard Design does not support any of Excels form controls, meaning they cannot be imported. While that is true, Dashboard Design does have some options that provide the same functionality. One is the Spinner component. The majority of Excels form controls have a counterpart (i.e., Check Box, Combo Box, List Box) in Dashboard Design.

Formatting Options

Excel provides a variety of formatting options for text and numeric data. Most of them are not available in Dashboard Design. The sections below discuss data that should be added to the spreadsheet so that it will be available in Dashboard Design and formatting that you should set up in Excel.

Titles And Labels

You have seen some of the Properties panel options in Dashboard Design. On the General view are several options for selecting title information from the spreadsheet for various parts of a component. Overall, it is a good idea to include as many of the titles and labels in the spreadsheet as possible. If for no other reason, Excel has a spell checker and Dashboard Design does not.

Getting Labels To Fit On A Dashboard

Excel provides several options to format labels in a spreadsheet when the labels are too wide for the axis, as shown at the top of Figure 5-37. Usually, this is an issue for months. I prefer the first option shown in the figure. It saves space because the month names are abbreviated. Many people prefer to use the second option in Excel.

Dashboard Design does not have options that replicate the last two options. On the X axis if you have enough space to make the chart large enough, you can get the titles in a vertical position, as shown in Figure 5-38. If you want to use the first option shown in Figure 5-37, but the spreadsheet will be used for other purposes, you can put the month names on a new tab. That way you can type in the abbreviated month names on the workbook that will be imported.

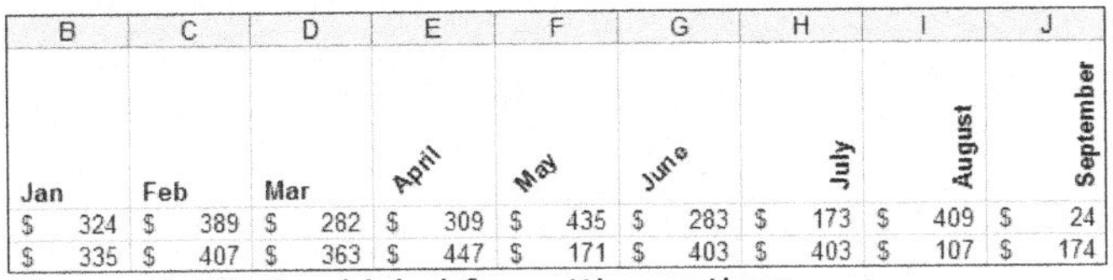

Figure 5-37 Excel label formatting options

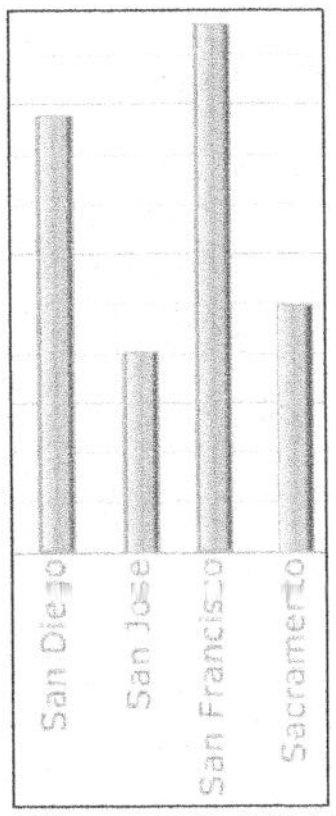

Figure 5-38 X axis labels

Using A Background Color In Spreadsheets

As you go through the exercises in this book, you will see that some cells in some of the spreadsheets have a background color. I take no credit for this great idea. These colored empty cells will be used to store the data selected by a component that will be displayed on the dashboard. This is helpful because hopefully, it will remind you that the cells are being used, so you should not put data or formulas in them.

You will see that the cells with a colored background that are at the top of the spreadsheet are used by components to pass data. This is how one component controls the data that is displayed in another component. Cells with a colored background that are below several rows of data are used to display a series of data on a component. This helps make the cells that have been reserved, so to speak, stand out on the spreadsheet.

Formatting Numbers

Excel provides more numeric formatting options than Dashboard Design. It is a good idea to format the numeric data in the spreadsheet as much as possible before importing it into a model.

While it is acceptable to use decimal points in Excel, as much as possible in my opinion, try to avoid them because decimal points are often hard to read in a dashboard. Commas on the other hand make the data easier to read in a dashboard. The dialog box in Figure 5-39 shows the formatting options in Excel.

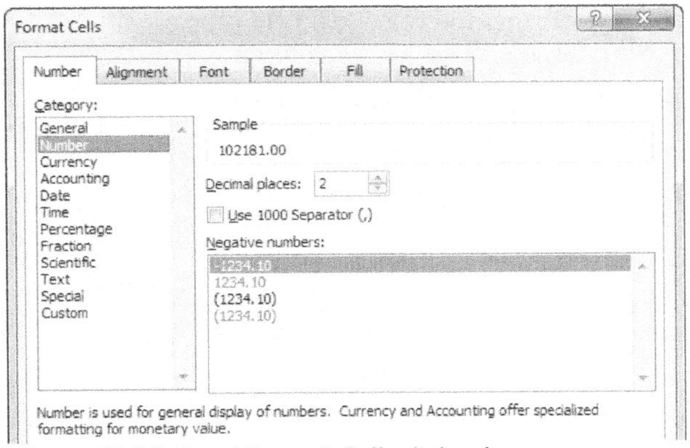

Figure 5-39 Excel Format Cells dialog box

Custom Numeric Formatting

Some of the numeric formatting that is supported in Excel does not have an equivalent formatting option in Dashboard Design.

This usually happens when a custom number format type is selected in Excel, as shown in Figure 5-40.

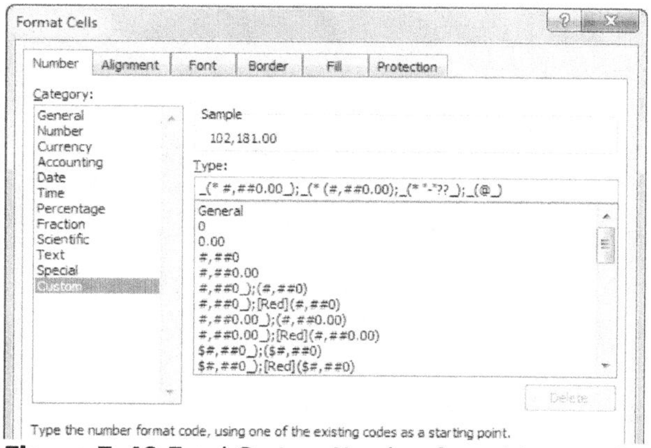

Figure 5-40 Excel Custom Number format type options

Conditional Formatting

Conditional formatting is the process of automatically changing the appearance of cells (like the background color of cells) or the values in cells (like changing the font size of the value in a cell) based on a condition that you set up. Without a doubt, Excel has the better tool set in my opinion, when it comes to conditional formatting. Excel allows you to create conditional formatting rules to change the color of cells, format bars on a chart and more. Figure 5-41 shows the conditional formatting options in Excel.

Dashboard Design has alerts, which support conditional formatting. Alerts are used to change the color of different parts of a component, based on whether the value in a field is below the target value, in the accepted target range or above the target value.

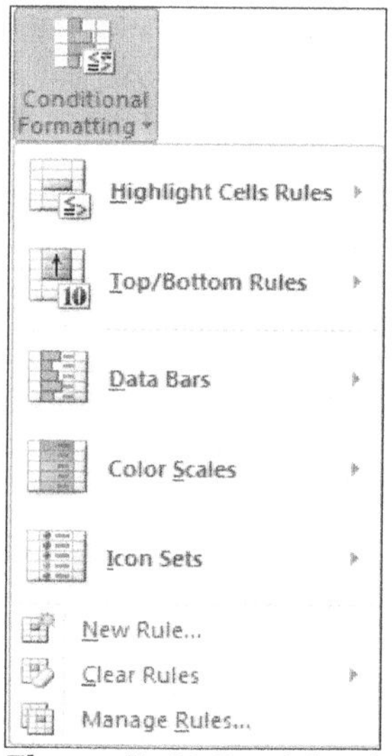

Figure 5-41 Excel Conditional Formatting options

SINGLE VALUE COMPONENTS

In this chapter you will learn about Single Value components and how to create dashboards that use the Single Value components listed below:

☑ Value component
☑ Dial component

CHAPTER 6

Overview

In this chapter you will learn about Single Value components. You will see that some options are the same for many Single Value components. Like the common options that you learned about in Chapter 4, each category of components has common options. They are covered at the beginning of a chapter instead of repeating them for each component that they apply to.

Single Value components are components that link to a single cell (of numeric data) in the spreadsheet. Figure 6-1 shows the types of Single Value components in Dashboard Design.

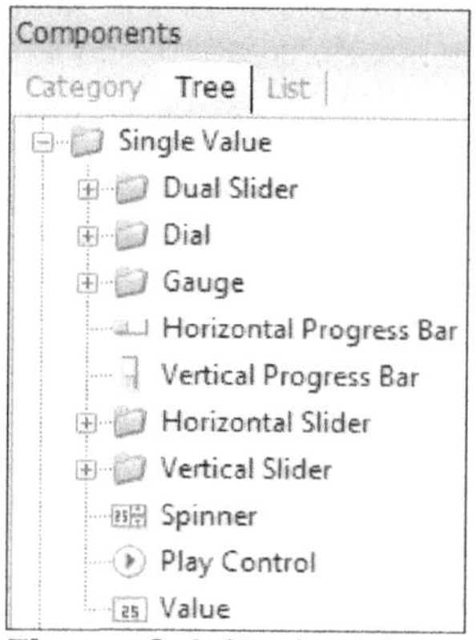

Figure 6-1 Single Value categories

Single Value Component Categories

As you will see, most Single Value components fall into at least one of the categories explained below.

① **INPUT COMPONENTS** allow the data that is linked to the component to be changed when the dashboard is run.

② **OUTPUT COMPONENTS** pass data to another component on the dashboard.

By default all Single Value components are output components, but some Single Value components are in both of the categories explained above. Table 6-1 explains the Single Value components. You can use some of the Single Value components interchangeably because they have the same functionality. When this is the case, my advice is to select the component that looks best for the data that will be displayed with the component.

Using Multiple Single Value Components

It is possible that you will need to link more than one Single Value component to the same cell in a dashboard. If this is the case and you use different minimum and maximum values for each Single Value component, some of them will reach the maximum value quicker then others. While the dashboard will function properly, the user may not notice that at least one of the components has reached the maximum, which means that accurate data may not be displayed in another component on the dashboard.

Component	Description
Dial	This component allows the user change the value in the linked cell. This action usually changes the values displayed in another component in the dashboard. Figure 6-2 shows a dial component. (1)
Slider	This component works the same as the dial component. (1)
Progress Bar	This component works the opposite of the dial and slider components because it displays a cells value instead of allowing the value to be changed. It has a read-only effect. The progress bar displays the linked value in comparison to the highest value in the cells that it is linked to. Figure 6-3 shows a progress bar component. (2)

Table 6-1 Single Value components explained

Component	Description
Gauge	This component is similar, in terms of functionality, to the progress bar component. The gauge also measures any change in the linked cell. Figure 6-4 shows a gauge component. This component can be used as an input or output component. It can also be set up to show multiple markers linked to different cells. This component is often for **WHAT-IF ANALYSIS**. (2)
Value	This component can be used as an input or output component because it represents a single cell. Figure 6-5 shows a value component.
Spinner	This component works the same as the dial component because it is used to change the value in another component. Figure 6-6 shows a spinner component. (1)
Play Control	This component allows the value in the linked cell to be increased or decreased in increments. (1)

Table 6-1 Single Value components explained (Continued)

(1) This component should be linked to a cell that has data that was typed into the spreadsheet, instead of a cell that has a formula if you want to use it as an input component.

(2) Use this component if the cell that is being linked to has a formula. Linking to a cell with a formula makes the component an output component. The value in a cell with a formula cannot be changed with a component because the value in the cell is calculated.

Figure 6-2 Dial component

Figure 6-3 Progress Bar component

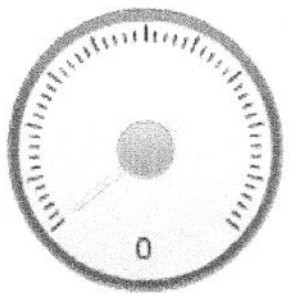

Figure 6-4 Gauge component

Figure 6-5 Value component

Figure 6-6 Spinner component

> If you link a component to the wrong type of cell, the component will not work as you expect. For example, if you link a dial component to a cell that has a formula, you will not be able to use the dial to select a value, thus making it an output component.

Single Value Component Options

The options explained in this section are common to the Single Value components that you just read about in Table 6-1. All of the options are not available for all Single Value components.

Common Single Value General View Options

The options on this view are used to link cells in a spreadsheet to a component on the model.

Figure 6-7 shows the General view options for a slider.

TITLE Type in the title or select the cell in the spreadsheet that has the title for the component. By default, the title is centered at the top of the component.

DATA Type in or select the cell in the spreadsheet that the component should be linked to. The gauge component does not have this option.

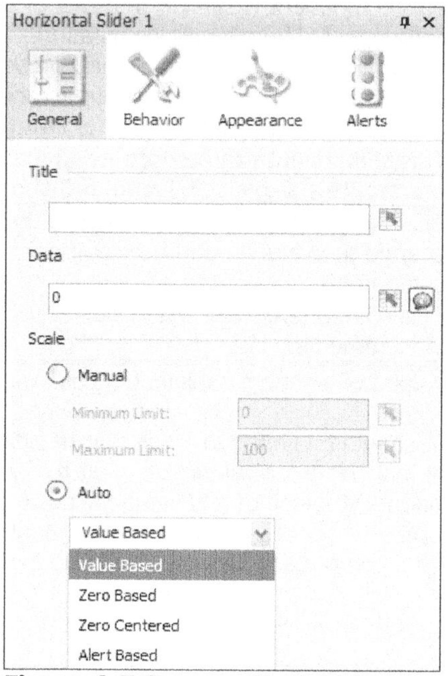

Figure 6-7 Common Single Value general view options

Scale Options

These options are used to set the initial minimum and maximum limits for the component.

① **MANUAL** This is the default option. Select this option when you want to select the minimum and maximum limit values.
② **AUTO** Select this option to have the minimum and maximum limits automatically calculated based on one of the options shown above in the drop-down list at the bottom of Figure 6-7. This option allows you to select one of the calculation options below.
③ **VALUE BASED** The limits are close to the value. This option is not available for these components: Dual Slider, Play Control, Spinner or Value.
④ **ZERO BASED** The range uses the value as the upper limit and zero as the lower limit. This means that the component can only display positive numbers.
⑤ **ZERO CENTERED** The range uses zero as the center value. This means that the component can display negative numbers.
⑥ **ALERT BASED** The range is based on the alert method selected.

Common Single Value Common Tab Options

Believe it or not, some of the options on this tab are used to limit data and functionality. Examples of limitations include adding a range of minimum and maximum values, as shown in Figure 6-8, or only allowing certain playback options.

Movement Options

The options in this section are used to select how the value increase and decrease increments are handled for the component, when the user interacts with the component.

Depending on the Single Value component that is selected, you will see that category name in front of the word movement on the Common tab.

For example, a slider component was selected in Figure 6-8, so the word slider is the first word of the section header. If a Progress Bar component is selected, you will see the word Progress, as shown in Figure 6-9. If a Dial or Gauge component is selected, you will see the word Needle, as shown in Figure 6-10.

INCREMENT Restricts values that the component can be increased by. For example, if this value is set to 100 (manually or if the component is bound to a cell), each increment on a component will represent an increase or decrease of 100. If you are entering percents in this field or any value field on any Common tab, they have to be entered in decimal format. For example, you have to type in .01 for 1% and .25 for 25%.

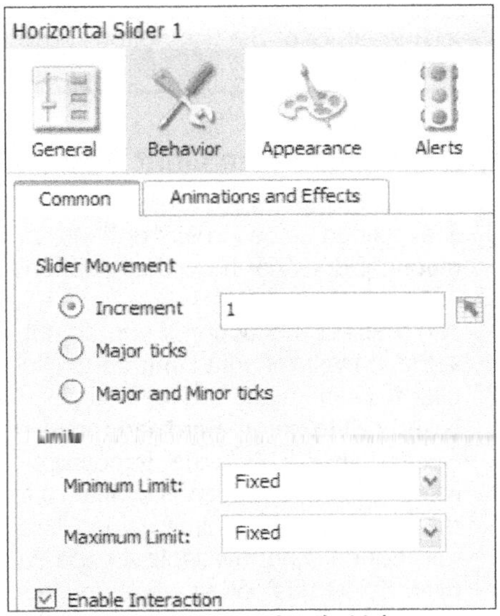

Figure 6-8 Common Single Value common tab options

MAJOR TICKS Select this option if you want the increase or decrease to only stop on the major tick marks on the component.

MAJOR AND MINOR TICKS Select this option if you want the increase or decrease to only stop on major and minor tick marks on the component.

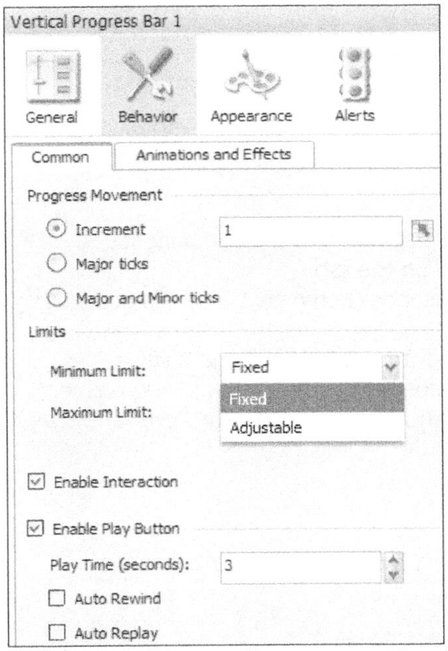

Figure 6-9 Progress Bar movement options

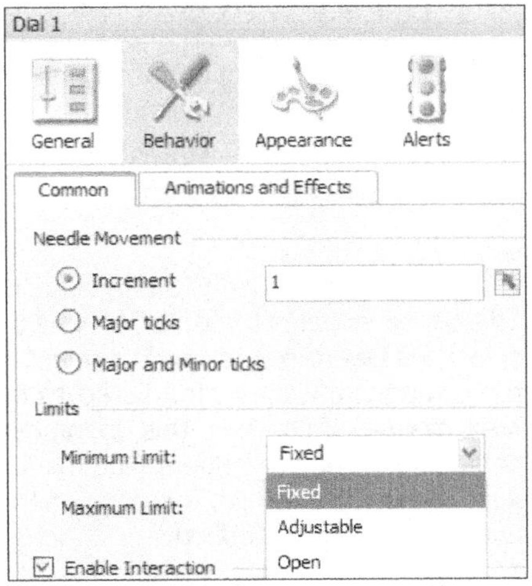

Figure 6-10 Dial movement options

Selecting either of the tick options prevents the ability to display or select values between any of the tick marks.

Minimum And Maximum Limit Options

As shown above in Figure 6-10, these two drop-down list fields have three options that can be selected, as explained below. These options control the values that users can select. The Play Control component does not have these options.

① **FIXED** Select this option if you do not want the value in the linked cell to be less than the value in the Minimum Limit option selected on the General view. This option prevents the user from changing the limit values. Select this option if you do not want the value in the linked cell to be greater than the value in the Maximum Limit option selected on the General view. This is the default option.

② **ADJUSTABLE** This option is similar to the Fixed option. The difference is that users can select the lower and upper limit values. Users cannot select a value greater than the maximum. This option is not available for the Value component.

③ **OPEN** Select this option when you want to select any number for the limit value, as long as the number does not conflict with the number for the other limit value. For example, you could select 10 for the minimum value and 20 for the maximum value, but you could not select 20 for the minimum value and 10 for the maximum value.

ENABLE INTERACTION Select this option to allow users to use the component.

Play Button Options (This option is not available in Presentation Design)

The options in this section of the Common tab are used to select the automation functionality for the component. These options are not available for the Dual Slider and Spinner components.

Figure 6-11 shows the Slider component with all of the play options selected and the minimum and maximum limits set to adjustable. The options shown at the bottom of Figure 6-9 are explained below.

Figure 6-11 Slider component with all of the play options selected

① **ENABLE PLAY BUTTON** Adds a play/start button to the beginning of the component. This option enables the other options in this section on the tab.

② **PLAY TIME (SECONDS)** Is used to select how many seconds (between 1 and 100 seconds) the component will run, from start to finish.

③ **AUTO REWIND** If checked, this option causes the slider to automatically go back to the beginning of the component (the minimum value) after it reaches the maximum value.

④ **AUTO REPLAY** If checked, the component will automatically continue to run, over and over, until it is manually stopped.

Common Single Value Layout Tab Options

The Layout tab options shown in Figure 6-12 are common to many Single Value components.

Ticks Options

The options in this section are used to add and customize the tick marks on a component like a progress bar or slider. Tick marks are the long and short lines on the component. Figure 6-13 illustrates the tick marks on a Dual Slider component.

ENABLE TICKS This option must be selected to display tick marks on the component. The markers on the component represent values.

AUTO SCALE This option automatically sets the scale spacing for the tick marks based on the data. This means that if the data changes, the scale will automatically change to accommodate the new values. (3)

MANUAL This option is used to customize the appearance of the tick marks by selecting one of the options below. (3)

① **NUMBER OF TICKS** Is used to select how many major and minor tick marks are displayed on the component.
② **SIZE OF DIVISIONS** Is used to select the space between the tick marks.

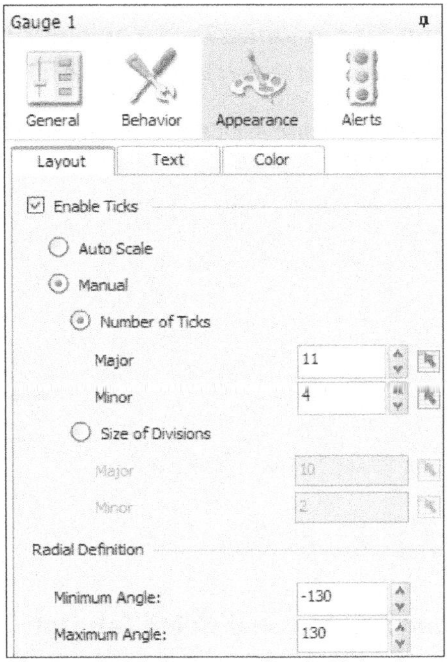

Figure 6-12 Common Single Value layout tab options

Number Of Ticks Options

MAJOR Is used to select how many primary (longer) tick marks are displayed on the component. A value from 2 to 21 can be entered for this option.

MINOR Is used to select how many secondary (shorter) tick marks are displayed on the component. Minor ticks are placed between two major tick marks. A value from 0 to 21 can be entered for this option.

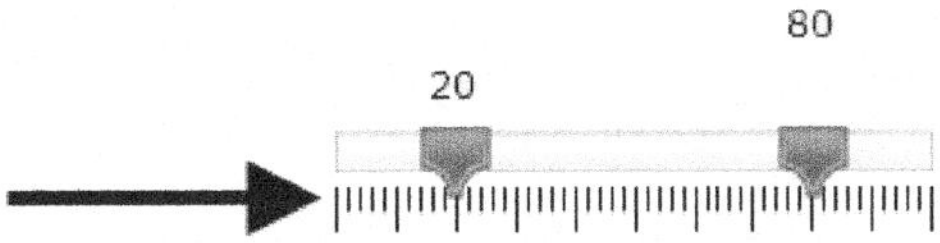

Figure 6-13 Tick marks illustrated

Size Of Divisions Options

MAJOR Is used to select the distance between the large (major) tick marks on the component. (4)

MINOR Is used to select the distance between the small (minor) tick marks on the component. The size of minor divisions is not dependent on the size of major divisions. (4)

(3) The Enable Ticks option must be selected to use this option.
(4) A value from zero to 100 can be entered in this option. Higher values create larger spaces between the tick marks.

The options shown earlier in Figure 6-12 are used to select the range of values for the needle on the component. The default range is -130° to 130°, but you can select the range that you need.

Radial Definition Options

MINIMUM ANGLE Is used to select the lowest number that the needle on the component can select. This option is not available if the Minimum Limit option on the Common tab is set to Open.

MAXIMUM ANGLE Is used to select the highest number that the needle on the component can select. This option is not available if the Maximum Limit option on the Common tab is set to Open.

Common Single Value Text Tab Options

The Text tab options shown in Figure 6-14 are common to many Single Value components.

LIMITS This option displays the lower and upper limits of the component, as illustrated in Figure 6-15. This option is not available for the Play Control and Value components.

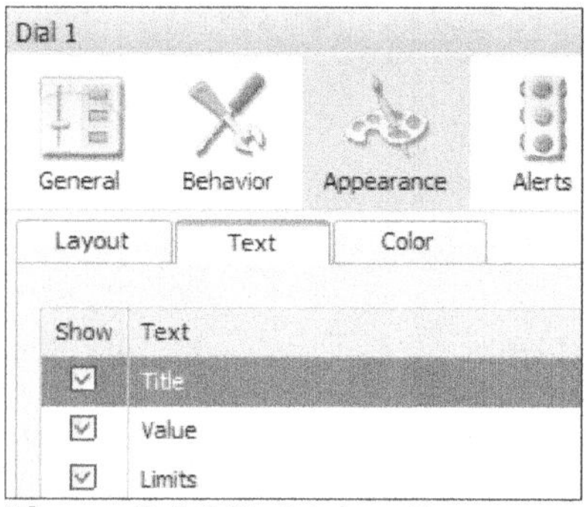

Figure 6-14 Text tab options

Figure 6-15 Lower and upper limits illustrated

Common Single Value Color Tab Options

The Color tab options shown in Figure 6-16 are common to many Single Value components.

MARKER COLOR Is used to change the color of the button on the slider.

TRACK COLOR Is used to change the default color of the bar that the button moves across on the component.

Ticks And Limits Options

TICK COLOR Is used to change the color of the tick marks on the component.

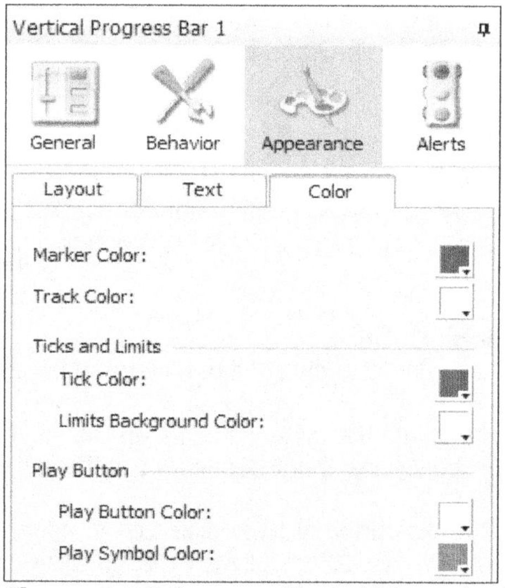

Figure 6-16 Common Single Value color tab options

LIMITS BACKGROUND COLOR Is used to change the background color of the values displayed from the Minimum and Maximum Limit options shown earlier in Figure 6-10. The Minimum or Maximum Limit option on the Common tab must be set to **ADJUSTABLE** for this option to be enabled on the Color tab.

Play Button Options

These options are only available if the Enable Play Button option on the Common tab is selected.

PLAY BUTTON COLOR Is used to change the background color of the Play button.

PLAY SYMBOL COLOR Is used to change the color of the symbol (which is usually an arrow) on the Play button.

Tips For Completing The Exercises In This Book

As you will see, many of the steps are the same for each model that you create. To avoid being extremely repetitive, the following tasks will not be repeated for each exercise.

① At the beginning of each exercise you should open a new model prior to starting step 1, unless instructed to open an existing model in step 1.
② When you see the instruction "Add the (name of) component", it means to add the component to the canvas. After you add a component to the canvas, you should open the Properties panel for the component that you added.
③ When instructed to open or save a file, look in or use the folder that you created.
④ Preview the model. If your model does not look like the one in the figure, you should go back and review the steps to make sure that you completed all of the tasks.
⑤ Unless specifically stated, you do not have to create (publish) the dashboard file for the remaining exercises in this book. In Chapter 16 you will learn how to publish dashboards in a variety of formats. For now, just save the model with the correct file name.
⑥ In the Option/Change To tables, like the one shown later in Exercise 6.1, step 3, you will see references to a single cell (A1, B5, etc.) or a cell range (A1:C5). This means to select the cell(s) in the spreadsheet for the option.
⑦ In some of the Option/Change To tables, you will see "Select this option" in the second column. This means that you should click in the box in front of the option, so that it has a check mark.
⑧ In some of the Option/Change To tables, you will see "Clear this option" in the second column. This means that you should remove the check mark from the option.

Format For The Exercises In This Book

At the beginning of this chapter, the common options for Single Value components were explained and illustrated. Before each exercise, the options that are unique for the components that will be used in the exercise will be explained.

For example, Exercise 6.1 uses the Value component. The options are explained right before the exercise starts. Many of the Properties panel screen shots (figures) will only display the options that will be explained.

Excel Spreadsheets

At the beginning of many exercises, you will see an Excel spreadsheet. The spreadsheet displays the data or part of the data that will be used to create the model. The reason that I display the data is to help you get a feel for how the data needs to appear in the spreadsheet for the components, which will hopefully help you to create the type of dashboard that you need, when you are on your own. The other reason that I show the data is because I am a firm believer that when you see something, it helps you to understand the concept better.

Value Component

This component is different from many of the other Single Value components because the user usually types in the value that this component uses to display the values in another component, like a chart. The Value component has the option of also using a play button, which will automatically increment the number in the Value component and display the corresponding data in another component on the dashboard. Remember that a Value component can only be linked to one cell in the spreadsheet.

Common Tab Options

The Value component common tab options shown in Figure 6-17 control the functionality of the Value component.

AUTO RESIZE Select this option if you want the Value component to automatically be resized to fit the number that is entered or displayed in the field.

MOUSE SENSITIVITY Is used to set how the mouse movements change the values that the component uses.

A low setting on this option means that small changes made by the mouse will increment the value of the component in small amounts, which means that the mouse is less sensitive.

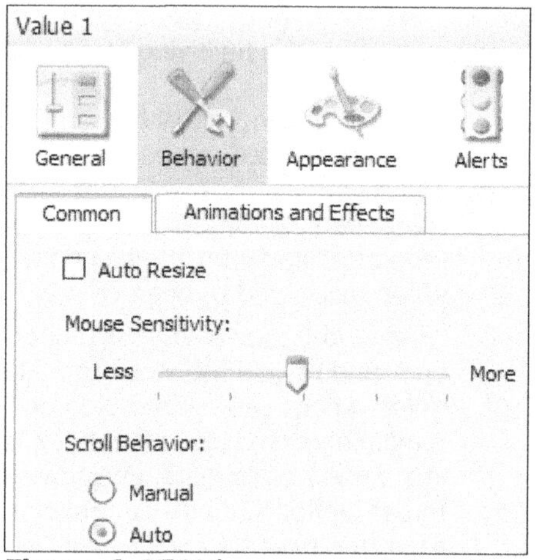

Figure 6-17 Value common tab options

A high setting on this option means that small changes made by the mouse will increment the value of the component in large amounts.

Scroll Behavior Options

These options are used to select how the mouse pointer can be used to change the value displayed in the component.

① Select the **MANUAL** option if you want the user to be able to drag the mouse pointer up or to the right of the component to change the value. This will increase the value that is displayed. Dragging the mouse pointer down or to the left will lower the value that is displayed. This option requires the user to continue moving the mouse pointer to display different values. This is the default option. The value will continues to change until the mouse stops moving, whether or not the mouse button is released.

② Select the **AUTO** option if you want the user to be able to drag the mouse pointer above or below the component to change the value. When the mouse button is pressed, the value continues to change without having to move the mouse. The value will continue to increase or decrease until the mouse button is released.

Layout Tab Options

The Value component layout tab options are shown in Figure 6-18.

The **SHOW BACKGROUND** option is used to display or hide the border around the component.

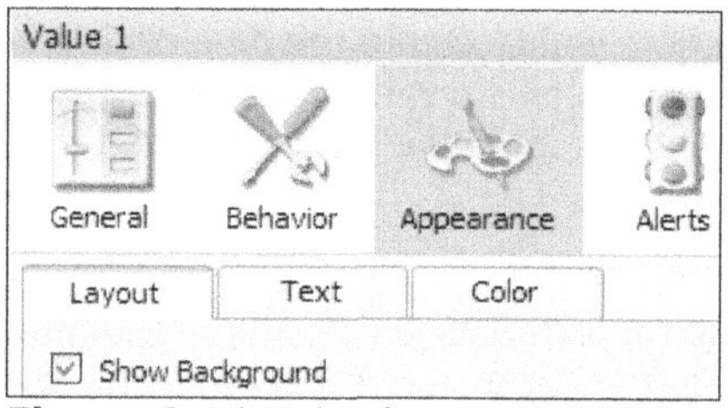

Figure 6-18 Value layout tab option

Color Tab Options

The Value component color tab options are shown in Figure 6-19.

BACKGROUND COLOR Is used to change the background color of the component.

Play Button Options

[See Common Single Value Color Tab Options, earlier in this chapter]

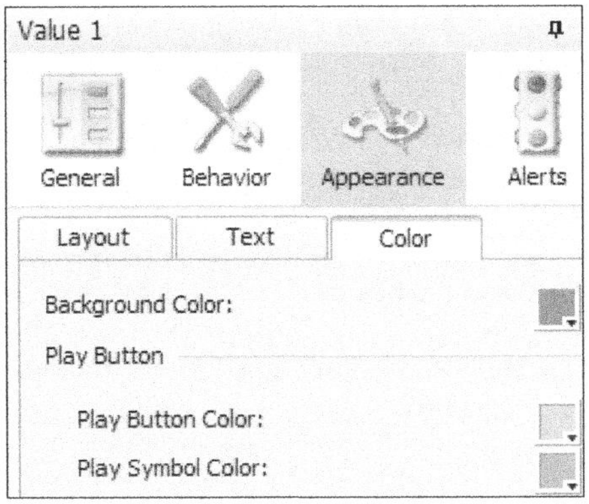

Figure 6-19 Value color tab options

Play Control Component

This component allows the user to select a numeric value by clicking on the buttons. The value is automatically incremented in equal intervals without the users input. The value selected is used to control what is displayed in another control. Like the Play Selector, there are 11 major and four minor tick marks, which cannot be changed.

> **Difference Between The Play Selector And Play Control**
> The difference between these components is that the Play Selector inserts a row or column of data from the spreadsheet into another row or column in the spreadsheet. The Play Control places the selected value into a cell.

Common Tab Options

The Play Control common tab options are shown in Figure 6-20.

AUTO PLAY If checked, the Play Control component will automatically start when the dashboard is run.

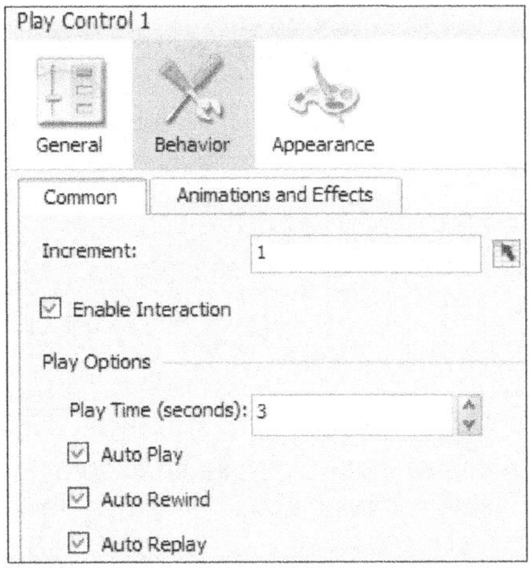

Figure 6-20 Play Control common tab options

> **How The Play Control Works**
> When clicked, the **PREVIOUS** and **NEXT** buttons are incremented or decreased by the value in the Increment field on the Common tab. When clicked, the **REWIND** and **FORWARD** buttons are incremented or decreased by four times the value in the Increment field.

Layout Tab Options

The Play Control layout tab options are shown in Figure 6-21.

SHOW REW/FWD If checked, this option adds the rewind and fast forward buttons to the play control.

SHOW PREV/NEXT If checked, this option adds the previous and next buttons to the play control.

SHOW SLIDER If checked, a slider will be added to the play control.

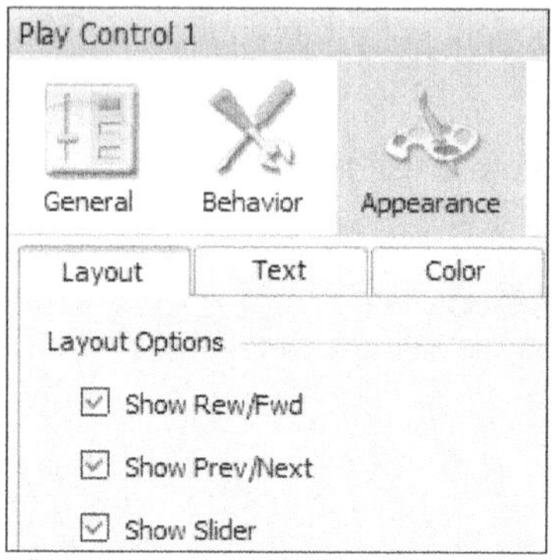

Figure 6-21 Play Control layout tab options

Text Tab Options

To keep the title and value data from over lapping on the dashboard, select a different position for each of them.

Exercise 6.1: Use The Value Component And Play Button Options

In this exercise you will add the Value component to a model. This will let the user enter the Unit price for a product, which will show how different price points affect the revenue for several stores. Figure 6-22 shows the data for this exercise.

	A	B	C	
1	**Price Sale Impact Over Total Revenues**			
2	Comparison by Store			
3				
4	Price per Unit	$ 45.00		
5				
6	Store Name	Quantity Sold	Revenues (Quantity * Price)	
7	Store A	350	$	15,750.00
8	Store B	125	$	5,625.00
9	Store C	245	$	11,025.00
10	Store D	88	$	3,960.00
11	Store E	188	$	8,460.00

Figure 6-22 Value component data

1. Save the dd_value_field file as `My value component.`

2. Add the Value component above the chart in the upper right corner.

3. On the General view, make the changes in the table.

Option	Change To
Title	A4
Data	B4
Minimum Limit (5)	0

(5) Setting the Minimum Limit option to zero prevents a negative number from being entered in the Value component field on the dashboard.

4. On the Common tab, make the changes in the table.

Option	Change To
Minimum Limit	Fixed
Maximum Limit	Open
Enable Play Button (6)	Select this option

(6) The Value Display sample dashboard that comes with Dashboard Design does not have this option enabled. I enabled it so that you can see how the Play Button options work.

5. Save the changes. The model should look like the one shown in Figure 6-23.

   If you see pound signs in the value component that you added to the model, as shown in Figure 6-24, make the component larger.

   Double-click in the Price per Unit field, then type in a different amount and press Enter. You will see the values in the chart change.

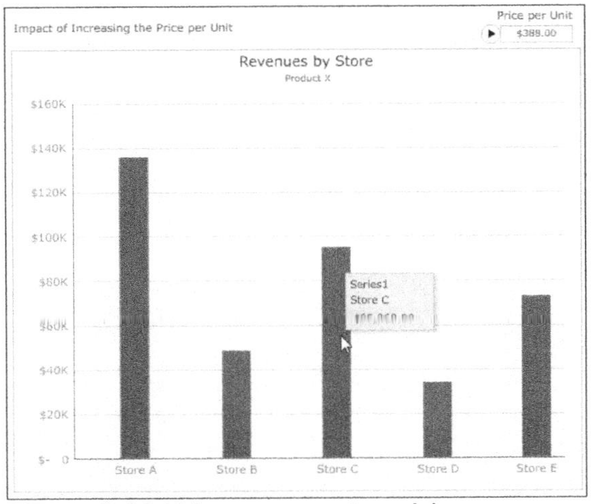

Figure 6-23 Value component model

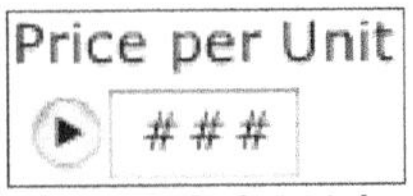

Figure 6-24 Value component that is too small

Earlier in Figure 6-22 you saw that cell B4 (the cell used in the Data option) has a value in it. This value will be displayed in the Value component by default when the dashboard is first opened. If cell B4 was empty in the spreadsheet, nothing would appear in the Price per Unit field when the dashboard is first opened.

The minimum value that can be entered in the field is zero, which may not be obvious to the user. In Exercise 14.4 you will modify a model just like this one to include a help message for this field.

6. Click the Play button. As the number in the Price per Unit field increases, notice that the values on the Y axis on the chart increase.

Dial Component

Common Tab Options

MOUSE SENSITIVITY [See Value Component Common Tab Options, earlier in this chapter]

If you have trouble moving the needle on the dial, it may be because by default, the **MOUSE TRACKING** option is set to **VERTICAL**, as shown in Figure 6-25. When this option is set to vertical, you can only move the mouse pointer up or down.

The **RADIAL** option allows the mouse pointer to use a circular movement.

Layout Tab Options

[See Common Single Value Layout Tab Options, earlier in this chapter]

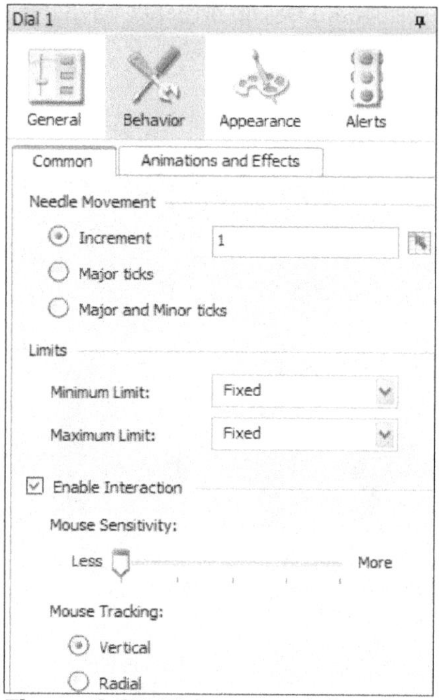

Figure 6-25 Dial common tab options

Color Tab Options

The Dial component color tab options are shown in Figure 6-26.

NEEDLE COLOR Is used to change the color of the needle on the dial.

GRIP COLOR Is used to change the border color on the dial.

BACKGROUND COLOR Is used to change the color of the face of the dial.

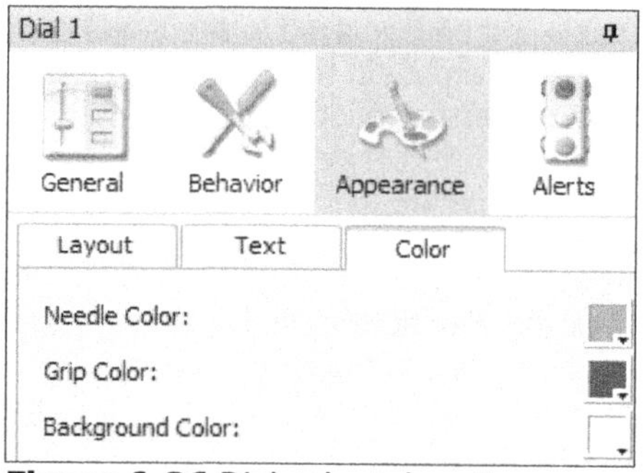

Figure 6-26 Dial color tab options

Exercise 6.2: Use The Dial Component

You have already created a dashboard that used a slider component as the input component. Dial and slider components can be used interchangeably. In this exercise you will add a dial component to the model that you created in Exercise 4.1.

1. Save the My slider model as `My dial component`.

2. Add the Dial component below the slider component, then make it larger.

3. On the General view, make the changes in the table.
   The Slider component has a maximum limit of 100. This means that using the Dial component will let the user see how income increases as the number of cars sold changes.

Option	Change To
Title	D4
Data	E4
Maximum Limit	250

4. On the Text tab, select the Show Limits option, illustrated in Figure 6-27.

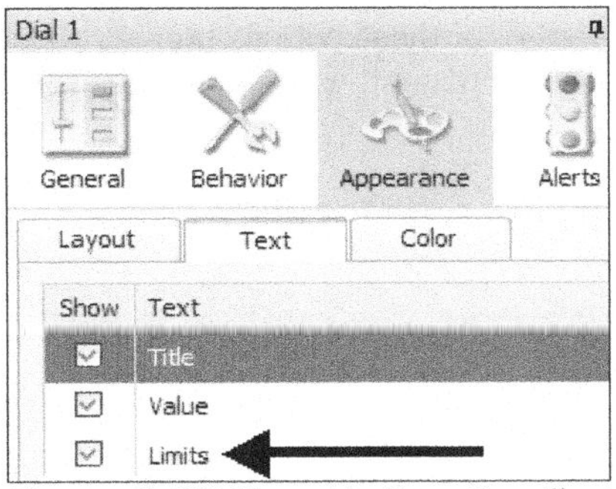

Figure 6-27 Show Limits option illustrated

5. On the Color tab, make the changes in the table.

Option	Change To
Needle Color	Red
Grip Color	Green

6. On the General view of the Horizontal Slider, change the Maximum Limit to 250.

7. Save the changes.

   If you click on the green part of the dial to increase the number of units sold, you will see that once you select a number greater than 138, all of the bars on the chart will have reached the top of the chart, as shown in Figure 6-28.

   That is because the chart has a maximum amount of $2.5 million. If this limitation was removed from the chart, the bars would not reach the top of the chart because the values on the Y axis would keep growing.

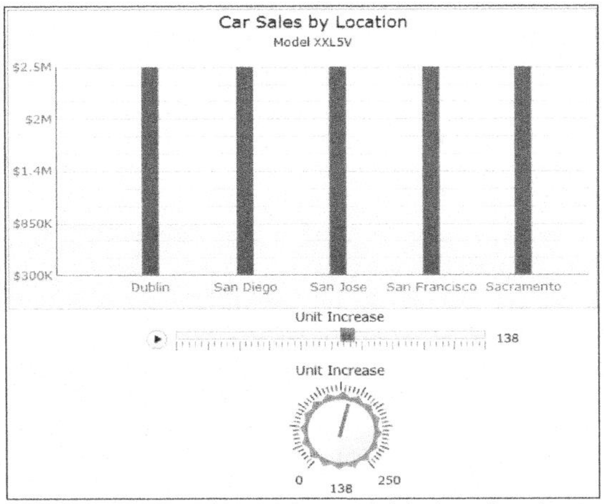

Figure 6-28 Dial component added to the chart

Horizontal And Vertical Slider Components

The Horizontal and Vertical Slider components have the same options on the Properties panel.

Dual Slider Component

Horizontal and vertical slider components only have one starting point. Dual sliders have two, as shown earlier in Figure 6-13. The numbers on the slider control the range of values (the starting and ending values) that will be displayed on another component. Each button can be moved left and right. The Dual Slider component does not support the play options that other slider components support.

General View Options

The Dual Slider general view options are shown in Figure 6-29.

Data Options

The values selected for these options are displayed on the component, as shown earlier in Figure 6-13.

LOW VALUE Is used to select the starting low value for the slider.

HIGH VALUE Is used to select the starting high value for the slider.

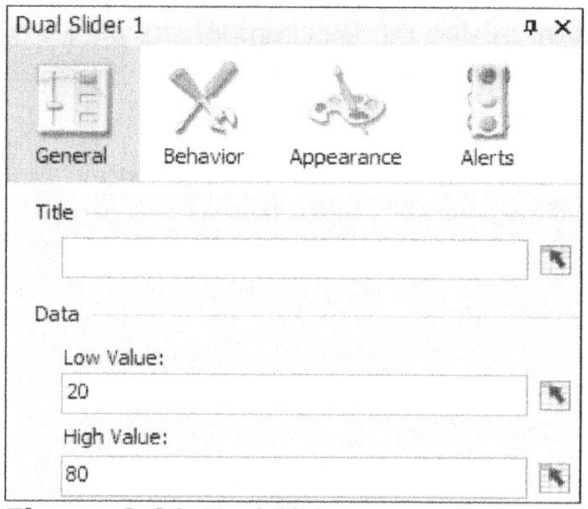

Figure 6-29 Dual Slider general view options

Text Tab Options

The Dual Slider text tab options are shown in Figure 6-30.

Format Selected Text Options

The low and high value offset options are used to position the low and high values on the dual slider.

Positive values shift the number to the right. Negative values shift the number to the left.

LOW VALUE OFFSET X Is used to shift the low value to the right or left on the slider.

HIGH VALUE OFFSET X Is used to shift the high value to the right or left on the slider.

LOW VALUE OFFSET Y Is used to shift the low value up or down on the slider.

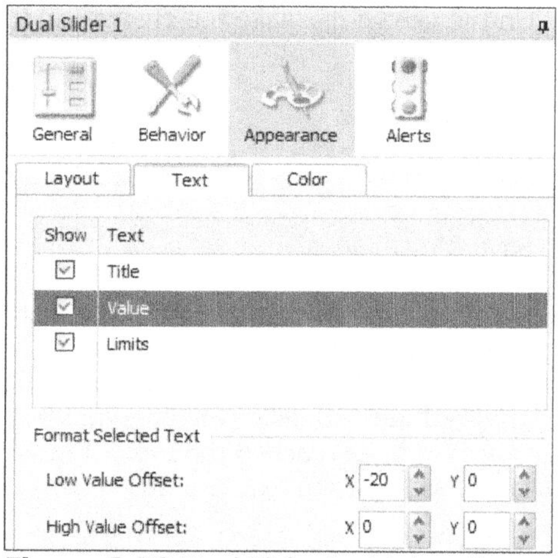

Figure 6-30 Dual Slider text tab options

HIGH VALUE OFFSET Y Is used to shift the high value up or down on the slider.

Color Tab Options

The Dual Slider color tab options are shown in Figure 6-31.

LOW MARKER COLOR Is used to change the color of the low value marker.

HIGH MARKER COLOR Is used to change the color of the high value marker.

TRACK COLOR Is used to change the color of the bar that the buttons slide across.

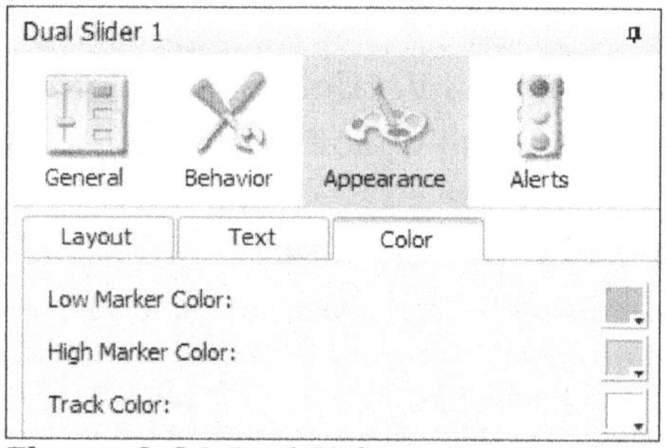

Figure 6-31 Dual Slider color tab options

Progress Bar Components

Select this component when you need to display how much of a task has been completed. The horizontal and vertical progress bar components have the same options on the Properties panel. This component is similar to the Slider component. The difference is that the Progress Bar component does not have a slider on the bar that can be used to change the value. Instead, the user has to drag the mouse pointer to change the value on the component.

Color Tab Options

The Progress Bar color tab options are shown in Figure 6-32.

MARKER COLOR Is used to change the fill color of the progress bar, as illustrated in Figure 6-33.

TRACK COLOR Is used to change the background color of the progress bar.

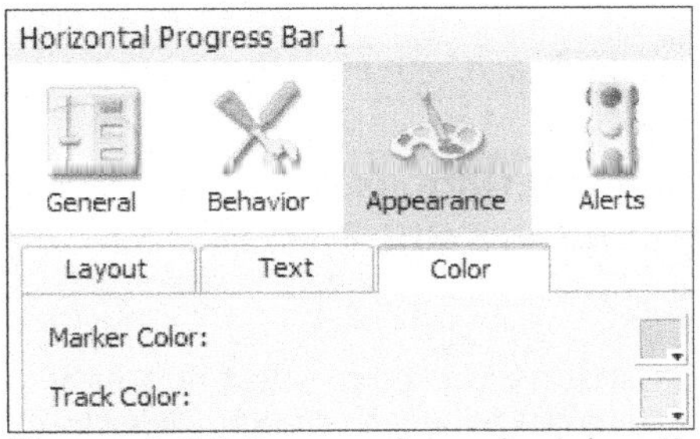

Figure 6-32 Progress bar color tab options

Figure 6-33 Marker color illustrated

Gauge Component

This component is similar to the Dial component.

General View Options

The Gauge general view options are shown in Figure 6-34.

The **BY RANGE** option is used to select the range of cells in the spreadsheet that have the data for the markers. A gauge component can be linked to several series of data and display multiple indicators on a single gauge, as shown in Figure 6-35. When displaying multiple indicators, the gauge can only be used to display values.

When a gauge component uses multiple series, they are added to the **BY INDICATORS** values. The By Indicators options are used to customize the markers. The options in the **TYPE** drop-down list shown in Figure 6-34 are used to select the type of marker for each range.

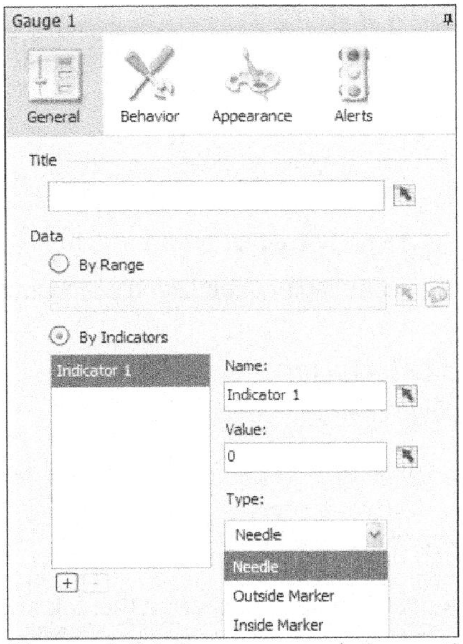

Figure 6-34 Gauge general view options

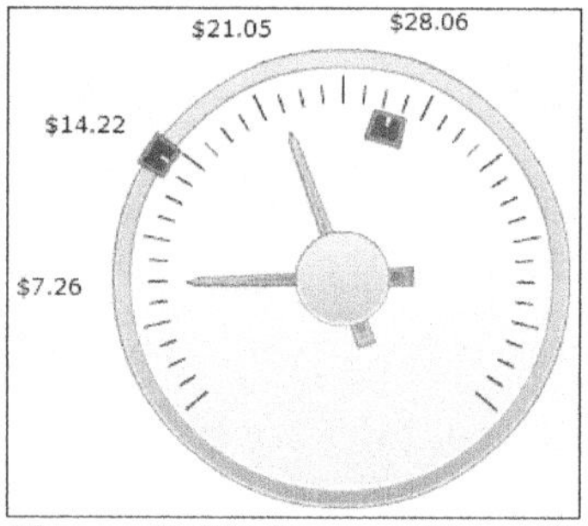

Figure 6-35 Gauge with multiple ranges

Common Tab Options

The Gauge common tab options are shown in Figure 6-36.

OBJECT ELASTICITY Is used to select how easy the needle moves. After moving the slider for this option to several positions, I did not notice any difference.

MOUSE SENSITIVITY [See Value Component Common Tab Options, earlier in this chapter]

MOUSE TRACKING [See Dial Component Common Tab Options, earlier in this chapter]

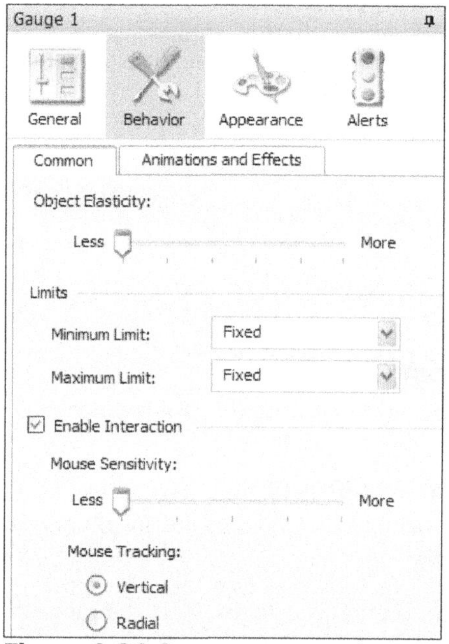

Figure 6-36 Gauge common tab options

Layout Tab Options

[See Common Single Value Layout Tab Options, earlier in this chapter]

Color Tab Options

The Gauge color tab options are shown in Figure 6-37.

FILL COLOR is used to select the color for each marker on the component.

FRAME COLOR Is used to change the color of the outer portion of the gauge.

CENTER COLOR Is used to change the color of the center (the circle) of the gauge.

BACKGROUND COLOR Is used to change the background color of the face of the gauge.

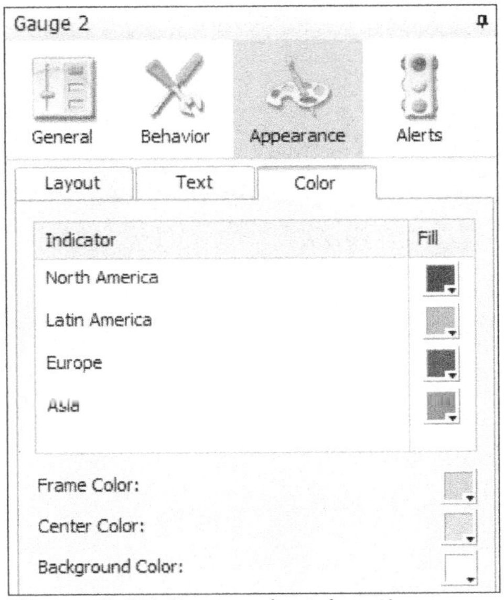

Figure 6-37 Gauge color tab options

Spinner Component

The Spinner component does not support the play options that other slider components support. This component is easier to use then slider components when it comes to selecting a specific value because the user clicks on the Up and Down buttons to select the value. This component has to be used to control another component.

General View Options

The Spinner general view options are shown in Figure 6-38.

TITLE A good use for this field is to inform the user what value the spinner represents.

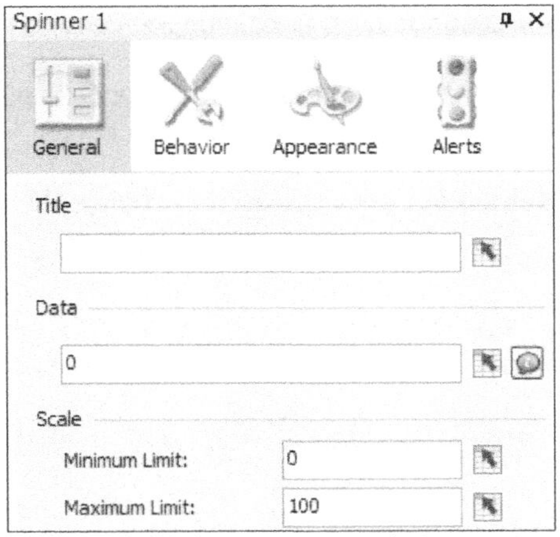

Figure 6-38 Spinner general view options

Color Tab Options

The Spinner color tab options are shown in Figure 6-39.

BACKGROUND COLOR Is used to change the background color of the spinner.

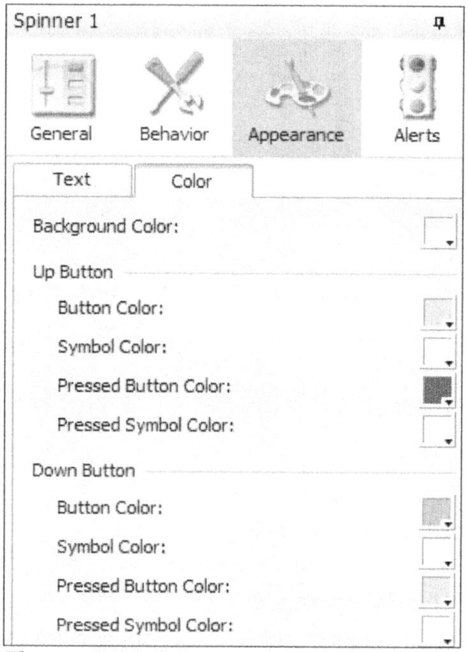

Figure 6-39 Spinner color tab options

Up Button Options

BUTTON COLOR Is used to change the default background color of the up arrow section of the component.

SYMBOL COLOR Is used to change the color of the up arrow when the dashboard is first displayed.

PRESSED BUTTON COLOR Is used to change the background color of the up arrow section of the component when the up arrow is clicked.

PRESSED SYMBOL COLOR Is used to change the color of the up arrow when the arrow is clicked.

Down Button Options

BUTTON COLOR Is used to change the default background color of the down arrow section of the component.

SYMBOL COLOR Is used to change the color of the down arrow when the dashboard is first displayed.

PRESSED BUTTON COLOR Is used to change the background color of the down arrow section of the component when the down arrow is clicked.

PRESSED SYMBOL COLOR Is used to change the color of the down arrow when the arrow is clicked.

CREATING CHARTS

In this chapter you will learn about the chart components. You will accomplish this by learning how to create the following types of charts:

- ☑ Line chart
- ☑ Pie chart
- ☑ Column chart
- ☑ Area chart
- ☑ Bubble chart
- ☑ Candlestick chart
- ☑ XY chart
- ☑ Radar chart
- ☑ Combination chart

Charts Overview

In previous chapters you saw a few charts, but there was not a lot of discussion about them. Based on the dashboards that have been presented so far in this book, hopefully it is evident that charts play a major role in dashboards. And as such, I feel that it is imperative that you understand as many of the chart options as possible. In this chapter you will learn to create a variety of charts, some of which will be used as the basis for exercises in future chapters.

Dashboard Design comes with 19 chart types, as explained in Table 7-1. If you have created charts in Crystal Reports or Excel, many of the chart types should be familiar. If you have not created charts before, you will find that Dashboard Design is pretty intuitive. Between that and the step-by-step instructions in this chapter, you will be able to select an appropriate chart type and create charts based on a series of data in the spreadsheet, opposed to all of the data in a spreadsheet, in no time.

Chart Type	This Chart Type . . .
Line	Shows trends and changes over a period of time. The markers across the bottom of the chart represent exact values. Line charts can have a single series of data, as shown in Figure 7-1 or multiple series of data, as shown in Figure 7-2.
Pie	Displays information for one point in time. Figure 7-3 shows sales by region. Each slice of the pie represents the percent for a different region. Pie charts show how the whole (100%) is divided.
OHLC and Candlestick	Is similar to bar charts. The difference is that the items for these charts usually do not touch the bottom of the chart because they are used to display stock data. OHLC stands for Open High Low Close. On an OHLC chart, the values are represented by **HASH MARKS**, as illustrated in Figure 7-4. The hash mark on the left of the bar represents the opening stock price and the hash mark on the right side of the bar represents the closing stock price. Figure 7-5 shows the same stock data on a Candlestick chart.
Column	Is similar to bar charts because they compare one or more items that are in a specific range of values or compares items over a period of time. This is probably the most used chart type.
Stacked Column	Shows each item as a percent of the total (vertically) in a specific range or over a period of time, as shown in Figure 7-6. Each item is displayed in a different color.
Bar	Shows differences between items over a period of time. Bar charts can plot more than one series of data as shown in Figure 7-7.
Stacked Bar	Shows each item as a percent of the total (horizontally) in a specific range or over a period of time. Each item on the bar is displayed in a different color.
Combination	Displays changes and the magnitude of the change over time. This change is usually illustrated by two chart types: A line chart and a column chart, as shown in Figure 7-8. This chart type is also known as a **TREND LINE** or **VARIANCE** chart. The major difference between line charts, column charts and combination charts is that a combination chart can use both columns and lines in the same chart and the other two chart types cannot.

Table 7-1 Chart types explained

Chart Type	This Chart Type . . .
Bubble	Compares a series of items based on the X axis, Y axis and Z value (item size), as shown in Figure 7-9. Bubble charts represent three numeric values. Together, the X and Y axis values determine where the bubble will be placed on the chart. The Z value is used to determine what size the bubble should be, which is based on a comparison of all of the values for each item on the chart. This chart type can be used for three dimensional analysis. Bubble charts allow more data to be added to a chart than XY charts. (1)
XY	Shows how two values are related (like month of year and order amount) and how a change in one value affects the other value, as shown in Figure 7-10. This chart type displays the correlation between the items. The XY chart type is similar to the bubble chart type because it uses the X and Y values to determine where to place the marker on the chart. The X and Y axis must display numeric data. If data like dates or months can be converted to numeric data, they can be used in this chart type. This chart type is also known as an **XY SCATTER** chart. (1)
Area	Shows how the data has changed over a period of time, as shown in Figure 7-11. Area charts are almost identical to stacked line charts. The difference is that area charts are filled in below the trend line, which emphasizes the magnitude of change. Area charts are probably best suited for a few groups (series) of data.
Stacked Area	Is similar to area charts. The difference is that stacked area charts display the differences in more than one series of data, as shown in Figure 7-12.
Radar	Compares sets of data relative to a center point and shows how far the data value is from the standard (the center point value), as shown in Figure 7-13. The data from the X axis is usually plotted in a circle and the Y axis values are plotted from the center of the circle out.
Filled Radar	Displays data the same way that a Radar chart does. The difference is that Filled Radar charts fill in each band with a different color to help illustrate the data, as shown in Figure 7-14.
Tree Map	Displays hierarchical data in a small area, as shown in Figure 7-15.
Horizontal Bullet	Displays data in a compact format. It charts a single performance value, which is represented by a horizontal bar marker against a comparative value. In the background of the chart is a range of values, as shown in Figure 7-16. The scale for each series can be customized individually. (2)
Vertical Bullet	Displays data in a compact format. It charts a single performance value, which is represented by a vertical bar marker against a comparative value. In the background of the chart is a range of values. The scale for each series can be customized individually. (2)
Sparkline	Is similar to OHLC and Candlestick charts because one dimensional series like low and high, start and end values can be displayed as markers on the chart. The range of values can be displayed as a colored background of the chart, as shown in Figure 7-17. This chart type uses very little space.

Table 7-1 Chart types explained (Continued)

(1) This chart type creates multi dimensional charts.
(2) This chart type can plot more than one series of data.

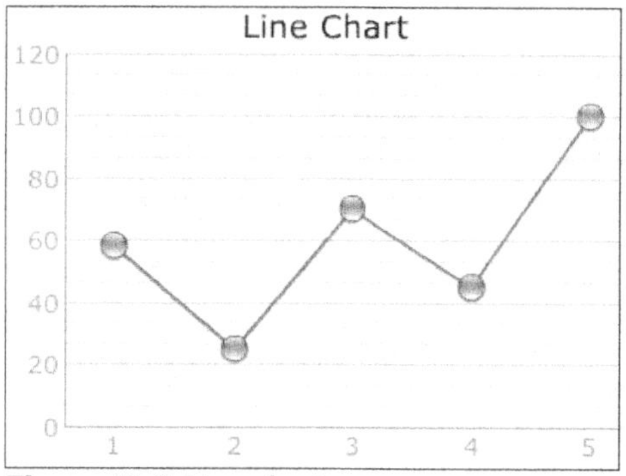

Figure 7-1 Line chart

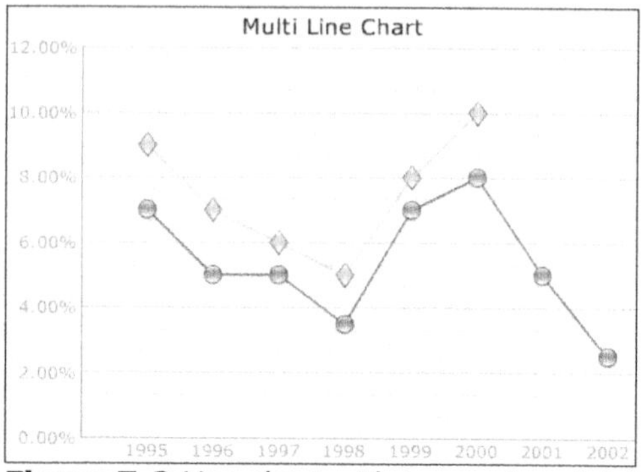

Figure 7-2 Line chart with two series of data

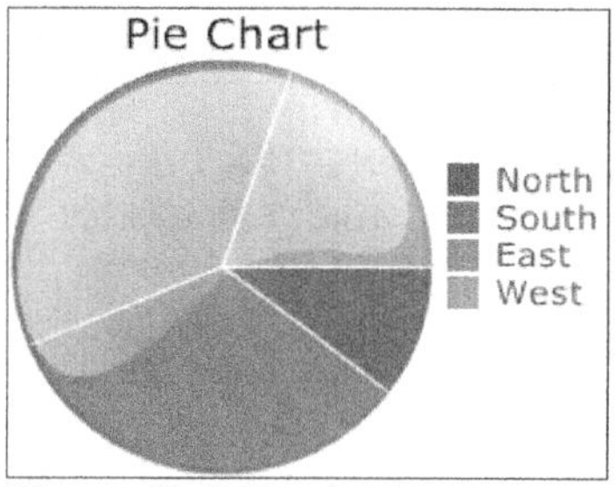

Figure 7-3 Pie chart

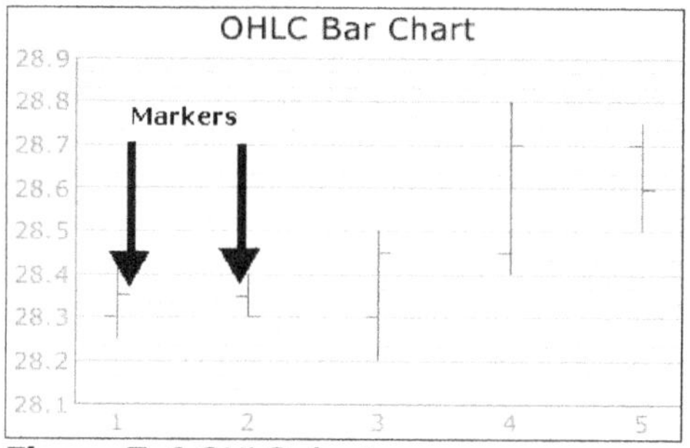

Figure 7-4 OHLC chart

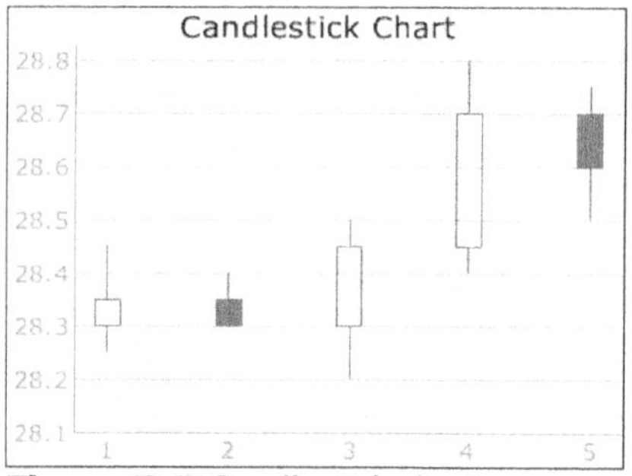

Figure 7-5 Candlestick chart

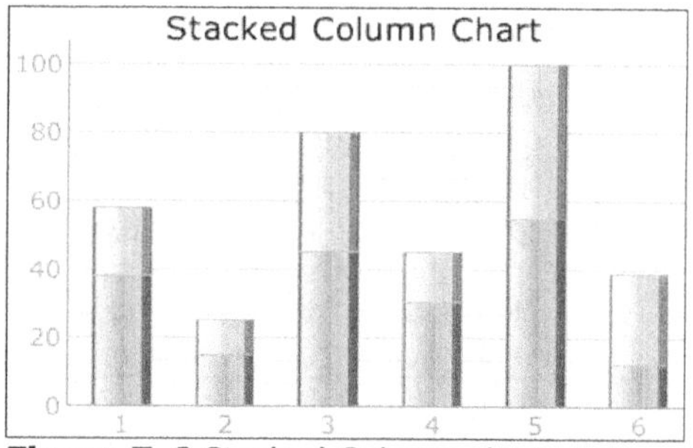

Figure 7-6 Stacked Column chart

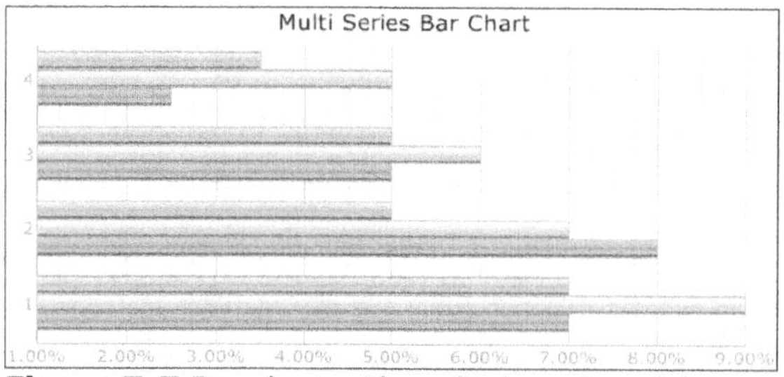

Figure 7-7 Bar chart with multiple series of data

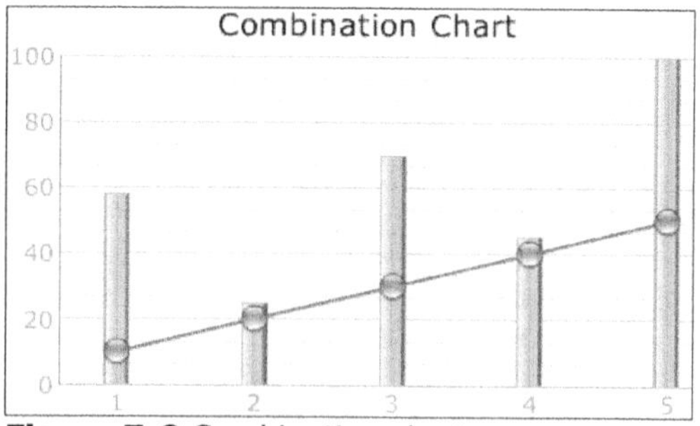

Figure 7-8 Combination chart

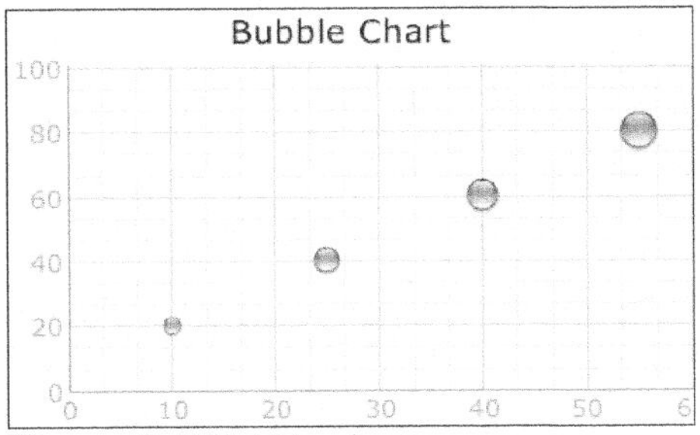

Figure 7-9 Bubble chart

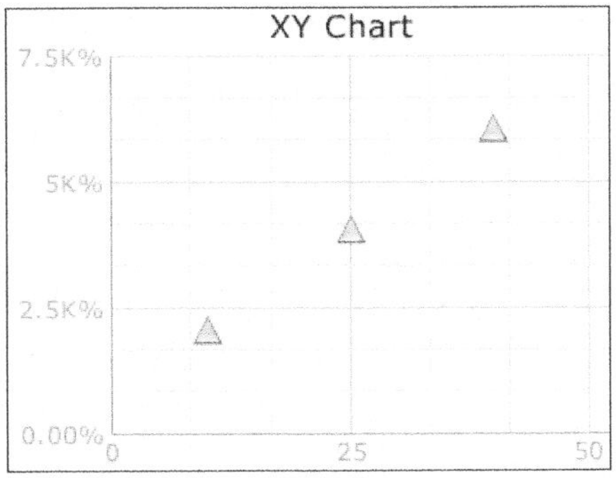

Figure 7-10 XY chart

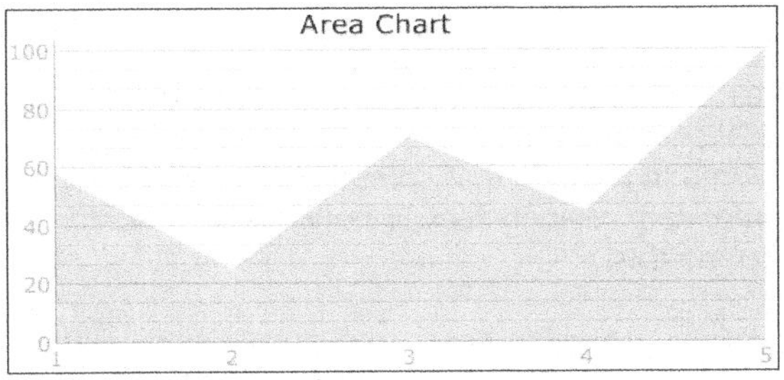

Figure 7-11 Area chart

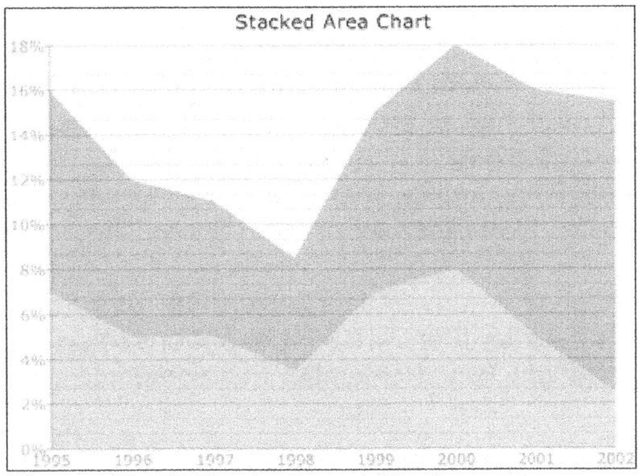

Figure 7-12 Stacked area chart

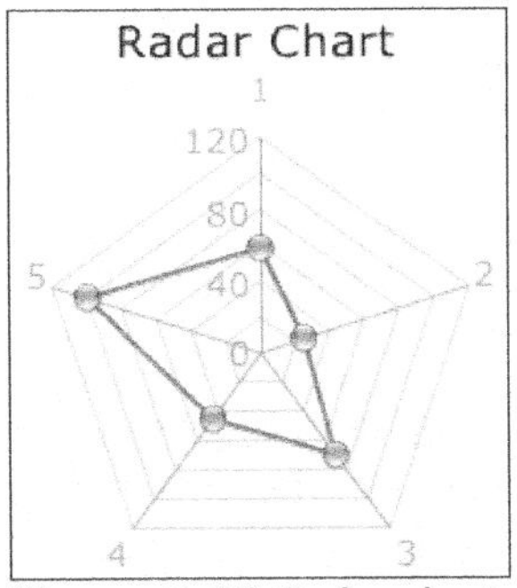

Figure 7-13 Radar chart

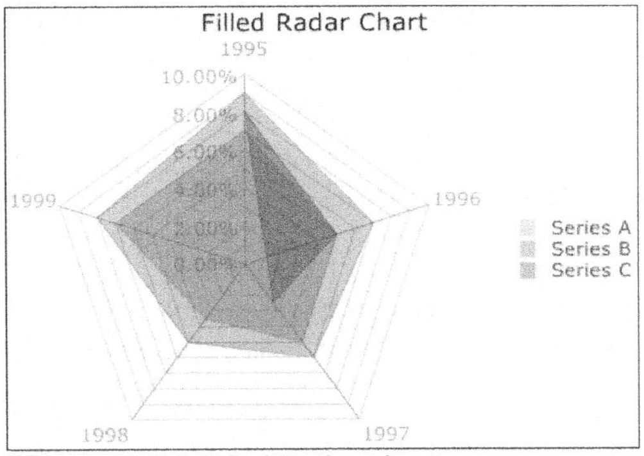

Figure 7-14 Filled Radar chart

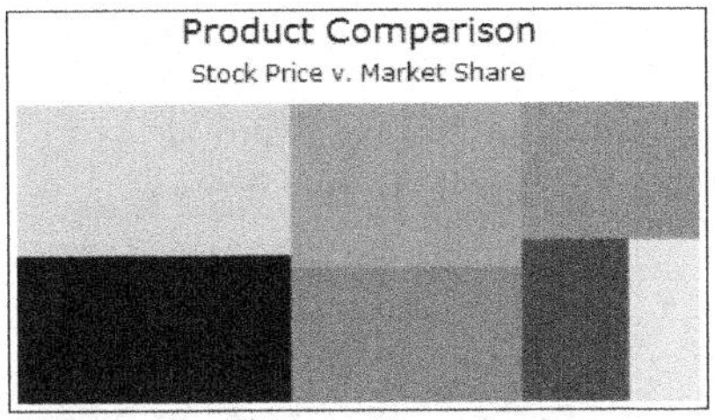

Figure 7-15 Tree Map chart

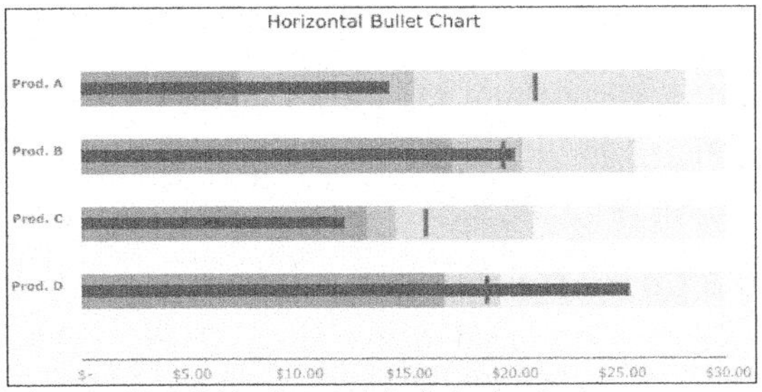

Figure 7-16 Horizontal Bullet chart

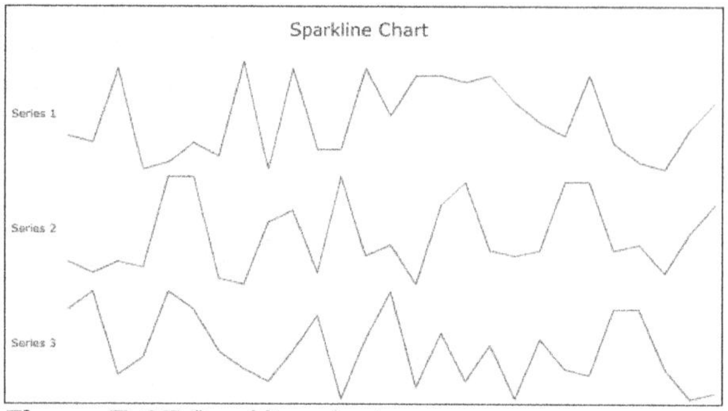

Figure 7-17 Sparkline chart

Why Charts Are Important

In addition to being able to format data in dashboards, charts present data in a graphical format, which often makes the data easier to understand because they visually display the relationship between the data. Charts also allow data to be presented in formats that spreadsheets cannot do as well. For example, charts can show trends over time, data relationships or how one set of data compares to another set of data. Spreadsheets cannot do this.

In Chapter 4 you created a basic chart. As you saw, it is very easy to get carried away when creating charts because there are a lot of options to select from. Try to create charts that present the data in a meaningful way. Remember that sometimes, less is more.

My Thoughts On Chart Design

The first thing that I want to say is that by no stretch of the imagination do I consider myself a chart design expert. I am only trying to help keep you from making some of the same poor chart design options that I made when I first started and that I have seen other people make.

As you will see in this chapter, creating a chart in Dashboard Design is relatively easy. When compared to Excels chart modification options, it may not seem like Dashboard Design provides as many options. That is true. Dashboard Design does not have as many chart formatting options, but trust me, there are enough for you to make a chart look something terrible <smile>.

I taught a technical writing class and one of the assignments had students create three charts to visually present data. Overall, the students did a good job on the charts. However, it was easy to tell which students had never created a chart before, because the charts exhibited at least one of the following issues:

① The wrong chart type was selected. **Newsflash**: Bar or column charts are not the best option for all types of data, especially data that shows trends or needs to show how data has changed over time.
② The values on the X and Y axes are backwards. Dollar amounts, quantity, percents, usually go on the Y axis, while time, dates and categories usually go on the X axis.
③ Not understanding the data that the chart is created from.

Selecting A Chart Type

There are two areas that need to be addressed before you start to create the chart: The chart type and the source of the data for the chart. The chart type is selected on the Components Browser. There is no way to change the chart type once it is added to the canvas. If you select the wrong chart type, you have to delete it and select another chart type. If you are not sure which chart type is the most appropriate, you can view the chart types on the Components Browser Category tab. This may help you figure out which chart type is best for the data, before linking cells to the chart. Charts should enhance the ability to understand the data and make it easy to see the differences in the data.

Like Excel, the data (a series) selected to create the chart in Dashboard Design must be in adjacent cells. While it is very easy to select a chart type, the important thing to remember is that you should select the chart type that will best represent the data. For example, if the goal of the chart is to show a comparison between items, a bar chart would be a good solution. Please do not get in the bad habit of only using bar or column charts for every dashboard. If you need to display more than one series of data, consider using one of the stacked chart types because they also support more than one series of data.

Chart Component Options

The sections that follow explain the options on the Properties panel that are common to charts.

Common Chart General View Options

Titles Options

The options in this section are used for the chart and axis titles, as shown in Figure 7-18.

CHART Displays text at the top of the chart. This is usually a brief description of the data on the chart. I noticed that on some chart types if this option is left blank, the plot area of a chart is displayed a little larger on the dashboard. When I do not want to use this option, I put the title in a Label component.

SUBTITLE Displays the text below the charts title. This option is used to provide more information about the data displayed on the chart.

CATEGORY (X) AXIS Type in or select the cell that has the title for the horizontal axis on the chart.

VALUE (Y) AXIS Type in or select the cell that has the title for the vertical axis on the chart.

Data Options

These options are used to select the range of data from the spreadsheet that will be displayed on the chart.

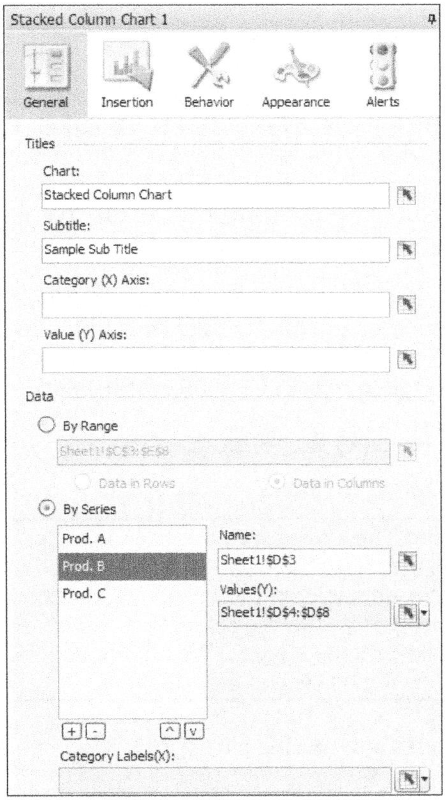

Figure 7-18 Common chart general view options

BY RANGE Is used to select the labels and data for the component. The cells selected for this option have to be next to each other. This option is not available for pie charts.

DATA IN ROWS or **DATA IN COLUMNS** Based on the cells selected for the By Range option, the rows or columns option will automatically be selected, based on the layout of data in the spreadsheet. If the option that is automatically selected is not what you need, select the other option. The first row or column of data in the range that you select is what will be used for the category (label) for the data. Figure 7-19 shows a series of data in rows. Figure 7-20 shows the same series of data in columns.

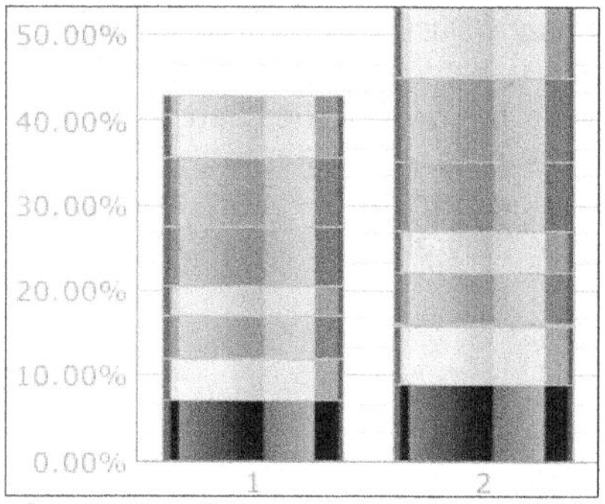

Figure 7-19 Data series displayed in rows

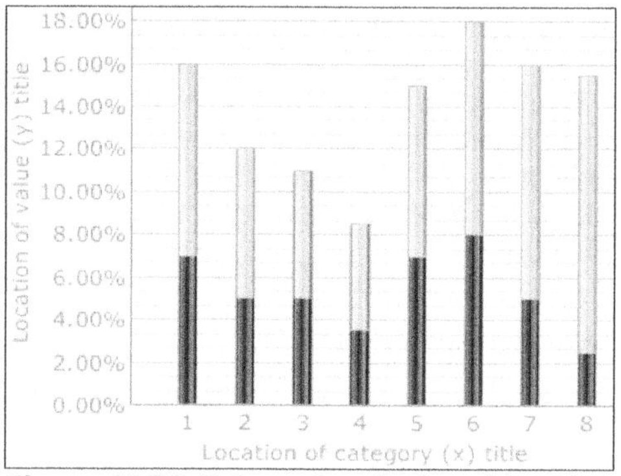

Figure 7-20 Data series displayed in columns

Series Options

The options in this section are used to modify the existing series for the chart, as well as, add new series, if needed. The options in this section provide more flexibility then the data options discussed above. Often, the options in this section are used to select ranges of cells that are not adjacent to each other in the spreadsheet, like the data options require.

BY SERIES Is used to add more series to the chart, edit existing series and delete series from the chart that are no longer needed.

NAME Is used to select a meaningful name for the series. It is not necessary to change the series name if there is only one or two series in the chart. This option does not print on the chart.

VALUES (Y) Is used to select the data for the series.

CATEGORY LABELS (X) Is used to select the cells for the labels that appear across the bottom of the chart.

> **Using The Category Labels (X) Option With The By Range Option**
> You may have the need to use the Category Labels option even though the By Range option discussed earlier in this chapter is not enabled. If that is the case, selecting the By Series option will enable the category labels option. You can select the cells for the labels, then reselect the By Range option. What you will notice is that the options that you selected in the By Range section are still there.

The **ADD SERIES BUTTON** (the plus sign) is used to add another series of data to the chart.

The **DELETE SERIES BUTTON** (the minus sign) is used to remove the selected series of data from the chart.

The **UP** and **DOWN BUTTONS** are used to change the order that the series of data are displayed in on the chart.

Common Chart Common Tab Options

Ignore Blank Cells Options

The options in this section are shown in Figure 7-21. They are used to select how the chart handles empty cells at the end of the data range.

IN SERIES Is used to stop empty cells that are after the last cell with data in the series, from being displayed on the chart.

IN VALUES Is used to stop empty cells that are after the last cell that has a value in the data range, from being displayed on the chart.

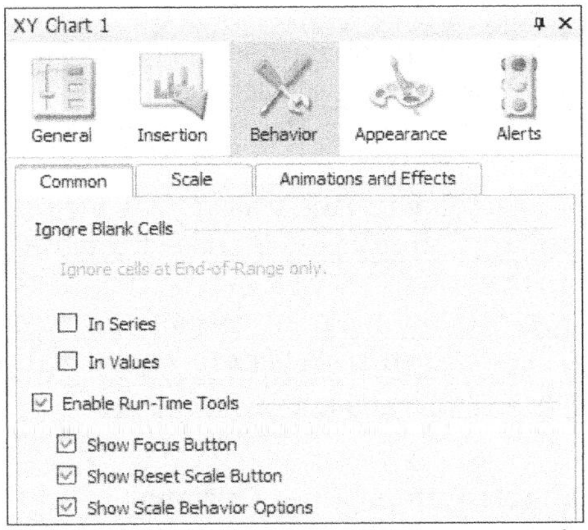

Figure 7-21 Common chart common tab options

Run-Time Tools Options

ENABLE RUN-TIME TOOLS If enabled, the options shown above in Figure 7-21 in this section allow the user some control over the scale behavior of charts. The three options explained below allow the scale of the chart to be changed by the person using the dashboard.

Keep in mind that you do not have complete control over the scale values that users will select. Charts that have run-time options enabled will display the icon shown in Figure 7-22.

Figure 7-22 Run-Time icon

① **SHOW FOCUS BUTTON** Allows the user to force the chart to be rescaled based on the data that is visible on the chart. This option enables the Force Chart Data button (the fourth button) on the menu shown in Figure 7-23.

② **SHOW RESET SCALE BUTTON** Allows the user to reset the scale back to what it was when the dashboard was first opened. This option enables the Reset Scale button (the fifth button) on the menu.

③ **SHOW SCALE BEHAVIOR OPTIONS** Allows the chart to be scaled, based on which of these buttons: Grow, Off and Auto (the first three buttons) on the menu shown in Figure 7-23 is selected after the data changes. Selecting this option allows the user to select the following scaling options: Auto Zoom Out, Manual (Y) and Auto (Y) axis.

Run-Time Menu

When the mouse pointer is hovered over the icon shown above in Figure 7-22, the menu shown in Figure 7-23 appears on the dashboard. Selecting the three options explained above cause some or all of the buttons on the menu to appear in the upper left corner of the chart.

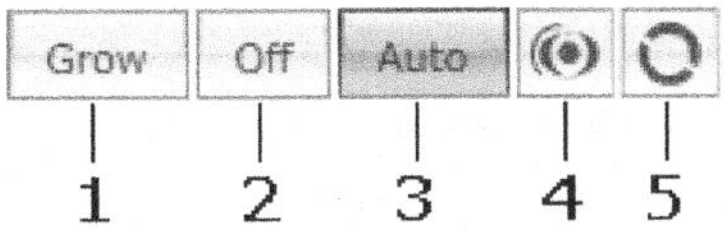

Figure 7-23 Run-Time menu

When the mouse pointer is hovered over a button, a tool tip appears that explains the purpose of the button. Table 7-2 explains the buttons on the menu. If you want to see how these options work, open the file dd_runtime_options.pdf.

Button	Description
1	Enables scale growth. Sets the scale behavior to Auto Zoom Out. This option allows the scale to grow when the data values increase. The scale will not shrink when the data values get smaller.
2	Disables scaling. The chart uses the minimum and maximum data points for the scale values even if the data changes.
3	Enables automatic scaling. Sets the scale behavior to auto. The minimum and maximum scale values will automatically adjust to include all of the data points.
4	Focus chart data. Forces the chart axes to be rescaled based on current data. This means that the chart keeps the scale even if the data changes going forward.
5	Resets chart scale back to what it was when the model was opened.

Table 7-2 Run-Time menu buttons explained

NEW Enable Range Slider Options

The options shown in Figure 7-24 are used to add a range slider to the chart. The purpose of this slider is to let the user view a portion of the data displayed on the chart (a specific data set), instead of all of the data. To select a specific data set, adjust the handle on either side of the slider.

When a range slider is added to a chart, a smaller version of the chart is displayed to the side or below the main chart with the range slider, as illustrated in Figure 7-25. The slider is used to let the use select a portion of the data to be displayed in the main chart.

The **BEGINNING RANGE VALUE** and **END RANGE VALUE** options are used to select a data position in the chart. You can type in the position or select it from the spreadsheet.

The **RANGE LABELS** are for the small chart associated with the range slider. Where the labels are placed depends on the number of data points and the number of labels.

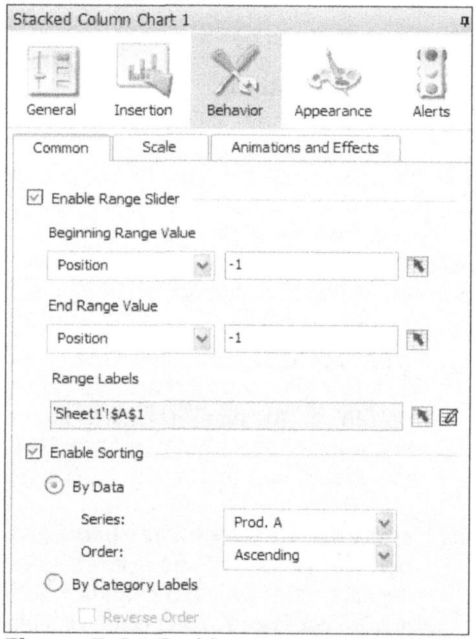

Figure 7-24 Enable Range slider and Enable Sorting options

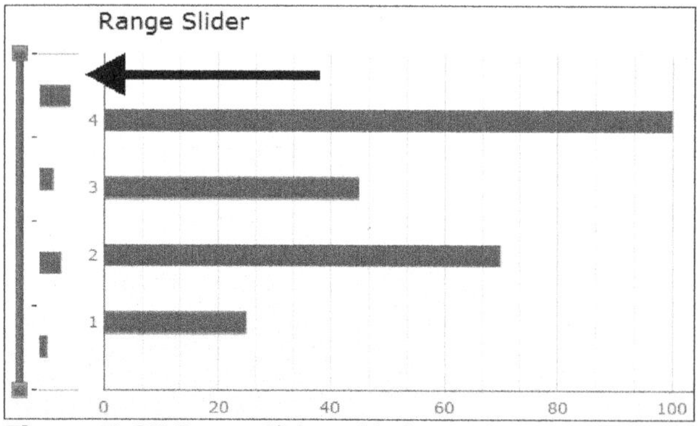

Figure 7-25 Range Slider added to a chart

Enable Sorting Options

The options shown earlier in Figure 7-24 are used to sort the values in the chart by a data series or by the category labels in the chart.

Common Chart Scale Tab Options

The options shown in Figure 7-26 are common to many chart components. The options on this tab control how the axis scale changes when the data changes. A scale is the range of values that the data must be in, to appear on the chart.

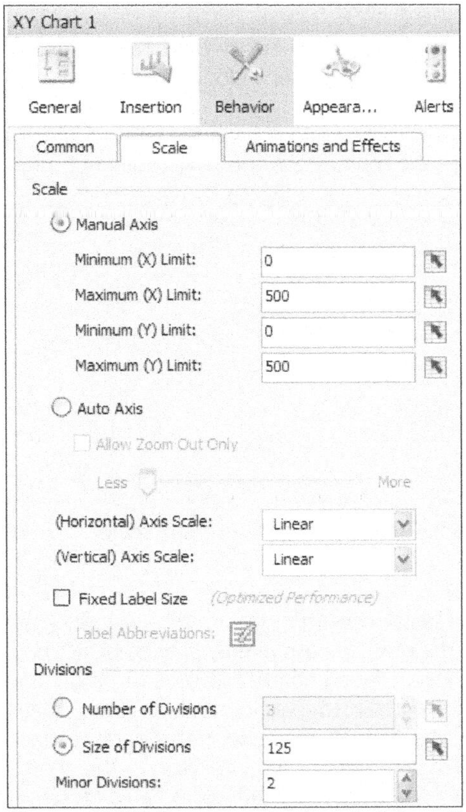

Figure 7-26 Common chart scale tab options

Manual Axis Options

These options are used to select the minimum and maximum values for the scale. The scale will not change when the data changes if these options are selected. The **MANUAL AXIS** option enables the X and Y Minimum and Maximum Limit options.

MINIMUM (X) LIMIT Is used to select the lowest value that will be displayed on the charts X axis.

MAXIMUM (X) LIMIT Is used to select the highest value that will be displayed on the charts X axis.

MINIMUM (Y) LIMIT Is used to select the lowest value that will be displayed on the charts Y axis.

MAXIMUM (Y) LIMIT Is used to select the highest value that will be displayed on the charts Y axis.

Auto Axis Options

Select this option to allow the axis scale to grow and shrink as the data changes. Selecting this option means that all values from the data source that meet the other criteria will be included on the chart.

ALLOW ZOOM OUT ONLY This option is only available if the Auto Axis option is selected. This option is used to select how much a scale can grow when the data changes. Use the slider shown in Figure 7-27 to adjust how much the scale can change. To the far right, the scale increases a lot. To the far left, the scale increases by a small amount.

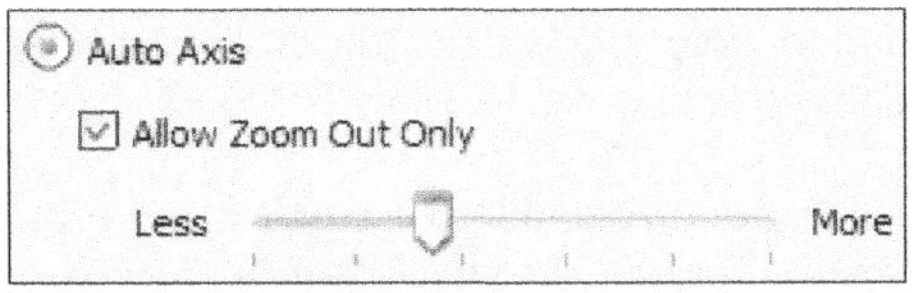

Figure 7-27 Allow Zoom Out Only option

The **(HORIZONTAL) AXIS SCALE** and **(VERTICAL) AXIS SCALE** options are used to select the type of interval (linear or logarithmic) that the scale on the chart will use. The options in these drop-down lists are explained below.

Linear And Logarithmic Scale Options

These options are important for charts that show trends, in particular trends that have a wide span of data. An example of a wide span of data would be the following data values: 10, 20, 5,000, 5,250, 6,125 and 7,500. If there were more high values on the chart, the low values will be difficult to see on the chart.

Figure 7-28 shows a chart that has the Y axis value set to linear. Figure 7-29 shows the same chart with the Y axis value set to logarithmic.

The **LOGARITHMIC** option provides a more accurate trend line in the chart because the spacing between the markers on the chart does not change.

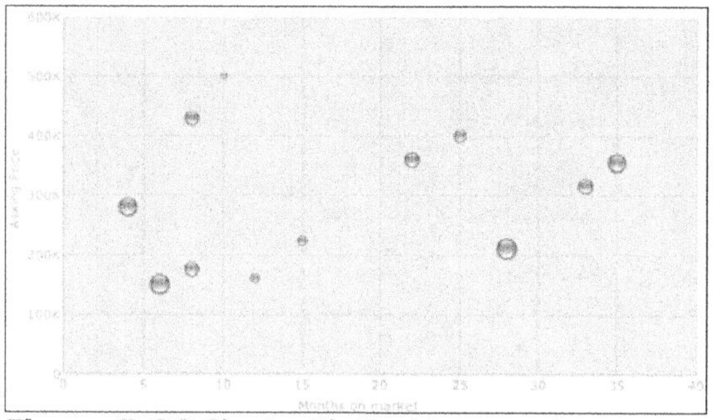

Figure 7-28 Chart with the Linear scale option

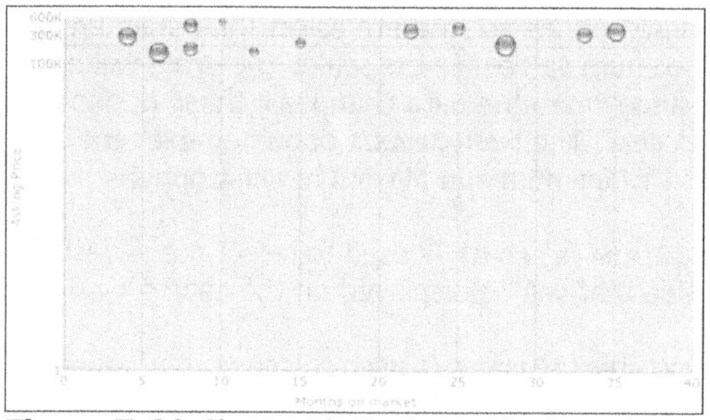

Figure 7-29 Chart with the Logarithmic scale option

① **LINEAR** uses intervals that are evenly spaced to create the scale for the axis. This means that the divisions are evenly spaced. This option allows the scale to resize itself based on the values being charted. This is the most common option to select.

② **LOGARITHMIC** uses intervals that are unevenly spaced. Divisions are plotted at intervals of the logarithm of the value, not the value itself, like linear does. Small values entered in the field force larger spaced intervals on the chart. Large values in the field force smaller spaced intervals on the chart. Select this option when the range of values displayed is large.

FIXED LABEL SIZE Check this option if you do not want the axis labels to be resized if the scale changes.

LABEL ABBREVIATIONS This option is only available if the Fixed Label Size option is checked. Clicking the Manual Edit button next to this option opens the dialog box shown in Figure 7-30.

The appropriate option in the **DISPLAYED SIGN** column will appear after the numbers on the Y axis on the chart. The option selected depends on the values on the scale for the axis. You can add or change the options on this dialog box as needed.

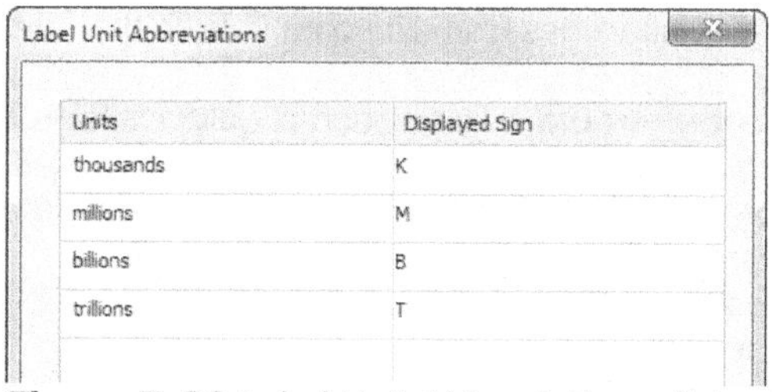

Figure 7-30 Label Unit Abbreviations dialog box

Divisions Options

The options in this section, shown earlier in Figure 7-26 are used to configure the gridlines and space between them. To use these options, the Manual Axis Scale option must be enabled.

NUMBER OF DIVISIONS Is used to select the number of major gridlines on the vertical axis. (3)

SIZE OF DIVISIONS Is used to select the distance (horizontally) between the divisions. The value entered in this field divides the range of values between the Minimum (X) Limit and Maximum (X) Limit values. For example, if the Minimum (X) Limit is zero and the Maximum (X) Limit is 1,000 and if the Size of Divisions option is set to 125, the values on the horizontal axis would be 0, 125, 250, 375, 500, etc. (3)

(3) These options cannot be selected at the same time.

MINOR DIVISIONS Is used to select the number of minor gridlines between each division on the horizontal and vertical axis.

Common Chart Layout Tab Options

The options on this tab are used to select backgrounds, borders, horizontal and vertical gridlines for the chart, as shown in Figure 7-31.

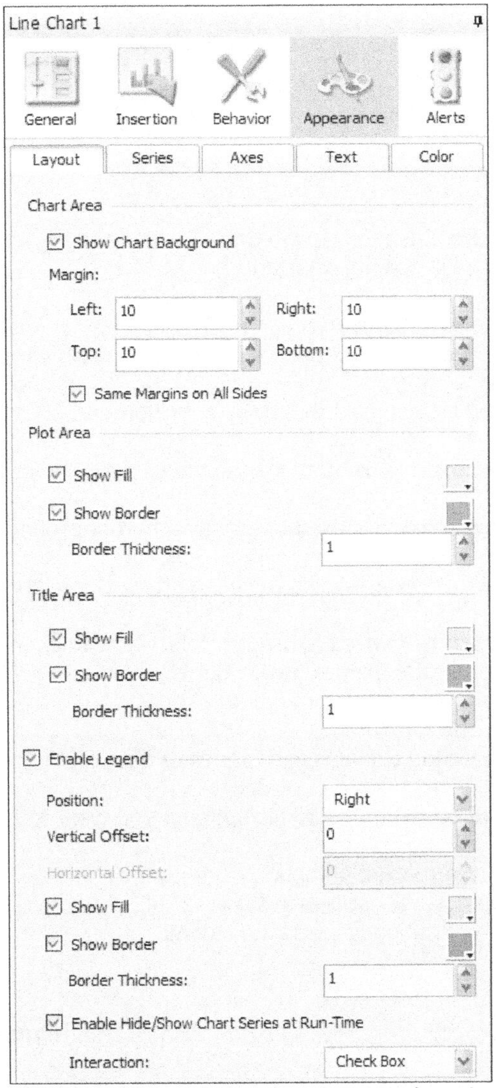

Figure 7-31 Common chart layout tab options

Chart Area Options

SHOW CHART BACKGROUND Check this option if you want to add a background to the chart. Because the default background color is white, if this option is checked, it will appear as a gray border instead of a color.

MARGIN The Left, Right, Top and Bottom options in this section are used to select the space between the outside of the plot area and the outer edges of the chart area. The smaller the number selected, the closer to the outer edge of the plot area the chart will be. As the chart expands, the larger the margin number is.

The **SAME MARGINS ON ALL SIDES** option if checked, requires all four margins to be the same size. If you change the size of one margin, the other three margins will automatically be changed.

Plot Area Options

The options in this section are for the center of the chart where the data is displayed.

SHOW FILL Is used to display a background color in the plot area. (4)

FILL COLOR Is used to change the background color for the plot area.

SHOW BORDER Is used to display a border around the plot area. (5)

BORDER COLOR Is used to change the color of the border around the plot area.

BORDER THICKNESS Is used to select how thick the border around the plot area is. The smaller the number, the thinner the border is.

Figure 7-32 shows a line chart with the **SHOW BORDER** and **SHOW FILL** options selected. The chart shown in Figure 7-32 has a border thickness of two. The chart shown in Figure 7-33 has a border thickness of five.

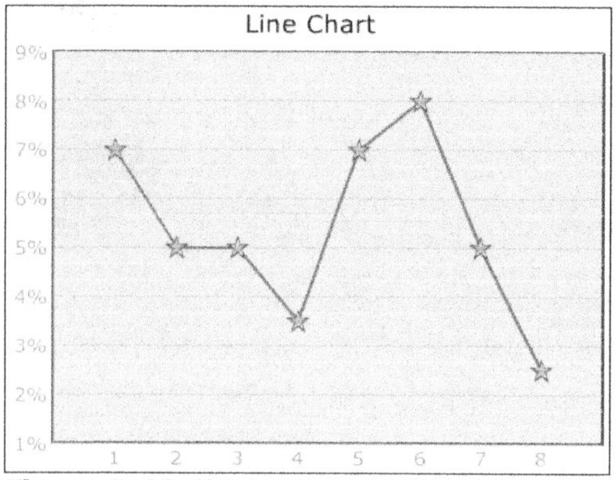

Figure 7-32 Chart with Show Border and Show Fill options selected

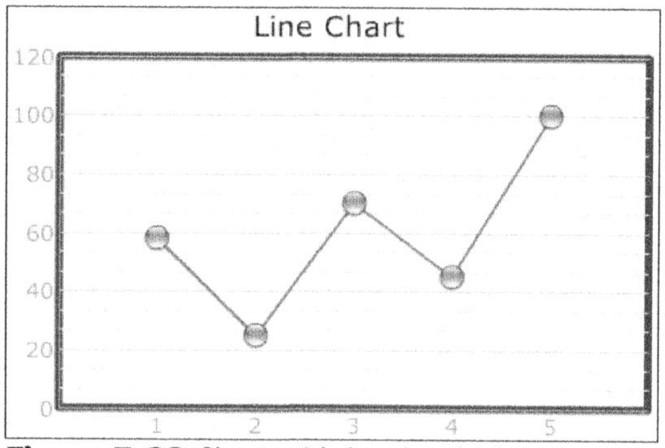

Figure 7-33 Chart with border thickness option increased

Title Area Options

The options in this section are used to configure the title section of the chart.

SHOW FILL Is used to display a background color in the title area. (4)

FILL COLOR Is used to change the background color in the title area.

SHOW BORDER Is used to display a border around the title area. (5)

BORDER COLOR Is used to change the color of the border around the title area.

BORDER THICKNESS Is used to select how thick the border around the title area is. The smaller the number, the thinner the border is.

Legend Options

The legend explains each series of data on the chart, as shown earlier in Figure 7-14.

ENABLE LEGEND Check this option if you want to display a legend with the chart.

POSITION Select an option from the drop-down list shown in Figure 7-34 as the location to place the legend.

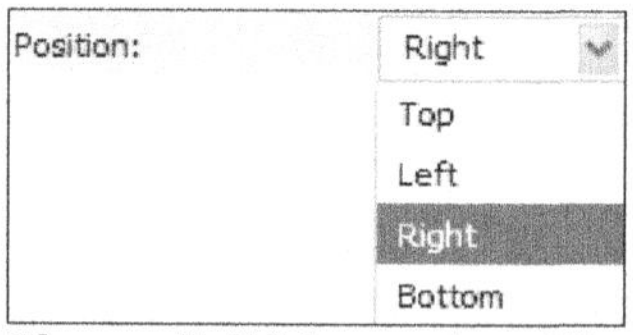

Figure 7-34 Legend position options

VERTICAL OFFSET Is used to shift the text up or down. This option is only available if the right or left option is selected in the Position drop-down list. Negative values shift the text down.

HORIZONTAL OFFSET Is used to shift the text right or left. This option is only available if the top or bottom option is selected in the Position drop-down list. Negative values shift the text left.

SHOW FILL Is used to display a background color in the legend. (4)

FILL COLOR Is used to change the background color of the legend.

BORDER COLOR Is used to change the color of the legends border.

SHOW BORDER Is used to display a border around the legend. (5)

BORDER THICKNESS Is used to select how thick the border around the legend is. The smaller the number, the thinner the border is.

NEW **ENABLE HIDE/SHOW CHART SERIES AT RUN-TIME** By default this option is selected. It lets the user display or hide a series of data on the chart.

If **CHECK BOX** is the selected Interaction option, a check box is added to the legend, as illustrated in Figure 7-35. If you click on a check box, the series of data will be hidden on the chart, as shown in Figure 7-36.

If **MOUSE CLICK** is the selected Interaction option, the user needs to click on the option in the legend to hide or display a series of data.

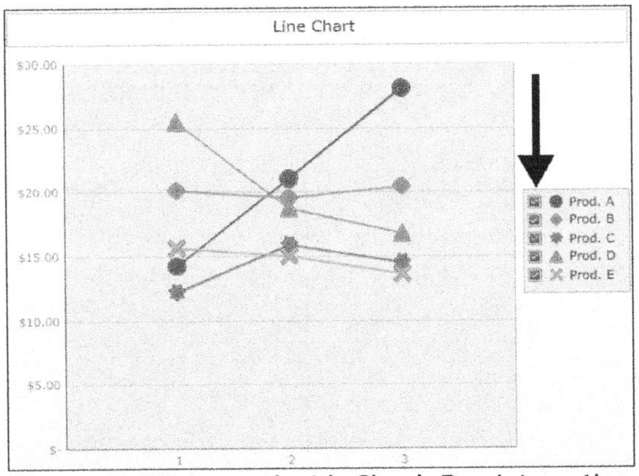

Figure 7-35 Legend with Check Box interaction enabled

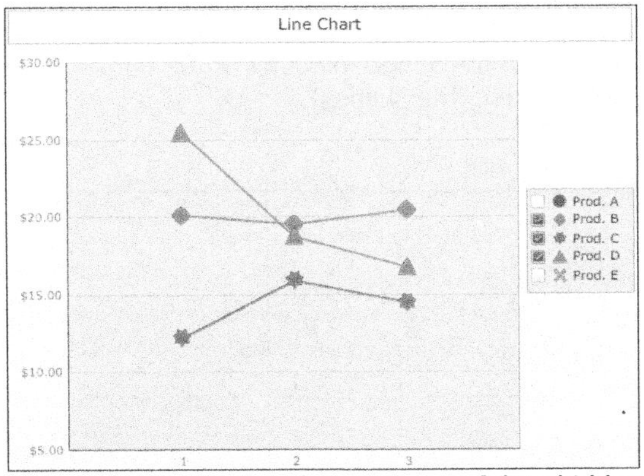

Figure 7-36 Chart with two series of data hidden

(4) The Show Fill option enables the Fill Color option in the same section.
(5) The Show Border option enables the Border Color and Border Thickness options in the same section.

Legends Overview

Adding a legend to a chart makes it easier to know what each series of data represents. The legend can be customized. When some parts of the chart like the shape of the marker is changed, it is also changed in the legend. You do not have to use column headings in the legend for the series name, you can type in the name for each series.

Common Chart Series Tab Options

Figure 7-37 shows the options on the Series tab. The options on this tab are used to format the data series.

SERIES Contains the names for the series of data that are being plotted on the chart. Select the series from the list that you want to make changes to. The names in this list come from the values that are created in the **NAME** field on the General view.

The options in the **SHAPE** drop-down list are used to select the shape (marker) for the data points for the series on the chart. Figure 7-38 shows a line chart without markers. In Figure 7-39, the diamond marker is selected.

LINE Is used to change the color of the line that connects the data points (markers) in the chart.

FILL Is used to change the color of the data point markers (the shapes).

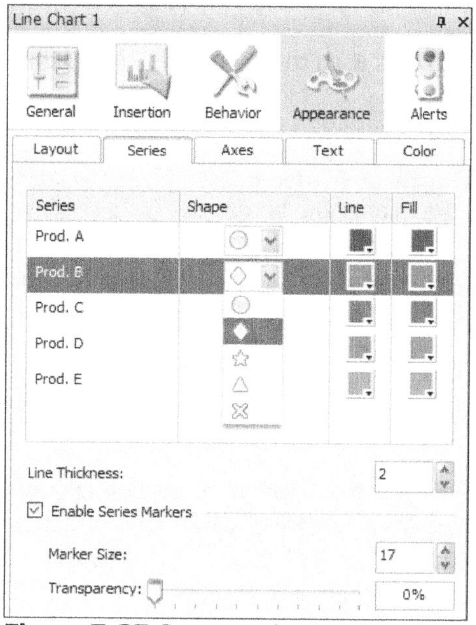

Figure 7-37 Common chart series tab options

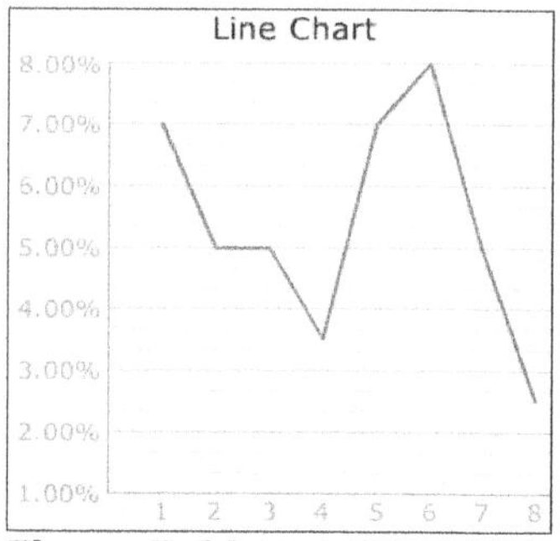

Figure 7-38 Line chart without markers

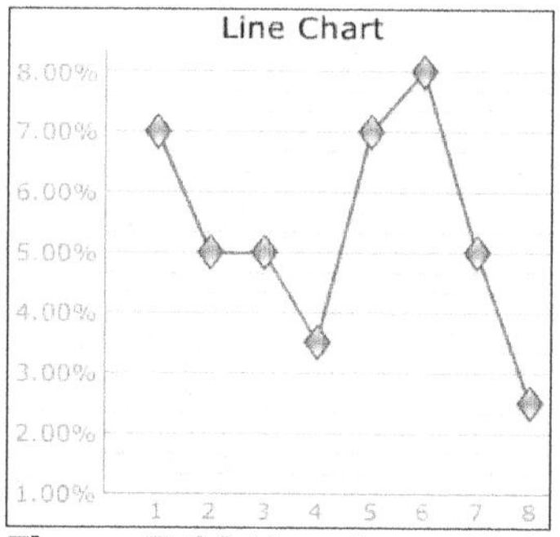

Figure 7-39 Line chart with markers

LINE THICKNESS Is used to select how thick (wide) the line is that connects the data points.

ENABLE SERIES MARKERS Select this option to display the markers (shapes) on the chart, if applicable.

MARKER SIZE Is used to select the size of the markers (shapes).

TRANSPARENCY [See Chapter 4, Transparency Option]

Common Chart Axes Tab Options

The options shown in Figure 7-40 are used to customize the color, thickness and tick marks on the Horizontal (X axis) and Vertical (Y axis) axes.

Figure 7-40 Common chart axes tab options

Vertical Axis Options

ENABLE VERTICAL AXIS Select this option to display the vertical axis line on the chart.

LINE COLOR Is used to change the color of the line on the vertical axis.

THICKNESS Is used to change the width of the line on the vertical axis.

SHOW MAJOR TICKS Select this option to display major (long) tick marks on the horizontal axis, where the major gridlines intersect on the vertical axis.

SHOW MINOR TICKS Select this option to display minor (short) tick marks between the major tick marks on the horizontal axis, where the minor gridlines intersect on the vertical axis.

Horizontal Axis Options

ENABLE HORIZONTAL AXIS Select this option to display the horizontal axis line on the chart.

LINE COLOR Is used to change the color of the line on the horizontal axis.

THICKNESS Is used to select the width of the line on the horizontal axis.

Horizontal Gridlines Options

The options in this section are used to display gridlines in the plot area section of the chart.

SHOW MAJOR GRIDLINES Select this option to display major gridlines on the horizontal axis.

MAJOR GRIDLINES COLOR Is used to change the color of the major gridlines on the chart.

MAJOR GRIDLINES THICKNESS Is used to select the thickness of the major gridlines. Figure 7-41 shows a chart with the Horizontal Gridlines Thickness option set to five.

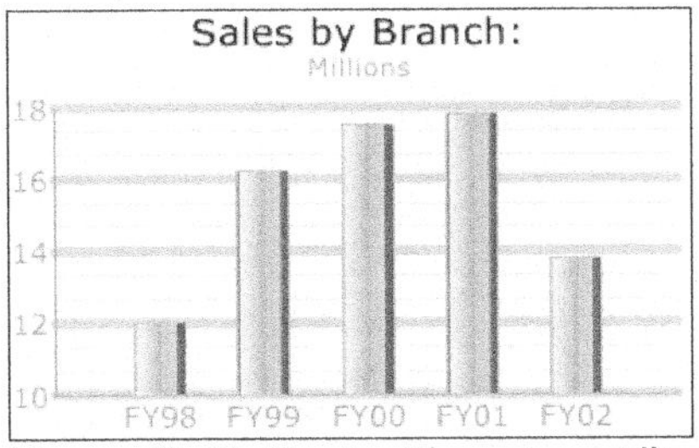

Figure 7-41 Chart with major gridlines value increased

SHOW MINOR GRIDLINES Select this option to display minor gridlines on the horizontal axis.

MINOR GRIDLINES COLOR Is used to change the color of the minor gridlines.

MINOR GRIDLINES THICKNESS Is used to select the thickness of the minor gridlines.

Common Chart Text Tab Options

The options shown in Figure 7-42 are used to modify the text on the chart. Check the box in the Show column for each text object that you want to appear on the chart.

When you click on an item in the Text column, the corresponding Format Selected Text options appear at the bottom of the tab. As shown in Figure 7-42, the legend will not appear on the chart because the Show option is not checked.

The **MOUSE-OVER VALUES** options are used to modify the text that is displayed when the mouse pointer is hovered over a part of the chart, as shown in Figure 7-43.

The **DATA LABELS** text options are used to select what content will be displayed for each marker on the chart.

The options in the **LABEL CONTAINS** section are used to select what content will appear next to the markers in the chart. More than one option can be selected. As shown at the bottom of the Figure 7-42, the series name and value will be displayed next to the markers for Product B. Figure 7-44 shows these options applied to the chart.

The options in the **LABEL SEPARATOR** drop-down list are used to select what will be placed between the data labels in the chart. The **CUSTOM** option lets you type in what you want. In Figure 7-44, the **NEW LINE SEPARATOR** option was selected. This stacks the data labels.

Figure 7-42 Common chart text tab options

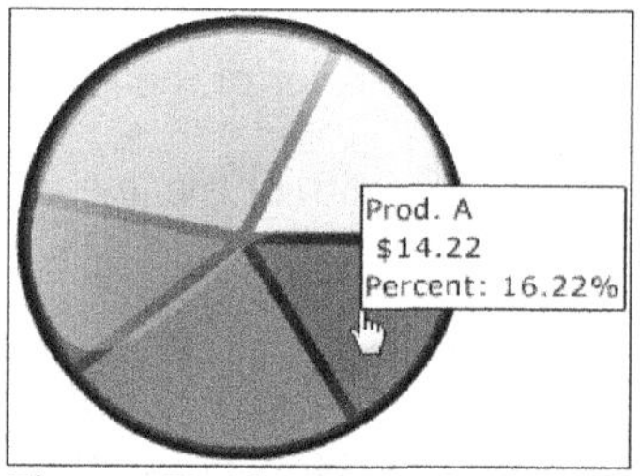

Figure 7-43 Mouse-Over Values displayed

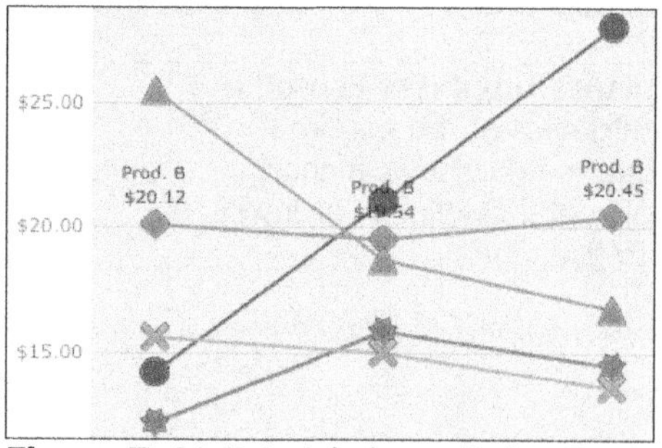

Figure 7-44 Data labels applied to Product B

Common Chart Color Tab Options

The options on this tab are used to change the color of various parts of the chart as shown in Figure 7-45.

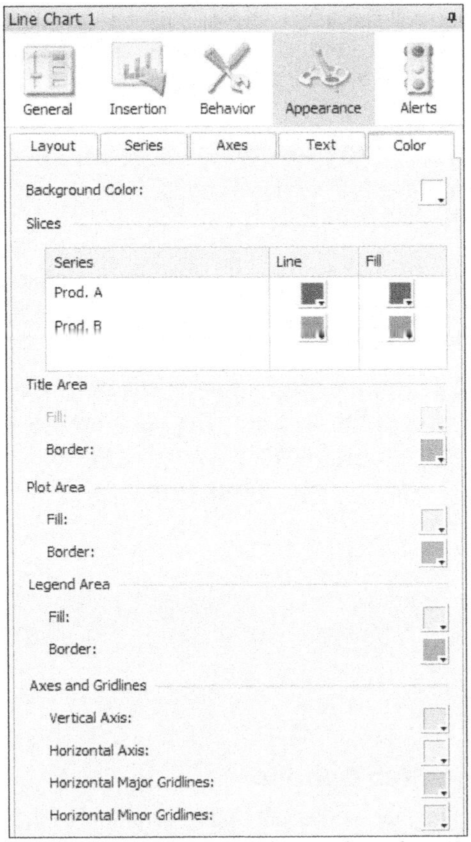

Figure 7-45 Common chart color tab options

BACKGROUND COLOR Is used to change the color of the background for the areas on the chart that do not have a color option.

> **Color Tab Options**
> The remaining options on this tab are duplicates of color options on other tabs, as indicated in Table 7-3. The options on the Color tab are only available if the corresponding Show Fill or Show Border option on the tab listed in the table is enabled. If you change the color on one tab, it is automatically changed on the other tab.
>
> For example, if you change the Show Border color in the Plot Area section on the Layout tab shown earlier in Figure 7-31, the Border option in the Plot Area section on the Color tab will automatically have the same color.

Color Tab Section	Tab
Slices	Series
Title Area	Layout
Plot Area	Layout
Legend Area	Layout
Axes and Gridlines	Axes

Table 7-3 Duplicate color tab options

Series, Title Area, Plot Area and Legend Area Options

[See Common Chart Series Tab Options, earlier in this chapter]

Axes And Gridlines Options

VERTICAL AXIS Is used to change the color of the line on the vertical axis. The Enable Vertical Axis option on the Axes tab must be enabled to use this option.

HORIZONTAL AXIS Is used to change the color of the line on the horizontal axis. The Enable Horizontal Axis option on the Axes tab must be enabled to use this option.

HORIZONTAL MAJOR GRIDLINES Is used to change the color of the horizontal major gridlines. The Show Major Gridlines option on the Axes tab must be enabled to use this option.

HORIZONTAL MINOR GRIDLINES Is used to change the color of the horizontal minor gridlines. The Show Minor Gridlines option on the Axes tab must be enabled to use this option.

Pie Chart Component

As you will see, each slice of a pie chart by default is a different color. Each slice represents a different piece of data. Each slice represents a percent of the pie. When percents need to be displayed in a chart, a pie chart is a good option.

General View Options

The Pie chart general view options are shown in Figure 7-46.

VALUES Is used to select the data for the chart. It is the same as the By Range option that many components have.

LABELS Is used to select the cells for the labels for each slice of the pie chart. This option works the same as the Category Labels (X) option.

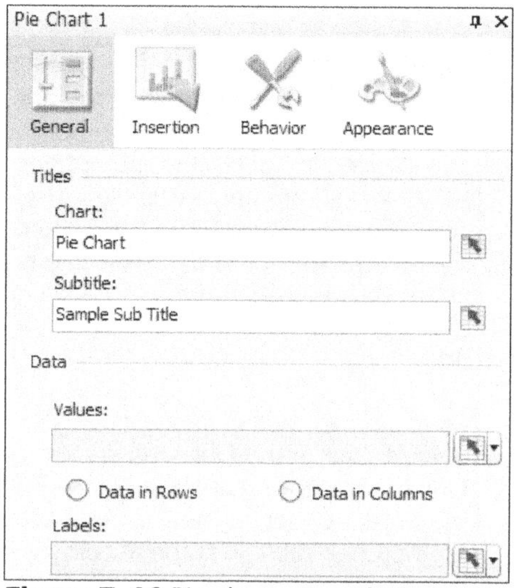

Figure 7-46 Pie chart general view options

Series Tab Options

The Pie chart series tab options are shown in Figure 7-47.

The options in the **DATA POINT** column contain all of the slices of the pie chart. Select the slice that you want to modify.

FILL Is used to change the color of a slice of the pie.

SHOW LINES If checked, lines will be placed between the slices on the chart. You can change the color and thickness of the line.

THICKNESS Is used to select the size of the line between the slices on the pie chart.

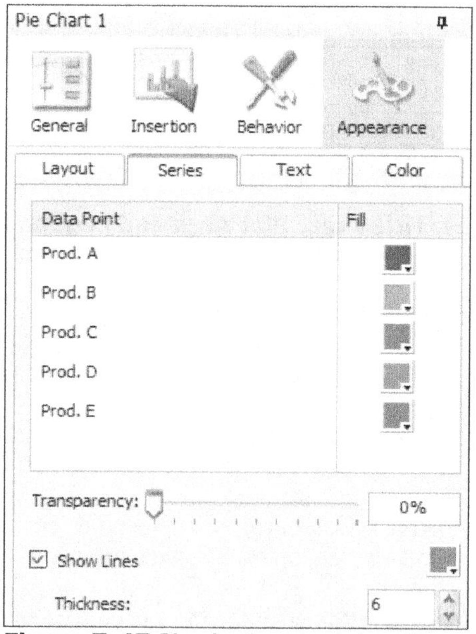

Figure 7-47 Pie chart series tab options

Color Tab Options

The Pie chart color tab options are shown in Figure 7-48. They are similar to the options on the Series tab.

LINE COLOR Is used to change the color of the line between the slices on the pie chart. The Show Lines option on the Series tab must be enabled to use this option.

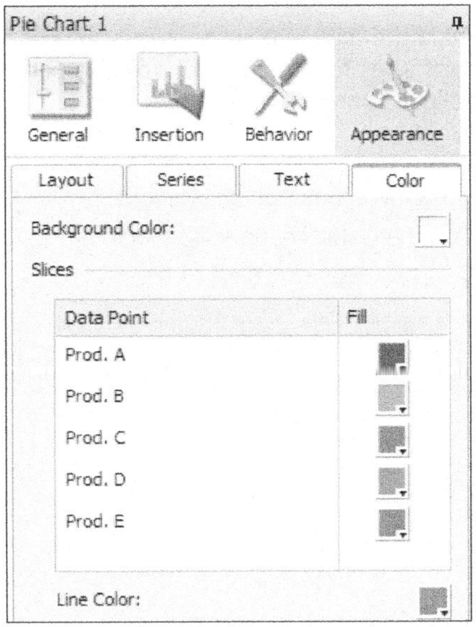

Figure 7-48 Pie chart color tab options

Exercise 7.1: Create The Revenues By Product Pie Chart

In this exercise you will create a pie chart that shows the revenue for several products in North America. Figure 7-49 shows the data for this exercise.

	A	B	C	D	E	F	G
1	Revenues By Product		Rev				
2							
3		Status List	Prod. A	Prod. B	Prod. C	Prod. D	Prod. E
4	North America		$ 14.22	$ 20.12	$ 12.18	$ 25.49	$ 15.64
5	Latin America		$ 21.05	$ 19.54	$ 15.88	$ 18.73	$ 15.02
6	Europe		$ 21.06	$ 20.45	$ 14.49	$ 16.78	$ 13.61
7	Asia		$ 12.25	$ 17.12	$ 20.99	$ 16.79	$ 12.07
8	Australia & Pacific		$ 15.36	$ 25.74	$ 13.17	$ 19.42	$ 12.70

Figure 7-49 Pie chart data

1. Import the Status List spreadsheet.
2. Add the Pie Chart component.
3. On the General view, make the changes in the table.

Option	Change To
Chart	A1
Subtitle	In North America
Values	C4:G8
Labels	C3:G3

4. On the Series tab, make the Data Point changes in the table.

Data Point	Change To
Prod. C	Red
Prod. E	Yellow

5. On the Text tab, change the **POSITION** of the legend to Bottom.

6. Save the model as `My pie chart.`

If you hold the mouse pointer over a slice of the chart, as shown in Figure 7-50, you will see the amount of sales for the product and the percent that the product represents of the total sales.
If the following changes were made on the Series tab, the chart would look like the one shown in Figure 7-51.

① Show Lines option selected.
② Line Color changed to black.
③ Thickness changed to 6.

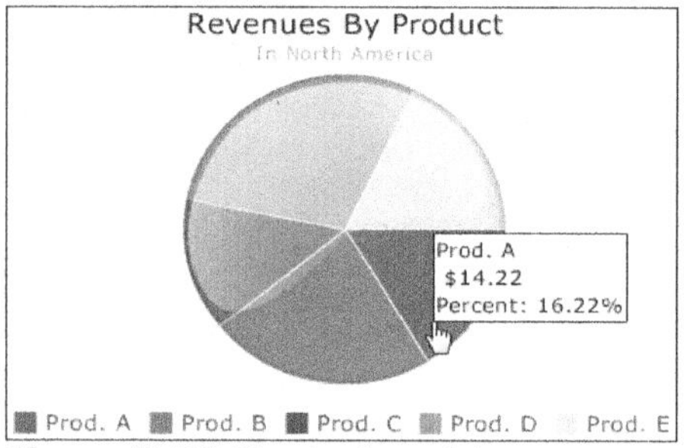

Figure 7-50 Pie chart model

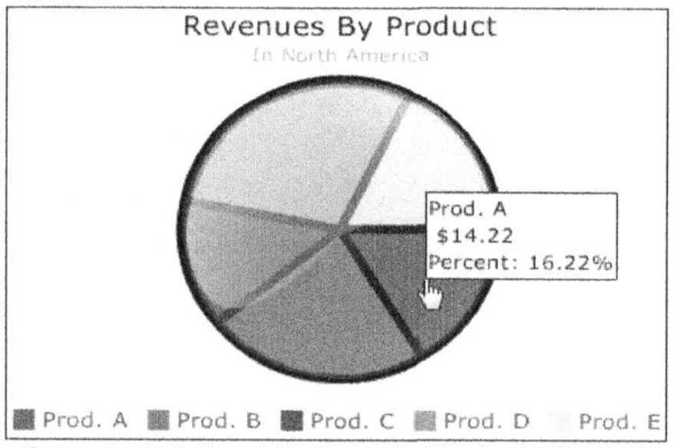

Figure 7-51 Pie chart with modified Series tab options

Bar And Column Chart Components

Bar and column charts are mostly used to compare values in a range. The only differences between bar and column charts is the direction that the bars are placed on the chart. Bar charts use vertical bars and column charts use horizontal columns. These chart types can be used interchangeably.
If space becomes an issue on the dashboard, keep in mind that bar charts use less space vertically and column charts use less space horizontally. The data on the X and Y axis is also switched.
You will learn how to create a bar chart in Exercise 13.2.

Bar Chart Component

General View Options

The Bar chart general view options are shown in Figure 7-52.

VALUE (X) AXIS Is used to select the cell that has the title for the horizontal axis (across the bottom) on the chart.

CATEGORY (Y) AXIS Is used to select the cell that has the title for the vertical axis (on the left side) on the chart.

SECONDARY VALUE (X) AXIS Is used to select the cell that has the title for the second horizontal axis on the chart. This option is only available when the Plot Series On Secondary Axis option on the General view is selected.

Figure 7-52 Bar chart general view options

The **BY SERIES** option on the General view has to be selected to use the Secondary Value (X) Axis option.

The **PLOT SERIES ON** options are used to select the axis to plot the series on.

Column Chart Component

General View Options

The Column chart general view options are very similar to the Stacked Column chart options shown earlier in Figure 7-18. The option that is different from the Stacked Column chart is explained below.

SECONDARY VALUE (Y) AXIS Is used to select the cell that has the title for the second vertical axis (on the right side) on the chart. This option is only available when the Plot Series On Secondary Axis option on the General view selected.

Scale Tab Options

The options shown in Figure 7-53 are used to control how the Y axis scale changes when the data changes.

MANUAL (Y) AXIS Select this option when you want to select the minimum and maximum limits and the number of major and minor divisions.

AUTO (Y) AXIS Select this option when you want the minimum and maximum limits and number of divisions to be selected automatically, based on the values. This means that the scale will shrink and grow when the data changes.

(Y) AXIS SCALE Is used to select how the major and minor divisions on the vertical axis are positioned.

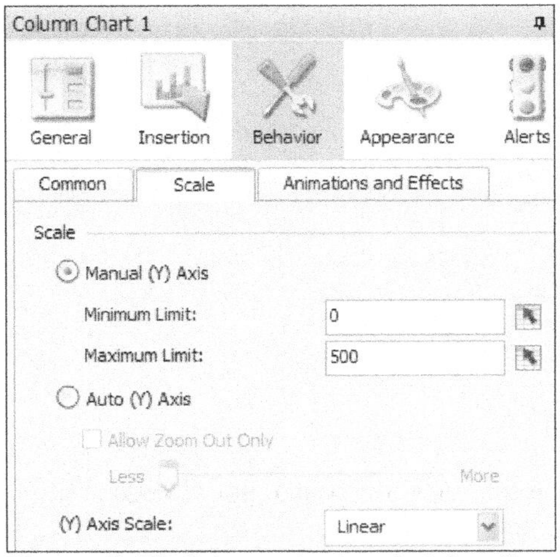

Figure 7-53 Column chart scale tab options

Series Tab Options

The Bar and Column chart series tab options are shown in Figure 7-54.

MARKER SIZE Is used to change the size of the bars or columns on the chart. The range of values for this option is 1 to 100.

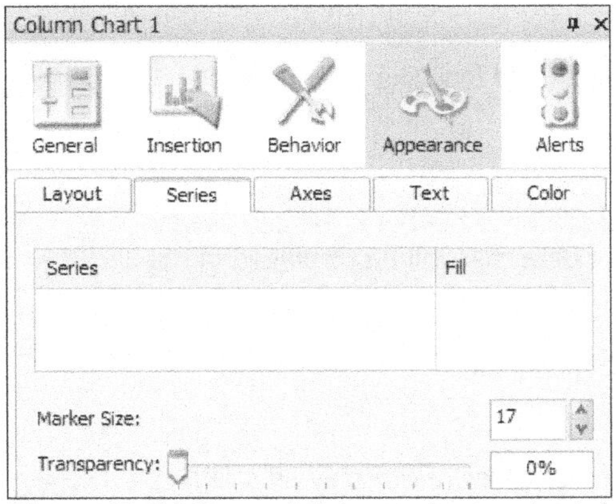

Figure 7-54 Bar and Column chart series tab options

> **Changing Marker Colors**
> Unlike pie charts where each series of data is a different color, all markers of a series of data have the same color by default. If you have the need to display the markers (based on the value) of a series with different colors, you can by using options on the Alerts view.

Exercise 7.2: Create The Sales By Branch Column Chart

In this exercise you will create a column chart. In Exercise 9.5 this chart will be connected to a List Box component.

The chart will display the sales for five fiscal years. Figure 7-55 shows the data for this exercise.

	A	B	C	D	E	F
1	Sales by Branch:					
2						
3		FY08	FY09	FY10	FY11	FY12
4	Atherton	$ 19.7	$ 17.1	$ 18.3	$ 14.8	$ 19.8
5	Berkeley	$ 14.4	$ 18.0	$ 16.4	$ 16.7	$ 19.3
6	Carmel	$ 18.8	$ 13.5	$ 18.7	$ 13.9	$ 15.7
7	Cupertino	$ 12.0	$ 16.2	$ 17.5	$ 17.8	$ 13.8
8	Freemont	$ 19.2	$ 15.6	$ 19.6	$ 15.9	$ 14.4
9	Irvine	$ 18.9	$ 14.6	$ 16.7	$ 12.1	$ 13.9
10	Milpitas	$ 18.7	$ 17.8	$ 14.0	$ 18.5	$ 13.7
11	Orange County	$ 17.0	$ 19.4	$ 17.1	$ 17.3	$ 17.3
12	San Francisco	$ 14.4	$ 14.0	$ 13.9	$ 15.4	$ 18.3
13						
14	Insert In Row:					

Figure 7-55 Column chart data

1. Import the List Box spreadsheet.

2. Add the Column Chart component.

3. On the General view, make the changes in the table.

Option	Change To
Chart	A1
Subtitle	Millions
By Range	B14:F14
Category Labels (X)	B3:F3

4. On the Scale tab, make the changes in the table.

Option	Change To
Manual (Y) Axis	Select this option
Maximum Limit	500
Auto (Y) Axis	Select this option

5. On the Series tab, change the Marker Size option to 25.

6. The chart should look like the one shown in Figure 7-56.

   The List Box component that you will add to this model later in the book will be used to select the data that will be displayed in the column chart.

   Save the model as `My list box selector.`

   Yes, the chart does not display any data. There is nothing wrong with the chart.

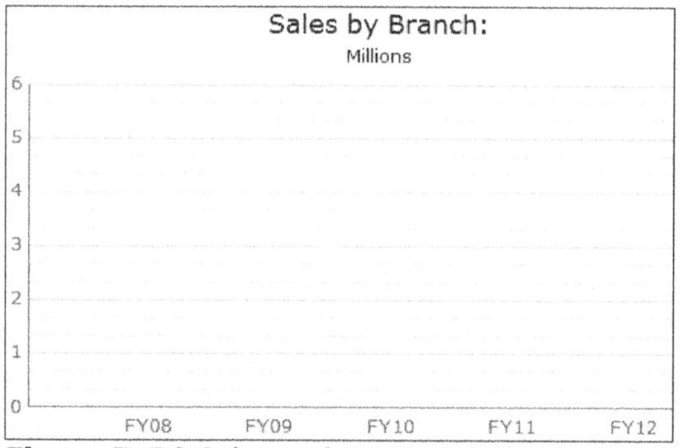

Figure 7-56 Column chart model

Exercise 7.3: Create A Revenues By Product Column Chart

In this exercise you will create a column chart that will be connected to the Play Selector component in Exercise 9.2.

The chart will display the product revenue for four quarters.

Figure 7-57 shows part of the data for this exercise.

	A	B	C	D	E	F
1		Revenues by Product				
2						
3			Q1	Q2	Q3	Q4
4		Product 1	$ 27.0	$ 34.6	$ 48.7	$ 54.8
5		Product 2	$ 43.3	$ 52.5	$ 33.5	$ 30.7
6		Product 3	$ 46.8	$ 23.1	$ 41.8	$ 50.9
⋮				⋮		
24		Product 21	$ 37.6	$ 52.5	$ 44.3	$ 29.8
25		Product 22	$ 45.2	$ 50.8	$ 46.4	$ 43.5
26						
27	Insert In Row:					

Figure 7-57 Column chart data

1. Import the Player Selector spreadsheet.
2. Add the Column Chart component.
3. On the General view, make the changes in the table. Selecting cell B27 for the subtitle will display the product name for the current row of data. This means that the subtitle will change on the dashboard each time a different product is selected.

Option	Change To
Chart	B1
Subtitle	B27
By Range	C27:F27
Category Labels (X)	C3:F3

4. On the Scale tab, make the changes in the table.

Option	Change To
Manual (Y) Axis	Select this option
Maximum Limit	500
Auto (Y) Axis	Select this option

5. On the Series tab, change the Marker Size option to 40.
6. The chart should look like the one shown in Figure 7-58.

   The chart does not display any values because no data has been added to cells C27:F27. The values will be added to these cells from the Play Selector component.

   Save it as `My play selector`.

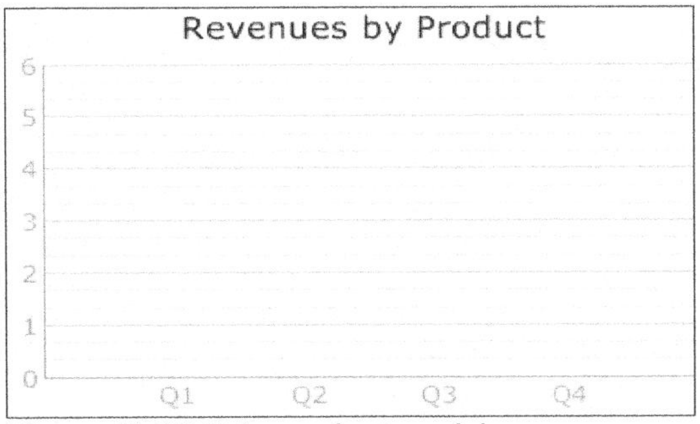

Figure 7-58 Column chart model

Exercise 7.4: Create A Chart For Historic Income

In this exercise you will create a chart that will display the historic data for a line item on the Income Statement. This chart will be used with the Spreadsheet Table component in Exercise 9.3. Figure 7-59 shows the data for this exercise.

	A	B	C	D	E	F	G	H	I	J	K	L
1	Income Statement				Historic Data							
2												
3												
4	Revenues	FY2013			**FY2005**	**FY2006**	**FY2007**	**FY2008**	**FY2009**	**FY2010**	**FY2011**	**FY2012**
5	Gross Sales	$ 12,000			12,600.00	13,104.00	13,628.16	14,173.29	14,740.22	15,329.83	15,943.02	16,580.74
6	Sales Return & Allowances	$ 125			131.25	136.50	141.96	147.64	153.54	159.69	166.07	172.72
7	Net Sales	$ 11,875			12,468.75	12,967.50	13,486.20	14,025.65	14,586.67	15,170.14	15,776.95	15,408.02
8	Cost of Good Sold	$ 5,666			5,949.30	6,187.27	6,434.76	6,692.15	6,959.84	7,238.23	7,527.76	7,828.87
9	Gross Profit	$ 6,209			6,519.45	6,780.23	7,051.44	7,333.49	7,626.83	7,931.91	8,249.18	8,579.15
10	Selling Expenses	$ 2,345			2,462.25	2,560.74	2,663.17	2,769.70	2,880.48	2,995.70	3,115.53	3,240.15
11	General & Admin.	$ 1,546			1,623.30	1,688.23	1,755.76	1,825.99	1,899.03	1,974.99	2,053.99	2,136.15
12	Operating Income	$ 2,318			2,433.90	2,531.26	2,632.51	2,737.81	2,847.32	2,961.21	3,079.66	3,202.85
13	Other Income / Expenses	$ 988			1,037.40	1,078.90	1,122.05	1,166.93	1,213.61	1,262.16	1,312.64	1,365.15
14	Income Before Interest & Taxes	$ 3,306			3,471.30	3,610.15	3,754.56	3,904.74	4,060.93	4,223.37	4,392.30	4,567.99
15	Interest Expenses & Taxes	$ 2,333			2,449.65	2,547.64	2,649.54	2,755.52	2,865.74	2,980.37	3,099.59	3,223.57
16	**Net Income**	**$ 973**			1,021.65	1,062.52	1,105.02	1,149.22	1,195.19	1,242.99	1,292.71	1,344.42
17												
18				Insert In								

Figure 7-59 Historic Income data

1. Import the Table spreadsheet.
2. Add the Column Chart component.
3. On the General view, make the changes in the table.

Option	Change To
Chart	A1
Subtitle	E1
By Range	E18:L18
Category Labels (X)	E4:L4

4. On the Scale tab, make the changes in the table.

Option	Change To
Manual (Y) Axis	Select this option
Maximum Limit	500
Fixed Label Size	Select this option
Auto (Y) Axis	Select this option

5. On the Series tab, change the Marker Size option to 25.
6. The chart should look like the one shown in Figure 7-60.

   Save the model as `My spreadsheet table.`

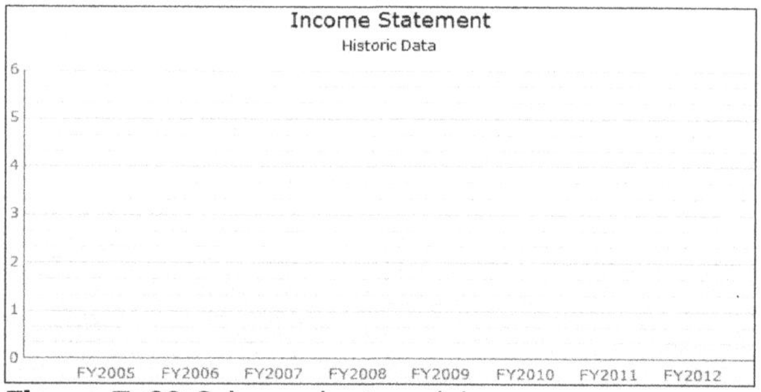

Figure 7-60 Column chart model

Exercise 7.5: Create A Line Chart

Line charts are similar to bar charts. You can refer back to the bar and column chart sections for explanations of the options. Line charts plot the values with data points instead of bars like column and bar charts do. The charts that you have created so far in this book have only displayed one series of data. In this exercise you will create a chart that displays two series of data: Market growth and sales growth. Figure 7-61 shows the data for this exercise.

	A	B	C	D	E	F	G	H	I
1	Sales Growth vs Market Growth								
2									
3		**2005**	**2006**	**2007**	**2008**	**2009**	**2010**	**2011**	**2012**
4	Market Growth	7.00%	5.00%	5.00%	3.50%	7.00%	8.00%	5.00%	2.50%
5	Sales Growth	9.00%	7.00%	6.00%	5.00%	8.00%	10.00%	11.00%	13.00%

Figure 7-61 Line chart data

1. Open a new model, then import the Line Chart spreadsheet.

2. Add the Line Chart component, then make the chart larger.

3. On the General view, make the changes in the table.

   When you are finished, two series of data should be on the chart, as shown in Figure 7-62.

Option	Change To
Chart	A1
Subtitle	Historic Trend
Category (X) Axis	Years
By Range	A4:I5
Category Labels (X)	B3:I3

Figure 7-63 shows the series data options on the General view. If you click the **ADD SERIES** button under the Series list box, you can add another series of data to the chart. If you click on an option in the Series list (i.e. Market Growth, Sales Growth), the data in the **NAME** and **VALUES (Y)** fields will change to display the values for the series that you selected.

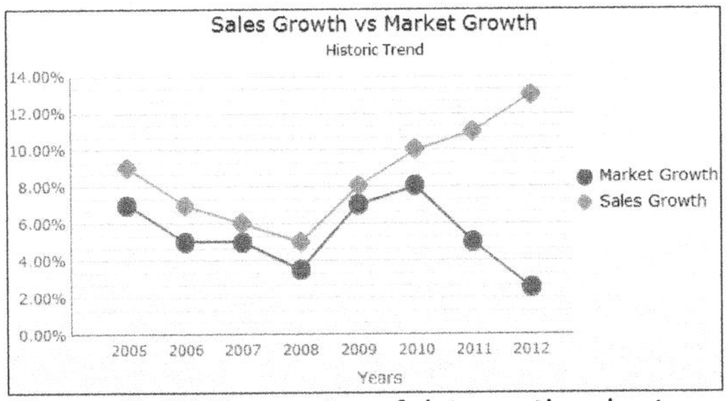

Figure 7-62 Two series of data on the chart

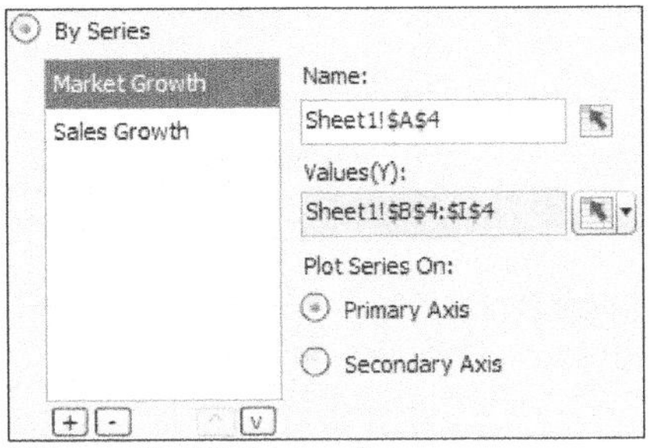

Figure 7-63 Series data

4. On the Scale tab, make the changes in the table.

Option	Change To
Manual (Y) Axis	Select this option
Maximum Limit	.40
Fixed Label Size	Select this option
Auto (Y) Axis	Select this option

5. On the Series tab, change the **MARKER SIZE** option to 14.

6. If the labels across the bottom of the chart are sideways, make the chart larger.

   The chart should look like the one shown in Figure 7-64.

   Save the model as `My line chart.`

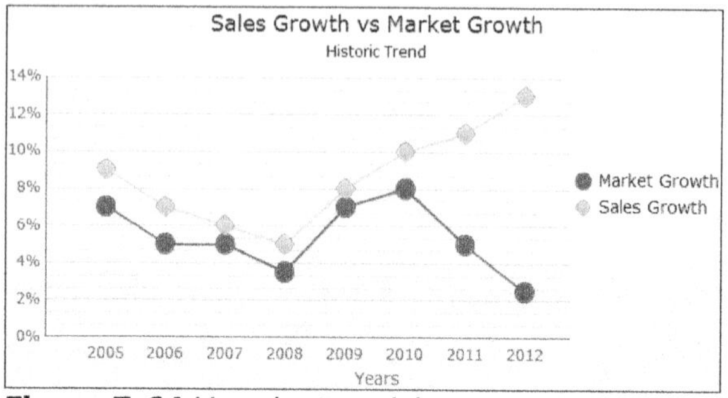

Figure 7-64 Line chart model

If the values on the Y axis had decimal places and you did not want them, you would have to remove them from the cell range B4:I5 in the spreadsheet shown earlier in Figure 7-61.

Modify The Chart

As you can see, the Sales Growth series is pink and may not stand out enough. In this part of the exercise, you will change the color for this series and make the markers larger and a different color.

1. On the Series tab, make the changes in the table.

Option	Change To
Marker Size	18
Series	Select Sales Growth
Line	Red
Fill	Red
Line Thickness	5

2. Save the changes.

   The chart should look like the one shown in Figure 7-65.

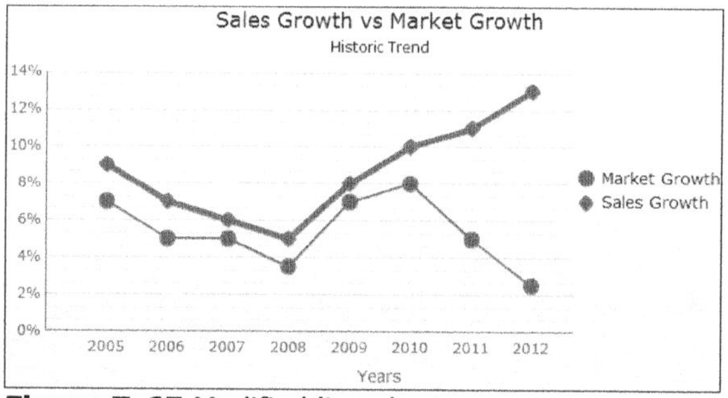

Figure 7-65 Modified line chart

ADVANCED CHARTS

In the previous chapter you learned about the chart types that are used the most. This chapter covers chart types that go beyond the basic chart requirements.

CHAPTER 8

Stacked Bar And Stacked Column Chart Components

The Stacked Bar and Stacked Column chart components have almost the same options on the General view. The stacked charts are similar to the bar and column charts that you learned about in the previous chapter. Figure 8-1 shows a Column chart. Figure 8-2 shows the same data in a Stacked Column chart.

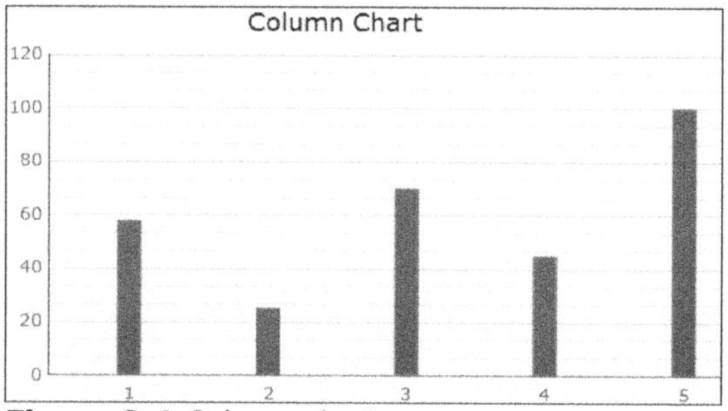

Figure 8-1 Column chart

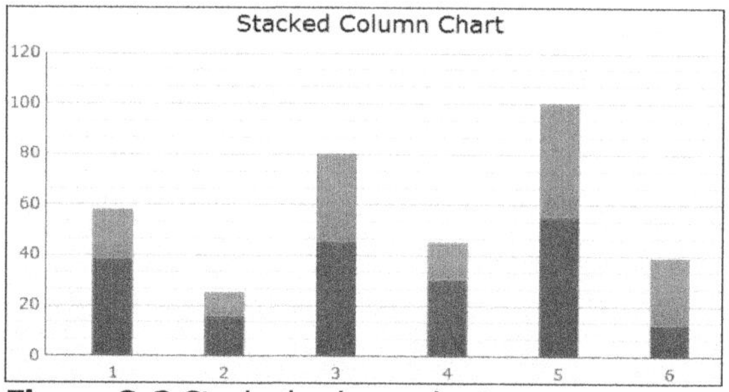

Figure 8-2 Stacked column chart

Stacked Column Chart Component

The differences that a Stacked Column chart has from a Column chart are explained below.

① A Stacked Column chart will only display one column per series.
② Each column is divided into segments. Each segment is a different color. Each color represents a different series of data.
③ The Stacked Column chart does not have the Secondary Value (Y) Axis option.
④ Stacked column charts can be used to compare totals over a period of time.

Series Tab Options

The Stacked Bar and Stacked Column chart series tab options are shown in Figure 8-3.

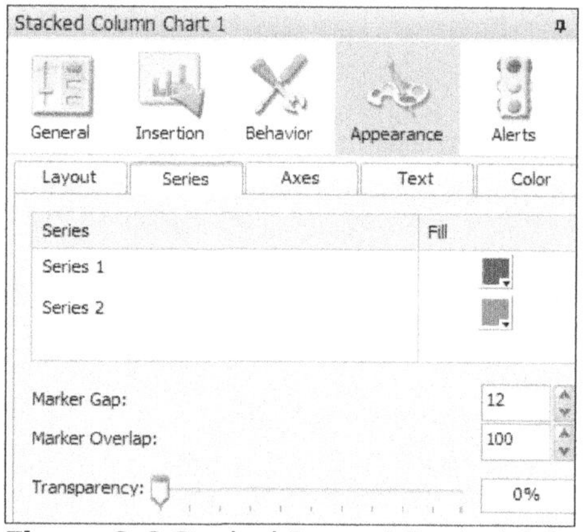

Figure 8-3 Stacked Bar and Stacked Column chart series tab options

MARKER GAP Is used to select the amount of space between the bars or columns on the chart.

Figure 8-4 shows this option set to 10.
Figure 8-5 shows this option set to 100. (1)

MARKER OVERLAP Is used to select how much each series on the bar or column are lined up.

Figure 8-5 shows this option set to 100.
Figure 8-6 shows this option set to 10.
Notice that the series for the column barely overlaps. Figure 8-7 shows this option set to 50. (1)

(1) The acceptable range for this option is 1 to 100.

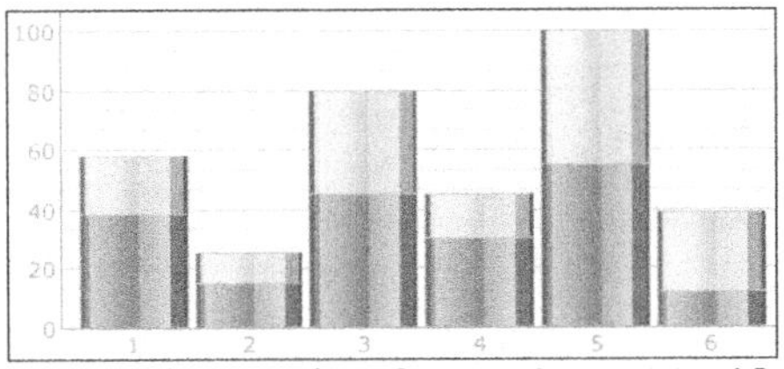

Figure 8-4 Marker Gap option set to 10

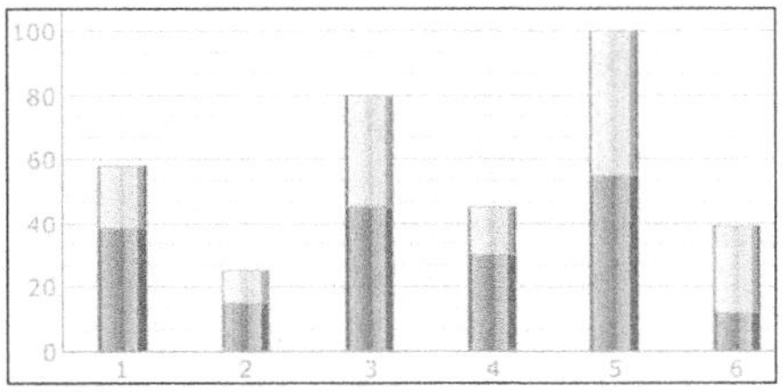

Figure 8-5 Marker Gap option set to 100 and Marker Overlap option set to 100

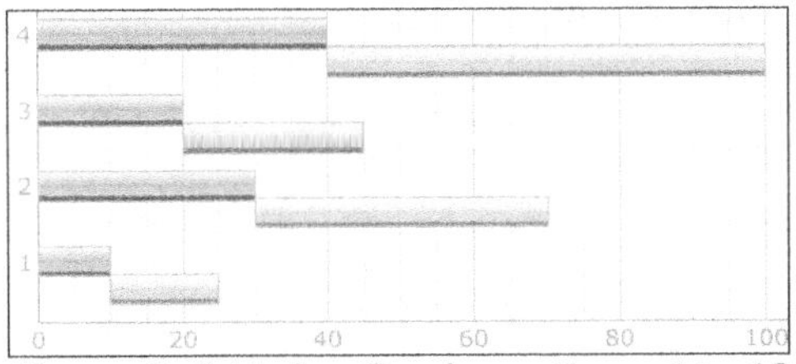

Figure 8-6 Marker Overlap option set to 10

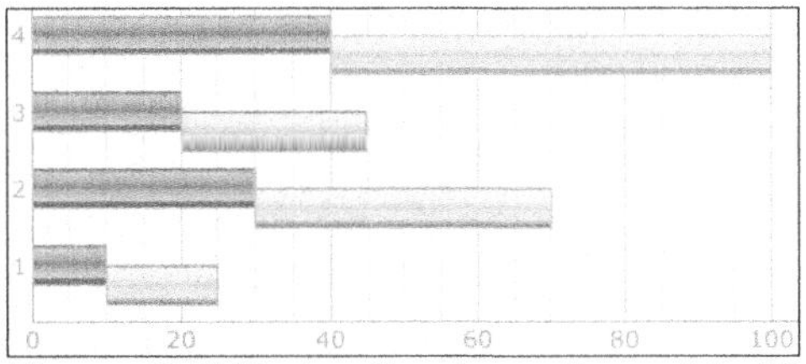

Figure 8-7 Marker Overlap option set to 50

Area And Stacked Area Chart Components

The Area and Stacked Area chart components have the majority of the same options on the Properties panel. Area charts do not have alert or drill-down functionality. One difference that Area charts have from other chart types is that the first value displayed is the minimum limit value on the Y axis, as shown later in the lower left corner of the chart in Figure 8-12. Other chart types use zero as the minimum limit value.

General View Options

The Area and Stacked Area chart general view options are shown in Figure 8-8.

SECONDARY VALUE (Y) AXIS Is used to select the cell that has the title for the second vertical axis on the chart. This option is only available when the Plot Series Secondary Axis option is selected on Area, Bar, Column, Combination and Line charts.

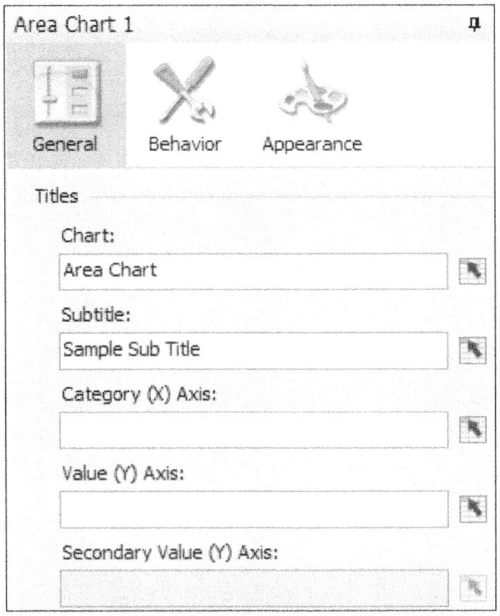

Figure 8-8 Area chart general view options

Exercise 8.1: Create An Area Chart

The area chart that you will create in this exercise will display two series of data from the spreadsheet: Internet and Mail Order, as shown in Figure 8-9.

	A	B	C
1	Customer Name	Internet	Mail Order
2	Psycho-Cycle	$52,809.11	$82,809.11
3	The Great Bike Shop	$15,218.09	$55,218.09
		⋮	
14	Fred's Bikes	$7,874.25	$874.25
15	Phil's Bikes	$27.00	$15,927.00

Figure 8-9 Area chart data

1. Import the dd_area_chart spreadsheet.

2. Add the Area Chart component.

3. On the General view, make the changes in the table. You should have the options shown in Figure 8-10.

Option	Change To
Chart	Sales Area Chart
Subtitle	Sources of Income
By Range	B2:C15
Series 1 Name	Internet
Series 2 Name	Mail Order
Category Labels (X)	A2:A15

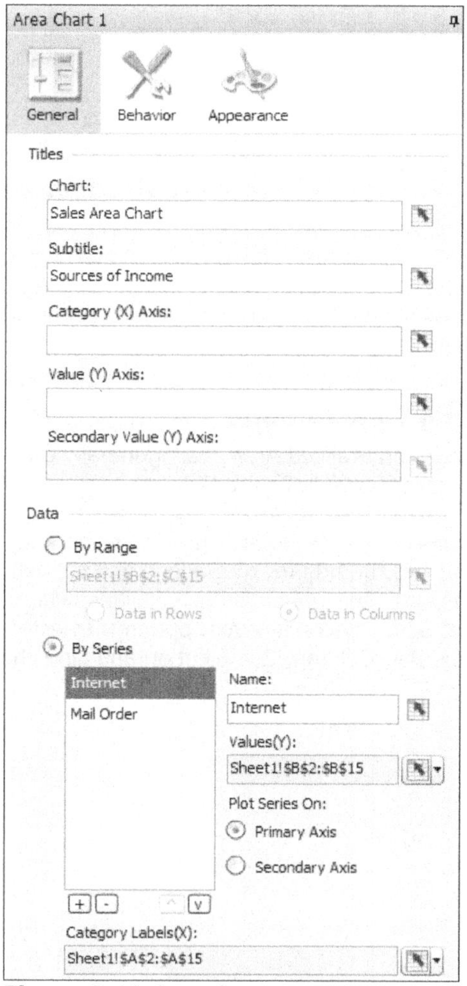

Figure 8-10 Area chart general view changes

4. On the Scale tab, make the changes in the table.

Option	Change To
Manual (Y) Axis	Select this option
Minimum Limit	500
Maximum Limit	100000
Fixed Label Size	Select this option
Auto (Y) Axis	Select this option

5. On the Series tab, make the changes in the table. You should have the options shown in Figure 8-11.

Series	Option	Change To
Internet	Fill	Navy blue
Mail Order	Fill	Red
Mail Order	Transparency	75

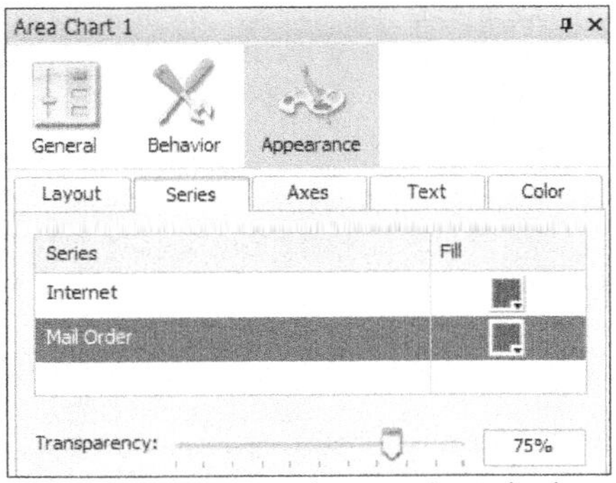

Figure 8-11 Area chart series tab changes

6. The chart should look like the one shown in Figure 8-12.

   Save the model as `My area chart.`

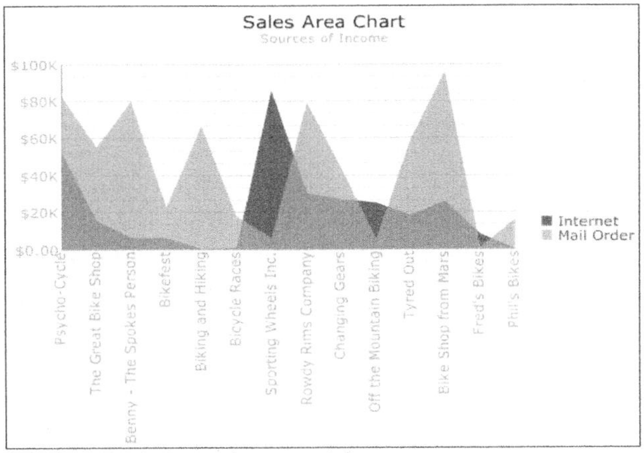

Figure 8-12 Area chart model

Bubble Chart Component

General View Options

The Bubble chart general view options are shown in Figure 8-13.

VALUE (X) AXIS Is used to select the cell that has the title for the horizontal axis on the chart.

VALUE (Y) AXIS Is used to select the cell that has the title for the vertical axis on the chart.

If the **BY RANGE** option is selected, three sequential rows or columns of data have to be selected for the X, Y and Z axes.

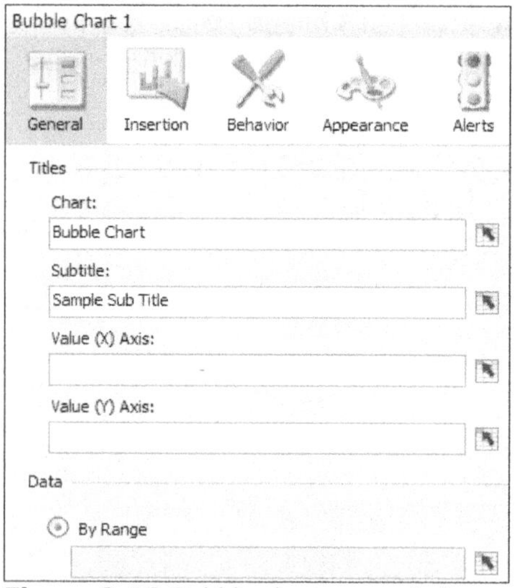

Figure 8-13 Bubble chart general view options

Series Tab Options

The Bubble chart series tab options are shown in Figure 8-14.

FILL Is used to change the color of the bubbles in the series.

MARKER SIZE Is used to select the size of the bubble.

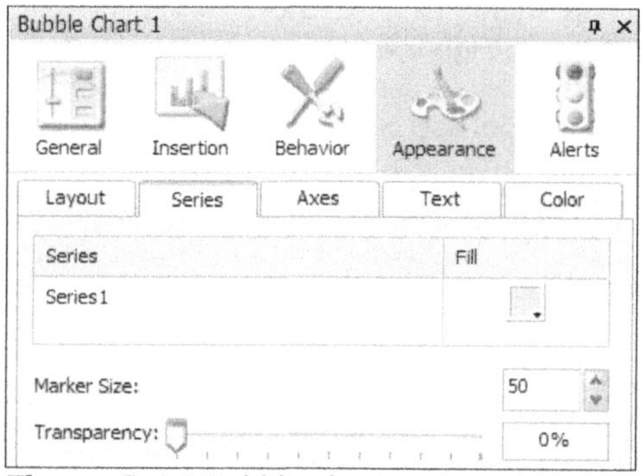

Figure 8-14 Bubble chart series tab options

Text Tab Options

The Bubble chart text tab options are shown in Figure 8-15.

NUMBER FORMAT options are used to select the label value for the X or Y axis, that you want to change the font or number format of, as illustrated in Figure 8-15.

SIZES This option (in the Number Format drop-down list) is used to change the font size of text that is displayed when the mouse pointer is hovered over a bubble on the chart, as shown in Figure 8-16.

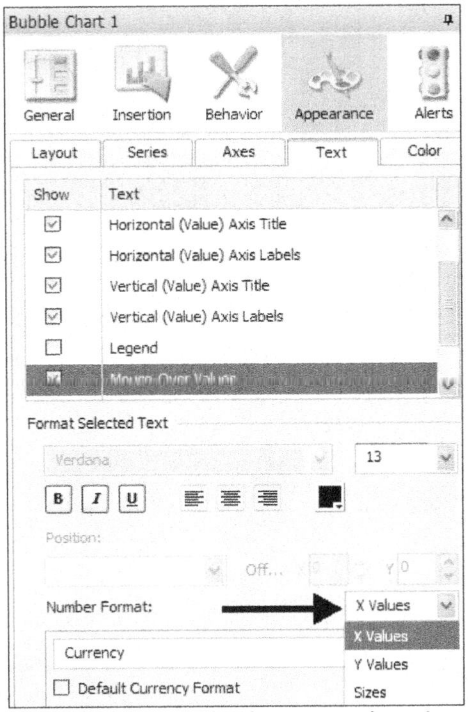

Figure 8-15 Bubble chart text tab options

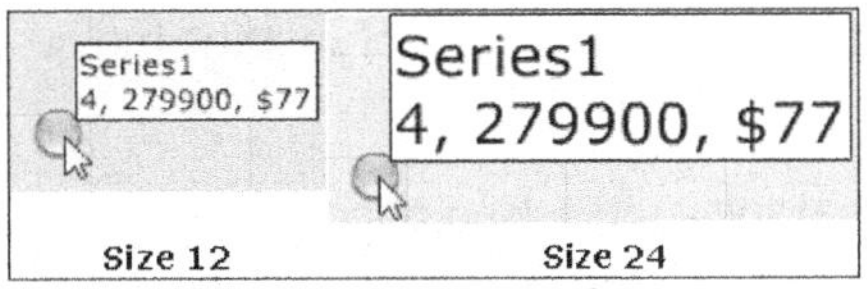

Figure 8-16 Sizes option font size set to 12 and 24

NEW The Bubble Chart has the label options illustrated at the bottom of Figure 8-17 for the data labels for series in the chart. Check the labels that you want to appear next to the marker in the chart for a specific series of data.

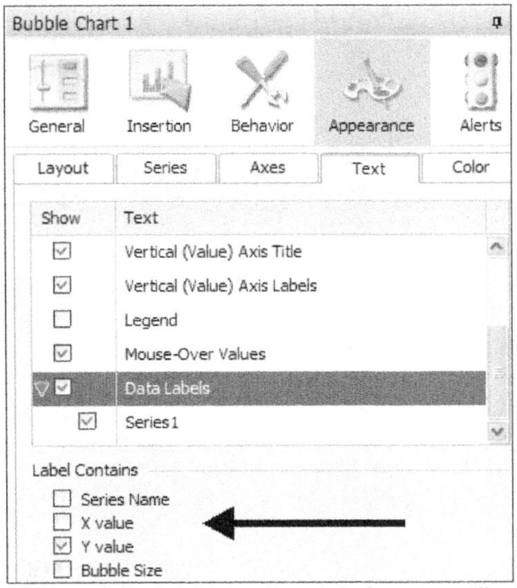

Figure 8-17 Bubble chart label options illustrated

Exercise 8.2: Create A Bubble Chart

In this exercise you will create a bubble chart that will display how long homes have been on the market. Bubble charts require numeric data for three axis. Figure 8-18 shows the data for this exercise.

The **X AXIS** will display the number of months the homes have been on the market.

The **Y AXIS** will display the asking price of the home.

The **Z AXIS** is used to calculate the size of the bubble for each column of data. The Qty column will be used for the Z axis. The larger the quantity, the larger the bubble will be.

	A	B	C
1	Months on market	Asking Price	Qty
2	35	$355,000	78
3	12	$160,000	19
4	6	$150,000	89
5	25	$400,000	36
6	28	$210,000	100
7	8	$175,000	47
8	22	$360,000	51
9	15	$223,000	22
10	33	$316,000	53
11	10	$500,000	10
12	8	$429,000	44
13	4	$279,900	77

Figure 8-18 Bubble chart data

1. Import the dd_bubble_chart spreadsheet.

2. Add the Bubble Chart component.

3. On the General view, make the changes in the table. You should have the options shown in Figure 8-19.

Option	Change To
Subtitle	Homes For Sale
Value (X) Axis	A1
Value (Y) Axis	B1
By Range	A2:C13

Figure 8-19 General view changes

4. On the Scale tab, make the changes in the table.

Option	Change To
Manual Axis	Select this option
Maximum (X) Limit	40
Minimum (Y) Limit	100000
Maximum (Y) Limit	600000
Fixed Label Size	Select this option
Auto Axis	Select this option

5. On the Animations and Effects tab, clear the Enable Data Animation option.

6. On the Layout tab, make the changes in the table.

Option	Change To
Plot Area Show Fill	Select this option
Title Area Show Border	Select this option

7. On the Axes tab, make the changes in the table.

Option	Change To
Vertical Show Minor Gridlines	Clear this option
Horizontal Show Minor Gridlines	Clear this option

8. The chart should look like the one shown in Figure 8-20.

   Save the model as `My bubble chart.`

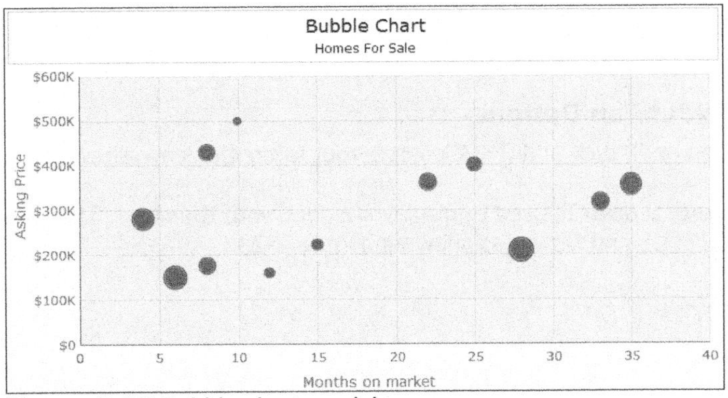

Figure 8-20 Bubble chart model

Unlike some other chart types, when the mouse pointer is hovered over an item on the chart (in this case a bubble on the chart), the information displayed does not indicate what the value represents, as shown earlier in Figure 8-16. A work around is to display the data in a grid or spreadsheet component on the model.

Candlestick And OHLC Chart Components

The Candlestick and OHLC chart components have the same options on the Properties panel. The difference between Candlestick and OHLC charts is how the bar looks. These chart types can be used interchangeably.

OHLC charts display the lowest and highest values on the vertical bar of one item over time. It is similar to bar and column charts. They do not have a **SECONDARY VALUE (Y) AXIS**. OHLC charts require four series of data (for the open, high, low and close values).

General View Options

The Candlestick and OHLC chart general view options are shown in Figure 8-21.

OPEN Is used to select the cells that have the opening price of the stock for the day.

HIGH Is used to select the cells that have the highest price of the stock for the day.

LOW Is used to select the cells that have the lowest price of the stock for the day.

CLOSE Is used to select the cells that have the closing price of the stock for the day.

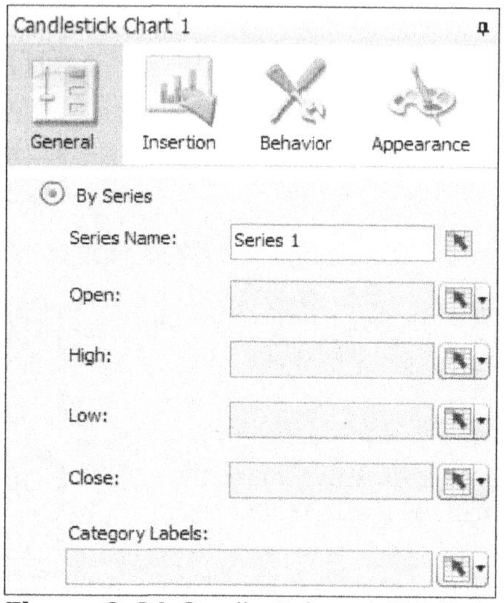

Figure 8-21 Candlestick and OHLC chart general view options

Layout Tab Options

The Candlestick and OHLC chart layout tab options are shown in Figure 8-22.

ENABLE LEGEND Is used to display a legend with the chart. The legend that is displayed only has two items: Up and Down, as shown in Figure 8-23.

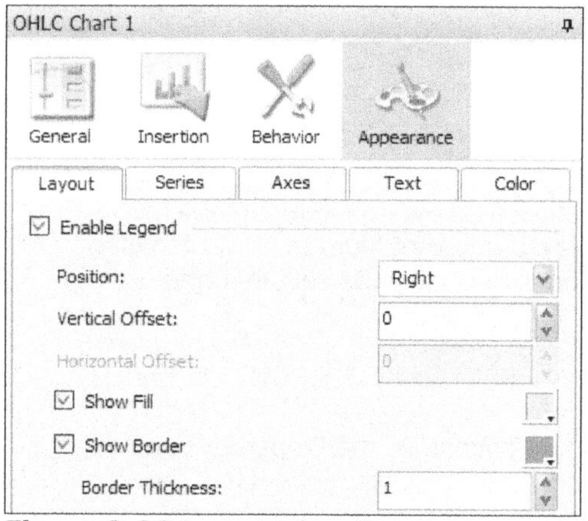

Figure 8-22 Layout tab options

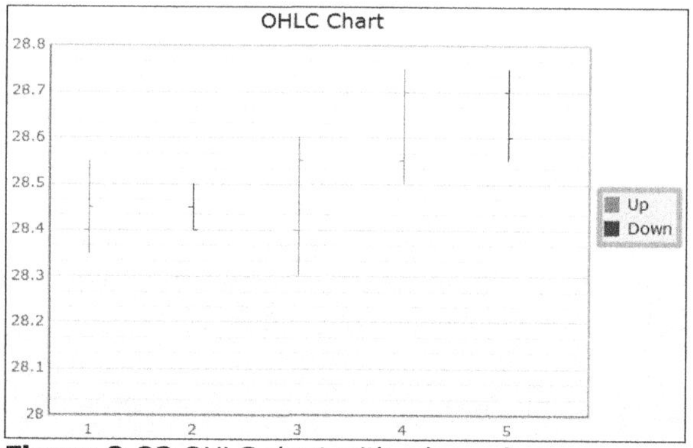

Figure 8-23 OHLC chart with a legend

Series Tab Options

The Candlestick and OHLC chart series tab options are shown in Figure 8-24. The options on this tab are used to change the colors of the bars on the chart and the markers on the legend.

POSITIVE COLOR Is used to change the series color when the close value is greater than the open value.

NEGATIVE COLOR Is used to change the series color when the close value is less than the open value.

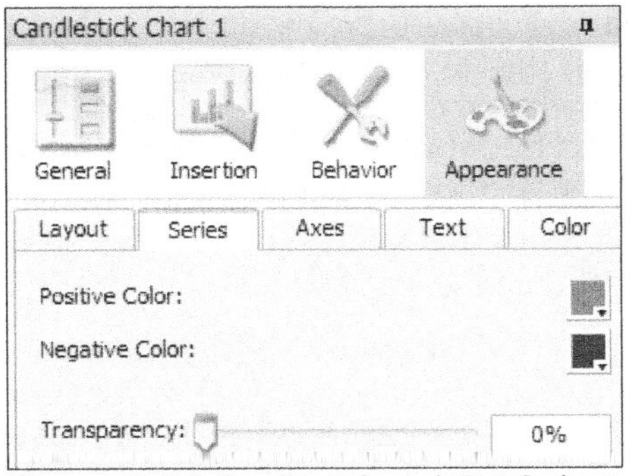

Figure 8-24 Candlestick and OHLC chart series tab options

Text Tab Options

The Candlestick and OHLC chart text tab options are shown in Figure 8-25.

The **MOUSE-OVER VALUES** number format options illustrated in Figure 8-25 are used to modify the values (Open, High, Low and Close) that are displayed when the mouse pointer is hovered over a part of the chart.

Figure 8-26 shows all four values with the currency formatting.

Figure 8-27 illustrates the high value changed to numeric formatting and the close value changed to percent formatting.

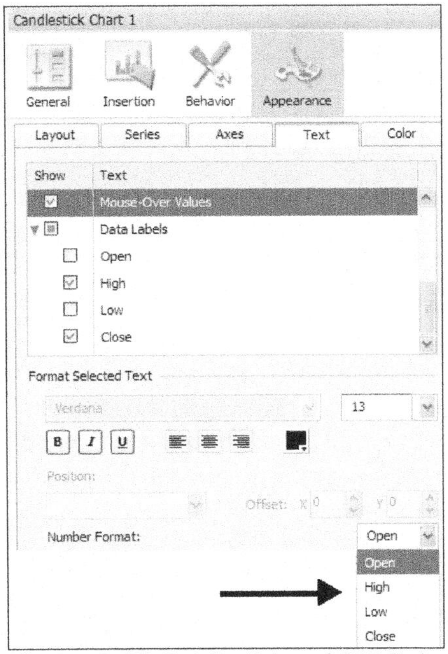

Figure 8-25 Candlestick and OHLC chart text tab options

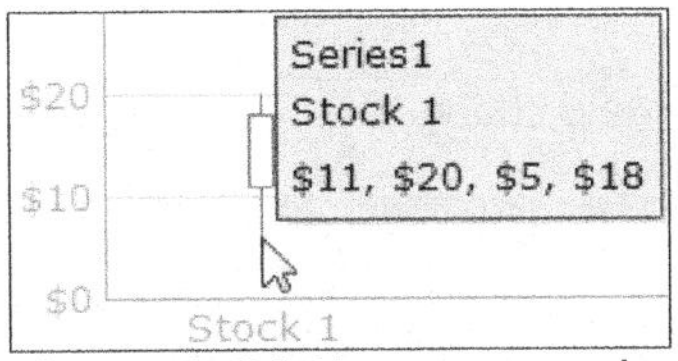

Figure 8-26 Mouse over values with currency formatting

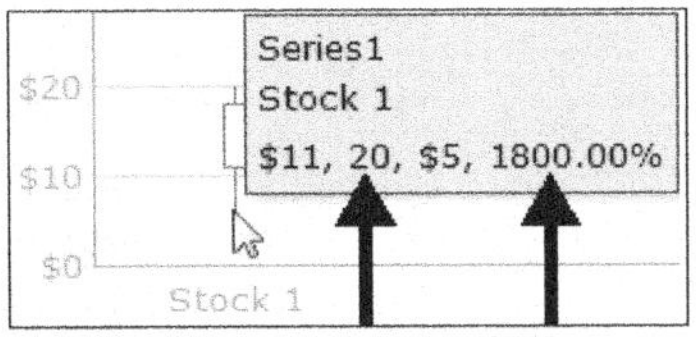

Figure 8-27 High and Close mouse over values with changed formatting illustrated

Exercise 8.3: Create A Candlestick Chart

Candlestick and OHLC charts are primarily used to display stock data. Each marker on the chart corresponds to one of the four values on the General view that were explained earlier. Figure 8-28 shows the data for this exercise.

	A	B	C	D	E	F
1		Stock 1	Stock 2	Stock 3	Stock 4	Stock 5
2	Open	$11	$55	$23	$44	$30
3	High	$20	$55	$60	$44	$68
4	Low	$5	$50	$23	$44	$45
5	Close	$18	$50	$60	$44	$65

Figure 8-28 Candlestick chart data

1. Import the dd_candlestick_chart spreadsheet.

2. Add the Candlestick Chart component. If you wanted to create an OHLC chart, you would select that chart component here and follow the rest of the instructions.

3. On the General view, make the changes in the table. You should have the options shown in Figure 8-29.

Option	Change To
Subtitle	5 Stocks
By Range	B2:F5
Category Labels	B1:F1

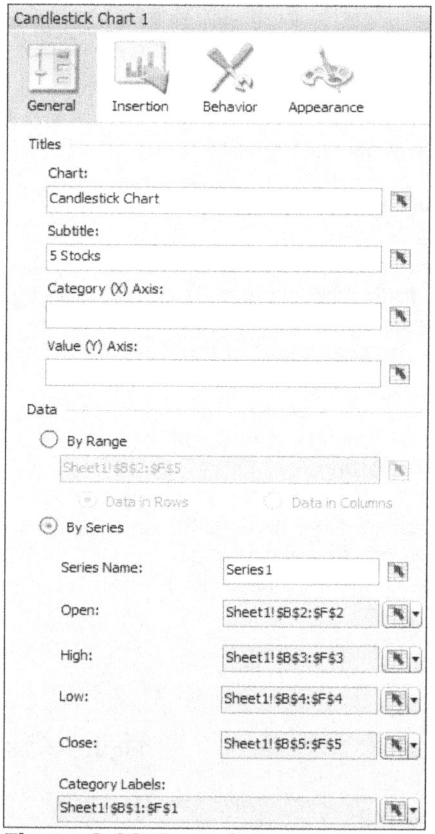

Figure 8-29 General view changes

4. On the Scale tab, make the changes in the table.

Option	Change To
Manual (Y) Axis	Select this option
Maximum Limit	70
Number of Divisions	5
Size of Divisions	10
Auto (Y) Axis	Select this option

5. On the Axes tab, clear the Show Minor Gridlines option.

6. The chart should look like the one shown in Figure 8-30.

   Save the model as
   `My candlestick chart.`

   The reason that Stock 2 is burgundy (a negative number) is because the closing price is lower than the opening price.

   The reason that Stock 4 is a line is because the closing price is the same as the other prices, as if there was no activity for the stock that day.

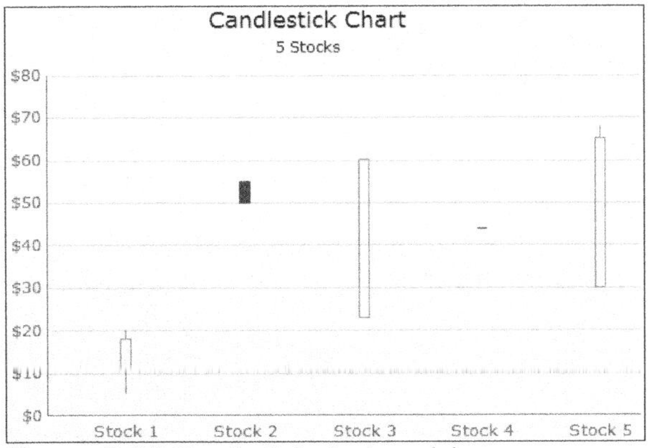

Figure 8-30 Candlestick chart model

XY Chart Component

XY charts resemble the line charts they both display the values. The visible difference is that XY charts do not have a connecting line between the data points. That is because the data points (values) may not be placed on the chart in the same order as the data is in the spreadsheet.

General View Options

[See Bubble Chart Component General View Options, earlier in this chapter]

Scale Tab Axis Options

[See Chapter 7, Common Chart Scale Tab Options]

Text Tab Options

[See Bubble Chart Component Text Tab Options, earlier in this chapter]

Exercise 8.4: Create An XY Chart

The XY chart that you will create in this exercise will display the sales amount and the number of orders per month. Figure 8-31 shows the data for this exercise.

Like the Bubble chart, the XY and Radar charts can use three rows or columns of data.

The difference is that only Bubble charts require all of the data to be numeric. Compare the data shown earlier in Figure 8-18 to the data shown in Figure 8-31.

	A	B	C
1	Month	Orders	Total Amount
2	Jan	4	$1,276.74
3	Feb	7	$1,784.75
4	Mar	20	$7,981.41
5	April	17	$5,879.70
6	May	15	$4,751.27
7	June	13	$12,546.12
8	July	25	$21,264.30
9	Aug	31	$31,019.40
10	Sept	26	$8,823.65
11	Oct	1	$819.55
12	Nov	24	$5,879.70
13	Dec	20	$2,378.35

Figure 8-31 XY chart data

1. Import the dd_xy_and_radar_chart spreadsheet.

2. Add the XY Chart component.

3. On the General view, make the changes in the table.

Option	Change To
Subtitle	Monthly Sales
Value (X) Axis	Number of sales
Value (Y) Axis	Total monthly sales amount
By Range	A2:C13

4. On the Scale tab, make the changes in the table.

Option	Change To
Manual Axis	Select this option
Maximum (X) Limit	30
Minimum (Y) Limit	100
Maximum (Y) Limit	40000
Fixed Label Size	Select this option
Auto Axis	Select this option

5. On the Series tab, open the **SHAPE** drop-down list and select Diamond.

6. On the Axes tab, clear the horizontal and vertical **SHOW MINOR GRIDLINES** options.

7. The chart should look like the one shown in Figure 8-32.

   Save the model as `My XY chart.`

   As you can see, it is difficult to know which diamond value is for which month of sales.

   In Exercise 14.5 you will modify this chart so that it will be easier to tell which marker is for which month.

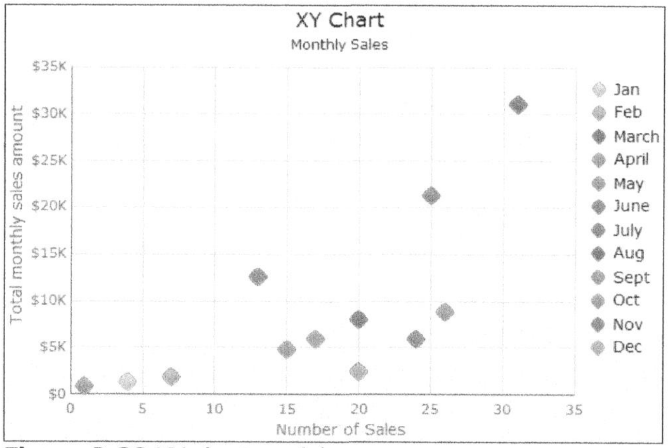

Figure 8-32 XY chart model

Radar And Filled Radar Chart Components

As you saw in Chapter 7, Figures 7-13 and 7-14, radar charts have a different look then the other charts. One reason is because they do not have a category axis option. Instead, they have vertical axis option. This axis starts from the center (the minimum value) of the chart and stop at the perimeter (the maximum value) of the chart. The number of data points that each series of data has determines the number of axes and sides of the polygon that the chart will have. The majority of options on the Properties panel for the Radar and Filled Radar chart components are the same.

For the most part these charts can be used interchangeably. The main differences between radar and filled radar charts is that filled radar charts do not have markers. Instead the data series are filled in with different colors.

Scale Tab Options

The options shown in Figure 8-33 are similar to the Common chart scale tab options, that were covered in Chapter 7. The differences are explained below.

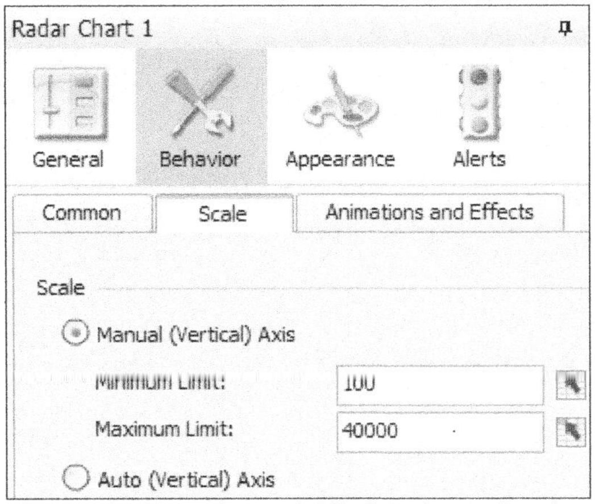

Figure 8-33 Radar and Filled Radar scale tab options

MANUAL (VERTICAL) AXIS Is used to select vertical fixed scale limits that will not change, even if the data changes.

AUTO (VERTICAL) AXIS Select this option if you want the vertical scale to adjust to accommodate the data values as they change.

Exercise 8.5: Create A Radar Chart

Radar charts function very similar to XY charts. In this exercise you will use the same spreadsheet that you used for the XY chart. [See Figure 8-31, earlier in this chapter]

1. Import the dd_xy_and_radar_chart spreadsheet.

2. Add the Radar Chart component.

3. On the General view, make the changes in the table.

Option	Change To
Subtitle	Monthly Sales
By Range	A2:C13
Series 1	Delete this series

4. On the Scale tab, make the changes in the table.

Option	Change To
Manual (Vertical) Axis	Select this option
Minimum Limit	100
Maximum Limit	40000
Fixed Label Size	Select this option
Auto (Vertical) Axis	Select this option

5. On the Series tab, open the Shape drop-down list and select Diamond, if it is not already selected.

6. On the Text tab, clear the **LEGEND** option if it is selected.

7. The chart should look like the one shown in Figure 8-34.

   Save the model as `My radar chart.`

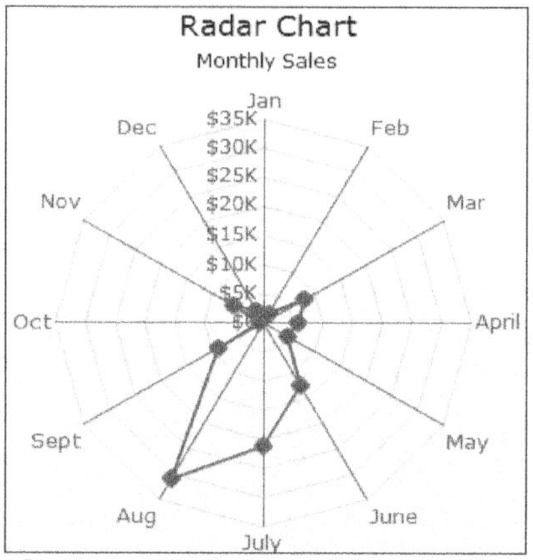

Figure 8-34 Radar chart model

Combination Chart Component

As you read in Chapter 7 in Table 7-1, Combination charts are used to plot two or more series of data, using different chart types in the same chart. When combined in one chart, a line and column chart is used to display a range of values with a trend line. There are some automatic default chart type selections that you should be aware of, as explained below. You can change the chart type of any series on the chart.

- ① The first series defaults to a column chart.
- ② The second series defaults to a line chart.
- ③ The third series and above, defaults to a column chart.
- ④ If the second series is deleted in a chart that has at least three data series, the third data series becomes the second data series and defaults to a line chart.

Series Tab Options

The Combination chart series tab options are shown in Figure 8-35.

TYPE Is used to select how the series of data should be represented on the chart, as a line or column. I think that this is a pretty cool feature to use.

Column Settings Options

The options in this section are used to configure the Column chart.

Line Settings Options

The options in this section are used to display and configure the markers for a Line chart.

ENABLE MARKERS Is used to display or hide the markers on the Line chart.

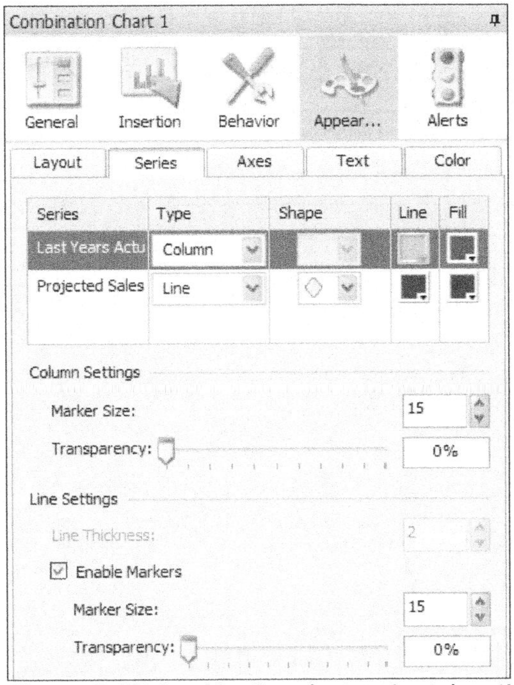

Figure 8-35 Combination chart series tab options for a line series type

Exercise 8.6: Create A Combination Chart

In this exercise you will create the Actual vs Projected model that you saw in Chapter 1. [See Chapter 1, Figure 1-4]

1. Import the dd_actual_vs_projected spreadsheet.

2. Add the Combination Chart component.

3. On the General view, make the changes in the table.

Option	Change To
Chart	A1
Subtitle	B3
By Range	B5:B8
Category Labels (X)	A5:A8

4. Add another series for the Last Years projected sales data, then rename the series, as shown in the table.

Series	New Name
Series 1	Last Years Actual Sales
Series 2	Projected Sales

5. On the Series tab, make the changes in the table.

Option	Change To
Select the Series	Last Years Actual Sales
Fill	Red
Select the Series	Projected Sales
Shape	Triangle
Line	Blue
Fill	Blue

6. On the Axes tab, clear the **SHOW MINOR GRIDLINES** option.

   The chart should look like the one shown in Figure 8-36.

   Save the model as `My combination chart.`

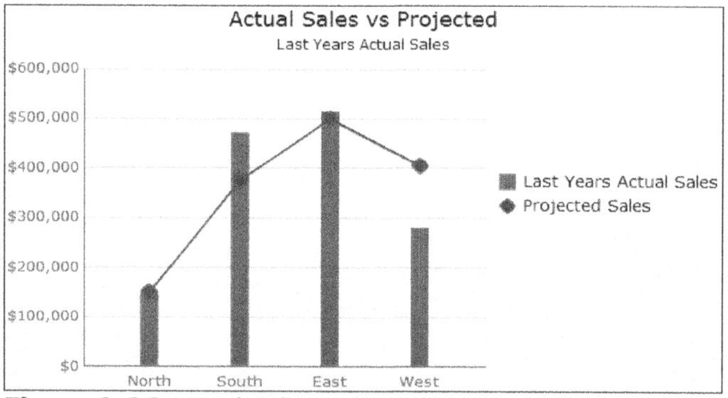

Figure 8-36 Actual Sales vs Projected chart

NEW Horizontal Bullet And Vertical Bullet Chart Components

The Horizontal Bullet and Vertical Bullet chart components have many of the same options on the Properties panel. The difference between Horizontal Bullet and Vertical Bullet charts is the direction of the bars. For the most part, these chart types can be used interchangeably.

General View Options

The Horizontal Bullet and Vertical Bullet chart general view options are shown in Figure 8-37.

HORIZONTAL (X) AXIS Is used to type in or select the content for the label on the x axis. The Vertical Bullet chart uses the **VERTICAL (Y) AXIS** option for the content for the label on the y axis.

LABEL Is used to type in or select the name for the series.

SUB-LABEL Is used to display a second label for the series, which will appear below the series label.

PERFORMANCE VALUE Is used to select the actual performance range of values.

COMPARATIVE VALUE Is used to select the target performance range of values.

SCALE VALUES Is used to select the range of values for the scale of the performance.

Scale Tab Options

The Horizontal Bullet and Vertical Bullet chart scale tab options are shown in Figure 8-38.

CONFIGURE SCALE BY SERIES Select this option when you have the need to create a different scale for a series, then select the series from the drop-down list.

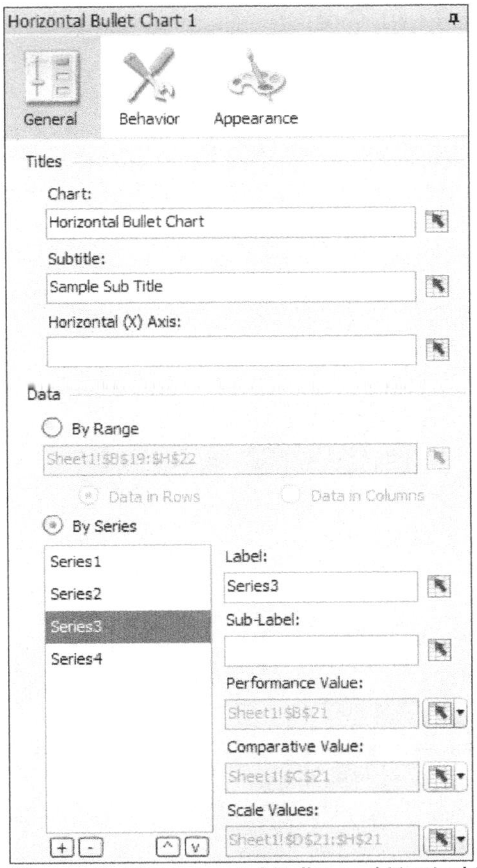

Figure 8-37 Horizontal Bullet and Vertical Bullet chart general view options

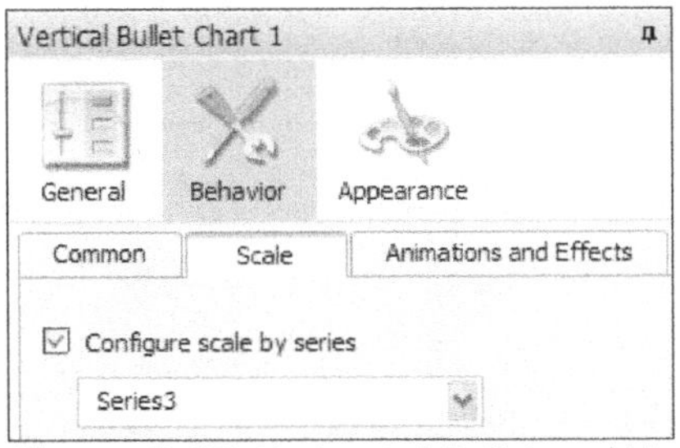

Figure 8-38 Horizontal Bullet and Vertical Bullet chart scale tab options

Series Tab Options

The Horizontal Bullet and Vertical Bullet chart series tab options are shown in Figure 8-39.

PERFORMANCE COLOR Is used to select the color for the actual performance values.

COMPARATIVE MARKER COLOR Is used to select the color for the target values.

SCALE HIGH COLOR Is used to select the color for the marker for the high value.

SCALE LOW COLOR Is used to select the color for the marker for the low value.

BAR SIZE Is used to change the size (width) of the bars on the chart.

PERFORMANCE MARKER SIZE Is used to select the size of the actual performance value marker.

COMPARATIVE MARKER SIZE Is used to select the size of the target data value marker.

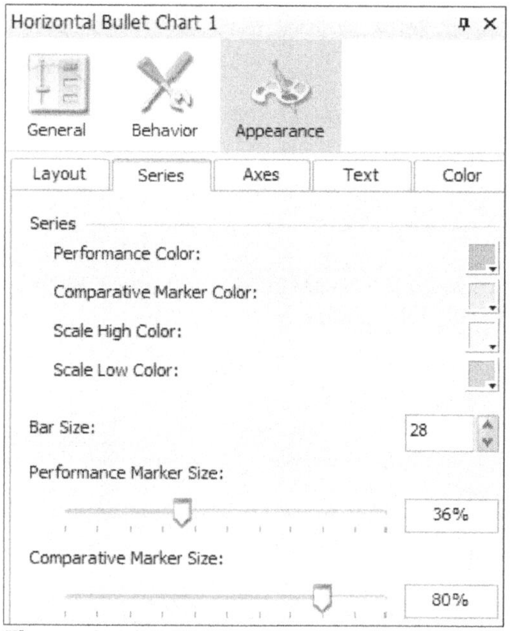

Figure 8-39 Horizontal Bullet and Vertical Bullet chart series tab options

Color Tab Options

The Horizontal Bullet and Vertical Bullet chart color tab options are shown in Figure 8-40.

Series Options

PERFORMANCE COLOR Is used to select the color of the actual performance values.

COMPARATIVE MARKER COLOR Is used to select the color for the target data value marker.

SCALE HIGH COLOR Is used to select the color for the marker for the high value.

SCALE LOW COLOR Is used to select the color for the marker for the low value.

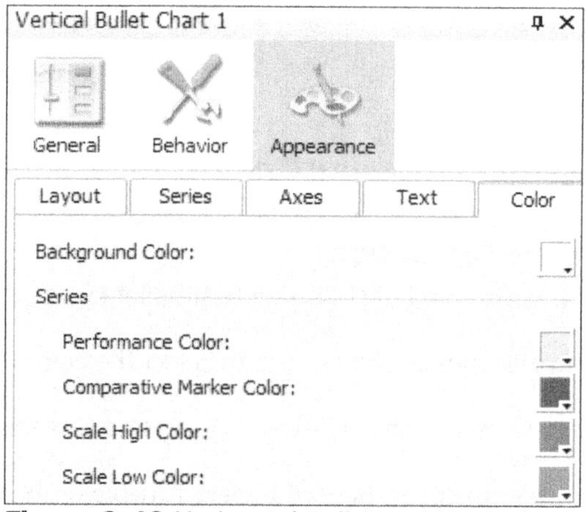

Figure 8-40 Horizontal Bullet and Vertical Bullet chart color tab options

CREATING MENU BASED DASHBOARDS

In this chapter you will learn how to create the following types of menu based dashboards.

- ☑ List Box
- ☑ Play Selector
- ☑ Spreadsheet Table
- ☑ Radio Button
- ☑ Combo Box
- ☑ Filter
- ☑ Label Based Menu

CHAPTER 9

Menu Components

Menus add another level of functionality to dashboards. Like the menus in Dashboard Design and other applications, the menus that you can add to a dashboard allow the user to select an option on the menu, which causes an action to happen. The action that usually happens in a dashboard is data being displayed. Different data will be displayed for each menu option or the same data is displayed in a different format, like a different chart type. The choices for each menu item come from one of two sources: From cells in the spreadsheet or you can type the menu items in.

Menus are selector components. Each item on the menu is linked to a cell or range of cells. This link is what controls the data that is displayed in another component on the dashboard.

Filter Data Using Selectors

Filtering data is a way to manage large amounts of data in a dashboard. Filtered data is a subset of all of the data that is selected for the dashboard. If you have a dashboard that displays data for all sales reps in a chart and you wanted to be able to display the data for one sales rep at a time, you could create a filter by using a selector component and link it to the chart component.

In Chapter 7 you created models that did not display any data. In this chapter, you will add a menu selector component to these models, so that the charts will display data.

Selector Components

You have seen some of the menu layouts that can be created in Dashboard Design or have used them in other software. Other selector component types that you will learn about may be brand new to you. The selector components are shown in Figure 9-1 and are explained below. The chapter that the component is covered in, is listed at the end of the description in brackets.

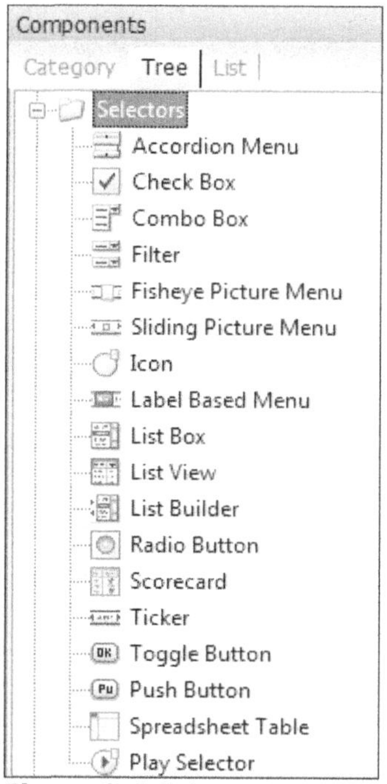

Figure 9-1 Selector components

In Chapter 5 you learned that the form controls in Excel are not available in Dashboard Design, but that some of the functionality of the form controls can be reproduced.

In Chapter 6 you learned about Single Value components, which only allow the component to be linked to one cell in the spreadsheet. You also learned that in that regard Single Value components are somewhat static, when compared to the functionality of selector components.

Selector components are used to link the component to several cells in the spreadsheet, which will give the dashboard a more dynamic and interactive effect. Selector components allow users pick an option from a list. This is how selector components can be used to create a variety of menus. The remainder of this section provides an overview of the selector components.

Accordion Menu

Creates a two level filter, based on the relationship of data in two fields, as shown in Figure 9-2. The item selected in the top level menu (Category 1, Category 2, etc.) controls (filters) the options that are displayed in the second level of the menu (the items for the selected category).

For example, if you need to display sales for a sales rep in a region. The top level menu would contain the regions.

Once a region is selected, the second level menu would be filtered to only display sales reps for the selected region. (1) [Chapter 13]

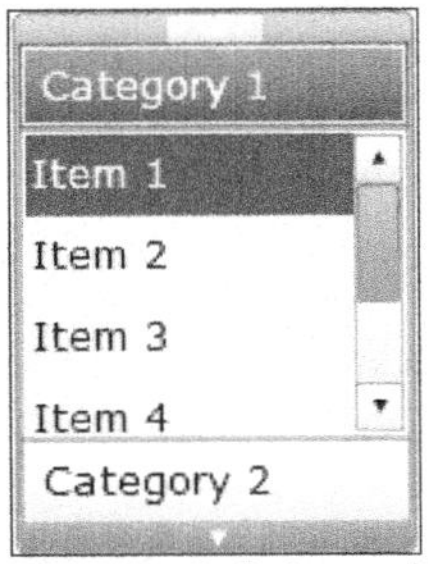

Figure 9-2 Accordion Menu component

Check Box
Toggles between two states: Checked (On), as shown in Figure 9-3 and Not Checked (Off). (2) [Chapter 14]

Figure 9-3 Check Box component

Combo Box
Creates a single level filter, as shown in Figure 9-4. This component ensures that duplicate records from the range of data that is selected are not displayed in the drop-down list. When the arrow is clicked, a drop-down list appears. An option from the list is selected and the corresponding data is displayed in another component on the dashboard. (3) [Chapter 9]

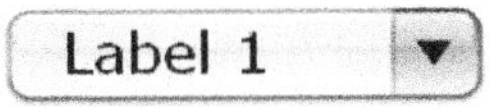

Figure 9-4 Combo Box component

Filter
Select this component when you need to filter on more than one value (column of data), as shown in Figure 9-5. The values displayed in the second filter are based on the value selected in the first filter, like the Accordion menu. [Chapter 9]

Figure 9-5 Filter component

Fisheye Picture Menu
Uses pictures or icons instead of text for the menu options, as shown in Figure 9-6. While the menu can support more than five images, keep in mind that all of the images will be displayed on the dashboard all the time.

Figure 9-6 Fisheye Picture Menu component

There is no option to make the menu smaller, in terms of the number of images that are displayed. This menu type may require more space than you have allocated for a menu.

Clicking on an image is how an option is selected. When an option on the menu is clicked, the data that is linked to the picture or icon is displayed in another component on the dashboard. The term Fisheye comes from a type of camera lens. (1) (3) [Chapter 13]

Icon
This component, as shown in Figure 9-7, has the same functionality as the Check Box. It can represent the value in one cell and be compared to a target value and change color accordingly. (2) (4) [Chapter 14]

Figure 9-7 Icon component

Label Based Menu

This menu type can be vertical, as shown in Figure 9-8, or horizontal, as shown in Figure 9-9. (3) [Chapter 9]

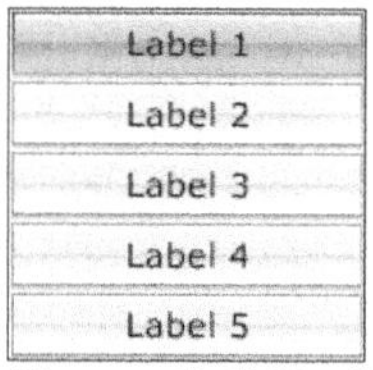

Figure 9-8 Vertical Label Based Menu component

Figure 9-9 Horizontal Label Based Menu component

List Box

Is similar to a Combo Box. The biggest difference is that the menu options are visible on the dashboard, as shown in Figure 9-10. The slider on the right side of the List Box indicates that there are more options that are currently not visible, that can be selected. (3) [Chapter 9]

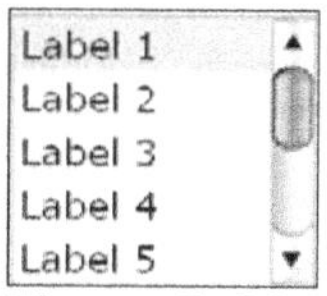

Figure 9-10 List Box component

List Builder

This component allows the user to build their own data set, as shown in Figure 9-11.

The data set that users create will be used as the data set for another component on the dashboard. (1) (3) [Chapter 15]

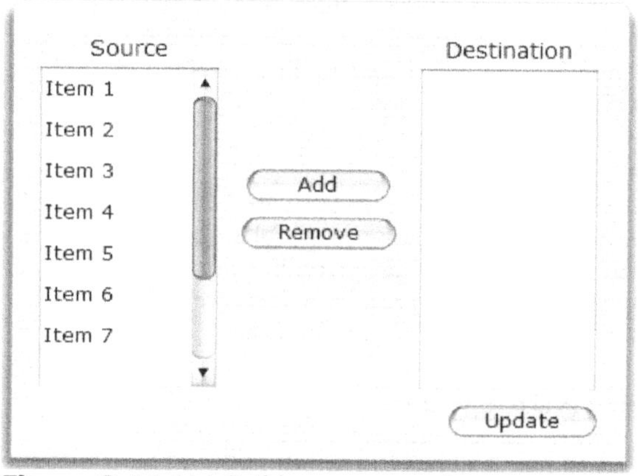

Figure 9-11 List Builder component

List View

The List View component shown in Figure 9-12 will remind you of a spreadsheet. The benefit that the List View component has over the Spreadsheet Table component is that it also allows the data to be sorted by the columns and the width of the columns can be adjusted by the user.

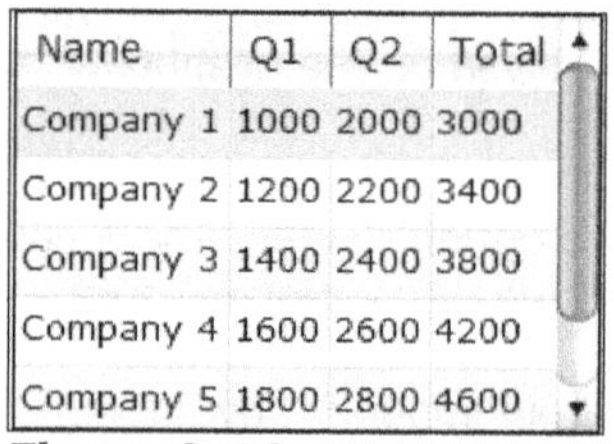

Figure 9-12 List View component

To sort by a column, click on the column heading. You will see an arrow, as illustrated in Figure 9-13.

The arrow indicates if the data in the column is sorted in ascending ▲ or descending ▼order.

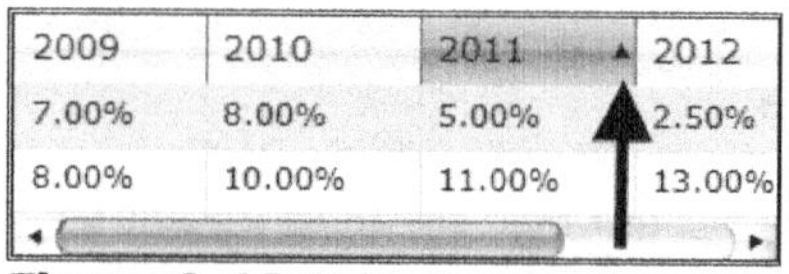

Figure 9-13 Column sorted

To change the column width, place the mouse pointer to the right of the column that you want to resize. You will see a double headed arrow. Drag the mouse in the direction that you want to resize the column to. [Chapter 9]

Play Selector
This component adds automation to the dashboard. Clicking the play button causes the data to be displayed in another component automatically. The controls on this component allow the user to pause or continue the data being displayed to the end of the animation.

The buttons shown in Figure 9-14 allow the data to be viewed one row or column at a time by clicking the Forward button or automatically by clicking the Play button. Table 9-1 explains the buttons.

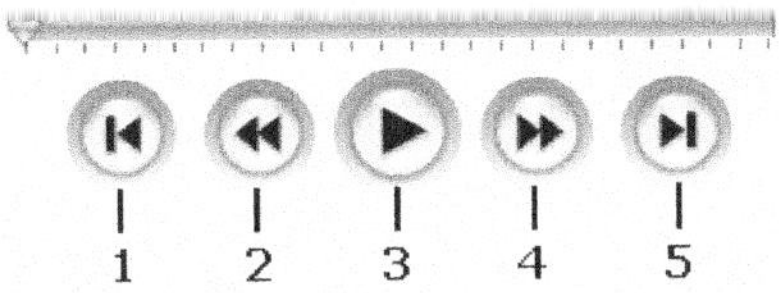

Figure 9-14 Play Selector component

Button	Description
1	Previous
2	Rewind
3	Play/Pause
4	Forward
5	Next

Table 9-1 Play Selector component buttons explained

The difference between the Play Button options that you learned about in Chapter 6 and the Play Selector is that the Play Button options are functionality that you can add to a component, like a slider. The Play Selector is a component. (1) (3) [Chapter 9]

Push Button
This component is used to set values in cells when clicked or reset values in Single Value components. The component shown in Figure 9-15 can also be used to create a pop-up window. [Chapter 14]

Figure 9-15 Push Button component

Radio Button
Allows one option to be selected from a group of options, as shown in Figure 9-16. This menu can also be placed horizontally. (3) [Chapter 9]

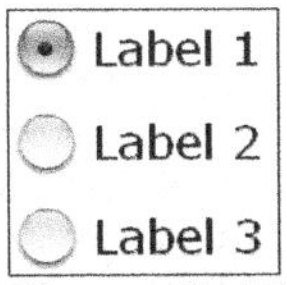

Figure 9-16 Radio Button component

Scorecard
This component is used to display alerts in a grid. The component shown in Figure 9-17 is similar to the List View component because the user can click on the column headings to sort the data. (3) [Chapter 10]

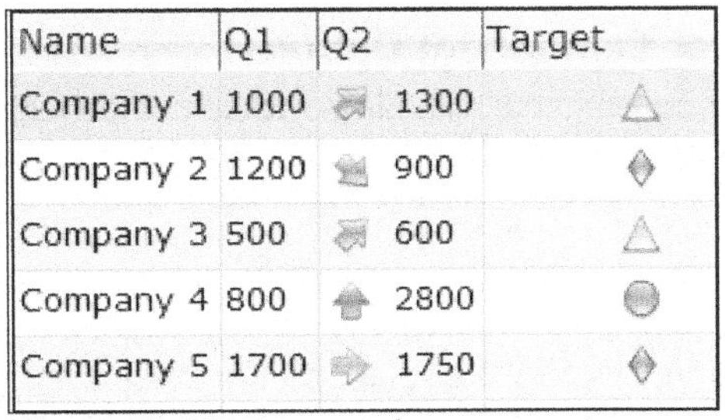

Figure 9-17 Scorecard component

Sliding Picture Menu
Is similar to a Fisheye Picture Menu because pictures or icons are used instead of text for the items on the menu.

This menu has arrows on the left and right that are used to scroll through the menu options, as shown in Figure 9-18.

Figure 9-18 Sliding Picture Menu component

This allows the menu to have more options while not taking up additional space on the dashboard. There is also an option to scroll through the pictures by holding the mouse pointer over them, like the Fisheye Picture Menu has. (1) (3) [Chapter 13]

Spreadsheet Table
The Spreadsheet Table component is similar to the List View component.

As shown in Figure 9-19, the Spreadsheet Table component displays the data from cells in a spreadsheet, just as they are. (3) (4) [Chapter 9]

Stores	State
# 210	CA
# 45	FL
# 88	NY
# 105	MD

Figure 9-19 Spreadsheet Table component

Ticker
This component displays scrolling text, as shown in Figure 9-20. It will remind you of the stock ticker that runs across the bottom of your TV. (3) [Chapter 10]

Figure 9-20 Ticker component

Toggle Button
The Toggle button component shown in Figure 9-21 has the on and off states like the Check Box has. (2) [Chapter 14]

Figure 9-21 Toggle Button component

(1) This component is not available in Presentation Design.
(2) The component is most often used to display and hide another component on the dashboard.
(3) This component can be set up to retrieve source data from multiple locations and insert the data into multiple destination locations.
(4) This component can be used as a display or selector component.

Selector Component Options

Selector components, like Single Value components, allow the user to interact with the dashboard to create what-if scenarios and other types of analysis. Selector components provide a lot of flexibility. The values that the selector component capture are usually used by another component on the dashboard.

For example, in the first dashboard that you created in this book, the slider component that you configured, controls the values that are displayed on the chart. [See Exercise 4.1] A Single Value component can only control one value. Selector components let the user select an item from a list. This causes the corresponding data for the selected item to be displayed in another component. In a way, selector components allow you to put multiple dashboards into one dashboard. The next few sections explain the common options that selector components have.

Common Selector General View Options

The common general view options for selector components are shown in Figure 9-22.

TITLE Like the chart (title) option, you can type in the title for a selector.

By default, the title will appear at the top of the component. If you want to change the location of the title, you can change it on the Text tab.

LABELS Is used to select the cell range for the row or column that has the name for each item in the menu. For example, in Figure 9-23, the names for the menu items would come from the range A4:A12.

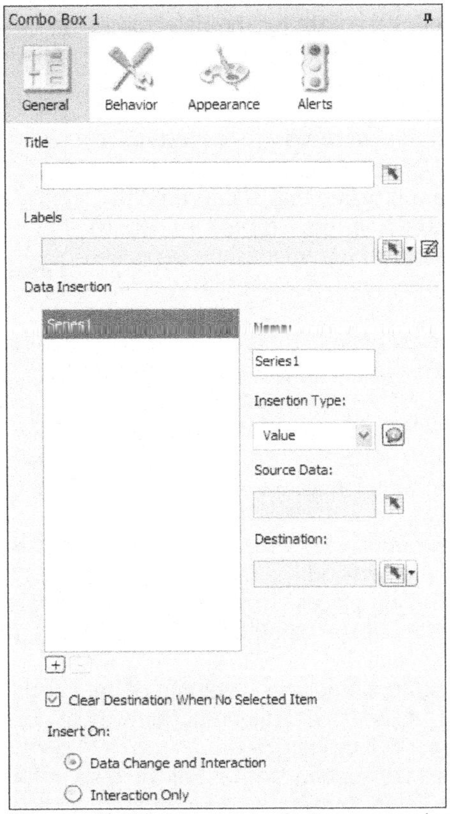

Figure 9-22 Common selector general view options

	A	B	C	D	E	F
1	Sales by Branch:					
2						
3		FY08	FY09	FY10	FY11	FY12
4	Atherton	$ 19.7	$ 17.1	$ 18.3	$ 14.8	$ 19.8
5	Berkeley	$ 14.4	$ 18.0	$ 16.4	$ 16.7	$ 19.3
6	Carmel	$ 18.8	$ 13.5	$ 18.7	$ 13.9	$ 15.7
7	Cupertino	$ 12.0	$ 16.2	$ 17.5	$ 17.8	$ 13.8
8	Freemont	$ 19.2	$ 15.6	$ 19.6	$ 15.9	$ 14.4
9	Irvine	$ 18.9	$ 14.6	$ 16.7	$ 12.1	$ 13.9
10	Milpitas	$ 18.7	$ 17.8	$ 14.0	$ 18.5	$ 13.7
11	Orange County	$ 17.0	$ 19.4	$ 17.1	$ 17.3	$ 17.3
12	San Francisco	$ 14.4	$ 14.0	$ 13.9	$ 15.4	$ 18.3
13						
14	Insert In Row:					

Figure 9-23 Data for menu labels

Depending on the component, the Manual Edit button will display a Labels dialog box with different options. For example, on the Combo Box component, the Labels dialog box displays options to create or change text labels. Clicking this button on the Toggle Button component displays status options. The Manual Edit button for the Labels option is not enabled for the Icon component.

Data Insertion Type Options

The options in this section of the General view are used to select the data for the Selector component. This section is the equivalent to the Data section for charts.

The options in the **INSERTION TYPE** drop-down list shown in Figure 9-24 are used to define the type of data or value that is delivered to the target destination (the Destination option). The seven insertion type options are explained below.

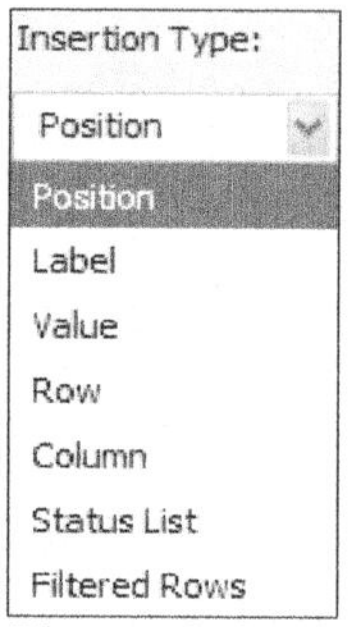

Figure 9-24 Insertion Type drop-down list options

① The **POSITION** option stores the location of the item selected. For example, Figure 9-25 shows a menu component on the left with five buttons. The table on the right is the data for the menu. If you selected the Label 3 menu option and the target cell is C5, a three would be placed in cell C5, the target cell, because Label 3 is in the third position on the menu. (5)

② The **LABEL** option stores the selected menu label name in the target field. If the Label 1 menu option shown in Figure 9-25 is selected and the target cell is C5, "Label 1" would be placed in cell C5. (5)

③ The **VALUE** option stores the actual value that the menu item points to. If the Label 2 menu option is selected and the menu range is B1:B5, the value 11 would be placed in cell C5.

④ The **ROW** option places a row of data in the target cells based on the option selected in the menu. If the Label 4 menu option was selected, the data in cells A4:B4 would be placed in the target cell range.

⑤ The **COLUMN** option places a column of data in the target cells based on the option selected in the menu. If the Label 2 menu option was selected, the values in cells B1:B5 would be placed in the target cell range.

⑥ The **STATUS LIST** option sets one of the cells in the target cell range to one and sets all of the other cells in the target cell range to zero. If the Label 3 menu option was selected, a 1 would be placed in the third cell of the target cell range and all of the other target cells would automatically be set to zero. The Status List option is primarily used with dynamic functionality. (5)

⑦ The **FILTERED ROWS** option is used to select rows of data that correspond to the (label) option that is selected. This option is not available when a selector component is configured to be used for multiple insertions.

(5) The Source Data field shown earlier in Figure 9-22 is not available if this option is selected.

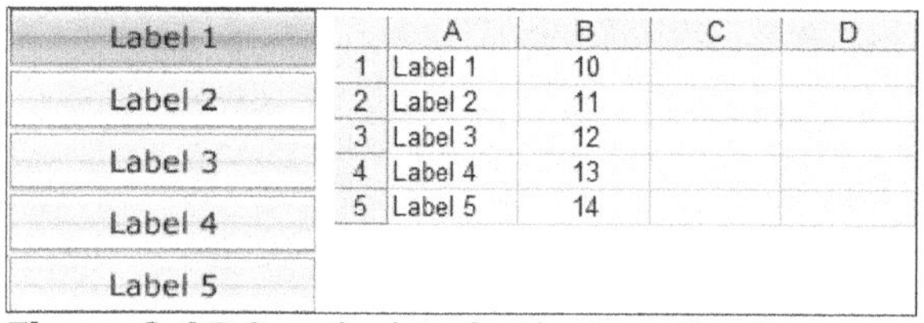

Figure 9-25 Sample data for the Insertion Type property

SOURCE DATA Is used to select the data for the selector component.

DESTINATION Is used to store where the selected data will be placed in the spreadsheet. This is the target cells. The cells selected for this option should be empty and not used for any purpose because each time an option on the menu is selected, the corresponding data will be placed in these cells.

For example, in Figure 9-23 shown earlier, if Orange County is selected in the menu, the data in cells B11:F11 will be placed in the cells in the Destination field.

NEW **CLEAR DESTINATION WHEN NO SELECTED ITEM** The data in the Destination field is deleted if this option is selected and the selector is in the "unchecked" (not selected) state. The data stays in the Destination field if this option is not selected. (6)

NEW Insert On Options

These options are used to select what action has to happen for the data to be inserted.

DATA CHANGE AND INTERACTION Select this option if you want the data to be inserted when the data changes or when the user makes a selection. (7)

INTERACTION ONLY Select this option if you only want data to be inserted when the user makes a selection. (7)

(6) This option is not available for the Icon, Play Selector, Push Button and Toggle Button components.
(7) This option is not available for the Icon, Push Button and Toggle Button components.

Common Selector Common Tab Options

The common tab options for selector components are shown in Figure 9-26.

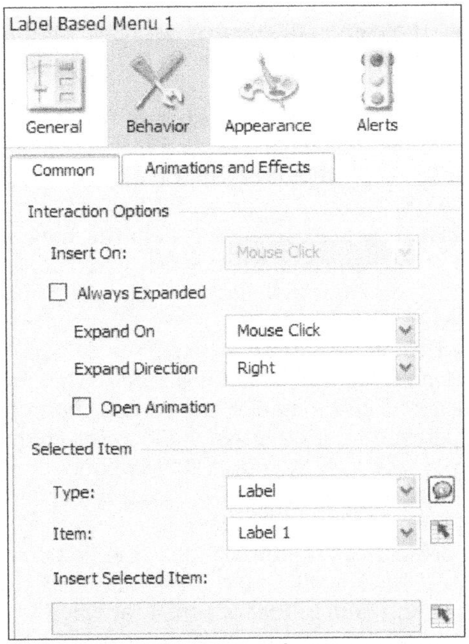

Figure 9-26 Common selector common tab options

Interaction Options

INSERT ON Is used to select how the component should recognize that an option on the menu has been selected that requires data to be displayed on another component. The two options are shown in Figure 9-27. (8)

① **MOUSE CLICK** Select this option if you want the user to click on a menu option to select it.
② **MOUSE OVER** Select this option if you want the user to use the mouse pointer to hover over a menu option to select it.

ALWAYS EXPANDED If checked, this option forces all of the labels on the menu to be displayed and it disables other options on the Common tab.

EXPAND ON Is used to select how the component should recognize that an option on the menu has been selected. (8)

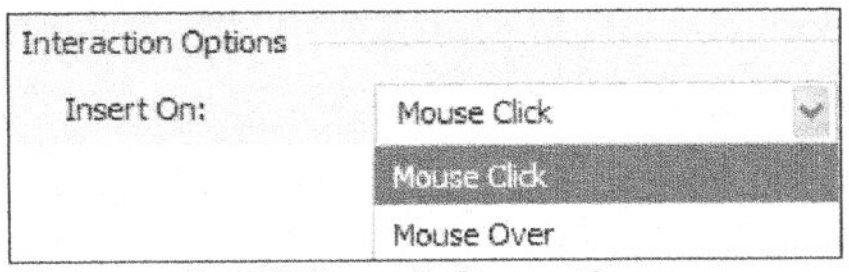

Figure 9-27 Insert On options

EXPAND DIRECTION Is used to select the direction that the menu will expand when it is opened. The options in this drop-down list change, based on the orientation of the menu. The options that appear for Label Based and Radio Button menus depend on what is selected in the **ORIENTATION** option on the General view. (8)

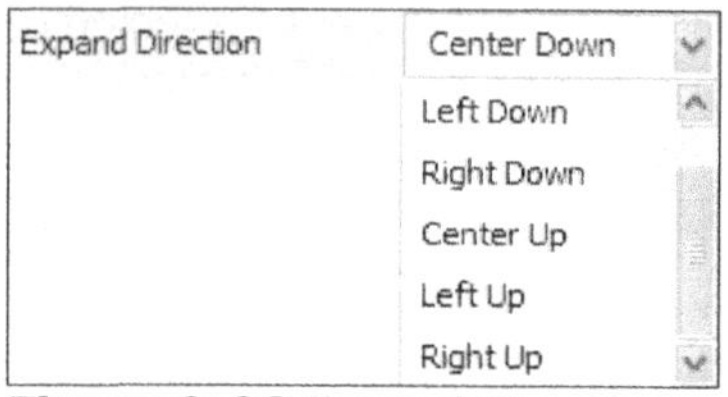

Figure 9-28 Expand Direction drop-down list options

Figure 9-28 shows the Expand Direction options for a Label Based Menu component with vertical orientation.

OPEN ANIMATION If checked, a brief animation will appear when the menu is opened or closed.

(8) This option is only available for the Label Based menu component.

Selected Item Options

The options in this section are used to select the default options for the component when the dashboard is first opened.

TYPE The options in this drop-down list are explained below. They are used to select the type of data that has to be matched. This will be used as the default selection. If no match is found, the selection is set to "None".

LABEL The data in the Source Data field on the General view is matched to the components labels. If the Source Data field is set to None, no item is selected.

POSITION The position of each item (for the component) is given a number, starting with one. The data in the Source Location match is matched to the position numbers. If the Source Data field is set to -1, an item is not selected.

DYNAMIC The position of each item (for the component) is given a number starting with zero. The data in the Source Location is first matched (compared) to the components labels. If a match is found, the data is matched to the position number. If no match is found, the first item is selected.

ITEM This option is used to select the default item of the component. You can select whether or not an item on the component is selected when the dashboard is first opened. For example, in Figure 9-25 shown earlier, the Label 1 menu option is selected. If you wanted the menu component to open and have the Label 4 option selected, you would select the Label 4 option from the Item drop-down list. If the **NO SELECTION** option is selected, no item is selected until the user selects it. The options in this drop-down list vary depending on the component.

The default for the Item option is the first entry in the list, but you can select any entry that you want. If you know that the users will select a certain option in the menu most of the time, you can change the Item to that option. That way, when the dashboard is first opened, the data for the option that they use most will automatically be displayed.

INSERT SELECTED ITEM Is used to select the location where to store the selected item value. If the selected item type option is set to Dynamic, the Insert Selected Item option is not available.

Common Selector Color Tab Options

The color tab options shown in Figure 9-29 are common to many selector components.

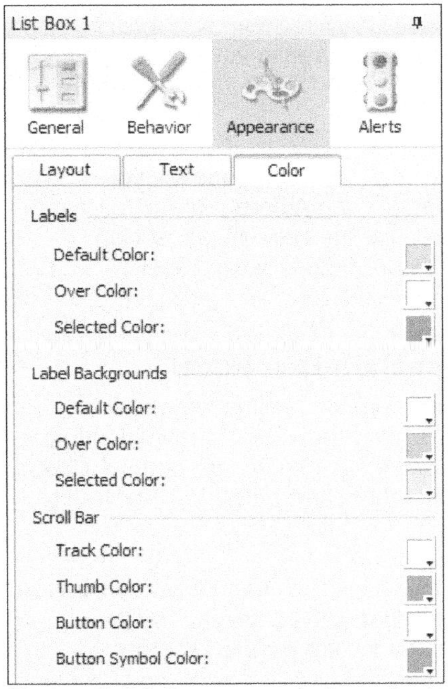

Figure 9-29 Common selector color tab options

Labels Options

DEFAULT COLOR Is used to change the color of the text on the component.

OVER COLOR Is used to change the color of the text when the mouse pointer is hovered over an option on the menu.

SELECTED COLOR Is used to change the text color of the option that is selected on the menu.

Label Backgrounds Options

DEFAULT COLOR Is used to change the background color of the menu (selector).

OVER COLOR Is used to change the background color used when the mouse pointer is hovered over an option on the menu.

SELECTED COLOR Is used to change the background color of the menu option that is clicked on.

Scroll Bar Options

TRACK COLOR Is used to change the background color of the scroll bar area on the component.

THUMB COLOR Is used to change the color of the scroll bar.

BUTTON COLOR Is used to change the background color behind the arrows on the scroll bar.

BUTTON SYMBOL COLOR Is used to change the color of the arrows on the scroll bar.

Exercise 9.1: Use The List Box Component

In this exercise you will add a List Box component to the model that you created in Exercise 7.2. The List Box will allow the user select the branch that they want to see the sales data for.

1. Open the My list box selector model.
2. Add the List Box component to the left of the chart.
3. On the General view, make the changes in the table.

   The data that will be added to the cells in the Destination option will be displayed on the chart. The data in the chart will change, based on the option that is selected in the List Box menu.

Option	Change To
Labels	A4:A12
Insertion Type	Row
Source Data	B4:F12
Destination	B14:F14

4. Save the changes, then preview the model.

   Select the Carmel branch in the List Box. The model should look like the one shown in Figure 9-30.

   When you first preview the model, you see the data for the Atherton branch. That is because the **ITEM** option, shown earlier in Figure 9-26 is set to Label 1.

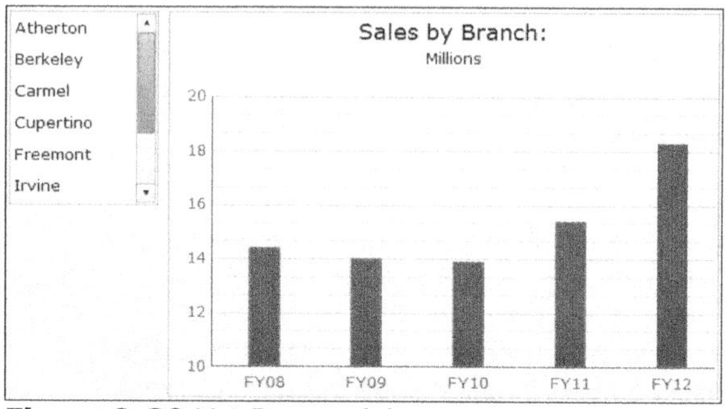

Figure 9-30 List Box model

Adding Animation To A Model

When used appropriately, animation can visually enhance charts in a dashboard. In my opinion, bar, column and combination charts are better suited for animation then other chart types, but feel free to experiment.

Many chart types have the **ENABLE DATA ANIMATION** option shown in Figure 9-31 selected by default. This component does not have a Text tab.

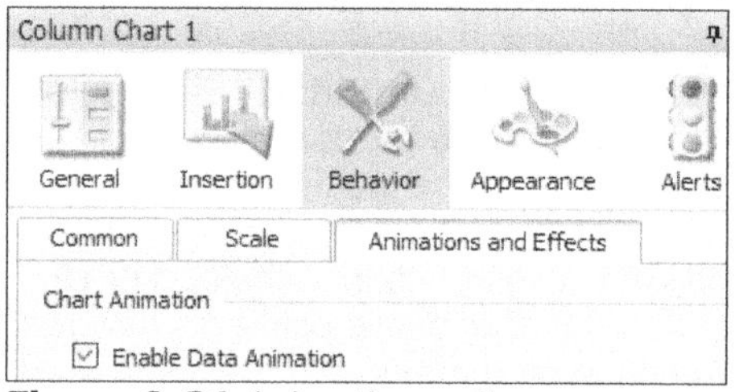

Figure 9-31 Animation option

Play Selector Component (This component is not available in Presentation Design)

This component will remind you of some of the buttons (Play, Rewind etc.) that are on a DVD player. The shape of the progress bar and the default major and minor ticks on this component cannot be customized. A benefit that the Play Selector component has over other components is that the user does not have to click on each item. This component will let the user view a large amount of data.

Layout Tab Options

The Play Selector layout tab options are shown in Figure 9-32.

SHOW BACKGROUND Is used to display or hide the background on the play selector.

SHOW PROGRESS INDICATOR If checked, a slider will be added to the play selector, as shown earlier at the top of Figure 9-14.

SHOW REW/FWD If checked, this option adds the rewind and fast forward buttons to the play selector.

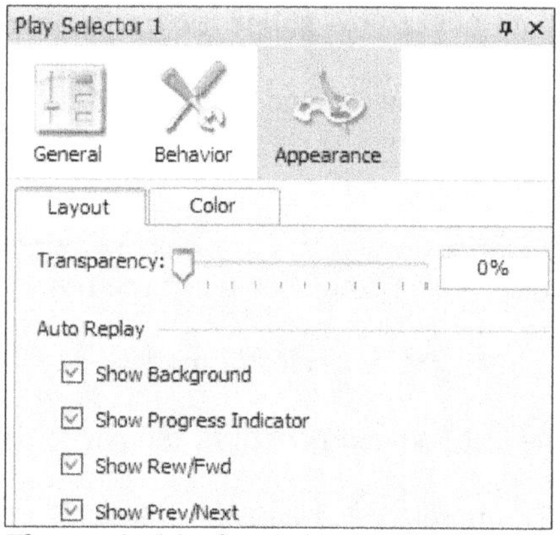

Figure 9-32 Play Selector layout tab options

SHOW PREV/NEXT If checked, this option adds the previous and next buttons to the play selector.

Color Tab Options

The Play Selector color tab options are shown in Figure 9-33.

BACKGROUND COLOR Is used to change the background color of the area behind the component.

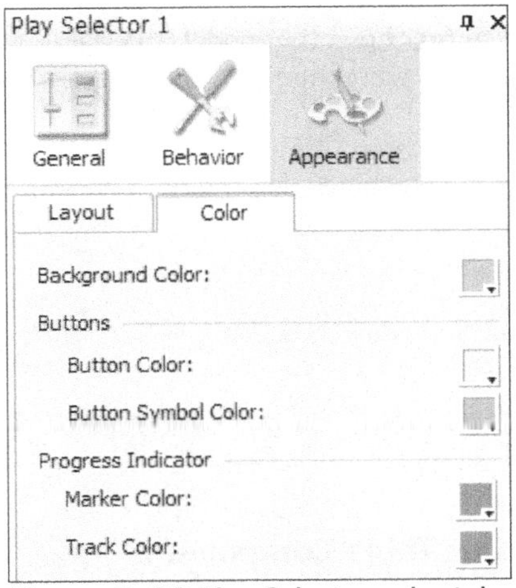

Figure 9-33 Play Selector color tab options

Buttons Options

BUTTON COLOR Is used to change the background color of the buttons on the play selector.

BUTTON SYMBOL COLOR Is used to change the color of the arrow on the play selector button.

Progress Indicator Options

The options in this section are applied to the progress bar indicator on the component.

MARKER COLOR Is used to change the color of the triangle that moves across the progress bar on the slider.

TRACK COLOR Is used to change the color of the bar and tick marks on the slider.

Exercise 9.2: Use The Play Selector Component

In this exercise you will add the Play Selector component to the My play selector model that you created in Exercise 7.3.

1. Open the My play selector model, then add the Play Selector component below the chart.

2. On the General view, make the changes in the table.

Option	Change To
Insertion Type	Row
Source Data	B4:F25
Destination	B27:F27

3. On the Common tab, make the changes in the table.

Option	Change To
Play Time	4
Item	Row 2

4. On the Layout tab, clear the Show Background option.

5. Save the changes.

   When you first open the model, the data for Product 2 is automatically displayed.

   Click the Forward button until you see Product 5. You should see the data shown in Figure 9-34.

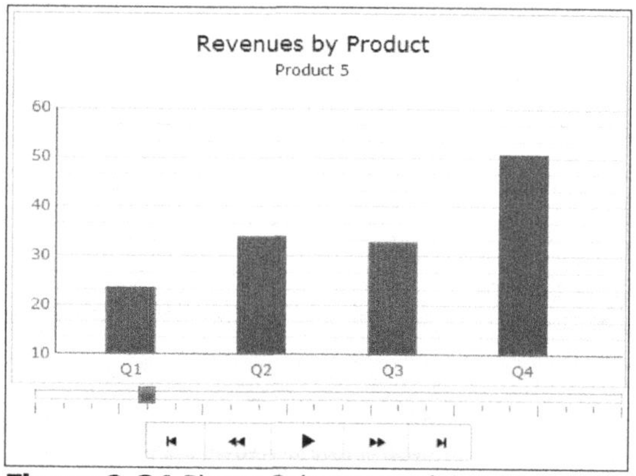

Figure 9-34 Player Selector model

Spreadsheet Table Component

This is one of three components that can be used to display data in a table layout on the dashboard. The other two components that provide similar functionality are the Grid and List View components. This component was formerly called the Table component. The Spreadsheet Table component does not have a Text tab.

> **Spreadsheet Table Component vs List View Component**
> The tips below may help you decide which of these components to use.
>
> ① The advantage that the Spreadsheet Table component has over the List view component is that it displays most of the size, color and formatting of the cells in the embedded spreadsheet. Bold and italic are not. Underlining works, but you may have to resize the component to see it.
>
> ② The columns in the Spreadsheet Table component cannot be resized, nor can the data be sorted.
>
> ③ The Spreadsheet Table does not have title or column headers.
>
> ④ If there is a large amount of data that is formatted in the embedded spreadsheet, use the List View component because the Spreadsheet Table component will take a performance hit because of the cell formatting that it has to process.

General View Options

The Spreadsheet Table general view options are shown in Figure 9-35.

DISPLAY DATA Is used to store the cells for the data that will be displayed in the table. The first row selected will be used as the column headings.

To use the Spreadsheet Table as a selector component, on the General view, click the **DISPLAY DATA** Bind button. Select the range of cells that will be used as the menu options, then set the **INSERTION TYPE** option to row.

The only insertion types that are available are: Position, Value and Row. [See Data Insertion Type Options, earlier in this chapter]

To use the Spreadsheet Table as a display component, select the range of cells that you want to display in the Display Data option.

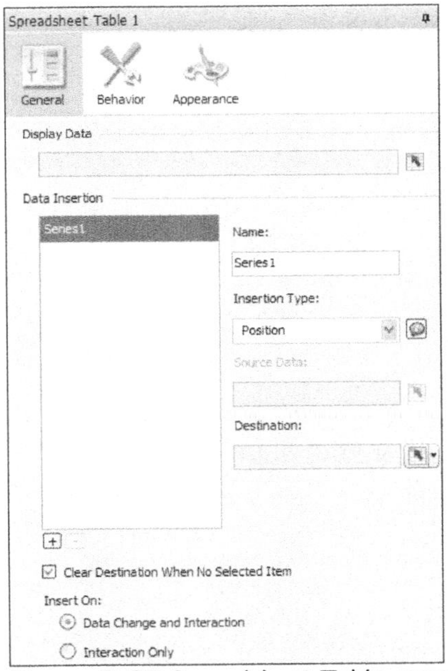

Figure 9-35 Spreadsheet Table general view options

Common Tab Options

The Spreadsheet Table common tab options are shown in Figure 9-36.

Row Selectability Options

The options in this section are used to select whether or not specific rows in the spreadsheet table can be selected by the user.

ROW If the check box illustrated in Figure 9-36 is cleared, none of the rows in the table can be selected. If you want a specific row (or rows) to not be selected, clear the check mark next to the row.

ENABLE SCROLL BARS If checked, scroll bars can be added to the spreadsheet table in one of the three ways listed below. These options are available for both (horizontal and vertical) scroll bars.

① **OFF** Is used to turn the scroll bar off.

② **ON** Will keep the scroll bar on all the time.

③ **AUTO** Will only display the scroll bar when needed.

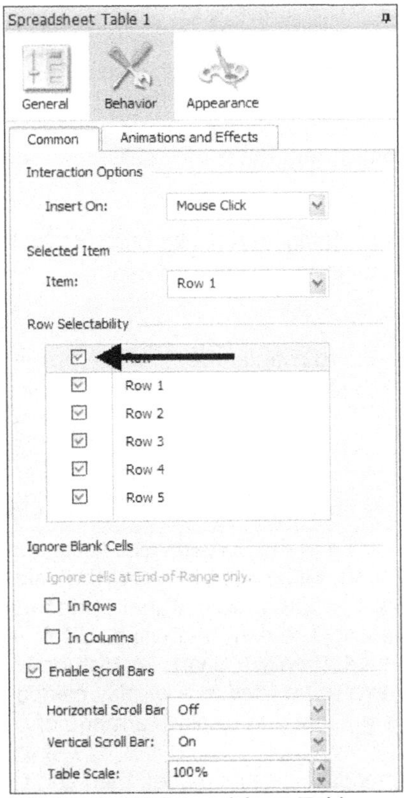

Figure 9-36 Spreadsheet Table common tab options

HORIZONTAL SCROLL BAR Is used to enable the scroll bar at the bottom of the table.

VERTICAL SCROLL BAR Is used to enable the scroll bar on the right side of the table.

TABLE SCALE Is used to change the scale (size) of the table.

Layout Tab Options

The Spreadsheet Table layout tab options are shown in Figure 9-37.

SHOW GRIDLINES Is used to display or hide gridlines on the component. If the embedded spreadsheet has gridlines for cells enabled, the gridlines will appear in the component, whether or not the Show Gridlines option is selected.

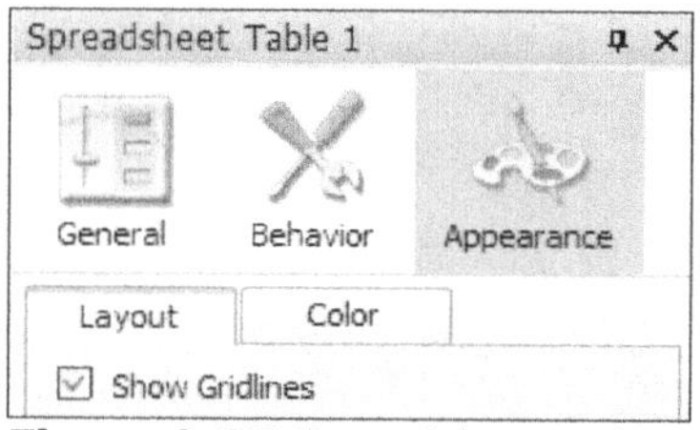

Figure 9-37 Spreadsheet Table layout tab options

Color Tab Options

The Spreadsheet Table color tab options are shown in Figure 9-38.

GRIDLINE COLOR Is used to change the color of the gridlines on the table.

Rows Options

The options in this section are used to change the background color of the rows when the mouse pointer is hovered over a row. The default row color comes from the source cells in the spreadsheet.

OVER COLOR Is used to change the background color when the mouse pointer is hovered over a row in the table.

SELECTED COLOR Is used to change the background color of the row that is selected.

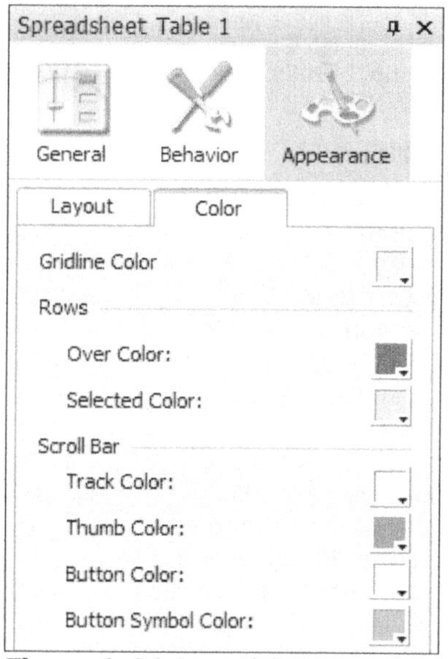

Figure 9-38 Spreadsheet Table color tab options

Exercise 9.3: Use The Spreadsheet Table Component

In this exercise you will add the Spreadsheet Table component to a model. The data in the spreadsheet table menu will be used to select the data that will be displayed in the chart. In this exercise, the data for the Spreadsheet Table component will come from the Income statement line items in the spreadsheet. The data that will be displayed in the chart is the fiscal data for several years. [See Exercise 7.4, Create A Chart For Historic Income] As you read earlier, the Spreadsheet Table component can also be used as a display component. When used as a display component, the table becomes a graphic that displays a range of cells from the spreadsheet.

1. Open the My spreadsheet table model, then add the Spreadsheet Table component to the left of the chart. Make the table larger.

2. On the General view, make the changes in the table.

Option	Change To
Display Data	A4:B16
Insertion Type	Row
Source Data	E4:L16
Destination	E18:L18

3. On the Common tab, change the **ITEM** option to Row 3, then save the changes.

When you select an option from the spreadsheet table menu shown on the left of Figure 9-39, the historic income data for the item that is selected is displayed in the chart. Notice that the Y axis (vertical) values on the chart change each time a different item in the menu is selected.

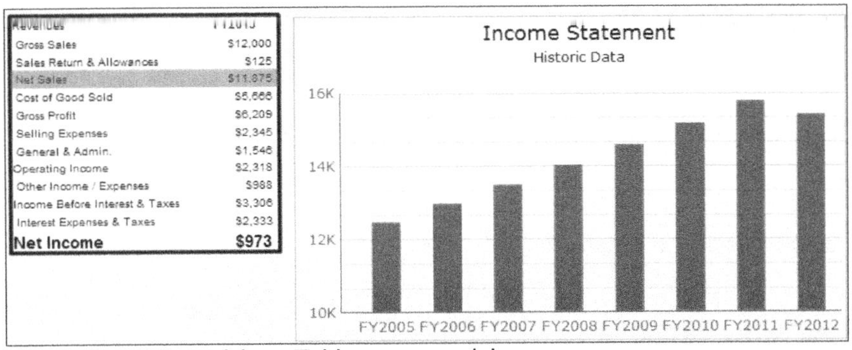

Figure 9-39 Spreadsheet Table menu model

If you wanted to add a scroll bar to the spreadsheet table, as shown in Figure 9-40, you would select the appropriate scroll bar options shown earlier in Figure 9-36.

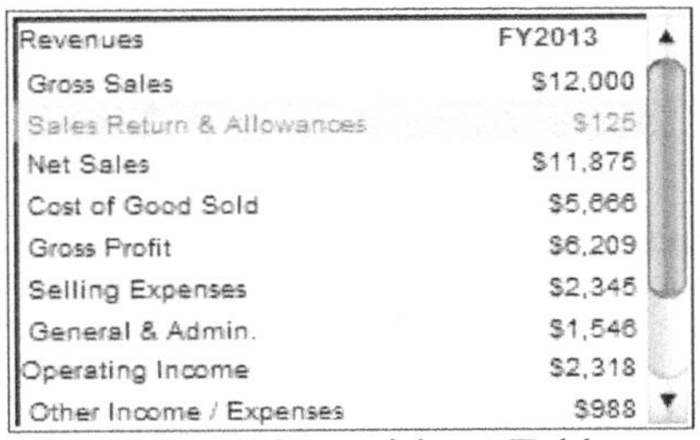

Figure 9-40 Spreadsheet Table component with a scroll bar

Radio Button Component

General View Options

The Radio Button general view options are shown in Figure 9-41.

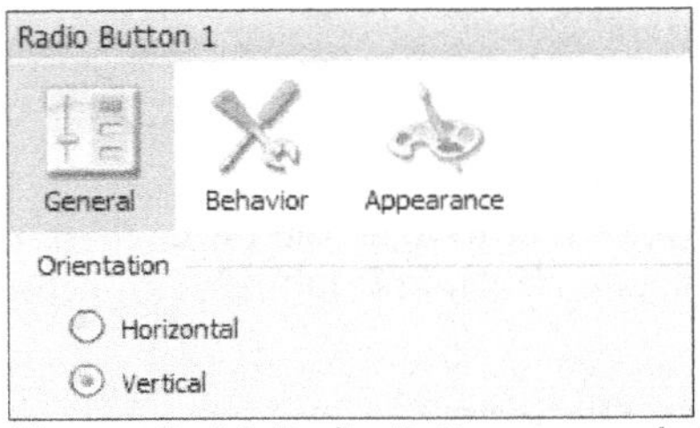

Figure 9-41 Radio Button general view options

Orientation Options

These options are used to select how the Radio Button menu will be displayed. They also control the items that are available in the **EXPAND DIRECTION** drop-down list on the common tab.

Common Tab Options

[See Common Selector Common Tab Options, earlier in this chapter]

Layout Tab Options

The Radio Button layout tab options are shown in Figure 9-42.

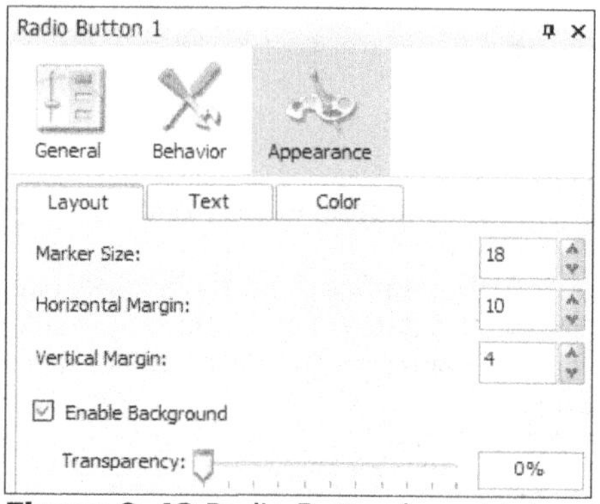

Figure 9-42 Radio Button layout tab options

MARKER SIZE Is used to change the size (between 1 and 300) of the radio buttons on the menu.

HORIZONTAL MARGIN Is used to select the amount of space between the left and right edge of the radio buttons.

VERTICAL MARGIN Is used to select the amount of space between the top and bottom edge of the radio buttons.

ENABLE BACKGROUND Is used to display or hide the background color of the menu.

Color Tab Options

The Radio Button color tab options are shown in Figure 9-43.

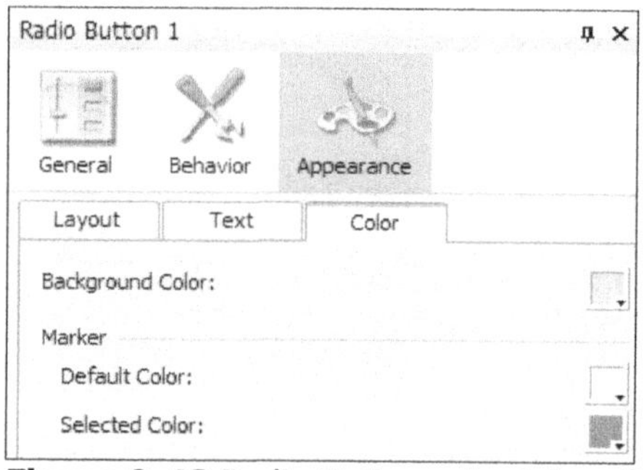

Figure 9-43 Radio Button color tab options

BACKGROUND COLOR Is used to change the background color of the menu.

Marker Options

DEFAULT COLOR Is used to change the border color of the radio buttons that are not selected.

SELECTED COLOR Is used to change the border color of the radio button that is selected.

Grid Component (This component is not available in Presentation Design)

The Grid component can be used as an input or output component. When used as an input component, the user can click in cells in the grid to type new values. If the user holds the left mouse button down in a cell and drags the mouse up or down, the value in the cell will increase or decrease. This table is not static like the one in the Spreadsheet Table component. It is used as an output component when you want to display the underlying data for another component on the dashboard in a traditional table layout.

Make sure that the cells in the grid are large enough to accommodate the largest value that will be displayed, otherwise, the table will look like the one shown in Figure 9-44.

1	##	3	4	5
2	4	6	8	##
3	6	##	12	15

Figure 9-44 Grid too small to support large values

General View Options

The Grid general view options are shown in Figure 9-45.

DATA Type in or select the cells in the spreadsheet that the component should be linked to. The values are displayed in the grid in the same order that they are in the spreadsheet. A value is displayed for each cell that is selected.

If the user changes the values in any of the cells selected in this field, the changed data is written back to the embedded spreadsheet.

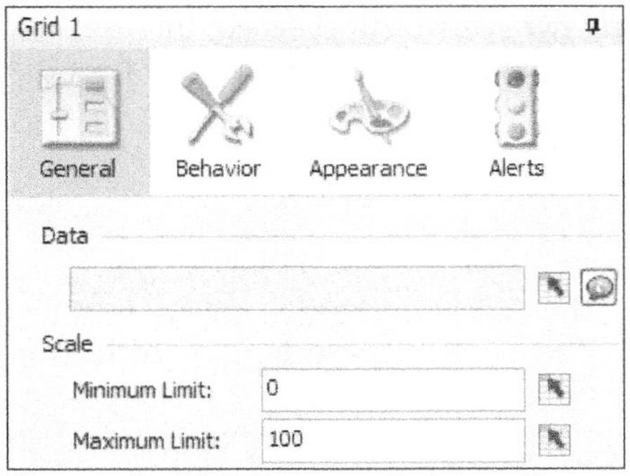

Figure 9-45 Grid general view options

Scale Options

The options in this section are used to limit the values that a user can enter into the cell range in the Data field. These options are not applied to values in the spreadsheet. If these values are outside of the range entered in the fields in this section, they will still appear in the grid.

MINIMUM LIMIT Is used to select the lowest value that a user can enter in the grid.

MAXIMUM LIMIT Is used to select the highest value that a user can enter in the grid.

Common Tab Options

The Grid common tab options are shown in Figure 9-46.

INCREMENT Is used to select how much the value will be increased or decreased by, each time the mouse is dragged up or down. (9)

Limits Options

MINIMUM LIMIT Is used to select the lowest value that will appear in the grid. The options in the drop-down list are explained below. (9)

① **FIXED** The user cannot select a value that will appear in the grid that is less than the Minimum Limit value that is selected on the General view.
② **OPEN** The user can select a value that will appear in the grid, as long as it is not greater than the Maximum Limit value that is selected on the General view. (10)

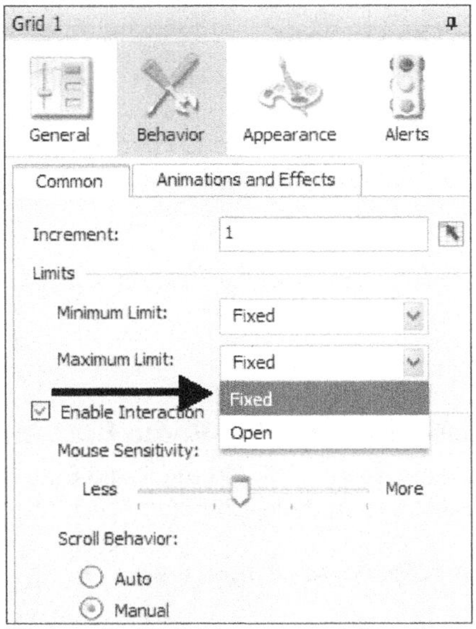

Figure 9-46 Grid common tab options

MAXIMUM LIMIT Is used to select the highest value that will appear in the grid. The options in the drop-down list are explained below. (9)

① **FIXED** The user cannot select a value that will appear in the grid that is greater than the Maximum Limit value that is selected on the General view.
② **OPEN** The user can select a value that will appear in the grid, as long as it is not less than the Minimum Limit value that is selected on the General view. (10)

ENABLE INTERACTION If checked, this option allows users to enter values in the grid. If the cells in the grid are linked to cells in the spreadsheet that have formulas, users will not be able to enter values in the grid.

Scroll Behavior Options
[See Chapter 6, Value Component Common Tab Options]

(9) The Enable Interaction option must be selected to use this option.
(10) If this option is selected, the corresponding option on the general view is disabled.

Layout Tab Options

The Grid layout tab options are shown in Figure 9-47. They are used to change the spacing on the grid.

VERTICAL MARGIN Is used to select the amount of space between the rows in the grid.

HORIZONTAL MARGIN Is used to select the amount of space between the columns in the grid.

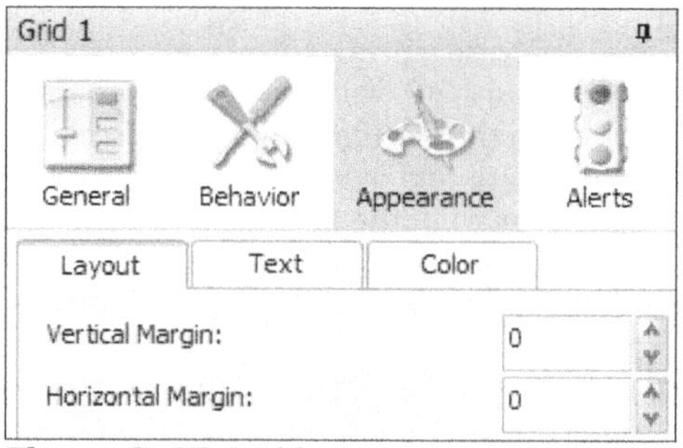

Figure 9-47 Grid layout tab options

Color Tab Options

The Grid color tab option is shown in Figure 9-48.

BACKGROUND COLOR Is used to change the background color of the grid.

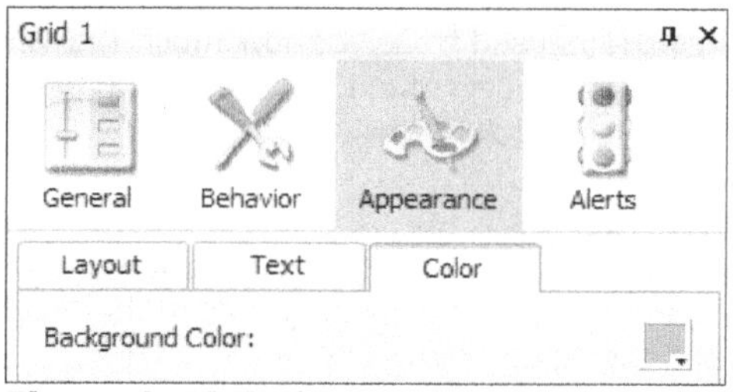

Figure 9-48 Grid color tab options

Exercise 9.4: Use The Radio Button And Grid Components

In this exercise you will add the Radio Button and Grid components to the model. The data for this model was shown earlier in Figure 9-23.

1. Open the dd_radio_button file.

2. Add the Radio Button component to the left of the chart.

3. Open the Other category folder in the Components Browser and add the Grid component below the chart. Make the grid component as wide as the titles on the horizontal axis on the chart.

4. Save the model as `My radio button menu`.

Select The Radio Button Options

1. On the General view, make the changes in the table.

Option	Change To
Labels	A4:A12
Insertion Type	Row
Source Data	B4:F12
Destination	B14:F14

2. If necessary, resize the Radio Button component so that all of the options are visible.

Select The Grid Options

1. On the General view, change the **DATA** option to B13:F14.

2. Save the changes.

   The model should look like the one shown in Figure 9-49.

   When you click on a city in the menu, the sales for the city will be displayed on the chart and in the grid below the chart.

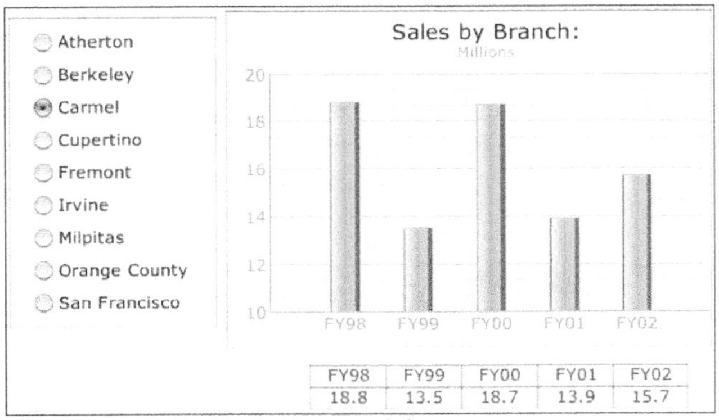

Figure 9-49 Radio Button model

If you wanted to add a background color to the grid, as shown in Figure 9-50, select the Background Color option shown earlier in Figure 9-48.

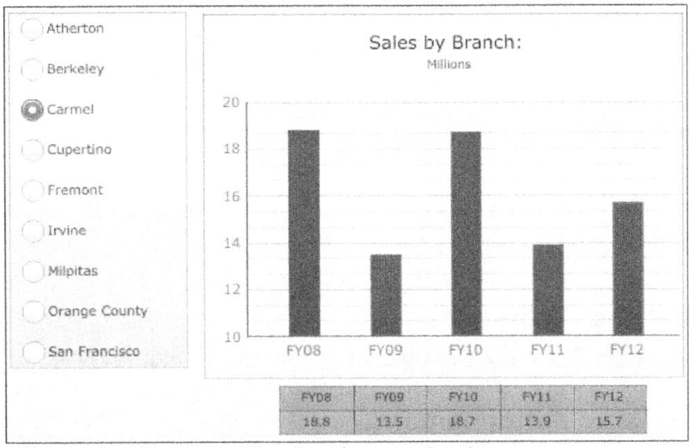

Figure 9-50 Grid with a background color

Combo Box Component

This component has the same functionality as the list box that you learned how to use in Exercise 9.1. The combo box component creates the drop-down list shown in Figure 9-51.

When an option in the drop-down list is selected, the corresponding data is displayed in another component like a chart or grid. The benefit that the combo box has over a list box is that it does not have to be expanded to accommodate a lot of options.

If the list has 10,000 items, it does not need any more space on the dashboard then a combo box that has 10 items. To demonstrate that list box and combo box have the same functionality, you will use the same model.

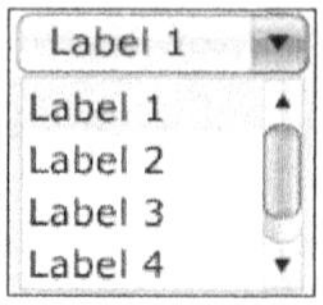

Figure 9-51 Combo Box drop-down list

Animations And Effects Tab Options

The options shown in Figure 9-52 are used to add animation and sound to a component.

DROP-DOWN ANIMATION Adds a slow opening effect to the combo box when it is first opened. I did not notice the difference when this option was enabled.

ENABLE SOUND Is used to play a sound when the drop-down list is first opened and when an option on the drop-down list is selected.

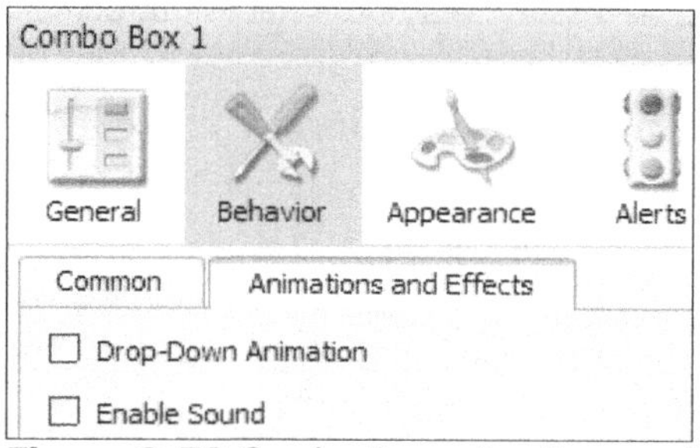

Figure 9-52 Combo Box animations and effects tab options

Layout Tab Options

The Combo Box layout tab options are shown in Figure 9-53.

NUMBER OF LABELS DISPLAYED Is used to select the maximum number of rows that are displayed in the drop-down list. Enter a number between 2 and 50. If the number of rows selected in the spreadsheet is greater than the number selected in this option, a scroll bar is automatically added to the drop-down list, as shown earlier in Figure 9-51.

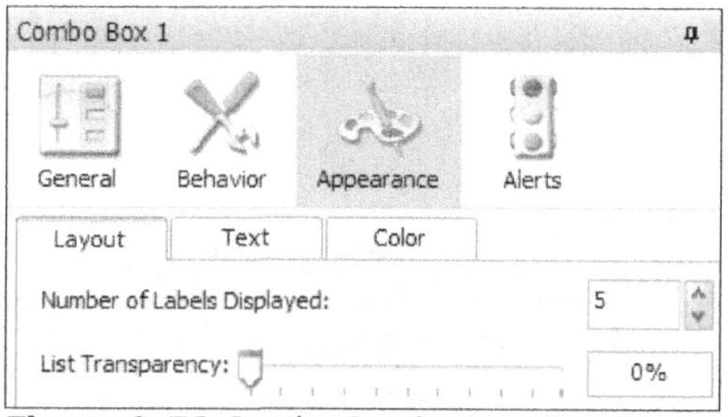

Figure 9-53 Combo Box layout tab options

LIST TRANSPARENCY Is used to make the selected item in the list and the selected roll over color lighter or darker.

Color Tab Options

The Combo Box color tab options are shown in Figure 9-54.

Drop-Down Button Options

The options in this section are used to change the colors for the arrow section of the drop-down list on the combo box.

BUTTON COLOR Is used to change the background color of the arrow.

ARROW COLOR Is used to change the color of the arrow on the label.

SELECTED BUTTON COLOR Is used to change the background color of the arrow section when the arrow is clicked.

SELECTED ARROW COLOR Is used to change the color of the arrow when the arrow is clicked.

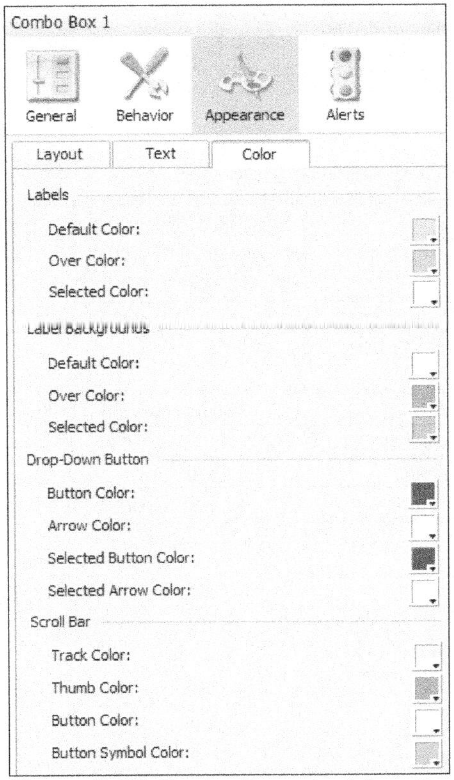

Figure 9-54 Combo Box color tab options

Exercise 9.5: Use The Combo Box Component

In this exercise you will add the Combo Box component to the model that you created in Exercise 7.2. The combo box will allow the user to select the branch that they want to see the sales data for.

Modify The Model

1. Save the My list box selector model as `My combo box`.
2. Delete the List Box component.
3. On the Chart Series tab, make the changes in the table.

Option	Change To
Fill	Red
Marker Size	10

4. Make the chart larger, then save the changes.

Add The Combo Box Component

1. Add the Combo Box component to the upper left corner of the chart.

2. On the General view, make the changes in the table.

Option	Change To
Labels	A4:A12
Insertion Type	Row
Source Data	B4:F12
Destination	B14:F14

3. On the Common tab, open the Item drop-down list and select Label 4.

4. On the Animations and Effects tab, make the changes in the table.

Option	Change To
Drop-Down Animation	Select this option
Enable Sound	Select this option

5. On the Layout tab, change the Number of Labels Displayed option to 4.

6. On the Color tab, make the changes in the table.

Option	Change To
Label Backgrounds Selected Color	Light yellow
Selected Arrow Color	Red
Thumb Color	Light green

7. Save the changes.

   Compare the model shown in Figure 9-55 to the model shown earlier in Figure 9-30.

   As you can see, the combo box takes up less space.

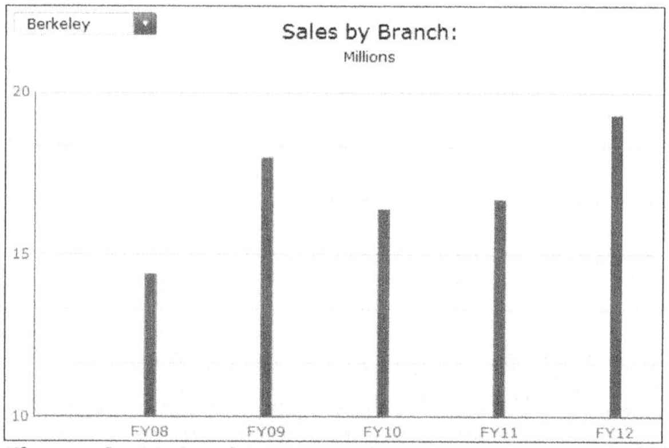

Figure 9-55 Combo Box model

Filter Component

This component usually contains at least two combo boxes, which is why you would use this component instead of the Combo Box component. While you can create multiple combo boxes for a dashboard that filter the data in the spreadsheet, you would have to write formulas that use the **VLOOKUP** function. Many of the Filter component options are the same as the combo box options. The options that are unique to this component are explained in the next few sections.

General View Options

The Filter general view options are shown in Figure 9-56.

TITLE Is used to select the cells that have the titles for the filter button. The titles can be changed by clicking the Manual Edit button. The range selected should be the same number of cells that the Number of Filters option is set to.

SOURCE DATA Is used to select the range of data, which includes the data for the labels. This means that the columns of data for the labels have to be the left most columns in the spreadsheet, as shown below in Figure 9-58.

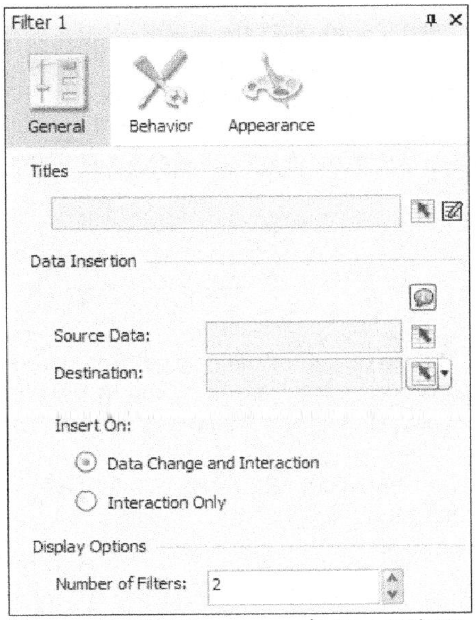

Figure 9-56 Filter general view options

Display Options

NUMBER OF FILTERS Is used to select the number of drop-down lists that the menu will have. The maximum number of filters is 10.

Layout Tab Options

The Filter layout tab options are shown in Figure 9-57.

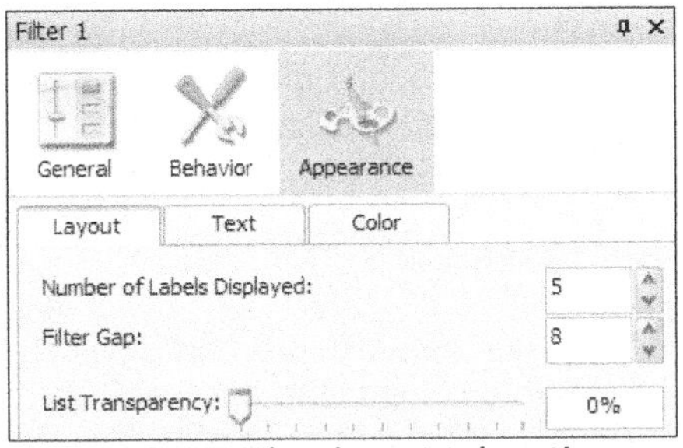

Figure 9-57 Filter layout tab options

NUMBER OF LABELS DISPLAYED [See Combo Box Layout Tab Options, earlier in this chapter]

FILTER GAP Is used to change the amount of space between the drop-down lists on the Filter component.

Exercise 9.6: Use The Filter Component

In this exercise you will add a Filter component that has three drop-down lists (for the product, sales rep and account type) to the model. Each list will allow the user to select options which control the data that is displayed in the chart. The option selected in the first filter will control the value in the second filter. The Filter component looks like the Combo Box component that you created in the previous exercise. Figure 9-58 shows the data for this exercise.

	A	B	C	D	E	F	G
1	Sales by Sales Representative						
2							
3	*Product*	*Sales Rep*	*Account Type*	Q1	Q2	Q3	Q4
4	Product 1	Sales Rep. 1	New Customer	$ 44.2	$ 64.4	$ 55.3	$ 50.7
5	Product 2	Sales Rep. 1	New Customer	$ 39.6	$ 38.3	$ 34.7	$ 47.2
6	Product 3	Sales Rep. 1	New Customer	$ 41.9	$ 66.8	$ 55.5	$ 54.2
7	Product 4	Sales Rep. 1	New Customer	$ 41.5	$ 66.9	$ 40.8	$ 59.4
8	Product 5	Sales Rep. 1	New Customer	$ 63.2	$ 40.2	$ 58.1	$ 46.7
9	Product 6	Sales Rep. 1	New Customer	$ 50.9	$ 44.3	$ 50.1	$ 51.9
10	Product 7	Sales Rep. 1	New Customer	$ 53.7	$ 54.8	$ 39.1	$ 54.7
11	Product 8	Sales Rep. 1	New Customer	$ 62.0	$ 58.7	$ 56.6	$ 62.6
12	Product 9	Sales Rep. 1	New Customer	$ 63.8	$ 37.6	$ 48.1	$ 53.3
13	Product 1	Sales Rep. 1	Existing Customer	$ 52.8	$ 43.5	$ 44.0	$ 63.6

Figure 9-58 Filter component data

1. Save the dd_filter file as `My filter drop-down list.`

2. Add the Filter component above the chart.

3. On the General view, make the changes in the table.

Option	Change To
Title	A3:C3
Source Data	A4:G26
Destination	D27:G27
Number of Filters	3

The **TITLE** option will display the name for each of the drop-down lists above the list. Each drop-down list created by the **NUMBER OF FILTERS** option will store the values for a different field, which is usually a column of data.

4. On the Layout tab, make the changes in the table.

Option	Change To
Number of Labels Displayed	4
Filter Gap	5

5. Make the Filter component as wide as the chart, then save the changes.

6. Open the Product drop-down list and select Product 2.

   Open the Account Type drop-down list and select New Customer.

   The model should look like the one shown in Figure 9-59.

   It appears that each drop-down list is a separate component, but that is not the case. It would be nice if each drop-down list could be sized individually.

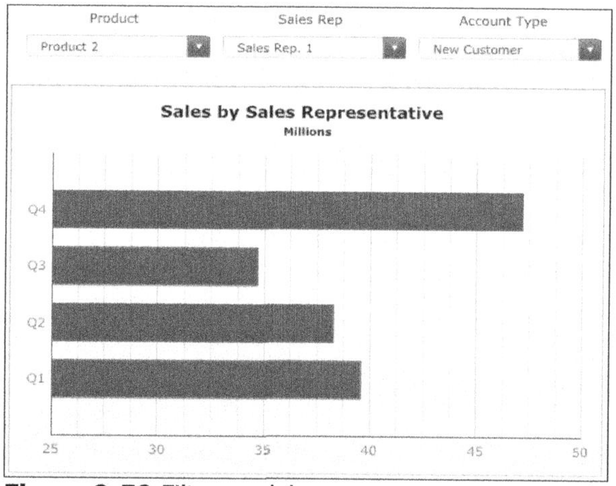

Figure 9-59 Filter model

List View Component

This component is used to view rows of data from the spreadsheet. It can only be used as a selector to insert a row of data for another component. The columns can be sorted and the column width can be adjusted.

General View Options

[See Spreadsheet Table Component General View Options, earlier in this chapter]

NEW The data that you select to display in the List View component can be configured. The **CONFIGURE COLUMNS** button shown in Figure 9-60 opens the dialog box shown in Figure 9-61. The options on this dialog box are used to configure the columns that will be displayed in the List View component.

Figure 9-60 List View general view options

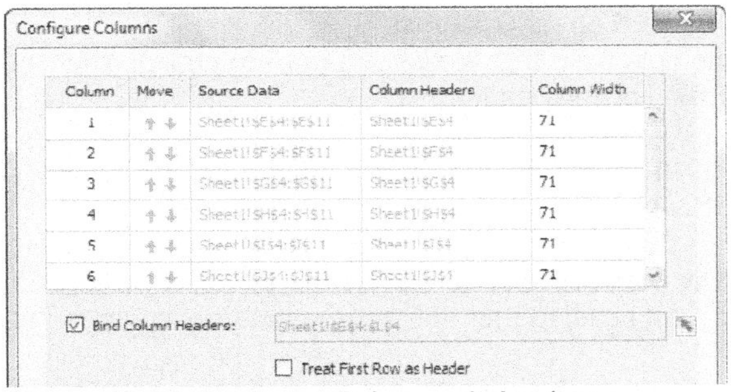

Figure 9-61 Configure Columns dialog box

Layout Tab Options

The List View layout tab options are shown in Figure 9-62.

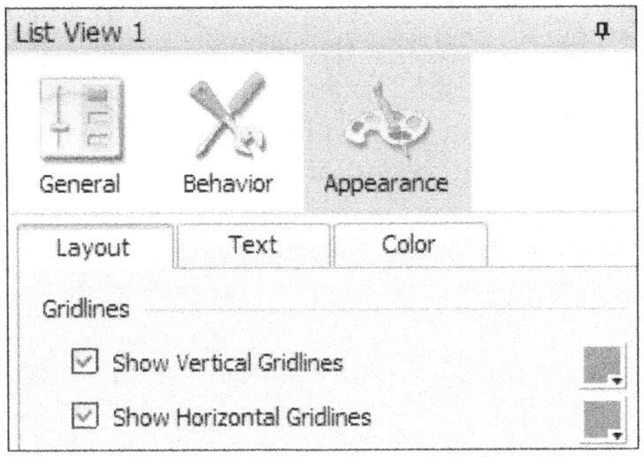

Figure 9-62 List View layout tab options

Gridlines Options

SHOW VERTICAL GRIDLINES Is used to add vertical gridlines to the table.

VERTICAL GRIDLINES FILL COLOR Is used to change the color of the vertical gridlines.

SHOW HORIZONTAL GRIDLINES Is used to add horizontal gridlines to the table.

HORIZONTAL GRIDLINES FILL COLOR Is used to change the color of the horizontal gridlines.

Text Tab Options

The List View text tab options are shown in Figure 9-63.

HEADER Displays a heading row for the grid.

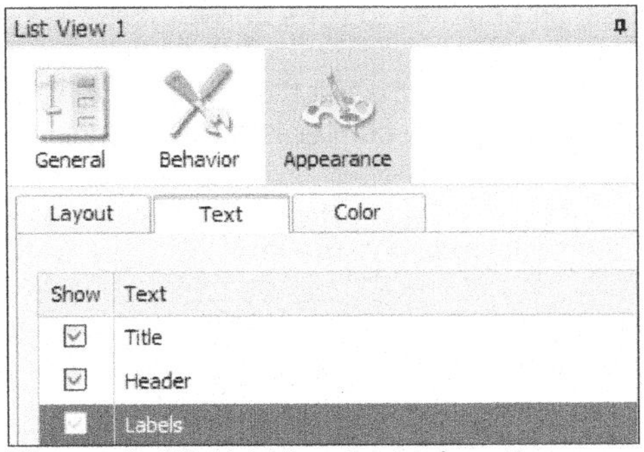

Figure 9-63 List View text tab options

Color Tab Options

The List View color tab options are shown in Figure 9-64.

BACKGROUND COLOR Is used to select the background color for the table. Most of the time, this color will appear as a border color for the table.

Header Labels Options

The options in this section are used to change the color of the column header text.

DEFAULT COLOR Is used to change the default color of the column headings.

OVER COLOR Is used to change the text color of the column heading that the mouse pointer is hovered over.

SELECTED COLOR Is used to change the text color of the column heading that is clicked on.

Header Background Options

The options in this section are used to change the background color of the column headings.

DEFAULT COLOR Is used to change the background color of the header section of the component.

SELECTED COLOR Is used to change the background color of the text of the column that is clicked on.

OVER COLOR Is used to change the background color of the column that the mouse pointer is hovered over.

Label Backgrounds Options

ROW 1 COLOR Is used to change the default background color of the even numbered rows in the table.

ROW 2 COLOR Is used to change the default background color of the odd numbered rows in the table.

OVER COLOR Is used to change the background color of the row that the mouse pointer is hovered over.

SELECTED COLOR Is used to change the background color of the selected row in the table.

Gridlines Options

The options in this section are applied to the lines between the rows and columns in the table. If the Show (Vertical of Horizontal) Gridlines options on the Layout tab are not selected, the gridlines options are not enabled on the Color tab. These options are also available for the Spreadsheet Table and Scorecard components.

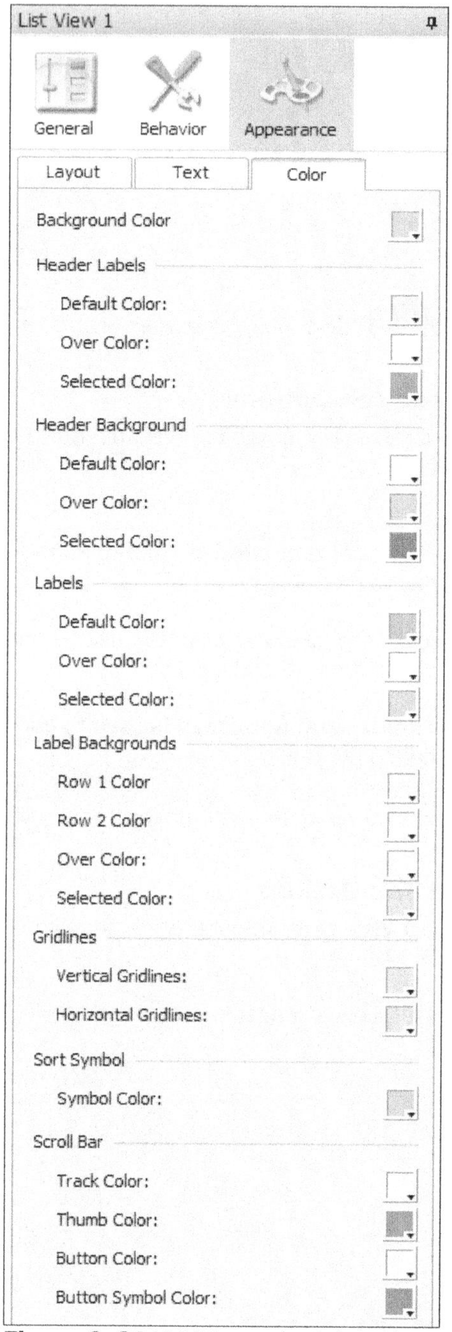

Figure 9-64 List View color tab options

VERTICAL GRIDLINES Is used to add vertical gridlines to the table.

HORIZONTAL GRIDLINES Is used to add horizontal gridlines to the table.

Sort Symbol Option

SYMBOL COLOR Is used to change the color of the arrow on the column that was used to change the sort order, as shown earlier in Figure 9-13. The symbol is not visible when designing the model. This option is only on the Scorecard and Ticker components.

Label Based Menu Component

If you need to display several charts in a small space, with easy access to all of the charts, using the Label Based Menu component is a good option. In terms of functionality, it will remind you of the Radio Button menu.

General View Options

[See Radio Button Component General View Options, earlier in this chapter]

Common Tab Options

The Label Based Menu common tab options were shown earlier in Figure 9-26.

INSERT ON This option is not available if the **ALWAYS EXPANDED** option on the common tab is not selected.

Layout Tab Options

The Label Based Menu layout tab options are shown in Figure 9-65.

BUTTON SEPARATION Is used to select the amount of space between each button on the menu.

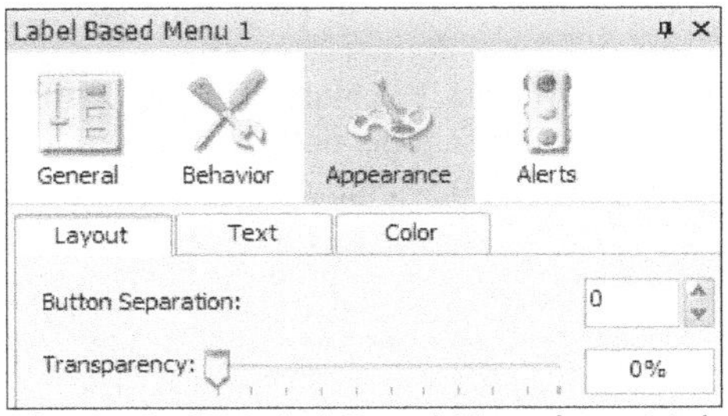

Figure 9-65 Label Based Menu layout tab options

Color Tab Options

The Label Based Menu color tab options are shown in Figure 9-66.

Labels Options

DEFAULT COLOR Is used to change the label color of the buttons.

OVER COLOR Is used to change the label color of the button when the mouse pointer is hovered over a button.

SELECTED COLOR Is used to change the label color of the button that is clicked on.

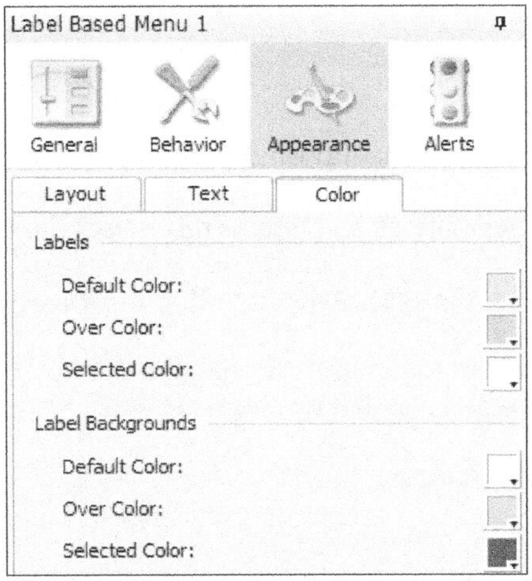

Figure 9-66 Label Based Menu color tab options

Label Backgrounds Options

DEFAULT COLOR Is used to change the background color of the buttons.

OVER COLOR Is used to change the background color of the button that the mouse pointer is hovered over.

SELECTED COLOR Is used to change the background color of the button that is clicked on.

Exercise 9.7: Use The Label Based Menu Component

In this exercise you will add the Label Based Menu component to a model that has five charts. When you open the model, you will only see one chart. The other four charts are behind the one that you see. You will learn how to layer several objects, later in the book. Each chart will be linked to a different button on the menu.

1. Save the dd_label_based_menu model as `My label based menu.`

2. Add the Label Based Menu component above the chart.

3. On the General view, make the changes in the table.

Option	Change To
Title	Clear this option
Insertion Type	Status List
Destination	B4:B8

4. On the General view, click the Manual Edit button at the end of the Labels field, then make the changes shown in Figure 9-67.

   Click OK.

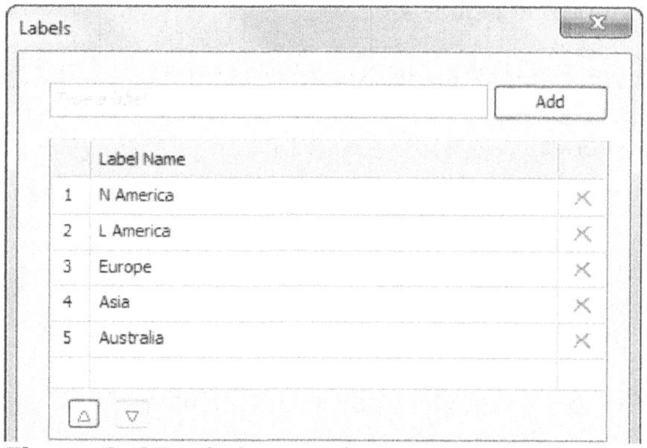

Figure 9-67 Label name changes

5. On the Common tab, open the Item drop-down list and select Label 3.

6. On the Animations and Effects tab, select the Enable Sound option.

7. On the Layout tab, change the Button Separation option to 5.

8. On the Color tab, make the changes in the table, in the Label Backgrounds section.

   Save the changes.

Option	Change To
Default Color	Light yellow
Over Color	Light green
Selected Color	Orange

As you click on each button, you will see a different chart.

The charts would look better if they had the region in the subtitle, instead of the word millions.

To change the subtitle, click on the chart in the Object Browser, then change the Subtitle option to the corresponding cell in the spreadsheet.

The Latin America chart should look like the one shown in Figure 9-68.

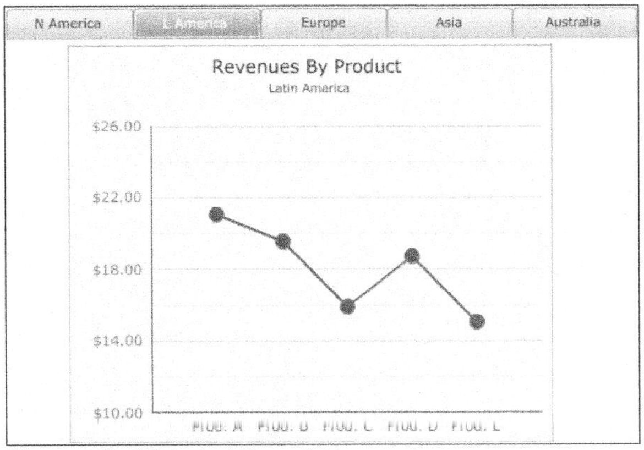

Figure 9-68 Label Based Menu

CREATING DASHBOARDS WITH ALERTS

In this chapter you will learn how to create dashboards that have the following types of alerts:

- ☑ Percent alerts
- ☑ Value alerts
- ☑ Selector alerts
- ☑ Ticker component with an alert

CHAPTER 10

Alerts Overview

Alerts are created to let the person using the dashboard know that a value has been reached in a field that they should be aware of. This is done by designing the item in a different color. Alerts can be informational, like 50 or more customers ordered a specific product. These limits are called by a variety of names including benchmarks, targets and thresholds. Alerts can also be used as a reminder. For example, an inventory dashboard could have an alert to indicate which products need to be reordered, based on the quantity on hand.

Alerts are not available for all components. Alerts are created with formulas that evaluate the conditions that you specify. The component used for the alert can only have one series of data. Selector and container components do not support alert functionality. A dashboard can have more than one alert. Alerts are only activated when the data is refreshed in the dashboard. There are two types of alerts that can be created: Value and Percent.

Alerts View Options

The options on the Alerts view shown in Figure 10-1 are used to create an alert.

ENABLE ALERTS To create an alert, this option has to be selected.

Alert Method Options

The options explained below determine how the alert will be processed.

AS PERCENT OF MAX VALUE [100] Select this option when you want the alert to use percents of the largest value in the range. This option can only be used for single value components.

AS PERCENT OF TARGET Select this option when you need to create a percentage alert that is based on specific target values. The **BIND** button at the end of this option is used to select the cell in the spreadsheet. Separate target vales can be created for each data point.

BY VALUE Select this option when the alert value is a number. You can select a value from the spreadsheet or you can enter the value manually. When this option is selected, the Use A Range, Enable Auto Colors and Low values are good options are automatically selected.

Alert Thresholds Options

The options in this section are used to select a range of values for the alert. The range can be selected from the spreadsheet or you can manually enter the range for each color by changing the From and To values. The options change depending on which alert method, value or percent is selected.

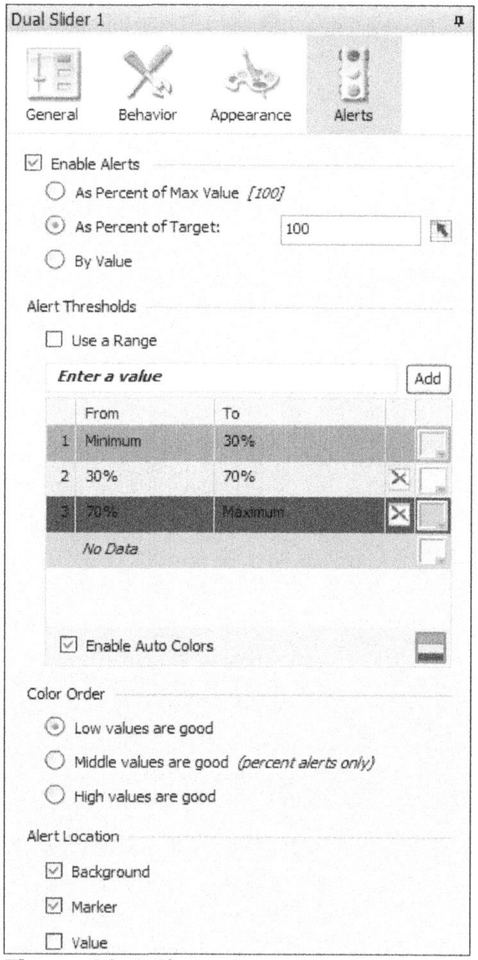

Figure 10-1 Alerts view options

By default, as shown above in Figure 10-1, there are three levels. You can add more levels if necessary. The threshold options are used to select specifics about the alert values including: Selecting the colors for the alert, the number of alerts and the values that will trigger the alerts.

The options in the grid determine which values will trigger the alert. The data is compared to the target values. Data that does not meet the target values selected here can trigger the alert, depending on which of the color order options are selected.

The **USE A RANGE** option must be enabled if you want to select the range levels for the alert from the spreadsheet.

The **ENTER A VALUE** field is used to type in a value.

The **BIND TO A RANGE** option illustrated in Figure 10-2 is used to select the range level values from the spreadsheet. Check the Use a Range option, then click the Bind button at the end of the field to select the cells in the spreadsheet.

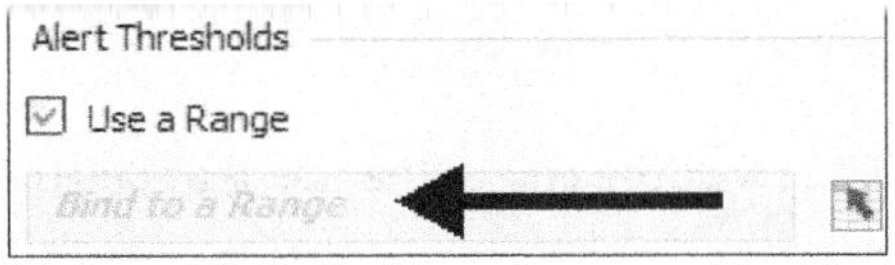

Figure 10-2 Bind to a Range option illustrated

How To Modify The Range Manually

To modify the range manually, follow the steps below.

1. Clear the Use a Range option.
2. Double-click on the value that you want to change, then type in the value that you want, as illustrated in Figure 10-3.

   Compare this to the value shown earlier in Figure 10-1.

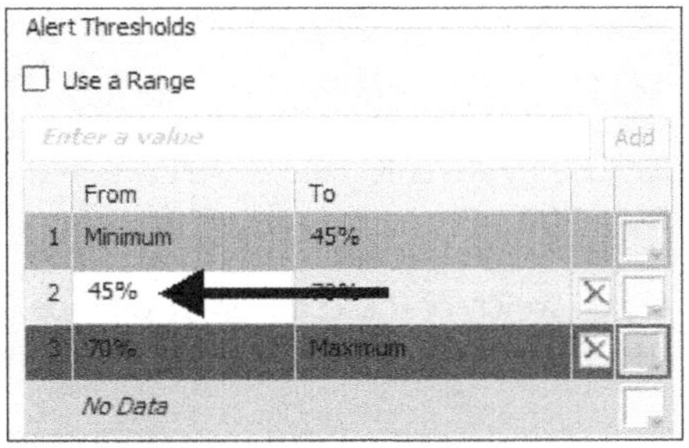

Figure 10-3 Range modified

You cannot change the Minimum and Maximum options.

How To Add A Range

To add a range, follow the steps below.

1. Clear the Use a Range option.
2. Type the starting value for the range that you want to create in the Enter a Value field (under the Use a Range option), shown in Figure 10-4.

Figure 10-4 Enter a value field

3. Click the **ADD** button. You will see the new range, as illustrated in Figure 10-5.

   Compare this to Figure 10-3 shown earlier.

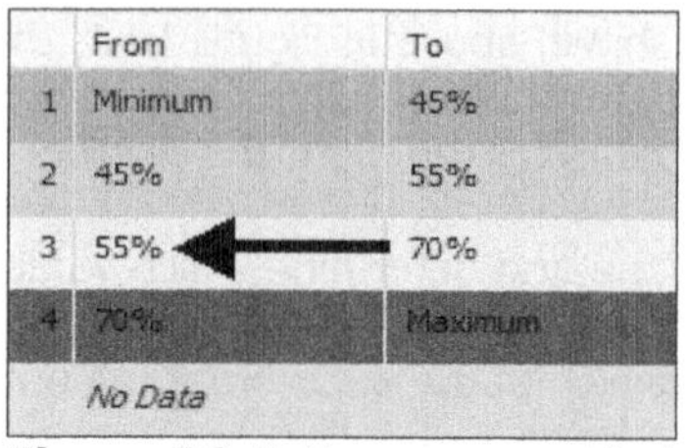

Figure 10-5 New range added

How To Delete A Range

To delete a range, follow the steps below.

1. Clear the Use a Range option.

2. Click the X at the end of the row that has the range that you want to delete, as shown earlier in Figure 10-3.

Default Alert Level Colors

By default, Dashboard Design creates three levels of alerts. Each level has a different color: Green for good, Yellow for satisfactory and Red for poor. The range of values that you select for each alert level should correspond to the data. For example, the range levels could be 0-60 red, 60-75 yellow and 75-100 green. You could select the following range levels: 0-63 red, 63-80 yellow, 80-100 green for the same data and still achieve the same results.

In both examples, if the range of values that you are expecting to see is greater than 75, the **HIGH VALUES ARE GOOD** option has to be selected to have the alert options display the data correctly. This is because by default, values that are in the green represent the good values. You can change the colors as needed.

Depending on which of the color order options (low values, middle values or high values) that you select, the colors will be in a different location on the component, as illustrated in Figures 10-6 to 10-8.

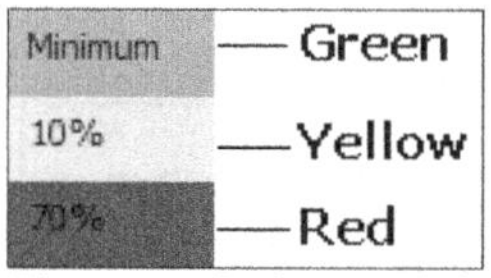

Figure 10-6 Low values are good default color order

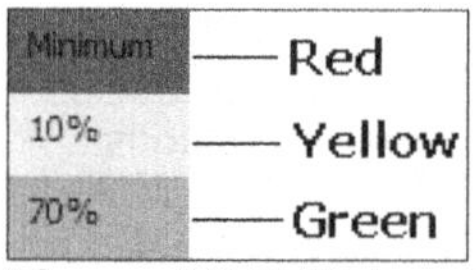

Figure 10-7 High values are good default color order

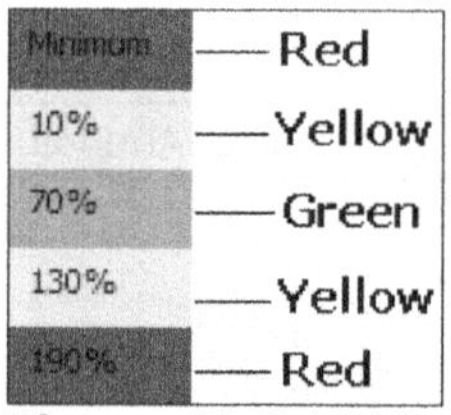

Figure 10-8 Middle values are good default color order

How To Manually Change The Range Colors

To change a color, follow the steps below.

1. Clear the Enable Auto Colors option.

2. Click on the Color Selector button at the end of the row that you want to change, as shown earlier in Figure 10-3. You will see the dialog box shown in Figure 10-9.

The **MORE ALERT COLORS** button opens the dialog box shown in Figure 10-10.

The **CHOOSE FONT COLOR** button also opens the dialog box shown in Figure 10-10. The color that you select will change the color of the font.

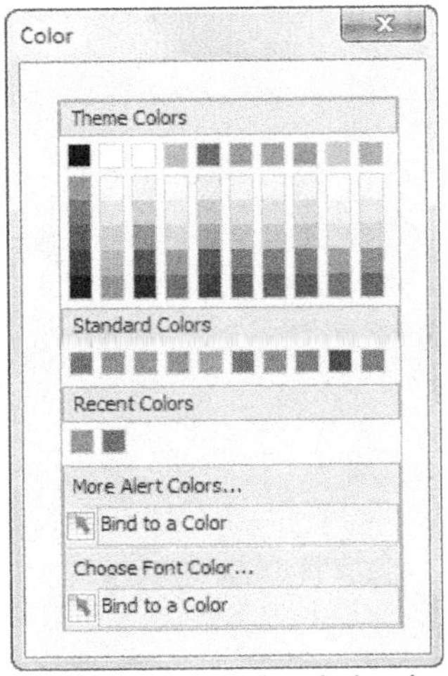

Figure 10-9 Color dialog box

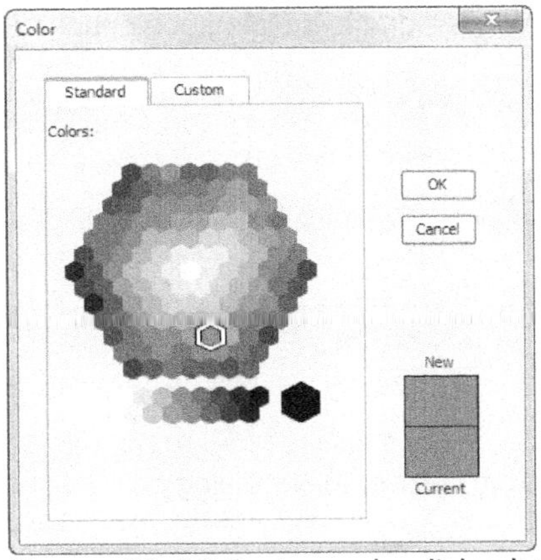

Figure 10-10 Custom color dialog box

Alert Thresholds Options (Continued)

The **NO DATA** option is used to change the color for any part of the component that does not have alert data. This option is not available for Single Value components.

ENABLE AUTO COLORS If this option is checked, the color for the values in the range cannot be changed individually. If necessary, clear this option, change the range colors, then check this option again.

ENABLE AUTO COLORS (button) This button is across from the Enable Auto Colors option, which must be selected to change the range colors. Clicking this button opens the dialog box shown in Figure 10-11. If you have created a custom gradient color scheme, you will see it in the Custom section of the dialog box. The options in the **BUILT-IN** section are pre configured gradient color schemes that you can select.

The **CREATE NEW GRADIENT** button opens the dialog box shown in Figure 10-12, which is used to create a custom gradient color scheme for the value range and fonts. If you click OK on this dialog box, the color scheme that you created will be saved and stored in the **CUSTOM** section on the Color dialog box, shown in Figure 10-11. The options are explained in Table 10-1.

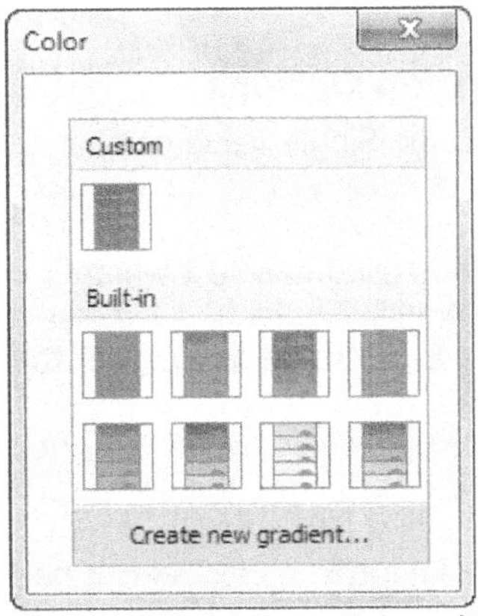

Figure 10-11 Auto Colors dialog box

Option	This Option . . .
2-Color Gradient	Will use two colors on the alert scale.
3-Color Gradient	Will use three colors on the alert scale.
Colors	Is used to select the fill and text color for each color on the scale.

Table 10-1 Custom color gradient dialog box options explained

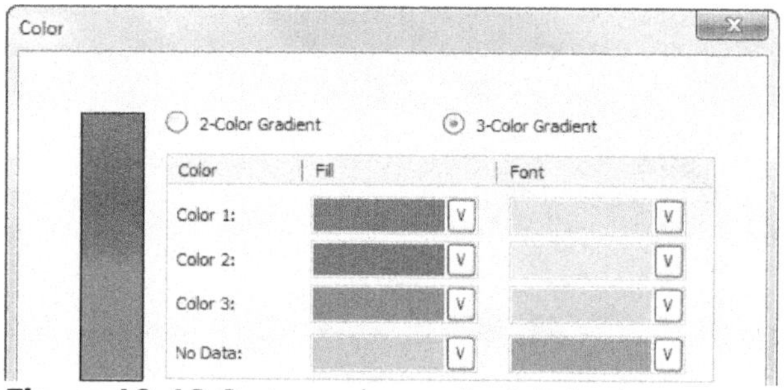

Figure 10-12 Custom color gradient dialog box

Color Order Options

The options explained below are used to select the alert criteria.

① **LOW VALUES ARE GOOD** Selecting this option means that data that is below the target value will not trigger the alert. Use this option when the good values are lower than the target value.

② **MIDDLE VALUES ARE GOOD (PERCENT ALERTS ONLY)** Selecting this option means that data that is close to the target will not trigger the alert. Use this option when the good values are close to the target value. This option is only available for percents.

③ **HIGH VALUES ARE GOOD** Selecting this option means that data that is greater than the target value will not trigger the alert. Use this option when the good values are higher than the target value.

Alert Location Options

(Applies to some Single Value components only) The options in this section are used to customize how alerts are displayed on the component.

BACKGROUND Is used to select whether or not the alert colors will be displayed on the background of the component. Figure 10-13 shows the gauge without any alert level display options selected. Figure 10-14 is the same gauge with the Background option selected.

MARKER Is used to select whether or not the needle will use the alert color, as shown in Figure 10-15. This option is what allows the slider to change colors or the needle on a gauge to change colors.

VALUE If checked, this option adds a background color to the value to display the alert color, as illustrated in Figure 10-16.

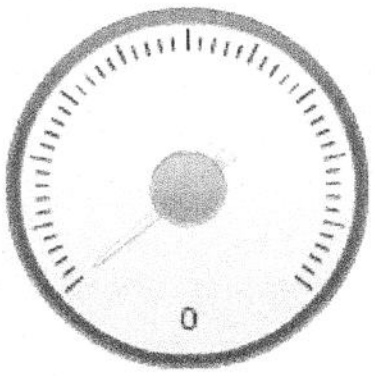

Figure 10-13 Gauge without any alert location options

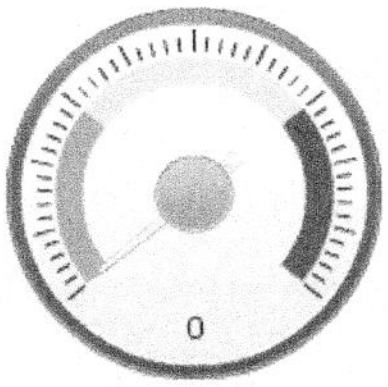

Figure 10-14 Background option selected

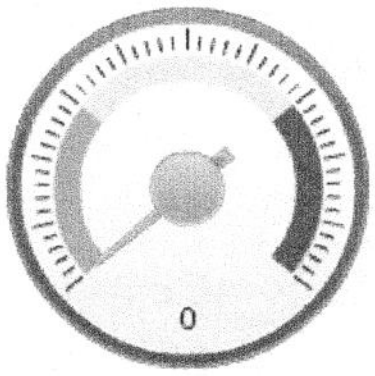

Figure 10-15 Marker option selected

Figure 10-16 Value option selected

Chart Component Alerts View Options

Figure 10-17 shows the chart alerts view options.

The options on the Alerts view that are different or are unique to charts are explained below.

The **AS PERCENT OF TARGET** option is used to type in or select the target value for the percent levels.

The Bind button is used to select the target range. Usually this value is 100. When creating a percent alert, you would enter a one in this field to represent 100%.

Clicking the Manual Edit button opens the dialog box shown in Figure 10-18. This is how you enter the **TARGET VALUES** for the low, middle and high value ranges that are needed for the alert.

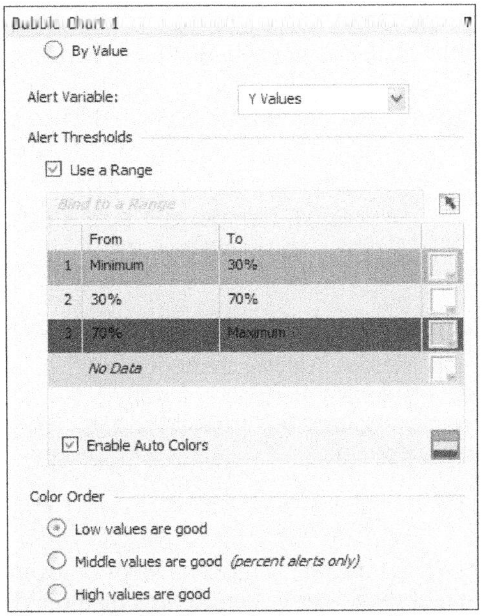

Figure 10-17 Chart alerts view options

ALERT VARIABLE Is used to select the X or Y axis values to trigger an alert. This option is only available for multi variable charts. Bubble and XY charts have multi variable functionality, because bubble charts require three variables (Size, X values and Y values), as shown in Figure 10-19 and XY charts require two variables to plot a point on the chart.

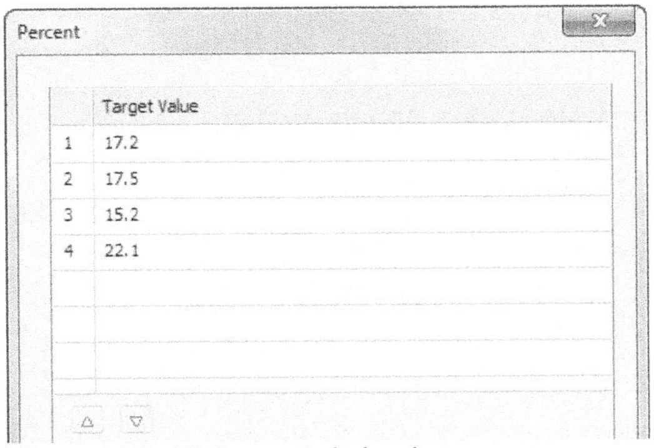

Figure 10-18 Percent dialog box

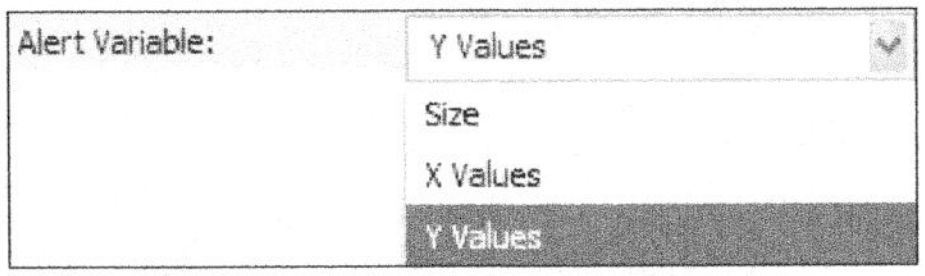

Figure 10-19 Alert Variable options

Components That Have Alerts

As you read earlier, not all components have alerts. Table 10-2 lists the components that have alert functionality.

Component Type	Components
Charts	Bar, Bubble, Column, Combination, Line, Radar, Stacked Bar, Stacked Column and XY.
Map	All map components.
Other	Grid.
Selectors	Combo Box, Icon, Label Based Menu, List Box, List Builder, Scorecard and Ticker.
Single Value	All components except the Play Control component.

Table 10-2 Components that have alerts

Charts that display multiple data series do not support alerts.

Scorecard Component And Alerts
Alerts can be enabled individually for different columns on a scorecard component.

Exercise 10.1: Create A Percent Alert Chart

In this exercise you will create a chart that has percent alerts for quarterly revenues. Figure 10-20 shows the data for this exercise.

	A	B	C	D	E
1	North America Revenues				
2				Actual Data	
3		Q1	Q2	Q3	Q4
4	Actual Values	$ 14.22	$ 20.12	$ 12.18	$ 25.49
5	Target	$ 17.20	$ 17.50	$ 15.20	$ 22.10

Figure 10-20 Alerts chart data

The Target amounts are the amount of revenue that a company wants to make. As you can see, some of the target values are less than the actual values (which would be good if the targets are realistic) and other target values are greater than the actual value. In most cases, this means that for the quarter, the company did not meet the projected target amount. On a chart that has alerts, quarters that fall into this category would be displayed in red, if the default alert colors are used.

1. Import the Alerts Charts spreadsheet.

2. Add the Column Chart component.

Select The Chart Options

1. On the General view, make the changes in the table.

Option	Change To
Chart	A1
Subtitle	Millions $
By Range	B4:E4
Category Labels (X)	B3:E3

2. On the Scale tab, make the changes in the table.

Option	Change To
Manual (Y) Axis	Select this option
Minimum Limit	10
Maximum Limit	30
Number of Divisions	4
Size of Divisions	5

3. On the Series tab, change the Marker Size option to 30.

Select The Alert Options

1. On the Alerts view, make the changes in the table.

Option	Change To
Enable Alerts	Select this option
As Percent of Target	Select this option
Target	B5:E5
High values are good	Select this option

2. If you open the Percent dialog box (click the Manual Edit button at the end of the As Percent of Target field) you will see the options shown earlier in Figure 10-18. If you look on the spreadsheet for this model, shown earlier in Figure 10-20, you will see that the values in the Target row are the same as the values in the Target Value column on the Percent dialog box.

Select The Range For The Alerts

Alert values need a range. The creator of this dashboard determined that the range values are as follows:

Red 0-90, means that the actual revenue is less than the target.
Yellow 90-110, means that the actual revenue is in the target range.
Green 110 +, means that the actual revenue is more than the target.

1. Change the values in the grid to match the ones shown in Figure 10-21.

	From	To
1	Minimum	90%
2	90%	110%
3	110%	Maximum

Figure 10-21 Alert range options

2. Save the model as `My alerts chart.`

   The model should look like the one shown in Figure 10-22.

   The alert colors let you know visually that in the first and third quarters, the actual revenue is less than the target revenue.

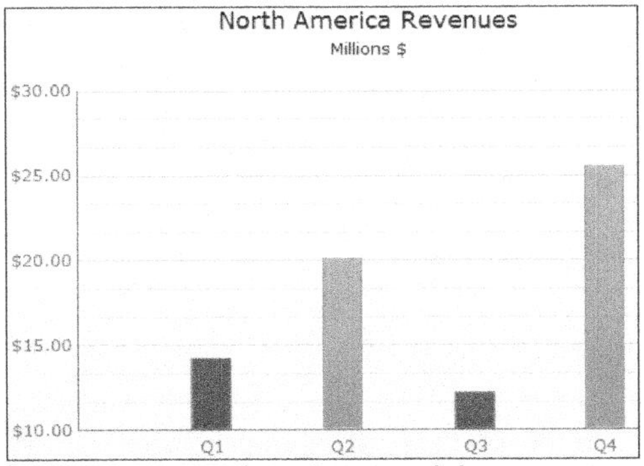

Figure 10-22 Alert chart model

The reason that you and I know what the colors represent is because we created the model. Users may not know this, which is why I think that it is a good idea to include what the colors represent on the dashboard. I can't imagine how confusing it would be for a user to understand a different set of alert colors on the next dashboard that you create, without including something to indicate what the colors represent.

Exercise 10.2: Create A Single Value Alert

The alert that you will create in this exercise will use three gauges to display actual balances versus the target balance. Figure 10-23 shows the data for this exercise.

	A	B	C	D
1	Summary Report			
2	Corporate Health Measures			
3				
4		Sales	Inventories	Cost of Goods Sold
5	Actual Value	$ 456.00	$ 78.00	$ 256.00
6	Target	$ 435.00	$ 54.00	$ 220.00

Figure 10-23 Single Value alert data

1. Import the Alerts Single Values spreadsheet.
2. Add the Gauge single value component, then add the Horizontal Slider component. Put it below the gauge.
3. Save the model as `My single value alerts`.

Select The Sales Gauge Options

In this part of the exercise you will set up three gauge components for sales, inventory and cost of goods sold. There is a column of data in the table for each gauge in each step. It will be easier to copy the first gauge after all of the options have been selected (in steps 1-4) and use it as the basis for the other two gauges, rather than create each gauge from scratch. As you go through each step, you only have to change what is different for the second and third gauge.

1. On the General view, make the changes in the table.

Option	Sales	Inventory	Cost of Goods
Title	B4	C4	D4
Data	B5	C5	D5
Minimum Limit	99	0	0
Maximum Limit	500	108	440

2. On the Common tab, make the changes in the table.

Option	All Gauges
Minimum Limit	Fixed
Maximum Limit	Fixed
Mouse Tracking	Radial

3. On the Layout tab, make the changes in the table.

Option	All Gauges
Manual	Select this option
Number of Major Ticks	11
Number of Minor Ticks	4
Minimum Angle	-130
Maximum Angle	130

4. On the Text tab, make the changes in the table, as illustrated in Figure 10-24.

Option	All Gauges
Show Value (Text)	Select this option
Offset X	0
Offset Y	35

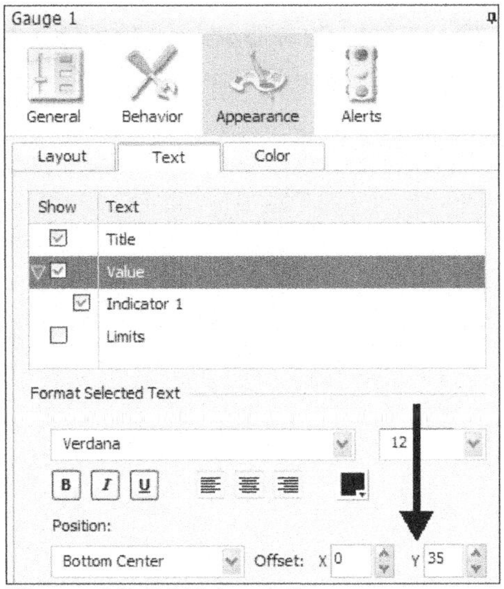

Figure 10-24 Value options

5. Make a copy of the Sales gauge component and place the copy to the right of the Sales gauge.
6. Repeat steps 1-4 above to set up the Inventory gauge.
7. Make a copy of the Sales gauge and place it to the right of the Inventory gauge.
8. Repeat steps 1-4 above to set up the Cost of Goods Sold gauge.
9. Save the changes.

Add The Alert Options

In this part of the exercise you will set up the alert functionality for the three gauge components that you just created.

Select The Alert View Options For The Sales Gauge

1. On the Alerts view, make the changes in the table.

Option	Change To
Enable Alerts	Select this option
As Percent of Target	Select this option
Target Value	B6
High values are good	Select this option
Background	Select this option
Marker	Select this option

2. Change the values in the grid to match the ones shown in Figure 10-25.

   0-80 red, 80-100 yellow, 100 green

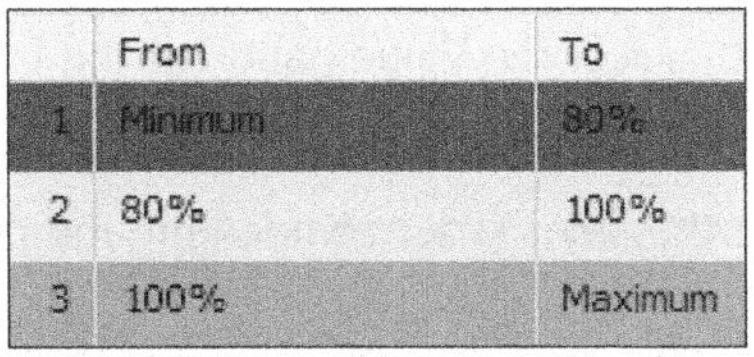

Figure 10-25 Sales range options

Select The Alert View Options For The Inventory Gauge

1. On the Alerts view, make the changes in the table.

Option	Change To
Enable Alerts	Select this option
As Percent of Target	Select this option
Target Value	C6
Middle values are good	Select this option

2. Change the values in the grid to match the ones shown in Figure 10-26.

   0-30 red, 30-70 yellow, 70-130 green, 130-170 yellow, 170+ red

	From	To
1	Minimum	30%
2	30%	70%
3	70%	130%
4	130%	170%
5	170%	Maximum

Figure 10-26 Inventory range options

Select The Alert View Options For The Cost Of Goods Sold Gauge

1. On the Alerts view, make the changes in the table.

Option	Change To
Enable Alerts	Select this option
As Percent of Target	Select this option
Target Value	D6
Low values are good	Select this option

2. Change the values in the grid to match the ones shown in Figure 10-27.

   0-74 green, 74-106 yellow, 106+ red

   Save the changes.

	From	To
1	Minimum	74%
2	74%	106%
3	106%	Maximum

Figure 10-27 Cost of Goods Sold range options

Set Up The Slider Component Options

In this part of the exercise you will set up three sliders, one for each gauge.

1. On the General view, make the changes in the table.

Option	Sales	Inventory	Cost of Goods
Data	B5	C5	D5
Minimum Limit	99	0	0
Maximum Limit	900	100	512

2. On the Common tab, select the Enable Play Button option.

3. On the Text tab, select the Value option at the top, then open the **POSITION** drop-down list and select Bottom Center.

4. Make a copy of the Sales slider component and place the copy to the right of the Sales slider.

5. Repeat steps 1-3 above to set up the Inventory slider by using the values in the Inventory column.

6. Make a copy of the Sales slider and place it to the right of the Inventory slider.

7. Repeat steps 1-3 above to set up the Cost of Goods slider by using the values in the Cost of Goods column.

8. Save the changes.

Finish And Test The Model

1. Add a Label Text component above the Inventory slider.

2. On the General view, type `Forecast` in the **ENTER TEXT** field.

3. On the Text tab, select the Center alignment option, then click the Bold button. Change the font size to 14.

4. Save the changes. The model should look like the one shown in Figure 10-28. Notice that the needle on each gauge changes color to match the section of the gauge that it is in. You can use the gauge as a selection tool just like you can use the slider.

   This means that you can move the needle on the gauge without using the slider.

   The play button on each slider can be started and stopped as needed.

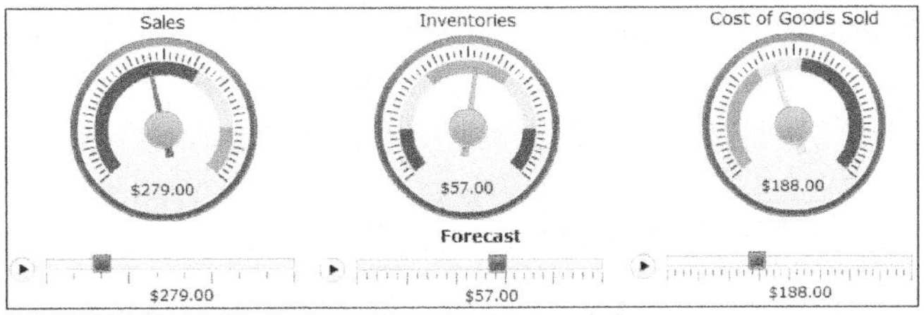

Figure 10-28 Single Value Alerts model

Selector Component Alerts

Alerts can be added to the following selector components: Combo Box, Label Based Menu, List Box, List Builder and Ticker. Components that have this functionality enabled, provide a visual representation of the value that is being displayed.

Selector Component Alerts View Options

Selector components that support alerts have the options explained below.

ALERT VALUES This option is used to select the range of values.

In the left column of the grid is an icon and check boxes, as illustrated in Figure 10-29. The check boxes are used to add an icon next to options on the component, as shown in Figure 10-30. The icons will change colors based on the alert values that are selected. If you only wanted to have the icon display a color for high values, you would clear the check mark from the rows in the grid for low and middle values.

> **Icon Component And Alerts**
> If the **ENABLE ALERTS** option shown in Figure 10-29 is selected, the Color option on the Color tab is disabled.

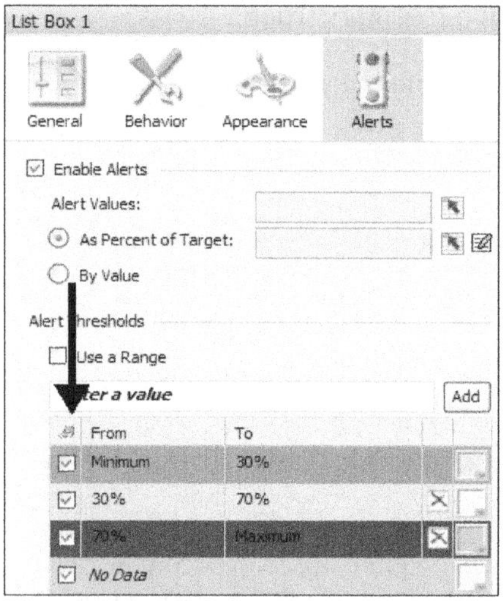

Figure 10-29 Selector component alert tab options

Figure 10-30 Alert icons added to selector component

Ticker Component

This component displays scrolling text from the spreadsheet horizontally. The Ticker component can be used as a display or selector component.

General View Options

The Ticker general view options are shown in Figure 10-31.

VALUE LABELS Is used to select the text that will be displayed on the component.

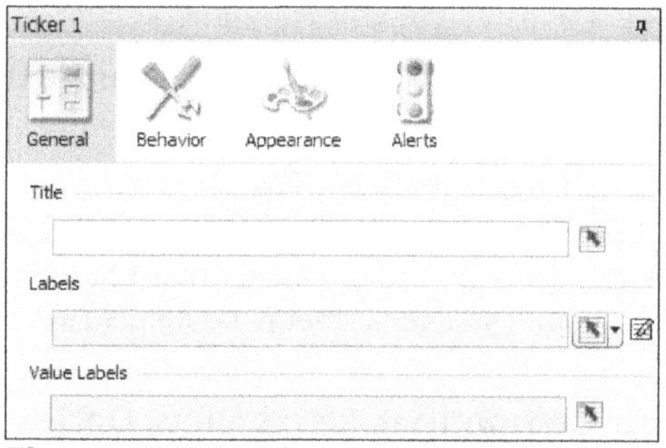

Figure 10-31 Ticker general view options

Common Tab Options

The Ticker common tab options are shown in Figure 10-32.

Ticker Options

ITEM SEPARATOR Is used to type in the character(s) that will be displayed between the items on the ticker.

SCROLL DIRECTION Is used to select the direction (left or right) that the information will scroll on the ticker.

SCROLL SPEED Use the slider to select how fast or slow the information on the ticker will scroll.

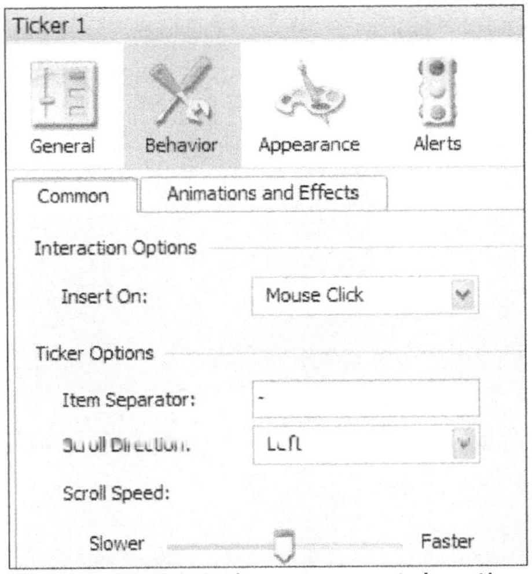

Figure 10-32 Ticker common tab options

Layout Tab Options

The Ticker layout tab option is shown in Figure 10-33.

SHOW TICKER BACKGROUND Is used to display a background color for the component.

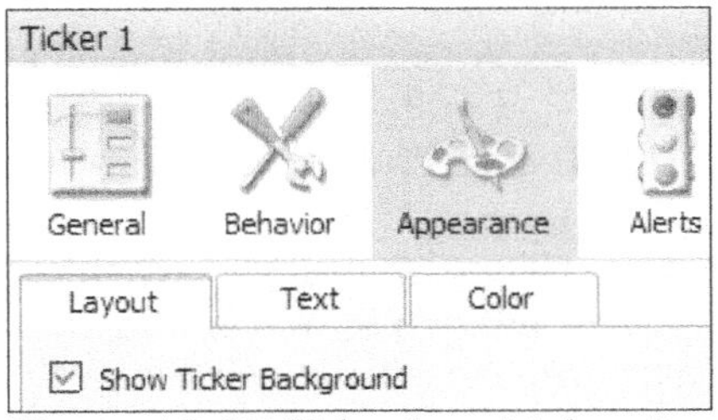

Figure 10-33 Ticker layout tab option

Text Tab Options

The Ticker text tab options are shown in Figure 10-34.

You may have noticed that you can manually change the width of the Ticker component, but not the height. The workaround to changing the height of the component is to increase the Labels font size.

DISPLAY VALUES Displays the data value for each item.

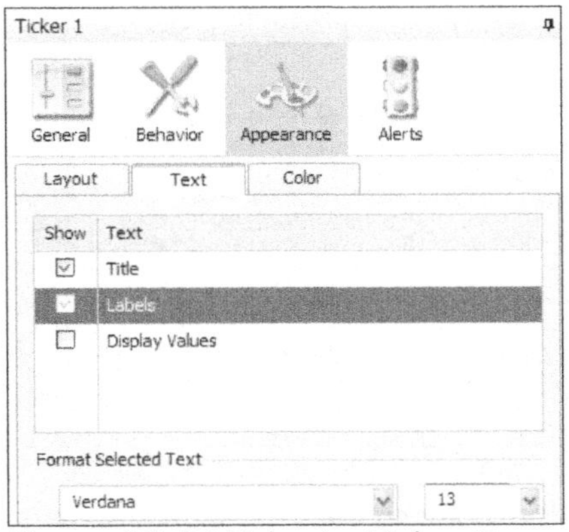

Figure 10-34 Ticker text tab options

Ticker Alert Functionality

Like the other components that support alert functionality and display different colors depending on the values, the Ticker component displays the colors in a different way. On this component, the alert value colors are displayed on an icon, which appears right before each value displayed on the ticker.

Color Tab Options

The Ticker color tab options are shown in Figure 10-35.

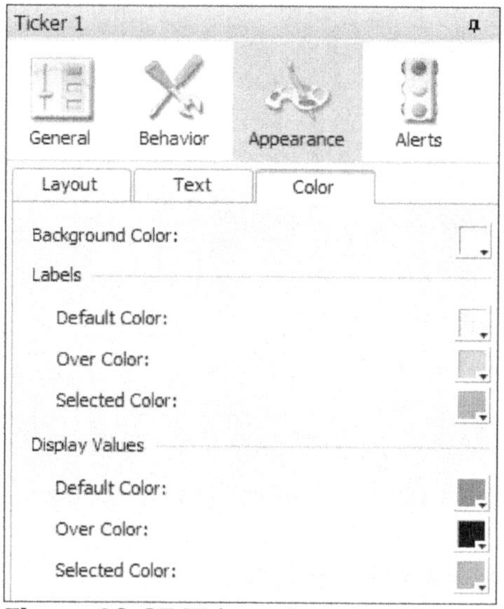

Figure 10-35 Ticker color tab options

BACKGROUND COLOR The **SHOW TICKER BACKGROUND** option on the Layout tab must be selected to select a background color.

Display Values Options

The color options for the labels are separate from the color options for the Display Values options.

DEFAULT COLOR Is used to change the color of the data displayed on the component.

OVER COLOR Is used to change the color of the data displayed on the component when the mouse pointer is hovered over it.

SELECTED COLOR Is used to change the color of the data displayed on the component when it is clicked on.

Exercise 10.3: Use The Ticker Component

In this exercise the Ticker component will be used as a selector component to display text and values for weekly sales by branch. When an item is clicked on the ticker, the corresponding daily sales data will be displayed on the chart. You will use the options on the Alerts tab to display different color buttons on the menu to indicate how the value compares to the target. Figure 10-36 shows the data for this exercise.

	A	B	C	D	E	F	G	H	I	J
1	**Ticker Insert In Row:**									
2										
3										
4										
5	**Actual Values**									**Targets**
6	Weekly Sales by Branch	Sun	Mon	Tue	Wed	Thu	Fri	Sat	Avg Sales	Avg Sales
7	Atherton	$ 19.70	$ 19.10	$ 18.30	$ 18.80	$ 19.80	$ 13.09	$ 19.96	$ 18.39	$ 18.00
8	Berkeley	$ 14.40	$ 18.00	$ 16.40	$ 16.70	$ 19.30	$ 19.16	$ 14.11	$ 16.87	$ 17.00
9	Carmel	$ 18.80	$ 13.50	$ 18.70	$ 13.90	$ 15.70	$ 15.23	$ 18.73	$ 16.37	$ 18.00
10	Cupertino	$ 12.00	$ 16.20	$ 17.50	$ 17.80	$ 13.80	$ 14.62	$ 18.27	$ 15.74	$ 17.00
11	Fremont	$ 19.20	$ 15.60	$ 19.60	$ 15.90	$ 14.40	$ 17.48	$ 18.14	$ 17.19	$ 16.00
12	Irvine	$ 18.90	$ 14.60	$ 16.70	$ 12.10	$ 13.90	$ 17.62	$ 12.34	$ 15.17	$ 16.00
13	Milpitas	$ 18.70	$ 17.80	$ 14.00	$ 18.50	$ 13.70	$ 15.77	$ 12.43	$ 15.84	$ 15.00
14	Orange County	$ 17.00	$ 19.40	$ 17.10	$ 17.30	$ 17.30	$ 15.93	$ 12.21	$ 16.61	$ 17.00
15	San Francisco	$ 14.40	$ 14.00	$ 13.90	$ 15.40	$ 18.30	$ 15.23	$ 17.06	$ 15.47	$ 15.00

Figure 10-36 Data for the ticker component

1. Save the dd_ticker model as `My ticker model.`

2. Add the Ticker component below the chart, then make it as wide as the chart.

Select The Ticker Options

1. On the General view, make the changes in the table.

Option	Change To
Labels	A7:A15
Value Labels	I7:I15
Insertion Type	Row
Source Data	A7:H15
Destination	A2:H2

2. On the Alerts view, make the changes in the table.

Option	Change To
Enable Alerts	Select this option
As Percent of Target	Select this option
Target Value	J7:J15
High values are good	Select this option

3. Change the values in the grid to match the ones shown in Figure 10-37.

   0-95 red, 95-100 yellow, 100+ green

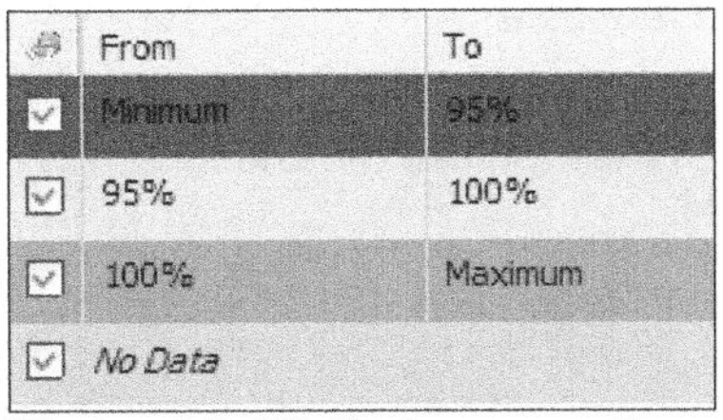

Figure 10-37 Alert range options

4. Enable the icons illustrated earlier in Figure 10-29 if they are not already selected.

   Save the changes.

   The ticker should scroll. Click on one of the branches in the ticker to display the daily sales for the branch in the chart, as shown in Figure 10-38.

   When you move the mouse pointer away from the ticker, it will scroll again.

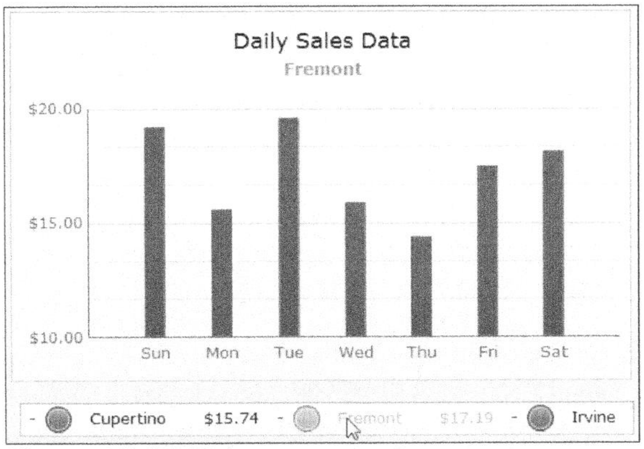

Figure 10-38 Ticker component

Exercise 10.4: Add Value Alert Functionality To The Label Based Menu Component

In this exercise you will learn how to add a value alert to a menu component. The model will display the daily sales for the product, by region, in a chart and the average sales for the product selected will be displayed on a gauge. Figure 10-39 shows the data for this exercise.

	A	B	C	D	E	F	G
1							
2		Region 1	Region 2	Region 3	Region 4		Average Sales
3	Product 1	$ 1.00	$ 9.00	$ 18.00	$ 16.00		$ 11.00
4	Product 2	$ 53.00	$ 74.00	$ 80.00	$ 92.00		$ 74.75
5	Product 3	$ 57.00	$ 7.00	$ 83.00	$ 60.00		$ 51.75
6	Product 4	$ 90.00	$ 71.00	$ 60.00	$ 40.00		$ 65.25
7	Product 5	$ 54.00	$ 36.00	$ 61.00	$ 23.00		$ 43.50
8	Product 6	$ 6.00	$ 9.00	$ 15.00	$ 14.00		$ 11.00
9	Product 7	$ 95.00	$ 62.00	$ 41.00	$ 84.00		$ 70.50

Figure 10-39 Value alert data

1. Save the dd_alert_selector model as `My alert selector`.

2. Add the Label Based Menu component to the left of the chart.

Select The Label Based Menu Component Options

1. On the General view, make the changes in the table.

   Resize the component as needed, so that seven buttons are showing.

Option	Change To
Labels	A3:A9
Insertion Type	Row
Source Data	A3:G9
Destination	A11:G11
Vertical	Select this option

2. On the Color tab in the Label Backgrounds section, make the changes in the table.

Option	Change To
Over Color	Beige
Selected Color	Brown

3. On the Alerts view, make the changes in the table.

Option	Change To
Enable Alerts	Select this option
Alert Values	G3:G9
By Value	Select this option
High values are good	Select this option

4. Change the values in the grid to match the ones shown in Figure 10-40.

   0-30 red, 30-70 yellow, 70+ green

   Enable the icons.

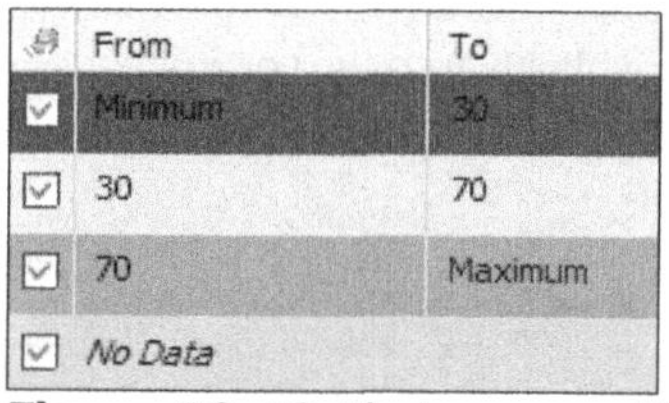

Figure 10-40 Alert range options

5. Save the changes.

   As you can see in Figure 10-41, each product on the menu has an alert level color button next to it. The colors will not change until either the data is modified or the alert level range is changed.

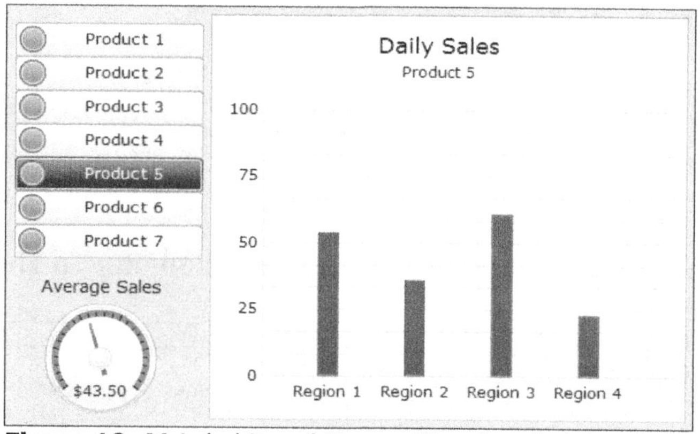

Figure 10-41 Label Based Menu with value alert functionality

NEW Scorecard Component

This component resembles the Grid component. The biggest difference is that the scorecard component uses symbols as visual alerts. Headers can be added to the columns to sort the data.

Common Tab Options

The Scorecard common tab options are shown in Figure 10-42.

ALLOW COLUMN SORTING If selected, users can sort the data by clicking on a column heading.

ROWS ARE SELECTABLE If selected, the scorecard component can be used as a selector component. This will allow users to click on a row of data that will be placed in the destination location.

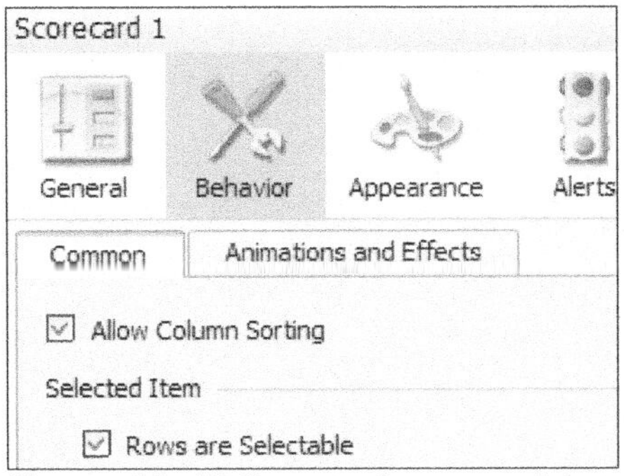

Figure 10-42 Scorecard common tab options

Color Tab Options

The Scorecard color tab options are shown in Figure 10-43. The majority of the options were covered in Chapter 9. [See Chapter 9, List View Component]

BORDER COLOR Is used to select the color for the border of the scorecard.

Rows Options

ROW COLOR Is used to select the default background color of the rows.

ALTERNATING ROW COLOR Is used to select the second background color for the rows. This color will appear in the background in every other row.

OVER COLOR Is used to change the background color of the row that the mouse pointer is hovered over.

SELECTED COLOR Is used to change the background color of the row that is clicked on.

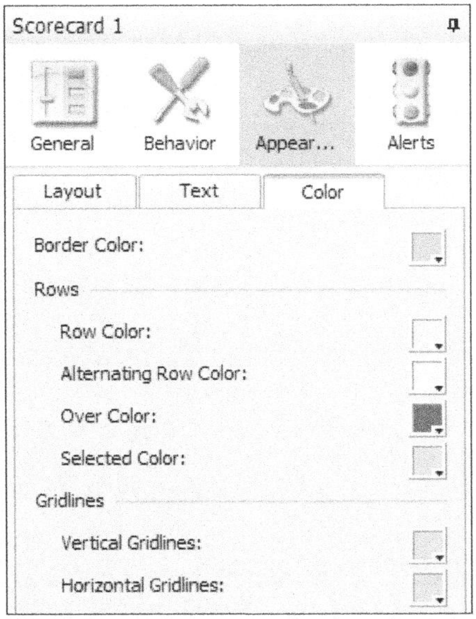

Figure 10-43 Scorecard color tab options

Gridlines Options

VERTICAL GRIDLINES Is used to change the color of the vertical gridlines in the grid.

HORIZONTAL GRIDLINES Is used to change the color of the horizontal gridlines in the grid.

MAP COMPONENTS

In this chapter you will learn how to use map components and how to configure a map to be used as an input selector.

CHAPTER 11

Overview

Map components display the data geographically, often by region, state or country. Dashboard Design has over 90 maps. There are different types of maps, including, country, region, province and more.

Each map has regions already set up. The characteristics of map components are:

① Maps show data for each region.
② Each region on a map can be used as a selector component to display data for that region in another component, like a chart, on the dashboard.
③ You can elect to have the data for each region appear when the mouse pointer is hovered over a region on the map.

How Do Map Components Work?

Overall, the map component gathers data differently then other components, even though the same options are used on the Properties panel. Depending on the map being used, the term region will refer to something different. On one map a region could refer to a state and on another map a region could refer to a country.

If you have an existing spreadsheet that has data by state or country for example, that you want to use to create a map, more than likely you will have to modify it before importing it into a model. The region names must be the first column of the spreadsheet.

One change that you may have to make is to create or edit the **REGION KEYS** in your spreadsheet. This could include changing the region names or adding region keys to the spreadsheet. For example, the USA (Continental) map uses the full state name as the region key, as shown in Figure 11-1.

If your spreadsheet currently uses the two character state abbreviations, you will not have to modify the spreadsheet, as long as the states are in the same order as shown in Figure 11-1.

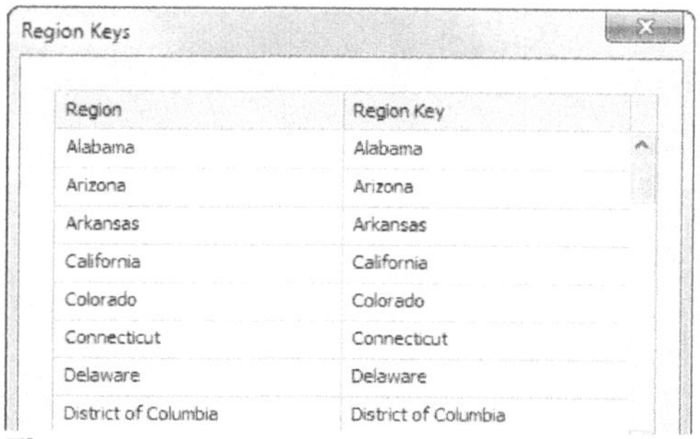

Figure 11-1 Region Keys dialog box

If you import your spreadsheet, the dialog box will look like the one shown in Figure 11-2, if you are using two character state abbreviations. Keep in mind that the values in the Region Key column is what will be displayed on the map. Figure 11-3 shows one state with a two character abbreviation and one state with the full name.

> The USA (Continental) map does not include Alaska or Hawaii. If you want a map with these states, select the USA map.

For a map to work, the region keys must be set up correctly because Dashboard Design links the data in a spreadsheet to a region in the map. By correctly, I mean that your data must be in the same order as it is in the Region Keys dialog box. Each region on the map has its own key. When the **SOURCE DATA, DISPLAY DATA** or **DESTINATION DATA** field is selected, the map component searches the first row or column of the cell range that is defined in the Region Key field for the codes. When the code is found, the data in the row or column is associated with the corresponding region on the map. It seems to me that there should be a way to let Dashboard Design know that the data in the spreadsheet is not in the same order as what the map component is expecting.

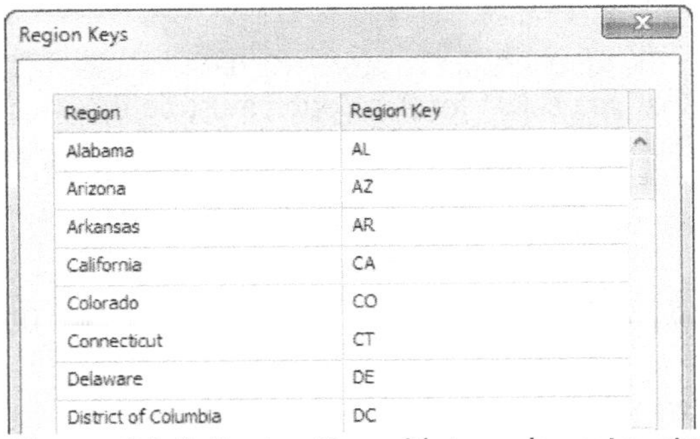

Figure 11-2 Region Key with two character state abbreviations

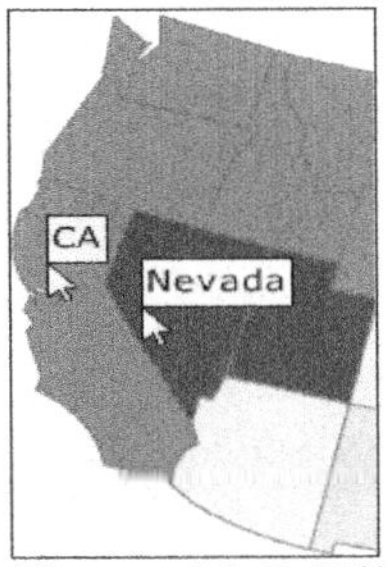

Figure 11-3 Differences in Region Keys

> **Default Region Keys**
> Dashboard Design comes with a spreadsheet that lists the default region keys for each map. The file is in the following location on your computers hard drive.
> C:\Program Files (x86)\SAP BusinessObjects\Xcelsius 4.0\Assets\Samples\User Guide Samples\Map Regions.xls Spreadsheet

Map Component

All of the map components have the options explained below.

General View Options

The Map general view options are shown in Figure 11-4.

TITLE Is used to enter the title for the map or select a cell in the spreadsheet that has the title. The default value for this field is the name of the map component.

REGION KEYS Is used to define the cell range for the codes for each region on the map.

There are two ways to select the region codes, as explained below.

① Select them from the spreadsheet.

② Click the Manual Edit button for the Region Keys option, then type in the region codes on the dialog box shown earlier in Figure 11-2.

DISPLAY DATA Is used to select the cells in the spreadsheet that have the region (on the USA map, this is the full state name) and the data for each state that should be displayed when the user clicks on a region on the map.

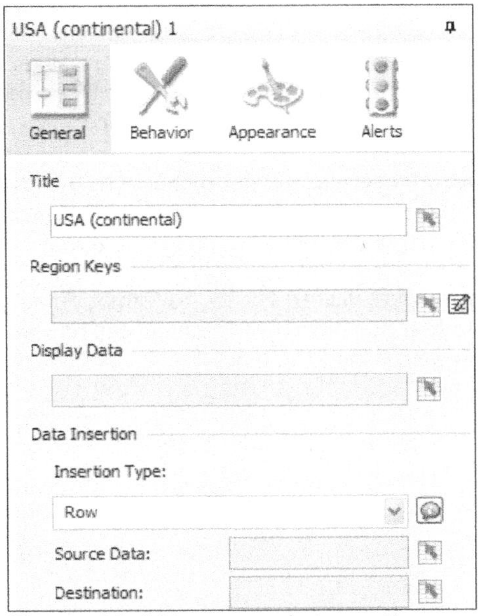

Figure 11-4 Map general view options

Data Insertion Options

INSERTION TYPE Is used to select how the region data should be added to the empty cells.

SOURCE DATA Is used to select the cells in the spreadsheet that have the regions and data for the map. This field configures the map to be used as a selector.

DESTINATION Is used to select a range of empty cells in the spreadsheet to store the data for the region that the user clicks on, on the map. The range that you select for this option must be the same (a row or column) as what is selected for the Insertion Type field.

Common Tab Options

The Map common tab options are shown in Figure 11-5.

Interaction Options

INSERT ON Is used to select how the component should recognize that an option on the map has been selected.

Default Selected Region Option

REGION Select the region that you want to be automatically selected when the dashboard is opened. The selected region will usually be a different color from all of the other regions on the map if you change the color for the Selected Color option on the Color tab.

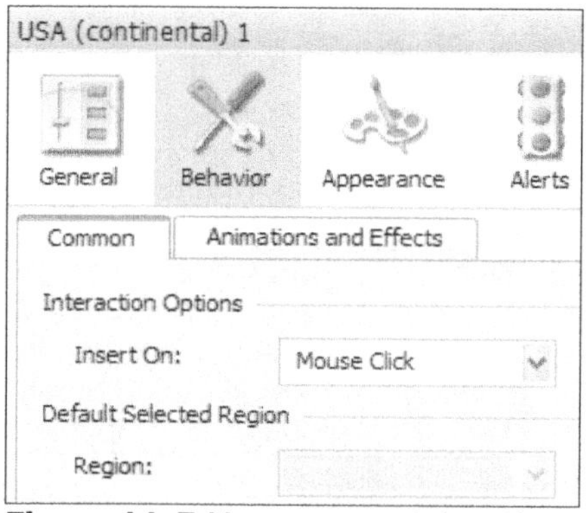

Figure 11-5 Map common tab options

Text Tab Options

The Map text tab options are shown in Figure 11-6.

Like charts, maps display mouse over values. They also display mouse-over labels when the mouse points to a region on the map.

MOUSE-OVER LABELS Is used to format the text that appears when the mouse is hovered over a section of the map.

MOUSE-OVER VALUES Is used to format numeric data that appears when the mouse is hovered over a section of the map.

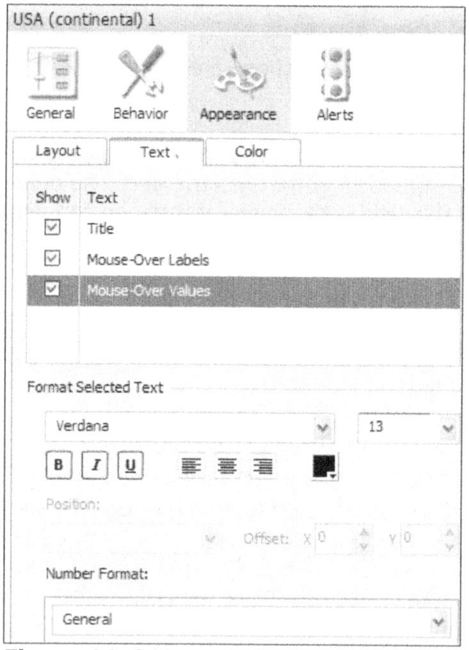

Figure 11-6 Map text tab options

Color Tab Options

The Map color tab options are shown in Figure 11-7.

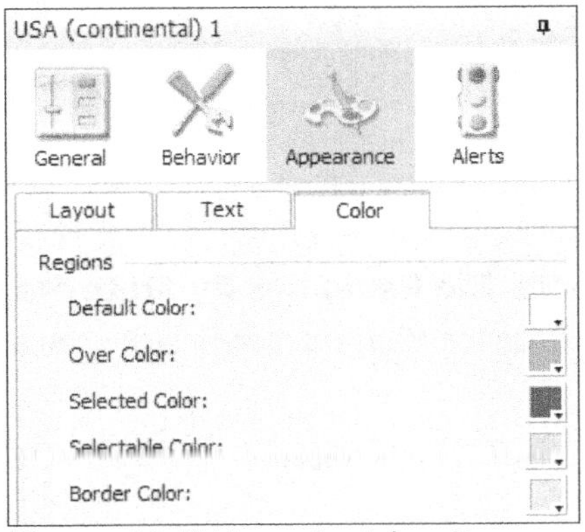

Figure 11-7 Map color tab options

Regions Options

The options in this section are used to customize the region colors on the map.

DEFAULT COLOR Is used to change the default color of regions that do not have source data.

OVER COLOR Is used to change the color of the region that the mouse pointer is hovered over.

SELECTED COLOR Is used to change the default color of the region that is clicked on.

SELECTABLE COLOR Is used to change the default color of regions that can be selected and have source data.

BORDER COLOR Is used to change the border color of the regions on the map.

Exercise 11.1: Create A Revenues By State Map

In this exercise you will create a map that displays the revenue when the mouse pointer is hovered over a region on the map. The map will also be used as an input selector for a chart. When a region is selected on the map, the corresponding data will be displayed in the chart below it. Figure 11-8 shows the data for this exercise.

	A	B	C	D	E	F	G	H	I	J	K	L
1	Revenues by State											
2												
3	Display Data Range			Source Data Range								
4	State	FY2012		State	FY2005	FY2006	FY2007	FY2008	FY2009	FY2010	FY2011	FY2012
5	Alabama	$ 31.66		Alabama	$ 28.23	$ 18.89	$ 21.89	$ 28.36	$ 24.85	$ 21.70	$ 20.21	$ 31.66
6	Arizona	$ 17.14		Arizona	$ 21.58	$ 17.11	$ 22.58	$ 24.11	$ 24.04	$ 19.27	$ 17.09	$ 17.14
7	Arkansas	$ 25.61		Arkansas	$ 17.64	$ 16.43	$ 22.96	$ 17.29	$ 25.74	$ 19.22	$ 19.23	$ 25.61
8	California	$ 23.92		California	$ 23.94	$ 23.93	$ 22.76	$ 26.20	$ 22.51	$ 17.74	$ 27.77	$ 23.92
9	Colorado	$ 17.69		Colorado	$ 16.45	$ 27.71	$ 28.40	$ 22.98	$ 18.13	$ 16.84	$ 26.13	$ 17.69
10	Connecticut	$ 28.93		Connecticut	$ 22.78	$ 20.08	$ 26.02	$ 28.89	$ 22.65	$ 20.15	$ 26.41	$ 28.93

Figure 11-8 State map data

1. Import the Map spreadsheet.

2. Save the model as `My USA map`.

Create The Chart

1. Add the Column Chart component near the bottom of the canvas.

2. On the General view, make the changes in the table.

    (1) To enable this option, select the **BY SERIES** option.

Option	Change To
Chart	A1
Subtitle	D55
Value (Y) Axis	Millions US
By Range	E55:L55
Category Labels (X) (1)	E4:L4

3. On the Scale tab, make the changes in the table.

Option	Change To
Manual (Y) Axis	Select this option
Maximum Limit	500
Auto (Y) Axis	Select this option

4. On the Series tab, change the Marker Size option to 30, then save the changes.

Create The Revenues By State Map

1. Open the Maps category folder, then add the USA (Continental) map component above the chart.
2. On the General view, make the changes in the table.

Option	Change To
Title	United States of America
Region Keys	A5:A53
Display Data	A5:B53
Insertion Type	Row
Source Data	D5:L53
Destination	D55:L55

3. On the Common tab, open the Region drop-down list and select Texas.

   Save the changes.

   When you click on a state in the map, the chart will display the revenue data by fiscal year for the state, as shown in Figure 11-9.

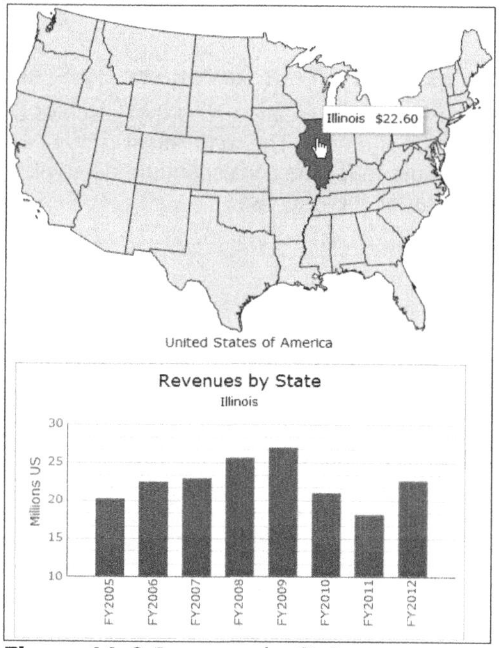

Figure 11-9 Revenues by State map

Mapping To Specific States

You do not have to provide data for all of the states on the map that you just created. The only requirement is that the states that you map to are adjoining states in the spreadsheet. Figure 11-10 shows a map with only 10 states (Delaware to Kentucky) that have data. If you click on or hold the mouse pointer over any other state, no information will be displayed.

To accomplish this, on the General view (of the Map Properties panel) I changed the Display Data option to A11:B20 and the Source Data option to D11:L20.

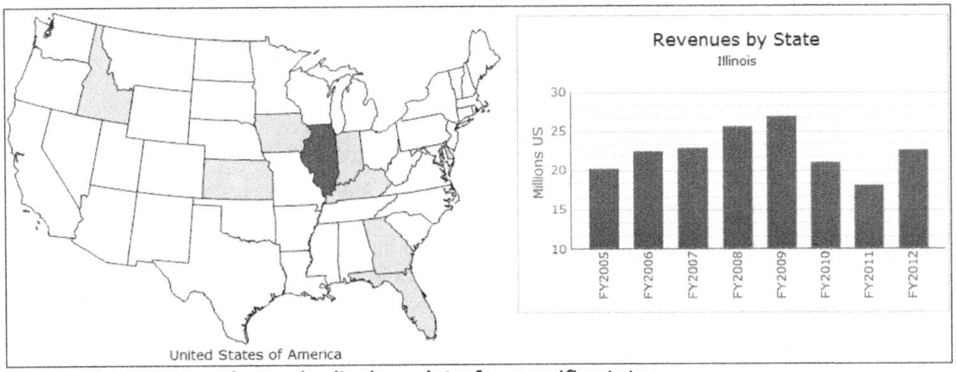

Figure 11-10 Map that only displays data for specific states

Exercise 11.2: Create A Map That Has Alerts

In this exercise you will create a map similar to the Revenues by State map that you created in Exercise 11.1.

The map that you will create will change the color of states on the map based on whether or not the annual fiscal year amount is below, above or within the target range.

Figure 11-11 shows the data for this exercise.

	A	B	C	D
1	Revenues by State			
2				
3	**Display Data Range**			
4		**Actual**		**Target**
5	**State**	FY2011	**State**	FY2011
6	Alabama	$ 31.66	Alabama	$ 28.00
7	Arizona	$ 17.14	Arizona	$ 27.90
8	Arkansas	$ 25.61	Arkansas	$ 19.88
9	California	$ 23.92	California	$ 19.85
10	Colorado	$ 17.69	Colorado	$ 21.30

Figure 11-11 Map with alerts data

1. Import the Alerts Map spreadsheet, then add the USA (Continental) map component.
2. Save the model as `My map with an alert.`
3. On the General view, make the changes in the table.

Option	Change To
Title	Revenue by State FY2011
Region Keys	A6:A54
Display Data	A6:B54
Insertion Type	Row

4. On the Text tab, change the Title font size to 18. Change the Position to Top Center.
5. On the Alerts view, select the following options: Enable Alerts and As Percent of Target.
6. Change the Target Value option to C6:D54.
7. Select the High values are good option.

8. Change the values in the grid to match the ones shown in Figure 11-12.

   0-50 red, 50-95 yellow, 95-100 green

	From	To
1	Minimum	50%
2	50%	95%
3	95%	Maximum

Figure 11-12 Alert range options

9. Save the changes. Your map should look like the one shown in Figure 11-13.
   Red represents states that the actual fiscal year revenue is below the target.
   Yellow represents states that the actual fiscal year revenue is in the acceptable target range.
   Green represents states that the actual fiscal year revenue is above the target range.

   If the alert levels were the following: 0-81 red, 81-98 yellow, 98-100 green, the map would look like the one shown in Figure 11-14.

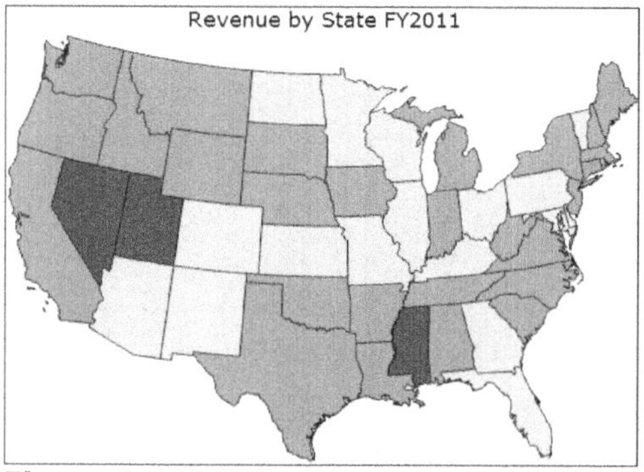

Figure 11-13 United States map with alerts

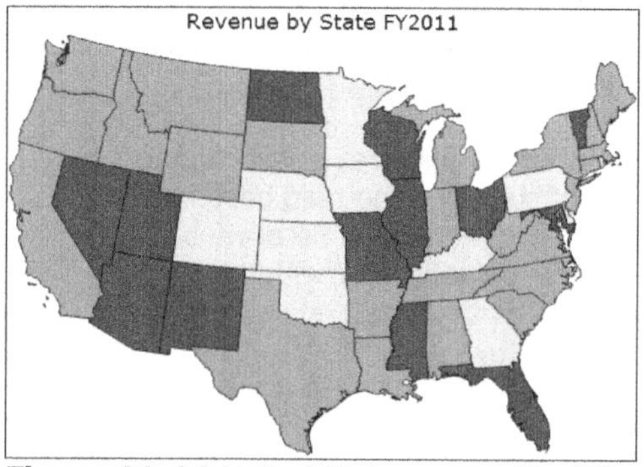

Figure 11-14 United States map with different alert level ranges

ENHANCING DASHBOARDS

In this chapter you will learn about the following types of components that are used to enhance the appearance of dashboards.

☑ Art and Backgrounds
☑ Text
☑ Web Connectivity
☑ Other

You will also learn how to refresh the data in a dashboard.

CHAPTER 12

Overview

You have created and edited a lot of models in this book. While they are effective and will get the job done, they could be enhanced to have a more professional look. That is the goal of this chapter, to discuss enhancement options and show you how to implement them. The options explained in this chapter are not a definitive list of enhancements. Hopefully though, they will be enough to bring out your creative side. The two things that I hope that you keep in mind are:

① More than likely you will not be the only person that will use or see the dashboard. That means that you should listen to what other people say about the functionality of the dashboard. Make sure that you have incorporated all of the requirements.

② While it is very easy to add every bell and whistle, it is a better idea to have as much consistency as possible from one dashboard to the next, especially if you are designing a series of dashboards for the same users. This includes tasks like putting the corporate logo in the same place on each dashboard or using the same color scheme for all of the dashboards in the series. If several dashboards contain alerts, I believe that it will be more helpful if they use the same colors to indicate low, middle and high values in each dashboard, unless users request different colors for a reason. That way, users will know what each color represents, when they use different dashboards.

Art And Backgrounds Components

These components are used to add more flair or personality if you will, to a dashboard to customize it. They are explained in Table 12-1.

Component	Description
Background	Adds a background image or color to the model.
Image Component	Allows JPG image or SWF files, animations, logos and videos to be imported into the model.
Rectangle	Adds a square to the model. This component is often used as a border around other components.
Ellipse	Adds an ellipse object to the model.
Horizontal Line	Adds a horizontal line to the model.
Vertical Line	Adds a vertical line to the model.

Table 12-1 Art and Backgrounds components explained

Background Component

In addition to using this component to add a visual effect to the dashboard, this component can be used to prevent the user from using a component on the dashboard. To accomplish this, place the background component over the component that you do not want to be used. On the General view, set the Background component transparency option to 100%, then select the Block Mouse Events option on the General view.

General View Options

The Background component general view options are shown in Figure 12-1.

BACKGROUND COLOR Is used to change the color of the background component. The default background color is determined by the color scheme of the dashboard. [See Chapter 16, Color Schemes]

BORDER SCALE Is used to adjust the width of the background components border.

BLOCK MOUSE EVENTS Is used to prevent the user from using other components on the dashboard. For this feature to work, the background component has to be layered on top of the components that you do not want the user to interact with.

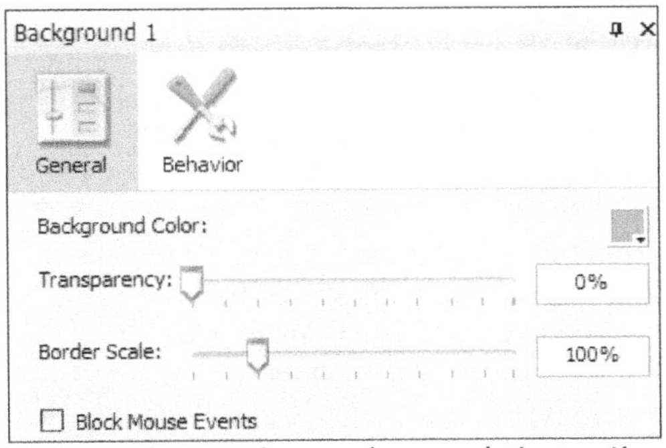

Figure 12-1 Background general view options

Exercise 12.1: Add A Background Component To A Model

In this exercise you will add a background component to a model that you already created.

1. Save the My filter drop-down list model as `My background`.
2. Add the Background component, then make it large enough to cover the two components already on the canvas.
3. On the General view of the background component, move the **BORDER SCALE** slider to the right, past the half way mark.
4. Right-click on the background component and select **SEND TO BACK**.
5. Resize and adjust the background component as needed.

   Save the changes.

   The model should look like the one shown in Figure 12-2.

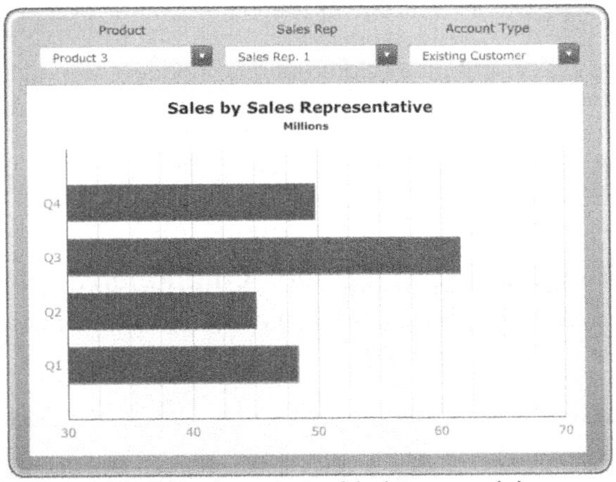

Figure 12-2 Background added to a model

Image Component

By default, the Image Component is an empty container. You have to add a file to it before it has any functionality. The following file types can be used with this component: JPG, SWF, GIF, BMP and PNG. If the model references an external file, Adobe security restrictions will automatically be enabled. When run from a computers hard drive, the file has to be made trusted.

General View Options

The Image component general view options shown in Figure 12-3 are used to select, import and configure the image.

As you read in Table 12-1, you can add images to a component, similar to how images are added to the Fisheye and Sliding Picture Menu components.

JPEG Or SWF Options

IMPORT BUTTON Is used to select the image file to be imported into the Image Component.

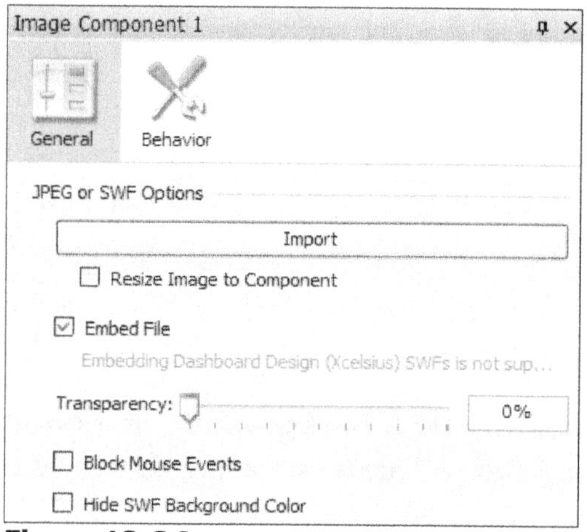

Figure 12-3 Image component general view options

> When SWF files are imported using the Image component, the SWF file is an external file. When the dashboard is exported, the SWF files that were imported are placed in a folder with the final dashboard.

RESIZE IMAGE TO COMPONENT If checked, the imported file will be resized to fit the size of the Image component. If this option is not checked, the image file will be displayed in its actual size.

EMBED FILE If checked, a copy of the image file will be embedded in the model.

BLOCK MOUSE EVENTS [See Background Component General View Options, earlier in this chapter] Mouse events are blocked for imported SWF files, even if this option is not enabled.

HIDE SWF BACKGROUND COLOR If checked, the background of the SWF file that will be imported, will be invisible.

Exercise 12.2: Use The Image Component

In this exercise you will add an Image Component to an existing model. This is how you would add a corporate logo to a dashboard.

1. Save the My background model as `My image model.`
2. Add the Image Component to the top of the canvas.
3. On the General view, click the Import button, then double-click on one of the image files in your folder.
4. Save the changes.

   You should see the image that you selected above the chart, as shown in Figure 12-4.

Figure 12-4 Image added to the model

Ellipse And Rectangle Components

These components are used to add shapes to a model. They have the same options on the Properties panel.

General View Options

The options shown in Figure 12-5 are used to customize the ellipse and rectangle components.

The options on this view are used to select whether or not the ellipse or rectangle border should be displayed, as well as, the thickness, transparency and color of the border.

ENABLE BORDER Select this option if you want the ellipse or rectangle to display a border.

COLOR Is used to change the color of the border of the component. (1)

THICKNESS Is used to change the width of the components border. (1)

TRANSPARENCY Is used to select how visible the border color is. (1)

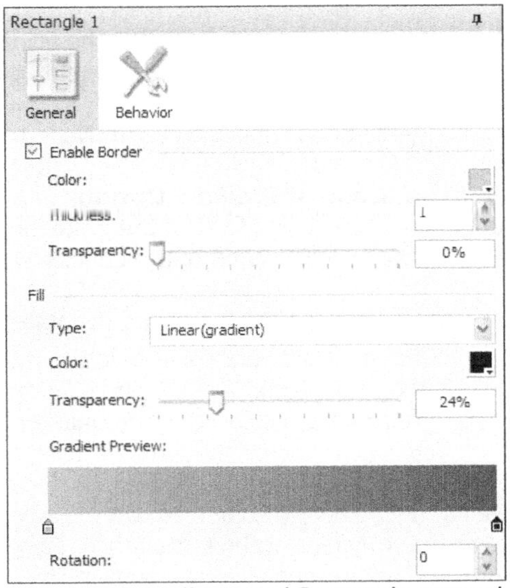

Figure 12-5 Ellipse and Rectangle general view options

(1) The Enable Border option must be enabled to use this option.

Fill Options

The options in this section are used to select the color and shading of the interior (background) of the component.

TYPE Is used to select one of the options shown in Figure 12-6. These options determine how the color is displayed in the ellipse or rectangle. The options are explained in Table 12-2.

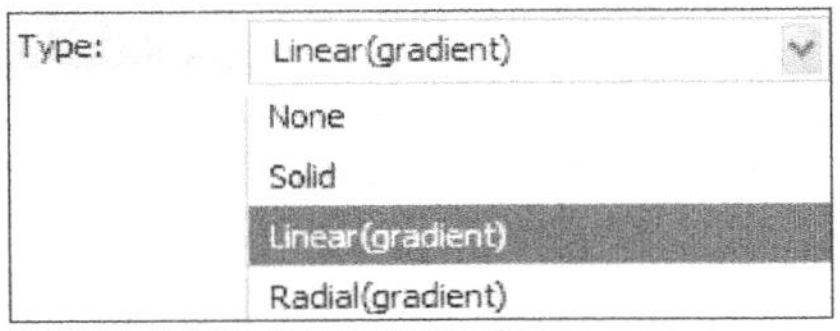

Figure 12-6 Type options

Type	Description
None	The shape will not have a fill color. The inside of the shape will be transparent.
Solid	The fill color is only one color.
Linear (gradient)	The fill color changes from side to side on the component. Selecting this option enables the Rotation option. (2)
Radial (gradient)	The fill color changes from the center to the edge of the component. The left marker is for the color in the center of the object. The marker on the right is for the color near the edge of the object. (2)

Table 12-2 Type (fill color) options explained

(2) Selecting this option enables the Gradient Preview option.

COLOR Is used to change a color of the interior of the ellipse or rectangle. (3)

TRANSPARENCY Is used to select how much of the interior area of the ellipse or rectangle the color should cover. Selecting zero will fill the interior to the border. (3)

GRADIENT PREVIEW Is used to display the transition between two or more colors. It is only enabled if Linear or Radial is selected in the Type drop-down list.

(3) The Type option cannot be set to None to use this option.

Using The Gradient Preview Option

In addition to being able to view the gradient color pattern, the following functionality is available in the gradient preview section of the general view.

① The triangle can be moved to rotate the gradient color.

② To add a gradient color, hold the mouse pointer over the location where you want to add the color. When you see the plus sign shown in Figure 12-7, click in the preview area.

③ To remove a color, drag the marker for the color away from the Gradient Preview box.

If you look closely on your computer screen you will see the color that each marker (the triangles at the bottom of Figure 12-7) represents is at the bottom of the triangle.

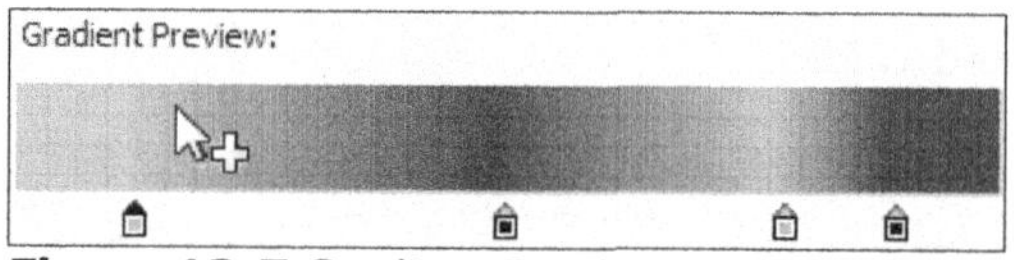

Figure 12-7 Gradient Preview section of the general view

ROTATION Is used to change how the Type (fill style) color is displayed. This option will remind you of the gradient options that many image software packages have. The Type option has to be set to Linear (gradient) to use this option.

Figure 12-8 shows the ellipse with the linear (gradient) Type option selected and the Rotation option set to 10.

Figure 12-9 shows the ellipse with the linear (gradient) Type option selected and the Rotation option set to 100.

Figure 12-10 shows the ellipse with the radial Type option selected.

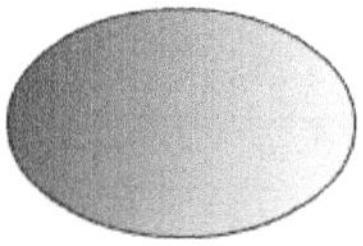

Figure 12-8 Ellipse with rotation set to 10

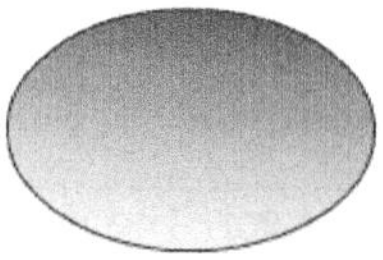

Figure 12-9 Ellipse with rotation set to 100

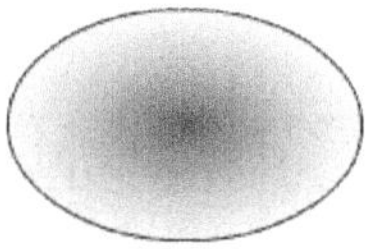

Figure 12-10 Ellipse with the radial type option selected

Resizing The Ellipse And Rectangle Components
If you want to resize these components and keep the ratio of the axes of the ellipse or the sides of the rectangle, hold down the Shift key when you resize the component.

Vertical And Horizontal Line Components

The Vertical Line and Horizontal Line components have the same options. These components are used to add lines to the model, usually to give the dashboard the appearance of having different sections.

General View Options

The vertical and horizontal line general view options are shown in Figure 12-11.

LINE COLOR Is used to change the border color.

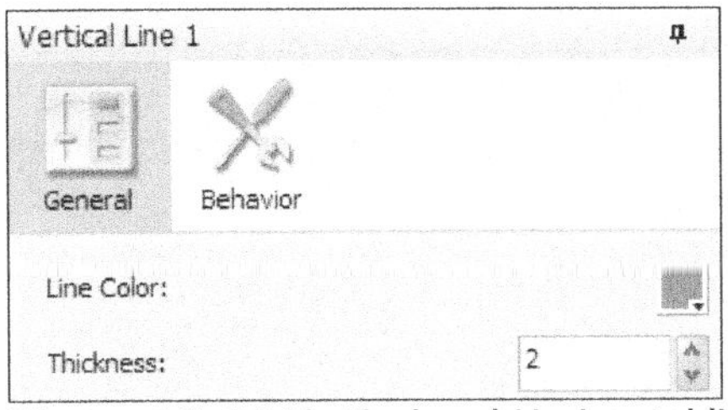

Figure 12-11 Vertical and Horizontal line general view options

Preventing User Input

Earlier in this chapter you read that the Background component could be used to prevent users from using a component. The other ways to prevent user input for single value components are explained below.

① Clear the **ENABLE INTERACTION** option on the Common tab on the components Property panel.
② **BIND THE COMPONENT** to a cell in the spreadsheet that has a formula.

Text Components

The components in this category are used to add free standing text and labels to the model. The values that are displayed in the **ENTER TEXT** option of text components do not change when the data in the model is updated. Table 12-3 explains both types of text components.

Component	Description
Input Text	Is used to let users type in the field.
Input Text Area	This component is similar to the Input Text component. The difference is that the user can type multiple lines of text in the field.
Label	Users cannot type in this field. An unlimited amount of text can be entered in the label. This component is often used to create titles and other information to display on the dashboard.

Table 12-3 Text component types explained

Input Text Area Component

General View Options

The Input Text Area general view options are shown in Figure 12-12.

Default Text Options

LINK TO CELL Is used to select the text from the spreadsheet that will be displayed in the Input Text field. Dynamic labels can be created by using formulas that update the data based on what the user selects.

ENTER TEXT Is used to type in the default text that will be displayed in the Input Text field on the model. Select this option if the text that you need to initially display is not in the spreadsheet.

ENABLE HTML FORMATTING If checked, text can be displayed in HTML format. The HTML tags shown in Figure 12-13 are the ones that you can use in Dashboard Design.

Data Insertion Options

INSERT DATA ON LOAD Is used to select the default text that will be added to the Destination option when the dashboard is run.

DESTINATION Is used to select the cell where the text will be added. The destination cells must be empty.

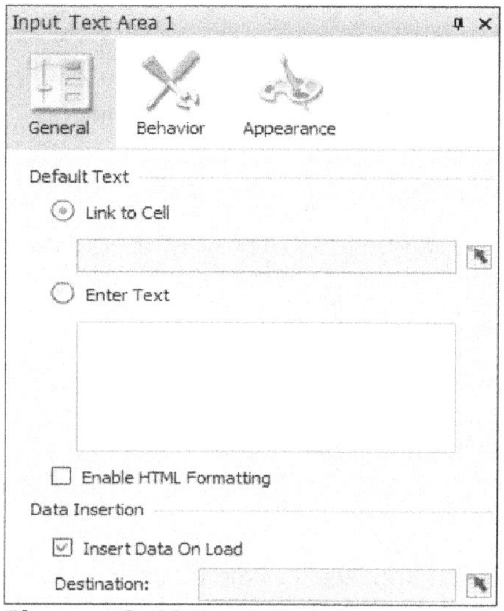

Figure 12-12 Input Text Area general view options

Anchor tag (<a>)
Bold tag (<b>)
Break tag (<br>)
Font tag (<font>)
Image tag (<img>)
Italic tag (<i>)
List item tag (<li>)
Paragraph tag (<p>)
Text format tag (<textformat>)
Underline tag (<u>)

Figure 12-13 HTML supported tags

Common Tab Options

The Input Text Area common tab options are shown in Figure 12-14.

Input Options

TREAT ALL INPUT AS TEXT If checked, the input from the user is treated as text. If not checked, the input is treated as numeric and can be used in formulas.

MAXIMUM NUMBER OF CHARACTERS Is used to enable and select the maximum number of characters that a user can enter in the field.

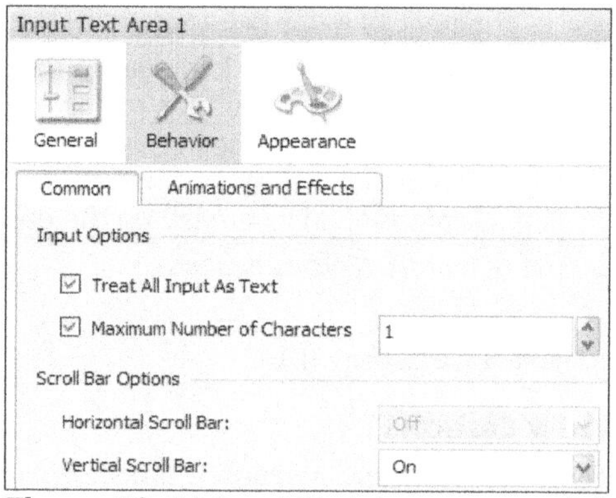

Figure 12-14 Input Text Area common tab options

Scroll Bar Options

The options in this section are used to add scroll bars if the text in the field is more than what the component can display. [See Chapter 9, Spreadsheet Table Component Common Tab Options]

Layout Tab Options

The Input Text Area layout tab options are shown in Figure 12-15.

WRAP TEXT If checked, text that is entered will automatically wrap to the next line if it is longer than the width of the component.

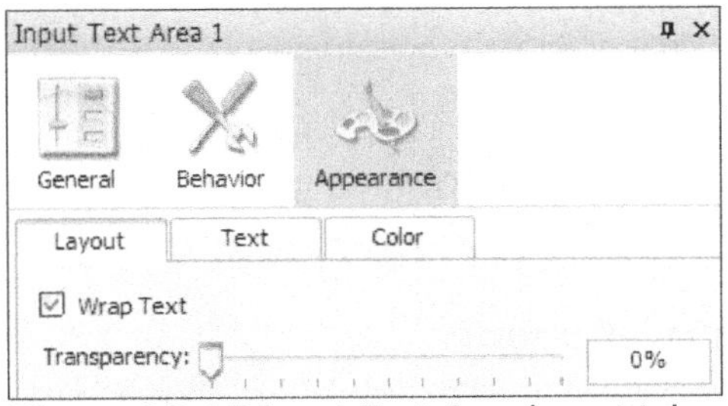

Figure 12-15 Input Text Area layout tab options

Web Connectivity Components

The components in this category allow Internet functionality to be added to a dashboard. Table 12-4 explains the Web Connectivity components.

Component	This Component . . .
URL Button	Is used to link to a web address when clicked.
Reporting Services Button	Is used to connect to a Reporting Services server (like Microsoft SQL Server Reporting Services) to select a report to use for the data of the model.
Slide Show	Creates a slide show that uses images and SWF files that are stored on the Internet. The files do not have to be imported into the model.
SWF Loader	Is similar to the Slide Show component because it loads SWF files from the specified URL without having to import the files.
Connection Refresh Button	Is used to allow users to refresh the data that is in the dashboard.

Table 12-4 Web Connectivity components explained

URL Button Component

General View Options

The URL Button general view options are shown in Figure 12-16.

LABEL Is used to select the cell or type in the text that will appear on the button.

URL Is used to select the web site that you want the button to open, when clicked. The button is updated automatically when the value in the cell changes.

NEW **ENCODE URL** Select this options if you want the special characters in the URL to be converted to ASCII format.

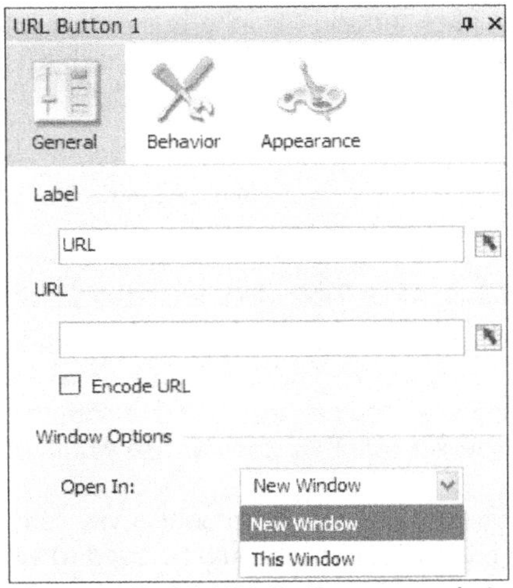

Figure 12-16 URL Button general view options

Window Options

The **OPEN IN** option is used to select whether or not the file or web site should be opened in a new browser window or in the browser window that is already open.

The **THIS WINDOW** option will open the link in the same window as the dashboard. This option does not provide a way to go back and view the dashboard with the data that was displayed before clicking the URL button.

Common Tab Options

The URL Button common tab options are shown in Figure 12-17.

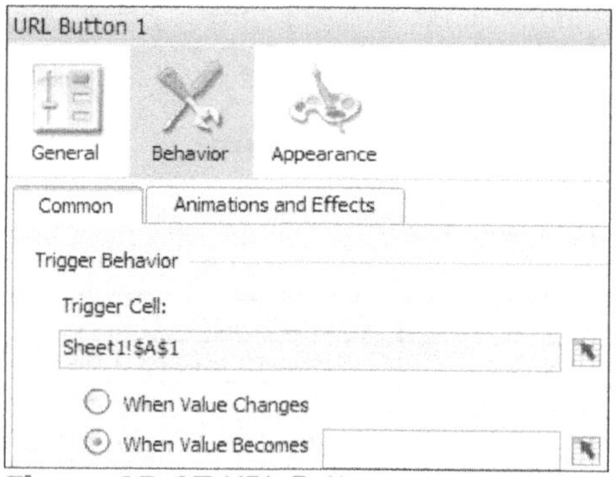

Figure 12-17 URL Button common tab options

Trigger Behavior Options

These options are used to have the web site open if a value is added (inserted) in a specific field or if the value in a field changes.

TRIGGER CELL Select the cell that will trigger the URL button. This means that the button will be activated (in this case, clicked) when the value in the cell that you select changes.

WHEN VALUE CHANGES Select this option if you want the URL Button to be activated when the value in the Trigger Cell field changes.

WHEN VALUE BECOMES Select this option if you want the URL Button to be activated when the value in the trigger cell is set to a specific value.

Layout Tab Options

The URL Button layout tab option is shown in Figure 12-18.

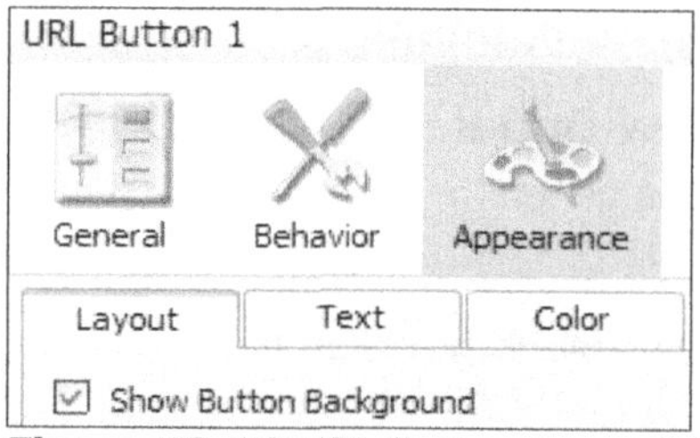

Figure 12-18 URL Button layout tab options

SHOW BUTTON BACKGROUND Clearing this option will make the button transparent, which means that only the text will appear. This will cause the label to look like a hyperlink.

Exercise 12.3: Use The URL Button Component

If there is information on a web site that would be helpful to the dashboard user or information that would enhance the dashboard, you can create a button that is linked to the web site or specific page on a web site. You can also use this component to link to a file (like a spreadsheet) on the Internet or a server. Another popular use would be to link to a PDF file.

In this exercise you will add web connectivity to the filter drop-down list model that you created. In this model, the URL Button could be used to view information about the products that the sales reps sell.

1. Save the My filter drop-down list model as `My URL product link`.

2. Move the chart down, then add the URL Button component right above the chart.

3. On the General view, make the changes in the table.

Option	Change To
Label	View Products Online
URL	http://www.tolanapublishing.com

You have to type the http:// or https:// in the URL field.

4. Make the button larger so that all of the text on it is visible.

5. Save the changes.

   The model should look like the one shown in Figure 12-19.

   If your computer is connected to the Internet and you click on the button, the web site that you typed in will open in a browser window.

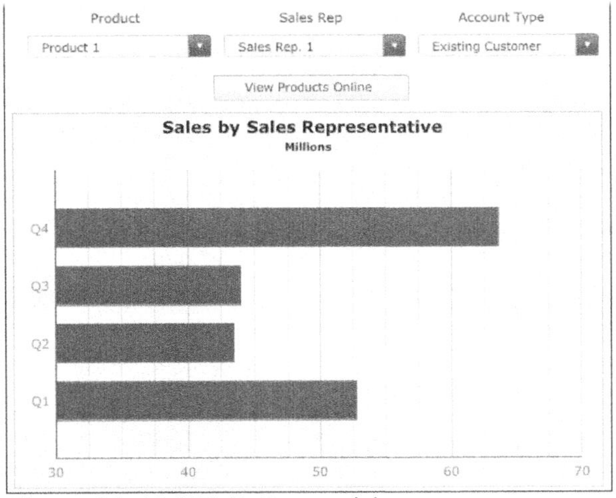

Figure 12-19 URL Button model

NEW Reporting Services Button Component

(This component is not available in Presentation Design)

General View Options

The Reporting Services Button general view options are shown in Figure 12-20.

LABEL Is used to enter the text that you want to appear on the button.

SELECT REPORT BUTTON Clicking this button opens the Select Report dialog box, which is used to select the report that has the data that you want to use to create the dashboard model.

Reporting Parameters Options

DISPLAY PARAMETERS AT RUN TIME Is used to display the reports parameters when the model is run.

USE SERVICE VALUES Is used to select the parameter that the report will use to retrieve the data.

LINK TO CELL Is used to select a cell in the spreadsheet embedded in the model that the report will use as the parameter value.

Data Mapping Options

The options in this section are used to map the data from the report to the model.

DEFAULT This option will use the default data maps.

ADVANCED Is used to set up the data maps by using one of the three options explained below.

① **MAPPED RANGES** The options in this list are the existing mapped ranges.
② **SELECTED COLUMNS** The options in this list are the columns of data for the mapped range that is selected. The Up and Down buttons will change the order of the columns. The X button deletes the column of data that is selected.
③ **NAME** Is used to type in a name for the selected range.

RANGE Is used to select the destination location in the embedded spreadsheet for the report data.

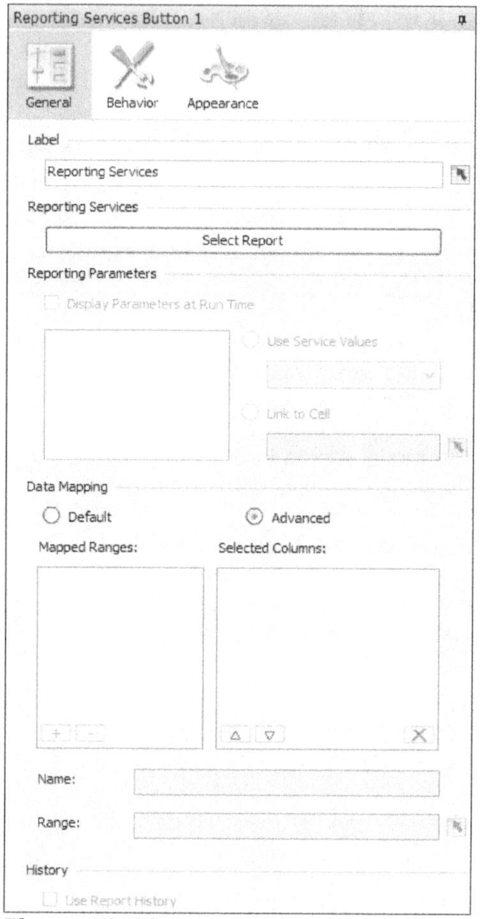

Figure 12-20 Reporting Services Button general view options

Common Tab Options

The Reporting Services Button common tab options are shown in Figure 12-21.

Refresh Options

REFRESH BEFORE COMPONENTS ARE LOADED If checked, the Reporting Services are loaded before the components are loaded at run time.

REFRESH EVERY If necessary, select the interval that the data should be refreshed automatically.

Load Status Options

LOADING MESSAGE Type in or select the cell in the spreadsheet that has the message to display when the query data connection is loading.

IDLE MESSAGE Type in or select the cell in the spreadsheet that has the message to display when the query data connection is idle.

INSERT IN Is used to select the cell to store the loading and idle messages.

ENABLE LOAD CURSOR If checked, a special cursor is displayed when the data from the report is loading.

DISABLE MOUSE INPUT ON LOAD If checked, user input is disabled while the data from the report is loading.

Trigger Behavior Options

[See URL Button Common Tab Options, earlier in this chapter]

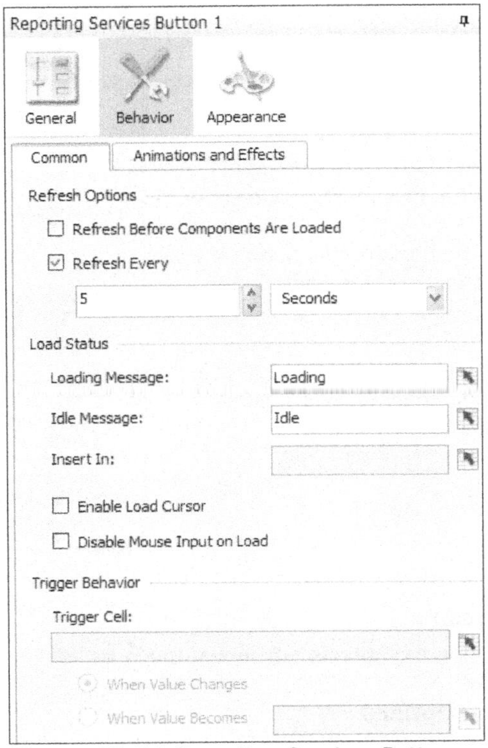

Figure 12-21 Reporting Services Button common tab options

Color Tab Options

The Reporting Services Button color tab options are shown in Figure 12-22.

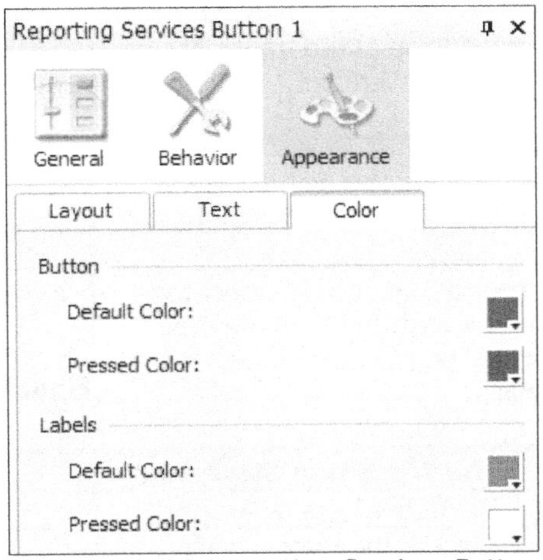

Figure 12-22 Reporting Services Button color tab options

Button Options

DEFAULT COLOR Is used to select the buttons background color.

PRESSED COLOR Is used to select the background color for the button when it is clicked.

Labels Options

DEFAULT COLOR Is used to select the color for the text on the button.

PRESSED COLOR Is used to select the color for the text on the button, when it is clicked.

Slide Show Component (This component is not available in Presentation Design)

This component is used to create a slide show of images or SWF movie files that are on the Internet. Each time the dashboard is run, the component will load the images or SWF files that are in the location listed in the URL option on the General view. The source files do not have to be imported.

General View Options

The Slide Show general view option is shown in Figure 12-23.

URL (JPEG OR SWF ONLY) Is used to type in or select the location of the files for the slide show.

BLOCK MOUSE EVENTS If checked, this option keeps the user from interacting with the Slide Show component.

APPLICATION DOMAIN This option is used to select which domain the Slide Show or SWF Loader model will be loaded into.

Figure 12-23 Slide Show general view options

Common Tab Options

The Slide Show common tab options are shown in Figure 12-24.

Transition Behavior Options

The options in this section are used to set the style and timing of the transition from one file to another.

TRANSITION TYPE Is used to select the effect that will appear between each file. The options in this drop-down list will remind you of the transitions in the presentation software PowerPoint.

EASING TYPE Is used to select how slow the slide show will open, close or both. The options are explained in Table 12-5.

TRANSITION TIME (SECONDS) Is used to select the time in seconds between each frame in the slide show. The transition will be smoother if the transition time is small.

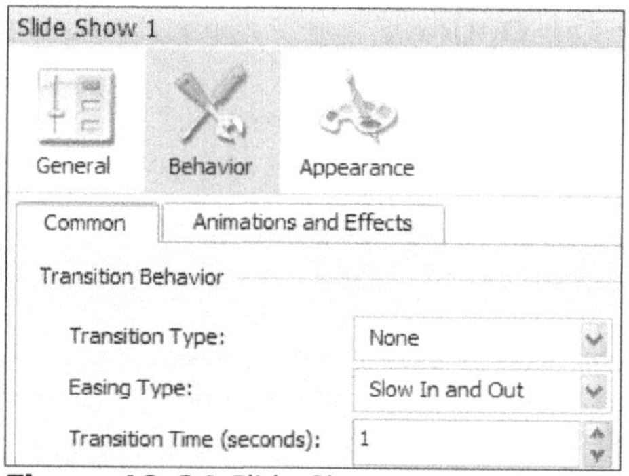

Figure 12-24 Slide Show common tab options

Easing Option	The Transition Starts . . .
Slow In	Slow, then gets faster.
Slow Out	Quickly, then slows down.
Slow In and Out	Slow and gets faster, then slows down.

Table 12-5 Easing Type options explained

Layout Tab Options

The Slide Show layout tab options shown in Figure 12-25 are used to select the size and alignment of the files that will be used in the slide show.

Image Options

SIZING METHOD Is used to select how the file fits in the frame of the Slide Show component. The options are explained in Table 12-6.

HORIZONTAL ALIGNMENT Is used to select how (on which edge horizontally) the image is aligned.

VERTICAL ALIGNMENT Is used to select how (on which edge vertically) the image is aligned.

Selecting both the horizontal and vertical alignment options allow you to select the part of the image that will be visible.

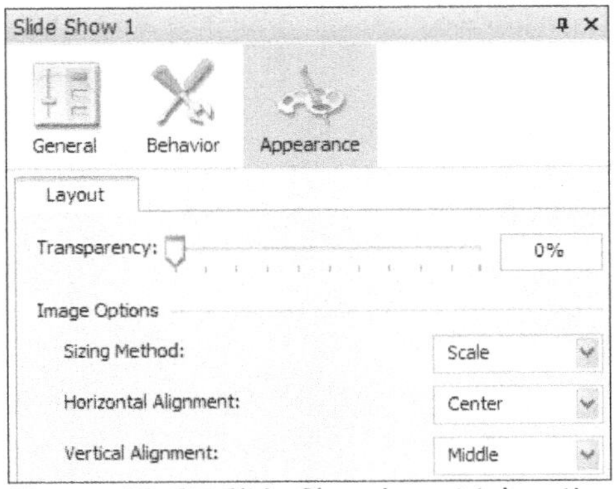

Figure 12-25 Slide Show layout tab options

Sizing Method	The Image Is . . .
Scale	Resized to fit in the Slide Show component without distortion. This is the default option.
Stretch	Stretched to the edge of the Slide Show component. The image can be distorted if this option is selected.
Original Size	Displayed at its actual size, even if it is larger than the box. This means that some of the image may not be displayed in the component.

Table 12-6 Sizing Method options explained

SWF Loader Component (This component is not available in Presentation Design)

This component loads SWF files from the URL that you select, which means that files do not have to be imported into the model first. This component has to have access to the URL and the file has to be available to load at run time. This component can be set up to load other models that are saved in a BOE. The SWF Loader component has better memory management then the Slide Show component.

The SWF Loader component has the same options as the Slide Show component.

Connection Refresh Button Component (This component is not available in Presentation Design)

The component is used to let the user manually refresh the connection that is linked to the button.

General View Options

The Connection Refresh Button general view options are shown in Figure 12-26.

AVAILABLE CONNECTIONS Displays a list of external data connections that can be refreshed when the button is clicked. Click in the box in front of each connection that you want to be refreshed.

LAUNCH DATA MANAGE BUTTON Opens the Data Manager dialog box. [See Chapter 2, Data Menu, Connections Option]

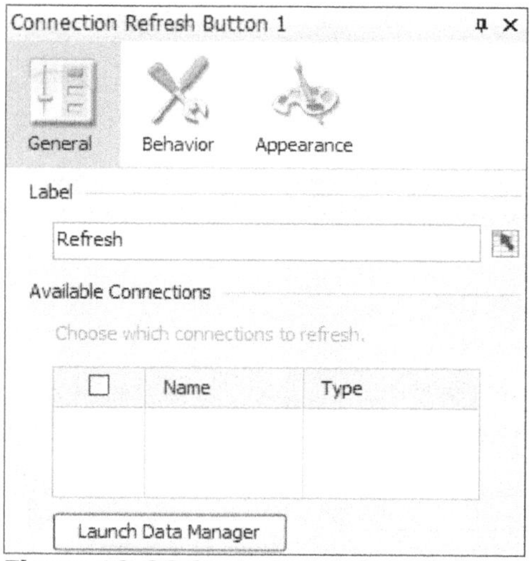

Figure 12-26 Connection Refresh Button general view options

Common Tab Options

The Connection Refresh Button common tab options are shown in Figure 12-27.

REFRESH AFTER COMPONENTS ARE LOADED If checked, the connections linked to this component are refreshed after the dashboard is first loaded.

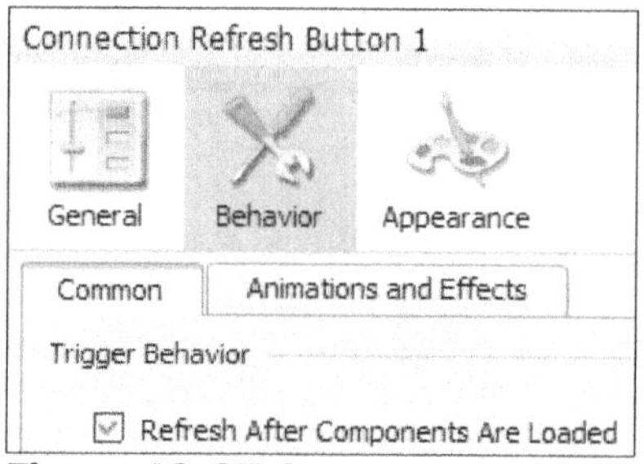

Figure 12-27 Connection Refresh Button common tab options

Other Components

The components in this category can be used to enhance dashboards in a variety of ways. Table 12-7 explains the components in this category.

Component	Description
Calendar	Is used as a selector component to use dates to select the data to display in another component in the dashboard. This component is covered in detail in Chapter 13.
Local Scenario Button	This component allows users to save the current view of the dashboard. This is helpful if the user wanted to save several what-if scenarios that they create. The saved scenarios can be run over and over, even after the dashboard has been closed.

Table 12-7 Other component types explained

Component	Description
Trend Icon	Plots how a value changes. The direction that the arrow points in changes, based on the value, as explained below: ⇒ The arrow points up if the value in the cell is positive. ⇒ The arrow points down if the value in the cell is negative. ⇒ If the value in the cell is zero, a symbol (usually a minus sign) is displayed instead of an arrow.
History	Is used to display the history of changes in a cell. (4)
Panel Set	Creates a series of panels that are used to navigate between the files in the dashboard.
Source Data	Is used to push data into other empty cells by changing the value in the Selected Item Index field, on the Common tab.
Trend Analyzer	Is used to add data points for a trend line to the model, based on the analysis of the data. (4)
Print Button	Is used to let the user print the dashboard.
Reset Button	Is used to let the user reset the dashboard to the way it was when it was first opened.
Grid	Creates a dynamic table that displays rows and columns of data. You can display the data exactly like it is in the spreadsheet or you can change the appearance of the data.

Table 12-7 Other component types explained (Continued)

(4) This component is covered in detail in Chapter 15.

Local Scenario Button Component

This component is used when users want to save their what-if analysis from a dashboard.
The Local Scenario Button component is unique in my opinion, for the two reasons explained below.

① This component allows users to save their what-if scenarios.

② Once you add the component to the model, your job is done because the component does not need to have any options changed for it to work. However, you can change the default options, if needed.

General View Options

The Local Scenario Button general view option is shown in Figure 12-28.

LABEL Type in or select the cell that has the text for the Local Scenario Button label.

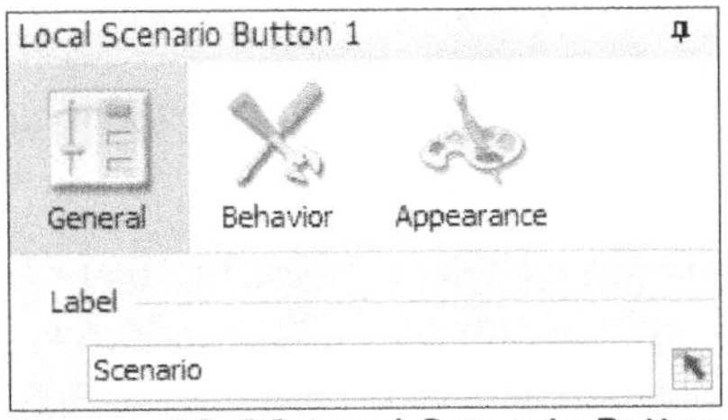

Figure 12-28 Local Scenario Button general view options

Layout Tab Options

The Local Scenario Button layout tab option is shown in Figure 12-29.

SHOW BUTTON BACKGROUND This option must be checked to change the background color options on the Color tab.

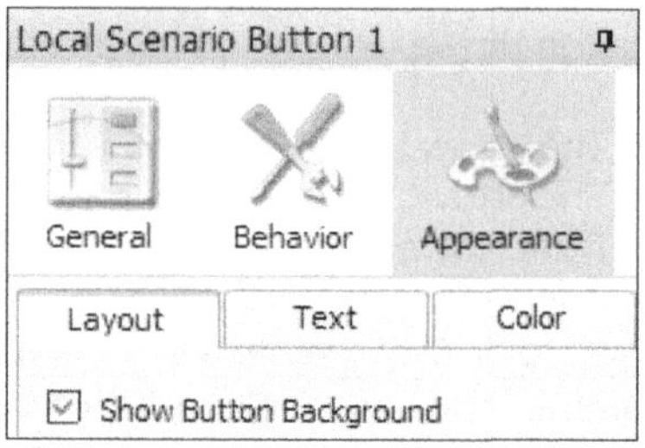

Figure 12-29 Local Scenario Button layout tab option

Color Tab Options

The Local Scenario Button color tab options are shown in Figure 12-30.

Button Options

DEFAULT COLOR Is used to select the background color of the scenario button.

SELECTED COLOR Is used to select the background color of the button when it is clicked.

Labels Options

DEFAULT COLOR Is used to select the color of the text on the scenario button.

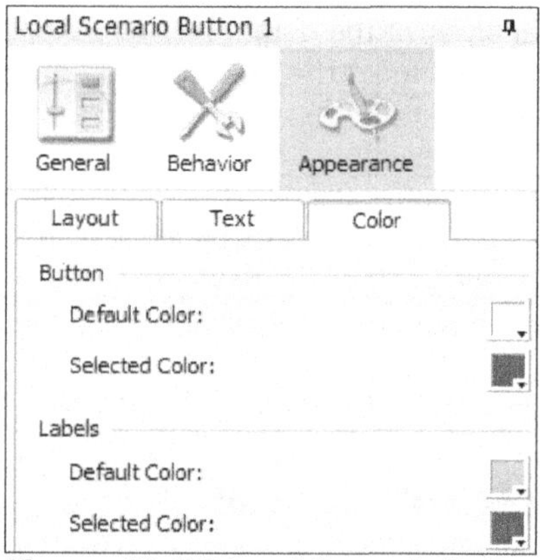

Figure 12-30 Local Scenario Button color tab options

SELECTED COLOR Is used to select the color of the text on the button when it is clicked.

Exercise 12.4: Use The Local Scenario Button Component

In this exercise you will add the Local Scenario Button component to a model. You will also learn how to create, save and load scenarios from a users perspective.

1. Save the My radio button model as `My local scenario button`.
2. Add the Local Scenario Button component above the upper right corner of the chart, then save the changes.
3. File ⇒ Export ⇒ PDF. Type `My scenario button dashboard` as the file name.

How To Create A Scenario

In this part of the exercise you will create and save scenarios, just like a user would.

1. Open the PDF file that you just created (in Adobe Acrobat or the free Adobe Reader).
2. Select the Carmel branch.

3. Click the Scenario button, then click the Save button, shown in Figure 12-31.

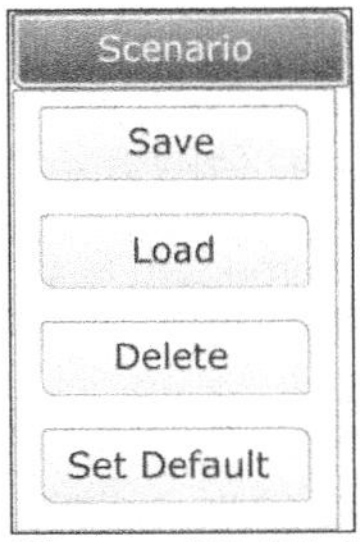

Figure 12-31 Local Scenario Button component on a model

4. Type `Carmel` in the field in the bottom left corner of Figure 12-32, then click the Save button.

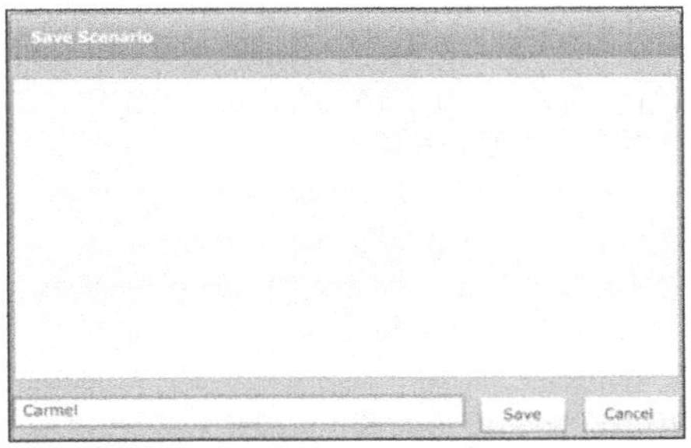

Figure 12-32 Save Scenario screen

5. Create and save a scenario for Irvine.

How To Load A Scenario

In this part of the exercise you will learn how to load saved scenarios from the dashboard (PDF) file. When a scenario is loaded it restores the model to the way it was, when the scenario was saved.

1. Click the Scenario button, then select Load.

2. Click on the Carmel scenario, then click the **LOAD** button shown in Figure 12-33. You will see the data for Carmel.

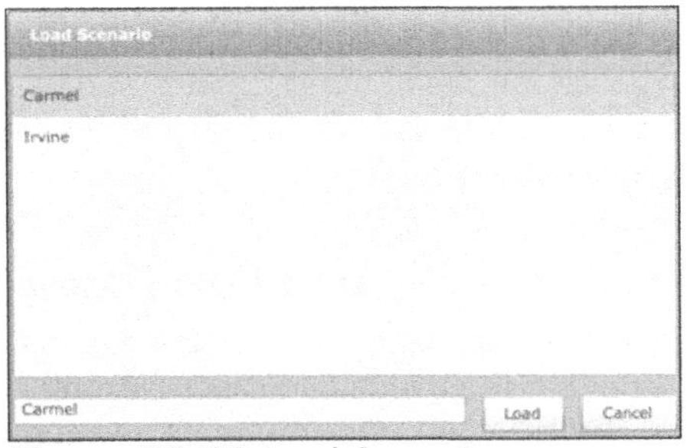

Figure 12-33 Load Scenario screen

> **Flash Player Impact On Local Scenarios**
> There is no limit to the number of scenarios that can be saved from a dashboard. The number of saved scenarios only becomes an issue if there is not enough hard drive space set aside for the Flash Player.

The scenarios are not saved with the dashboard. This means that if one person uses the dashboard on multiple computers, each computer will only have the scenarios that were saved on that computer.

Each scenario that is saved, creates a file. Over time the files can build up. You can delete them from the dashboard or you can delete them manually. The path below is where the saved scenario files are stored. The temporary folder name is usually all caps with two numbers in the folder name.

C:\Users\Your Username\AppData\Roaming\Macromedia\Flash Player\#SharedObjects\
<Temporary Folder Name>\localhost\<object name.sol>

Trend Icon Component

This output component is for a single numeric value and is used to track the value in one cell and display a different color and arrow direction depending on how the value has changed. The trend icon will remind you of an alert.

General View Options

The Trend Icon general view options shown in Figure 12-34 are used to select the data and customize the colors for the three value options that Trend Icons can display.

DATA Is used to select the value that the trend icon will represent. If the value in the cell is greater than zero, the component will display an up arrow. If the value is less than zero, the component displays a down arrow. If the value is zero, a symbol is displayed, usually a minus sign.

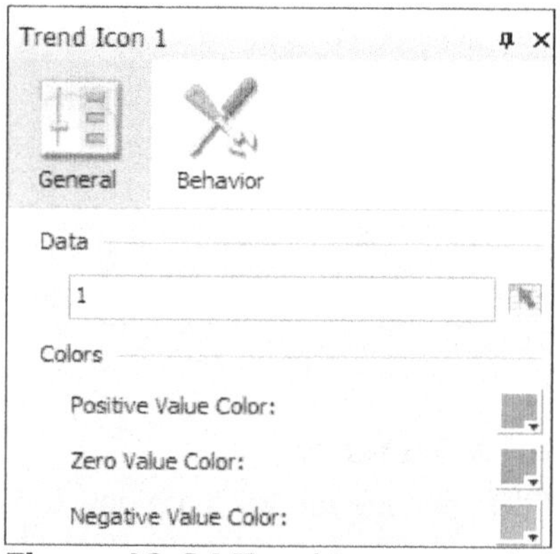

Figure 12-34 Trend Icon general view options

Colors Options

POSITIVE VALUE COLOR Is used to change the background color of the icon if the value is greater than zero.

ZERO VALUE COLOR Is used to change the background color of the icon if the value is zero.

NEGATIVE VALUE COLOR Is used to change the background color of the icon if the value is less than zero (a negative number).

Exercise 12.5: Use The Trend Icon Component

In this exercise you will modify the Single Value alerts model by adding the Trend Icon component. The data range that the gauge and slider currently use is all positive. To demonstrate how the trend icon changes, based on negative numbers and zero, the value range on the slider has to be changed.

Set Up The Trend Icon

1. Save the My single value alerts model as `My trend icon`.

2. Add the Trend Icon component to the middle of the sales gauge to cover the button that is there.

3. On the General view, select cell B5 for the Data field.

Modify The Sales Slider Options

In this part of the exercise you will modify the sales slider to accommodate negative numbers.

1. On the General view of the Sales slider, change the Minimum Limit option to `-100`.

2. On the Text tab, make the changes in the table for the Value option.

   These changes are necessary because you want the zero dollar amount illustrated at the bottom of Figure 12-35, to be displayed and not just display a dollar sign.

Option	Change To
Number Format	Currency
Negative Values	-$1,234.21
Decimal Places	2
Prefix	Select this option. The $ should be visible.

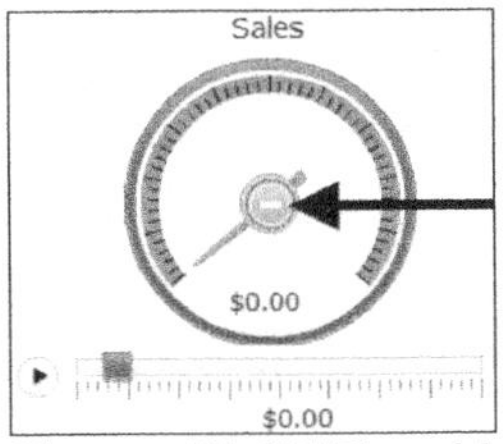

Figure 12-35 Trend icon and gauge components not displaying a zero amount

Modify The Sales Gauge Options

In this part of the exercise you will modify the sales gauge to accommodate negative numbers.

1. On the Text tab, make the changes in the table for the Value option.

Option	Change To
Number Format	Currency
Negative Values	-$1,234.21
Decimal Places	2
Prefix	Select this option. The $ should be visible.

2. Save the changes.

Notice that when you preview the model and the slider is all the way to the left, that it and the gauge display a negative number. Also notice that the trend icon is red and pointing down, as illustrated in Figure 12-36.

When the slider reaches zero, the trend icon changes to a minus sign and displays the zero dollar amount, as illustrated above in Figure 12-35.

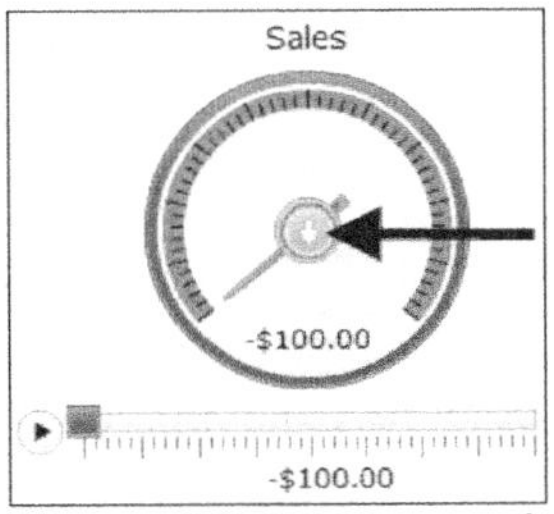

Figure 12-36 Gauge, slider and trend icon displaying a negative number

Panel Set Component (This component is not available in Presentation Design)

This component provides navigation between dashboards and image files through frames in the panel set in the dashboard.

General View Options

The Panel Set general view options shown in Figure 12-37 are used to select a layout and select the files that will be attached to each panel.

TITLE Is used to type in or select a cell from the spreadsheet for the heading that will appear above the panel set.

PANEL TITLES Is used to type in or select cells from the spreadsheet for the headings that will appear on each panel of the panel set. The number of titles should equal the number of dashboards and image files that you will add to the panel set, unless you do not want each panel to have a title. The Manual Edit button opens the dialog box shown in Figure 12-38. You can type in the titles for each panel.

LAYOUT Is used to select what you want the panel set dashboard to look like. There are over 25 layouts that you can select from. Select a layout that has the number of panels for the number of dashboards and image files that you will add to the panel set.

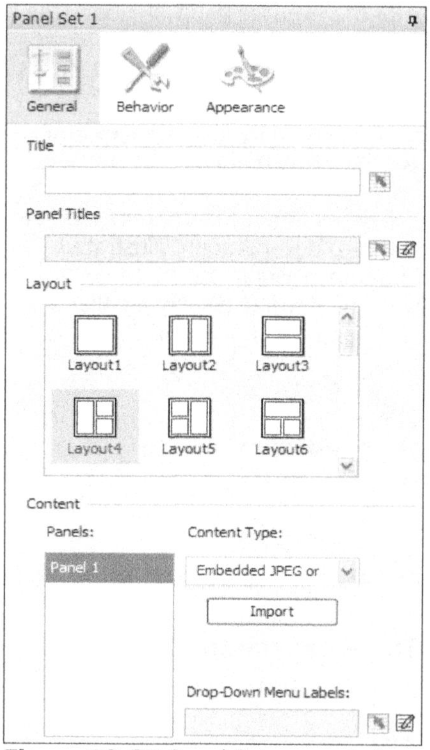

Figure 12-37 Panel Set general view options

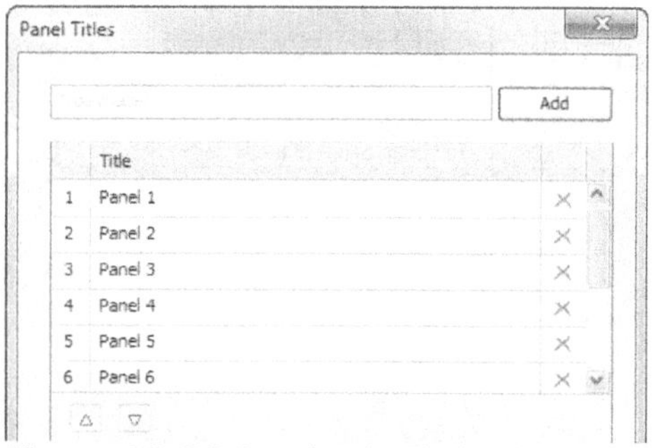

Figure 12-38 Panel Titles dialog box

Content Options

PANELS Is used to select the panel that the JPG or SWF file will be linked to or the panel that you need to modify.

CONTENT TYPE Is used to select how the file will be linked to the panel. The options are explained below.

① **NONE** Select this option if you want to leave the selected panel empty.

② **EMBEDDED JPEG OR SWF** Select this option to embed (save) the JPG or SWF file that is imported. (5)

③ **BY URL** Select this option to link a file to the panel. Selecting this option displays the options shown in Figure 12-39. The **URLS** field is used to enter the location of the file. The **MANUAL EDIT** button opens the dialog box shown in Figure 12-40. The number after "URL" in the Title bar (illustrated in the figure) on the dialog box represents the panel that is currently selected. You can use this dialog box to type in the URL.

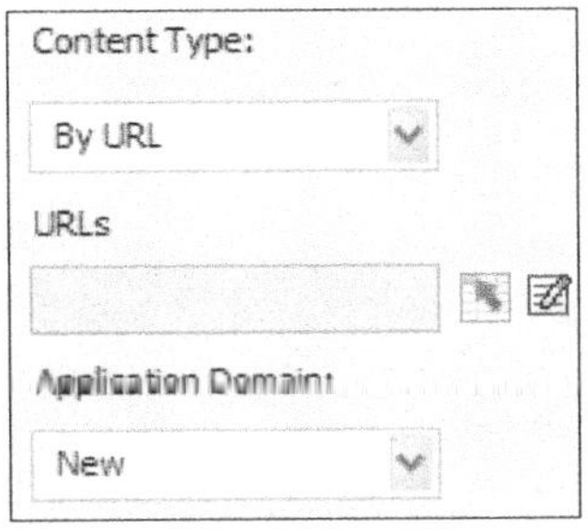

Figure 12-39 By URL content type options

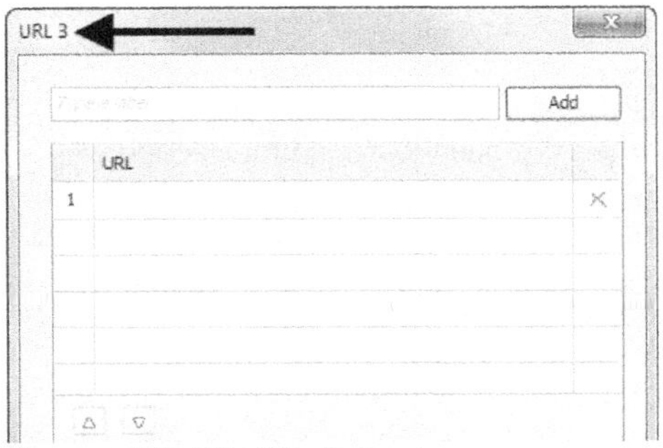

Figure 12-40 URL dialog box

> **By URL Option Tip**
> The URL's can be in a spreadsheet or you can type them into the embedded spreadsheet.

IMPORT BUTTON Is used to select the file that you want to embed in the panel.

DROP-DOWN MENU LABELS Is used to select or type in a label for the file that is linked or embedded in the selected panel. The Manual Edit button opens the dialog box, which you can use to enter or edit the label for the file in the panel.

(5)

> **Cannot Import Dashboard Design SWF Files**
> Believe it or not, by default SWF files created in Dashboard Design cannot be imported into a panel set. This does not make sense to me. If you select a Dashboard Design SWF file, you will see the message shown in Figure 12-41.

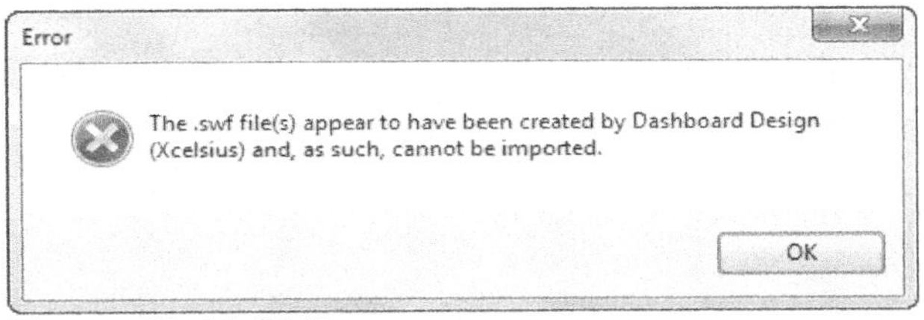

Figure 12-41 SWF error message

Common Tab Options

The Panel Set common tab options are shown in Figure 12-42.

Panel Behavior Options

ENABLE MAXIMIZE BUTTON If checked, a Maximize button will be added to the upper right corner of each panel. This will allow the user to expand one of the panels in the set to cover the other panels temporarily. Clicking the Maximize button again will restore the panel back to its original size. This is helpful when there is a need to see a specific data set enlarged on the screen.

ZOOM SPEED The slider is used to select how fast or slow the panels are expanded or contracted.

Selected Item Options

The options in this section are used to select the default files that will be displayed for each panel in the panel set when it is first opened. For example, if the panel set uses the Layout 4 option, you can select a default item to be displayed for each of the three panels in the layout.

PANEL Is used to select which panel will be displayed when the dashboard is first opened.

ITEM Is used to select the file that will be displayed from the panel selected (in the Panel field above) when the dashboard is first opened.

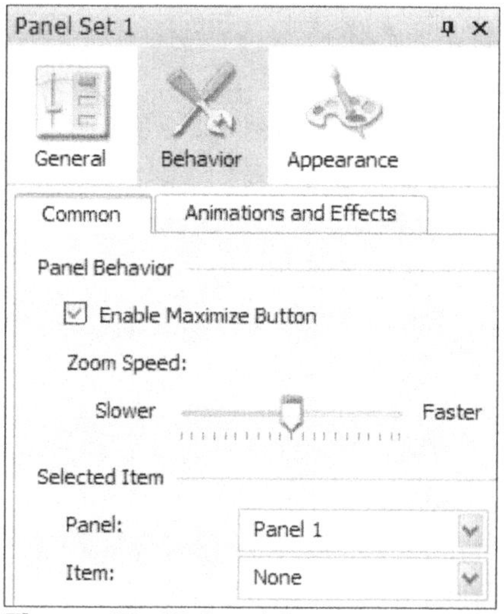

Figure 12-42 Panel Set common tab options

Layout Tab Options

The Panel Set layout tab options are shown in Figure 12-43.

SHOW PANEL HEADERS If checked, this option will display the header and title, as well as, a drop-down menu for each panel in the component.

NUMBER OF LABELS DISPLAYED Is used to select the maximum number of labels that will be displayed by default in the drop-down list for each panel. If the number entered in this field is less than the number of labels that will be displayed, a vertical scroll bar will automatically be added to the drop-down list.

BACKGROUND TRANSPARENCY Type in a value or use the slider to set the transparency of the panel set background.

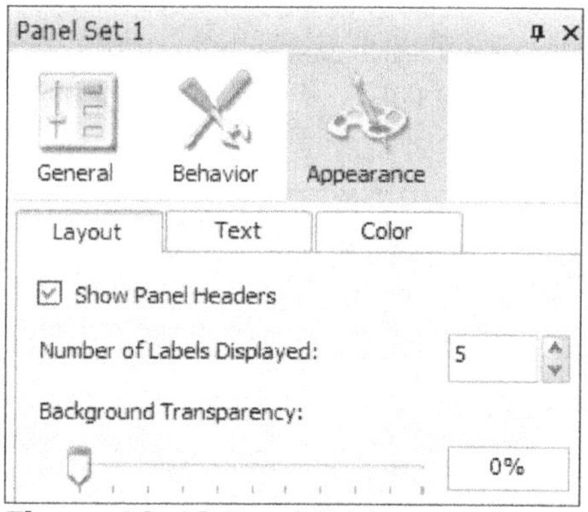

Figure 12-43 Panel Set layout tab options

Color Tab Options

The Panel Set color tab options are shown in Figure 12-44.

BACKGROUND COLOR Is used to select the background color for the panel set. This option covers everything outside of each panel in the layout.

PANEL BACKGROUND COLOR Is used to change the background color of the panels. The color is for all of the panels in the layout that you selected.

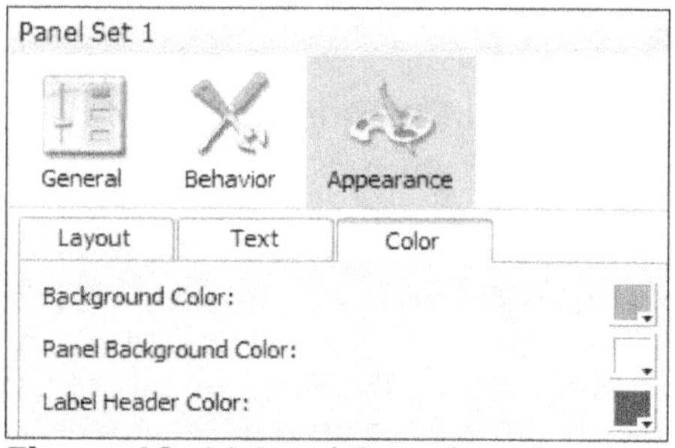

Figure 12-44 Panel Set color tab options

LABEL HEADER COLOR Is used to change the background color of the title bar (header) for each panel in the layout.

Source Data Component (This component is not available in Presentation Design)

Unlike the majority of other components, you cannot see this component on the dashboard. It is used to put data in other cells of the spreadsheet by changing the index.

General View Options

The Source Data general view options are shown in Figure 12-45.

Data Insertion Options

INSERTION TYPE Is used to select the type of information that is added, as explained in Table 12-8.

SOURCE DATA Is used to select the cells of the source data in the spreadsheet.

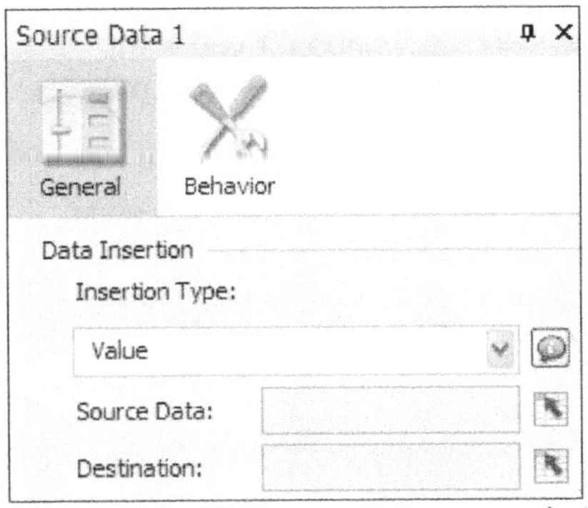

Figure 12-45 Source Data general view options

Option	This Option Will Insert The . . .
Value	Value from one cell.
Row	Values from a row of data.
Column	Values from a column of data.

Table 12-8 Insertion Type options explained

Common Tab Options

The Source Data common tab option is shown in Figure 12-46.

SELECTED ITEM INDEX Is used to select the cell that will bind the Selected Index of the Source Data component to the spreadsheet. If the value in the cell selected changes, the index will be updated.

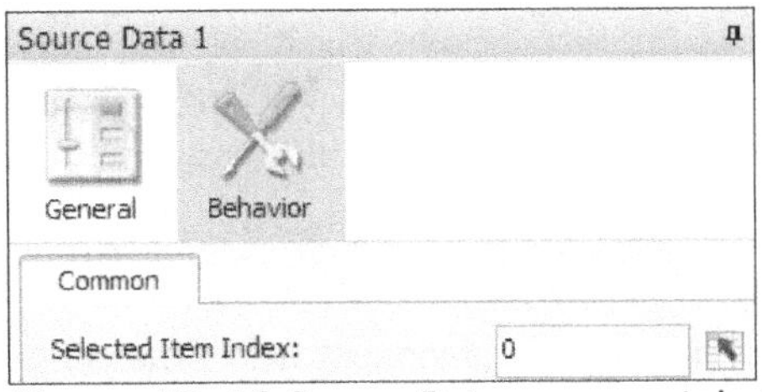

Figure 12-46 Source Data common tab option

Print Button Component

This component is used to allow the user to print the dashboard. The Print Button will appear on the dashboard when the dashboard is printed. It is probably a good idea to make the button as small as possible and put it in a place that does not detract from the appearance of the dashboard.

Common Tab Options

The Print Button common tab options are shown in Figure 12-47.

Print Scale Options

The options in this section are used to select how the dashboard will be scaled, if it is printed.

SCALE TO Is used to select the percent that the dashboard should be resized to when it is printed.

SCALE TO FIT PAGE Select this option if you want the dashboard to be resized to print on one page. It is probably best to select this option.

Many printers today have an option to scale what will be printed. If the Scale To option is selected, it may not allow your printers scaling options to function properly.

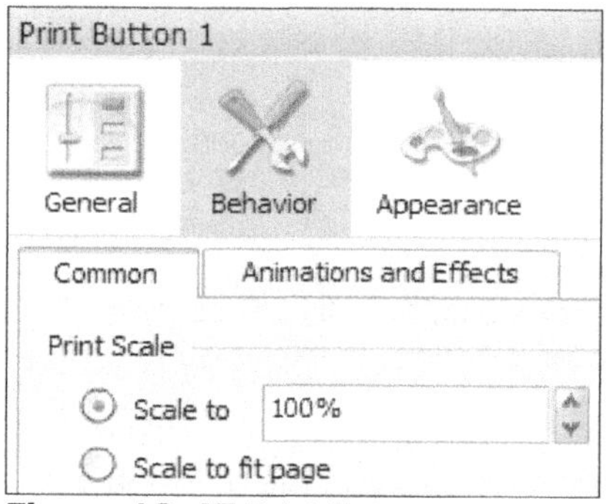

Figure 12-47 Print Button common tab options

Layout Tab Options

The Print Button layout tab options are shown in Figure 12-48.

SHOW BUTTON BACKGROUND Is used to set the transparency level for the background of the button.

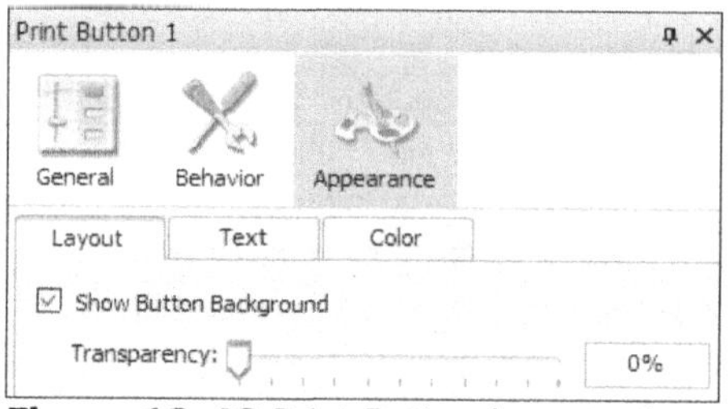

Figure 12-48 Print Button layout tab options

Exercise 12.6: Use The Print Button Component

In this exercise you will add the Print Button component to a model.

1. Save the My filter drop-down list model as `My print button`.
2. Add the Print Button component below the chart.
3. On the General view, type `Print It` in the Label option.
4. On the Common tab, select the Scale to fit page option.
5. Save the changes. When you click the Print button, you should see the Print dialog box. Select the printer that you want to print to and the preferences, if necessary.

For testing purposes, you should either print or preview the dashboard in portrait and landscape. This will let you know which layout is best for the dashboard, so that you can tell the users.

Reset Button Component

This component is used to allow the person using the dashboard to reset the options back to the way they were when the dashboard was first opened. This button has the same options on the Properties panel that the Print Button has.

Exercise 12.7: Use The Reset Button Component

In this exercise you will add the Reset Button component to a model.

1. Save the My filter drop-down list model as `My reset button`.

2. Add the Reset Button component below the chart.

3. On the General view, type `Reset the options` in the Label option. Make the button large enough to display all of the text.

4. Save the changes.

Test The Reset Button

1. Select Product 4 and Sales Rep 2, as shown in Figure 12-49.

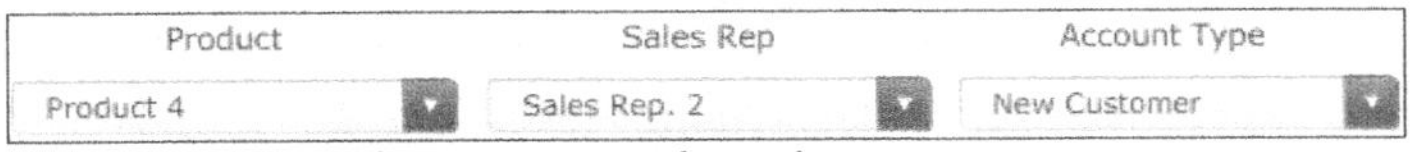

Figure 12-49 Filter options selected

2. Click the Reset button. The options for the first two filters should have been reset to what they were when the dashboard was first opened. The Account Type filter option was not reset because New Customer is the only option in the drop-down list.

If there was more data in the model that would force a selection in each drop-down list, you would see that all of the values would be reset as you expect.

Refreshing Data In A Dashboard

Earlier in this book you learned that once you import data from the spreadsheet, any changes made to the layout of the spreadsheet or data changes are not automatically added to the model. More than likely, the majority of dashboards that are created need to have the data refreshed from time to time.

Reasons To Refresh Data

There are several reasons to refresh the data, including the following:

① The data in the data source has changed.
② The layout has changed, meaning that at least some data in the spreadsheet is in different cells.
③ Rows or columns of data have been added or deleted.

Refresh Data Options

There is more than one way to refresh the data, as explained below.

① Use the Export Settings option. This is the easiest option, but as the dashboard developer, you will always have to refresh the data for the users.
② Use the Data Manager. This option requires more work for you to set up, but you can add the Connection Refresh Button component to the dashboard, which will allow the user to refresh the data on their own.

Export Settings Options

As stated earlier, this is the easiest option to update data in a dashboard. The Data Manager is used to connect to a variety of databases, including XML compliant databases. If you need to update data in a model but do not know XML or do not want to learn it (Don't feel bad, I didn't want to learn XML either), the Export Settings option may fit your needs.

If users will need to update the data in the dashboard, using the Export Settings options will make the process easier because you will not have to import the spreadsheet with the data changes. The options replace data in the model from an external spreadsheet either the original spreadsheet or a different spreadsheet. This option does not recognize new rows or columns of data and the options for the component are not changed. The exception to this is if components have the Ignore Blank Cells options enabled.

For example, if the user needs to see the most current data in the dashboard every Tuesday, have them update the spreadsheet before you export the model on Tuesday. During the export process, the options on the Export Settings dialog box are checked to see if the spreadsheet that was originally used to create the model should be used or if a different spreadsheet should be used. During the export process, the spreadsheet listed on the Export Settings dialog box is used to update the data for the dashboard.

Exercise 12.8: Use The Export Settings Options

The steps below show you how to refresh data in a spreadsheet.

1. Save the dd_actual_vs_projected model as `My refreshed data.`

Figure 12-50 shows the current data that the dashboard is using. Figure 12-51 shows the data after it has been modified. Only the Projected Sales amounts have been changed.

	A	B	C
1	Actual Sales vs Projected		
2			
3		Last Years Actual	Projected Sales
4			
5	North	$147,000	$150,000
6	South	$472,000	$375,000
7	East	$515,000	$500,000
8	West	$280,000	$405,000

Figure 12-50 Current spreadsheet data

	A	B	C
1	Actual Sales vs Projected		
2			
3		Last Years Actual	Projected Sales
4			
5	North	$147,000	$425,000
6	South	$472,000	$576,000
7	East	$515,000	$225,000
8	West	$280,000	$345,000

Figure 12-51 Spreadsheet data after changes

Figure 12-52 shows the current model before the data is updated.

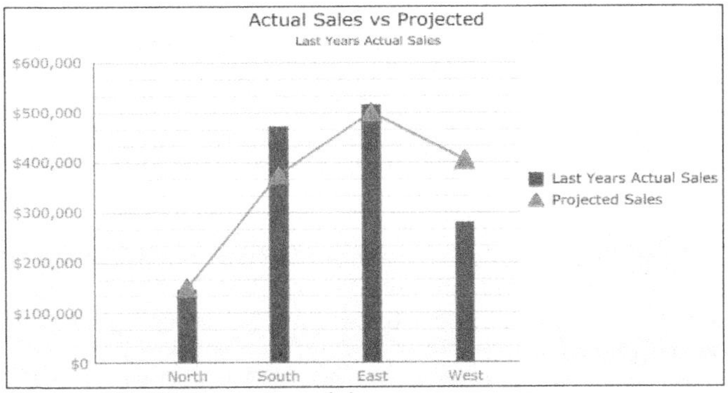

Figure 12-52 Current model

2. File ⇒ Export Settings.

3. Select the **USE ANOTHER EXCEL FILE** option.

4. Click the Browse button, then double-click on the dd_projected_sales spreadsheet.

   You should see the spreadsheet that you selected, as shown in Figure 12-53.

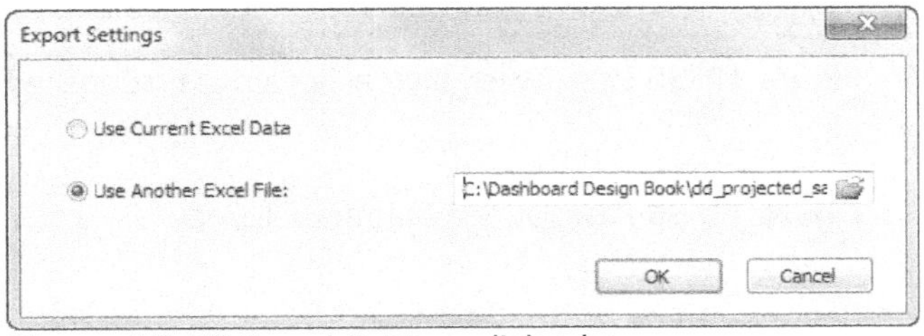

Figure 12-53 Export Settings dialog box

5. Click OK, then save the changes.

   The chart should look like the one shown in Figure 12-54.

   When you compare it to the chart shown earlier in Figure 12-52, you will see that the Projected Sales values have changed.

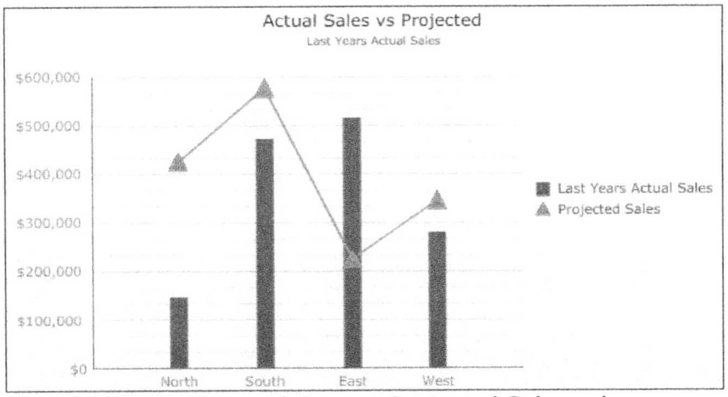

Figure 12-54 Changed Current Projected Sales values

How To Make The Label Based Menu Smaller

In Exercise 9.7 you created a Label Based Menu. The menu takes up a lot of space because it stays expanded. You can shrink the menu so that only one button is displayed by default. If the dashboard has a lot of components, only displaying one button will save space. You could make the changes below to have the menu display like the one shown in Figure 12-55 when the dashboard is first opened.

1. On the General view, enter a brief description of the menu in the **TITLE** option. This is what will appear on the button.
2. On the Common tab, clear the **ALWAYS EXPANDED** option. If necessary, change the **EXPAND DIRECTION** option to right.
3. Make the menu button the size shown in Figure 12-55.

When you click the menu button shown in Figure 12-55, the rest of the menu will be displayed, as shown in Figure 12-56. Once you select an option on the menu, the menu will automatically go back to only displaying one button.

Figure 12-55 Menu when the dashboard is first opened

Figure 12-56 Menu after a button is clicked

ADVANCED MENUS AND CHARTS

In this chapter you will learn how to create the menus and charts listed below.

- ☑ Accordion menu
- ☑ Calendar
- ☑ Fisheye Picture menu
- ☑ Sliding Picture menu
- ☑ Drill down chart
- ☑ Tree Map chart

CHAPTER 13

Overview

While the menu and chart components that you will learn how to create in this chapter may be a bit more complicated to understand, the value that they add to dashboards is well worth the effort.

Accordion Menu Component (This component is not available in Presentation Design)

In Chapter 9 you learned that Accordion menus filter data based on the option selected in the menu. Components like the Accordion menu are designed to support a lot of menu options. The items in the menu are grouped by categories that you create. Each category has several items.

General View Options

The Accordion Menu general view options shown in Figure 13-1 are used to create the categories and items for the menu.

Data Insertion Options

INSERTION TYPE The options in this drop-down list are used to define the type of data or value that is placed in the Destination field.

DESTINATION Is used to store the data for the item selected in the menu. The cells selected for this option should be empty.

Insert On Options

[See Chapter 9, Common Selector General View Options]

CATEGORIES Is used to create the top level of each section of the menu. Click on the Plus sign button below the list to add categories.

The values in the **NAME** field are the category names on the menu. This option is used to select the name for the item that is selected in the Categories list.

Figure 13-1 Accordion Menu general view options

The values in the **LABELS** field are the items for the category selected in the Name field.

The values in the **SOURCE DATA** field is the range of data for the menu.

CATEGORY NAME DESTINATION Is used to select the destination cells for the menu category.

Common Tab Options

The Accordion Menu common tab options shown in Figure 13-2 are used to control how menu items open and close.

Interaction Options

SLIDE SPEED Is used to select how fast or slow the categories on the menu expand.

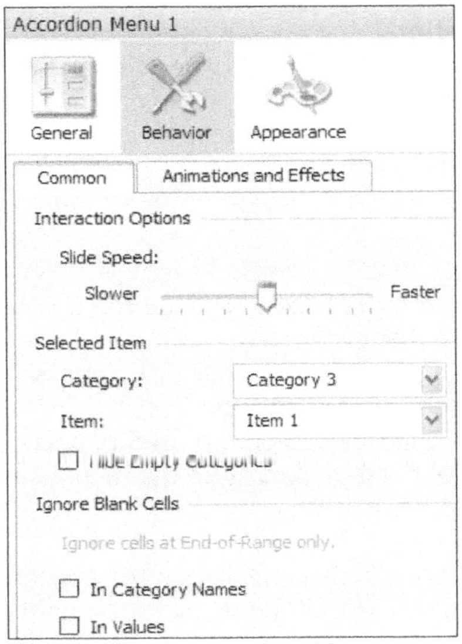

Figure 13-2 Accordion Menu common tab options

Selected Item Options

CATEGORY Is used to select the category that will be displayed (selected) when the dashboard is opened. The category selected, filters the options that are available in the Item drop-down list.

ITEM Is used to select the item that is displayed when the dashboard is opened. The options in this list correspond to the category that is selected.

HIDE EMPTY CATEGORIES Is used to keep categories that do not have any items from being displayed on the menu.

Ignore Blank Cells Options

The options in this section are used to select how the menu handles empty cells at the end of the data range.

IN CATEGORY NAMES Is used to stop empty cells that are after the last cell with data in the series, from being displayed on the menu.

IN VALUES Is used to stop empty cells that are after the last cell with data in the range, from being displayed on the menu.

Color Tab Options

The Accordion Menu color tab options are shown in Figure 13-3.

BACKGROUND COLOR Is used to change the background color of the menu where the navigation buttons are.

Category Names Options

The options in this section are used to change the color of the category buttons on the menu shown in Figure 13-4.

DEFAULT COLOR Is used to change the text color of the categories that are not selected on the menu.

OVER COLOR Is used to change the text color when the mouse pointer is hovered over a category on the menu.

SELECTED COLOR Is used to change the text color of the category that is selected.

Category Background Options

The options in this section are used to change the color of the background of the category buttons.

DEFAULT COLOR Is used to change the background color of the categories that are not selected.

OVER COLOR Is used to change the background color of the category that the mouse pointer is hovered over on the menu.

SELECTED COLOR Is used to change the background color of the category that is selected.

Label Options

DEFAULT COLOR Is used to change the text color of the items that are not selected on the menu.

OVER COLOR Is used to change the text color when the mouse pointer is hovered over an item on the menu.

SELECTED COLOR Is used to change the text color of the item that is selected.

Label Background Options

The options in this section are used to change the color of the item section of the menu shown in Figure 13-4.

DEFAULT COLOR Is used to change the background color of the items that are not selected on the menu.

OVER COLOR Is used to change the color when the mouse pointer is hovered over an item on the menu.

SELECTED COLOR Is used to change the background color of the item that is selected.

Buttons Options

The options in this section are used to change the color of the arrow at the top and bottom of the Accordion menu.

BUTTON COLOR Is used to change the background color of the arrow buttons.

SYMBOL COLOR Is used to change the default color of the arrow.

PRESSED BUTTON COLOR Is used to change the background color of the arrow button when it is clicked.

PRESSED SYMBOL COLOR Is used to change the color of the arrow when it is clicked.

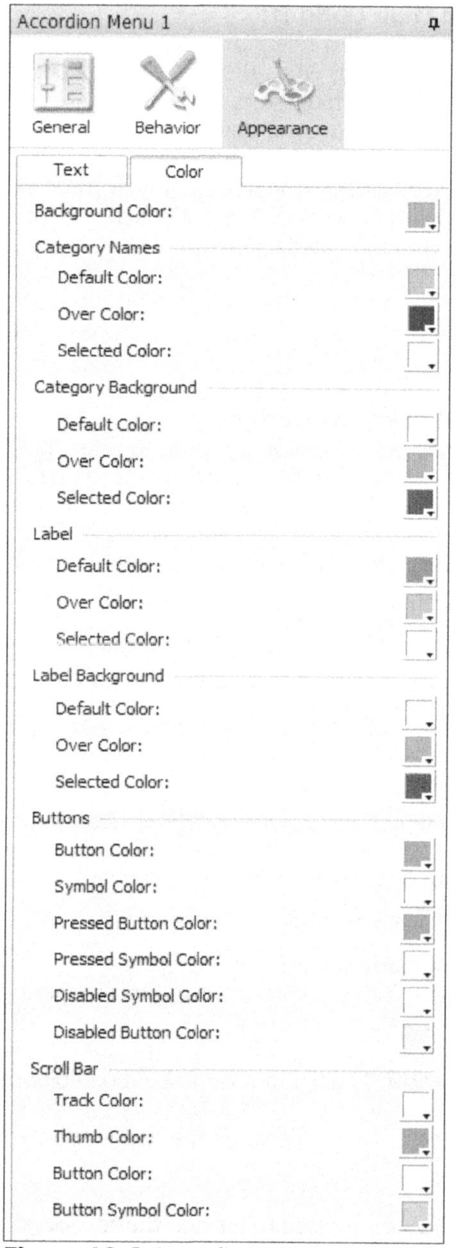

Figure 13-3 Accordion Menu color tab options

DISABLED SYMBOL COLOR Is used to change the color of the arrow when clicking on the arrow will not display any more categories or items on the menu.

DISABLED BUTTON COLOR Is used to change the background color of the arrow button when clicking on the arrow will not display any more categories or items on the menu.

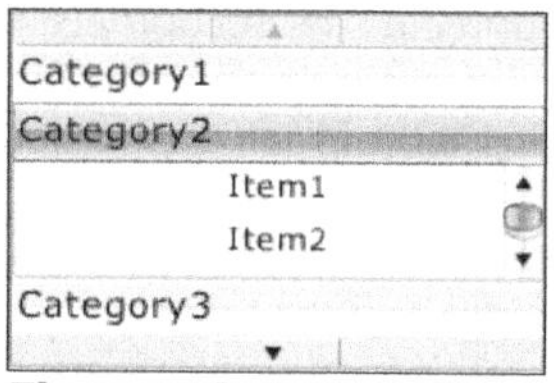

Figure 13-4 Accordion menu

Scroll Bar Options

The items in this section are used to change the color of the scroll bar on the menu.

TRACK COLOR Is used to change the scroll bar slider background color.

THUMB COLOR Is used to change the color of the slider on the scroll bar on the menu.

BUTTON COLOR Is used to change the background color of the button on the scroll bar.

BUTTON SYMBOL COLOR Is used to change the color of the arrow on the scroll bar.

Exercise 13.1: Use The Accordion Menu Component

In this exercise you will design an Accordion menu that will be used to select a sales rep. When the sales rep is selected, their sales for the year will be displayed in a chart. Figure 13-5 shows the data for this exercise.

	A	B	C	D	E	F	G	H	I	J	K	L	M
1	Title	ion Label Menu											
2	Subtitle	Available in X4											
3			The Accordion Label Menu is a list of text label items that can expand to reveal sub-items within the group or category, and can be										
4	Bottom Text												
5													
6	Sales Rep 1	$ 324	$ 389	$ 282	$ 309	$ 435	$ 283	$ 173	$ 409	$ 24	$ 394	$ 444	$ 69
7													
8	Xcelsius- East Region	Jan	Feb	Mar	Apr	May	Jun	Jul	Aug	Sep	Oct	Nov	Dec
9	Sales Rep 1	$ 324	$ 389	$ 282	$ 309	$ 435	$ 283	$ 173	$ 409	$ 24	$ 394	$ 444	$ 69
10	Sales Rep 2	$ 335	$ 407	$ 363	$ 447	$ 171	$ 403	$ 403	$ 107	$ 174	$ 106	$ 455	$ 41
11	Sales Rep 3	$ 431	$ 28	$ 322	$ 112	$ 260	$ 273	$ 136	$ 442	$ 340	$ 25	$ 217	$ 481
12	Sales Rep 4	$ 499	$ 63	$ 318	$ 330	$ 325	$ 158	$ 370	$ 14	$ 73	$ 161	$ 198	$ 460
13	Sales Rep 5	$ 118	$ 418	$ 14	$ 17	$ 274	$ 46	$ 486	$ 195	$ 23	$ 476	$ 318	$ 92
14	Sales Rep 6	$ 250	$ 97	$ 167	$ 496	$ 213	$ 420	$ 256	$ 276	$ 98	$ 279	$ 473	$ 53
15	Sales Rep 7	$ 76	$ 332	$ 435	$ 443	$ 130	$ 147	$ 272	$ 381	$ 473	$ 174	$ 119	$ 68
16	Sales Rep 8	$ 333	$ 440	$ 474	$ 260	$ 362	$ 160	$ 11	$ 91	$ 317	$ 481	$ 120	$ 57

Figure 13-5 Accordion Menu data

1. Import the Accordion Menu spreadsheet.
2. Add the Accordion Menu component to the left side of the canvas, then add the Column Chart component to the right of the menu. Make the menu and chart the same length.
3. Save the model as `My accordion menu`.

Select The Chart Options

1. On the General view, make the changes in the table.

Option	Change To
Chart	A6 (1)
Subtitle	Thousands $
By Range	B6:M6
Category Labels (X)	B8:M8

(1) The data in this cell will change when a different option is selected on the menu.

2. On the Scale tab, make the changes in the table.

Option	Change To
Manual (Y) Axis	Select this option
Maximum Limit	500
Auto (Y) Axis	Select this option

3. On the Series tab, change the Marker Size option to 15.

Select The Accordion Menu Options

1. On the General view, make the changes in the table.

Option	Change To
Insertion Type	Row
Destination	A6:M6

The range of cells selected for the Destination field should either be empty in the spreadsheet or contain data that can be overwritten because the range will be used to store the selections made on the Accordion menu. As you saw when you selected the cells for the Destination option, the range of cells was not empty. The values that you see in the range are for the sales rep whose data will be displayed by default.

2. On the General view, add the categories in the table by clicking the plus sign button below the **CATEGORIES** list box. You should have the options shown in Figure 13-6.

Name	Labels	Source Data
A8	A9:A16	A9:M16
A19	A20:A35	A20:M35
A39	A40:A62	A40:M62
A65	A66:A97	A66:M97

The Name column contains the regions.

The range in the Labels column will display the sales reps for the region.

The Source Data column contains the sales reps monthly sales for a region.

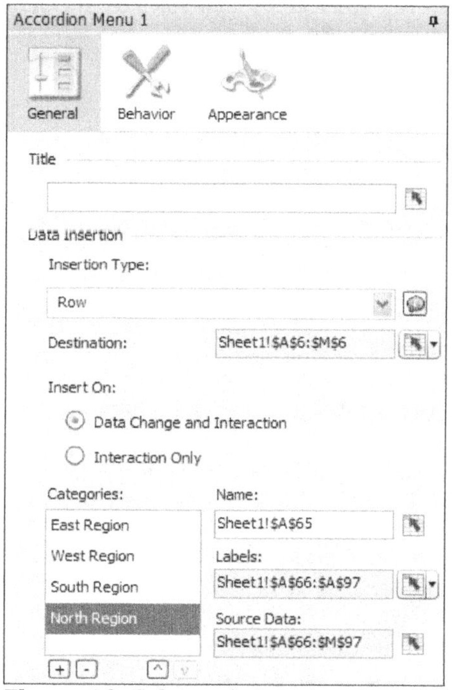

Figure 13-6 General view changes

3. On the Common tab, make the changes in the table. You should have the options shown in Figure 13-7.

Option	Change To
Category	Category 3
Item	Item 5

4. On the Animations and Effects tab, select the Enable Sound option.

5. Save the changes. When an item in the menu is selected, the corresponding sales rep data is displayed in the chart. Click on the West region in the menu, then select Sales Rep 12. The model should look like the one shown in Figure 13-8. When you select an option in the menu, you should hear a clicking sound.

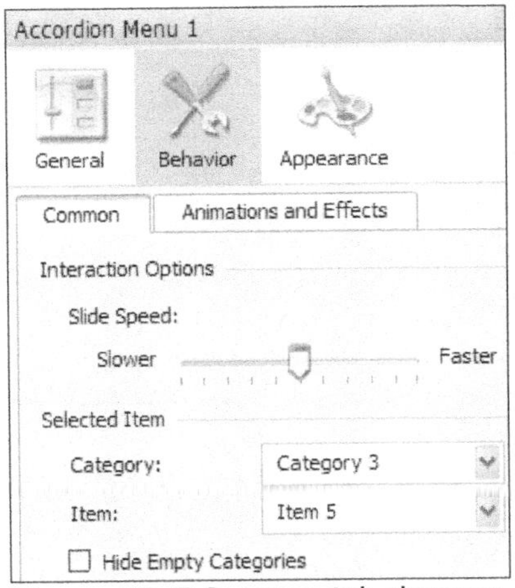

Figure 13-7 Common tab changes

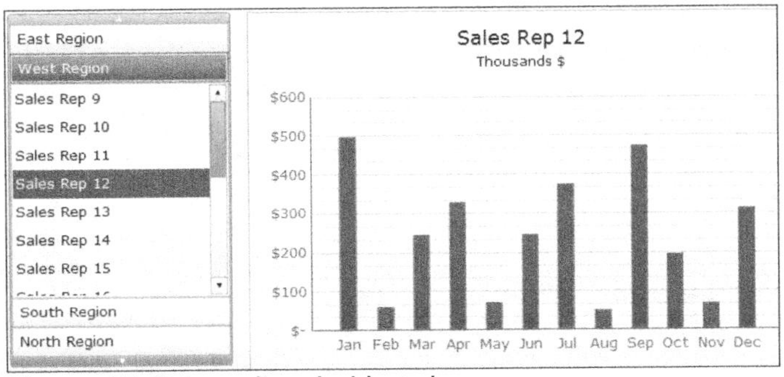

Figure 13-8 Accordion dashboard

> If the number of items in the Accordion menu is longer than the space allocated for the menu, a scroll bar is automatically added, as shown above in Figure 13-8. The arrow at the top and bottom of the menu lets the user know that there are additional menu options that are not visible.

Modify The Menu Options

The easiest way to change the category names is to change them in the spreadsheet and then re-import the spreadsheet. Yes, you can make the changes in the copy of the spreadsheet that was imported into the model. If you make the changes in that copy and later need to refresh the spreadsheet data, the changes that you make could be over written, depending on how the data is refreshed.

Calendar Component (This component is not available in Presentation Design)

The Calendar component shown in Figure 13-9 is used to select the date that will be used to display data in the another component on the dashboard.

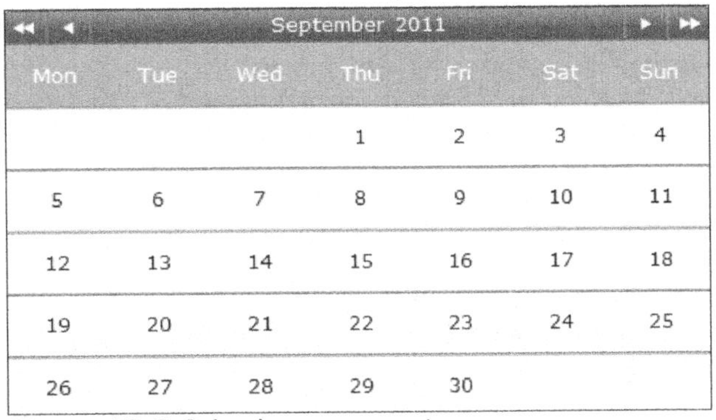

Figure 13-9 Calendar component

There are two ways to select the date range for the calendar component, as explained below.

① Limit the range of dates that can be selected by setting a minimum and maximum value for the month and year.
② Do not put any limits on the dates that can be viewed.

General View Options

The Calendar general view options are shown in Figure 13-10.

TITLE A good use for this field is to inform the user what date they should select.

Data Insertion Options

The options in this section are used to select how the calendar will respond when it is clicked on.

INSERTION TYPE Select the **DAY** or **DATE** option from the drop-down list to indicate the format of the date that will be inserted.

DESTINATION Is used to select the cell that the date will be placed in.

MONTH DESTINATION Is used to select the empty cell for the month.

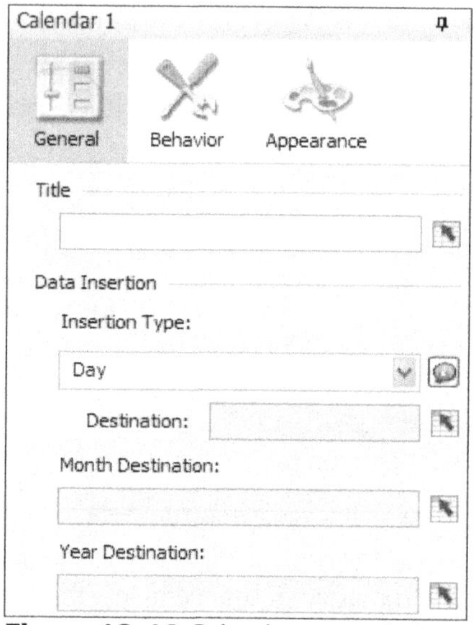

Figure 13-10 Calendar general view options

YEAR DESTINATION Is used to select the empty cell for the year.

Common Tab Options

The Calendar common tab options are shown in Figure 13-11. The options on this tab are used to set the default date and date range for the calendar. I find it easier to type in the day, month and year options, then it is to select them from the spreadsheet. That and the spreadsheet data is probably not in an appropriate format for the options on this tab <smile>.

Default Date Options

The options shown in this section are used to select the day, month and year that are displayed when the dashboard is first opened.

USE CURRENT DATE Select this option if you want the calendar to display the current date each time the dashboard is first opened.

USE CUSTOM DATE Select the date that will be displayed in the calendar when the dashboard is first opened.

The **DAY, MONTH** and **YEAR** options are used to select the day, month and year that is displayed and selected on the calendar when the dashboard is first opened.

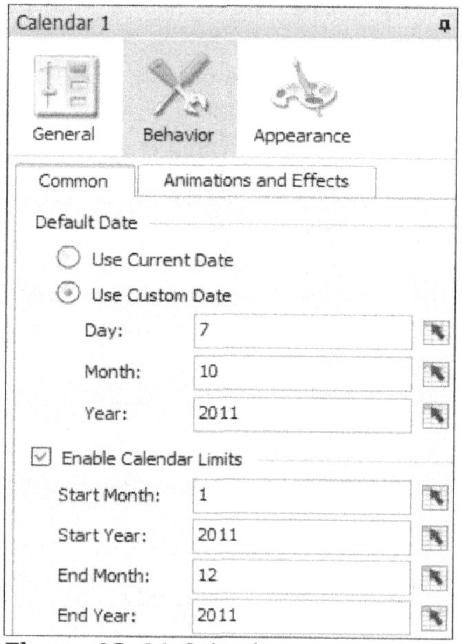

Figure 13-11 Calendar common tab options

Calendar Limits Options

The options in this section are used to select a specific date or range of dates that the user can select on the calendar. Notice that there is no option to select a specific day of the month.

ENABLE CALENDAR LIMITS This option must be checked to select a date range for the calendar.

The **START MONTH** and **START YEAR** options are used to select the first month and year that can be accessed on the calendar.

The **END MONTH** and **END YEAR** options are used to select the last month and year that can be accessed on the calendar.

Color Tab Options

The Calendar color tab options are shown in Figure 13-12.

BACKGROUND COLOR Is used to change the background color of the calendar. Depending on the theme that is selected, the results will vary. Figure 13-13 shows the background color option applied to the calendar using the Halo theme. Figure 13-14 shows the background color option applied to the calendar using the Nova theme.

MONTH COLOR Is used to change the background color of the month and year headings at the top of the calendar.

DAY OF THE WEEK COLOR Is used to change the background color of the days of the week at the top of the calendar.

Date Text Options

The options in this section are used to change the color of the text for the dates in the month.

DEFAULT COLOR Is used to change the color of the inactive dates in the grid portion of the calendar.

OVER COLOR Is used to change the color of the dates in the grid portion of the calendar when the mouse is hovered over a date.

SELECTED COLOR Is used to change the color of the default day selected on the common tab.

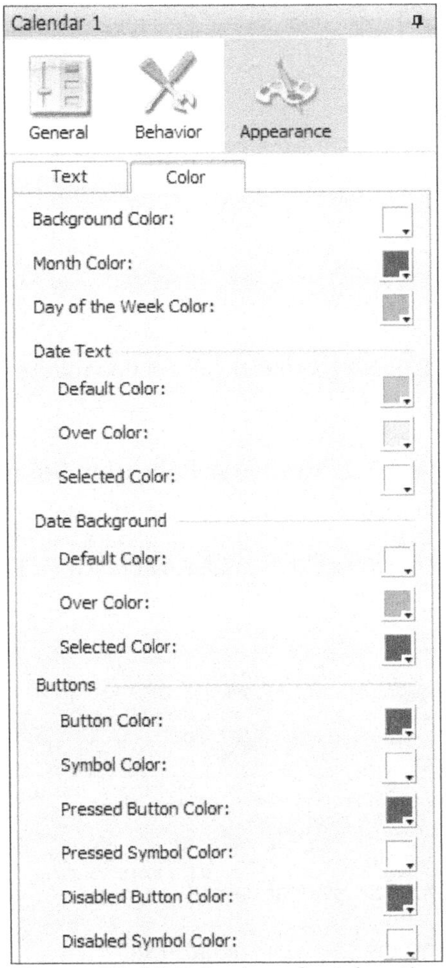

Figure 13-12 Calendar color tab options

Date Background Options

The options in this section are used to change the color of the area behind the dates.

DEFAULT COLOR Is used to change the background color of the days that are not selected. This is one of the options that do not work the same for all themes. This option works using the Elan theme, but not with the Nova theme.

OVER COLOR Is used to change the color that is displayed when the mouse pointer is hovered over a day in the calendar.

SELECTED COLOR Is used to change the background color of the day that is clicked on.

Buttons Options

DISABLED SYMBOL COLOR Is used to change the color of an arrow that is at the beginning or end of the calendar range. This means that clicking on the arrow will not display another month.

DISABLED BUTTON COLOR Is used to change the background color of an arrow that is at the beginning or end of the calendar range. This means that clicking on the arrow will not display another month.

Figure 13-13 Background color option using the Halo theme

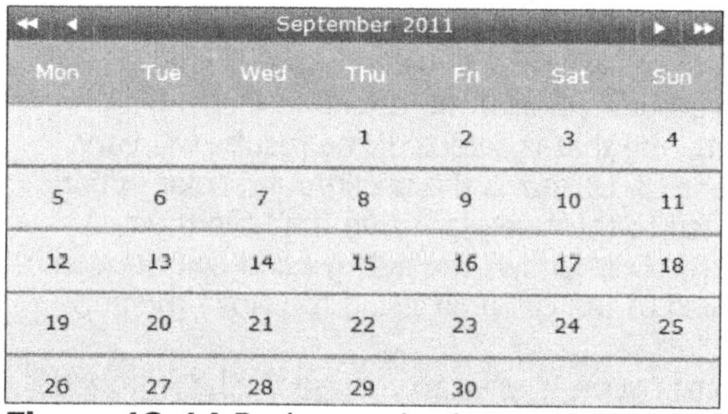

Figure 13-14 Background color option using the Nova theme

Exercise 13.2: Create A Calendar Dashboard

The calendar that you will set up in this exercise will be used as an input component to display the daily sales in a bar chart. This dashboard will allow the user select a day in July 2011 in the calendar and then see the sales by branch for the day that was selected. Figure 13-15 shows the data for this exercise.

	A	B	C	D	E	F	G	H	I	J
1										
2	Calendar Insert In Cell	7/1/2011								
3	Chart Data Range	$12.54	$12.65	$17.24	$10.79	$18.06	$15.98	$24.22	$9.92	$23.02
4	Chart Subtitle	7/1/2011								
5										
6										
7	Daily Sales by Branch	Atherton	Berkeley	Carmel	Cupertino	Fremont	Irvine	Milpitas	Orange Cc	San Franc
8	7/1/2011	$12.54	$12.65	$17.24	$10.79	$18.06	$15.98	$24.22	$9.92	$23.02
9	7/2/2011	$11.02	$14.63	$17.33	$10.35	$20.13	$15.54	$23.61	$8.93	$22.00
10	7/3/2011	$12.77	$12.24	$19.50	$9.85	$19.43	$14.29	$22.50	$9.47	$23.10

Figure 13-15 Calendar data

1. Import the Calendar spreadsheet.
2. Add the Calendar component, then add the Bar Chart component below the calendar. Make both of the components larger.
3. Save the model as `My calendar`.

Select The Bar Chart Options

1. On the General view, make the changes in the table.

Option	Change To
Chart	A7
Subtitle	B4 (2)
By Range	B3:J3
Series Name	B4
Category Labels (Y)	B7:J7

(2) Selecting this cell means that a different date will be displayed in the Subtitle field on the bar chart each time a date is selected in the calendar.

2. On the Scale tab, make the changes in the table.

Option	Change To
Manual (X) Axis	Select this option
Maximum Limit	500
Auto (X) Axis	Select this option

3. On the Series tab, change the Marker Size option to 15.

The **FILL** option shown in Figure 13-16 is used to change the color of the bars for the series for the chart.

Change the Fill color option to a color that you like.

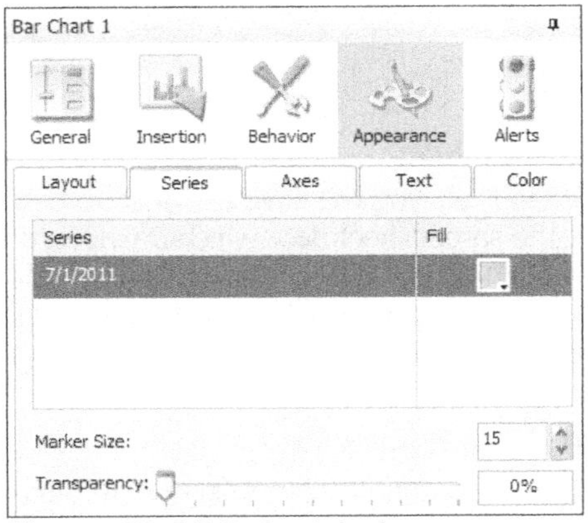

Figure 13-16 Series tab changes

Select The Calendar Options

1. On the General view, make the changes in the table.

Option	Change To
Insertion Type	Date
Destination	B2

2. On the Common tab, make the changes in the table.

In this exercise the user can only select a day in July 2011.

You should have the options selected that were shown earlier in Figure 13-13.

Option	Change To
Use Custom Date	Select this option
Day	1
Month	7
Year	2011
Enable Calendar Limits	Select this option
Start Month	7
Start Year	2011
End Month	7
End Year	2011

3. Save the changes.

   The model should look like the one shown in Figure 13-17.

   When you click on a date in the calendar, the corresponding daily branch sales will be displayed in the bar chart.

   The keyboard arrow keys work with the Calendar component.

   If you hold the mouse pointer over a bar in the chart, as shown at the bottom of the figure, you will be able to see the exact amount of the sales for the branch, for the date that is selected.

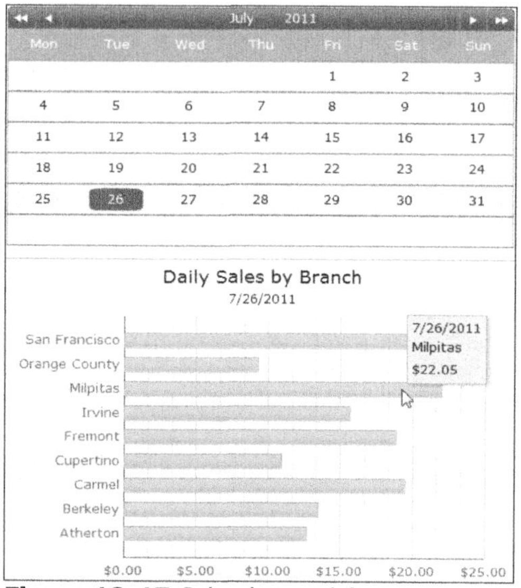

Figure 13-17 Calendar model

External Files

More than likely you will have the need to use an external file for a dashboard that you create. Unlike the spreadsheet data which Dashboard Design automatically embeds a copy of, you have the option of embedding other types of external files. Having the ability to incorporate external files into a model opens up a lot of possibilities for a dashboard. The next two sections discuss the external file types that you can use.

Nested Flash Files

The most interesting external file option to me is the ability to import a Flash file that was not created in Dashboard Design into a model. This means that once you compile the model, the dashboard will have two SWF files. If this is something that you plan to do, if possible, embed all of the objects in the SWF file that you want to import into the model, so that you do not have to put a copy of any of the external files in the folder that the model uses for external file.

This is not a requirement. The reason to embed the objects is because the model can only look in one folder for files that are referenced. If the SWF file references files in a folder named SWF/Images and you import the SWF file into a model, the model can only look in the folder that the model is saved in. This is where the files for the imported SWF file would have to be moved to, so that the model can find them.

Embedding Files

A good rule of thumb to follow in deciding whether or not to embed a file is who the user group is and how they will use the dashboard. If the user group will primarily use the dashboard on a desktop computer you can probably get away with not embedding the external files. Why? Because people tend not to move desktop computers around. If the user group will use the dashboard on a laptop, to me, that means that it is very possible that the dashboard could be used in a conference room, on a airplane or in a convention center, all of which may not have access to the server that the external files would be stored on.

The decision to embed files should be done on a dashboard by dashboard basis. Like a lot of things in life, there are advantages and disadvantages of embedding external files, as explained below. Depending on the environment that a dashboard will be used in, there could be more advantages or disadvantages than those discussed here.

Advantages Of Embedding Files

① The person using the dashboard does not need to have access to a server because all of the files needed are saved in the dashboard file.
② Embedded files maintain their state (on or off) when hidden, using the dynamic visibility options.
③ Dynamic visibility functionality is faster because objects do not have to be reloaded.

Advantages Of Not Embedding Files

① The model does not have to be recompiled if a change is made to an external file.
② Load times are shorter because the external files are only loaded when needed. If all of the files are saved in the dashboard file, they are all loaded, whether or not they are accessed when the dashboard is run.
③ Run time performance can increase because external files are unloaded if dynamic visibility functionality is enabled to hide the files.

Picture Menus (These components are not available in Presentation Design)

Believe it or not, the Fisheye and Sliding Picture Menus are very similar to the other types of menus like the ticker, that you have already learned how to create because you use the component to select a value. They have many of the same options that other selector components have. The main difference is that image files are used for the menu items instead of text. The steps required to create a Fisheye or Sliding Picture Menu are basically the same.

What Is The Difference Between Fisheye And Sliding Picture Menus?

There are some differences between these two picture menu components, as explained below.

① By default, the Fisheye Menu component displays all of the images that are used to create items on the menu. If you are using a lot of images, which makes the final display size of the dashboard larger than you need it to be, use the Sliding Picture Menu component.
② The Sliding Picture Menu component can be resized horizontally. Neither menu can be resized vertically.
③ The Sliding Picture Menu component has an option that controls the number of images that are displayed in the menu. This picture menu has arrows that are used to scroll through the pictures, one at a time or several at a time. The Sliding Picture Menu component is better suited for menus that have a lot of images or if you need to control the display size of the menu.

Picture Menu Components

As stated earlier, the Fisheye and Sliding Picture Menu components are very similar. Options specific to each component are explained later in this chapter.

Common Picture Menu General View Options

The general view options shown in Figure 13-18 are used to select and configure the image files.

LABELS If you want to change the Label names from what they are in the spreadsheet, click the Manual Edit button next to the Labels option to change the name, as shown in Figure 13-19.

Images Options

The options in this section are used to add images to the component. Keep in mind that the order that the images are imported in is the order that they will be displayed in.

EMBEDDED Is used to add a copy of the image to the model, so that it will always be available.

BY URL Is used to select the range of cells that contain image locations. The location of each image is stored in a cell in the spreadsheet. The images do not have to be on a web server to use this option. This option can be used to point to images on your computers hard drive (not the best option) or on a network or shared drive. Keep in mind when using the By URL option that if the images are on a hard drive of any type and the drive is not working (is down), the images will not be available when the dashboard is run.

IMPORT BUTTON Is used to select the image files to embed.

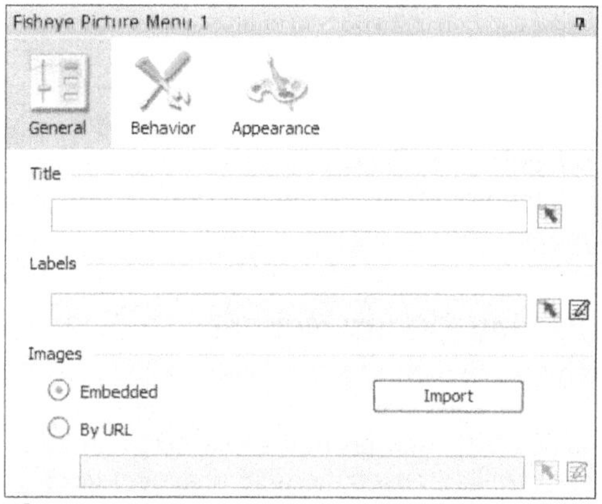

Figure 13-18 Common Picture Menu general view options

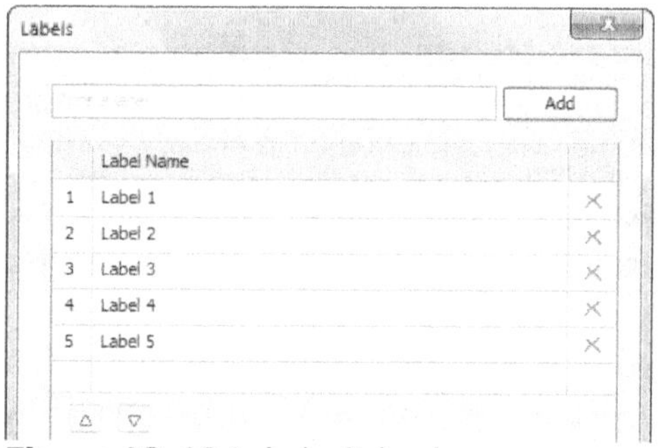

Figure 13-19 Labels dialog box

How To Determine Which Image Option Is Best

This decision should be made on a case by case basis. If the embedded option is selected and the images change, the model will have to be exported again and the dashboard will have to be redistributed. The options below are my summary of how to select the appropriate image option.

① Select the **EMBEDDED** option if there are a small number of images or the images will not need to be changed on a regular basis.

② Select the **URL** option if there are a lot of images or the images will change on a regular basis. With this option, when an image file changes, the model does not have to be exported again, unless the file name or location of an image changes.

Common Picture Menu Layout Tab Options

The layout tab options shown in Figure 13-20 are used to customize the image size, margins, colors and thumbnail background. The spacing is in pixels.

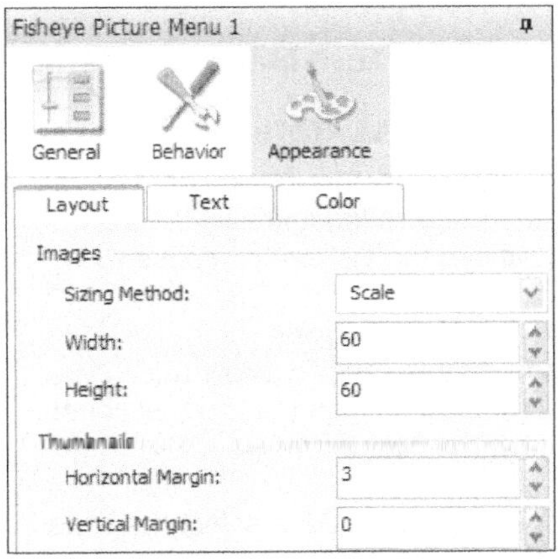

Figure 13-20 Common Picture Menu layout tab options

Images Options

The options in this section are used to resize the images for the menu.

The **SIZING METHOD** option is used to select how the image will be sized. The two options are explained below.

① **SCALE** Select this option to reduce the image to fit in the thumbnail area. The image may be smaller than the thumbnail area.
② **STRETCH** Select this option to resize the image to fit in the thumbnail area.

WIDTH Is used to select the width that the image will be resized to.

HEIGHT Is used to select the height that the image will be resized to.

Thumbnails Options (Layout Tab)

The options in this section determine how much space is above, below and between the images on the menu.

HORIZONTAL MARGIN The smaller the number, the closer together the images are, from left to right.

VERTICAL MARGIN The larger the number, the more space there is above and below the images.

Common Picture Menu Color Tab Options

The color tab options shown in Figure 13-21 are used to change the color of parts of the menu.

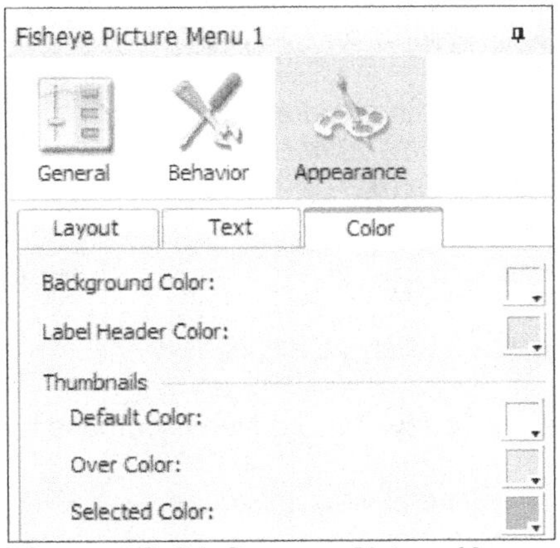

Figure 13-21 Common Picture Menu color tab options

BACKGROUND COLOR Is used to change the background color behind the images on the menu.

LABEL HEADER COLOR Is used to change the color of the title bar at the top of the menu. The color of the label text is selected on the Text tab (Select the Labels Text option).

Thumbnails Options (Color Tab)

DEFAULT COLOR Is used to change the color behind the image when the dashboard is first opened.

OVER COLOR Is used to change the color behind the image when the mouse pointer is hovered over an image.

SELECTED COLOR Is used to change the color behind the image when the image is clicked on.

Fisheye Picture Menu Component (This component is not available in Presentation Design)

Common Tab Options

The Fisheye Picture Menu common tab options shown in Figure 13-22 are specific to the Fisheye component.

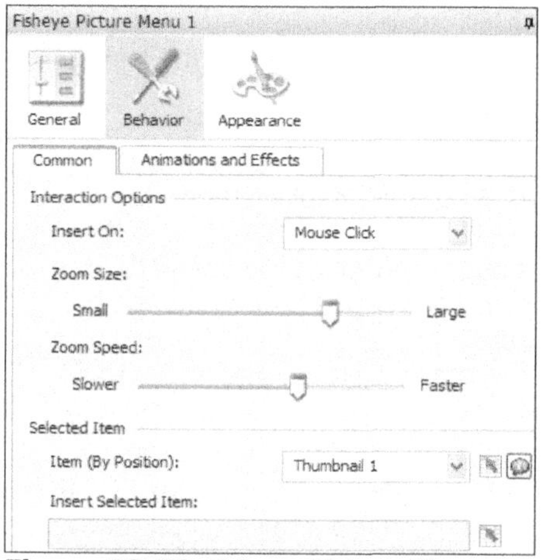

Figure 13-22 Fisheye Picture Menu common tab options

Interaction Options

ZOOM SIZE Is used to select the magnification when the mouser pointer is hovered over an image.

ZOOM SPEED Is used to select the speed of the popup effect when the mouse pointer is hovered over an image.

Selected Item Options

ITEM (BY POSITION) Is used to select which image file (from the images section on the general view) is selected when the dashboard is first opened.

INSERT SELECTED ITEM [See Chapter 9, Selected Item Options]

Exercise 13.3: Create A Fisheye Picture Menu Dashboard

The Fisheye Menu that you will create in this exercise will display the sales by product for five years.

The options on the menu are the products. Figure 13-23 shows the data for this exercise.

	A	B	C	D	E	F
1	**Insert In Range**					
2						
3						
4	**Actual Data**					
5	Sales by Product	FY08	FY09	FY10	FY11	FY12
6	Enterprise Software	$19.7	$17.1	$18.3	$14.8	$19.8
7	Developer Tools	$14.4	$18.0	$16.4	$16.7	$19.3
8	Consumer Software	$18.8	$13.5	$18.7	$13.9	$15.7
9	Services	$12.0	$16.2	$17.5	$17.8	$13.8
10	Support	$19.2	$15.6	$19.6	$15.9	$14.4
11	Training	$18.9	$14.6	$16.7	$12.1	$13.9

Figure 13-23 Fisheye Picture Menu data

1. Save the dd_fisheye model as `My fisheye menu.`

2. Add the Fisheye Picture Menu component above the chart.

3. On the General view, make the changes in the table.

   The labels are the product names.

Option	Change To
Labels	A6:A11
Insertion Type	Row
Source Data	A6:F11
Destination	A2:F2

How To Embed Image Files

The image files that you will use in this exercise are different then the ones in the sample model that comes with Dashboard Design because the image files that are used in the sample are not included with the software.

1. On the General view, select the **EMBEDDED** option, then click the Import button.

2. Click the **CLICK TO ADD IMAGES** button on the dialog box, then navigate to the folder where the images are. In this exercise navigate to your folder, if necessary.

3. Click on the image1.jpg file.

   Press and hold down the Shift key, then click on the image6.jpg file.

   Six image files should be highlighted, as shown in Figure 13-24.

   If the image does not clearly represent the product, the button image should have the name of the product to help the user know what item the button will display.

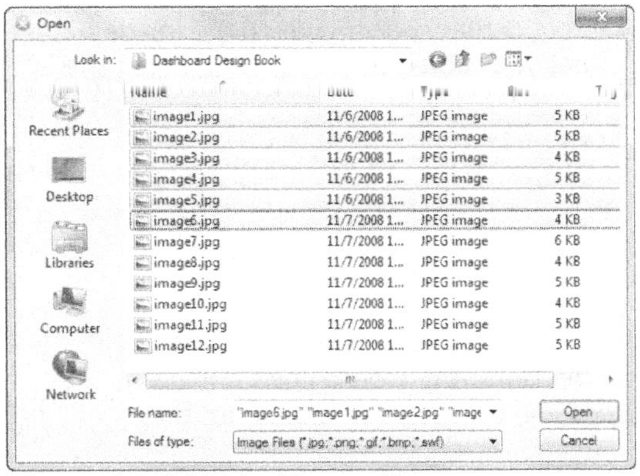

Figure 13-24 List of image files

4. Click the Open button.

   Make sure that the images are in the correct order.

   If they are not in the correct order, click on a file name, then click the Up and Down buttons, illustrated in Figure 13-25, to put the image files in the correct order.

   Click OK.

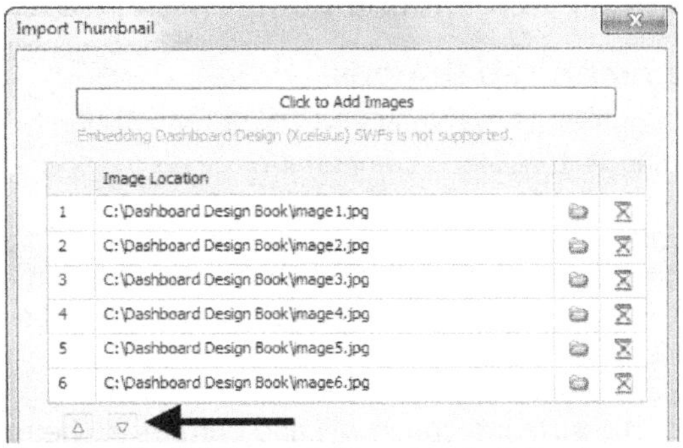

Figure 13-25 Import Thumbnail dialog box

Finish Selecting The Fisheye Picture Menu Options

1. On the Common tab, change the Item (By Position) option to Thumbnail 3.

2. On the Layout tab, make the changes in the table.

Option	Change To
Sizing Method	Scale
Width	70
Height	70
Horizontal Margin	10
Vertical Margin	10

3. On the Color tab, change the Label Header Color option to a color that you like.

4. Save the changes.

   The model should look like the one shown in Figure 13-26.

   When you click on an image in the menu, the text on the title bar at the top of the menu will display the product name.

   The chart will display the data for the product that corresponds to the image that you clicked on.

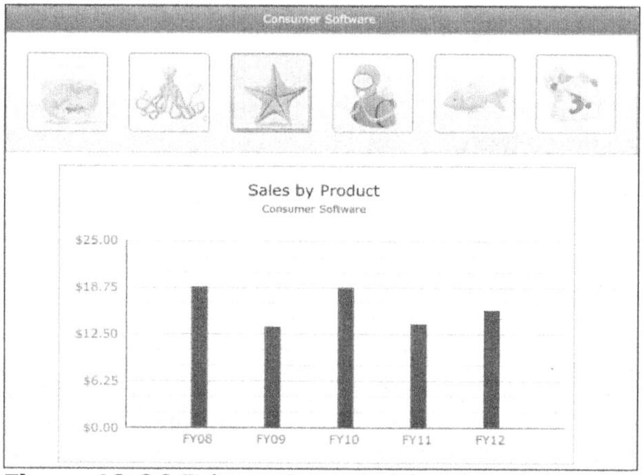

Figure 13-26 Fisheye Menu model

5. Hold the mouse pointer over an icon. It should look like the one shown in Figure 13-27.

   The closer the mouse pointer is to the middle of the image, the larger the image will appear.

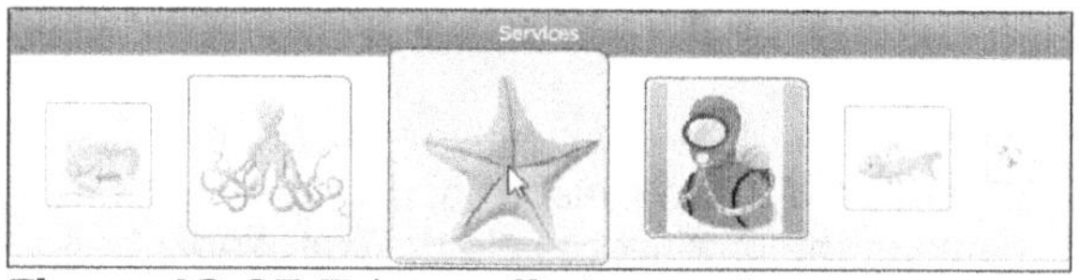

Figure 13-27 Fisheye effect on an Image

Sliding Picture Menu Component (This component is not available in Presentation Design)

Common Tab Options

The options shown in Figure 13-28 are specific to the Sliding Picture Menu component.

SLIDER METHOD Is used to select the how the images will be scrolled through on the menu when the menu is not wide enough to display all of the images. The two options are explained below.

① The **BUTTONS** option will add buttons to the menu that the user has to click on to view the images that are not currently visible on the menu.
② The **MOUSE** option uses the mouse pointer to scroll through the images in the direction that the mouse pointer moves. If the mouse pointer moves to the left on the menu, the first images will be displayed.

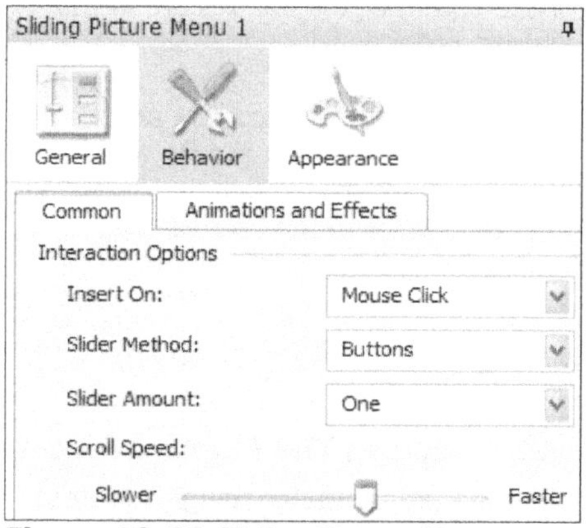

Figure 13-28 Sliding Picture Menu common tab options

SLIDER AMOUNT Is used to select if the scroll is one image at a time or one page at a time. A page is equal to the number of images that are initially displayed on the menu. For example, if four images are initially displayed on the menu, when the arrow is clicked or the mouse pointer moves to the right, the next four images are displayed.

SCROLL SPEED Is used to select how fast or slow the menu scrolls.

Color Tab Options

The options shown in Figure 13-29 that are specific to the Sliding Picture Menu are explained below.

Buttons Options
[See Accordion Menu Component Color Tab Options, earlier in this chapter]

DISABLED BUTTON COLOR Is used to change the background color of the arrow when clicking on the arrow will not display any more menu options.

DISABLED SYMBOL COLOR Is used to change the color of the arrow when clicking on the arrow will not display any more menu options.

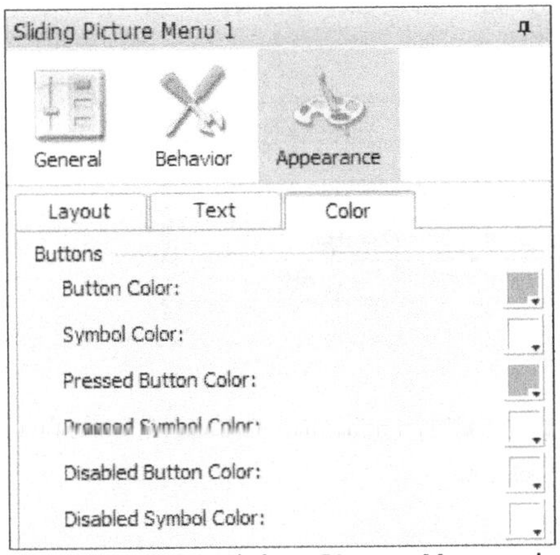

Figure 13-29 Sliding Picture Menu color tab options

Exercise 13.4: Create A Sliding Picture Menu Dashboard

In this exercise the Sliding Picture Menu will be used to select the product that you want to see the sales for, by clicking on the button on the menu that represents the product. The data for this model is the same as the Fisheye Picture Menu, shown earlier in Figure 13-23.

1. Save the dd_sliding_picture model as `My sliding picture`.

2. Add the Sliding Picture Menu component above the chart.

Select The Sliding Picture Menu Options

1. On the General view, make the changes in the table.

Option	Change To
Labels	A6:A11
Insertion Type	Row
Source Data	A6:F11
Destination	A2:F2

2. Follow the steps in the "How To Embed Image Files" section in the Fisheye Picture Menu exercise, earlier in this chapter to add the images to the Sliding Picture menu. Use image files 7 to 12 for this exercise.

3. On the Common tab, make the changes in the table. You should have the options shown in Figure 13-30.

Option	Change To
Insert On	Mouse click
Slider Method	Buttons
Slider Amount	Page
Item (By Position)	Thumbnail 2

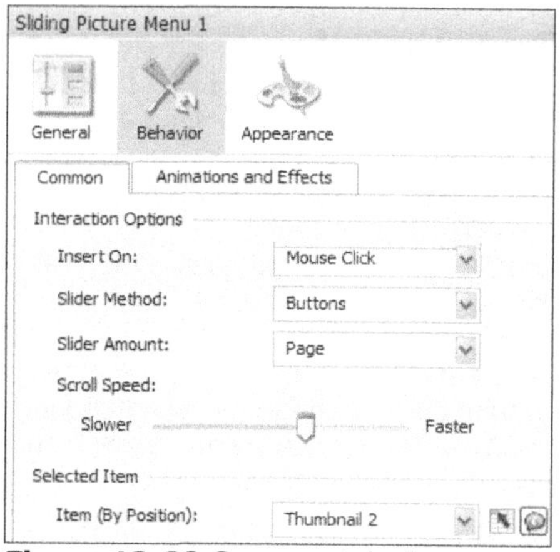

Figure 13-30 Common tab changes

4. On the Layout tab, make the changes in the table. You should have the options shown in Figure 13-31.

Option	Change To
Sizing Method	Scale
Width	80
Height	80
Horizontal Margin	10
Vertical Margin	0

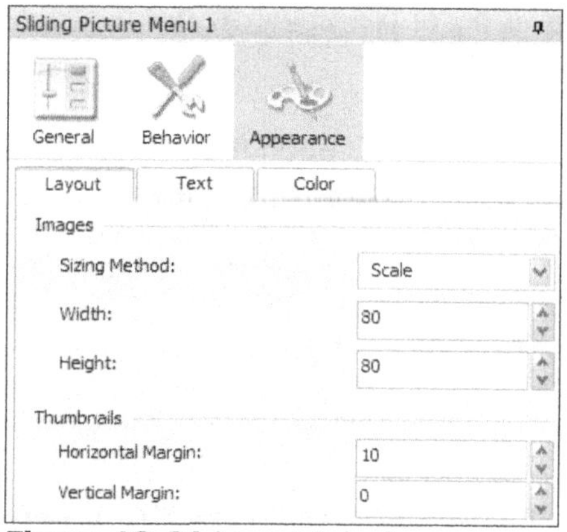

Figure 13-31 Layout tab changes

5. Save the changes.

   The model should look like the one shown in Figure 13-32.

   If you click on the right arrow button, you will see the next set of images.

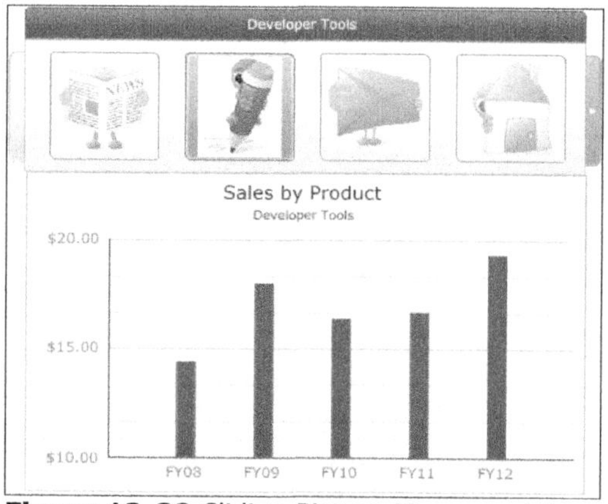

Figure 13-32 Sliding Picture Menu model

Drill Down Overview

Drill down options add additional functionality to charts. When this feature is implemented, users can click on a part of the chart and view the detailed information that was used to summarize that specific part of the chart. A chart that has drill down functionality mimics a selector component because the chart is used to select the data that is displayed in another component on the dashboard.

Drilling down to view detail data is helpful when performing analysis to show related information. Three items are needed to add drill down functionality to a chart, as explained below.

① Aggregated data. This is accomplished by creating a dashboard because dashboards can present aggregated summary data.
② Detail data. This is the data that will be displayed when the chart or table is drilled down on. The component used to display the detail data does not have to be a chart.
③ A link between the chart or table and its related detailed data.

> Area, Stacked Area, Radar, Filled Radar, Sparkline, Horizontal and Vertical Bullet are the only chart types that do not have drill down capabilities.

Insertion View Options

This view is only available for charts that have more than one series of data. Figure 13-33 shows the Insertion view options for a combination chart. Figure 13-35 shows the Insertion view options for a Candlestick chart. The options are explained below.

Combination Chart Insertion View Options

The options shown in Figure 13-33 are used to configure drill down functionality for a combination chart. The options on this view determine what happens when a section of the chart is selected to be drilled down on. The options may look familiar from the selector component options that you learned about.

ENABLE DATA INSERTION Must be selected if you want to add drill down functionality to the chart. This option is only available after the data on the General view has been selected. This open is per series, even though only one insertion type can be selected for a chart. A different Default Selection item can be selected for each series of data.

SERIES NAME DESTINATION Is used to select the cell where the series name is added.

INSERTION TYPE Is used to select the structure of the data that is added when a selection is made.

SERIES Is used to select the series of data to configure the drill down options for.

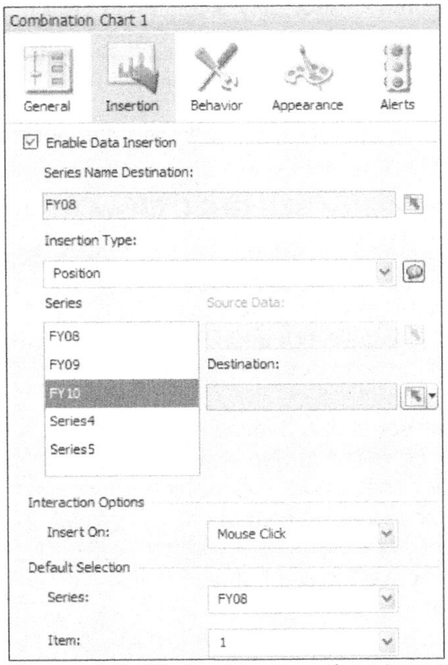

Figure 13-33 Combination chart insertion view options

SOURCE DATA Is only available if the Insertion Type option is set to rows or columns. This option is used to select the range of data to display on the chart.

DESTINATION Is used to select the cells where the source data will be added.

Figure 13-34 shows the insertion type options. The options are explained in Table 13-1, as they relate to chart drill down functionality. In Chapter 9, these options were explained from the perspective that the component is a selector component.

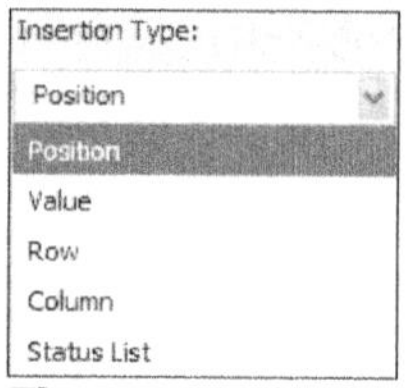

Figure 13-34 Chart Insertion Type options

Default Selection Options

The options in this section are used to select what values will be displayed on the chart when it is first opened. The default is the first item or value.

The **SERIES** drop-down list contains all of the series of data that the chart has. Select the series that you want displayed when the dashboard is first opened.

The **ITEM** drop-down list is used to select the value that will be displayed when the dashboard is first opened. You have to select an option. If you do not want a value displayed when the dashboard is opened, select the **NO SELECTION (-1)** option.

Option	Select This Option To . . .
Position	Display the position of the slice that is clicked on.
Value	Display the actual value of the selected slice.
Row	Display a row of data from a two-dimensional range in the source data. (3)
Column	Display a column of data from a two-dimensional range in the source data. (3)
Status List	Control the dynamic visibility of other components on the dashboard.

Table 13-1 Chart insertion type options explained

(3) This option causes the chart component to function like a selector component.

Candlestick And OHLC Chart Insertion View Options

The options shown in Figure 13-35 are used to configure drill down functionality for the Candlestick and OHLC chart components.

VALUE SET Is only available if the Insertion Type option is set to Value. The options (open, high, low and close) shown in the figure are used to select which stock price the chart should drill down on.

[See Chapter 8, Candlestick And OHLC Chart General View Options]

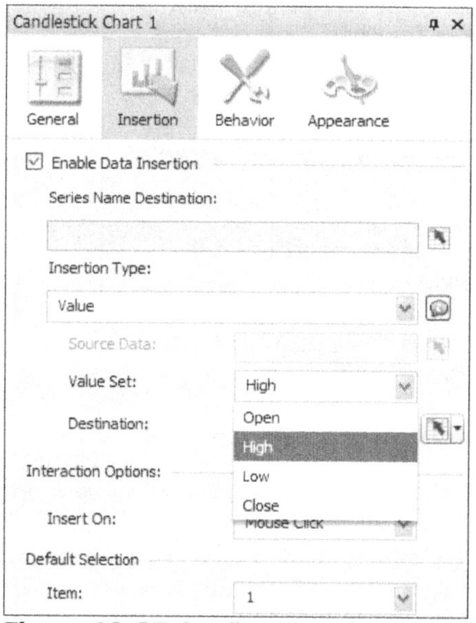

Figure 13-35 Candlestick and OHLC chart insertion view options

Exercise 13.5: Create A Drill Down Chart Dashboard

In this exercise you will add two charts to the model. You will add a pie chart that will be used to select a branch. Once selected, the sales data for the branch will be displayed in the column chart. Figure 13-36 shows the data for this exercise.

	A	B	C	D	E	F	G	H	I	J	K	L	M	N
1	**Insert In Range**													
2														
3														
4	**Actual Data**													
5	Sales by Branch	Jan	Feb	Mar	Apr	May	Jun	Jul	Aug	Sep	Oct	Nov	Dec	Totals
6	Atherton	$4.6	$3.0	$6.9	$5.4	$6.8	$9.0	$4.3	$5.6	$8.3	$8.9	$6.5	$3.0	$72.1
7	Berkeley	$13.0	$8.3	$11.3	$10.7	$8.8	$9.9	$7.8	$10.1	$7.1	$10.2	$10.0	$8.6	$115.8
8	Cupertino	$6.0	$6.4	$6.5	$5.5	$7.0	$6.1	$5.2	$7.8	$7.2	$5.0	$4.8	$5.9	$73.5
9	Fremont	$8.5	$6.2	$7.3	$9.7	$8.3	$11.0	$7.3	$9.5	$7.6	$6.1	$6.9	$8.8	$97.3
10	Milpitas	$9.9	$8.5	$9.2	$5.6	$8.1	$9.6	$9.3	$9.4	$5.7	$7.5	$5.9	$5.2	$93.9
11	San Francisco	[illegible]	[illegible]	[illegible]	[illegible]	[illegible]	[illegible]	[illegible]	[illegible]	$26.7	$29.0	$28.2	$29.4	$332.3

Figure 13-36 Drill down chart data

1. Import the Drill Down Chart spreadsheet.
2. Add the Pie chart component, then add the Column Chart component below it.
3. Save the model as `My drill-down chart.`

Select The Pie Chart Options

1. On the General view, make the changes in the table.

Option	Change To
Chart	A5
Subtitle	Clear this option
Values	N6:N11
Labels	A6:A11

2. On the Series tab, make the changes in the table.

Option	Change To
Show Lines	Select this option
Show Lines Color Selector	Black
Thickness	4

Select The Drill Down Options For The Pie Chart

The pie chart will be used as a selector. The user will click on a slice of the pie and the corresponding sales data for the branch will be displayed in the column chart. The pie chart will have the drill down options.

1. On the Insertion view, make the changes in the table. You should have the options shown in Figure 13-37.

   Save the changes.

Option	Change To
Enable Drill Down	Select this option
Insertion Type	Row
Source Data	A6:M11
Destination	A2:M2
Item	3

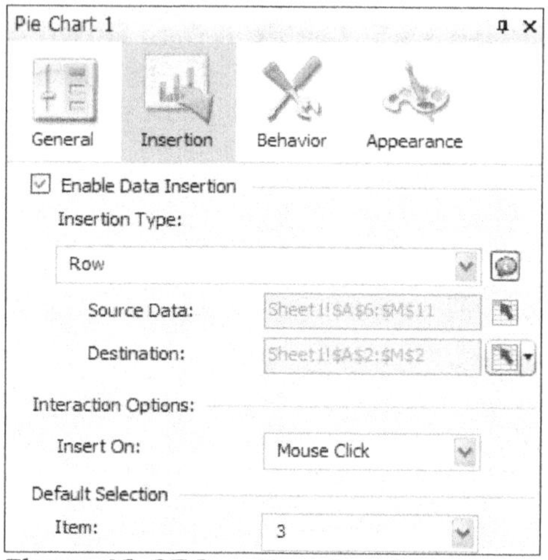

Figure 13-37 Insertion view changes

Select The Column Chart Options

The column chart will be used to display the detail information for the slice of the pie that is selected.

1. On the General view, make the changes in the table.

Option	Change To
Chart	A2
Subtitle	Monthly Sales
Values (Y)	B2:M2
By Range	B2:M2
Category Labels (X)	B5:M5

2. On the Scale tab, make the changes in the table.

Option	Change To
Manual (Y) Axis	Select this option
Maximum Limit	500
Auto (Y) Axis	Select this option

3. Save the changes.

   If you hold the mouse pointer over the San Francisco slice of the pie chart, you will see the information shown at the top of Figure 13-38.

   If you click on the San Francisco slice of the pie chart, you will see the monthly sales in the column chart for San Francisco.

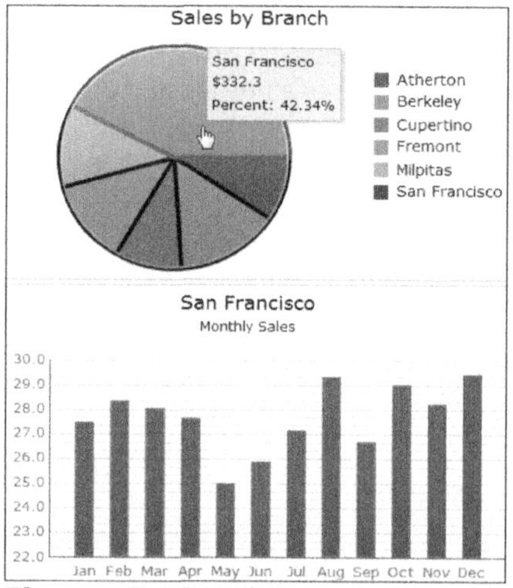

Figure 13-38 Drill down chart model

Tree Map Component

Tree map charts are used to display hierarchical data in a small space. Each data point is represented by a rectangle on the chart. The color intensity and size of the rectangles are determined by the data. The rectangles are automatically arranged by size, then by color. The smaller the size of the rectangle and the lighter the color of the rectangle, represents lower values.

This chart type is similar to an XY chart because it is used to analyze two measures. The one difference between these two chart types is that Tree Maps do not support alerts.

General View Options

The Tree Map general view options are shown in Figure 13-39.

DISPLAY LABELS Is used to select the text values that will be displayed when the mouse pointer is hovered over a block on the chart.

VALUES (SIZE) Is used to select the values that create the size of the rectangles for the series of data.

VALUES (COLOR INTENSITY) Is used to select the values that create the color intensity (for the rectangles) for the series of data.

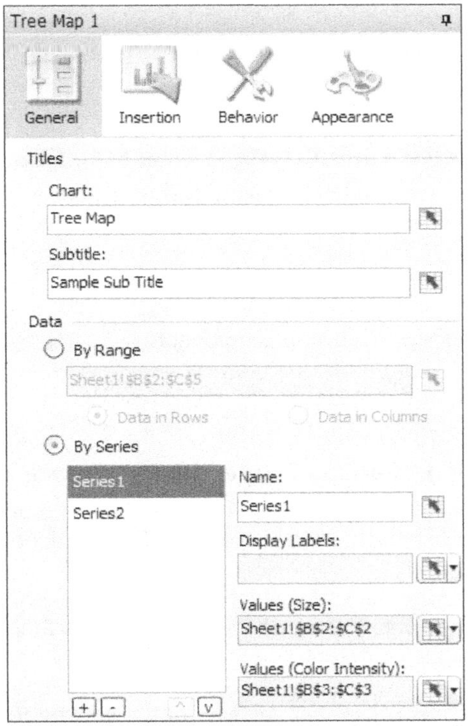

Figure 13-39 Tree Map general view options

Series Tab Options

The Tree Map series tab options are shown in Figure 13-40.

HIGH COLOR Is used to change the high intensity color (high values) for the series.

LOW COLOR Is used to change the low intensity color (low values) for the series.

Similar to the gradient spectrum range that the ellipse and rectangle components support, the low and high color options are used to create the color spectrum for the series of data.

Usually, a dark color is selected for the high color option and a light color option is selected for the low color. Based on the colors that you select, the color for each rectangle is automatically calculated, so that each color is in the range of colors that you selected.

SHOW LINES Is used to display a line around each rectangle on the Tree Map. Click the Color Selector button to select the color for the line for the series of data.

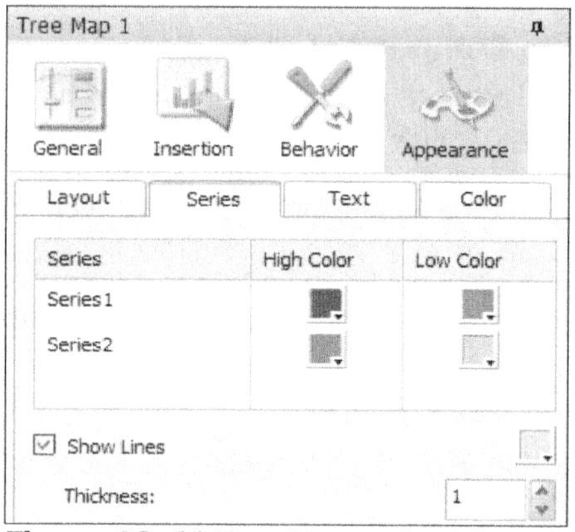

Figure 13-40 Tree Map series tab options

Exercise 13.6: Create A Tree Map Chart

In this exercise you will learn how to create a Tree Map chart that compares the price and market share of seven products.

1. Import the Tree Map spreadsheet.
2. Add the Tree Map component.
3. Save the model as `My tree map`.

Use The Canvas Properties To Create A Background

In Chapter 3 you learned about the canvas properties. In this part of the exercise you will use these properties to create a background for the model.

1. On the General view of the Canvas Properties panel, open the Type drop-down list and select Gradient. This is not the type that the sample Tree Map model used. I wanted to do something slightly different.
2. Select colors that you like for the **BACKGROUND COLOR 1** and **2** options.

Select The Options For The Tree Map

1. On the General view, make the changes in the table.

Option	Change To
Chart	Product Comparison
Subtitle	Stock Price vs Market Share

2. On the General view, create the series in the table. The values in this table will be displayed when the mouse pointer is hovered over a rectangle on the chart.

Option	Change To
Display Labels	B3:B9
Values (Size)	C3:C9
Values (Color Intensity)	D3:D9

3. On the Series tab, make the changes in the table.

Option	Change To
High Color	Black
Low Color	Light Gray

4. Save the changes. Your chart should look like the one shown in Figure 13-41.

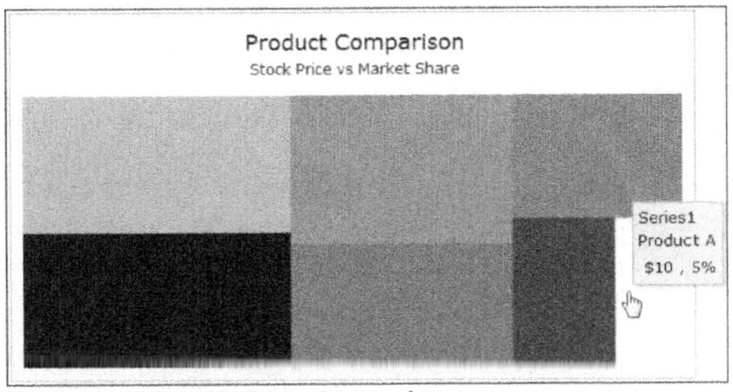

Figure 13-41 Tree Map chart

How To Read A Tree Map Chart

The rectangle in the upper left corner of the chart is the largest because it represents the largest price. The color is light because Product D has a low percent of the market share. Product A that is illustrated above in Figure 13-41 has the lowest price and the lowest market share.

NEW Sparkline Chart Component

Use this chart type when you need to display a one dimensional series of numeric data in a small space. Sparkline charts also support multiple series of data. Like Candlestick and OHLC charts, low values, high values, start values and end values data points can be displayed as markers on the chart. A normal range of data can be displayed as a colored background in the chart.

General View Options

The Sparkline chart general view options are shown in Figure 13-42.

HEADER LABELS Is used to select the labels that will be displayed next to each series on the chart.

Common Tab Options

The Sparkline chart common tab options are shown in Figure 13-43.

NORMAL RANGE AREA Is used to enable the range of normal values to be displayed in the background of the chart.

AUTO Select this option to have the normal range based on the range of data.

MANUAL Select this option to have the normal range based on specific low and high values that you can type in or select in the embedded spreadsheet.

NORMAL RANGE LOW Is used to select the low value for the range.

NORMAL RANGE HIGH Is used to select the high value for the range.

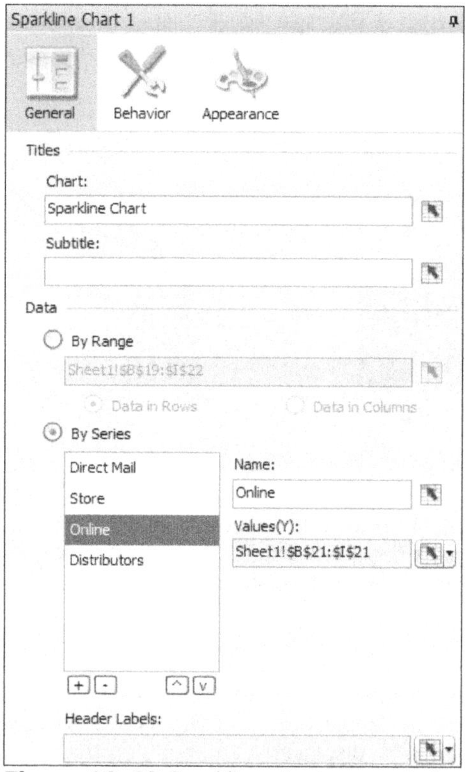

Figure 13-42 Sparkline chart general view options

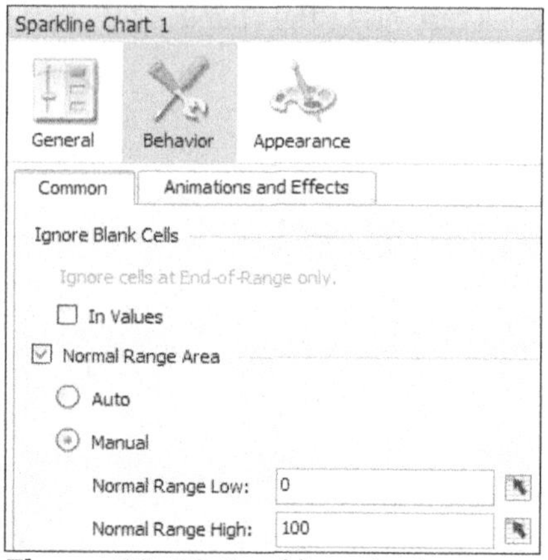

Figure 13-43 Sparkline chart common tab options

Layout Tab Options

The Sparkline chart layout tab options are shown in Figure 13-44.

HORIZONTAL GAP Is used to select the amount of space that will be between the plot area and series labels.

VERTICAL GAP Is used to select the amount of space that will be between each series of data.

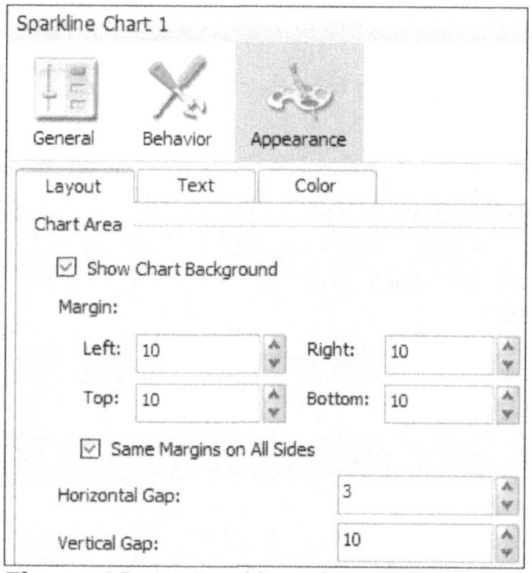

Figure 13-44 Sparkline chart layout tab options

Text Tab Options

The Sparkline chart text tab options are shown in Figure 13-45.

These options are used to display and hide labels and values on the chart. Figure 13-46 illustrates the series and header labels.

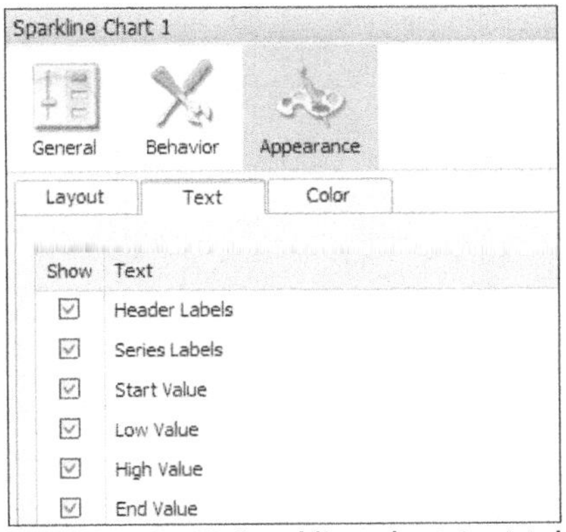

Figure 13-45 Sparkline chart text tab options

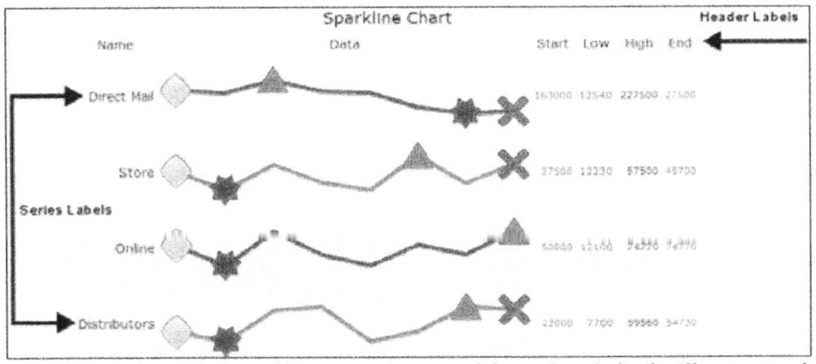

Figure 13-46 Sparkline series and header labels illustrated

Color Tab Options

The Sparkline chart color tab options are shown in Figure 13-47.

NORMAL RANGE COLOR Is used to select the color for the normal range that will be displayed as the colored background of the chart.

NORMAL RANGE TRANSPARENCY Is used to select how visible the normal range background color will be.

Line Colors Options

The options in this section are used to select the line color for each series of data.

Markers Options

The options in this section are used to display or hide markers. If displayed, the markers shape and fill color can be changed.

Figure 13-47 Sparkline chart color tab options

ADVANCED FUNCTIONALITY

In this chapter you will learn about the following advanced functionality topics.

- ☑ Dynamic Visibility
- ☑ Password protecting a dashboard
- ☑ Use components to display and hide other components on a dashboard

Overview

The topics covered in this chapter are not required to create most dashboards. Learning about the topics in this chapter will help you determine if they would enhance the dashboards that you create.

Dynamic Visibility

By now you have seen the dynamic visibility options on the Common tab of the Properties panel more times than you can remember. I hope that you are not annoyed that I waited until now to cover this topic. Hopefully, you will find the "cool" factor of this feature, worth the wait.

Simply put, dynamic visibility gives you the option of controlling when components are displayed or hidden on the dashboard. The models that you have created in this book so far have not had an overwhelming number of components. But have no fear, users will ask for dashboards that need a lot more components. There is but so much space available that you can use to display the components in a size that does not cause eye strain.

If you remember, you had to make the charts larger than the default size so that the values on the horizontal axis were easier to read. Usually, you can fit two or three charts plus a few selectors without a lot of sizing issues. If you have looked at the sample dashboards you have seen what I consider the best use of screen real estate for dashboards. Never mind the fact that they also look great. The graphics that are used on many of the sample dashboards on the web site are custom. I cannot tell you the number of hours that it takes to create dashboards that look like those from scratch, when you include the time to design the graphics.

If you do not have the time or artistic ability to create those dashboards, the dynamic visibility options allow you to include all of the components to meet the dashboard requirements, look good and have some "wow" functionality thrown in for good measure. I will say this about dynamic visibility, when I first started learning this software, there was not (and still is not) a lot of "how to" information for the software. Many people, including moiré, have spent countless hours trying to figure out what each option could be used for. I had no idea that the two dynamic visibility options shown in Figure 14-1 could provide so much functionality! These options control when the component will be displayed on the dashboard. A group of components can be controlled by these options. The two options shown in Figure 14-2 are on the Animations and Effects tab. The Entry Effect options are often used with the dynamic visibility options.

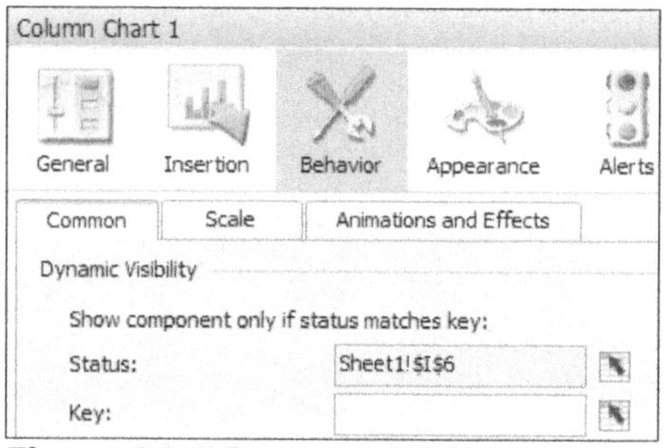

Figure 14-1 Dynamic Visibility options

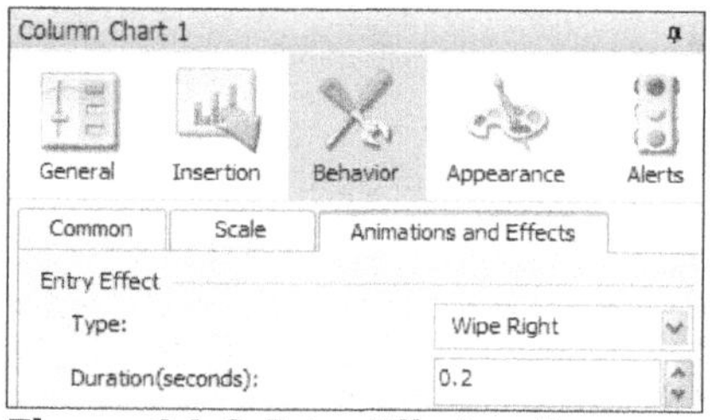

Figure 14-2 Entry Effect options

Common Tab Dynamic Visibility Options

STATUS This is the option that Dashboard Design uses to determine if dynamic visibility is to occur for a component. This option is used to select the cell that is the trigger, to determine whether or not the component is visible. If there is no cell in this field, the Key option is ignored.

KEY This option contains the value that the cell referenced in the Status field must match for the component to be displayed on the dashboard. This means that the operator is "Equal to" and cannot be changed. If the value in this field matches, the component is displayed. If not, the component stays hidden. The default value for this field is "1". Most of the time, you will not have to change this value. The number one signifies that the option is "on" and zero or any other value indicates that the option is "off". This field is case sensitive.

Animations And Effects Tab Options

Entry Effect Options

TYPE The options in this drop-down list are used to select how the component should become visible. The default option is **NONE**, which will display the component without any animation. The other options in the drop-down list add animation to the component as explained below.

① **FADE-IN** Select this option if you want the component to first appear semi-transparent and slowly become solid.
② **WIPE RIGHT** Select this option if you want the component to appear at full height, then grow to its full width.
③ **WIPE RIGHT DOWN** Select this option if you want the component to appear gradually until it becomes its full size.

DURATION (SECONDS) This option is used to select how long (in seconds), the option selected in the Type field takes to complete. The range of values that can be entered in this field are zero to 10. This option is not available if the Entry Effect option is set to None.

Applying Dynamic Visibility Functionality To Multiple Components
What may not be obvious is that dynamic visibility functionality can be applied to multiple components on a dashboard. This will allow several components to be displayed or hidden at the same time. There are two ways to set the dynamic visibility options for multiple components, as explained below.
① Hold down the CTRL key, then click on each of the components that you want to apply the same dynamic visibility options to.
② Group the components that you want to apply the same dynamic visibility options to.

Check Box Component

The Check Box component is often used to display and hide another component on the dashboard.

General View Options

The Check Box general view options are shown in Figure 14-3.

SOURCE DATA Is used to select the empty cells for the two states (on and off) of the Check Box component. Keep in mind that the first cell that you select is used for the "unselected" state (off) of the button. The second cell is for the "selected" state (on) of the button.

DESTINATION Is used to select one empty cell in the spreadsheet that the value in one of the source data cells will be inserted into.

The Manual Edit button across from the Source Data option opens the dialog box shown in Figure 14-4. You can change the values in the Source Data column if necessary, by double-clicking on the value.

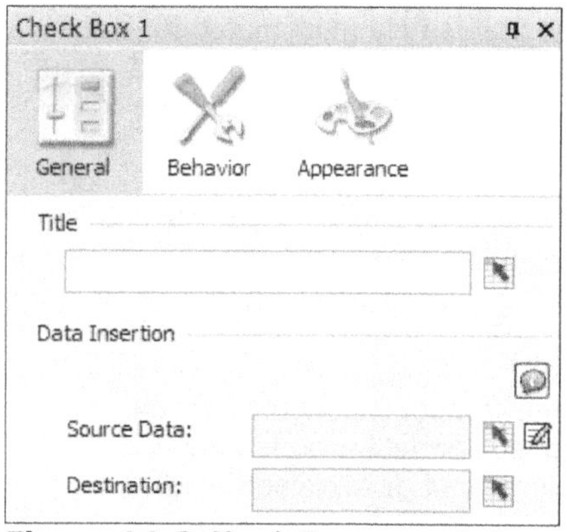

Figure 14-3 Check Box general view options

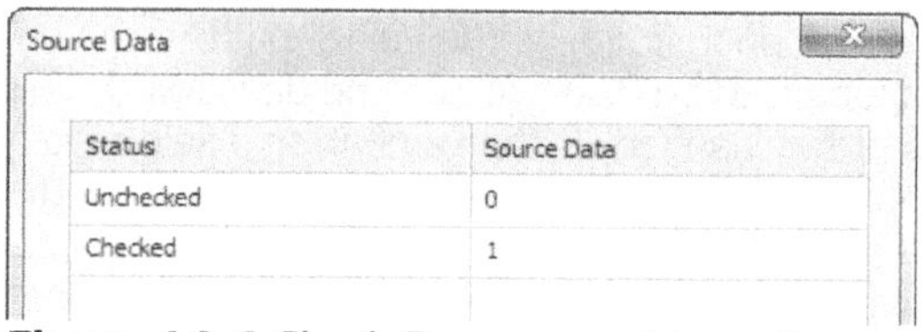

Figure 14-4 Check Box source data options

Common Tab Options

The Check Box common tab options are shown in Figure 14-5.

ITEM The options in the drop-down list are used to select if the check box does or does not have a check mark when the dashboard is first opened.

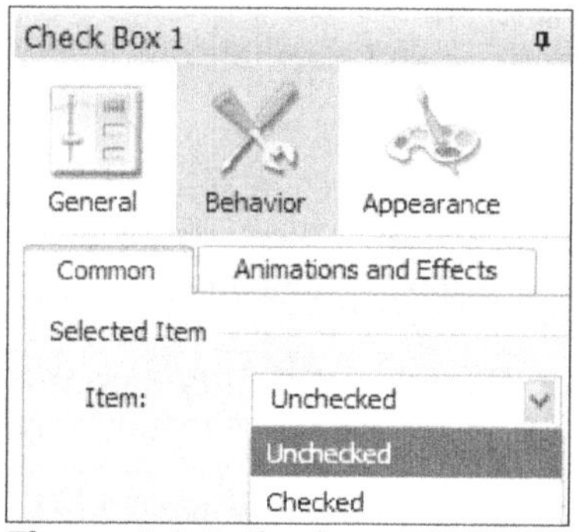

Figure 14-5 Check Box common tab options

Color Tab Options

The Check Box color tab options shown in Figure 14-6 are used to change the background color of the check box.

UNCHECKED COLOR Is used to change the background color when the check box is not checked.

CHECKED COLOR Is used to change the background color when the check box is checked.

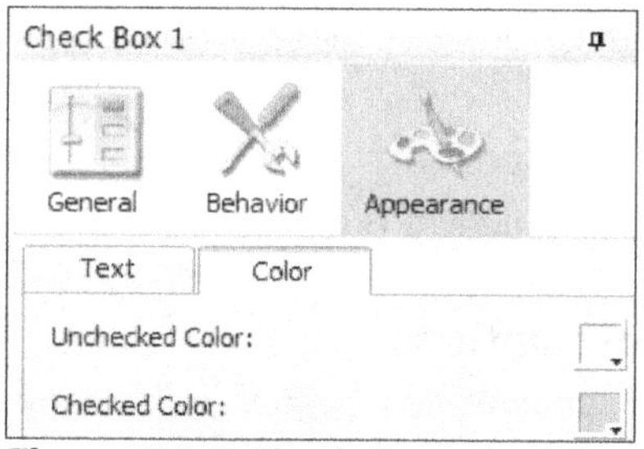

Figure 14-6 Check Box color tab options

Exercise 14.1: Use The Check Box Component To Display And Hide A Chart

If the dashboard has several components and appears somewhat crowded or if there is something like a chart that does not always have to be displayed on the dashboard, you can hide it. To accomplish this, you will add the check box component so that the user can display or hide a chart as needed. Other components like the Icon and Toggle Button can also be used to display or hide another component.

1. Save the My line chart model as `My check box chart.`

2. Add the Check Box component above the upper left corner of the chart, then make the check box larger.

Select The Check Box Component Options

1. On the General view, make the changes in the table.

Option	Change To
Title	View Chart
Destination	A7

2. On the Common tab, open the Item drop-down list and select **UNCHECKED**. Selecting this option means that when the dashboard is first opened, the check box will be visible.

Select The Line Chart Component Options

1. On the Common tab, make the changes in the table.

Option	Change To
Status	A7 (1)
Key	1

(1) This is the link between the check box and the chart to determine if the chart will be hidden or displayed when the button is clicked.

2. Save the model and preview it.

   Click the **VIEW CHART** button. You should see the chart.

   The model should look like the one shown in Figure 14-7.

   If you click the View Chart button again, the chart will be hidden.

Figure 14-7 Check Box model

Input Text Component

Common Tab Options

The Input Text common tab options are shown in Figure 14-8.

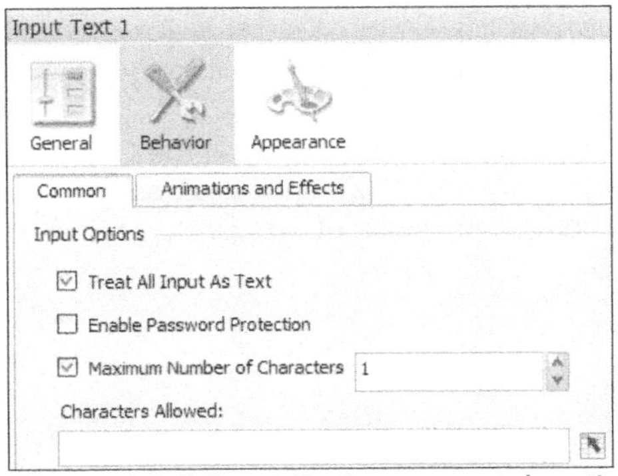

Figure 14-8 Input Text common tab options

Input Options

ENABLE PASSWORD PROTECTION Selecting this option causes asterisks to be displayed instead of the password when it is typed in the field.

MAXIMUM NUMBER OF CHARACTERS Is used to enable the maximum number of characters that can be entered into the field.

NUMBER OF CHARACTERS Is used to select the maximum number of characters that can be entered for the password. Select a number that is at least the length of the password that will be used for the dashboard.

CHARACTERS ALLOWED Type in or select the characters that cannot be entered into the field. If this field is left blank, all characters can be entered in the field.

Color Tab Options

The Input Text color tab option is shown in Figure 14-9.

BACKGROUND COLOR Is used to change the background color of the interior section of the Input Text field.

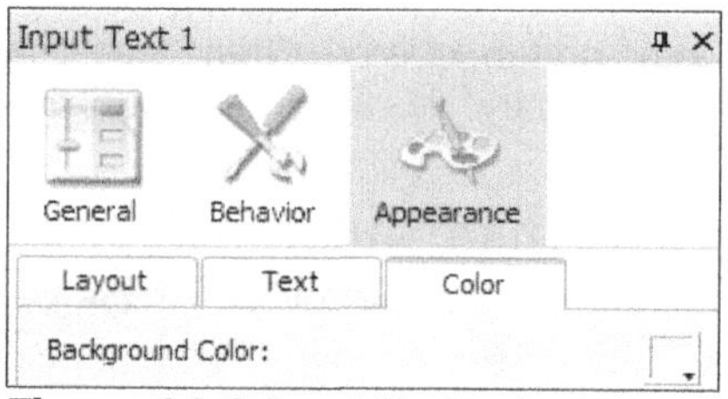

Figure 14-9 Input Text color tab option

Exercise 14.2: Adding Password Protection To A Dashboard

There may be times when you want to restrict some people from viewing a dashboard or part of a dashboard. Usually, this is because the data is sensitive in nature. This type of functionality can be implemented using the Dynamic Visibility options. In addition to using these options, the components on the dashboard that you want to protect have to be grouped.

In this exercise you will add password protection to a model. Users will have to enter the correct password before the dashboard will be displayed. While this exercise applies the protection to all of the components on the dashboard, you can set the protection for some components and allow access to other components all the time.

Group The Components For Password Protection

The components that have to be password protected have to be added to the same group, so that a password can be added to them. If there are several components on the model and only some of the components require protection, you have to select the components that you want password protected when the dashboard is first opened and add them to the same group. Only components in the group that have a component with dynamic visibility enabled, will be hidden when the dashboard is first opened.

1. Save the My filter drop-down list model as `My password protection.`

2. Select both of the components in the Object Browser, then right-click and select **GROUP**, as illustrated in Figure 14-10.

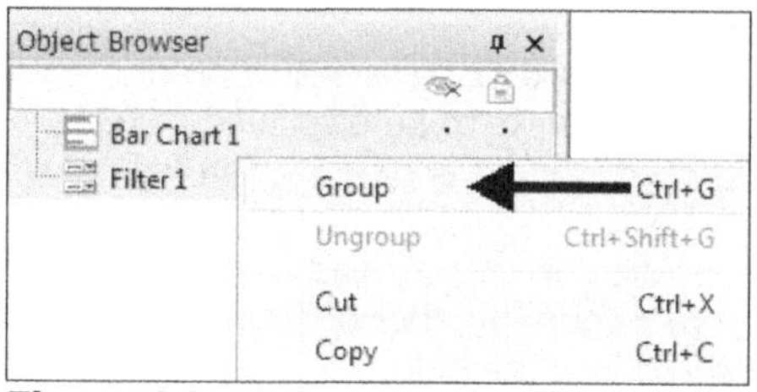

Figure 14-10 Group option illustrated

Select The Password Options

In this part of the exercise you will select the Status and Key options for the group. In this exercise the Key field will store the password.

1. Right-click on the group in the Object Browser and select Properties. You will see the Dynamic Visibility options.

2. On the Common tab, (this should be the only tab) make the changes in the table. You should have the options shown in Figure 14-11.

Option	Change To
Status	H1 (2)
Key	Mypassword1 (3)

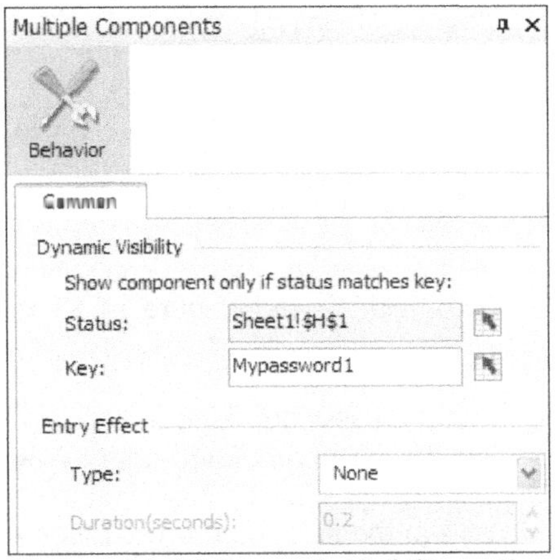

Figure 14-11 Dynamic Visibility options for the group

(2) You can use any empty cell in the spreadsheet for this option.
(3) The password is case sensitive because the Key field is case sensitive.

If you select the objects individually in the group instead of selecting the group, you will see that the Properties panel name changes to **MULTIPLE COMPONENTS**, as shown above in Figure 14-11.

3. If necessary, move the components down so that there is room to add a component at the top of the model.

Select The Input Text Component Options

This component will be used to enter the password. While not done in this exercise, you should add another Input Text component to the model that informs the user to enter the password in the field, otherwise, they may not know what the field is for.

1. Add the Input Text component above the filter component. Make the Input Text component wider.

2. On the General view, make the changes in the table.

Option	Change To
Enter Text	Enter the password
Destination	H1 (4)

(4) You have to select the same cell for this option that you selected for the Status option for the group.

3. On the Common tab, make the changes in the table. You should have the options selected that are shown in Figure 14-12.

Option	Change To
Enable Password Protection	Select this option
Maximum Number of Characters	Select this option
Number of characters	11

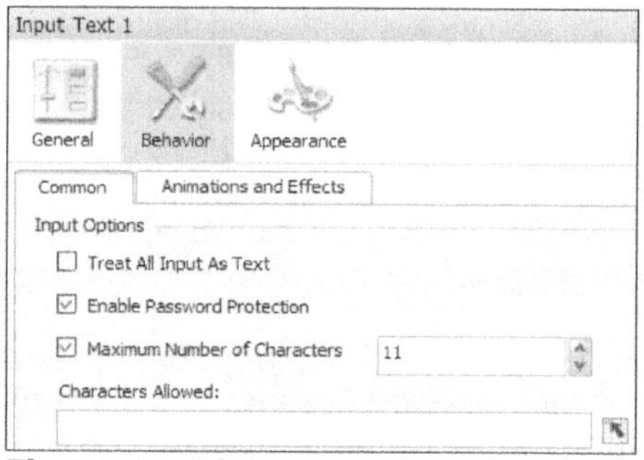

Figure 14-12 Input Text common tab changes

Test The Model

1. Save the changes and preview the model. You should only see the password field shown in Figure 14-13 on the model.

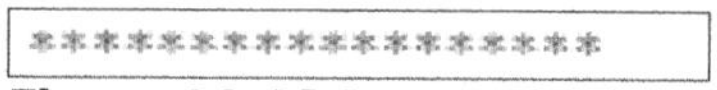

Figure 14-13 Password field

2. Type `testmodel` in the Password field, then press Enter. This is not the correct password, so the other components in the group are not displayed.

3. Type `Mypassword1` in the field, then press Enter. You should now see the rest of the model.

Toggle Button Component

This component is similar to the Check Box component because it uses two states, which are often used to display and hide another component on the dashboard.

Color Tab Options

The Toggle Button color tab options are shown in Figure 14-14.

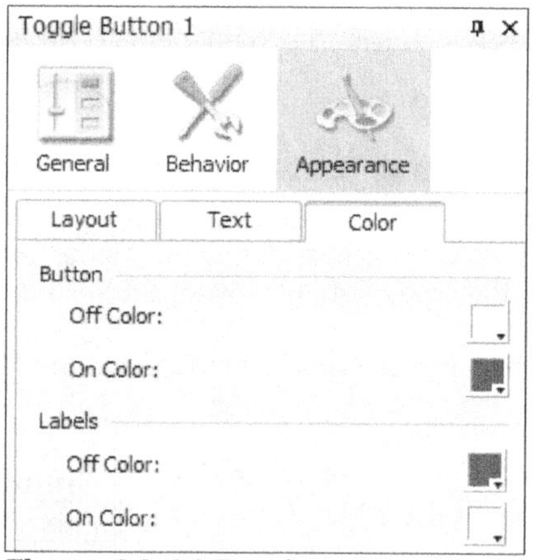

Figure 14-14 Toggle Button color tab options

Button Options

OFF COLOR Is used to change the background color when the button is not clicked.

ON COLOR Is used to change the default background color.

Labels Options

OFF COLOR Is used to change the default color of the text on the button.

ON COLOR Is used to change the color of the text when the button is clicked.

Exercise 14.3: Use The Toggle Button Component

Toggle buttons are used to display or hide an object on the dashboard. If you look at the chart in Figure 14-15, you see that it plots four series of data: Market Growth, Sales Growth, East Region and West Region. This chart may look familiar because you created part of it in Exercise 7.5. I added two series of data to the spreadsheet and chart.

As you can see, it is somewhat difficult to see each series of data on the chart shown in Figure 14-15.

If you added toggle buttons to the model, you could hide one or all of the series of data as needed, to make the chart easier to read.

Figure 14-15 Line chart with four series of data

1. Save the dd_toggle_button model as `My toggle button`.
2. Add the Toggle Button component above the chart on the left.
3. On the General view, change the Destination option to L4.
4. On the Common tab, change the Item option to On.

How To Customize The Text On A Button

By default, the text on a Toggle button is "On". If there is only one toggle button on the dashboard this may not be a problem because once the user clicked on it, they could tell what was hidden. This is not a good design choice though. There are two options for changing the text on a button, as explained below.

① **USE THE LABELS FIELD ON THE GENERAL VIEW** If the text that you want to put on the button is in the spreadsheet, add the cell to the Labels field.

② **USE THE LABELS DIALOG BOX** If you do not want to use data in the spreadsheet or the text that you want to use is not in the spreadsheet, select this option. A benefit that the Labels dialog box has is that you can change the text that is displayed for the on and off states of the button.

How To Create A Custom Label For A Toggle Button

1. On the General view, click the Manual Edit button at the end of the Labels field.
2. Click in the **OFF** Label Name field, then type `Show Market Growth`.
3. Click in the **ON** Label Name field, then type `Hide Market Growth`.
4. You should have the options shown in Figure 14-16. Click OK.

   Make the button wider so that you can see all of the text.

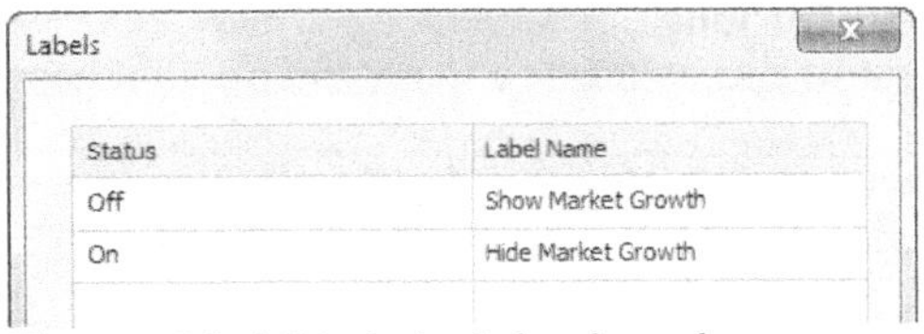

Figure 14-16 Labels dialog box changes

5. Save the changes, then preview the model. If you click the button, you will see that the market growth trend line in the chart disappears. If you click the button again the market growth trend line will reappear.

Add The Other Buttons

In this part of the exercise you will create buttons for the other three trend lines in the chart. To do that, you will copy the existing button and only change what is necessary.

1. Right-click on the toggle button that you just created, then select **COPY**.
   Right-click on the canvas and select **PASTE**.
   Move the new button to the right of the first button.

2. Make two more copies of the button.

3. Select the options in the table below for each of the three buttons.

Option	Button 2	Button 3	Button 4
Label Off	Show Sales Growth	Show East Region	Show West Region
Label On	Hide Sales Growth	Hide East Region	Hide West Region
Destination	L5	L6	L7

4. Save the changes.

   The model should look like the one shown in Figure 14-17.

   When you click the buttons, lines in the chart will disappear or reappear.

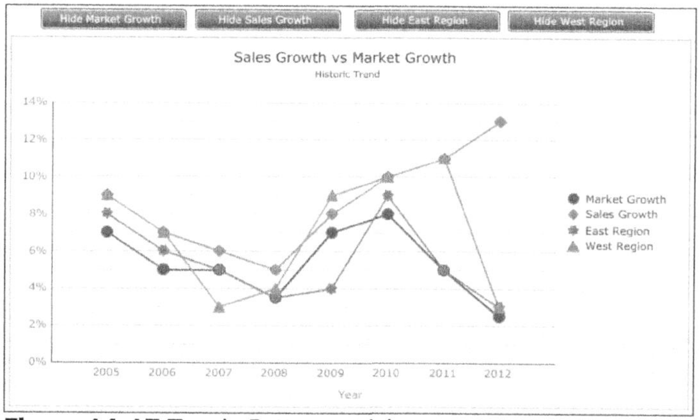

Figure 14-17 Toggle Button model

Label Component

General View Options

The Label general view options are shown in Figure 14-18.

Text Options

LINK TO CELL Is used to select the cell that has the text for the label.

APPLY CELL FORMATTING If clicked, this button will apply the formatting from the spreadsheet to the label.

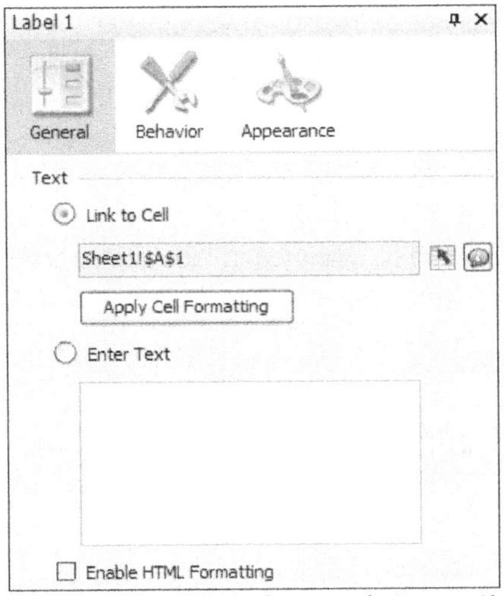

Figure 14-18 Label general view options

Layout Tab Options

The Label layout tab options are shown in Figure 14-19.

WRAP TEXT If checked, the text will wrap to the next line of the label, as needed.

Label Background Options

DRAW BORDER ON Is used to select which sides of the label will display a border.

SHOW BORDER Is used to add a border to sides of the label. (5)

BORDER THICKNESS Is used to select the thickness for the border. (5)

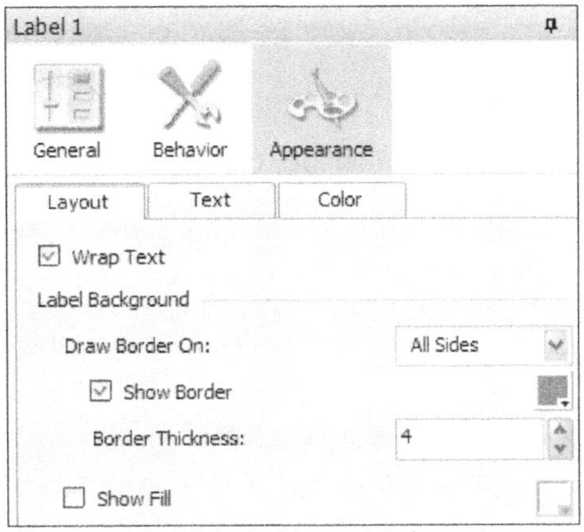

Figure 14-19 Label layout tab options

SHOW FILL Is used to enable the Fill Color option to the right.

FILL COLOR Is used to display a background color. The fill color can also be selected on the Color tab. If selected, the label will have a solid background.

(5) This option is applied to the sides selected in the Draw Border On option.

Exercise 14.4: Adding Help To A Dashboard

In Exercise 6.1 you created a dashboard that used a value component to get information from the user. This information is used to select the data to display on the chart. There are options about the field that a user may not know about. One way to help the people using the dashboard is to provide help, right on the dashboard.

Don't worry, the type of help that you will learn how to create will not detract from your visual master piece. In the previous exercise, you used a toggle button to display and hide series of data on the chart. In this exercise you will use a toggle button to display a help message for the Price per Unit field.

Create The Help Button

In this part of the exercise you will create the button that will be used to display and hide the help window that you will create later in this exercise.

1. Save the dd_help_button model as `My help button`.
2. Add the Toggle Button component to the left of the Price per Unit label.
3. On the General view, change the Destination option to E1.
4. Open the Labels dialog box for the Labels field, then change the Off Label Name to `Close`.

   Change the On Label Name to `Help`, as shown in Figure 14-20, then click OK.

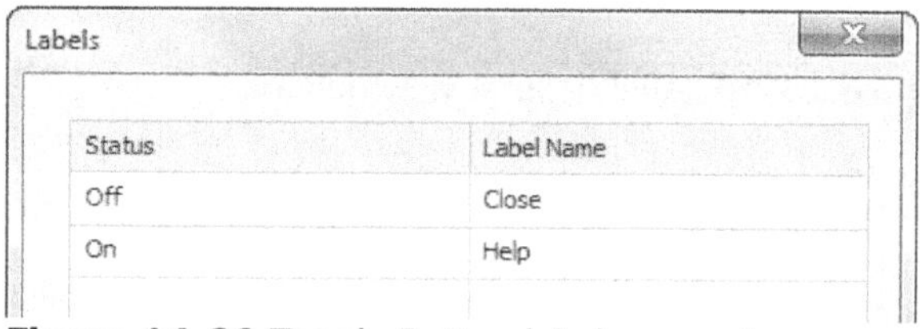

Figure 14-20 Toggle Button label name changes

5. On the Common tab, change the Item option to On.
6. On the Animations and Effects tab, select the Enable Sound option.
7. On the Color tab, select complementary colors for the button **OFF COLOR** and **ON COLOR** options. These options will change the color of the button when it is clicked.

Create The Help Window

1. Add the Label component below the Price per Unit field.
2. On the General view, type a brief message in the **ENTER TEXT** field that will help the person using the dashboard know what to enter in the field.

   My message is shown in Figure 14-21.

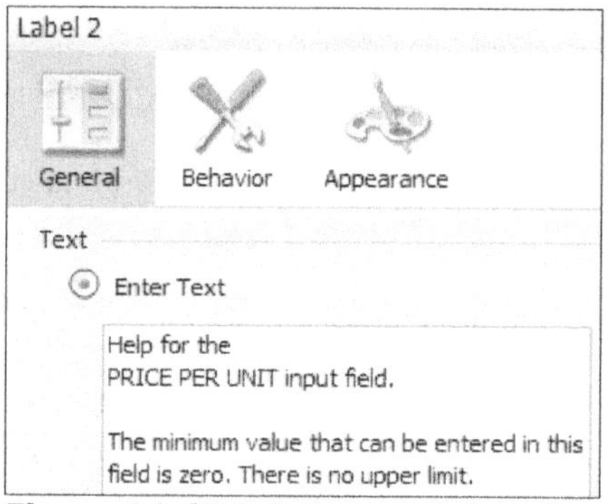

Figure 14-21 Label general view changes

3. On the Common tab, make the changes in the table. You should have the options shown in Figure 14-22.

Option	Change To
Vertical Scroll Bar	On
Status	E1
Key	0

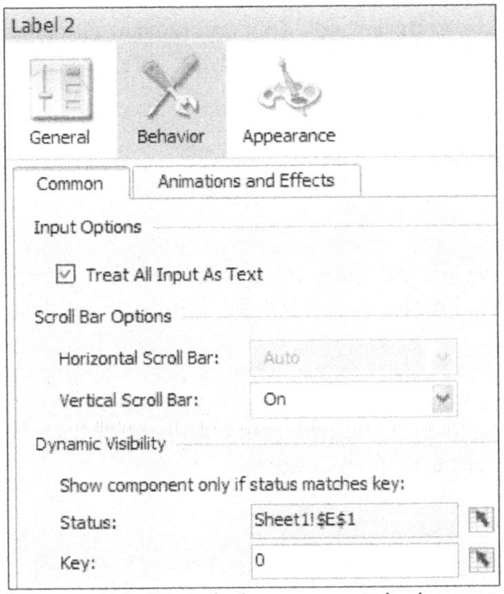

Figure 14-22 Label common tab changes

4. On the Layout tab, make the changes in the table.

Option	Change To
Show Border	Select this option
Border Thickness	1
Show Fill	Select this option
Show Fill (Color)	Light yellow

5. On the Text tab, change the Show Text font size option to 12.

6. On the Color tab, change the color of the **TRACK COLOR** option to a color that goes with the yellow background.

7. Resize the Label component so that the scroll bar is displayed properly, then save the changes.

8. When you first preview the model, it should look like the one shown in Figure 14-23. When you click the Help button, you should see the help message that you entered, as shown in Figure 14-24. When you click the Close button, the help window will close.

Figure 14-23 Help button added to the model

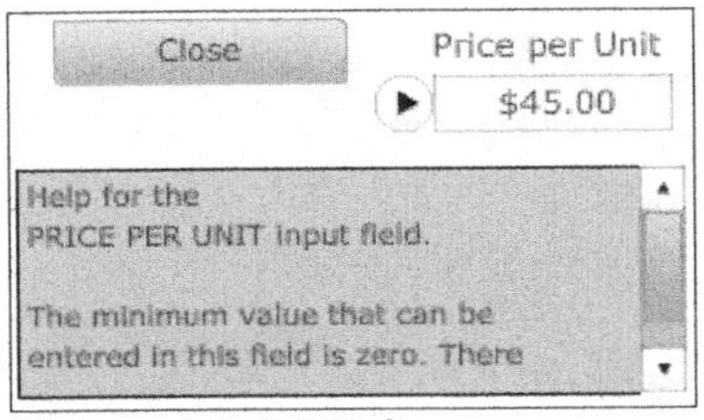

Figure 14-24 Help message

NEW Push Button Component

The Push Button component can be used to create a pop-up window when the button is clicked. This component can also be used to add data each time that it is clicked. For example, it can be used to let users restore a single value component to its default value without resetting all of the values in the model. This component can be configured to set the value of one or more cells to specific values. The majority of options for this component are the same as the Toggle button.

Layout Tab Options

The Push Button layout tab options are shown in Figure 14-25.

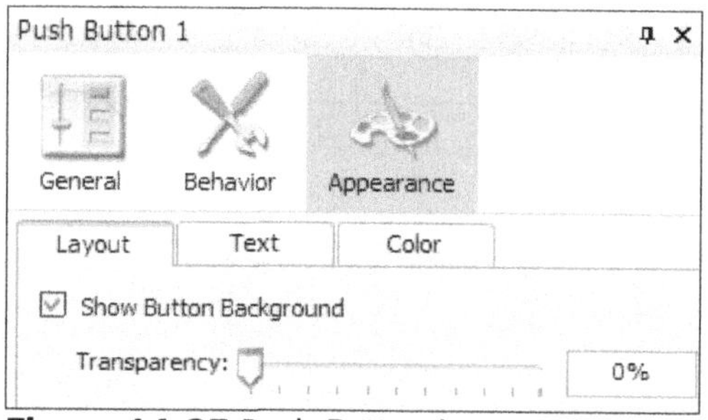

Figure 14-25 Push Button layout tab options

SHOW BUTTON BACKGROUND Select this option if you want the background of the button to be visible.

TRANSPARENCY If the Show Button Background option is selected, the Transparency options can be used to adjust the transparency for the background of the button.

Exercise 14.5: Revise The XY Chart

In Exercise 8.4 you created an XY chart. The problem in my opinion, is that it is hard to tell which diamond marker is for which month of sales on the chart. To fix this, the data for each month needs to be created individually, as its own series.

1. Save the My XY chart model as `My XY chart revised`.
2. On the General view in the By Series section, make the changes in the table.

Option	Change To
Name	Jan
Values (X)	B2
Values (Y)	C2

3. Click the **PLUS** sign button, then add the series of data in the table.

Option	Change To
Name	Feb
Values (X)	B3
Values (Y)	C3

The chart should look like the one shown in Figure 14-26.

Notice that the legend now has the month names. After you add all 12 series, you can change the symbol and/or color of the symbol for each month individually.

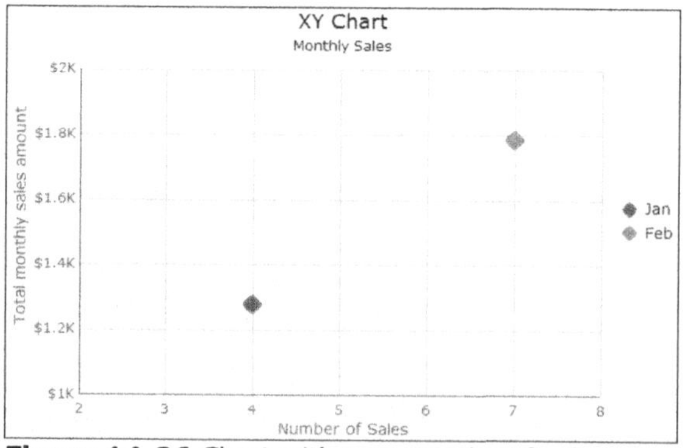

Figure 14-26 Chart with two months of sales shown in the legend

4. Repeat step three for each of the remaining months.

Customize The Markers

In this part of the exercise you will select a shape for each data series, which is each month.

1. On the Series tab, select Feb.
2. Select a symbol from the options illustrated in Figure 14-27.

   Change the color for the symbol.

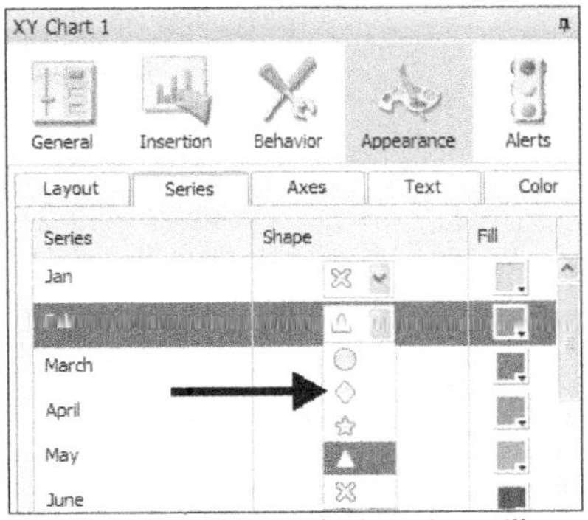

Figure 14-27 Symbol options illustrated

3. Repeat the steps above for each month. The goal is to make each month different on the chart. You can use the same symbol for all 12 months and select a different color for each month or any combination of symbols and colors that you want, as long as each month on the chart is uniquely represented.
4. Save the changes.

   Figure 14-28 shows the options that I selected.

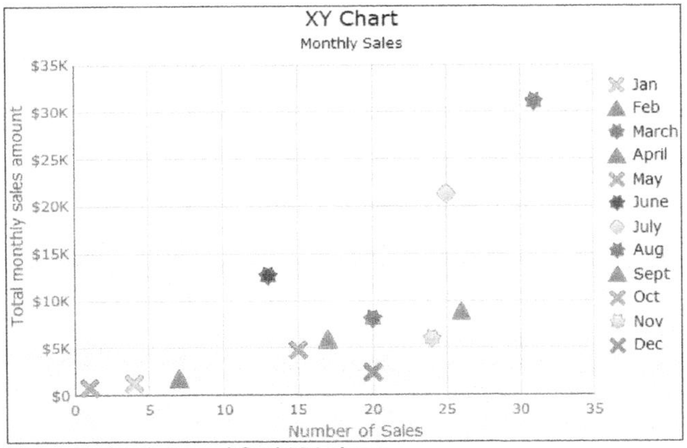

Figure 14-28 Modified XY chart

Displaying Multiple Charts

There will be times when a dashboard will require that more than one chart be displayed. There are several options available, including displaying all of the charts on the dashboard at the same time, displaying one or two charts at a time or letting the user select which chart they want to see.

Figure 14-29 shows five charts, displayed on the dashboard. While this layout meets the users needs, it may not be very pleasing to the eye. To display several charts on a dashboard at the same time may mean that you have to reduce their size. This could make the charts difficult to read. In Exercise 14.1 you added a Check Box component to the dashboard to display or hide a chart. You can link more than one chart to the same Check Box, by setting the Display Status option on multiple charts to the same value.

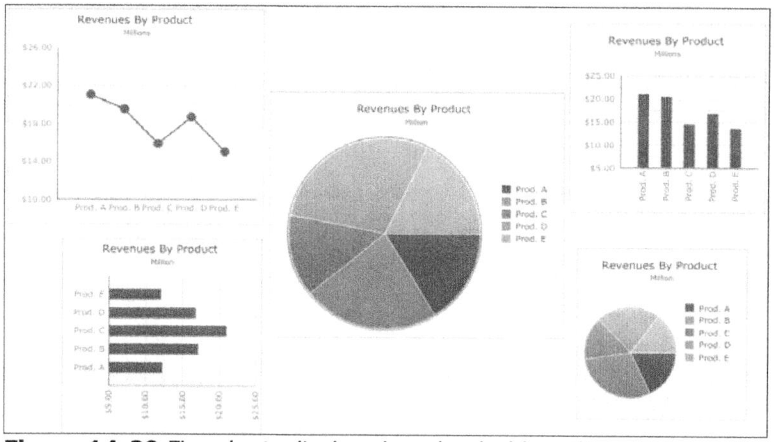

Figure 14-29 Five charts displayed on the dashboard

A Better Layout For Multiple Charts

Believe it or not, the five charts shown above in Figure 14-29 came from one of the sample dashboards that come with Dashboard Design.

1. Open the Samples dialog box.

2. Open the Status List model and preview it. If you click on each menu option, you will see a different chart.

If you go into design mode, it appears as though there is only one chart.

If you look in the Object Browser shown in Figure 14-30, you will see that there are five charts. These are the same five charts shown above in Figure 14-29.

Yes, all five charts were created from data in the same spreadsheet, which is shown in Figure 14-31.

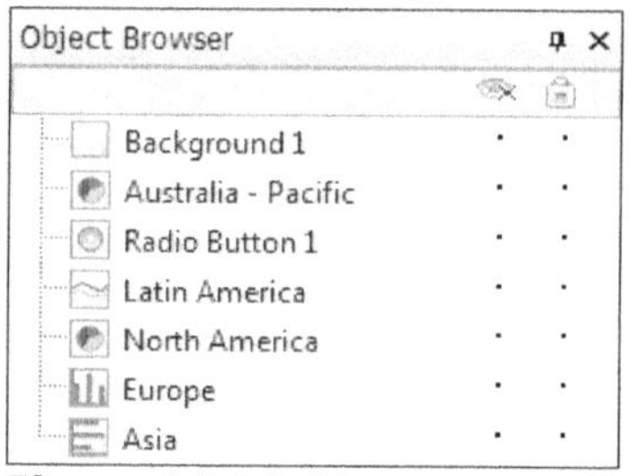

Figure 14-30 Object Browser with five charts

	A	B	C	D	E	F	G	H
1	Revenues By Product		Rev					
2								
3		Status List	Prod. A	Prod. B	Prod. C	Prod. D	Prod. E	Chart Type
4	North America		$ 14.22	$ 20.12	$ 12.18	$ 25.49	$ 15.64	Pie Chart
5	Latin America		$ 21.05	$ 19.54	$ 15.88	$ 18.73	$ 15.02	Line Chart
6	Europe		$ 21.06	$ 20.45	$ 14.49	$ 16.78	$ 13.61	Column Chart
7	Asia		$ 12.25	$ 17.12	$ 20.99	$ 16.79	$ 12.07	Bar Chart
8	Australia & Pacific		$ 15.36	$ 25.74	$ 13.17	$ 19.42	$ 12.70	Pie Chart

Figure 14-31 Data for the five charts

Icon Component

This component can be used to display and hide another component on the dashboard. This component can also be used to show (indicate) the status of a value and display whether or not the value is acceptable. This is useful if the dashboard needs to display several components on an as needed basis. By default, when an icon component is added to the model, the Alerts tab options are enabled. If the icon does not need alert functionality you can disable this option. Disabling the alerts also allows the color of the icon to be changed.

General View Options

The Icon general view options are shown in Figure 14-32.

DISPLAY VALUE Is used to select the value (cell) that will be displayed as a tool tip when the mouse pointer is hovered over the component. The value selected should be numeric. If a numeric value is not selected, a zero will be displayed.

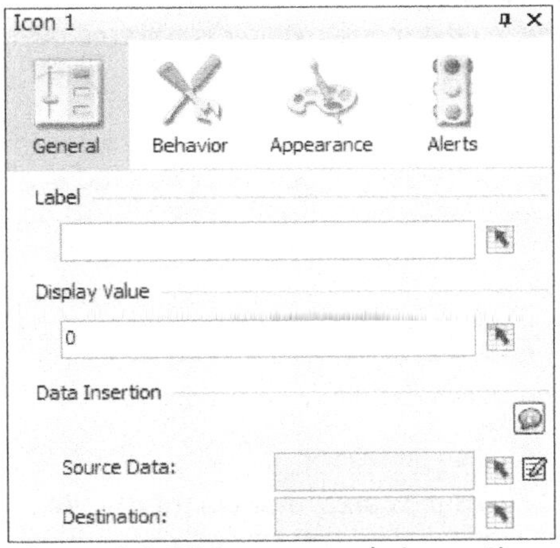

Figure 14-32 Icon general view options

If you will use the Icon component as an on/off button, leave the Label and Display Value fields empty.

Layout Tab Options

The Icon layout tab options are shown in Figure 14-33.

SHOW ON/OFF This option is selected by default. It is used to change the appearance of the icon when it is on (hovered over) and off (not hovered over). The icon will have a different color for each state (on and off).

If this option is not enabled, all of the following are true.

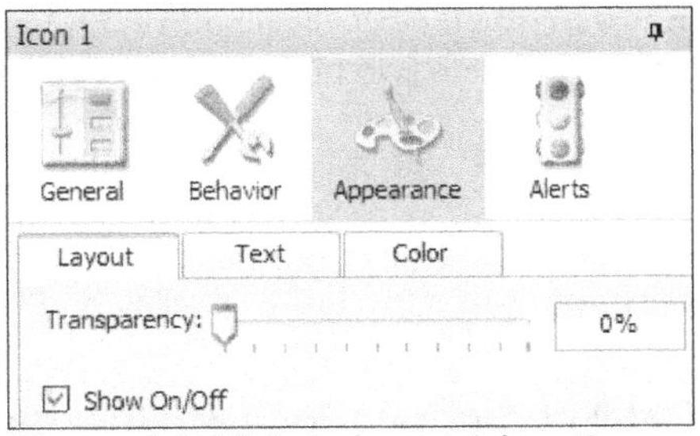

Figure 14-33 Icon layout tab options

① This component can be used as a display component, which means that it can't be clicked on.
② The color of the icon will not change if this option is not enabled.
③ You can set the default color for the off state on the Color tab if the alert functionality is not enabled.
④ If you do not want the on color to be used to calculate the alert colors, enable the alerts option, then clear the Show On/Off option.

Text Tab Options

The Icon text tab options are shown in Figure 14-34.

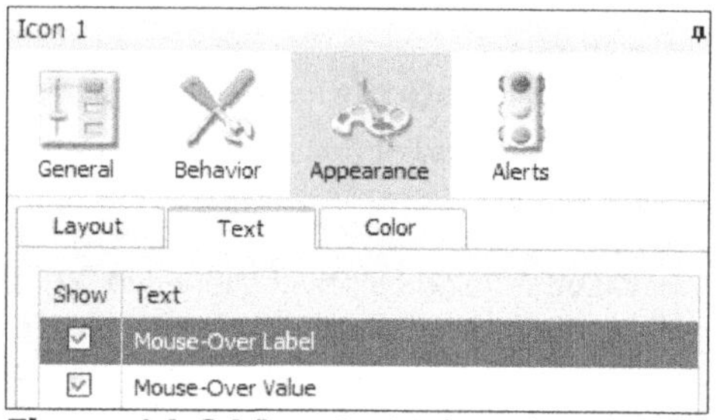

Figure 14-34 Icon text tab options

MOUSE-OVER LABEL Is used to display the label in a tooltip when the mouse pointer is hovered over the icon.

MOUSE-OVER VALUE Is used to display a value in a tooltip when the mouse pointer is hovered over the icon.

Color Tab Options

The Icon color tab options are shown in Figure 14-35.

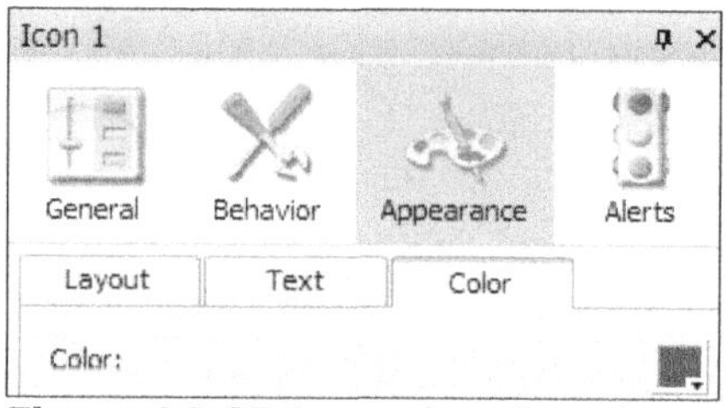

Figure 14-35 Icon color tab options

COLOR Is used to change the color of the icon. To enable this option, you have to clear the Enable Alerts option on the Alerts view.

Exercise 14.6: Display And Hide Charts Using The Icon Component

In this exercise you will place an icon on two states on the map. The icon components will be used to display and hide two of the charts shown earlier in Figure 14-29.

1. Save the dd_map_with_icons_model as `My icons model`.

If you look in the Object Browser you will see that three charts are hidden. After you complete this exercise, you can add icons to display and hide these charts also, if you want to.

Select The Options For The Nevada Icon Component

1. Add the Icon component to the state of Nevada on the map.

2. On the General view, make the changes in the table.

Option	Change To
Label	A4
Display Value	A2 (6)
Destination	B4

(6) I noticed that if I left the Display Value option empty, a zero would automatically be added to the field and would be displayed when the mouse pointer was hovered over an icon. Selecting a cell that had no data made the problem go away.

3. On the Common tab, make the changes in the table.

Option	Change To
Insert On	Mouse Over
Item	Unselected

4. On the Alerts view, clear the Enable Alerts option.

5. On the Color tab, change the color option to red.

Select The Options For The Florida Icon Component

1. Add an Icon component to the state of Florida on the map.

2. On the General view, make the changes in the table.

Option	Change To
Label	A7
Display Value	A2
Destination	B7

3. On the Common tab, make the changes in the table.

Option	Change To
Insert On	Mouse Over
Item	Unselected

4. On the Alerts view, clear the Enable Alerts option.

5. On the Color tab, change the color option to green.

6. Save the changes.

   If you hold the mouse pointer over the icon on the state of Florida, you will see the chart shown in Figure 14-36.

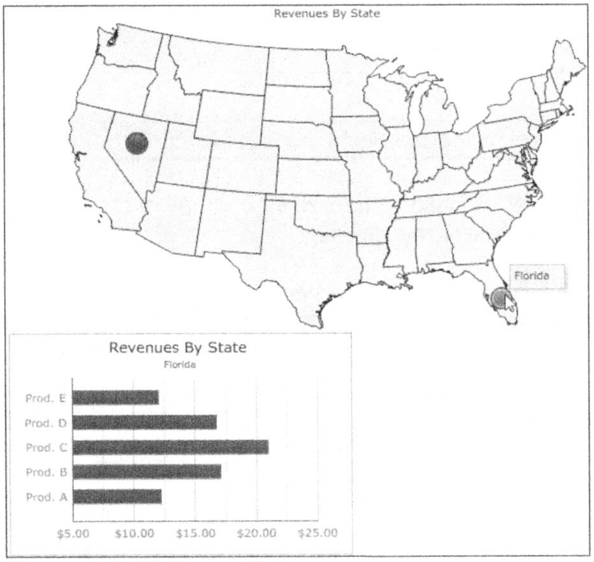

Figure 14-36 Map with icons

Exercise 14.7: Use A Menu To Display And Hide Charts

In this exercise you will start off with the model shown earlier in Figure 14-29. When you finish this exercise, you will have the Status List sample model that you viewed earlier.

As you saw earlier in Figure 14-29, the charts are not the same size. They have to be the same size to achieve the layout that you previewed. The other main task is to set up the dynamic visibility options.

Select The Dynamic Visibility Options

1. Save the dd_multiple_charts model as `My multiple charts menu`.

As you saw earlier in Figure 14-31, Column B in the spreadsheet is being used to check the status of each chart. The cells in Column B will be used to control when each chart is displayed.

2. On the Common tab, make the changes in the table for each chart.

   (**Hint:** You will see the chart name at the top of the Properties panel.)

Chart Name	Status
North America	B4
Latin America	B5
Europe	B6
Asia	B7
Australia	B8

Resize The Charts

The pie chart in the middle of the model is the size that all of the other charts should be.

1. Click on the pie chart in the middle of the model, then press and hold down the CTRL key.

> Remember that the format options use the first component selected as the one that the others will be compared to and changed to match.

2. Click on each of the other charts.

> You can also select the charts by clicking on them in the Object Browser.

3. Format ⇒ Make Same Size ⇒ Both. All of the charts should be the same size as the pie chart in the middle of the canvas.

4. One by one, drag a chart and place it directly on top of the pie chart in the middle. The order that you place them in is not important. If they are not lined up exactly right, they will not be displayed properly in the dashboard. Save the changes.

> If you have trouble aligning the charts, select all of the charts, then Format ⇒ Align. Select the option that will align them. The Left and Top align options worked best for me.

Create The Menu

In this part of the exercise you will add the Radio Button component and attach each chart to an option on the menu.

1. Add the Radio Button component to the left of the charts.

2. On the General view, make the changes in the table.

Option	Change To
Labels	A4:A8
Insertion Type	Status List
Destination	B4:B8

3. On the Layout tab, make the changes in the table.

Option	Change To
Marker Size	17
Horizontal Margin	8
Vertical Margin	1

4. Resize the menu so that all of the items are visible, then save the changes.

Set Up The Background And Label Components

1. Add the Background component to the canvas, then resize it so that it is large enough to cover the other components.
2. Right click on the background and select **SEND TO BACK**.
3. Add the Label component above the menu.
4. On the General view in the Enter Text field, type `Status List Example`.
5. On the Text tab, select the Center option, then click the Bold button.

   Save the changes.

   Your model should look like the one shown in Figure 14-37.

   When you select an option on the menu, the corresponding chart should appear.

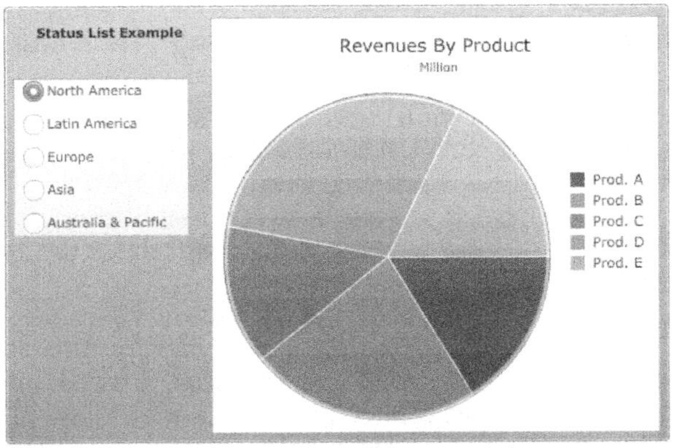

Figure 14-37 Status List example model

> **Using Unrelated Data In The Same Dashboard**
> What I hope that you gained from the previous exercise is that you could put unrelated types of data in the same spreadsheet and create a chart for each data set, if you will. For example, you could put the data from Exercises 14.1 to 14.5 on different sheets (tabs) in an Excel workbook, or you can put the data for all of the exercises on the same sheet, in the Excel workbook. This would allow you to create the same charts that you did in those exercises and combine them into one dashboard.

Exercise 14.8: Use A Spreadsheet That Has Multiple Tabs Of Data

In the tip box above, I explained working with a spreadsheet that had multiple tabs of data. In this exercise you will import the spreadsheet and create a chart.

1. Import the dd_multiple_tabs spreadsheet.
2. Add the Line Chart component. Make the chart larger. When working with a spreadsheet that has multiple tabs, the biggest difference is remembering to select the correct tab.

3. On the General view, make the changes in the table. Click on the Line_Chart tab in the spreadsheet before selecting a cell. Figure 14-38 shows the **SERIES** section on the General view. As illustrated, notice that the spreadsheet tab name is part of the data path.

Option	Change To
Chart	A1
Subtitle	Historic Trend
Category (X) Axis	Years
By Range	A4:I5
Category Labels (X)	B3:I3

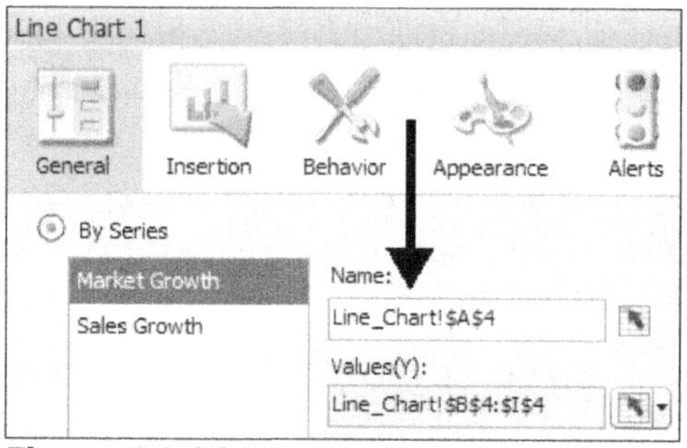

Figure 14-38 Series options

4. Save the model as `My multiple tab model`.

Exercise 14.9: Create A Legend Using The Image Component

In Exercise 14.4 you used the Toggle Button component to display or hide another component on the dashboard. As you know, when you create a chart, you have the option of displaying a legend. If your dashboard contains a lot of components, you may decide to not display a legend for space reasons. The only time that the options on a legend change is if the structure of the data for a chart changes. For example, if you create a chart that displays data for three products and then six months later you add three more products to the chart, the structure has changed, which means the legend will change.

In this exercise you will use the Check Box component to display and hide the legend for a chart. You will not use the legend that is automatically created with the chart. You will use an image of the legend, which I have created for you. Using an image of the legend will allow you to place the legend any place on the canvas that you want, even over another component, because the visibility of the legend will be controlled by the check box.

Create The Pie Chart

1. Save the dd_hidden_legend as `My hidden legend`.

2. On the Series tab, select the colors for the countries in the table.

Data Point	Color
Australia	Orange
Japan	Light green
Canada	Red
England	Teal
Italy	Purple
Germany	Light blue

Select The Legend Options

1. Add the Image component.

   Place it partially over the orange slice of the chart, as shown in Figure 14-39.

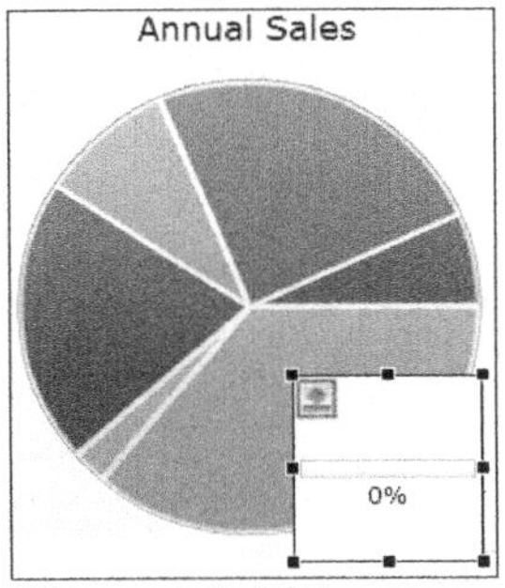

Figure 14-39 Image component added to the model

2. On the General view, click the Import button, then double-click on the legend.jpg file.
3. On the Common tab, make the changes in the table.

Option	Change To
Status	C2
Key	1

4. On the Animations and Effects tab, select a Type.
5. Save the changes.

Select The Check Box Options

1. Add the Check Box component right below the word Sales in the chart title.
2. On the General view, make the changes in the table.

Option	Change To
Title	Show Legend
Destination	C2

3. On the Color tab, change the Unchecked Color option to a color that you like.

Preview The Model

1. Save the changes.
2. When you click the Show Legend button, the legend will appear, as shown in Figure 14-40.

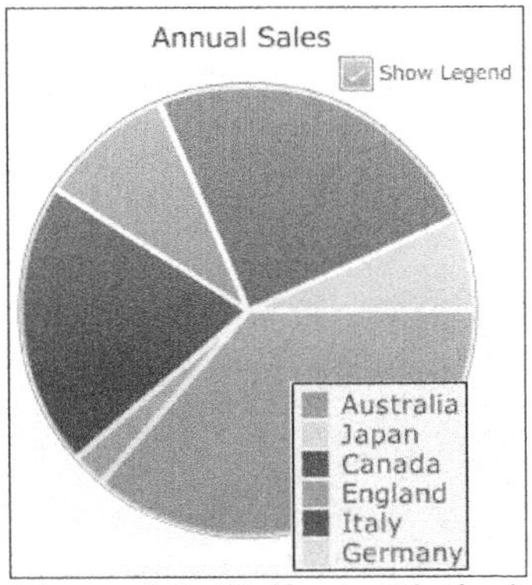

Figure 14-40 Chart with the legend as an image

ADVANCED COMPONENTS

In this chapter you will learn about Dual Axis charts and the following components:

- ☑ Filtered Rows
- ☑ Panel Container
- ☑ Tab Set
- ☑ List Builder
- ☑ History
- ☑ Trend Analyzer

CHAPTER 15

Overview

In this chapter you will learn how to use some of the components and features that I consider advanced. Keep in mind that "advanced" does not mean extremely difficult.

Dual Axis Charts

This type of chart is used to plot data on a primary and secondary axis. The following chart types support dual axis functionality: Area, Bar, Column, Combination, Line, Stacked Area, Stacked Bar and Stacked Column.

General View Options

Plot Series On Options

Figure 15-1 shows the Plot Series On options on the General view. They are used to select which axis the series of data is plotted on.

PRIMARY AXIS Select this option to plot the series on the left vertical axis.

SECONDARY AXIS Select this option to plot the series on the right vertical axis.

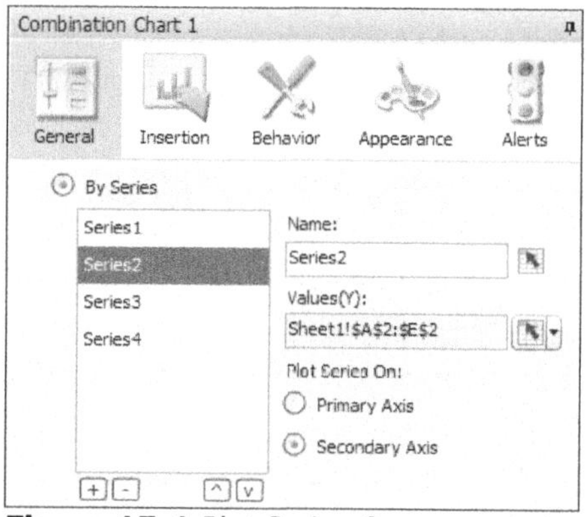

Figure 15-1 Plot Series On general view options

Scale Tab Options

Charts that have a secondary axis have two scale tabs, called **PRIMARY SCALE** and **SECONDARY SCALE**, as shown in Figure 15-2.

Both tabs have the same options that the Scale tab has.

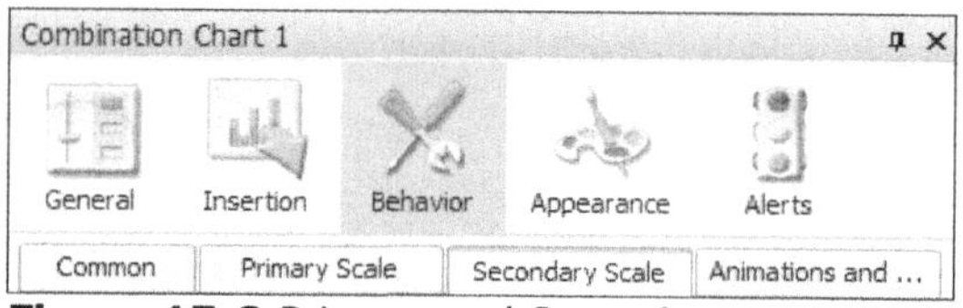

Figure 15-2 Primary and Secondary scale tabs

Axes Tab Options

Like the Scale tab options, there are two Axes tabs for dual axis charts.

The **PRIMARY AXES TAB** has the Enable Horizontal Axis options shown in Figure 15-3.

The **SECONDARY AXES TAB** does not.

[See Chapter 7, Common Chart Axes Tab Options]

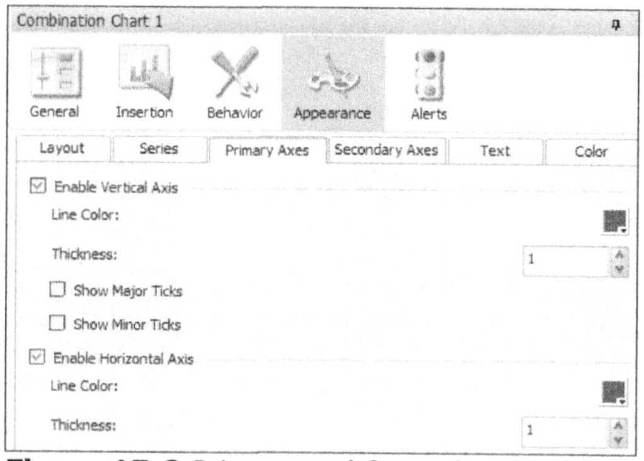

Figure 15-3 Primary and Secondary Axes tabs

Color Tab Options

Each axis on dual axis charts have options in the Axes and Gridlines section on the Color tab, as shown in Figure 15-4.

The Axes tab that the option is on, is in parenthesis.

The **HORIZONTAL AXIS** option is only on the Primary Axes tab.

[See Chapter 7, Common Chart Color Tab Options]

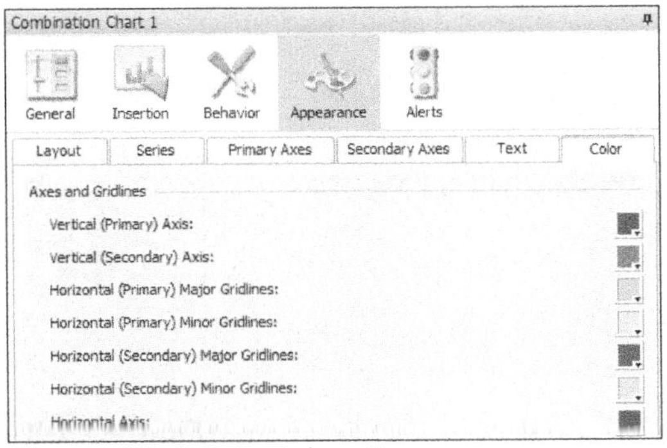

Figure 15-4 Color tab options

Exercise 15.1: Create A Dual Axis Chart

In this exercise you will learn how to create a chart that plots the price and volume (quantity) on the vertical axis and the weeks on the horizontal axis.

1. Save the dd_dual_axis_chart model as `My dual axis chart.`

2. Add the Combination Chart component.

3. On the General view, make the changes in the table.

Option	Change To
Chart	Stock Price vs Volume
Subtitle	7/16/11 - 10/26/11
Category (X) Axis	Week Ending
Value (Y) Axis	Price
Category Labels (X)	A2:A18

Create The Primary And Secondary Axis

1. Click the By Series button, then create the series in the table.

Option	Change To
Name	B1
Values (Y)	B2:B18
Plot Series On	Primary Axis

2. Create the series in the table.

Option	Change To
Name	C1
Values (Y)	C2:C18
Plot Series On	Secondary Axis

3. On the General view, type `Volume` in the Secondary Value (Y) Axis field.

Select The Remaining Options

1. On the Secondary Scale tab, select the Fixed Label Size option.

2. On the Series tab, change the Enable Marker Size option to 8.

   Save the changes.

   The chart should look like the one shown in Figure 15-5.

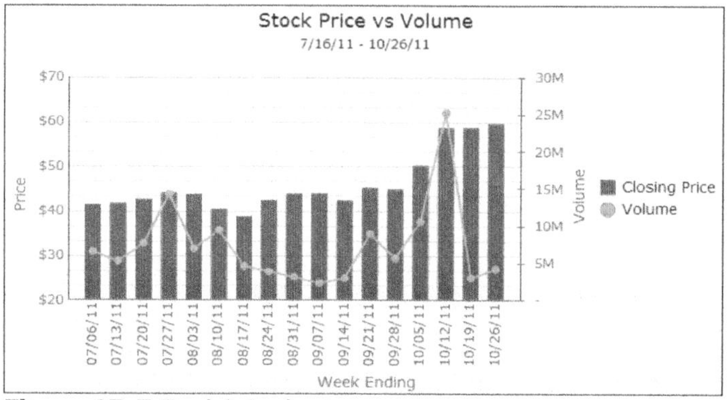

Figure 15-5 Dual Axis chart

Filtered Rows

In Chapter 9 you read about the filtered rows Insertion Type option. The selector component has a range of cells linked to the component. Each label on the selector component will only retrieve the rows of data that correspond to the label. What makes this option useful is that all of the rows of data that are associated to the label do not have to be above and below each other in the spreadsheet. Figure 15-6 shows some of the data that will be used in this exercise.

Rows 3, 4 and 8 are for the same item. Using the Filtered Rows option will allow these rows of data to be associated to the keyboard option on the selector component.

When the keyboard option on the selector component is selected, these records will be displayed on the chart, even though the rows of data are not next to each other in the spreadsheet.

	B	C	D	E
2	Date of Purchase		Quantity	Item
3	1/8/11		14	Keyboard
4	1/9/11		22	Keyboard
5	1/13/11		10	Desktop
6	1/18/11		11	Laptop
7	2/5/11		10	Laptop
8	2/6/11		9	Keyboard

Figure 15-6 Data for a filtered row model

Exercise 15.2: Create A Filtered Rows Model

1. Save the dd_filtered_rows model as `My filtered rows.`

2. Add the Radio Button component to the left of the chart.

3. On the General view, make the changes in the table.

Option	Change To
Labels	E3:E78
Insertion Type	Filtered Rows
Source Data	B3:E78
Destination	G3:J25

4. Save the changes. The model should look like the one shown in Figure 15-7. If you select the keyboard option, you will see the three rows of data shown above in Figure 15-6 on the chart, as well as, the other rows of data for keyboards.

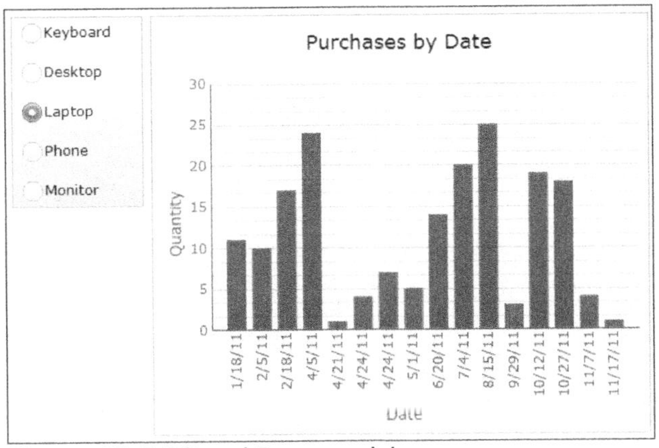

Figure 15-7 Filtered Rows model

Ignore Blank Cells Options

The options shown in Figure 15-8 are used to control how charts handle blank cells at the end of the data range.

IN SERIES Is used to stop empty series that are after the last cell with data in the series from being displayed on the chart.

IN VALUES Is used to stop empty values that are after the last cell that has a value in the data range from being displayed on the chart.

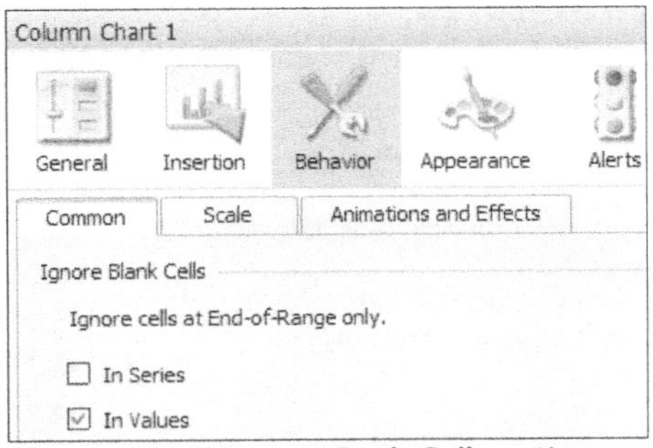

Figure 15-8 Ignore Bank Cells options

These options are helpful when an unknown number of series or values need to be displayed in the chart. For example, if there are four months of data currently in the data source and you know that the user will add data for another eight months, you could set up the 12 month range now and select the In Series or In Values option now, instead of having to modify the model later.

The reverse is also true. If the spreadsheet currently has 12 rows of data and the user deleted three rows of data that are no longer needed, the chart options do not have to be changed to keep the empty rows of data from being displayed on the chart.

Exercise 15.3: Use The Ignore Blank Cells Options

In this exercise you will create a sales per day chart that is based on the data shown in Figure 15-9. As you see, there are days in some months that do not have data at the end of the month. Without the Ignore Blank Cells options, you would have to create each series separately. If the data were to be filled in the empty cells shown in Figure 15-9, without these blank cells options, you would have to change the data range on the Properties panel.

C	AD	AE	AF	AG	AH
	27	28	29	30	31
January	$ 5,000	$ 16,000	$ 10,000	$ 12,000	$ 10,000
February	$ 18,000	$ 19,000			
March	$ 11,000	$ 16,000	$ 7,000	$ 18,000	$ 8,000
April	$ 18,000	$ 14,000	$ 14,000	$ 9,000	
May	$ 9,000	$ 7,000	$ 13,000	$ 7,000	$ 20,000
June	$ 20,000	$ 15,000	$ 18,000	$ 17,000	
July	$ 16,000	$ 8,000	$ 11,000	$ 11,000	$ 14,000
August	$ 6,000	$ 7,000	$ 10,000	$ 10,000	$ 11,000
September	$ 17,000	$ 7,000	$ 14,000	$ 19,000	
October	$ 20,000	$ 16,000	$ 13,000	$ 11,000	$ 12,000
November	$ 18,000	$ 18,000	$ 7,000	$ 7,000	
December	$ 8,000	$ 16,000	$ 19,000	$ 13,000	$ 18,000

Figure 15-9 Data with empty cells at the end of rows

1. Save the dd_ignore_blank_cells model as `My ignore blank cells chart.`
2. Add the Column chart component, then make it larger.
3. Add the Combo Box component to the upper right corner of the chart.

Select The Combo Box Options

The Combo Box component will be filled with the months of the year.

1. On the General view, make the changes in the table.

Option	Change To
Labels	C3:C14
Insertion Type	Row
Source Data	C3:AH14
Destination	C16:AH16

2. On the Common tab, select Label 1 in the Item drop-down list.

Select The Column Chart Options

1. On the General view, make the changes in the table.

Option	Change To
Chart	Daily Sales
Subtitle	C16
Category (X) Axis	Day of the month
Name	Daily Sales
Values (Y)	D16:AH16
Category Labels (X)	D2:AH2

2. On the Common tab, check the In Values option.
3. Save the changes. If you look at the data shown earlier in Figure 15-9, you will see that there is no data for the 29th, 30th and 31st of February. That is because the month only has 28 days. If you select Feb from the Combo Box you will not see those days on the chart shown in Figure 15-10 like you do the chart shown in Figure 15-11.

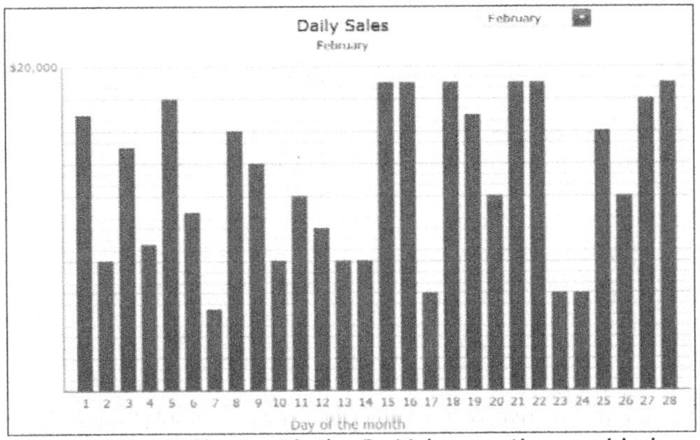

Figure 15-10 Chart with the In Values option enabled

The reason that you see the dates without any data in Figure 15-11 is because I cleared the **IN VALUES** option on the Common tab.

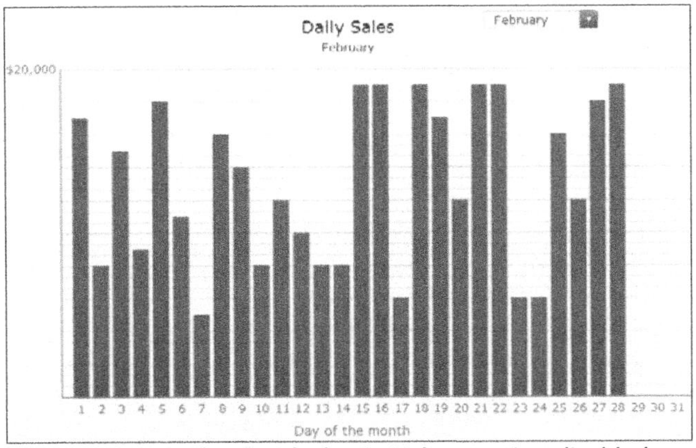

Figure 15-11 Chart with the In Values option disabled

Containers Components

The Containers components are used to display more than one other component. There are four container components: Canvas, Panel, Panel 2 and Tab Set.

Components in the container can be changed, moved or deleted, as if they were one component. Like groups, components that are added to the Container component are organized in the Object Browser, as shown in Figure 15-12.

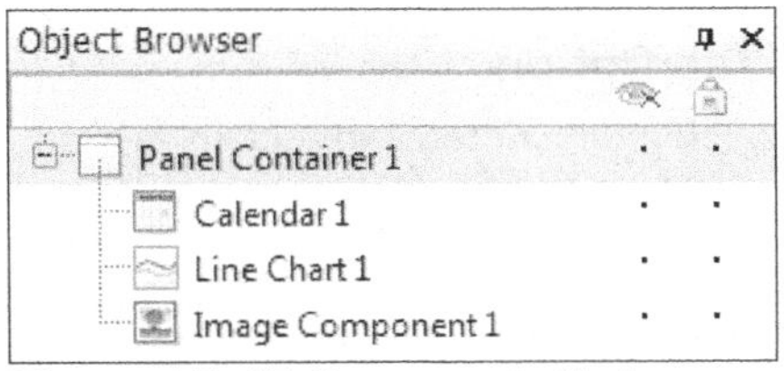

Figure 15-12 Components that were added to the Container component

This component type is helpful if you need to display several components in a small space on the dashboard or you have the need to display or hide several of the components on the dashboard at the same time.

Components added to a container component inherit the dynamic visibility options of the container component. This means that all of the components in the container can be hidden and displayed at the same time. Keep in mind that if using a container component to display and hide other components that there is no way to hide or remove the borders and header that the container component has.

Panel Container Component (This component is not available in Presentation Design)

General View Options

The Panel Container general view options are shown in Figure 15-13.

TITLE Is used to type in a title for the container or select a cell in the spreadsheet that has the title.

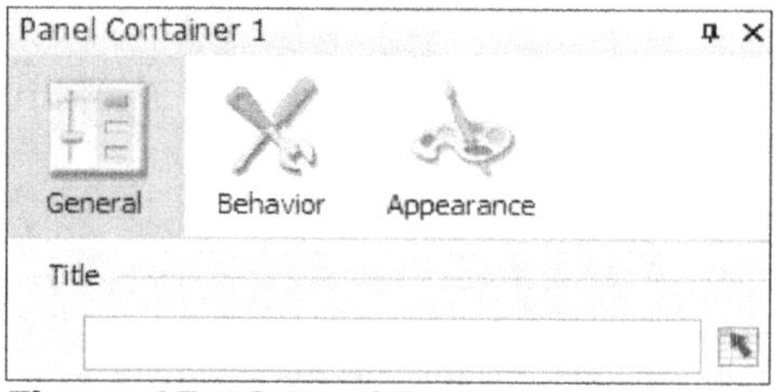

Figure 15-13 Panel Container general view options

Common Tab Options

The Panel Container common tab options are shown in Figure 15-14.

Scroll Bar Options
The options in the drop-down list are used to select when the horizontal and vertical scroll bars appear on the Panel Container. The drop-down list options are explained below.

AUTO If the contents of the canvas are more than its width (for the horizontal scroll bar) or more than its height (for the vertical scroll bar).

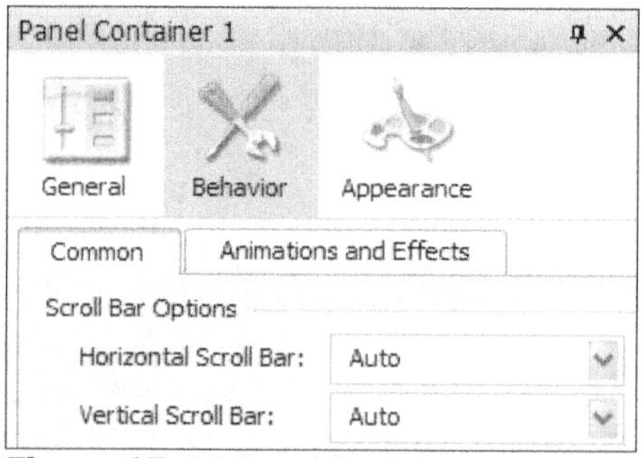

Figure 15-14 Panel Container common tab options

ON The scroll bar will always appear on the container, whether or not its needed.

OFF The scroll bar will never appear on the container, whether or not its needed.

Color Tab Options

The Panel Container color tab options are shown in Figure 15-15.

BACKGROUND COLOR Is used to change the background color of the interior portion of the panel.

PANEL COLOR Is used to change the border color of the panel.

Scroll Bar Options
TRACK COLOR Is used to change the background color of the scroll bar area.

THUMB COLOR Is used to change the color of the scroll bar.

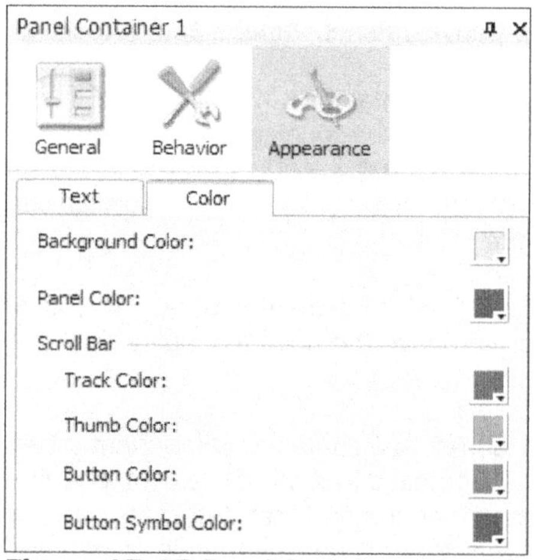

Figure 15-15 Panel Container color tab options

BUTTON COLOR Is used to change the color behind the symbol on the scroll bar.

BUTTON SYMBOL COLOR Is used to change the color of the symbol on the scroll bar.

Exercise 15.4: Use The Panel Container Component

In this exercise you will create a panel container model that will display other components.

1. Open a new model and save it as `My panel container`.
2. Add the Panel Container component, then make the component larger.
3. On the General view, type `My Container Panel` in the Title field.
4. On the Common tab, change the Horizontal Scroll Bar option to Off.

Add The Components To The Container

1. Add the Pie Chart component to the top of the container, then make the chart smaller so that it fits in the container.

At this point you would select the chart properties. If you were going to add several components, you would have to put the data for all of the components in the same spreadsheet.

2. Add the Horizontal Line component below the chart. Make the line almost as wide as the interior of the container.
3. Add the Image component below the horizontal line, then resize it to fit the interior of the container. Make the component longer.
4. On the General view, select the Resize Image to Component option.
5. Import the My Slider dashboard.swf file into the Image component.
6. If necessary, resize the Panel Container to fit the other components.

View The Panel Container And Object Browser

1. Save the changes. The model should look like the one shown in Figure 15-16. If you scroll down, you will be able to see the other components in the Panel Container.
2. Click on the plus sign next to the Panel Container in the Object Browser. You should see the options shown in Figure 15-17.

You are not limited to only using a Panel Container in the model. You can add components that are not in the Panel Container, as shown in Figure 15-18. Compare the options in the Object Browser shown in Figure 15-19 to the ones shown in Figure 15-17.

The exercise that you just completed did not use a spreadsheet that had data. You can use a spreadsheet that has data when the model will use other components.

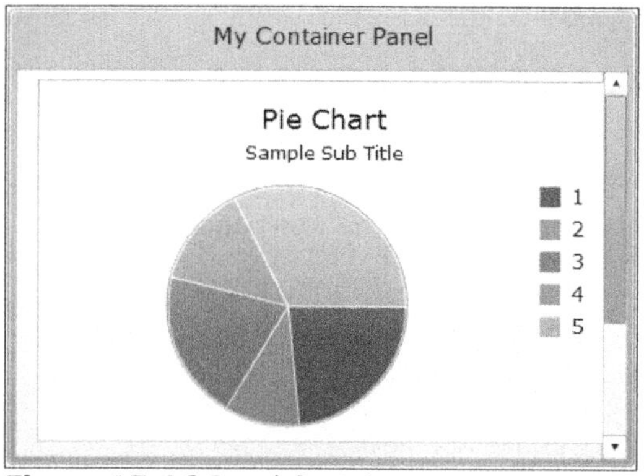

Figure 15-16 Panel Container

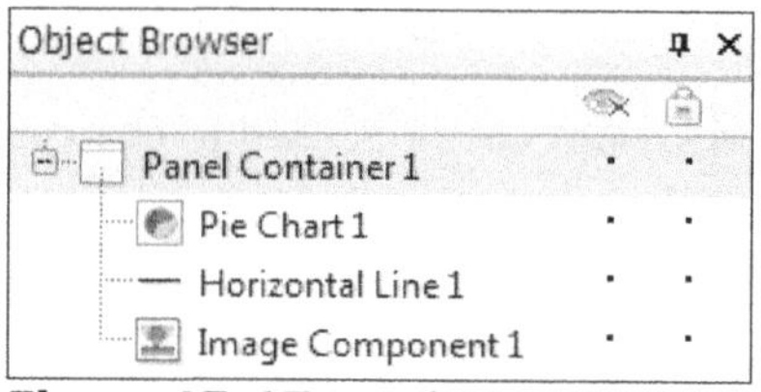

Figure 15-17 Panel Container components in the Object Browser

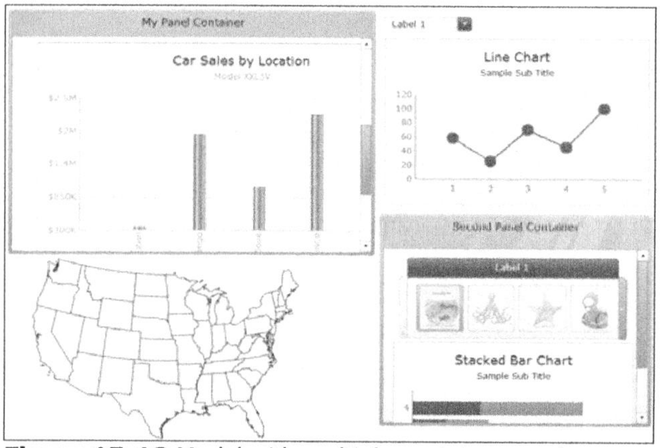

Figure 15-18 Model with multiple containers and components

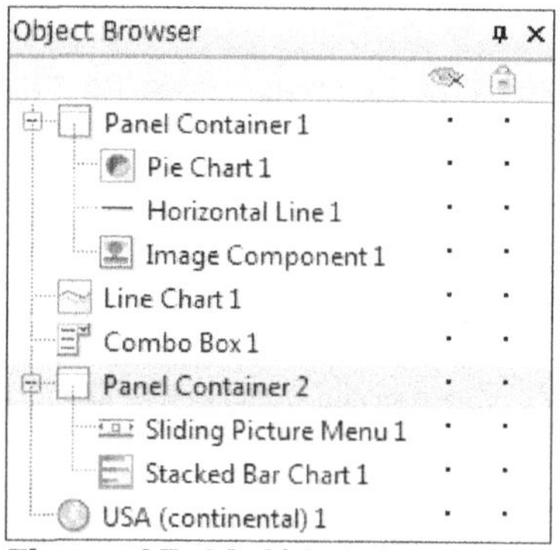

Figure 15-19 Object Browser with multiple containers and components

Panel Container 2 Component (This component is not available in Presentation Design)

This component has the same functionality as the Panel Container component. The only difference is how the container looks.

Canvas Container Component (This component is not available in Presentation Design)

This component is similar to the Panel Container component. The difference is that the Canvas Container component does not have border, background and title options like the Panel Container has.

When the model is run, the Canvas Container is invisible, which gives the components in the container the appearance of being free floating, as shown in Figure 15-20. I added color to the scroll bars on purpose, so that you could see part of the Canvas Container.

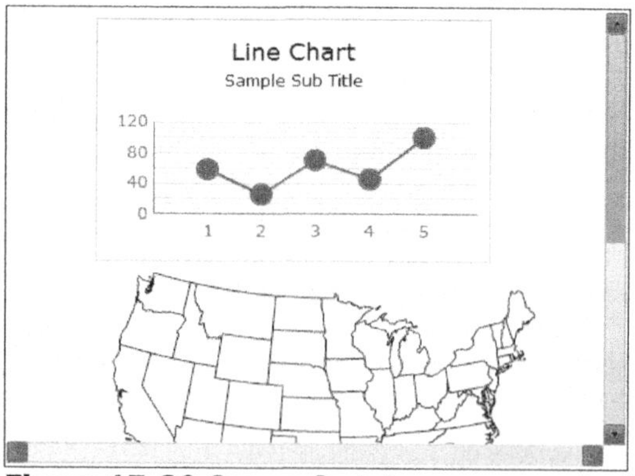

Figure 15-20 Canvas Container component with scroll bars

Tab Set Component (This component is not available in Presentation Design)

This container component is similar to the panel container component that you learned about in the previous exercise. Subgroups of tabs cannot be created in this component. One difference is the use of the tabs across the top of the component. Another difference is that each tab can be linked to a different data set.

The other difference is that Tab Sets have a Properties panel which uses a sub component called the Canvas, which has its own Properties panel. Components that you add to the tab set are automatically placed in a canvas.

Figure 15-21 shows a tab set with five canvases. In each canvas there is a different chart. This hierarchy allows you to customize each tab individually.

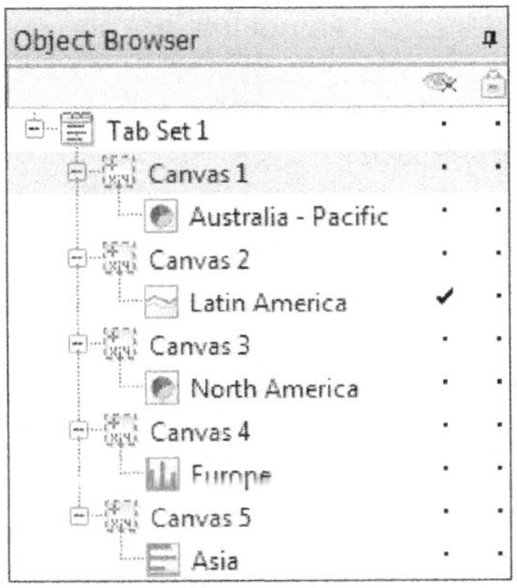

Figure 15-21 Tab Set layout in the Object Browser

Tab Set Properties

The options on this Properties panel are used to configure the tabs at the top of the component.

The plus and minus buttons shown at the top of Figure 15-22 are used to add and remove tabs. These buttons are not displayed when the dashboard is run. If you delete a tab, all of the components on the tab are also deleted.

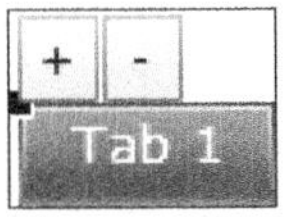

Figure 15-22 Tab Set buttons

General View Options

The Tab Set general view option is shown in Figure 15-23.

TAB ALIGNMENT Is used to select the placement of the tabs.

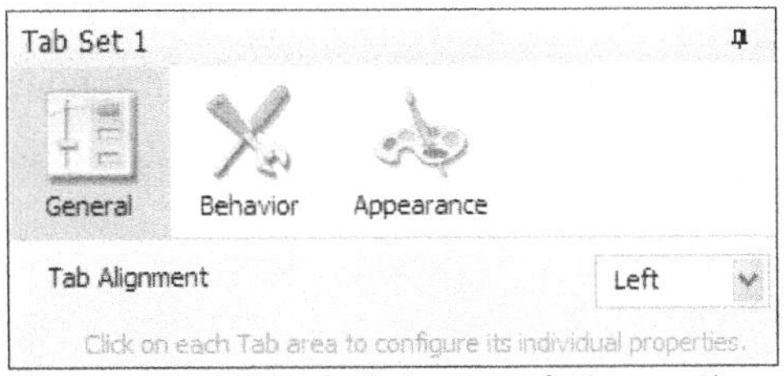

Figure 15-23 Tab Set general view option

Common Tab Options

The Tab Set common tab options are shown in Figure 15-24. These options can be applied to each tab on the Tab Set. The option on this tab is used to select the tab that is displayed when the dashboard is opened.

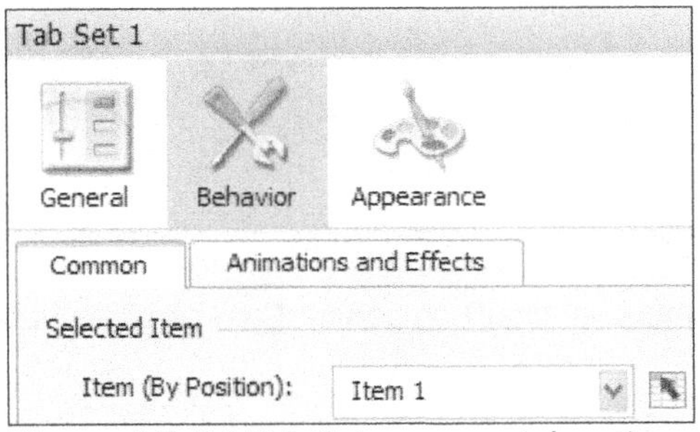

Figure 15-24 Tab Set common tab options

Color Tab Options

The Tab Set color tab options are shown in Figure 15-25.

BACKGROUND COLOR Is used to change the color of the bar below the tabs.

Tab Backgrounds Options

DEFAULT COLOR Is used to change the background color of the tabs.

OVER COLOR Is used to change the background color of the tab when the mouse pointer is hovered over the tab.

SELECTED COLOR Is used to change the background color of the tab that is clicked on.

Labels Options

DEFAULT COLOR Is used to change the color of the text on the tabs.

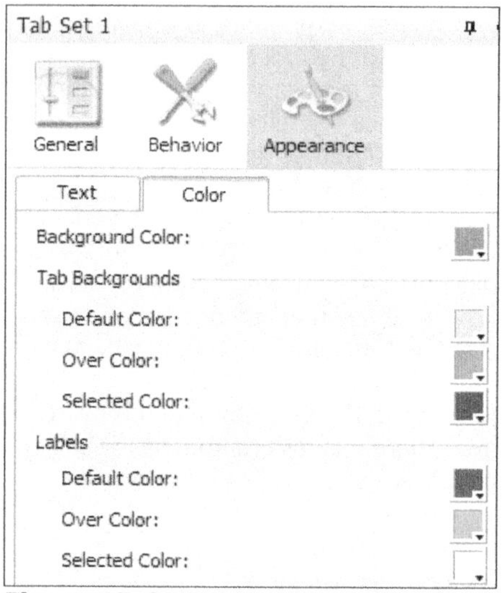

Figure 15-25 Tab Set color tab options

OVER COLOR Is used to change the color of the text on the tab when the mouse pointer is hovered over the tab.

SELECTED COLOR Is used to change the color of the text on the tab when it is clicked on.

Canvas Panel

The options on the Canvas panel are used to configure the canvas, which is the empty space below the tabs. Each tab has its own canvas. This is not the Canvas Container component that was covered earlier in this chapter. Click in the Tab Set component to display this panel.

General View Options

The Canvas general view option is shown in Figure 15-26.

LABEL Is used to create the text for the tab.

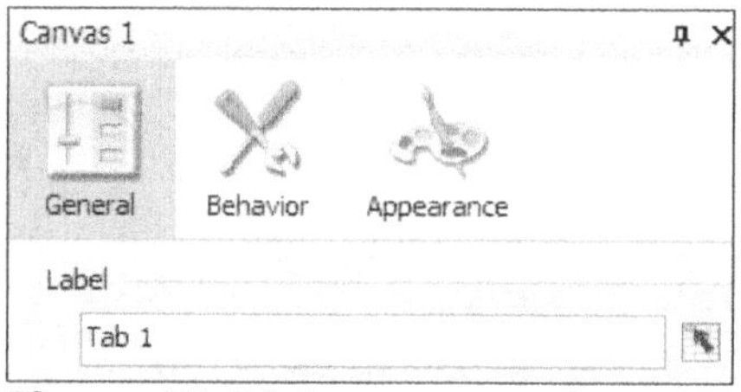

Figure 15-26 Canvas general view option

Behavior View Options

The Canvas behavior view options are shown in Figure 15-27.

[See Panel Container Component Common Tab Options, earlier in this chapter]

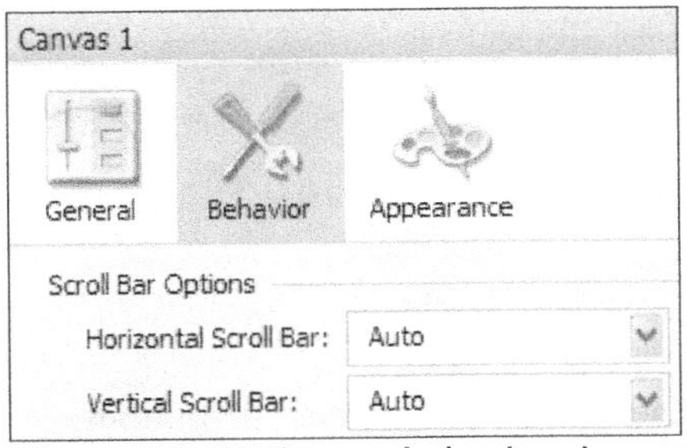

Figure 15-27 Canvas behavior view options

Appearance View Options

The Canvas appearance view options shown in Figure 15-28 are used to customize the tab for the canvas.

BACKGROUND COLOR Is used to change the background color of the container portion of the tab set.

Scroll Bar Options

The options are used to set the color for the Button, Button Symbol, Thumb and Track parts of the scroll bar. [See Panel Container Component Color Tab Options, earlier in this chapter]

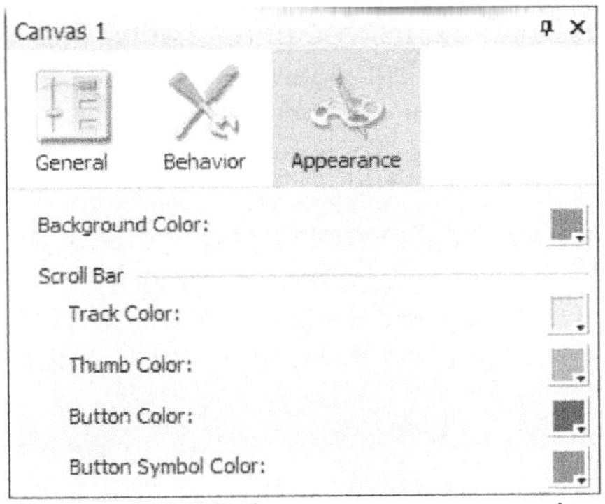

Figure 15-28 Canvas appearance view options

Exercise 15.5: Create A Tab Set Model

1. Save the dd_tab_set model as `My tab set`.
2. Add the Tab Set component, then make the component larger.

Create The Tabs

1. In the Object Browser, click on the plus sign in front of the Tab Set component.
2. Click on the icon in front of the Canvas 1 option to display the Properties panel.
3. On the General view, type `Australia - Pacific` in the Label field.
4. Click on the Tab Set in the Object Browser, then click the Plus button above the Tab Set on the canvas.
5. Type `Latin America` in the Label field on the dialog box shown in Figure 15-29, then click OK.

   You may have to scroll down to see this dialog box.

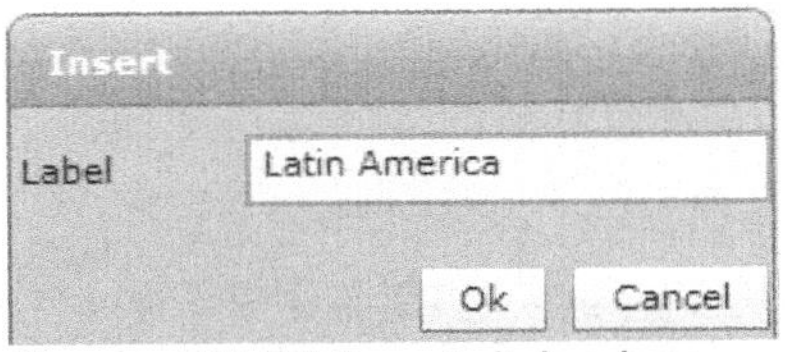

Figure 15-29 Insert dialog box

6. Repeat the steps above to create the following tabs: North America, Europe and Asia.

7. If necessary, make the tab set wider so that all of the text on each tab is visible, as shown in Figure 15-30, then save the changes.

Figure 15-30 Tabs created

Add Components To The Tabs

In this part of the exercise you will add the components to each tab. You could create them from scratch by clicking on a canvas option in the Object Browser and then add and customize the component.

The spreadsheet at the bottom of the workspace should look familiar because you have used it to create charts already. Instead of recreating the same charts, you can copy them from another model and paste them into this model. When I have the need to copy and paste components between models, I open another instance of Dashboard Design, then open the model that has the components that I want to copy.

1. Open another instance of Dashboard Design, then open the My multiple charts menu model.
2. In the Object Browser, right-click on the North America map and select Copy, then click on the instance of Dashboard Design that has the Tab Set component.
3. Click on the North America tab, then right-click on the container and select Paste.
4. Drag the chart into the container and resize as needed. Make sure that the chart is under the Canvas 3 section in the Object Browser, then click on the chart in the Object Browser.
5. On the Common tab, delete the data in the Status and Key fields by clicking the Bind button and clearing the data on the Select a Range dialog box, then click OK.
6. Repeat the steps above to copy and paste the charts in the table. The name of the chart is not kept when it is pasted into a model. When you are finished, the Object Browser should look like the one shown in Figure 15-31.

Chart	Canvas
Australia	1
Latin America	2
Europe	4
Asia	5

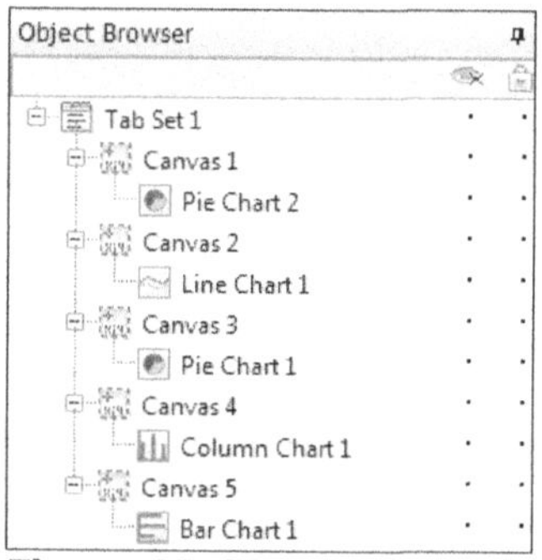

Figure 15-31 Tab Set Object Browser

7. Save the changes. When you click on each tab in the Tab Set, you will see a different chart. If you wanted to have a specific tab be displayed when the dashboard is first opened, select it from the Item drop-down list on the Common tab of the Tab Set Properties panel.

8. Close the second instance of Dashboard Design.

List Builder Component (This component is not available in Presentation Design)

So far, you have selected the data set for each model. In the real world, users will give you input on the data for the dashboard.

If you have ever created reports for users you are already use to them asking for several variations of the same report.

The List Builder component, shown in Figure 15-32 is used to allow the person running the dashboard to create their own data set, which will allow them to see several variations of the same data.

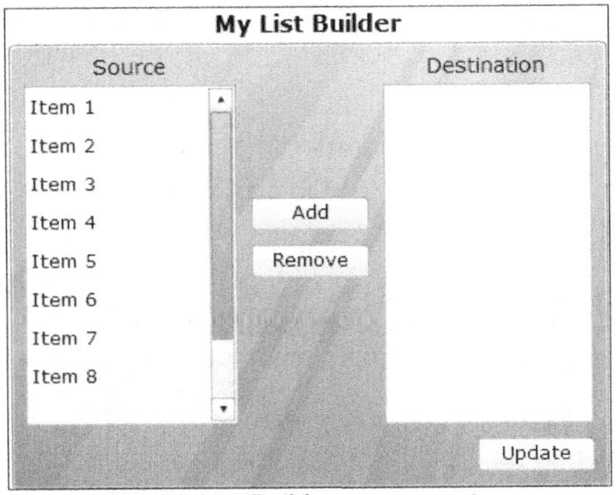

Figure 15-32 List Builder component

While you create the options for the users to select from, they can use this component to select the specific data that they want to see. Unlike other components, the List Builder component allows the user to select more than one option.

General View Options

The List Builder general view options are shown in Figure 15-33.

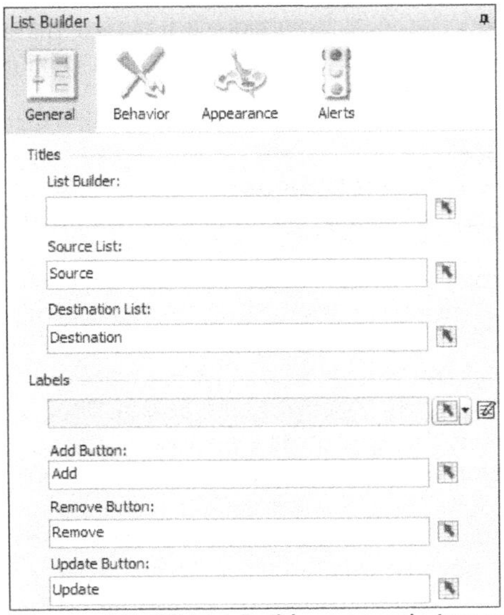

Figure 15-33 List Builder general view options

Titles Options

LIST BUILDER Is used to select a title that will appear above the component, as shown above in Figure 15-32. The title is My List Builder.

SOURCE LIST Is used to select the titles for the list box on the left of Figure 15-32 above. (1)

DESTINATION LIST Is used to select the titles for the list box on the right of Figure 15-32 above. (1)

Labels Options

LABEL Is used to select the label names for the items in the Source List. As shown above in Figure 15-32, the default values for this field is Item 1, Item 2, etc.

ADD BUTTON Is used to select the text for the Add button shown earlier in Figure 15-32. This button allows the user to move items from the Source List to the Destination List. (1)

REMOVE BUTTON Is used to select the text for the Remove button shown earlier in Figure 15-32. This button allows the user to move items from the Destination List to the Source List. (1)

UPDATE BUTTON Is used to select the text for the Update button shown earlier in Figure 15-32. When the user clicks this button, the data for the items in the Destination List are retrieved and used to filter the data displayed in another component on the dashboard. (1)

(1) The value that you see for this field in Figure 15-33 is the default for the option, but you can change it.

Common Tab Options

The List Builder common tab options are shown in Figure 15-34.

TYPE Is used to select the type of data that has to be matched to select the default option. [See Chapter 9, Selected Items Options]

ITEM(S) Is used to select the items that will be added to the Destination list. The items are not added until the user clicks the Update button.

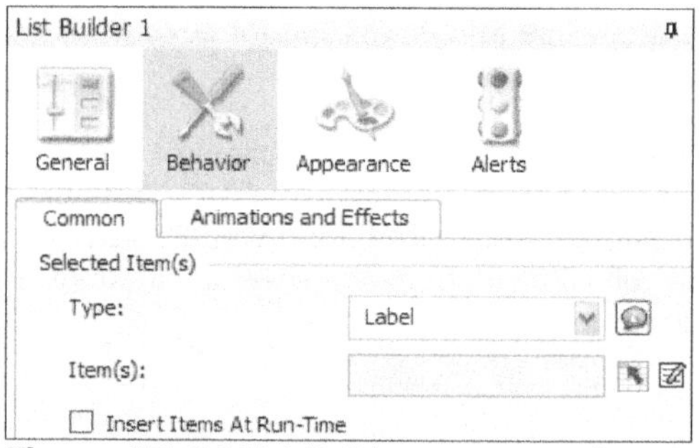

Figure 15-34 List Builder common tab options

INSERT ITEMS AT RUN-TIME If checked, this option will add the items in the Items List to the destination cells when the dashboard is first opened.

Color Tab Options

The List Builder color tab options are shown in Figure 15-35. Because this component does not have a Layout or Series tab, the Color tab is the only tab used to change colors.

BACKGROUND COLOR Is used to change the background color for the component.

Source List Labels Options

DEFAULT COLOR Is used to change the text color of the items in the Source List.

OVER COLOR Is used to change the text color of the item in the Source List that the mouse pointer is hovered over.

SELECTED COLOR Is used to change the text color of the item in the Source List that is clicked on.

Source List Backgrounds Options

DEFAULT COLOR Is used to change the background color of the items in the Source List.

OVER COLOR Is used to change the background color of the item in the Source List that the mouse pointer is hovered over.

SELECTED COLOR Is used to change the background color of the item in the Source List that is clicked on.

Destination List Labels Options

DEFAULT COLOR Is used to change the text color of the items in the Destination List.

OVER COLOR Is used to change the text color of the item in the Destination List that the mouse pointer is hovered over.

SELECTED COLOR Is used to change the text color of the item in the Destination List that is clicked on.

Destination List Backgrounds Options

DEFAULT COLOR Is used to change the background color of the items in the Destination List.

OVER COLOR Is used to change the background color of the item in the Destination List that the mouse pointer is hovered over.

SELECTED COLOR Is used to change the background color of the item in the Destination List that is clicked on.

Buttons Options

The options in this section are for the Add, Remove and Update buttons on the List Builder component, shown earlier in Figure 15-32.

BUTTON COLOR Is used to change the color of the buttons on the component.

BUTTON LABEL COLOR Is used to change the color of the text on the buttons.

PRESSED BUTTON COLOR Is used to change the background color when a button is clicked.

PRESSED BUTTON LABEL COLOR Is used to change the text color when a button is clicked.

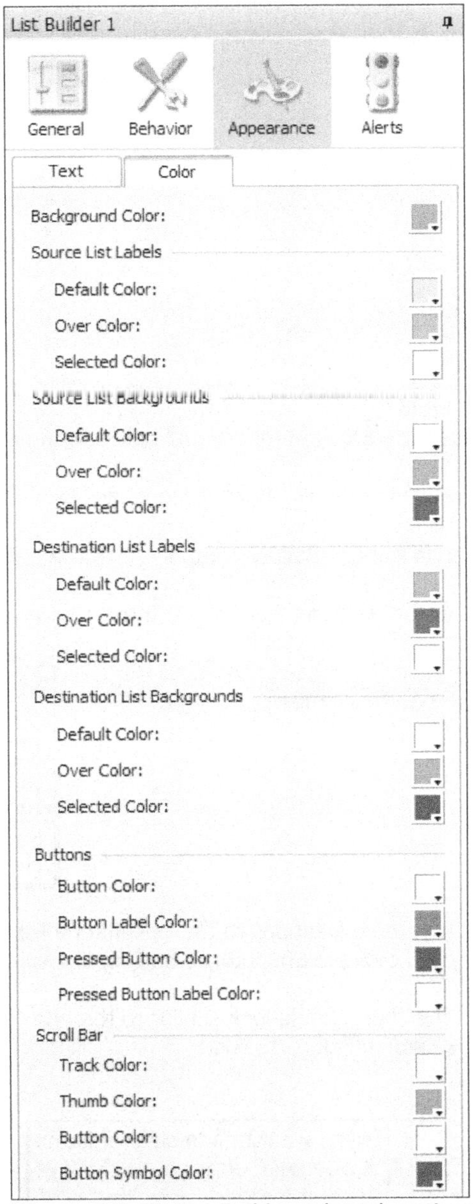

Figure 15-35 List Builder color tab options

Exercise 15.6: Use The List Builder Component

In Exercise 9.4, you used the Radio Button component to select one location to display the sales for the branch. Using the List Builder, the user will be able to select more than one branch and have the sales for each branch displayed on the same chart, like you saw in Exercise 14.3.

In this exercise, the List Builder component will contain all of the locations in the Source List. The user will select the locations that they want to see the sales data for by adding them to the Destination List. When the Update button is clicked, the Line chart will display the sales for each location in the Destination List on the List Builder on one chart. Figure 15-36 shows some of the data that will be used in this exercise.

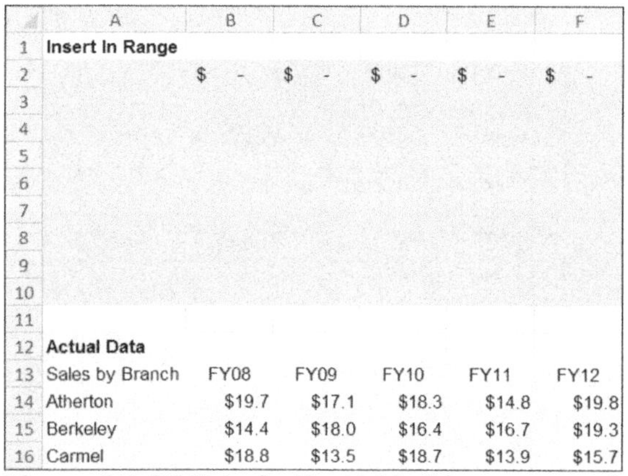

	A	B	C	D	E	F
1	**Insert In Range**					
2		$ -	$ -	$ -	$ -	$ -
3						
4						
5						
6						
7						
8						
9						
10						
11						
12	**Actual Data**					
13	Sales by Branch	FY08	FY09	FY10	FY11	FY12
14	Atherton	$19.7	$17.1	$18.3	$14.8	$19.8
15	Berkeley	$14.4	$18.0	$16.4	$16.7	$19.3
16	Carmel	$18.8	$13.5	$18.7	$13.9	$15.7

Figure 15-36 Data for the List builder component

1. Save the dd_list_builder model as `My list builder`.
2. Add the List Builder component to the top of the canvas.
3. On the General view, make the changes in the table.

   Save the changes.

Option	Change To
Source List	Select the location(s)
Labels	A14:A22
Add Button	>>
Remove Button	<<
Update Button	Show Chart
Insertion Type	Row
Source Data	A14:F22
Destination	A2:F10

4. Add three locations to the Destination list, then click the Show Chart button.

   The chart should look similar to the one shown in Figure 15-37.

> If you want to add several items at one time, after you click on the first location, press and hold down the CTRL key, then click on the other locations that you want, before clicking the Add button.

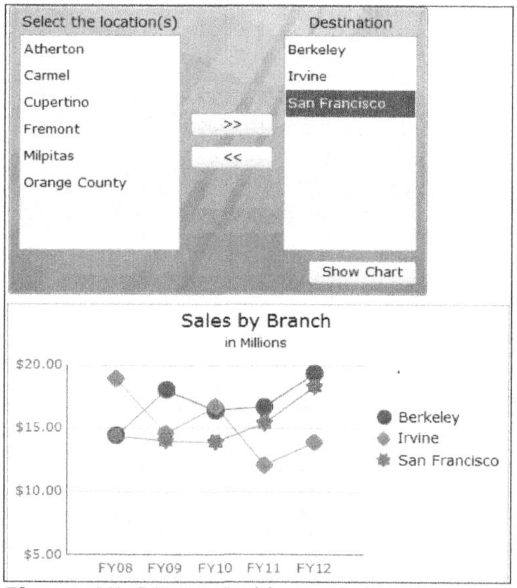

Figure 15-37 List Builder and chart

History Component (This component is not available in Presentation Design)

This component is used to track the changes of a cell in the spreadsheet. The cell is linked to the History component which displays the values in the cell, each time the value changes. The History component is not visible on the dashboard. This means that the component can be placed anywhere on the dashboard.

General View Options

The History general view options are shown in Figure 15-38.

DATA Is used to select the cell that you want to track.

Insertion Options

DATA DESTINATION Is used to select the cells that the history data will be inserted into. The number of cells selected in this option is how many (history) data changes can be displayed, usually on a chart. Once the limit is reached, the oldest changes are removed as new changes are added.

WHEN VALUE CHANGES Select this option if you want to capture/display all changes in the cell selected in the Data option.

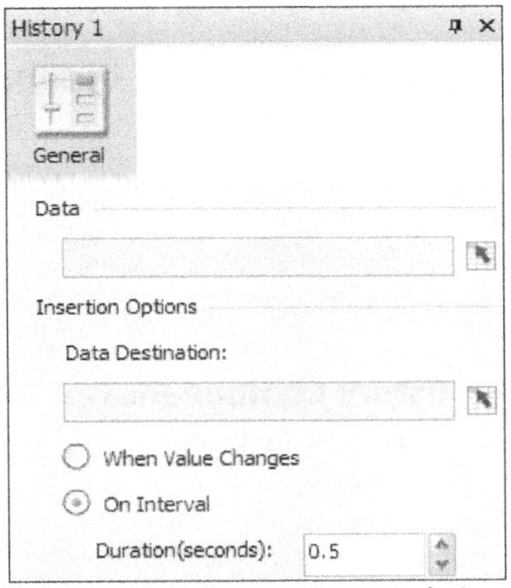

Figure 15-38 History general view options

ON INTERVAL Select this option if you want the cell changes (history) to be tracked at scheduled intervals in seconds, even if no changes have been made to the cells being tracked.

DURATION (SECONDS) Select how frequently the cell should be checked for changes.

Exercise 15.7: Use The History Component

In this exercise you will add and configure the components explained below. The chart is used to display the changes that are recorded by the History component. Figure 15-39 shows the data for this exercise.

① The Play Selector component will use fixed data points from the values in the spreadsheet.
② The Spreadsheet Table component will display the fixed data point values from the spreadsheet as they appear on the chart.
③ The History component records each change in the selected cell. (Cell A1)

	A	B	C	D	E
1					Values
2					4
3					16
4					36
5					64
6					100
7					64
8					36
9					16
10					4

Figure 15-39 Data for this exercise

1. Save the dd_history model as `My history component and chart.`
2. Add the Play Selector component below the chart, then add the Spreadsheet Table component below the Values label.
3. Add the History component below the Spreadsheet Table, across from the Play Selector.

Select The Play Selector Options

1. On the General view, make the changes in the table.

Option	Change To
Insertion Type	Row
Source Data	E2:E10
Destination	A1

2. On the Common tab, select the Auto Play option.

Select The Spreadsheet Table Options

1. On the General view, make the changes in the table.

Option	Change To
Display Data	B1:B10
Insertion Type	Position

2. On the Common tab, clear the check mark next to the Row option.

Select The History Component Options

1. On the General view, make the changes in the table.

Option	Change To
Data	A1
Data Destination	B1:B10
When Value Changes	Select this option

Test The Model

1. Save the changes.

   The chart displays the numbers from the values list on the right, as shown in Figure 15-40.

   The Play Selector was set to continuously play. Notice that the History component is not visible.

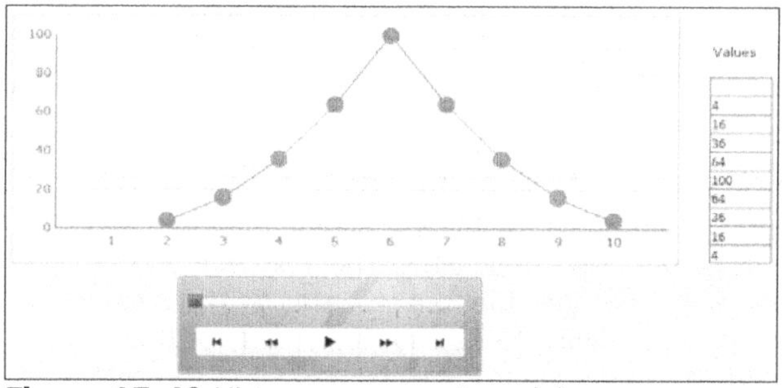

Figure 15-40 History component model

Trend Analyzer Component (This component is not available in Presentation Design)

This component is used to analyze data and present the analysis in a trend line. It is not visible on the dashboard. This component can also be configured to forecast future trends and display the forecasted data in a component. It is more powerful then the Trend Icon component because it reads numeric data and generates a trend analysis algorithm. The output is then placed in a row or column in the embedded spreadsheet. Unlike most components, the Trend Analyzer component only has one tab.

General View Options

The Trend Analyzer general view options shown in Figure 15-41 are used to select the data to be analyzed and select how to display the analysis in a trend line.

DATA Is used to select the cells that have the data that will be analyzed.

Trend/Regression Type Options

USE BEST FIT Select this option if you want Dashboard Design to select the analysis type that is best for the data.

SELECT A TYPE Select this option if you want to select one of the five analysis types explained in Table 15-1. The type of data being used for analysis determines the type of trend line that you should use.

ORDER (POLYNOMIAL ONLY) Is used to select a value between two and six for the polynomial analysis type.

Insertion Options

ANALYZED DATA DESTINATION Is used to select empty cells in the spreadsheet to store the analyzed data.

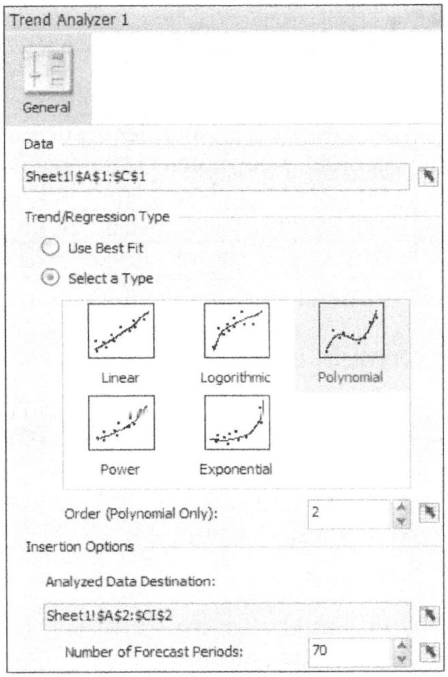

Figure 15-41 Trend Analyzer general view options

NUMBER OF FORECAST PERIODS Is used to enter the number of periods that you want to forecast. You can also bind this field to a cell in the spreadsheet by clicking the Bind button. This option is available if the number of cells in the Analyzed Data Destination field is greater than the number of cells in the Data field.

MORE OPTIONS Clicking on this link (shown above in Figure 15-41) displays the options shown in Figure 15-42. These options are used to add more analysis information to the spreadsheet.

EQUATION TYPE DESTINATION Is used to add the type of equation that was used to analyze the data.

EQUATION DESTINATION Is used to select the location for the equation that was used to analyze the data.

R^2 VALUE DESTINATION Is used to select the location for the R^2 value of the analysis. The R^2 value is how much of a variation in the data can be attributed to the trend line.

F VALUE DESTINATION Is used to select the location for the F value (a random variable) of the analysis.

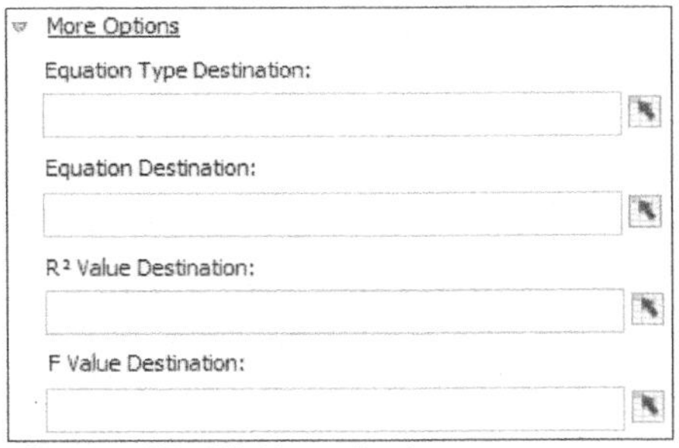

Figure 15-42 More Options

Types Of Trend Lines

Trend Line	Is Used When The . . .
Linear	Data points look like a line. It is often used for forecasting. Linear trend lines show values that increase or decrease at a steady pace.

Table 15-1 Types of trend lines explained

Trend Line	Is Used When The . . .
Logarithmic	Change in data increases or decreases fast, then levels off. Select this option if you are doing probability analysis.
Polynomial	Data fluctuates. An order 2 polynomial trend line usually only has one curve. An order 4 polynomial trend line usually has three curves. Select this option if you want to analyze gains and losses.
Power	Data increases at a specific rate. (2)
Exponential	Data rises or falls at increasing higher rates. (2)

Table 15-1 Types of trend lines explained (Continued)

(2) This option cannot be used if the data has a zero or negative numbers.

Exercise 15.8: Use The Trend Analyzer Component

In this exercise the Trend Analyzer component will be used to analyze stock data and select the best way to plot the data on a trend line.

A combination chart is used to display the trend analysis data plotted against a column chart. Figure 15-43 shows some of the data for this exercise.

	A	B	C	D	E	F
1	Stock Price Trend Analysis					
2		45		Date	Price	Analyzed Trend Data
3				2010 - January	$ 14.00	
4				2010 - February	$ 20.00	
5				2010 - March	$ 10.00	
6				2010 - April	$ 29.00	

Figure 15-43 Data for this exercise

1. Save the dd_trend_analyzer model as `My trend analyzer chart.`

2. Add the Trend Analyzer component to the upper right corner of the chart.

3. On the General view, make the changes in the table.

Option	Change To
Data	E3:E26
Use Best Fit	Select this option
Analyzed Data Destination	F3:F26

Save the changes.

The chart should look like the one shown in Figure 15-44.

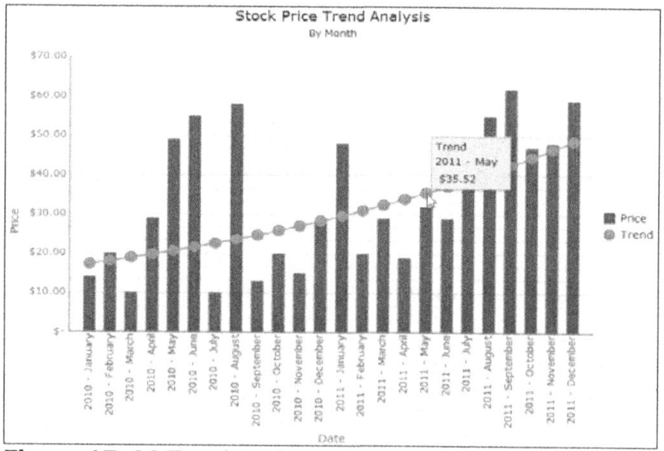

Figure 15-44 Trend Analyzer chart

CUSTOMIZATION AND EXPORTING OPTIONS

In this chapter you will learn about the following three types of customization options:

- ☑ Themes
- ☑ Color Schemes
- ☑ Templates

You will also learn how to export models to several dashboard formats.

CHAPTER 16

Customization Options

In Chapter 12 enhancement techniques were discussed that are applied to individual components on dashboards. In this chapter you will learn about the customization options that are applied to the Dashboard Design workspace and an entire dashboard.

If you have had to sit through what many, including myself, call boring PowerPoint presentations, keep all of the features of the presentation that made you cringe in the front of your brain, so that you do not wind up designing a dashboard that looks just like a presentation that was painful for you to look at <smile>.

I know that I have spent more time trying to figure out why the person used so many fonts on each slide and why the layout did not seem appropriate for the large amount of data, then I did paying attention to the actual information in the presentation. If you understand what I am talking about, this is your time to shine.

Themes

In prior versions of this software, themes were called **SKINS**. Dashboard Design comes with nine themes. Themes are used to change the appearance of components. Themes provide an easy way to customize a dashboard. Each theme has a different look, feel and color scheme which you can modify. Themes also store visual effects, font and font styles. Nova is the default theme.

Clicking the Themes button on the Themes toolbar displays the themes shown in Figure 16-1.

Format ⇒ Theme, opens the dialog box shown in Figure 16-2.

Figures 16-3 to 16-5 show the same set of components (Combination chart, Accordion menu and Grid) in three themes. As you can see, the same components have a different look under each theme.

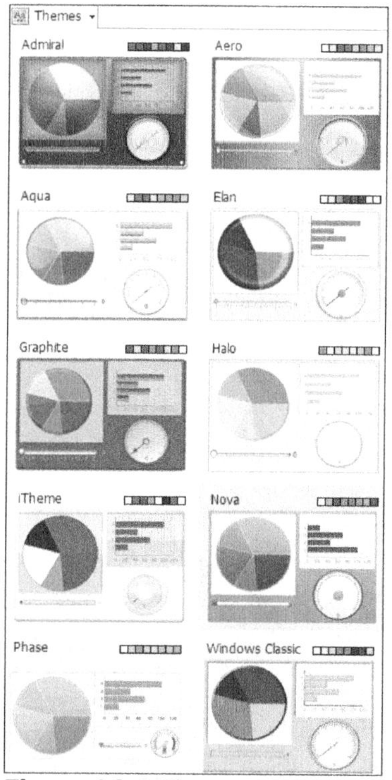

Figure 16-1 Themes

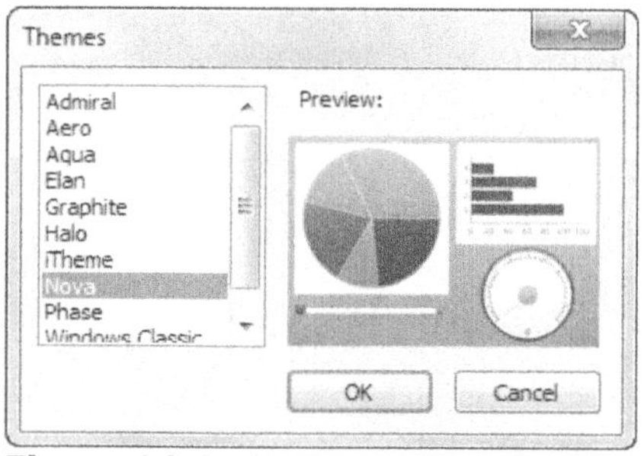

Figure 16-2 Themes dialog box

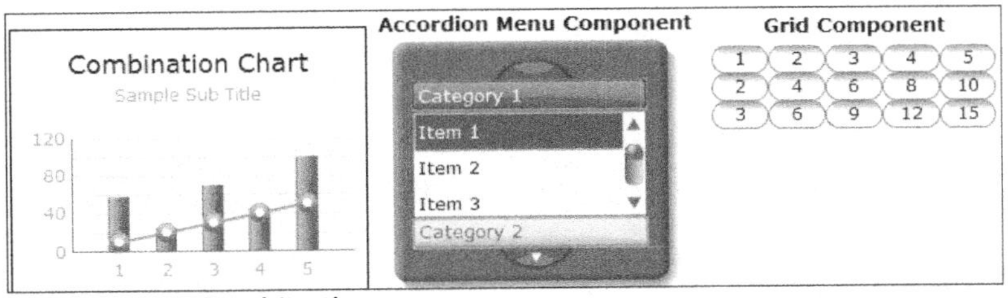

Figure 16-3 Graphite theme

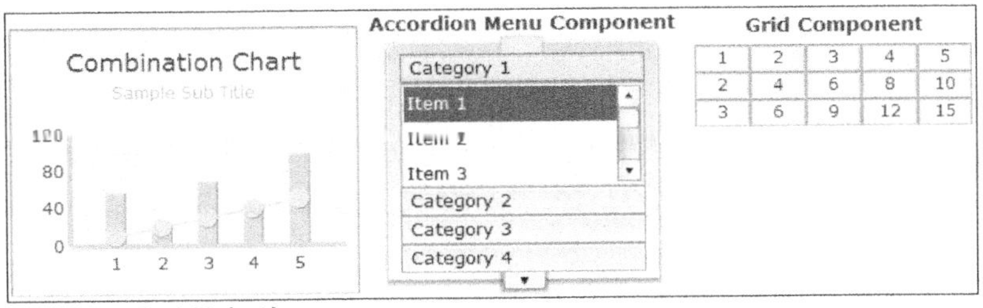

Figure 16-4 Halo theme

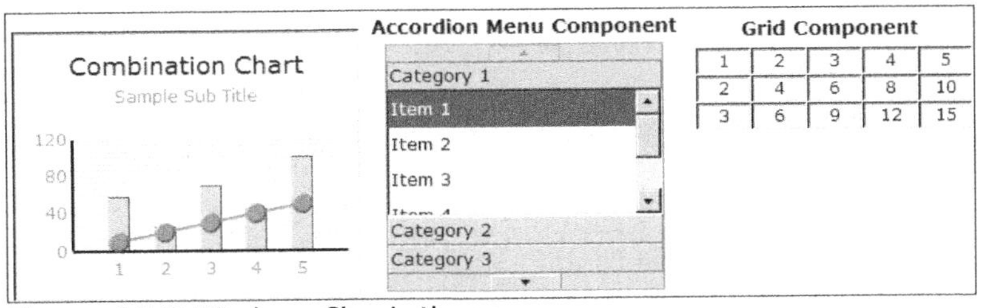

Figure 16-5 Windows Classic theme

What I noticed is that all themes do not have the same number of options per component type. For example, the Aqua theme has the four progress bars shown in Figure 16-6 and the Graphite theme only has the two progress bars shown in Figure 16-7.

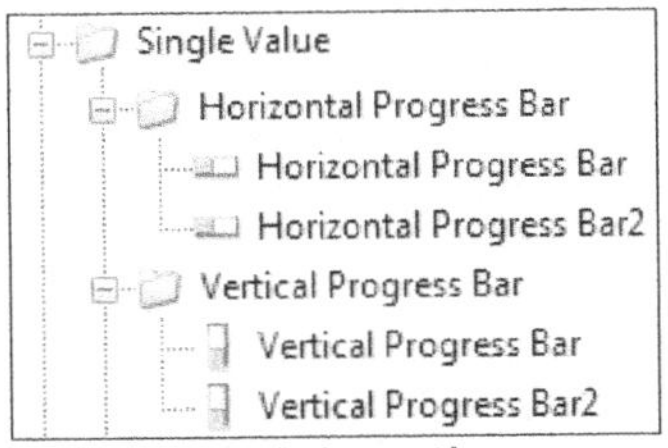

Figure 16-6 Aqua theme progress bar options

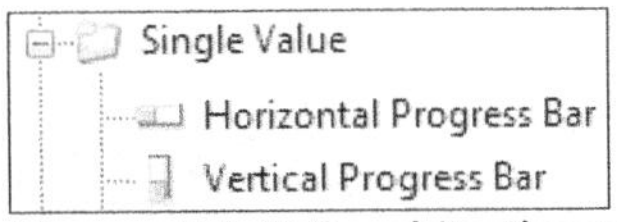

Figure 16-7 Graphite theme progress bar options

Changing Themes
If you create a dashboard with one theme and later want to use a different theme on the dashboard, you could get unexpected results when the new theme is applied. For example, if the dashboard currently uses the Gauge 4 component in the Aqua theme and you change the dashboard to use the Aero theme, the gauge component in the dashboard would go from the one shown in Figure 16-8 to the one shown in Figure 16-9. The reason this will happen is because the Aqua theme has four gauge components and the Aero theme only has two gauge components.

Figure 16-8 Aqua theme gauge 4 component

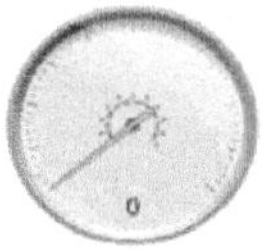

Figure 16-9 Aero theme gauge component

> **Selecting A Default Theme**
> If you find that you use a particular theme over and over, you can make it the default theme by following the steps below.
>
> 1. File ⇒ Preferences.
> 2. Click on the Document option.
> 3. In the default Theme list, select the theme that you want to use as the default, then click OK.

Exercise 16.1: How To Change The Theme Of A Model

In this exercise you will change the theme of a model.

1. Save the My radio button menu as `My new theme background`.

2. Format ⇒ Theme. Select Graphite, then click OK.

3. Delete the rectangle around the model.

4. Add the Background 4 component, then resize the background so that it covers the other components.

5. On the General view of the background component, change the Transparency to 25%.

6. On the General view of the Canvas Properties panel, make the changes in the table.

Option	Change To
Type	Solid Color
Background Color	White

7. Save the changes.

   The model should look like the one shown in Figure 16-10.

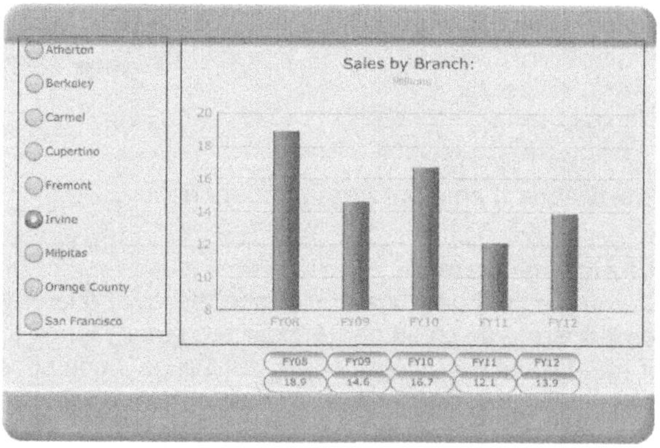

Figure 16-10 Model with a Graphite theme background

> **Themes Can Resize Components**
> If you apply a different theme to the model, depending on the components in the model, the size of the components will change. You may need to manually resize some of the components if the theme is changed after the components have been added to the model.

Color Schemes

Color Schemes replace the **GLOBAL STYLES** functionality in previous versions of the software. They are used to change the color pattern of a dashboard. Each color scheme is a collection of appearance options that are used to change the default colors for components. Color Schemes do not change text formatting or fonts.

You have learned how to change the color of parts of a component. The Color Schemes tool contains several schemes that can easily be applied to a model. You can also change the color for an individual item in a color scheme.

In addition to being able to apply the color scheme to new models that you create, color schemes can also be applied to existing models. If you open a model that has a color scheme that is not on the computer that you are currently using, the model will still open and have the color scheme that it was created with. Color Schemes do not change the alert, font or text formatting.

While it may be necessary to select a custom color after applying a color scheme, keep the following in mind, especially when using a color scheme other than the default color scheme. If you find yourself creating a custom color for several components on a regular basis in the model, you should consider creating your own custom color scheme, because you can save it and apply it to the components. Figure 16-11 shows the built in color schemes. The **CURRENT THEME COLORS** option is the one applied to the dashboard that is currently displayed on your computer screen.

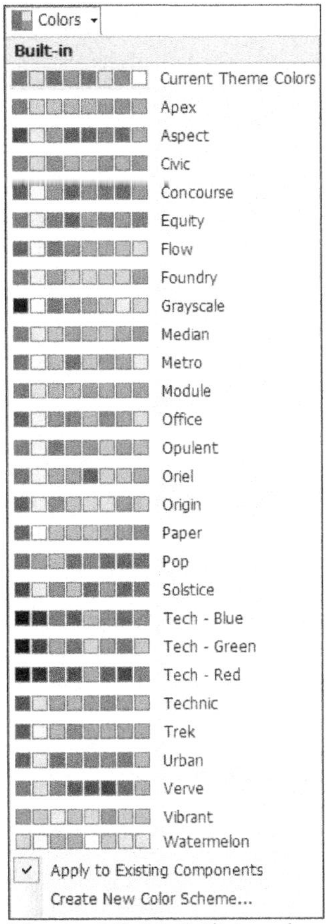

Figure 16-11 Built in color schemes

Format ⇒ Color Scheme, opens the dialog box shown in Figure 16-12. The built in color schemes can be modified if they are saved with a new name.

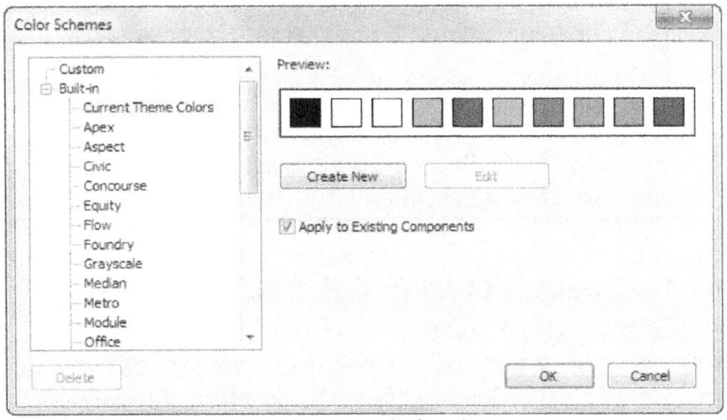

Figure 16-12 Color Schemes dialog box

Using Color Schemes

There are two ways to apply a color scheme to a model, as explained below.

① **TO THE CURRENT MODEL ONLY** Open the model that you want to apply the color scheme to, then click the Colors button on the Themes toolbar.

② **TO ALL NEW MODELS** Change the default Color Scheme option on the Preferences dialog box. [See Chapter 3, Preferences - Document Options]

Exercise 16.2: Apply A Different Color Scheme To A Model

In this exercise you will apply a different color scheme to the model shown in Figure 16-13.

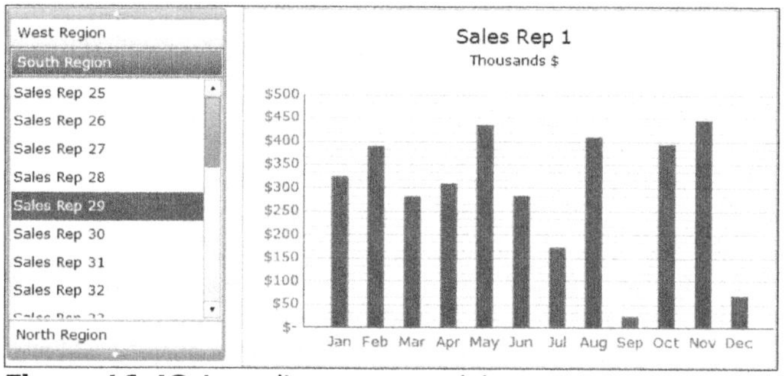

Figure 16-13 Accordion menu model

1. Save the My accordion menu model as `My new color scheme.`

2. Click the Colors button on the Themes toolbar, then select the **OPULENT** color scheme.

   Save the changes.

   The model should look like the one shown in Figure 16-14.

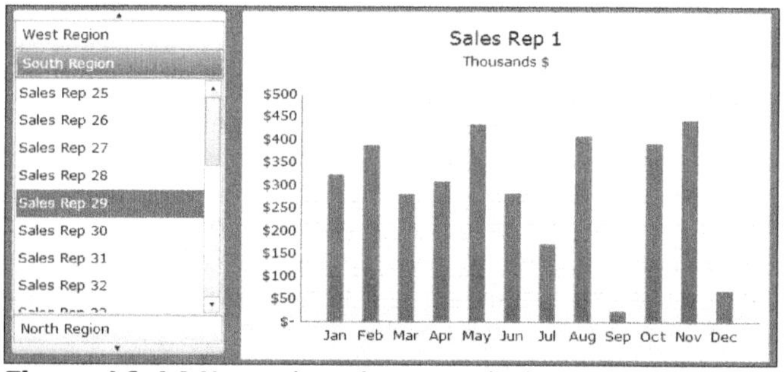

Figure 16-14 New color scheme applied to a model

> **Selecting A Default Color Scheme**
> If you find that you use a particular color scheme over and over, you can make it the default color scheme by following the steps below.
>
> 1. File ⇒ Preferences.
> 2. Click on the Document option.
> 3. In the Default Color Scheme list, select the color scheme that you want to use as the default, click Apply, then click OK.

How To Create A Custom Color Scheme

The good thing about creating your own color scheme is that if one of the color schemes that comes with Dashboard Design has many of the colors that you want to use, select that color scheme before opening the Custom Color Scheme dialog box. That way you will only have to change a few colors. Like the built in color schemes, the ones that you create are available for all themes.

1. Select the **CREATE NEW COLOR SCHEME** option at the bottom of the Colors button, shown earlier in Figure 16-11 or click the **CREATE NEW** button on the Color Schemes dialog box shown earlier in Figure 16-12.

   You will see the dialog box shown in Figure 16-15.

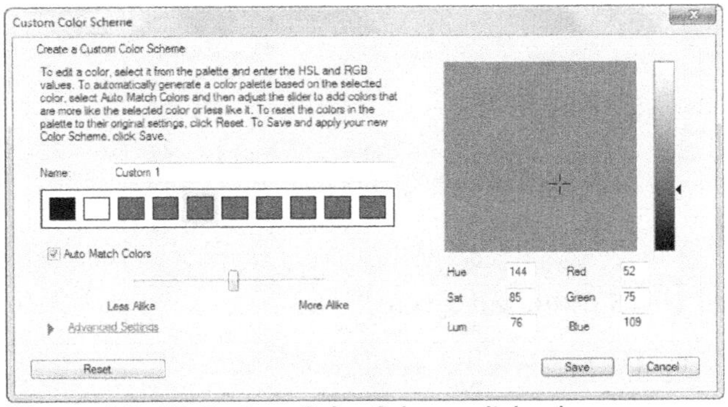

Figure 16-15 Custom Color Scheme dialog box

2. Type in a name for the custom color scheme. I use my first name for options like this because that makes it easier for me to recognize what I created.

Advanced Setting Options

Clicking on the **ADVANCED SETTINGS** link shown above in Figure 16-15, expands the Custom Color Scheme dialog box, as shown in Figure 16-16.

The options on the Buttons, Charts, Single Value and Scroll Bars tabs, shown in Figures 16-17 to 16-20 should look familiar from the options on the Properties panel.

The colors selected on the Custom Color Scheme dialog box are the default colors that you see with the color options on the Properties panel.

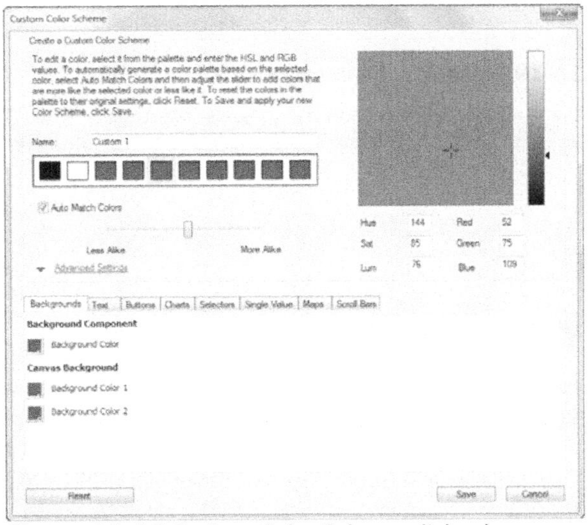

Figure 16-16 Custom Color Scheme dialog box expanded

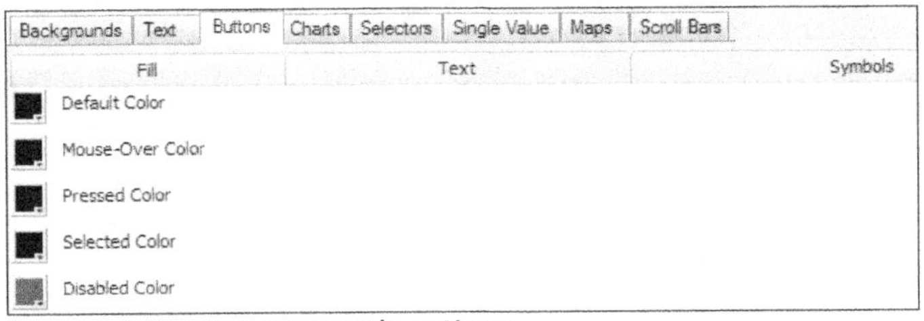

Figure 16-17 Buttons tab options

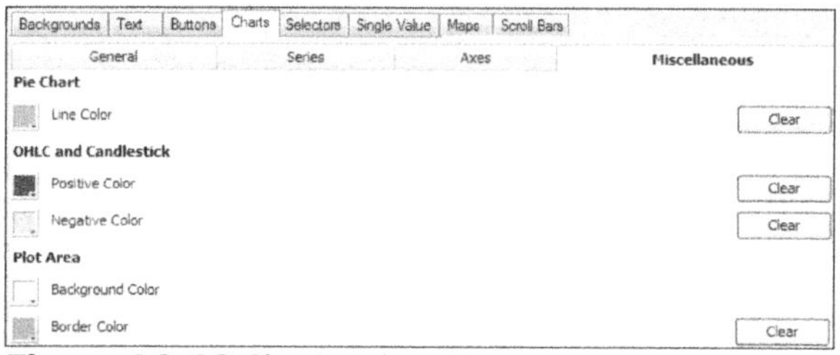

Figure 16-18 Charts tab options

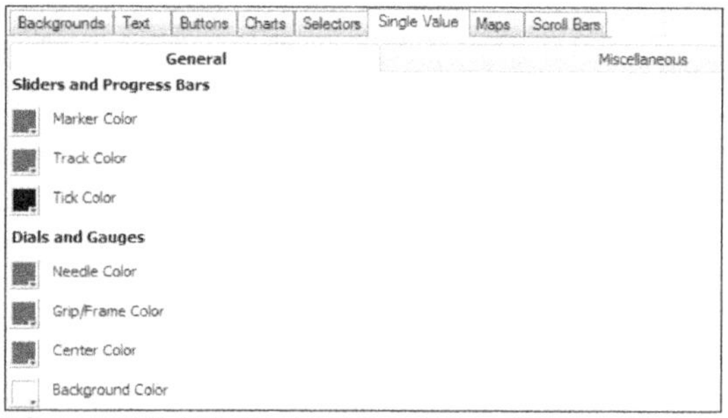

Figure 16-19 Single Value tab options

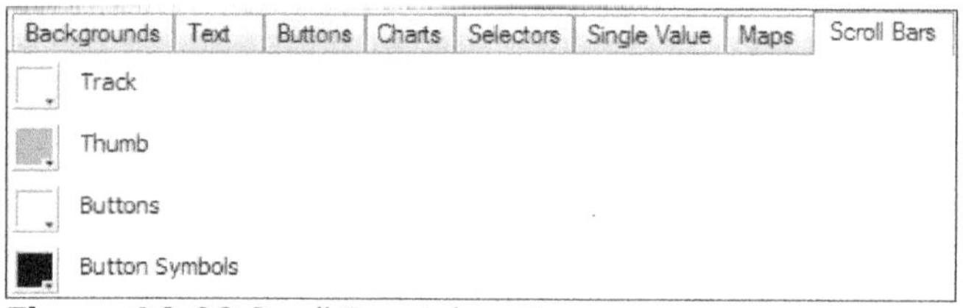

Figure 16-20 Scroll Bars tab options

The **CLEAR** button is used to reset the color of a single option that you change. In Figure 16-18 shown earlier, three of the color options were changed.

The **RESET** button is used to reset all of the changes that you made on the tab.

The **SAVE** button is used to save your custom color scheme. Custom color schemes are displayed at the top of the options on the Colors button, as illustrated in Figure 16-21 and in the Custom section on the Color Schemes dialog box, as illustrated in Figure 16-22.

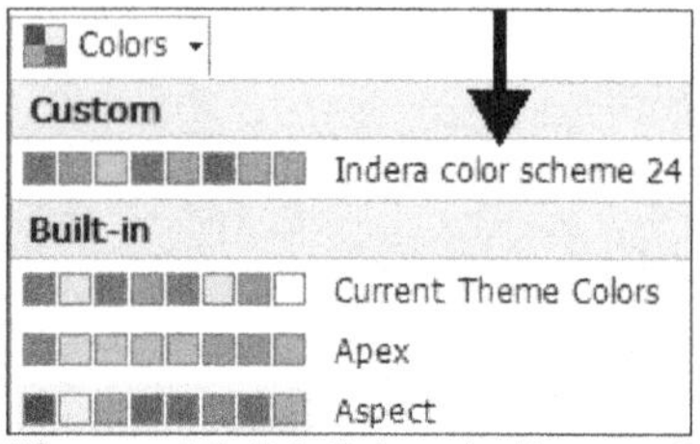

Figure 16-21 Colors button custom section illustrated

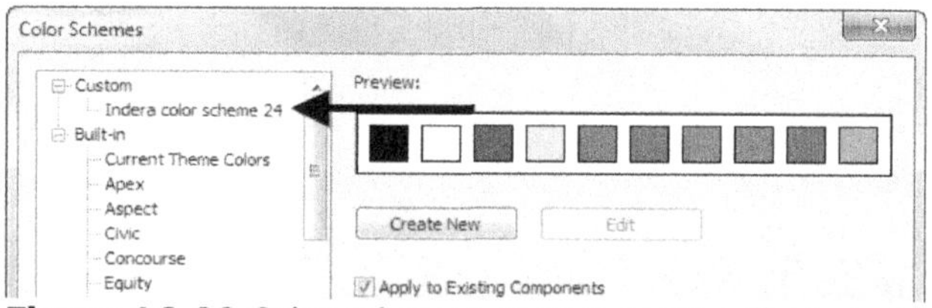

Figure 16-22 Color schemes custom section illustrated

If you want to keep all of the changes, type in a name for the color scheme, then click the **SAVE** button. The color schemes are stored in this location.

C:\Users\YourUsername\AppData\Roaming\XcelsiuscustomThemes\

> **Let Dashboard Design Help You Create A Custom Color Scheme**
> If you want some help selecting the colors for the scheme, select the main color that you want to use on the Custom Color Scheme dialog box, then select the **AUTO MATCH COLORS** option. This will cause Dashboard Design to create a color scheme based on the main color that you selected. You can adjust the color scheme by moving the bar between the **LESS ALIKE** and **MORE ALIKE** options shown earlier in Figure 16-15. Clear the Auto Match Colors option if you want to change a specific color in the scheme.

Exercise 16.3: Using A Custom Color Scheme On A Different Computer

If you need to work on a model on a computer that does not have the custom color scheme that you created or need, you have to copy the color scheme file to the other computer.

The custom color file is saved in an **.XML** file, as illustrated in Figure 16-23. I created the custom color scheme dd_my_customcolor, illustrated in the figure.

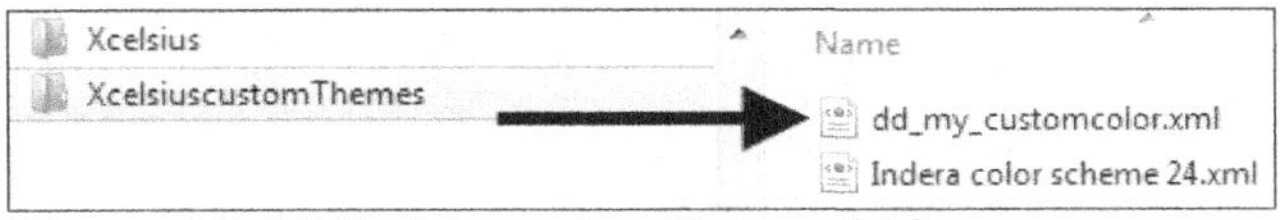

Figure 16-23 XcelsiuscustomThemes folder

This is the file that you would copy to another computer. Follow the steps below to copy this color scheme to your computer.

1. Close Dashboard Design.
2. In Windows Explorer, copy the dd_my_customcolor file in your folder to the XcelsiuscustomThemes folder. The path for the folder is shown in Figure 16-24.

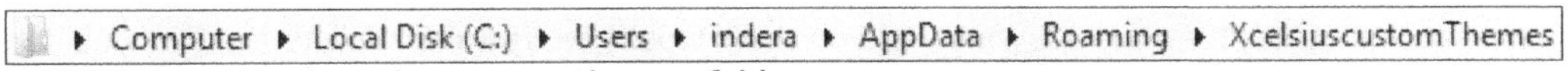

Figure 16-24 Path to the custom themes folder

3. Open Dashboard Design, then save the My single value alerts model as `My custom color`.
4. Open the Colors drop-down list and select the custom color scheme that you just copied, as shown in the Custom section of Figure 16-25.

   You should see the new color scheme applied to the model. Yes, it is very colorful.

   Save the changes.

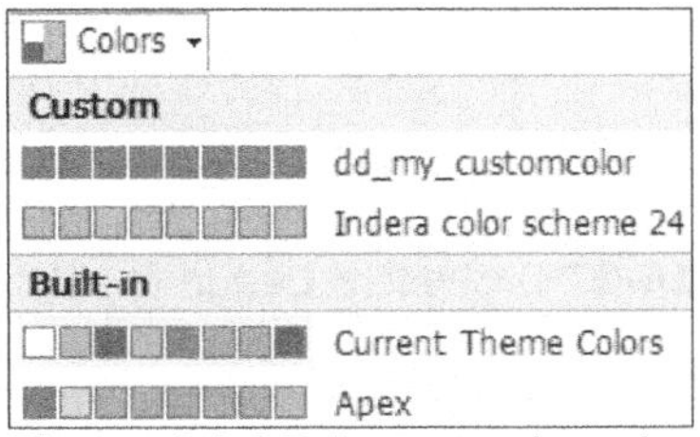

Figure 16-25 Custom color scheme

Templates

Dashboard Design has several templates that you can use to create the look and feel of the dashboard. Templates can save you time because you do not have to create the layout for the model from scratch. Templates cannot be applied to an existing model.

File ⇒ Templates, opens the dialog box shown in Figure 16-26. What is interesting about templates is that they are interactive on the dialog box, which means that you can click on a component displayed in the **PREVIEW** section and use it like you would use a dashboard. Templates that are not in the Template folder have setup instructions and sample data in the spreadsheet that will help you set up the data in your own spreadsheet to work with the template.

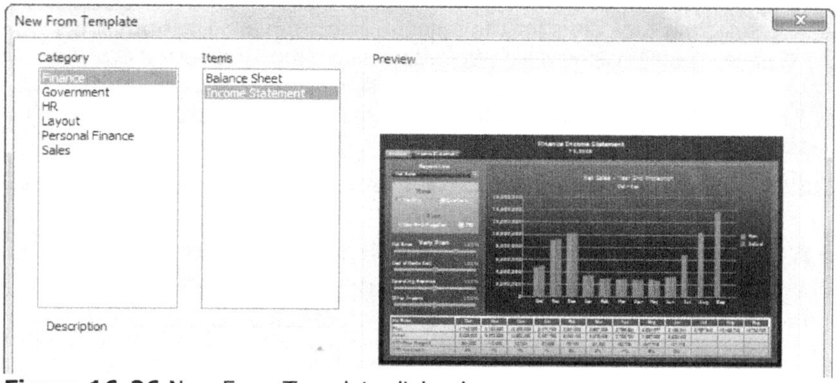

Figure 16-26 New From Template dialog box

Template Folders

The default template folder is named template. The first list on the New From Template dialog box is named **CATEGORY**. Each category is a folder on your computers hard drive. In addition to being able to create your own templates, you can create your own folders.

One use that comes to mind for creating your own folders is if you create dashboards for different departments in a company or if you create dashboards for different clients. The folders would allow you to keep the templates organized.

How To Create Your Own Template

If you create a model that has a layout that you think would be useful for future models, you can save it as a template by following the steps below.

1. Open the model that you want to save as a template, then File ⇒ Save As.

2. Navigate to the **TEMPLATE** folder shown in the path in Figure 16-27, or a template folder that you created.

Figure 16-27 Dashboard Design template folder

3. Type in the name for the template, then press Enter. If you open the New From Template dialog box, you should see the template that you created.

Make The Template Interactive

If you want your template to be interactive in the New From Template dialog box, follow the steps below. When you open the New From Template dialog box, select the folder in the Category list that your template is in.

1. Open the template that you created, then File ⇒ Export ⇒ Flash (SWF).
2. Navigate to the folder that you saved the template in.
3. Type in the same file name that you used for the template, then press Enter.

Exporting

Exporting models is important because it is how you can share the dashboard with other people that do not have Dashboard Design installed. This book has shown you how to create a lot of models, but you have only exported a model to a Flash file to create a dashboard. The next few sections cover all of the exporting options. Keep in mind that each export option creates a SWF file and then adds the SWF file to the export format that you select. Each export format retains all of the functionality that the model has.

The next to last step that I do before exporting the model is resizing the canvas, so that it is the right size for the dashboard. [See Chapter 3, Resize The Canvas] Exporting the model is the last step in creating the dashboard that will be distributed to users.

What may not be obvious is that the dashboard can be copied and pasted to another file.
For example, when you export the model to PowerPoint, a file is created that has one slide that contains the dashboard. If you are creating a larger presentation, you can copy the slide with the dashboard to another PowerPoint file, by right-clicking on the slide that you want to copy. Open the presentation file that you want to copy it to. Select the slide that you want to paste it on, then right-click and select Paste. The same is also true for other export options.

Exporting Tip
If the images have not been embedded in the model, when you export a **SLIDING PICTURE MENU** model, the SWF file has to be exported to the same folder as the image files that the menu uses, so that the images will load properly.

Open the model that you want to create the dashboard for, before following the instructions below. Some of the export options will create two files: the SWF file and the export file type that you selected, as shown in Figure 16-28.

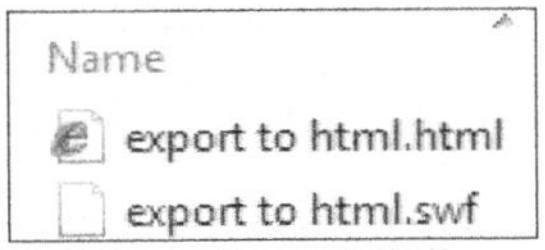

Figure 16-28 HTML export files

Export To Flash (This option is not available in Presentation Design)

This export option creates a SWF file. The benefit of using this export option is that the file is not dependent on the computers operating system. This means that it can be run from any computer. The Flash Player is usually used to view the dashboard file created from this export option.

1. File ⇒ Export ⇒ Flash (SWF). You will see the Export dialog box.
2. Navigate to the folder where you want to save the dashboard file.
3. Type in the name for the Flash file, then press Enter or click the Save button. The dashboard in Flash format will be created.

Export To Adobe AIR (This option is not available in Presentation Design)

This export option creates an Adobe Integrated Runtime (AIR) application. This is a stand alone file that can be run under multiple operating systems. This export option only supports PNG image files.

1. File ⇒ Export ⇒ AIR.

   You will see the dialog box shown in Figure 16-29 if you do not have the free Flex Builder 3 SDK installed.

   Clicking on the Download Here link will open the web page that has the free Software Developer Kit (SDK).

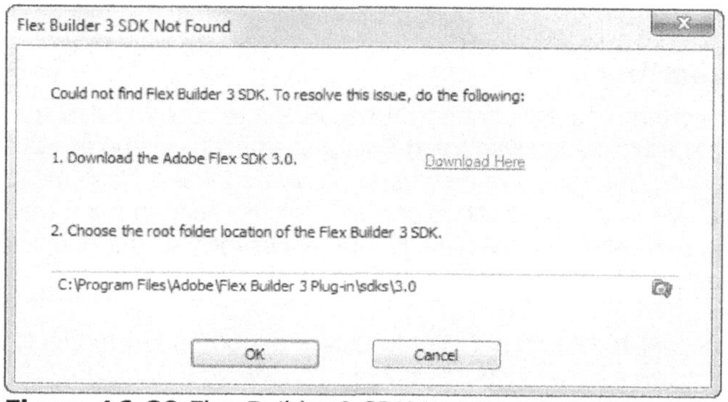

Figure 16-29 Flex Builder 3 SDK Not Found dialog box

The free Adobe AIR Player is required to run exported AIR files. You can download the Player from http://get.adobe.com/air/.

Export To HTML (This option is not available in Presentation Design)

This export option creates an HTML file (a web page) that automatically loads the SWF file.
In Chapter 1, I explained file naming conventions that will come into play with this export option.
The SWF and HTML files that are created will have the same file name. It is best to use a file name that does not have spaces. You can rename the HTML file after it is created. If necessary, if you need to rename the SWF file, you will have to change the code in the HTML file to point to the new name of the SWF file.

1. File ⇒ Export ⇒ HTML. You will see the Save As dialog box.
2. Navigate to the folder where you want to save the dashboard files.
3. Type in the name for the HTML file, then press Enter or click the Save button. The HTML dashboard file will be created.

Export To PowerPoint

This export option adds the SWF file to a new Microsoft PowerPoint file. Like any other PowerPoint file, one with a dashboard can be emailed. Keep in mind that if the exported file is viewed in the Edit mode in PowerPoint that it could appear blank.

1. File ⇒ Export ⇒ PowerPoint Slide. You will see the Save As dialog box.
2. Navigate to the folder where you want to save the dashboard files.
3. Type in the name for the PowerPoint file, then press Enter or click the Save button.
   The PowerPoint dashboard file will be created and automatically displayed in PowerPoint.

Export To Outlook (This option is not available in Presentation Design)

This export option automatically adds the SWF file to a Microsoft Outlook email message that you can email to someone.

1. File ⇒ Export ⇒ Outlook. A Outlook email window will open. The SWF file will be attached to the email automatically.

Export To Word

This export option adds the SWF file to a Microsoft Word document. The dashboard is embedded in a Word document as a Shockwave Flash object, opposed to being linked, like it is in PowerPoint and Outlook. Keep in mind that because the dashboard is embedded, the file size of the Word document can be large.

1. File ⇒ Export ⇒ Word. You will see the Save As dialog box.
2. Navigate to the folder where you want to save the dashboard file.
3. Type in the name for the Word file, then press Enter or click the Save button. The Word dashboard file will be created.

Export To A PDF File

This export option adds the SWF file to an Adobe PDF file. All of the functionality created in the model works in the dashboard in the PDF file.

There are two Acrobat formats that you can select from to export to: Acrobat 6 and Acrobat 9. The Export to PDF option on the toolbar only exports to the Acrobat 9 format. If you want to export to Acrobat 6 format, use the PDF export option on the File menu.

The PDF export option only exports to the portrait orientation. Landscape orientation is currently not supported.

1. File ⇒ Export ⇒ PDF. You will see the Save As dialog box.
2. Navigate to the folder where you want to save the dashboard file.
3. Type in the name for the PDF file, then press Enter or click the Save button. The PDF dashboard file will be created.

The End!

If you are reading this paragraph, I hope it means that you have completed all of the exercises in this book. If so, congratulations because you have covered a lot of material. If some topics seem a little fuzzy right now, that is to be expected. Hopefully you have gained some valuable dashboard design creation skills and techniques. I hope that you enjoyed the book.

INDEX

C

D

E

F

G

H

M

N

T

U

V

W

X

Y

Z